Manual of Civil Ap

Manual of Civil Appeals

Second Edition

Editor in Chief
The Rt Hon Lord Justice Brooke
Vice-President, Court of Appeal (Civil Division)

General Editors

David di Mambro LLB (Lond), MCIArb, Fellow of the Society for Advanced Legal Studies, Barrister, Lamb Chambers
Appointed to Civil Procedure Rule Committee with effect from September 2004
Louise di Mambro LLB (Lond), Barrister
Deputy Master, Civil Appeals Office

Contributing Editors

Master David Gladwell LLM (Exon), Dip Intellectual Property Law (Lond), Barrister, CEDR Accredited Mediator
Head of the Civil Appeals Office and Master in the Court of Appeal, Civil Division
Brendan Keith
Clerk of the Judicial Office and Taxing Officer, House of Lords

Members of the LexisNexis Group worldwide

United Kingdom	LexisNexis UK, a Division of Reed Elsevier (UK) Ltd, Halsbury House, 35 Chancery Lane, LONDON, WC2A 1EL, and 4 Hill Street, EDINBURGH EH2 3JZ
United Kingdom	LexisNexis UK, a Division of Reed Elsevier (UK) Ltd, 2 Addiscombe Road, CROYDON CR9 5AF
United Kingdom	LexisNexis IRS, member of the Eclipse Group Ltd, 18–20 Highbury Place, LONDON N5 1QP
United Kingdom	LexisNexis UK, a Division of Reed Elsevier (UK) Ltd, 4 Hill Street, EDINBURGH EH2 3JZ and Halsbury House, 35 Chancery Lane, LONDON WC2A 1EL
Argentina	LexisNexis Argentina, BUENOS AIRES
Australia	LexisNexis Butterworths, CHATSWOOD, New South Wales
Austria	LexisNexis Verlag ARD Orac GmbH & Co KG, VIENNA
Canada	LexisNexis Butterworths, MARKHAM, Ontario
Chile	LexisNexis Chile Ltda, SANTIAGO DE CHILE
Czech Republic	Nakladatelství Orac sro, PRAGUE
France	Editions du Juris-Classeur SA, PARIS
Germany	LexisNexis Deutschland GmbH, FRANKFURT and MUNSTER
Hong Kong	LexisNexis Butterworths, HONG KONG
Hungary	HVG-Orac, BUDAPEST
India	LexisNexis Butterworths, NEW DELHI
Ireland	LexisNexis, DUBLIN
Italy	Giuffrè Editore, MILAN
Malaysia	Malayan Law Journal Sdn Bhd, KUALA LUMPUR
New Zealand	LexisNexis Butterworths, WELLINGTON
Poland	Wydawnictwo Prawnicze LexisNexis, WARSAW
Singapore	LexisNexis Butterworths, SINGAPORE
South Africa	LexisNexis Butterworths, DURBAN
Switzerland	Stämpfli Verlag AG, BERNE
USA	LexisNexis, DAYTON, Ohio

First published in 2000

© Reed Elsevier (UK) Ltd 2004

Published by LexisNexis UK

All rights reserved. No part of this publication may be reproduced in any material form (including photocopying or storing it in any medium by electronic means and whether or not transiently or incidentally to some other use of this publication) without the written permission of the copyright owner except in accordance with the provisions of the Copyright, Designs and Patents Act 1988 or under the terms of a licence issued by the Copyright Licensing Agency Ltd, 90 Tottenham Court Road, London, England W1T 4LP. Applications for the copyright owner's written permission to reproduce any part of this publication should be addressed to the publisher.

Warning: The doing of an unauthorised act in relation to a copyright work may result in both a civil claim for damages and criminal prosecution.

Crown copyright material is reproduced with the permission of the Controller of HMSO and the Queen's Printer for Scotland. Parliamentary copyright material is reproduced with the permission of the Controller of Her Majesty's Stationery Office on behalf of Parliament. Any European material in this work which has been reproduced from EUR-lex, the official European Communities legislation website, is European Communities copyright.

A CIP Catalogue record for this book is available from the British Library.

ISBN 0 406 97582 5

Typeset by Columns Design Ltd, Reading, Berkshire
Printed and bound in Great Britain by Hobbs the Printers Ltd, Totton, Hampshire

Visit LexisNexis UK at www.lexisnexis.co.uk

Foreword

The first edition of this Manual was published in September 2000, when the new CPR appellate procedures had been in place for quite a short time. We have now had four years' experience of them, and these four years have generated a volume of practical guidance which it is not always very easy for judges, practitioners and lay litigants to locate.

This second edition sets out under one cover not only the relevant rules and Practice Directions, but also a lot of this practical guidance. This takes the form of extracts from relevant judgments, whether or not they have found their way into the regular series of law reports. The volume also includes chapters relating to appeals to the House of Lords, applications to the courts in Luxembourg and Strasbourg, and alternative dispute resolution (when seen from an appellate perspective).

The publication of this edition of the Manual also coincides with the introduction of significant changes to the Practice Direction to CPR Part 52. These changes are largely concerned with the way in which documents are presented to an appeal court in advance of an appeal hearing. They include the creation of explicit costs sanctions against those who do not comply with the requirements of the Practice Direction. They should, therefore, be regarded as required reading for everyone who is concerned in any way with the prosecution of appeals at any level within our civil justice system.

Henry Brooke
Vice-President
Court of Appeal (Civil Division)
May 2004

Contents

Foreword v
Table of Statutes xi
Table of Statutory Instruments xiii
Table of Cases xix

Chapter 1 Introduction 1
   Scope and Application of the New Regime 1
   Terminology 2
   The Main Features of the Appeals Regime 5
   Appeals to the Court of Appeal 6
   Routes of Appeal 7

Chapter 2 An Appeal Court's Methods and its Power to Interfere 12
   Review or rehearing 12
   The grounds on which an appeal may be allowed 19
   Appeals founded on an error of law 22
   Appeals against findings of fact 31
   Appeals in respect of the exercise of a discretion 44
   New evidence or change of circumstances as a ground of appeal 47
   Serious procedural or other irregularity resulting in injustice 53
   Infringement of Art 6 of Sch 1 to the Human Rights Act 1998: 'Right to a fair trial' 54

Chapter 3 Routes of Appeal 57
   Access to Justice Act 1999 (Destination of Appeals) Order 2000 57
   Small claims 58
   Fast track claims 59
   Part 8 claims 60
   Contempt of court and committal orders 61
   Multi-track claims and specialist proceedings 62
   Second appeals 64
   Costs 66
   Original or ancillary order 67
   Assignment of appeals to the Court of Appeal 67

Family proceedings	69
Insolvency proceedings	69
Access to Justice Act 1999	71
Access to Justice Act 1999 (Destination of Appeals) Order 2000	75

Chapter 4 Procedure — 78

General rules about appeals	80
CPR 52.1 Scope and interpretation	80
CPR 52.2 Parties to comply with the practice direction	82
CPR 52.3 Permission	82
CPR 52.4 Appellant's notice	89
CPR 52.5 Respondent's notice	91
CPR 52.6 Variation of time	94
CPR 52.7 Stay	96
CPR 52.8 Amendment of appeal notice	98
CPR 52.9 Striking out appeal notices	99
CPR 52.10 Appeal court's powers	104
CPR 52.11 Hearing of appeals	106
CPR 52.12 Non-disclosure of Part 36 offers and payments	110
Special provisions applying to the Court of Appeal	112
CPR 52.13 Second appeals to the court	112
General notes on appeals and applications to the Court of Appeal	115
CPR 52.14 Assignment of appeals to the Court of Appeal	118
CPR 52.15 Judicial review appeals	120
CPR 52.16 Who may exercise the powers of the Court of Appeal	121
Provisions about reopening appeals	122
CPR 52.17 Reopening of final appeals	122
Practice Direction 52	124

Chapter 5 Miscellaneous Points of Practice — 182

Striking out of appeal notice: abuse of process	182
Change of solicitor	183
Discontinuance of proceedings in the lower court	184
Appeals against consent orders	184
Bankruptcy of appellant	185
Master in the Court of Appeal, Civil Division	185
Dismissal list hearings in the Court of Appeal	186
Enforcement of appeal order	186

Chapter 6 Documents — 187

The appellant's notice	187
Appellant's documents	196
Skeleton arguments	203
Transcripts of judgment	205
Service of the appellant's notice	207
Amendment of appeal notice	208
Applications for permission to appeal	209

Respondent's submissions on application for permission to appeal	212
Documents for the appeal hearing	213
Respondent's notices, skeleton arguments and documents	215
Summary assessment of costs	221
Appeal hearings in the Court of Appeal	221
Disposing of applications or appeals by consent	227

Chapter 7 Alternative Dispute Resolution — 231

Introduction: The CPR and ADR	231
Power of the court to compel the parties to participate in ADR	233
Sanctions for refusing to participate in ADR	236
The Court of Appeal scheme	243
Useful addresses	244

Chapter 8 Appeals to the House of Lords — 245

Introduction	245
Leave to appeal	246
Appeals	252
Procedural table	268

Chapter 9 Applications to the ECtHR and ECJ — 309

Introduction	309
The European Court of Human Rights	311
Court of Justice of the European Communities	315

Appendix 1 Forms — 319

Appellant's notice (N161)	320
Guidance notes on completing the appellant's notice (N161A)	328
Respondent's notice (N162)	340
Request for dismissal of an appellant's notice (253)	348
Request for dismissal of an appellant's notice (254A)	349
General form of request for dismissal of an application (254B)	350

Appendix 2 Case Law — 351

Aoun v Bahri and Angelou	352
Barings plc (in liquidation) and another v Coopers & Lybrand (a firm) and others	358
Beedell v West Ferry Printers Ltd	365
CIBC Mellon Trust Co and others v Mora Hotel Corp NV and another	368
Clark (Inspector of Taxes) v Perks and other applications	387
Contract Facilities Ltd v Rees' Estate	404
Electra Private Equity Partners and others v KPMG Peat Marwick (a firm) and others	416
Foenander v Bond Lewis & Co	424
Great Future International Limited and others v Sealand Housing Corporation and others	431

Hammond Suddards Solicitors v Agrichem International Holdings Ltd	437
Hertfordshire Investments Ltd v Bubb and another	446
Hunt v Peasegood	454
Jolly v Jay	461
Sarah Lloyd Jones and others v T Mobile (UK) Ltd	473
Koller v Secretary of State for the Home Department	478
Milward v Three Rivers District Council	481
Owusu v Jackson and others	485
R (on the application of Nine Nepalese Asylum Seekers) v Immigration Appeal Tribunal	487
Shire v Secretary of State for Work and Pensions	493
Slot and another v Isaac	495
Southern & District Finance Plc v Turner	500
Tanfern Ltd v Cameron-MacDonald and another	510
Unilever plc v Chefaro Proprietaries Ltd and other appeals	526

Index 535

Table of Statutes

Paragraph numbers in **bold** type indicate where the act is set out in part or in full

A

Access to Justice Act 1999 ..... 3.29, 3.45, 4.7
  s 11 .... 8.72
  54 .... 1.1, **3.45**, 4.1, 4.15
    (4) 3.5, 3.9, 3.11, 3.15, 3.16, 3.25, 3.35, 4.16
    (5) 1.3
    (6) 4.115
  55 ...... 1.1, 1.4, 3.5, 3.7, 3.12, 3.16, 3.25, 3.26, 3.27, 3.28, 3.30, 3.34, **3.46**, 4.1, 4.14, 4.43, 4.89, 4.90
    (1) 1.3, 1.4
  56 .... 1.1, 1.9, 3.1, **3.47**, 4.1
  57 .... 1.1, 1.12, 3.19, 3.36, 3.37, **3.48**, 4.1, 4.112
    (1) 3.36
    (2) 3.37
  58 .... **3.49**
  59 .... **3.50**
  60 .... **3.51**
  106 .... 3.43
  Sch 15
    Pt III 3.43
Administration of Justice Act 1960
  s 13 .... 3.1, 3.17, 3.18
    (2) 3.19
Administration of Justice Act 1969 ...... 8.12
  s 1 .... 8.15
  12 .... 8.9, 8.10
    (3)(a), (b) 8.11, 8.13
  13 .... 8.9
    (1) 8.13
  14 .... 8.9
  15 .... 8.9
    (3) 8.15

Administration of Justice (Appeals) Act 1934
  s 1(1) 8.5
    (2) proviso 8.7
Aircraft and Shipbuilding Industries Act 1977
  Sch 7
    para 9(2) 8.16
Appellate Jurisdiction Act 1876
  s 3(2) 8.16
  4 .... 8.7
  11 .... 8.2
Arbitration Act 1996
  s 67 .... 4.6
  69 .... 3.27, 4.6, 4.14
    (2), (3) 4.6
    (8) 3.27, 4.6, 8.5

B

Banking Act 1987
  s 31(4) 8.16
Building (Scotland) Act 1959
  s 16(3) 8.16

C

Caravan Sites and Control of Development Act 1960
  s 32(2)(b) 8.16
Children Act 1989
  s 25 .... 1.7, 3.22, 3.24
Companies Act 1985 .... 1.9, 3.20, 3.21
Companies Act 1989 .... 1.9, 3.21
County Courts Act 1984
  s 5 .... 3.1
  77(6) 4.5

Court of Session (Scotland)
Act 1988
  s 40(1)(b) 8.16
    41(2) 8.7

Courts Act 1971
  s 24 .... 3.1

Crown Proceedings Act 1947
  s 17 .... 4.27

E

Employment Protection
  (Consolidation) Act 1978 .... 2.19

Employment Rights Act 1996 .... 2.19

Estate Agents Act 1979
  s 7(6) 8.16

European Communities Act 1972
  s 3(1) 9.4, 9.9

H

Housing Act 1985 .... 8.5

Housing Act 1996 .... 1.6, 2.90
  s 152 .... 3.13
    204(1) 3.28
    204A 3.28, 4.89
      (1) 4.89

Human Rights Act 1998 ...... 4.28, 8.3, 8.34,
                                                          8.84, 9.4
  s 2(1) 9.4, 9.9
    3(1) 2.90
  Sch 1 .... 2.90
    art 6 .... 2.16, **2.84**, 2.87
    art 6(1) 2.86

I

Inheritance (Provisions for Family
  and Dependants) Act 1975 .... 3.21

Insolvency Act 1986
  s 375 .... 3.43

Insolvency Act 1986 − *contd*
  s 375(2) 3.43

J

Judicature (Northern Ireland)
  Act 1978
  s 42 .... 8.5
    45(3) 8.15

L

Law of Property Act 1925
  s 146 .... 2.58

N

Nationality, Immigration and
  Asylum Act 2002
  s 78 .... 4.47

S

Supreme Court Act 1981
  s 18(1)(c) 3.21, 4.7
    51 .... 4.68
    54 .... 4.107
      (3) 4.107

T

Town and Country Planning
  Act 1990 .... 2.32

Tribunals and Inquiries Act 1992
  s 11 .... 3.28
    (7)(d) 8.16

Transport Act 1985
  s 9(9) 8.16

U

Unfair Contract Terms Act 1977 .... 2.51
  s 11 .... 2.51, 4.89

Table of Statutory Instruments

Paragraph numbers in **bold** type indicate where the rule is set out in part or in full

A

Access to Justice Act 1999
(Destination of Appeals)
Order 2000, SI 2000/1071 ..... 1.2, 1.3, 1.9,
3.1, 3.18, 3.39, **3.53**, 4.3,
4.7
art 1 .... 1.3, **3.53**
(2)(c) 1.3, 3.21, 3.23
(3) 1.3, 3.21, 3.23
(4)(a) 3.39
(b)(i) 3.1, 3.18, 3.43
(ii) 3.1
2 .... 3.33, **3.54**
3 .... **3.55**
(1) 3.6, 3.11, 3.16
(2) 3.2, 3.8, 3.14
4 .... 3.13, 3.20, 3.21, **3.56**
5 ..... 3.5, 3.7, 3.9, 3.10, 3.12,
3.15, 3.16, 3.26, 3.27,
3.33, 3.34, **3.57**, 4.89
(a) 3.33
6 .... **3.58**
7 .... **3.59**
8 .... **3.60**

C

Civil Procedure (Amendment No 2)
Rules 2000, SI 2000/940 .... 3.32

Civil Procedure (Amendment No 4)
Rules 2003, SI 2003/2113 .... 4.118

Civil Procedure Rules 1998,
SI 1998/3132
Pt 1 .... 2.11, 2.89, 7.1
r 1.1 .... 2.60
(1) 7.1

Civil Procedure Rules 1998, SI 1998/3132 – *contd*
Pt 1 – *contd*
(2) 2.11
1.2(b) 2.90
1.4(2)(e) 7.1
Pt 2
r 2.1 .... 4.58, 4.67, 5.1
(2) 1.2
PD 2B
para 11.1(d) 1.10
Pt 3 .... 1.5, 4.67
r 3.1(2)(a) 4.40
3.3(4) 4.58, 4.59, 5.1
3.9 .... 4.42
Pt 7 .... 1.2, 1.10, 2.12, 3.13, 3.20
Pt 8 .... 1.2, 1.9, 1.10, 2.12, 3.13
r 8.9(c) 1.10, 3.13
PD 8B 3.13
Pt 15
r 15.11(4) 2.47
Pt 16
PD 16 .... **6.3A**
para 15.1 .... 4.28, **6.3A**
15.2 .... **6.3A**
Pt 19
PD 19 .... 4.27, **6.3B**
para 6.1–6.6 .... **6.3B**
Annex **6.3C**
Pt 23 .... 4.46, 4.49, 5.2, 6.6, 8.82
r 23.2 .... 5.2
23.8 .... 4.15
23.11 .... 4.15
Pt 24 .... 3.23
r 24.2 .... 4.14, 7.4
Pt 25 .... 4.56
r 25.1 .... 6.6
25.13 .... 4.56
25.15 .... 4.63, 6.6
(1), (2) 4.56
Pt 27
r 27.12, 27.13 .... 3.3

Table of Statutory Instruments

Civil Procedure Rules 1998, SI 1998/3132 – contd
Pt 31 .... 2.88
Pt 36 .... 4.85, 4.86, 6.11
Pt 40
   PD 40B 8.82
Pt 42 .... 5.2
   r 42.2(6) 5.2
   42.3 .... 5.2
Pt 44 .... 6.38
   r 44.3(2) 7.4
      (a) 7.4
      (4) 7.4
   44.4 .... 8.84
   44.5 .... 7.1
      (3) **7.1**
   PD 44
      para 13 .... 6.38
Pt 47
   r 47.21 .... 3.32
   47.23 .... 2.2, 3.32
   Section VIII 1.2
Pt 52 .... 1.1, 1.2, 1.7, 1.8, 2.2,
                2.3, 2.7, 2.11, 2.13, 3.3,
                3.4, 3.32, 3.38, 3.39,
                3.43, 4.1, 4.14, 4.65,
                4.70, 4.97, 4.110, 4.114
   r 52.1 .... 3.21, **4.4**, 4.5, 4.6, 4.7
      (2) 2.2
         (b) 3.32, 3.33
      (3)(a), (b) 1.3
         (c) 1.3, 2.1
         (e) 1.3
      (4) 2.7
   52.2 .... **4.9**
   52.3 .... 1.7, 3.1, 3.8, 3.11, 3.14,
                3.16, 3.22, 3.24, **4.11**,
                4.15, 4.16
      (1) 3.17, 4.35
         (a) 3.19
         (b) 4.14
      (2) 1.7, 4.46
         (a) 1.7
      (3) 1.7, 4.15
      (4) 1.7, 3.5, 3.9, 3.11, 3.15,
                3.16, 3.25, 4.15, 4.20
      (5) 1.7
      (6) 1.7, 4.33, 6.23
         (a) 4.14
   52.4 .... **4.25**, 6.4, 6.5
      (2) 4.27
         (a) 1.7, 4.27, 4.39, 6.5
         (b) 4.39

Civil Procedure Rules 1998, SI 1998/3132 – contd
Pt 52 – contd
   52.5 .... **4.31**, 4.102, 4.106, 6.29
      (2), (3), (5) 4.34
      (6) 4.35
   52.6 .... 4.19, 4.27, 4.29, **4.38**,
                4.40, 4.41
   52.7 .... **4.45**
      (b) 4.47
   52.8 .... 1.7, 4.36, **4.50**, 4.101
   52.9 .... **4.55**, 4.63
      (1) 4.57
         (a) 4.58
         (c) 4.61
   52.10 .... 2.73, **4.64**, 5.1
      (1) 1.7, 2.61, 4.65
      (2) 4.65
         (c) 2.7
      (3), (4) 4.65
   52.11 .... 2.7, 2.73, 2.78, **4.69**
      (1) **2.1**, 2.4, 2.7, 4.70
         (b) 1.7, 2.5, 2.7, 2.79
      (2) 2.7, **2.62**, 2.68, 2.71
         (a) 4.76
         (b) 1.7, 4.81
      (3) 1.7, 2.4, **2.11**, 2.55, 4.70,
                4.71, 4.75
         (a) 2.35, 6.2
         (b) 2.81, 6.2
      (4) 2.54
      (5) 4.54, 4.82
   52.12 .... **4.84**, 4.85, 6.11
      (1) 4.86
      (2), (3) 4.85, 6.11
   52.13 .... 3.19, 3.25, 3.26, 3.27,
                3.34, 4.14, **4.88**
      (2) 4.33, 6.23
   52.14 .... 1.12, 3.19, 3.37, 3.37,
                4.111, 4.112
      (2) 3.37
   52.15 .... 1.7, **4.113**, 6.4, 6.5
   52.16 .... 4.53, **4.115**, 5.7, 6.51
      (2) 4.41, 4.116, 5.7
      (3) 4.116, 5.7
   52.17 .... **4.117**, 4.118, 4.120
   PD 52 ...... 1.7, 1.8, **1.11**, 3.38, 4.10,
                4.97, 4.98, **4.122**, 6.1
      para 1.1 .... 4.122
         2.1 .... 4.122
         2.2 .... 1.2, 3.39, 4.122
         2A.1 .... 1.11, 3.21, **4.122**
         2A.2–2A.4 .... 3.21, **4.122**

Civil Procedure Rules 1998, SI 1998/3132 – *cont*
Pt 52 – *cont*
  PD 52 – *contd*
    2A.5 .... **1.11**, **4.122**
    2A.6 .... 1.11, **1.12**, 3.21, **4.122**
    3.1 .... 4.122, 6.2
    3.2 .... 4.18, **4.122**, **6.2**
    4.1–4.4 .... 4.12, **4.122**
    4.5 .... 4.12, 4.17, **4.122**
    4.6 .... 4.12, 4.13, **4.122**
    4.7 .... 4.12, 4.13, **4.122**
    4.8 .... 1.7, 4.12, **4.122**
    4.9 .... 4.12, **4.122**
    4.10 .... 4.12, **4.122**
    4.11, 4.12 ...... 4.12, 4.20, **4.122**, **6.20**
    4.13–4.14 .... 4.12, 4.20, **4.122**, **6.20**
    4.14A 4.20, **4.122**, **6.20**
      (1), (2) **6.20**
    4.15, 4.16 ...... 4.12, 4.21, **4.122**, **6.20**
    4.17 .... 4.12, 4.20, **4.122**, **6.21**
    4.18 .... 4.12, 4.22, **4.122**, **6.22**
      (2) 6.22
    4.19–4.21 .... 4.12, 4.22, **4.122**, **6.22**
    4.22 .... **6.23**
    4.23, 4.24 .... 4.33, **4.122**
    5.1 .... 4.26, **4.122**, **6.1**
    5.1A 4.28, **4.122**, **6.3**
      (1)–(3) **6.3**
    5.1B **4.122**, **6.3**
    5.2 .... 4.26, 4.27, 4.40, 4.42, **4.122**
    5.3 .... 4.26, 4.27, 4.40, **4.122**
    5.4 .... 4.26, 4.27, **4.122**, **6.8**
    5.5 .... 4.26, 4.46, 4.49, **4.122**, 6.6, 6.34
    5.6 ..... 4.26, 4.28, 4.100, **4.122**, 6.7, 6.8, 6.9
      (1), (2) **6.12**
    5.6A 1.7, 3.38, 6.7, 6.8
      (1)–(3) 6.13
    5.7 .... 4.26, **4.122**, 6.13
    5.8 .... 4.26, **4.122**, 6.9
      (1)–(5) **6.14**
    5.8A-5.8D 3.4
    5.9 .... 1.7, 4.26, 4.52, 4.101, **4.122**
      (1)–(3) **6.15**
    5.10 .... 4.26, **4.122**, 6.15, 6.29

Civil Procedure Rules 1998, SI 1998/3132 – *cont*
Pt 52 – *cont*
  PD 52 – *contd*
    (1)–(5) **6.16**
    (6) 4.97, **6.16**
    5.11 .... 4.26, **4.122**, 6.16
    5.12 ..... 4.26, 4.100, **4.122**, 6.17
      (1)–(4) **6.17**
    5.13 .... **6.17**
    5.14 ..... 4.26, 4.100, **4.122**, 6.17
    5.15–5.18 .... 4.26, **4.122**, 6.17
    5.19 .... 1.7, 4.26, 4.27, 4.39, **4.122**, 6.4, **6.5**
    5.20 .... 4.26, **4.122**, 6.4
    5.21 .... 1.8, 4.26, 4.102, **4.122**
      (1), (2) **6.18**
    5.22 .... 1.8, 4.26, 4.33, 4.102, **4.122**, **6.18**, 6.23
    5.23, 5.24 .... 4.26, **4.122**, 6.18
    5.25 .... 1.7, 4.26, 4.51, 4.52, 4.54, 4.101, **4.122**, 6.19
    6.1 .... **4.122**
    6.2 .... 4.104, **4.122**, 6.24
    6.3 .... **4.122**, 6.24
    6.3A(1) **6.27**
      (2) 6.22, **6.27**
    6.4 .... **4.122**, **6.25**
    6.5 .... 4.105, **4.122**, **6.25**
    6.6 .... **4.122**, **6.26**
    7 .... 4.106, **4.122**
    7.1 .... 4.32, **4.122**, **6.29**
    7.2 .... 4.32, 4.35, **4.122**, **6.29**
    7.3 .... 4.32, **4.122**
      (1) **6.29**
      (2) 4.35, **6.29**
    7.3A **4.122**, **6.29**
    7.4 .... 4.32, **4.122**, **6.31**
    7.5 .... 4.32, 4.36, 4.36, **4.122**, **6.31**
    7.6 .... 1.7, 4.32, 4.35, 4.36, 4.52, 4.101, **4.122**, 6.32
    7.7 .... 4.32, **4.122**
    7.7(1) **6.32**
      (2) 4.36, **6.32**
    7.7A **4.122**
      (1), (2) **6.32**
    7.7B **4.122**, **6.32**
    7.8 .... 4.32, 4.36, **4.122**, **6.33**
    7.9 .... 4.32, 4.49, **4.122**, **6.34**
    7.10 .... 4.32, 4.36, **4.122**
      (1), (2) **6.35**
    7.11, 7.12 .... 4.32, **4.122**, **6.36**

Civil Procedure Rules 1998, SI 1998/3132 – cont
  Pt 52 – cont
    PD 52 – contd
      7.13 .... 4.32, **4.122**, **6.37**
      8.1–8.14 .... **4.122**
      8A.1 .... **4.122**
      9.1 .... 2.7, 4.70, **4.122**
      10.1 .... 3.38, 4.98, **4.122**
      11.1 .... 4.46, **4.122**, **6.6**, **6.34**
      11.2 .... 4.102, **4.122**, **6.6**, **6.34**
      12.1 .... 4.80, **4.122**, **6.52**
      12.2 .... **6.52**
      12.3, 12.4 .... **6.52**
      13.1 .... 4.80, **4.122**, 6.51, **6.53**
      13.2 .... **6.54**
      13.3 .... **6.55**
      13.4 .... **6.56**
      13.5 .... **6.57**
      14.1 .... 4.109, **4.122**, **6.38**
      14.2 .... 4.109, **4.122**, **6.38**
      15.1 .... 4.96, 4.98, **4.122**
        (1) **6.8**
        (2) 4.102, **6.8**
      15.2 ..... 4.96, 4.98, 4.116, **4.122**, 5.7, **6.28**
      15.3 .... 4.96, 4.98, **4.122**, **6.28**
      15.4 .... 4.96, 4.97, 4.98, **4.122**, **6.13**
        (1)–(12) **6.13**
      15.5 ..... 4.96, 4.98, 4.116, **4.122**
      15.6 ..... 4.96, 4.98, 4.106, **4.122**, **6.33**
      15.7 ..... 4.96, 4.98, 4.108, **4.122**
      15.8 ..... 4.96, 4.98, 4.108, **4.122**
      15.9 ..... 4.96, 4.98, 4.108, **4.122**, **6.39**
      15.9A **6.40**
      15.10 .... 4.96, 4.98, 4.116, **4.122**, **6.41**
      15.11 ..... 4.96, 4.98, **4.122**, **6.42**
      15.11A **4.122**, **6.43**
      15.11B **6.44**
        (2) 4.96, 4.97
      15.11C **4.122**, **6.50**
      15.12 ..... 4.96, 4.98, **4.122**, **6.45**
      15.13 ..... 4.96, 4.98, **4.122**, **6.45**
      15.14 ..... 4.96, 4.98, **4.122**, **6.45**
      15.15 ..... 4.96, 4.98, **4.122**, **6.46**
      15.16, 15.17 ... 4.96, 4.98, **4.122**, **6.47**
      15.18 ..... 4.96, 4.98, **4.122**, **6.48**

Civil Procedure Rules 1998, SI 1998/3132 – cont
  Pt 52 – cont
    PD 52 – contd
      15.19–15.21 ... 4.96, 4.98, **4.122**, **6.49**
      16.1, 16.2 .... **4.122**
      17.1 .... **4.122**
        (2) 2.7
      17.2 .... 4.14, **4.122**
      17.3–17.6 .... **4.122**
      18.1–18.18.20 .... **4.122**
      20.1–20.3 .... **4.122**
      21.1 .... 4.98, **4.122**
        (3) 4.27
      21.2, 21.3 .... 4.98, **4.122**
      21.4 .... 4.8, 4.27, 4.44, 4.66, 4.98, **4.122**
      21.5, 21.6 .... 4.98, **4.122**
      21.7 .... 4.91, 4.98, **4.122**
      21.8, 21.9 .... 4.98, **4.122**
      21.10 .... 4.91, 4.98, **4.122**
      21.11 .... 4.98, **4.122**
      22.1–22.8 .... **4.122**
      23.1–23.9 .... **4.122**
      24.1–24.3 .... **4.122**
      25.1 .... 4.121, **4.122**
      25.2–25.7 .... **4.122**
  Pt 54 .... 2.7, 2.18
  Pt 57 .... 1.9, 3.21
    Section I 1.9, 1.10, 3.20
    Section II 1.9, 3.20
    Section III 1.9, 3.20
    Section IV 3.21
  Pt 58 .... 1.9, 1.10, 3.20, 3.21
  Pt 59 .... 1.9, 1.10, 3.20, 3.21
  Pt 60 .... 1.9, 1.10, 3.20, 3.21
  Pt 61 .... 1.9, 1.10, 3.20, 3.21
  Pt 62 .... 1.9, 1.10, 3.20, 3.21
  Pt 63 .... 1.9, 1.10, 3.20, 3.21
  Pt 68 .... 9.11, 9.12, 9.13
    r 68.2 .... 9.11
  Sch 1 RSC
    Ord 67
      r 6(2) 5.2
  Additional Practice Directions
    PD – Insolvency Proceedings
      Pt 4
        para 17.4, 17.8–17.23 .... 3.43
    PD – Protocols
      para 2.1 .... 7.4

F

Family Proceedings Rules 1991,
SI 1991/1247 .... 3.40

S

Supreme Court Fees Order 1980,
SI 1980/821
Schedule
Fee 9.1 .... 4.99

Supreme Court Fees Order 1980, SI
1980/821 – *contd*
Schedule – *contd*
9.1(c) 4.104, 4.105
9.2 .... 4.99

Table of Cases

References in the right-hand column are to chapter and paragraph number and references to set out cases in the appendices are in **bold** type.

A

AEI Rediffusion Music Ltd v Phonographic Performance Ltd (No 2). See Phonographic Performance Ltd v AEI Redifussion Music Ltd
Ager v Ager [1998] 1 All ER 703, [1998] 1 WLR 1074, [1998] 3 FCR 355, [1998] 1 FLR 506, [1998] Fam Law 253, [1997] All ER (D) 127, CA 5.9
Akerhielm v De Mare [1959] AC 789, [1959] 3 All ER 485, [1959] 3 WLR 108, 103 Sol Jo 527, PC 2.36
Allmänna Svenska Elektriska A/B v Burntisland Shipbuilding Co Ltd [1951] 2 Lloyd's Rep 493, 69 RPC 63, CA 2.50
Antaios Cia Naviera SA v Salen Rederierna AB, The Antaios [1985] AC 191, [1984] 3 All ER 229, [1984] 3 WLR 592, [1984] 2 Lloyd's Rep 235, 128 Sol Jo 564, [1984] LS Gaz R 2776, HL 2.24
Aoun v Bahri [2002] EWCA Civ 1141, [2002] All ER (D) 511 (Jul) 4.48, **A2.1**
Armagas Ltd v Mundogas SA, The Ocean Frost [1985] 1 Lloyd's Rep 1; on appeal [1986] AC 717, [1985] 3 All ER 795, [1985] 3 WLR 640, [1985] 1 Lloyd's Rep 1, 129 Sol Jo 362, [1984] LS Gaz R 2169, CA; affd [1986] AC 717, [1986] 2 All ER 385, [1986] 2 WLR 1063, [1986] 2 Lloyd's Rep 109, 2 BCC 99,197, 130 Sol Jo 430, [1986] LS Gaz R 2002, [1986] NLJ Rep 511, HL 2.45, 2.46
Asiansky Television v Bayer Rosin (a firm) [2001] EWCA Civ 1792, [2002] CPLR 111, [2001] All ER (D) 271 (Nov) 2.5, 2.6, 4.72
Assicurazioni Generali SpA v Arab Insurance Group (BSC) [2002] EWCA Civ 1642, [2003] 1 All ER (Comm) 140, [2003] 1 WLR 577, [2003] Lloyd's Rep IR 131, [2003] 03 LS Gaz R 34, [2002] All ER (D) 177 (Nov) 2.53, 4.73
Athletic Union of Constantinople v National Basketball Association (No 2) [2002] EWCA Civ 830, [2002] 3 All ER 897, [2002] 1 WLR 2863 .... 4.6
A-G v Birmingham, Tame and Rea District Drainage Board [1912] AC 788, 11 LGR 194, 76 JP 481, 82 LJ Ch 45, [1911–13] All ER Rep 926, 107 LT 353, HL 2.76
Australia and New Zealand Banking Group Ltd v Société Générale [2000] 1 All (Comm) 682, CA 4.18
Azimi v London Borough of Newham (2001) 33 HLR 51 .... 1.6, 3.28, 4.89

B

B (a minor) (rejection of expert evidence), Re [1996] 3 FCR 272, sub nom B (care: expert witness), Re [1996] 1 FLR 667, [1996] Fam Law 347, CA 2.20

B (children: non-accidental injury), Re [2002] EWCA Civ 902,
[2002] 2 FCR 654, [2002] 2 FLR 599, [2002] Fam Law 655, [2002] All
ER (D) 452 (May) 4.2
Balani (Hiro) v Spain (Application 18064/91) (1994) 19 EHRR 566,
ECtHR 2.26
Banks v Cox (17 July 2000, unreported), CA 2.67
Barings plc (in liquidation) v Coopers & Lybrand (a firm)
[2002] EWCA Civ 1155, [2002] All ER (D) 278 (Jul) 4.57, A2.2
Barnet London Borough Council v Hurst [2002] EWCA Civ 1009,
[2002] 4 All ER 457, [2003] 1 WLR 722, [2003] HLR 244,
[2002] 36 LS Gaz R 39, [2002] NLJR 1275, [2002] All ER (D) 260
(Jul) 1.7, 3.18
Bartlam v Evans. See Evans v Bartlam
Beedell v West Ferry Printers Ltd [2001] EWCA Civ 400, [2001] ICR
962, (2001) Times, 5 April, [2001] All ER (D) 177 (Mar) 4.57, A2.3
Bell Electric Ltd v Aweco Appliance Systems GmbH & Co KG
[2002] EWCA Civ 1501, [2003] 1 All ER 344, [2002] All ER (D) 460
(Oct) 4.63
Bellenden (formerly Satterthwaite) v Satterthwaite [1948] 1 All ER
343, CA 2.57
Benmax v Austin Motor Co Ltd [1955] AC 370, [1955] 1 All ER 326,
[1955] 2 WLR 418, 72 RPC 39, 99 Sol Jo 129, HL 2.49, 2.50, 2.51, 2.52
Bhamjee v Forsdick (No 2) [2003] EWCA Civ 1113, [2004] 1 WLR 88,
[2003] 36 LS Gaz R 41, [2003] All ER (D) 429 (Jul) 4.2, 4.58, 5.1
Biogen Inc v Medeva plc [1997] RPC 1, 38 BMLR 149, HL 2.50
British Telecommunications plc v Sheridan [1990] IRLR 27, CA 2.20
Bulled v Khayat [2002] EWCA Civ 804 .... 4.2, 4.15

C

CEL Group Ltd v Nedlloyd Lines UK Ltd [2003] EWCA Civ 1871,
(2004) Times, 2 January 4.87
CG v United Kingdom (Application 43373/98) 34 EHRR 31, (2002)
Times, 4 January, ECtHR 2.83
CIBC Mellon Trust Co v Mora Hotel Corpn [2002] EWCA Civ 1688,
[2003] 1 All ER 564, [2003] 03 LS Gaz R 30, [2002] All ER (D) 270
(Nov) 4.68, A2.4
CMA CGM SA v Beteiligungs-Kommanditgesellschaft MS Northern
Pioneer Schiffahrtgesellschaft mbH & Co [2002] EWCA Civ 1878,
[2003] 1 All ER (Comm) 204, [2003] 3 All ER 330, [2003] 1 WLR
1015, [2003] 1 Lloyd's Rep 212, [2003] 09 LS Gaz R 28, [2002] All ER
(D) 286 (Dec) 4.6
Cable & Wireless plc v IBM United Kingdom Ltd [2002] EWHC 2059
(Comm), [2002] 2 All ER (Comm) 1041, [2002] NLJR 1652, [2003]
BLR 89, [2002] All ER (D) 277 (Oct) 7.2, 7.3
Cachia v Faluyi [2001] EWCA Civ 998, [2002] 1 All ER 192,
[2001] 1 WLR 1966, [2001] 29 LS Gaz R 39, [2002] PIQR P39, 145
Sol Jo LB 167, [2001] All ER (D) 299 (Jun) 2.90
Calden (Administrator of Calden's Estate v Dr Nunn and Partners
[2003] EWCA Civ 200, [2003] All ER (D) 265 (Feb) 4.17
Claims Direct Test Cases [2002] EWCA Civ 428, [2002] PIQR Q152,
(2002) Times, 4 April, [2002] All ER (D) 286 (Mar) 3.38, 4.112

Clark (Inspector of Taxes) v Perks [2000] STC 1080, [2000] 4 All ER 1,
[2001] 1 WLR 17, [2000] All ER (D) 1187 ... 1.12, 3.20, 3.28, 3.37, 4.3, 4.89, 4.112, **A2.5**
Coghlan v Cumberland [1898] 1 Ch 704, 67 LJ Ch 402, 78 LT 540, CA 2.38
Colley v Council for Licensed Conveyancers [2001] EWCA Civ 1137,
[2001] 4 All ER 998, [2002] 1 WLR 160, [2001] NPC 116,
[2001] 31 LS Gaz R 31, [2001] 30 EGCS 115, [2001] NLJR 1249, 145
Sol Jo LB 201, [2001] All ER (D) 216 (Jul) 4.14
Colonial Securities Trust Ltd v Massey [1896] 1 QB 38, 65 LJQB 100,
44 WR 212, 40 Sol Jo 83, 73 LT 497, 12 TLR 57, CA 2.36
Contract Facilities Ltd v Estate of Rees [2003] EWCA Civ 1105, 147
Sol Jo LB 933, [2003] All ER (D) 415 (Jul) 4.63, 4.68, **A2.6**
Cooke v Secretary of State for Social Security [2001] EWCA Civ 734,
[2002] 3 All ER 279, [2001] All ER (D) 175 (Apr) 3.30, 4.91
Cooper v Floor Cleaning Machines [2003] EWCA Civ 1649,
[2003] 43 LS Gaz R 32, [2003] All ER (D) 322 (Oct) 2.30
Corenso v Burnden Group (2003) LTL, 21 August 7.6
Council of Civil Service Unions v Minister for the Civil Service
[1985] AC 374, [1984] 3 All ER 935, [1984] 3 WLR 1174, [1985] ICR
14, 128 Sol Jo 837, [1985] LS Gaz R 437, sub nom R v Secretary of
State for Foreign and Commonwealth Affairs, ex p Council of Civil
Service Unions [1985] IRLR 28, HL 2.22
Coventry, Re, Coventry v Coventry [1980] Ch 461, [1979] 2 All ER 408,
[1979] 2 WLR 853, 123 Sol Jo 406; affd [1980] Ch 461,
[1979] 3 All ER 815, [1979] 3 WLR 802, 123 Sol Jo 606, CA 2.51
Cowl v Plymouth City Council [2001] EWCA Civ 1935, [2002] 1 WLR
803, (2002) Times, 8 January, [2001] All ER (D) 206 (Dec) 7.2, 7.3
Culver (infant) v Beard [1938] 2 KB 292n, [1937] 1 All ER 301, 81 Sol
Jo 156, CA 2.23
Curwen v James [1963] 2 All ER 619, [1963] 1 WLR 748, 107 Sol Jo
314, CA 2.76

D

D (child), Re (FAFMF 99/1102) (8 November 1999, unreported) 4.100
Daniels v Walker [2000] 1 WLR 1382, [2000] All ER (D) 608, CA 2.89
Deg-Deutsche Investitions und Entwicklungsgesellschaft mbH v Koshy
[2001] EWCA Civ 79, [2001] 3 All ER 878, [2001] 09 LS Gaz R 40,
(2001) Times, 6 February, 145 Sol Jo LB 36, [2001] All ER (D) 225
(Jan) 2.79
Designers Guild Ltd v Russell Williams (Textiles) Ltd [2001] 1 All ER
700, [2000] 1 WLR 2416, [2001] FSR 113, [2000] All ER (D) 1950,
[2001] IP & T 277, HL 2.52
Dobie v Burns International Security Services (UK) Ltd
[1984] 3 All ER 333, [1985] 1 WLR 43, [1984] ICR 812, [1984] IRLR
329, 128 Sol Jo 872, CA 2.21
Dominion Trust Co v New York Life Insurance Co [1919] AC 254, 88
LJPC 30, 119 LT 748, PC 2.48
Donaldson v Wilson [2004] EWCA Civ 123 .... 4.22
Dunnett v Railtrack plc (in railway administration) [2002] EWCA Civ
303, [2002] 2 All ER 850 .... 7.1, 7.3
Du Pont (EI) De Nemours & Co v ST Dupont [2003] EWCA Civ 1368,
147 Sol Jo LB 1207, [2004] IP & T 559, [2003] All ER (D) 185 (Oct) 2.3, 2.7
Dyson Ltd v Registrar of Trademarks (2003) Times, 23 May 4.74

E

E v Secretary of State for the Home Department [2004] EWCA Civ 49,
  [2004] 07 LS Gaz R 35, 148 Sol Jo LB 180, [2004] All ER (D) 16
  (Feb) 2.34, 2.72
Eagil Trust Co Ltd v Pigott Brown [1985] 3 All ER 119, CA 2.24, 2.25
Eckersley v Binnie (1987) 18 Con LR 1, CA 2.41
Edwards (Inspector of Taxes) v Bairstow [1956] AC 14, [1955] 3 All ER
  48, [1955] 3 WLR 410, 36 TC 207, 34 ATC 198, 48 R & IT 534,
  [1955] TR 209, 99 Sol Jo 558, L(TC) 1742, HL 2.22, 2.52
Egerton v Jones [1939] 2 KB 702, [1939] 3 All ER 889, 108 LJKB 857,
  83 Sol Jo 688, 161 LT 205, 55 TLR 1089, CA 2.58
Electra Private Equity Partners v KPMG Peat Marwick [2001] 1 BCLC
  589, [1999] All ER (D) 415, CA 2.66, 2.70, A2.7
Engineers' and Managers' Association v Advisory, Conciliation and
  Arbitration Service (No 2) [1979] 3 All ER 227, [1979] 1 WLR 1113,
  [1979] ICR 637, [1979] IRLR 246, 123 Sol Jo 353, CA; revsd
  [1980] 1 All ER 896, [1980] 1 WLR 302, [1980] ICR 215,
  [1980] IRLR 164, 124 Sol Jo 202, HL 2.76, 2.77
English v Emery Reimbold & Strick Ltd [2002] EWCA Civ 605,
  [2002] 3 All ER 385, [2003] IRLR 710, [2002] All ER (D) 302 (Apr) 2.25, 4.78
Evans v Bartlam [1937] AC 473, [1937] 2 All ER 646, 106 LJKB 568, 81
  Sol Jo 549, 53 TLR 689, sub nom Bartlam v Evans 157 LT 311, HL 2.7, 2.14

F

F (a minor), Re [1992] 1 FCR 167, [1992] 1 FLR 561, [1992] Fam Law
  330, CA 5.5
Fieldman v Markovic (2001) Times, July 4 .... 4.22
Flannery v Halifax Estate Agencies Ltd (t/a Colleys Professional
  Services) [2000] 1 All ER 373, [2000] 1 WLR 377,
  [1999] 13 LS Gaz R 32, [1999] NLJR 284, [1999] BLR 107, CA 2.25
Foenander v Bond Lewis & Co [2001] EWCA Civ 759, [2001] 2 All ER
  1019, [2002] 1 WLR 525, [2001] NLJR 890, [2001] All ER (D) 286
  (May) 1.5, 3.35, 4.43, 4.92, A2.8
Fowler de Pledge (a firm) v Smith [2003] EWCA Civ 703,
  [2003] 30 LS Gaz R 31, [2003] All ER (D) 261 (May) 2.10, 4.3, 4.92

G

G v G [1985] 2 All ER 225, [1985] 1 WLR 647, [1985] FLR 894,
  [1985] Fam Law 321, 129 Sol Jo 315, HL 2.13, 2.57, 4.75
Gabriel v Kirklees Metropolitan Council [2004] EWCA Civ 345, [2004]
  All ER (D) 462 (Mar) 2.30
Garcia Ruiz v Spain (2001) 31 EHRR 589 .... 2.26
Garratt v Saxby [2004] EWCA Civ 341, 148 Sol Jo LB 237, [2004] All
  ER (D) 302 (Feb) 4.86, 6.11
Gill v London Borough of Southwark (8 May 2000, unreported), CA 5.5
Glannibanta, The (1876) 1 PD 283, 24 WR 1033, sub nom The Transit
  3 Asp MLC 233, 2 Char Pr Cas 18, 34 LT 934, CA 2.37
Golding v Wharton Saltworks Co (1876) 1 QBD 374, 24 WR 423, 34
  LT 474, CA 2.56

Table of Cases xxiii

Goode v Martin [2001] EWCA Civ 1899, [2002] 1 All ER 620,
[2002] 1 WLR 1828, [2002] NLJR 109, (2002) Independent,
16 January, [2001] All ER (D) 167 (Dec) 2.90
Government of Sierra Leone v Davenport [2002] EWCA Civ 230, [2002]
All ER (D) 160 (Jan) 3.17
Gow v Harker [2003] EWCA Civ 1160, [2003] 38 LS Gaz R 35, [2003]
All ER (D) 12 (Aug) 2.46
Grace Shipping Inc and Hai Nguan & Co v C F Sharp & Co (Malaya)
Pte Ltd [1987] 1 Lloyd's Rep 207, PC 2.45
Grant v Kent County Council [2003] EWCA Civ 1917 .... 4.23
Grayan Building Services Ltd (in liquidation), Re [1995] Ch 241,
[1995] 3 WLR 1, [1995] 1 BCLC 276, [1995] BCC 554, 138 Sol Jo LB
227, CA 2.51
Great Future International Ltd v Sealand Housing Corpn
[2003] EWCA Civ 682, [2003] All ER (D) 365 (May) 4.67, **A2.9**
Gregory v Turner [2003] EWCA Civ 183, [2003] 2 All ER 1114,
[2003] 1 WLR 1149, [2003] All ER (D) 267 (Feb) 4.16

H

H (children) (application for rehearing), Re [2003] EWCA Civ 345,
[2003] All ER (D) 222 (Mar) 4.120
Hackney London Borough Council v Driscoll [2003] EWCA Civ 14 .... 2.8
Hadmor Productions Ltd v Hamilton [1983] 1 AC 191, [1982] 1 All ER
1042, [1982] 2 WLR 322, [1982] ICR 114, [1982] IRLR 102, 126 Sol
Jo 134, HL 2.14, 2.61, 2.73, 2.76
Halsey v Milton Keynes General NHS Trust [2004] EWCA Civ 576,
[2004] NLJR 769, 148 Sol Jo LB 629, [2004] All ER (D) 125 (May) 7.2, 7.3, 7.4
Hamilton v Al-Fayed (No 4) [2001] EMLR 15 .... 2.69
Hammond Suddard Solicitors v Agrichem International Holdings Ltd
[2001] EWCA Civ 2065, [2001] All ER (D) 258 (Dec) 4.23, 4.46, 4.61, 4.63, **A2.10**
Hampshire County Council v Gillingham (22 June 2000,
unreported), CA 1.7, 3.18
Harvey Shop Fitters Ltd v ADI Ltd [2003] EWCA Civ 1757, (2003)
Times, 26 November 4.92
Heath v Tang [1993] 4 All ER 694, [1993] 1 WLR 1421, CA 5.6, 8.71
Helle v Finland (Application 20772/92) (1997) 26 EHRR 159, ECtHR 2.26
Henry Boot Construction (UK) Ltd v Malmaison Hotel
(Manchester) Ltd [2001] QB 388, [2001] 1 All ER 257, [2000] 3 WLR
1824, [2000] 2 All ER (Comm) 960, [2000] 2 Lloyd's Rep 625, 72 Con
LR 1, [2000] NLJR 867, [2000] BLR 509, CA 3.27, 4.6
Hertfordshire Investments Ltd v Bubb [2000] 1 WLR 2318, [2000] All
ER (D) 1052, CA 2.68, 2.71, **A2.11**
Herefordshire and Worcester County Council v Neale [1986] IRLR
168, CA 2.22
Hertsmere Borough Council v Harty [2001] EWCA Civ 1238 .... 4.57, 4.108
Hickey v Marks (6 July 2000, unreported), CA 2.15
Hitco 2000 Ltd, Re [1995] 2 BCLC 63, [1995] BCC 161 .... 2.51
Hontestroom, SS v SS Sagaporack [1927] AC 37, 95 LJP 153, 17 Asp
MLC 123, 136 LT 33, 42 TLR 741, [1927] All ER Rep Ext 831, 25 Ll
L Rep 377, HL 2.39, 2.45
Hunt v Peasegood (2000) Times, 20 October, CA 4.57, **A2.12**

Hurst v Leeming [2002] EWHC 1051 (Ch), [2003] 1 Lloyd's Rep 379,
[2002] All ER (D) 135 (May) 7.3
Hyams v Plender [2001] 2 All ER 179, [2001] 1 WLR 32, [2000] All ER
(D) 1361, CA 3.9, 3.11, 3.15, 3.16, 3.25

I

Indrakumar v Secretary of State for the Home Department
[2003] EWCA Civ 1677, 147 Sol Jo LB 1366, [2003] All ER (D) 188
(Nov) 2.55

J

J (a child) [2001] EWCA Civ 1813 .... 4.20
JL v Finland No 32526/1996 .... 9.7
Jenkins v BP Oil UK Ltd. See Clark (Inspector of Taxes) v Perks
Jennings v Cairns [2003] EWCA Civ 1935, (2003) Times, 26 November 4.97
Jolly v Jay [2002] EWCA Civ 277, [2002] All ER (D) 104 (Mar) 3.35, 4.15, 4.33, 4.93,
6.23, A2.13
Jones v MBNA International Bank (30 June 2000, unreported), CA 4.18, 4.54, 4.82
Jordan v Jordan [1992] 2 FCR 701, [1993] 1 FLR 169, [1993] Fam Law
204, CA 4.40

K

Khoo Sit Hoh v Lim Thean Tong [1912] AC 323, 81 LJPC 176, 106 LT
470, PC 2.42
King v Read and Slack [1999] 1 FLR 425, [1999] Fam Law 90, CA 1.7, 3.18
Knight v Clifton [1971] Ch 700, [1971] 2 All ER 378, [1971] 2 WLR
564, 115 Sol Jo 60, CA 2.24
Koller v Secretary of State for the Home Department [2001] EWCA Civ
1267 .... 3.30, 4.91, **A2.15**
Koua Poirrez v France (40892/98, 30 September 2003) 9.1

L

Ladd v Marshall [1954] 3 All ER 745, [1954] 1 WLR 1489, 98 Sol Jo
870, CA 2.34, 2.65, 2.72
Lake v Lake [1955] P 336, [1955] 2 All ER 538, [1955] 3 WLR 145, 99
Sol Jo 432, CA 4.18
Lane v Esdaile [1891] AC 210, 60 LJ Ch 644, 40 WR 65, 64 LT 666, HL 8.5
Langdale v Danby [1982] 3 All ER 129, [1982] 1 WLR 1123, 126 Sol Jo
537, [1982] LS Gaz R 1258, HL 2.65
Lim Poh Choo v Camden and Islington Area Health Authority
[1980] AC 174, [1979] 2 All ER 910, [1979] 3 WLR 44, 123 Sol Jo
457, HL 2.76
Lloyd Jones v T Mobile (UK) Ltd [2003] EWCA Civ 1162,
[2003] 39 LS Gaz R 39, [2003] NLJR 1308, 147 Sol Jo LB 1027,
[2003] All ER (D) 561 (Jul) 4.13, 4.23, **A2.14**
Lloyds TSB Bank plc v Hayward [2002] EWCA Civ 1813, [2002] All ER
(D) 161 (Dec) 2.28

M

Madray v Madray [2001] EWCA Civ 524 .... 4.94
Mahomed v Morris [2000] 2 BCLC 536, [2001] BCC 233,
  [2000] 07 LS Gaz R 41, [2000] All ER (D) 193, CA 4.20, 4.83
Major v Lamyman [2003] EWCA Civ 1701, [2003] All ER (D) 443
  (Nov) 4.95
Mangan v Metropolitan Electric Supply Co [1891] 2 Ch 551, 65 LT 202,
  7 TLR 553, CA 2.57
Matlaszek v Bloom Camillion (a firm) [2003] EWCA Civ 154, [2003] All
  ER (D) 38 (Feb) 4.118
Maxwell v Keun [1928] 1 KB 645, 97 LJKB 305, [1927] All ER Rep
  335, 72 Sol Jo 48, 138 LT 310, 44 TLR 100, CA 2.57
Michael v Miller [2004] EWCA Civ 282, 148 Sol Jo LB 387, [2004] All
  ER (D) 399 (Mar) 7.6
Miller v Allied Sainiff (UK) Ltd (2000) Times, 31 October 5.3
Milward v Three Rivers District Council (25 October 2000,
  unreported), CA 4.3, A2.16
Miriki v General Council of the Bar [2001] EWCA Civ 1973,
  [2002] ICR 505, (2002) Times, 22 January, [2001] All ER (D) 364
  (Dec) 4.18
Mitchell (George) (Chesterhall) Ltd v Finney Lock Seeds Ltd [1983] QB
  284, [1983] 1 All ER 108, [1982] 3 WLR 1036, [1983] 1 Lloyd's Rep
  168, 126 Sol Jo 689, [1982] LS Gaz R 1144, CA; affd [1983] 2 AC
  803, [1983] 2 All ER 737, [1983] 3 WLR 163, [1983] 2 Lloyd's Rep
  272, [1983] Com LR 209, HL 2.51
Montgomerie & Co Ltd v Wallace-James [1904] AC 73, 73 LJPC 25,
  [1900–03] All ER Rep 926, 90 LT 1, HL 2.48
Muman v Nagasena [1999] 4 All ER 178, [2000] 1 WLR 299, CA 7.3
Murphy v Stone Wallwork (Charlton) Ltd [1969] 2 All ER 949,
  [1969] 1 WLR 1023, 113 Sol Jo 546, HL 2.74, 2.77

N

Napp Pharmaceutical Holdings Ltd v Director General of Fair Trading
  [2002] EWCA Civ 796, [2002] 4 All ER 376, 64 BMLR 165, 69
  BMLR 69, [2002] All ER (D) 31 (Jul) 3.30, 4.91
Nasser v United Bank of Kuwait [2001] EWCA Civ 556,
  [2002] 1 All ER 401, [2002] 1 WLR 1868, [2001] All ER (D) 146
  (Apr) 4.56
Nathan v Smilovitch [2002] EWCA Civ 759, [2002] All ER (D) 573
  (May) 4.57
Norman v King [1946] 1 All ER 339, 39 BWCC 1, CA 2.23

O

Okta Crude Oil Refinery AD v Moil-Coal Trading Co Ltd
  [2003] EWCA Civ 617 .... 4.57
Ord v Upton (as trustee to the property of Ord) [2000] Ch 352,
  [2000] 1 All ER 193, [2000] 2 WLR 755, [2000] 01 LS Gaz R 22,
  [1999] NLJR 1904, 144 Sol Jo LB 35, [2000] BPIR 104, CA 5.6

Owusu v Jackson (t/a Villa Holidays Ball-Inn Villas) [2002] EWCA Civ
877, [2003] PIQR 186, [2002] All ER (D) 130 (Jun) 4.27, 6.4, 9.15, **A2.17**
Ocean Frost, The. See Armagas Ltd v Mundogas SA, The Ocean Frost

P

Paragon Finance plc v Noueiri [2001] EWCA 1114 .... 4.107
Parker v Hutchings [2004] EWCA Civ 254 .... 4.119
Paulson v Bandegani [2001] EWCA Civ 1274 .... 4.2
Pepin v Watts [2001] CPLR 9, CA 4.89
Philosophy Inc v Ferretti Studio Srl [2002] EWCA Civ 921, [2003] RPC
287, [2002] All ER (D) 72 (Jun) 4.33
Phonographic Performance Ltd v AEI Rediffusion Music Ltd
[1999] 2 All ER 299, [1999] RPC 599, sub nom AEI Rediffusion
Music Ltd v Phonographic Performance Ltd (No 2) [1999] 1 WLR
1507, 143 Sol Jo LB 97, [1999] EMLR 335, CA 2.59
Piggott Bros & Co Ltd v Jackson [1992] ICR 85, [1991] IRLR 309, CA 2.22
Plymouth City Council v Hoskin [2002] EWCA Civ 684, [2002] CP Rep
55 .... 4.3
Poplar Housing and Regeneration Community Association Ltd v
Donoghue [2001] EWCA Civ 595, [2001] Fam Law 588, [2002] QB 48,
[2001] 4 All ER 604, [2001] 3 WLR 183, [2001] 3 FCR 74,
[2001] 2 FLR 284, 33 HLR 823, [2001] 19 LS Gaz R 38,
[2001] 19 EGCS 141, 145 Sol Jo LB 122, [2001] All ER (D) 210 (Apr) 4.27
Poshokhov v Russia (No 63486/2000) 9.6
Powell v Streatham Manor Nursing Home [1935] AC 243, 104 LJKB
304, [1935] All ER Rep 58, 79 Sol Jo 179, 152 LT 563, 51 TLR
289, HL 2.37
Practice Direction (Civil Litigation: Case Management) [1995] 1 WLR
262, [1995] 1 All ER 385 .... 7.5
Practice Direction (Court of Appeal: Procedure) [1995] 1 WLR 1191,
[1995] 3 All ER 850 .... 7.5
Practice Direction (Court of Appeal: Procedure) [1999] 2 All ER 490,
[1999] 1 WLR 1027, CA 3.29
Practice Statement (Commercial Court) (Alternative Dispute
Resolution) [1994] 1 WLR, [1994] 1 All ER 34 .... 7.5
Pridding v Secretary of State for Work and Pensions [2002] EWCA Civ
306, [2002] All ER (D) 30 (Mar) 4.42
Purdy v Cambran [1999] CPLR 843. CA 2.67

Q

Quilter v Mapleson (1882) 9 QBD 672, 47 JP 342, 52 LJQB 44, 31 WR
75, 47 LT 561, CA 2.75

R

R v Criminal Injuries Compensation Board, ex p A [1999] 2 AC 330,
[1999] 2 WLR 974, [1999] COD 244, 143 Sol Jo LB 120, HL 2.34
R (on the application of Burkett) v Hammersmith and Fulham London
Borough Council [2002] UKHL 23, [2002] 3 All ER 97,
[2002] 1 WLR 1593, [2002] All ER (D) 363 (May) 4.114

R (Idubo) v Home Secretary [2003] EWCA Civ 1203 .... 4.15
R (on the application of nine Nepalese asylum seekers) v Immigration
   Appeal Tribunal [2003] EWCA Civ 1892, [2004] All ER (D) 94 (Jan) 4.59, 5.1, A2.18
R (on the application of Werner) v IRC [2002] EWCA Civ 979,
   [2002] STC 1213 .... 4.114
R (on the application of Alconbury Developments Ltd) v Secretary of
   State for the Environment, Transport and the Regions [2001] UKHL
   23, [2003] 2 AC 295, [2001] 2 All ER 929, [2001] 2 WLR 1389, 82 P
   & CR 513, [2001] 2 PLR 76, 151 NLJ 727, (2001) Times, 10 May, 145
   Sol Jo LB 140, [2001] All ER (D) 116 (May) 2.34
R v Secretary of State for Foreign and Commonwealth Affairs,
   ex p Council of Civil Service Unions. See Council of Civil Service
   Unions v Minister for the Civil Service
R (on the application of Gunn) v Secretary of State for the Home
   Department [2001] EWCA Civ 891, [2001] 3 All ER 481,
   [2001] 1 WLR 1634, [2001] 27 LS Gaz R 38, [2001] NLJR 936, 145
   Sol Jo LB 160, [2001] All ER (D) 120 (Jun) 4.109
R (on the application of Pharis) v Secretary of State for the Home
   Department [2004] EWCA Civ 654, [2004] All ER (D) 353 (May) 4.47
R (on the application of Sezek) v Secretary of State for the Home
   Department [2001] EWCA Civ 795, [2002] 1 WLR 348,
   [2001] Imm AR 657, [2001] All ER (D) 336 (May) 4.66
R v Secretary of State for Trade and Industry, ex p Eastaway
   [2001] 1 All ER 27, [2000] 1 WLR 2222, 144 Sol Jo LB 282, HL 4.114
R (on the application of Sivasubramaniam) v Wandsworth County
   Court [2002] EWCA Civ 1738, [2003] 2 All ER 160, [2003] 1 WLR
   475, [2003] 03 LS Gaz R 34, [2002] All ER (D) 431 (Nov) 4.16
Reef Trade Mark. See South Cone Inc v Bessant (t/a Reef)
Riniker v University College London [2001] 1 WLR 13, CA 3.35
Robert v Momentum Services Ltd [2003] EWCA Civ 299,
   [2003] 2 All ER 74, [2003] 1 WLR 1577, [2003] 14 LS Gaz R 29,
   [2003] All ER (D) 125 (Feb) 4.42
Robert Horne Group plc v Ablett [2003] EWCA Civ 1310 .... 4.33
Robinson v Fernsby [2003] EWCA Civ 1820, 148 Sol Jo LB 59, [2003]
   All ER (D) 414 (Dec) 4.27
Runa Begum v Tower Hamlets London Borough Council [2003] UKHL
   5, [2003] 2 AC 430, [2003] 1 All ER 731, [2003] 2 WLR 388,
   [2003] LGR 205, [2003] HLR 448, [2003] 13 LS Gaz R 28, 147 Sol Jo
   LB 232, [2003] All ER (D) 191 (Feb), 14 BHRC 400 .... 2.7

S

Savage v Adam [1895] WN 109 .... 2.36
Sayers v Clarke Walker (a firm) [2002] EWCA Civ 645, [2002] 3 All ER
   490, [2002] All ER (D) 189 (May) 4.27, 4.42, 6.4
Scott v Shipp [2001] CPLR 5, CA 4.89
Sengupta v Holmes [2002] EWCA Civ 1104, (2002) Times, 19 August 4.83
Seray-Wurie v Hackney London Borough Council (No 2) [2002] EWCA
   Civ 909, [2002] 3 All ER 448, [2003] 1 WLR 257,
   [2002] 33 LS Gaz R 21, [2002] All ER (D) 199 (Jun) 4.118
Sevenoaks Stationers (Retail) Ltd, Re [1991] Ch 164, [1991] 3 All ER
   578, [1990] 3 WLR 1165, [1991] BCLC 325, [1990] BCC 765, 134 Sol
   Jo 1367, CA 2.51

Sewell v Electrolux Ltd (1997) Times, 7 November, CA 2.31
Shire v Secretary of State for Work and Pensions [2003] EWCA Civ
  1465, [2003] 42 LS Gaz R 32, [2003] All ER (D) 211 (Oct) 4.54, 4.82, **A2.19**
Skrine & Co v Euromoney Publications plc [2001] EWCA Civ 1479,
  [2001] All ER (D) 134 (Oct), CA 4.18
Slot v Isaac [2002] EWCA Civ 481, [2002] All ER (D) 197 (Apr) 4.20, **A2.20**
South Cone Inc v Bessant (t/a Reef) [2002] EWCA Civ 763, [2003] RPC
  101, [2002] All ER (D) 426 (May) 2.52, 4.79
Southern and District Finance plc v Turner [2003] EWCA Civ 1574, 147
  Sol Jo LB 1362, [2003] All ER (D) 112 (Nov) 1.5, 2.10, 4.2, **A2.21**
Storer v British Gas Plc [2000] 2 All ER 440, [2000] 1 WLR 1237,
  [2000] ICR 603, [2000] IRLR 495, CA 2.83
Subesh v Secretary of State for the Home Department [2004] EWCA
  Civ 56, [2004] All ER (D) 326 (Mar) 2.55
Swain v Hillman [2001] 1 All ER 91, [2000] PIQR P51, (1999) Times,
  4 November, CA 4.14

T

Tanfern Ltd v Cameron-MacDonald [2000] 2 All ER 801,
  [2000] 1 WLR 1311, [2000] All ER (D) 654, CA 2.4, 2.7, 2.13, 2.82, 3.29, 3.33, 4.71,
  4.75, **A2.22**
Tasyurdu v Secretary of State for the Home Department [2003] EWCA
  Civ 447, (2003) Times, 16 April 4.108
Taylor v Lawrence [2002] EWCA Civ 90, [2003] QB 528,
  [2002] 2 All ER 353, [2002] 3 WLR 640, [2002] 12 LS Gaz R 35,
  [2002] NLJR 221, 146 Sol Jo LB 50, [2002] All ER (D) 28 (Feb) 4.118
Thompson v Metropolitan Police Comr [1998] QB 498, [1997] 2 All ER
  762, [1997] 3 WLR 403, [1997] NLJR 341, CA 7.3
Three Rivers District Council v Bank of England [2001] UKHL 16,
  [2001] 2 All ER 513, [2001] All ER (D) 269 (Mar) 4.14
Todd v Adam [2002] EWCA Civ 509, [2002] 2 All ER (Comm) 97,
  [2002] 2 Lloyd's Rep 293, [2002] All ER (D) 121 (Apr) 2.7
Toriga (Ruiz) v Spain (Application 18390/91) (1994) 19 EHRR 553,
  ECtHR 2.26
Transit, The. See Glannibanta, The
Turner v Haworth Associates [2001] EWCA Civ 370, [2001] All ER (D)
  309 (Feb) 4.59, 5.1

U

Unilever plc v Chefaro Proprietaries Ltd and other appeals
  [1995] 1 All ER 587, [1995] 1 WLR 243, [1994] NLJR 1660,
  [1995] 1 FLR 1102n, CA 4.108, 4.122, **A2.23**
Utaniko Ltd v P & O Nedlloyd BV [2003] EWCA Civ 174,
  [2003] 1 Lloyd's Rep 265, (2003) Times, 21 February 4.87

V

Van Aken v Camden London Borough Council [2002] EWCA Civ 1724,
  [2003] 1 All ER 552, [2003] 1 WLR 684, [2003] HLR 481,
  [2002] 42 LS Gaz R 38, [2002] All ER (D) 170 (Oct) 4.27

Van de Hurk v Netherlands (Application 16034/90) (1994) 18 EHRR
481, ECtHR 2.26

W

Watt (or Thomas) v Thomas [1947] AC 484, [1947] 1 All ER 582, [1947]
LJR 515, 176 LT 498, 63 TLR 314, 1947 SC 45, HL 2.44
Webb v United Kingdom (1997) 24 EHRR CD 2.26
Westminster City Council v O'Reilly [2003] EWCA Civ 1007,
[2004] 1 WLR 195, [2003] 34 LS Gaz R 31, 147 Sol Jo LB 817, [2003]
All ER (D) 26 (Jul) 4.7
Wilkinson v S [2003] EWCA Civ 95, [2003] 2 All ER 184, [2003] 1 WLR
1254, [2003] 1 FCR 741, [2003] 12 LS Gaz R 29, 147 Sol Jo LB 178,
[2003] All ER (D) 23 (Feb) 3.17
Wilsher v Essex Area Health Authority [1988] AC 1074, [1988] 1 All ER
871, [1988] 2 WLR 557, 132 Sol Jo 418, [1988] 15 LS Gaz R 37,
[1988] NLJR 78, HL 2.40
Wray (Solicitor), Re (1887) 36 Ch D 138, 56 LJ Ch 1106, 36 WR 67, 57
LT 605, 3 TLR 708, CA 2.57

X

X v Germany 25 DR 240 (1981) 2.26

Y

Yell Ltd v Garton [2004] EWCA Civ 87, 148 Sol Jo LB 180, [2004] All
ER (D) 80 (Feb) 4.108
Yorke (MV) Motors v Edwards [1982] 1 All ER 1024, [1982] 1 WLR
444, 126 Sol Jo 245, HL 8.45
Yuill v Yuill [1945] P 15, [1945] 1 All ER 183, 114 LJP 1, 89 Sol Jo 106,
172 LT 114, 61 TLR 176, CA 2.43

CHAPTER 1

Introduction

Scope and Application of the New Regime	1.1
Terminology	1.3
The Main Features of the Appeals Regime	1.7
Appeals to the Court of Appeal	1.8
Routes of Appeal	1.9

SCOPE AND APPLICATION OF THE NEW REGIME

1.1 Part 52 of the CPR came into force on the 2 May 2000 and brought with it one of the biggest procedural changes since the first implementation of the CPR. It provides a uniform procedure for appeals in the county courts, the High Court and the Civil Division of the Court of Appeal and it complements the extensive changes made to the regime for appeals by ss 54–57 of the Access to Justice Act 1999.

This work principally addresses the bringing of appeals under the CPR regime but does contain chapters relating to appeals to the House of Lords and to proceedings in the courts at Luxembourg and Strasbourg.

1.2 There are a few exclusions from the scope of the new Pt 52.
- Part 52 does not apply to appeals in family proceedings in the county courts and in the High Court; these will continue to be regulated by the Family Proceedings Rules. Part 52 does, however, apply to appeals to the Court of Appeal from decisions made in family proceedings: CPR 2.1(2) and PD 52 para 2.2.

2   *Introduction*

- Appeals against decisions of authorised court officers in detailed assessment proceedings are made to a costs judge or a district judge of the High Court under Section VIII of CPR Pt 47[1].
- A significant feature of the regime is that the level of the court to which the appeal is to be made will depend not simply upon the level of judge who made the order or upon the court in which the judge sat but, to a large extent, will depend upon the type of proceedings – namely – the track to which they had been allocated and whether they were commenced by claim form under Pt 7 or the alternative procedure under Pt 8.

1   See the Access to Justice Act 1999 (Destination of Appeals Order) 2000, SI 2000/1071; see also CPR 52.1(2) and PD 52, para 2A.5.

TERMINOLOGY

1.3   The regime cannot be discussed without some of the terms which it uses being explained.

An *appeal* includes an appeal by case stated (Access to Justice Act 1999, s 54(5) and CPR 52.1(3)(a)).

The *lower court* means the court, tribunal or other person or body from whose decision an appeal is brought (CPR 52.1(3)(c)).

The *appeal court* means the court to which the appeal is made (CPR 52.1(3)(b)).

A *respondent* means:
(1)   a party other than the appellant who was a party to the proceedings in the lower court and who is affected by the appeal; and
(2)   a person who is permitted by the appeal court to be a party to the appeal (CPR 52.1(3)(e)).

The *route of appeal* means the appeal court prescribed by an Order made under s 56 of the Access to Justice Act 1999 for the hearing of an appeal in a particular class of case. The relevant Order is the Access to Justice Act 1999 (Destination of Appeals Order) 2000, SI 2000/1071, referred to throughout this work as the 'Destination of Appeals Order'.

A *final decision* (for the purpose of establishing the appropriate route of appeal) is a decision which would finally determine the entire proceedings (subject to any appeal or the assessment of costs) whichever way the court decided the issues before it[1].

A decision which is made at the conclusion of part of a hearing or trial which has been split into parts and would, 'if made at the conclusion of that hearing or trial, have been a final decision' is treated as a final decision for these purposes[2]. Where, for example, a trial is split in relation to the issues of liability and quantum, an order on liability made at the end of the trial on liability will be a final decision for this purpose.

Decisions made on an application for a strike-out or for summary judgment are not, however, final decisions for this purpose[3].

A *second appeal* is an appeal where the decision being appealed was itself made on appeal[4].

1   Arts 1(2)(c) and 1(3) Destination of Appeals Order.
2   Art 1(3) Destination of Appeals Order.
3   Art 1 Destination of Appeals Order.
4   S 55(1) Access to Justice Act 1999 and see para 1.4 below.

1.4 In **general** terms and provided permission has been given, an appellant may appeal – once – any decision (that is, any decision other than a decision of the appeal court dismissing or allowing the appeal).

There are, however, severe restrictions on a party's ability to appeal a decision by an appeal court allowing or dismissing an appeal.

Such appeals are *second appeals* and all second appeals are made to the Court of Appeal. Permission for a second appeal must be and can only be obtained from the Court of Appeal itself[1]. There is a stricter test for such appeals: a second appeal may be made only if the Court of Appeal considers that the appeal raises an important point of principle or practice or there is some other compelling reason for that court to hear it[2].

1   S 55(1) Access to Justice Act 1999.
2   S 55 Access to Justice Act 1999.

1.5 Not every appeal from a decision of an appeal court is necessarily a *second appeal*, even where the effect of the appeal court's decision is that the appeal is at an end. For example:

- An appeal court hears an application to extend the time for filing an appeal notice; it is the first time that that application had been before the court; it dismisses the application without considering the merits of the appeal and, consequently, it is effectively dismissing the appeal; any appeal in respect of the decision not to extend time is a 'first appeal' in the sense that the decision refusing an extension of time has not previously been the subject-matter of an appeal[1];
- An appeal court dismisses an appeal; it makes an order that the appellant pay the costs of the appeal; any appeal in respect of the decision to dismiss the appeal would be a second appeal but an appeal in respect of the order to pay costs is a 'first appeal' in the sense that the decision that

those costs be paid has not previously been the subject-matter of an appeal; subject to permission being given, the order to pay the costs of the appeal may be appealed[2].

The court to which an appeal court's decision is being appealed, for the purpose of establishing whether the appeal before it is a 'first' or 'second' appeal, will focus on the substance of the decision being appealed: where, as in the first of the above examples, an application is made to the appeal court to extend the time for appealing and the appeal court – without considering the merits of the appeal itself – refuses to exercise its discretion to extend time and the appeal fails for that reason, then an appeal from the decision to refuse to extend time is a 'first appeal' and – subject to the giving of permission may be appealed; where, however, on an application to extend time for filing the appeal notice, the appeal court considered the merits of the appeal and, having considered the merits, dismissed the appeal, then any appeal from that decision is a 'second appeal'[3].

1 *Foenander v Bond Lewis & Co* [2001] EWCA Civ 759 (paras 17 and 19) (see **para A2.2**); *Southern & District Finance plc v Turner* [2003] EWCA Civ 1574 (paras 32 and 33). If the proposed appeal lacks merit, the preferable course for the appeal court to take is to consider the merits and either to refuse permission to appeal (where it has not yet been obtained) or to dismiss the appeal, as appropriate. The appeal court hearing an application to extend time should be mindful of the fact that its decision in respect of such an application may be appealed (subject to permission to appeal being given); where the appeal has merit then any injustice to the respondent caused by delay on the part of the appellant in conducting his appeal may be avoided by the giving of limited permission to appeal or by the appeal court's imposing conditions under its case management powers in CPR Pt 3.
2 *Foenander v Bond Lewis & Co* [2001] EWCA Civ 759 (paras 17 and 19) (see **para A2.2**); [2002] 1 WLR 525; [2001] 2 All ER 1019; *Southern & District Finance plc v Turner* [2003] EWCA Civ 1574 (paras 32 and 33).
3 *Foenander v Bond Lewis & Co* [2001] EWCA Civ 759 (paras 17 and 19) (see **para A2.2**); *Southern & District Finance plc v Turner* [2003] EWCA Civ 1574 (paras 32 and 33).

1.6 It must be noted that, because the definition of '*lower court*'[1] includes a person or body making a decision which may appear to be a purely administrative matter, an appeal from such a decision to a court will itself be an appeal – even though that may be the first occasion that the matter comes before a court; consequently, any further appeal thereafter will be a '*second appeal*'; it can only be made to the Court of Appeal and only if the stringent criteria for second appeals are fulfilled. For example: under the Housing Act 1996, a homeless person may request a local housing authority to review his eligibility for assistance and, if dissatisfied with its decision, he may appeal on a point of law to the county court under s 204 of that Act; any appeal from the decision of the county court Judge is not made to a single Judge of the High Court (the usual route for an appeal from a decision of a county court Judge); it is a second appeal and can only be brought in the Court of Appeal[2].

1 See **para 1.3** above.
2 *Azimi v London Borough of Newham* [2001] 33 HLR 569, CA.

THE MAIN FEATURES OF THE APPEALS REGIME

1.7 As with nearly all the provisions in the CPR, Pt 52 is supplemented by its own Practice Direction. The Practice Direction also prescribes the two forms which are required to be used under Pt 52: the appellant's notice (Form N161) and the respondent's notice (Form N162). Some of the more significant features of CPR Pt 52 and its Practice Direction are as follows:

- The time limit for filing an appellant's notice is only **14 days** after the date of the decision appealed against, unless a longer period is directed by the lower court. Where the lower court directs a different period under CPR 52.4 (2)(a), that period should not normally exceed **28 days**: CPR PD 52 para 5.19. If the decision under appeal is in respect of a decision made on **judicial review** then the appellant's notice must be filed within **7 days** of the decision: CPR 52.15.
- The appeal notice should set out the grounds of appeal. It should be comprehensive (but nevertheless succinct) as, at the hearing, the appellant will only be allowed to rely upon matters contained in his notice; he will only be allowed to rely upon other grounds with permission; such permission generally will only be given in circumstances where there is no prejudice to the other party or in exceptional circumstances. Although permission is required to amend an appeal notice[1], the skeleton argument[2] included within the appeal notice may be amended or amplified without permission: CPR 52.8 and CPR PD 52 paras 5.9 and 7.6.
- An appellant is expected to file the appeal bundle with his appellant's notice. A transcript of judgment should accompany the notice: PD 52 para 5.6A. A copy of the transcript should, therefore, be obtained immediately that the decision to appeal is made.
- All appeals from the decision of a judge in a county court or the High Court require permission to appeal except where the appeal is against a committal order, a refusal to grant habeas corpus or a secure accommodation order made under s 25 of the Children Act 1989: CPR 52.3[3].
- The judge who made the decision which is being appealed may himself give permission to appeal at the hearing at which the decision being appealed was made if he considers that an appeal has a real prospect of success or that there is some other compelling reason for the appeal to be heard: CPR 52.3(6) and 52.3(2)(a). If the judge who made the decision does not give permission at the hearing at which the decision to be appealed was made then the appeal court may give it: CPR 52.3(3). If the appeal court refuses permission without holding a hearing, the appellant may seek a hearing within seven days of service of the notice of refusal: CPR 52.3(5). If no application for permission was made to the court which made the order then the application for permission is to be made to the appeal court and should be contained in the appeal notice: CPR 52.3(2).

6 *Introduction*

- Where – after hearing an application for permission – the appeal court refuses permission to appeal, there is no right of appeal against that decision: Access to Justice Act 1999, s.54 (4), CPR 52.3 (3) and (4) and PD 52 para 4.8.
- Every appeal (whether from a district judge to a circuit judge or from a master to a High Court judge or otherwise) will be limited to a review of the decision under appeal unless the practice direction makes different provision or the appeal court (i.e. the court to which the appeal is made) considers that a rehearing should be held in the interests of justice: CPR 52.11(1)(b). Rehearings are quite rare[4].
- The court will review the decision on the basis of the evidence given at the original hearing. No new evidence will be admitted unless the court orders otherwise (CPR 52.11(2)(b)); the adducing of new evidence is only permitted for good reason[5].
- If the decision of the judge is wrong or unjust because of a serious procedural or other irregularity, then the appeal will be allowed: CPR 52.11(3). The judge hearing the appeal has all the powers of the judge of the lower court and may make a wide variety of orders: CPR 52.10(1).

1   PD 52 paras 5.25.
2   There are extensive provisions in the PD in relation to the form and content of the skeleton argument: see **Chapter 6, para 6.16** below.
3   For guidance from the Court of Appeal on this complex issue refer to: *Barnet LBC v Hurst* [2002] EWCA Civ 1009, [2003] 1 WLR 722; [2002] 4 All ER 45, *King v Read and Slack* [1999] 1 FLR 425, CA and *Hampshire County Council v Gillingham, CA* (Unreported, 22 June 2000). See **Chapter 3, paras 3.17–3.18** below.
4   See **Chapter 2, paras 2.3–2.7** below.
5   See **Chapter 2, paras 2.62–2.72** below.

APPEALS TO THE COURT OF APPEAL

1.8   CPR Pt 52 and its Practice Direction apply to appeals to the Court of Appeal. In relation to appeals to the Court of Appeal, particular points to note are:

- *Practice Direction 52*: there are special provisions, which apply only to the Court of Appeal.
- *Sealing and service*: the Court of Appeal seals an appeal notice. Service on the respondent takes place after filing. Unlike the lower courts, the Court of Appeal does **not** effect service; the parties must effect service themselves: CPR PD 52 para 15.1(2). Where the appellant's notice contains an application for permission to appeal, the appellant must serve the notice on the respondent but the respondent need not take any action until such time as permission has been given: CPR PD 52 para 5.21–5.22.

ROUTES OF APPEAL

1.9 The most complicated feature of the regime is the concept of 'routes of appeal' provided by the Destination of Appeals Order[1]. The Order (which is made under s 56 of the Access to Justice Act 1999) provides a different route of appeal for certain county court decisions in that, instead of being made to the Court of Appeal as was previously the case, the appeal will be made to a single High Court judge.

The court to which an appeal is made is principally governed by four factors:
(1) the track to which the claim was allocated;
(2) whether the claim was:
   a. commenced under CPR Pt 7; or
   b. brought in specialist proceedings (that is, under the Companies Acts 1985 or 1989 or proceedings to which Sections I, II or III of CPR Pt 57 or any of CPR Pts 58–63 apply); or
   c. commenced **and** continued by using the alternative method under CPR Pt 8;
(3) the nature of the decision under appeal: is it final or interim[2]?
(4) the level of judge making the decision under appeal.

1 See *'route of appeal'* in **para 1.3** above.
2 See *'final decision'* in **para 1.3** above.

1.10 The position is summarised in the table below. In the table:
(1) all claims are assumed either:
   (a) to have been commenced under CPR Pt 7; or
   (b) to be specialist proceedings under the Companies Acts 1985 or 1989 or proceedings to which Sections I, II or III of CPR Pt 57 or any of CPR Pts 58–63 apply – unless otherwise stated;
(2) references to a circuit judge include a recorder or an assistant recorder and a district judge who is exercising the jurisdiction of a circuit judge with the consent of the parties and the permission of the designated civil judge in respect of that case[1].

COURT	TRACK/ NATURE OF CLAIM	JUDGE WHO MADE DECISION	NATURE OF DECISION UNDER APPEAL	APPEAL COURT
County	Small	District judge	any	Circuit judge in county court

COURT	TRACK/ NATURE OF CLAIM	JUDGE WHO MADE DECISION	NATURE OF DECISION UNDER APPEAL	APPEAL COURT
County	Small	Circuit judge	any	Single judge of the High Court
County	Fast/Multi-track	District judge	case management decision	Circuit judge in county court
County	Fast/Multi-track	District judge	grant or refusal of interim relief (for example, an interim payment)	Circuit judge in county court
County	Fast	District judge	final	Circuit judge in county court
County	Multi-track	District judge	final (for example, assessment of damages)	Court of Appeal
County	Fast/Multi-track	Circuit judge	case management decision	Single judge of the High Court
County	Fast/Multi-track	Circuit judge	grant or refusal of interim relief (for example, an injunction)	Single judge of the High Court

Routes of appeal

COURT	TRACK/ NATURE OF CLAIM	JUDGE WHO MADE DECISION	NATURE OF DECISION UNDER APPEAL	APPEAL COURT
County	CPR Pt 8 (not allocated to any track/simply treated as allocated to the multi-track under CPR 8.9(c)) (but see 'cases where normal route not appropriate', below)	Circuit judge	final	Single judge of the High Court (but see 'cases where normal route not appropriate', below)
County	CPR Pt 8 (specifically allocated to the multi-track by an order made by the lower court)	Circuit judge	final	Court of Appeal
County	Multi-track (other than claim commenced and continuing under CPR Pt 8)	Circuit judge	final	Court of Appeal
High Court	Multi-track	Master or district judge sitting in a district registry	case management decision	Single judge of the High Court
High Court	Multi-track	Master or District Judge sitting in a District Registry	grant or refusal of interim relief (for example, an interim payment)	Single judge of the High Court

10 Introduction

COURT	TRACK/ NATURE OF CLAIM	JUDGE WHO MADE DECISION	NATURE OF DECISION UNDER APPEAL	APPEAL COURT
High Court	Multi-track	Master or District Judge sitting in a District Registry	final (for example, assessment of damages)	Court of Appeal
High Court	Multi-track	High Court judge	case management decision	Court of Appeal
High Court	Multi-track	High Court judge	grant or refusal of interim relief (for example, an interim injunction)	Court of Appeal
High Court	Multi-track	High Court judge	final	Court of Appeal

1   See PD 2B para 11.1(d).

Summary or detailed assessment of costs/enforcement of a final decision

1.11   Practice Direction 52 (para 2A.5) provides that:

'An order made:
(a)   on a summary or detailed assessment of costs; or
(b)   on an application to enforce a final decision
is not a 'final decision' and any appeal from such an order will follow the appeal routes set out in the table in PD 52 para 2A.1.'

That table is set out below:

PD 52: para 2A.1

Decision of:	Appeal made to:
District judge of a county court	Circuit judge
Master or district judge of the High Court	High Court judge
Circuit judge	High Court judge
High Court judge	Court of Appeal

Cases where normal route is not appropriate

1.12 In cases where the normal route of appeal is not considered to be appropriate, s 57 of the Access to Justice Act 1999 enables the 'lower court' judge or the Master of the Rolls to direct that the appeal be heard by the Court of Appeal. Under CPR 52.14 the lower court may exercise this power where it considers that the appeal would raise an important point of principle or practice or there is some other compelling reason for the Court of Appeal to hear it (see PD 52 para 2A.6)[1].

This power is, however, to be used sparingly[2].

1   'PD 52 para 2A.6

(1) Where the decision to be appealed is a final decision in a Pt 8 claim treated as allocated to the multi-track under rule 8.9(c) the court to which the permission application is made should, if permission is given, and unless the appeal would lie to the Court of Appeal in any event, consider whether to order the appeal to be transferred to the Court of Appeal under rule 52.14.

(2) An appeal against a final decision on a point of law in a case which did not involve any substantial dispute of fact would normally be a suitable appeal to be so transferred (see also paragraph 10.1).'

2   *Jenkins v BP Oil UK Ltd*, CA (1 September 2000, unreported); see *Clark v Perks* [2001] 1 WLR 17, 30; [2001] 4 All ER 1 (see **para A2.5**).

CHAPTER 2

An Appeal Court's Methods and its Power to Interfere

Review or rehearing	2.1
The grounds on which an appeal may be allowed	2.11
Appeals founded on an error of law	2.17
Appeals against findings of fact	2.36
Appeals in respect of the exercise of a discretion	2.56
New evidence or change of circumstances as a ground of appeal	2.62
Serious procedural or other irregularity resulting in injustice	2.81
Infringement of Art 6 of Sch 1 to the Human Rights Act 1998: 'Right to a fair trial'	2.84

REVIEW OR REHEARING

2.1 CPR 52.11(1) provides that:

> 'Every appeal will be limited to a review of the decision of the lower court[1] unless:
> (a) a practice direction makes different provision for a particular category of appeal; or
> (b) the court considers that in the circumstances of an individual appeal it would be in the interests of justice to hold a rehearing.'

[1] 'Lower court' means the court, tribunal or other person or body from whose decision an appeal is brought: CPR 52.1(3)(c).

2.2 No further help is provided in relation to the difference between a review and a rehearing, except that para 9 of the Practice Direction to CPR Pt 52 makes express provision in relation to one situation in which a rehearing will be ordered:

> 'The hearing of an appeal will be a rehearing (as opposed to a review of the decision of the lower court) if the appeal is from the decision of a minister, person or other body and the minister, person or other body–
> (1) did not hold a hearing to come to that decision; or
> (2) held a hearing to come to that decision, but the procedure adopted did not provide for the consideration of evidence.'[1]

1   CPR 47.23 prescribes that an appeal to a judge from a decision of an authorised costs officer is by way of rehearing but the rules in CPR Pt 52 do not apply to such an appeal: see CPR 52.1(2).

2.3 Perhaps as a result of this lack of clarity, the difference between a review and a rehearing has caused a good deal of difficulty in practice, and it was not until May LJ's judgment in *E I Du Pont de Nemours & Co v ST Dupont*[1] that there was for the first time a clear description of the way in which the draftsman of CPR Pt 52 had absorbed into one place a number of different earlier appellate regimes, and in so doing had altered the meaning of the word 'rehearing' from that adopted in some earlier contexts.

1   [2003] EWCA Civ 1368.

2.4 Much earlier – in fact only ten days after the new regime came into force – Brooke LJ, in his comprehensive judgment in *Tanfern Ltd v Cameron-MacDonald*[1] (see **para A2.22**) (with which Lord Woolf MR and Peter Gibson LJ agreed) provided early guidance on the effect of CPR 52.11(1) and (3):

> '30. As a general rule, every appeal will be limited to a review of the decision of the lower court. This general rule will be applied unless a practice direction makes different provision for a particular category of appeal, or the court considers that in the circumstances of an individual appeal it would be in the interests of justice to hold a rehearing (r 52.11(1)) ...
>
> 31. This marks a significant change in practice, in relation to what used to be called 'interlocutory appeals' from district judges or masters. Under the old practice, the appeal to a judge was a rehearing in the fullest sense of the word, and the judge exercised his/her discretion afresh, while giving appropriate weight to the way the lower court had exercised its discretion in the matter. Under the new practice, the decision of the lower court will attract much greater significance. The appeal court's duty is now limited to a review of that decision, and it may only interfere in the quite limited circumstances set out in r 52.11(3).'

1   [2000] 2 All ER 801, [2001] 1 WLR 131, CA.

2.5 Additional assistance was furnished In *Asiansky Television plc v Bayer Rosin*[1] where Clarke LJ referred to the question whether an appeal should proceed by way of review or by way of rehearing, and said:

> '10. There was some debate before us as to what criteria should be used to decide that question. However for my part I do not think that it is desirable to fetter the wide discretion which Rule 52.11(1)(b) gives to the court. As I read the rule, it contemplates that in the ordinary case the appeal will be by way of review, but provides for the court to hold a rehearing if it 'considers that in the circumstances of the individual [appeal] it would be in the interests of justice' to do so. Since the circumstances of individual cases may be almost infinitely variable, it is not in my judgment appropriate to lay down criteria to be satisfied before the appeal court holds a rehearing. All will depend on the particular circumstances of the case.'[2]

1   [2001] EWCA Civ 1792; [2002] CPLR 111.
2   See also Jonathan Parker LJ in *Audergon v La Baguette Ltd* [2002] EWCA Civ 10, [2002] *The Times*, 31 January, endorsing this approach..

2.6 In the same case Dyson LJ said (at para 81):

> ' ... [T]here may be cases where it is difficult or impossible to decide an appeal justly without a rehearing; for example, if the judgment of the lower court is so inadequately reasoned that it is not possible for the appeal court to determine the appeal justly without a rehearing; or if there was a serious procedural irregularity in the court below so that, for example, the appellant was prevented from developing his case properly. But where the decision of the lower court is adequately reasoned and there has been no such procedural irregularity, it should usually be possible for the appeal court to determine the appeal by review and not rehearing.'

2.7 This early guidance has now been authoritatively supplemented in the *Dupont* case by May LJ, who was a member of the Civil Procedure Rules Committee at the time the provisions of CPR Part 52 were being formulated and approved. He said:

> '85. In considering the nature of an appeal, certain questions intrinsically arise. Will the appeal court start all over again as if the lower court had never made a decision? Will the appeal court hear the evidence again? What weight is to be given to the decision of the lower court? Will the appeal court admit fresh evidence and, if so, upon what principles? To what extent and upon what principles will the appeal court interfere with

the decision of the lower court? These and related questions are not answered simply by labelling the appeal process as a review or a rehearing.

86. The Civil Procedure Rules are a new procedural code. Reference to the former Rules of the Supreme Court and the County Court Rules and to authorities decided under them may be instructive, but will not necessarily be determinative of the meaning and effect of the new Civil Procedure Rules. In this instance, it is, in my view, informative to see in outline what the former position was, not least because it has contributed to some present confusion.

87. Under Order 59 rule 3 of the Rules of the Supreme Court an appeal to the Court of Appeal was by way of rehearing. In addition, the general powers of the court in Order 59 rule 10(2) gave restrictive powers to receive further evidence on questions of fact in these terms:

> " ... in the case of an appeal from a judgment after trial or hearing of any cause or matter on the merits, no such further evidence (other than evidence as to matters which have occurred after the date of the trial or hearing) shall be admitted except on special grounds."

The court also had a power to draw inferences of fact.

88. Order 55, which applied generally to statutory appeals to the High Court, provided in rule 3(1) that an appeal to which that order applied should be by way of rehearing. By rule 7(2), the court hearing the appeal had power to receive further evidence on questions of fact, but without the restriction in Order 59 rule 10(2). The court again had power to draw inferences of fact ... The expression "rehearing" was also used in RSC Order 104 rule 19(14) in relation to an appeal to the court from a decision of the Comptroller under the Patents Acts.

89. These provisions for a rehearing were not however references to a rehearing "in the fullest sense of the word" as noted by Brooke LJ in paragraph 31 of his judgment in *Tanfern Limited v Cameron-MacDonald* [2000] 1 WLR 1311 at 1317. Brooke LJ was there referring to High Court appeals from a Master or Registrar to a Judge in Chambers under Order 58 rule 1. On those appeals, the judge treated the matter as though it came before him for the first time. The parties were able to bring forward fresh evidence which had not been before the Master unconstrained by restrictions applicable to the Court of Appeal. The judge hearing the appeal was able to exercise any discretion afresh. As Lord Atkin said in *Evans v Bartlam* [1937] AC 473 at 478:

> "I wish to state my conviction that where there is a discretionary jurisdiction given to the Court or a judge the judge in Chambers is

in no way fettered by the previous exercise of the Master's discretion. His own discretion is intended by the rules to determine the parties' rights: and he is entitled to exercise it as though the matter came before him for the first time. He will, of course, give the weight it deserves to the previous decision of the Master: but he is in no way bound by it."

90. Rehearings on appeal under RSC Orders 55 and 59 were well understood not to extend to rehearings in the fullest sense of the word. The court did not hear the case again from the start. It reviewed the decision under appeal giving it the respect appropriate to the nature of the court or tribunal, the subject matter and, importantly, the nature of those parts of the decision making process which were challenged.

91. The former provisions for appeals in the county court were in Order 37 of the County Court Rules. Order 37 rule 6 provided for appeals from a district judge to a judge in terms which did not stipulate the nature of the hearing. Order 37 rule 1 contained an anomalous power, useful in practice, enabling a judge in any proceedings tried without a jury to order a rehearing where no error of the court at the hearing was alleged.

92. Rule 52 of the Civil Procedure Rules draws together a very wide range of possible appeals. It applies, not only to the Civil Division of the Court of Appeal, but also to appeals to the High Court and county courts. It encompasses, not only appeals where the lower court was itself a court, but also statutory appeals from decisions of tribunals, ministers or other bodies or persons. Within the court system, it applies to an appeal from a district judge to a circuit judge, just as it applies to an appeal from a High Court Judge to the Court of Appeal. Subject to rule 52.1(4) and paragraph 17.1(2) of the practice direction, it applies to a wide variety of statutory appeals where the nature of the decision appealed against and the procedure by which it is reached may differ substantially. It does not apply (other than on an appeal) to judicial review, which is the subject of Part 54.

93. It is accordingly evident that rule 52.11 requires, and in my view contains, a degree of flexibility necessary to enable the court to achieve the overriding objective of dealing with individual cases justly. But as Mance LJ said on a related subject in *Todd v Adam* [2002] EWCA Civ 509, it cannot be a matter of simple discretion how an appellate court approaches the matter.

94. As the terms of rule 52.11(1) make clear, subject to exceptions, every appeal is limited to a review of the decision of the lower court. A review here is not to be equated with judicial review. It is closely akin to, although not conceptually identical with, the scope of an appeal to the

Court of Appeal under the former Rules of the Supreme Court. The review will engage the merits of the appeal. It will accord appropriate respect to the decision of the lower court. Appropriate respect will be tempered by the nature of the lower court and its decision making process. There will also be a spectrum of appropriate respect depending on the nature of the decision of the lower court which is challenged. At one end of the spectrum will be decisions of primary fact reached after an evaluation of oral evidence where credibility is in issue and purely discretionary decisions. Further along the spectrum will be multi-factorial decisions often dependent on inferences and an analysis of documentary material ...

96. Submissions to the effect that an appeal hearing should be a rehearing are often motivated by the belief that only thus can sufficient reconsideration be given to elements of the decision of the lower court. In my judgment, this is largely unnecessary given the scope of a hearing by way of review under rule 52.11(1). Further the power to admit fresh evidence in rule 52.11(2) applies equally to a review or rehearing. The scope of an appeal by way of review, such as I have described, in my view means that the scope of a rehearing under rule 52.11(1)(b) will normally approximate to that of a rehearing "in the fullest sense of the word" such as Brooke LJ referred to in paragraph 31 of his judgment in *Tanfern*. On such a rehearing the court will hear the case again. It will if necessary hear evidence again and may well admit fresh evidence. It will reach a fresh decision unconstrained by the decision of the lower court, although it will give to the decision of the lower court the weight that it deserves. The circumstances in which an appeal court hearing an appeal from within the court system will decide to hold such a rehearing will be rare, not least because the appeal court has power under rule 52.10(2)(c) to order a new trial or hearing before the lower court. Circumstances in which the hearing of an appeal will be a rehearing are described in paragraph 9 of the Part 52 practice direction. This refers to some statutory appeals where the decision appealed from is that of a person who did not hold a hearing or where the procedure did not provide for the consideration of evidence. In some such instances, it might be argued that the appeal would in effect be the first hearing by a judicial process, and that a full rehearing was necessary to comply with Article 6 of the European Convention on Human Rights – but see *Runa Begum v Tower Hamlets LBC* [2003] 2 WLR 388. This apart, it will be rare for the court to consider that the interests of justice require a rehearing in the fullest sense of the word. All other appeals to which rule 52.11 applies will be limited to a review capable of extending in an appropriate case to the extent which I have described ...

98. Thus, in so far as "rehearing" in rule 52.11(1)(b) may have something of a range of meaning, at the lesser end of the range it merges with that of "review". At this margin, attributing one label or the other is a semantic exercise which does not answer such questions of substance as arise in any appeal.'

2.8 The importance of appeal courts' clearly identifying what type of rehearing has been ordered was highlighted in 2003 by three cases in which uncertainty arose in relation to the appropriate appeal route to be taken by a party dissatisfied by the result of a 'rehearing'. In *Hackney LBC v Driscoll (No 1)*[1] the Court of Appeal had earlier allowed a second appeal, and directed that the matter should be remitted to a different circuit judge for rehearing. The Court envisaged that the same circuit judge would not only hear the defendant's application to set aside the possession order which was the subject of his appeal, but that case management directions would be given so that, if the possession order was set aside, the same judge could consider the new situation at the same hearing.

[1] [2003] EWCA Civ 614.

2.9 If the Court of Appeal's order had accurately expressed its intention, it would have stated that the appeal was being remitted to a circuit judge to rehear as a first appeal, and that if the appeal was successful, the same circuit judge would have proceeded as a judge at first instance to consider the legal effect of the new situation. As it was, the Court's order did not reflect this intention and, when a circuit judge refused to set the possession order aside, it was unclear whether he had made that decision as a judge at first instance (in which case appeal would lie to the High Court) or as an appeal court (in which case a second appeal could only lie to the Court of Appeal).

2.10 Comparable difficulties arose in *Fowler de Pledge v Smith*[1] when Brooke LJ ended his judgment by saying:

'It would be wrong to leave this appeal without stressing how important it is that appeal courts, at all levels, should make clear on the face of their orders for a rehearing whether they are ordering a rehearing at appeal court level (in which case any subsequent appeal would be a second appeal) or whether they are ordering a rehearing of the original application at first instance. This is the second time this year in which litigants' time was wasted while an appeal went to and fro between the High Court and the Court of Appeal looking for a home. On the other occasion this court had set aside an order of a circuit judge sitting as an appeal court, but it did not make it clear whether the rehearing it was ordering was a rehearing of the appeal or a rehearing of the original application. If there is clarity in the appeal court's order directing a rehearing, we should have no more cases of later appeals wandering about looking for a home.'[2]

1   [2003] EWCA Civ 703.
2   See also *Southern & District Finance plc v Turner* [2003] EWCA Civ 1574, para 21 for another example of the same problem (see **para A2.21**).

THE GROUNDS ON WHICH AN APPEAL MAY BE ALLOWED

2.11

CPR 52.11(3) provides that:

'The appeal court will allow an appeal where the decision of the lower court was:
(a)   wrong; or
(b)   unjust because of a serious procedural or other irregularity in the proceedings in the lower court.'[1]

It must be remembered and emphasised that the overriding objective in Pt 1 applies to Pt 52 in just the same way as it applies to any other rule in the CPR. This means that an appeal court, just like a lower court, has to be concerned with the need to save expense, to deal with the case in a proportionate manner, to deal with it expeditiously and fairly, and to allot to it an appropriate share of the court's resources (and no more)[2]. Its obligation to take these considerations into account provide it with some of the tools it needs to enable it to deal with each case justly.

1   For the definitions of 'appeal court' and 'lower court' see **para 1.3**.
2   See CPR 1.1(2).

2.12 These grounds for interference apply to all appeals under the CPR appellate regime[1] irrespectively of the nature or amount of the claim; the nature of the proceedings[2]; the nature of the decision or direction being appealed; the identity of the 'court' which made the decision under appeal; and the identity of the court to which the appeal is being made.

On the other hand, the route the appeal will take and the identity of the court which will hear the appeal will be governed by such considerations and, in particular, by the nature of the proceedings[3].

1   They do not apply to appeals to the House of Lords, for which see **Chapter 8**.
2   That is, whether they have been issued under Pt 7 or Pt 8, or the track to which they have been allocated.
3   See **Chapter 1, paras 1.9–1.11** above.

2.13 Neither Pt 52 nor its Practice Direction provide guidance in respect of the meaning of these grounds. In *Tanfern* (see **para 2.4** above) Brooke LJ summarised the position in these terms:

> '32. The first ground for interference speaks for itself. The epithet "wrong" is to be applied to the substance of the decision made by the lower court. If the appeal is against the exercise of a discretion by the lower court, the decision of the House of Lords in *G v G* [1985] 2 All ER 225, [1985] 1 WLR 647 warrants attention. In that case Lord Fraser of Tullybelton said:
>
>> "Certainly it would not be useful to inquire whether different shades of meaning are intended to be conveyed by words such as 'blatant error' used by Sir John Arnold P in the present case, and words such as 'clearly wrong', 'plainly wrong' or simply 'wrong' used by other judges in other cases. All these various expressions were used in order to emphasise the point that the appellate court should only interfere when it considers that the judge of first instance has not merely preferred an imperfect solution which is different from an alternative solution which the Court of Appeal might or would have adopted, but has exceeded the generous ambit within which a reasonable disagreement is possible." (See [1985] 2 All ER 225 at 229, [1985] 1 WLR 647 at 652.)
>
> 33. So far as the second ground for interference is concerned, it must be noted that the appeal court only has power to interfere if the procedural or other irregularity which it has detected in the proceedings in the lower court was a serious one, and that this irregularity caused the decision of the lower court to be an unjust decision.'

2.14 Under the CPR appellate regime an appeal court may only interfere, so far as the merits of the matter are concerned, if in its view the opinion of the decision under appeal was 'wrong'. What does the word 'wrong' mean in this context? The old appellate regime did not contain – either by statute or by rule – any provision in respect of the nature of grounds for appeal[1]. The jurisdiction of the Court of Appeal was and remained statutory but it was said that 'there is in the statute no restriction upon the jurisdiction of the Court of Appeal'[2].

Similarly, in *Hadmor Productions Ltd v Hamilton*[3] (a decision concerning an order made by a lower court in the exercise of its discretion where no procedural error was identified, which contains dicta of general application), Lord Diplock said:

> 'The function of the appellate court is initially one of review only. It may set aside the judge's exercise of his discretion on the ground that it was based upon a misunderstanding of the law or of the evidence before him or upon an inference that particular facts existed or did not exist, which,

although it was one that might legitimately have been drawn upon the evidence that was before the judge, can be demonstrated to be wrong by further evidence that has become available by the time of the appeal; or upon the ground that there has been a change of circumstances after the judge made his order that would have justified his acceding to an application to vary it.'

He added that there might also be a class of case in which, while not being able to classify the error, an appeal court might conclude that the judge's decision was so aberrant that it must be set aside upon the ground that no reasonable judge regardful of his duty to act judicially could have reached it.

1   With the exception of the provision for appeals in relation to small claims in the County Court Rules.
2   Lord Atkin in *Evans v Bartlam* [1937] AC 473, 480, HL.
3   [1983] 1 AC 191, 220, HL.

2.15 Because the new appellate regime covers such a wide range of decisions – from a conventional judgment by a judge in a private law action to a decision by a tribunal or other body whose rulings are susceptible to a statutory appeal – it is necessary to be careful not to be overly prescriptive in identifying how a decision may be so 'wrong' that an appeal court may interfere with it. In particular, the same appellate regime embraces cases where appeal lies on fact or law, and also cases where appeal lies on a matter of law alone. The link between the old regime and the new regime was aptly described by May LJ in *Hickey v Marks*[1] in these terms:

'The principle for the future will be that, since the Civil Procedure Rules are a new procedural code, the former body of authority will not apply, although of course the intrinsic persuasiveness of all relevant considerations, including, if they arise, those which were considered persuasive under the former procedure, will be capable of contributing to a just result.'

1   6 July 2000, unreported, CA.

2.16 For the purposes of analysis, this chapter considers the previous case law in the context of the new regime by reference to the following categories or headings:

(1)   appeals founded on an error of law;
(2)   appeals against a finding of fact (where such an appeal lies);
(3)   appeals in respect of the exercise of a discretion;
(4)   appeals involving new evidence or a change of circumstances;
(5)   appeals involving a serious procedural or other irregularity resulting in injustice;

(6) appeals involving a violation of a Convention right – particularly the right contained in Art 6 of Sch 1 to the Human Rights Act 1998 (right to a fair trial).

APPEALS FOUNDED ON AN ERROR OF LAW

Scope and nature of ground

2.17 There is not a large body of case law devoted to identifying the meaning of 'an error of law' in the context of an appeal from the judgment of a civil court. Most appeals in respect of errors of law are concerned with matters such as (by way of example) the correct interpretation and application of a statute, the interpretation of documents such as a contract or a trust deed, or the effect and application of case law. The judgment of the appeal court in such cases will inevitably focus upon the particular issue of law which is the subject matter of the case under appeal; the court's power to intervene in such a case has generally been clear, obvious and taken for granted; there would have been scarcely any debate in respect of the power of the appeal court to intervene in such a case.

2.18 The language of error or misdirection of law, however, also encompasses a decision where there is either no evidence to support a finding of fact or where the decision of the lower court is simply perverse[1]. This is a familiar ground of challenge in judicial review cases under CPR Pt 54 and in statutory appeals where appeal lies only on points of law. A challenge on these bases is likely to require not only a detailed analysis of the reasoning of the lower court or tribunal but also of the evidence that was before it. More recently, a failure to give reasons, or any adequate reasons, has also emerged as a discrete ground of appeal[2]. An error of law also arises in those cases where a judge has failed to resolve conflicts of evidence or opinion that are central to the issues he has to resolve. In the context of statutory appeals, a mistake of fact that gives rise to unfairness may also in some contexts be classified as an error of law. These five different categories of error of law are analysed in the following sections.

1   For appeals on the basis that the court drew incorrect inferences from the found facts see **paras 2.43–2.46** below.
2   It is unnecessary to examine closely whether the decision of the lower court can properly be said to be wrong if the appeal court cannot identify the reasons for the material findings in the judgment, or whether this failure should be categorised as furnishing an unjust result because of a serious procedural irregularity. In each case the judgment will be set aside.

Absence of evidence to support a finding of fact

2.19 Before 1999 there did not exist any appreciable body of case law in relation to civil appeals where there was no evidence to support a finding of fact, or where the decision was perverse, because they only arose for distinct treatment in those cases where appeal lay only on a point of law. However, because the jurisdiction of the Employment Appeal Tribunal ('EAT')[1] has always been limited in this way, there are some helpful dicta in a number of appeals from the EAT to the Court of Appeal which define the scope of an error of law in the context of the Employment Protection (Consolidation) Act 1978 (now replaced by the Employment Rights Act 1996)[2]. These dicta provide a useful insight into the approach of the Court of Appeal to these types of errors of law.

1   And of the Court of Appeal on appeal from the EAT.
2   An appeal to the EAT, and to the Court of Appeal thereafter, is limited to an appeal on a point of law alone.

2.20 The absence of evidence to support a particular finding of fact is an error of law. In *British Telecommunications plc v Sheridan*, Lord Donaldson MR stated[1] that:

'On all questions of fact, the industrial tribunal is the final and only judge ... The Employment Appeal Tribunal can indeed interfere if it is satisfied that the tribunal has misdirected itself as to the applicable law, or, if there is no evidence to support a particular finding of fact, since the absence of evidence to support a particular finding of fact has always been regarded as a pure question of law.'

Similarly, although it is open to a trial judge to substitute his views for those of expert witnesses, he may not do so without some evidence to support his conclusions and he must give his reasons for disagreeing with their conclusions or recommendations[2].

1   [1990] IRLR 27, 30, at para 35, CA.
2   *Re B* [1996] 3 FCR 272, [1996] 1 FLR 667, CA per Butler-Sloss LJ.

Perverse Decision

2.21 A decision which is perverse – even though it cannot precisely be demonstrated how the reasoning of the lower court is incorrect – will give rise to an error of law. In *Dobie v Burns International Security Services (UK) Ltd*, Sir John Donaldson MR said[1]:

'All that this court or the EAT can do is to consider whether there has been an error of law on one of two alternative bases. The first basis is that the tribunal has given itself a direction on law and is wrong ... The alternative basis—which is almost a *Wednesbury* basis—is that no reasonable tribunal could have reached that conclusion on the evidence and, since *ex hypothesi* all industrial tribunals are reasonable tribunals, it must follow that, although we cannot detect what it is, there has been a misdirection of law.'

1   [1984] IRLR 329, 332, at para 17, CA; [1985] 1 WLR 43; [1984] 3 All ER 333, 337.

2.22 A decision of a court can only be characterised as perverse and, therefore, to amount to an error of law if that decision was not a permissible option. This approach is, however, adopted by the court with the greatest care. In *Hereford and Worcester County Council v Neale*[1] May LJ had suggested that if an industrial tribunal did not misdirect itself on the law, neither the EAT nor the Court of Appeal should disturb their decision unless one could say in effect: 'My goodness, that was certainly wrong'. In *Piggott Bros & Co Ltd v Jackson* Lord Donaldson said[2]:

'I accept, as I must, the exposition of May LJ. Indeed, it has the added authority of, I think, being derived, albeit expressed in more homely terms, from the speech of Lord Diplock in *R v Secretary of State for Foreign and Commonwealth Affairs, ex p Council of Civil Service Unions* [1985] IRLR 28 at p 36 where he said that a decision which was plainly wrong could found an application for judicial review and that it was no longer necessary to resort to Viscount Radcliffe's explanation in *Edwards v Bairstow*[3] of irrationality as raising an inference of law.

Nevertheless, it is an approach which is not without its perils. A finding of fact which is unsupported by **any** evidence clearly involves an error of law. The Tribunal cannot have directed itself, as it should, that its findings need **some** evidence to support them. The danger in the approach if May LJ is that an appellate court can very easily persuade itself that, as it certainly would not have reached the same conclusion, the tribunal which did was "certainly wrong". Furthermore, the more dogmatic the temperament of the judges concerned, the more likely they are to take this view. However, this is a classic *non sequitur*. It does not matter whether, with whatever degree of certainty, the appellate court considers that it would have reached a different conclusion. What matters is whether the decision under appeal was a permissible option. To answer that question in the negative in the context of employment law, the EAT will almost always have to identify a finding of fact which was unsupported by **any** evidence or a clear misdirection in law by the industrial tribunal. If it cannot do this, it should re-examine with the greatest care its preliminary conclusion that the decision under appeal was not a permissible option and has to be characterised as "perverse".' [The emphasis in bold type is Sir John Donaldson's].

1   [1986] IRLR 168.
2   [1991] IRLR 309, 312, at para 17.
3   [1956] AC 14, [1955] 3 All ER 48, HL.

The duty to give reasons

2.23 In the old case law – exemplified by authorities such as *Culver v Beard*[1] and *Norman v King*[2] which go back to the days before the Court of Appeal could be sure of obtaining a reliable note of what the judge had said, and when there was not the same emphasis as there is today on the importance of a judge giving reasons for his decision – a presumption was developed that the judge in the lower court had been right and the appellant had to show that he was wrong. Under CPR appellate practice the same result is achieved by the new rule that an appeal court may only interfere where the decision of the lower court was wrong.

1 [1937] 1 All ER 301, 304 CA.
2 [1946] 1 All ER 339, CA, per Lord Greene MR at 340H.

2.24 It can now be said that it is an error of law for a judge to fail to give any or any adequate reasons for his decision. In *Eagil Trust Co Ltd v Pigott-Brown*[1], the Court of Appeal held that a judge must give reasons for his decision although these reasons need not be elaborate and the particularity required will vary according to the circumstances of the case. Griffiths LJ said:

'The next general observation I want to make is as to the judge's duty to give his reasons for his decision. A professional judge should, as a rule, give reasons for his decision. I say 'as a general rule' because in the field of discretion there are well-established exceptions. The most obvious and frequently used is the exercise of the judge's discretion on costs. As a general rule the judge gives no reasons for the way in which he is exercising his discretion on costs, although if he were to make an unusual award of costs, it is clearly desirable that he should give his reasons for doing so. Another recent example of the judge not being required to give his reasons is when he refuses leave to appeal to the Court of Appeal, having refused leave to appeal from an arbitrator (see Lord Diplock in *Antaios Cia Naviera SA v Salen Rederierna AB, The Antaios*[2]).

Apart from such exceptions, in the case of discretionary exercise, as in other decisions on facts or law, the judge should set out his reasons, but the particularity with which he is required to set them out must depend on the circumstances of the case before him and the nature of the decision he is giving. When dealing with an application in chambers to strike out for want of prosecution, a judge should give his reasons in sufficient detail to show the Court of Appeal the principles on which he has acted and the reasons that have led him to his decision. They need not be elaborate. I cannot stress too strongly that there is no duty on a judge, in giving his reasons, to deal with every argument presented by counsel in support of his case. It is sufficient if what he says shows the parties and, if need be, the Court of Appeal the basis on which he has acted, and if it be that the judge has not dealt with some particular argument but it can be seen that there are grounds on which he would have been entitled to reject it, this court should assume that he acted on those grounds unless the appellant can point to convincing reasons leading to a contrary conclusion (see Sachs LJ in *Knight v Clifton*[3]).'

1   [1985] 3 All ER 119, 122A, CA. This case was concerned with the exercise of a discretion but is of general application.
2   [1984] 3 All ER 229, 237, [1985] AC 191, 205.
3   [1971] 2 All ER 378, 392–393, [1971] Ch 700, 721.

2.25   There was a period following the decision of the Court of Appeal in *Flannery v Halifax Estate Agencies Ltd*[1] when appellants regularly relied on a failure to give any reasons, or any adequate reasons, as a substantive ground of appeal. This tendency was checked by the later decision in *English v Emery Reimbold & Strick Ltd*[2] where Lord Phillips MR said:

> '18. In our judgment, these observations of Griffiths LJ [in *Eagil Trust*] apply to judgments of all descriptions. But when considering the extent to which reasons should be given it is necessary to have regard to the practical requirements of our appellate system. A Judge cannot be said to have done his duty if it is only after permission to appeal has been given and the appeal has run its course that the court is able to conclude that the reasons for the decision are sufficiently apparent to enable the appeal court to uphold the judgment. An appeal is an expensive step in the judicial process and one that makes an exacting claim on judicial resources. For these reasons permission to appeal is now a nearly universal prerequisite to bringing an appeal. Permission to appeal will not normally be given unless the applicant can make out an arguable case that the Judge was wrong. If the judgment does not make it clear why the Judge has reached his decision, it may well be impossible within the summary procedure of an application for permission to appeal to form any view as to whether the Judge was right or wrong. In that event permission to appeal may be given simply because justice requires that the decision be subjected to the full scrutiny of an appeal.
>
> 19. It follows that, if the appellate process is to work satisfactorily, the judgment must enable the appellate court to understand why the Judge reached his decision. This does not mean that every factor which weighed with the Judge in his appraisal of the evidence has to be identified and explained. But the issues the resolution of which were vital to the Judge's conclusion should be identified and the manner in which he resolved them explained. It is not possible to provide a template for this process. It need not involve a lengthy judgment. It does require the Judge to identify and record those matters which were critical to his decision. If the critical issue was one of fact, it may be enough to say that one witness was preferred to another because the one manifestly had a clearer recollection

of the material facts or the other gave answers which demonstrated that his recollection could not be relied upon.

26. Where permission is granted to appeal on the grounds that the judgment does not contain adequate reasons, the appellate court should first review the judgment, in the context of the material evidence and submissions at the trial, in order to determine whether, when all of these are considered, it is apparent why the Judge reached the decision that he did. If satisfied that the reason is apparent and that it is a valid basis for the judgment, the appeal will be dismissed. This was the approach adopted by this Court, in the light of *Flannery*, in *Ludlow v National Power PLC* 17 November 2000 (unreported). If despite this exercise the reason for the decision is not apparent, then the appeal court will have to decide whether itself to proceed to a rehearing, or to direct a new trial.'

1   [2000] 1 All ER 273, [2000] 1 WLR 377.
2   [2002] EWCA Civ 605, [2002] 3 All ER 385, [2002] 1 WLR 2409, CA. In *Bessant v South Cone Inc* Robert Walker LJ cited para 19 in the *English* judgment and commented that an appeal court should not treat a judgment or written decision as containing an error of principle simply because of its belief that the judgment or decision could have been better expressed: 'The duty to give reasons must not be turned into an intolerable burden.'

2.26 In *English* the Court of Appeal authoritatively considered the jurisprudence of the Court and the Commission at Strasbourg[1] which touched on a court's duty to give decisions. It concluded that the critical issue in each case was whether the form of the judgment in question was compatible with a fair trial. Where a judicial decision affected the substantive rights of the parties Strasbourg jurisprudence required a reasoned decision. In contrast, there were some judicial decisions, such as interlocutory decisions in the course of case management, where fairness did not demand that the parties should be informed of the reasoning underlying them. The Strasbourg Commission had also recognised that there were some circumstances in which the reason for the decision would be implicit from the decision itself. In such cases art 6 would not be infringed if the reason for the decision was not expressly spelt out by the judicial tribunal.

1   *Ruiz Torija v Spain* (1994) 19 EHRR 553 at para 29; *Garcia Ruiz v Spain* (2001) 31 EHRR 589; *Van de Hurk v The Netherlands* (1994) 18 EHRR 481 at para 59; *Hiro Balani v Spain* (1994) 19 EHRR 566; *Helle v Finland* (1997) 26 EHRR 159 at para 60; *X v Federal Republic of Germany* [1981] 25 DR 240; *Webb v UK* [1997] 24 EHRR CD 73.

2.27 So far as orders for costs were concerned, the Court of Appeal in *English* considered that for a judge to give no reasons for his decision in respect of costs could only comply with art 6 if his reasons were clearly implicit from the circumstances in which the award was made. Where the reason for an order as to costs was not obvious, the judge should explain why he or she made the order. This explanation could usually be brief. The court suggested that the

Failure to resolve conflicts of evidence or opinion that are central to the issues in the case

2.28 A judge should not decide a case without making clear findings of fact where this is necessary in order to resolve a central issue in the case. It is not permissible for the judge simply to state that the evidence is uncertain; he must, as best he can, resolve the conflict of evidence and make a finding. The judgments in *Lloyds TSB Plc v Hayward*[1] provide a good example of contemporary judicial techniques in this respect, Jonathan Parker LJ said:

> '65. Where an issue of fact arises which is peripheral to the dispute which the court is required to resolve, and the evidence in relation to that issue is equivocal, the trial judge may well take the view that it is unnecessary to deal with that issue. It is, after all, a trite proposition that a trial judge is not required to resolve every dispute of fact which may arise in the course of the trial. But where, as here, the issue as to when the Thomas note was prepared, far from being peripheral, is central to the issue which the court was required to resolve (that is to say the issue whether the requirement for a replacement guarantee was agreed at the 23 September meeting or introduced for the first time thereafter) the judge ought in my judgment to have tackled the issue head on and made a finding about it. His failure to do so leads me to the conclusion that his finding that the requirement for a replacement guarantee was agreed at the 23 September meeting is fundamentally flawed.'

1 [2002] EWCA Civ 1813.

2.29 Dame Elizabeth Butler-Sloss P said in the same case:

> '84. All trial judges face, from time to time, extreme difficulty in deciding issues during the hearing of a case. Some issues are not of sufficient importance to make it necessary for them to be resolved one way or other. A decision on other issues may have a real and substantial bearing on the outcome of the case. The question when the 'Thomas note' was prepared is, in my judgment, in the latter category. The witnesses were relying on their recollections of more than seven years before and a contemporary written note was possibly of great significance and could well assist in the difficult task of deciding between conflicting accounts given by the Bank witnesses and Mr Hayward about the 23 September meeting. If it was written after the 23 September, it had the potential to provide considerable support for the account given by Mr Hayward and was central to the main issue to be decided by the court, that is to say, the issue whether the

requirement for a replacement guarantee was agreed at the 23 September meeting or was raised after the 23 September. The issue as to the date when the 'Thomas note' was written became, therefore, one that, in my judgment, had to be resolved and could not properly be sidelined. The judge recognised ... that the 'Thomas note' was consistent with Mr Hayward's case. He had a duty to make a finding as to the date and decide whether the contemporary written evidence did or did not support Mr Hayward's case. His failure to do so fatally undermines his finding that the requirement for a replacement guarantee was agreed at the 23 September meeting and therefore his judgment cannot stand.'

2.30 In *Cooper v Floor Cleaning Machines*[1] the Court of Appeal held that, except in the most exceptional cases, it was incumbent on a judge hearing an action for negligence to analyse the evidence and decide which party's case was more likely to be correct. It was not permissible for him to decide that the only fair decision was that neither party had discharged the onus, on the balance of probabilities, of proving its claim or counterclaim against the other party.

1   [2003] EWCA 1649; [2003] *The Times* 24 October, CA. Similarly, a failure by a trial judge to make sufficiently detailed and thorough findings of fact (where this is necessary in order for the judge then to be able properly to apply legal principle) may result in the judgment being set aside and a re-trial ordered: *Gabriel v Kirklees Metropolitan Council* [2004] EWCA Civ 345; [2004] The Times 12 April (a case concerning duty of care owed by occupier of site in relation to actions of trespassing children throwing rubble from that site at pedestrians on adjacent highway).

2.31 Similarly, if there are conflicting expert opinions, the judge must resolve the conflict and give proper reasons for his decision. He cannot abdicate this responsibility by simply deciding that the claimant has not discharged the burden of proof[1].

1   *Sewell v Electrolux Ltd*, 8 October 1997 (unreported); (1997) The Times, 7 November, CA.

Statutory appeals: incorrect basis of fact giving rise to unfairness

2.32 There are numerous statutes which provide for decisions (generally of an administrative nature) to be made by an appointed individual or by a tribunal and which then further provide for an appeal on a 'point of law'[1] from such a decision to be made to some other tribunal or to a court. Examples include: a decision of the Secretary of State when deciding an appeal under the Town and Country Planning Act 1990, various decisions under immigration and asylum legislation (which is currently in a state of transition), decisions of the Criminal Injuries Compensation Authority, and various decisions made by the Secretary of State under the education legislation.

1   Or a statutory quashing order.

2.33 In some of these statutory contexts the parties share an interest in co-operating to achieve the correct result. Thus a planning authority has a public interest, shared with the Secretary of State, in ensuring that development control is carried out on the correct factual basis. In the field of education, a local education authority and the Secretary of State have a shared interest in a decision being made on correct information as to what is practical. In the asylum field, the Secretary of State has a shared interest with the appellant and the immigration appellate authorities in ensuring that decisions are reached on the best information. There has been an ongoing debate in recent years about the circumstances in which a mistake of fact that gives rise to unfairness could be properly categorised as 'an error of law' such as to permit the court to interfere.

2.34 In *E v Secretary of State for the Home Department*[1], Carnwath LJ said at paras 66 and 91:

'66. In our view, the time has now come to accept that a mistake of fact giving rise to unfairness is a separate head of challenge in an appeal on a point of law, at least in those statutory contexts where the parties share an interest in co-operating to achieve the correct result. Asylum law is undoubtedly such an area. Without seeking to lay down a precise code, the ordinary requirements for a finding of unfairness are apparent from the above analysis of *CICB*[2]. First, there must have been a mistake as to an existing fact, including a mistake as to the availability of evidence on a particular matter. Secondly, the fact or evidence must have been 'established', in the sense that it was uncontentious and objectively verifiable. Thirdly, the appellant (or his advisers) must not been have been responsible for the mistake. Fourthly, the mistake must have played a material (not necessarily decisive) part in the Tribunal's reasoning.

...

91. In summary, we have concluded in relation to the powers of this Court:
   (i) an appeal to this Court on a question of law is confined to reviewing a particular decision of the Tribunal ...
   (ii) such an appeal may be made on the basis of unfairness resulting from 'misunderstanding or ignorance of an established and relevant fact' (as explained by Lord Slynn in *CICB*[3] and *Alconbury*[4]);
   (iii) the admission of new evidence on such an appeal is subject to *Ladd v Marshall*[5] principles, which may be departed from in exceptional circumstances where the interests of justice require.'

1 [2004] EWCA Civ 49, Lord Phillips MR, Mantell LJ and Carnwath LJ.
2 *R v Criminal Injuries Compensation Board, ex p A* [1999] 2 AC 330, HL per Lord Slynn at 344–345.
3 *R v Criminal Injuries Compensation Board, ex p A* [1999] 2 AC 330.

4   R (on the application of Alconbury Developments Ltd) v Secretary of State for the Environment, Transport and the Regions [2003] 2 AC 295, [2001] UKHL 23 para 53.
5   Ladd v Marshall [1954] 1 WLR 1489; [1954] 3 All ER 745; see **paras 2.62–2.72** below.

2.35 It is far too early to say whether this newly found principle in the public law field can be carried across in some form or other to the field of private law. In private law, it is up to the parties to put before the court the evidence of fact on which they seek to rely. If the judge analyses that evidence incorrectly, then an appeal court can interfere because he was wrong within the meaning of CPR 52.11(3)(a). In public law, there is a public interest in the decision-maker not making a wrong decision where he was mistaken in relation to some 'established fact' (which may emerge for the first time before the appeal court). If that mistake gave rise to unfairness and the appellant had not contributed to it, then the appeal court may interfere. In private law, however, the party seeking to adduce evidence of an 'established fact' for the first time before an appeal court would first have to persuade the court that it was just to admit the fresh evidence, and it may be more difficult for it to do so[1].

1   For the power of an appeal court to interfere with a decision on the basis of evidence not before the lower court, see **paras 2.62–2.72** below..

APPEALS AGAINST FINDINGS OF FACT

Pre-CPR practice: the presumption that the lower court was correct

2.36 In any appeal under the former appellate regime where the decision of the lower court was being challenged on the basis that a finding of fact was wrong, the Court of Appeal operated on the presumption that the decision of the court below was right. It was for the appellant to displace this presumption[1]. If the appeal court was in any doubt, it would not disturb the decision of the lower court (*Savage v Adams*[2] and *Colonial Securities Trust Ltd v Massey*[3]). In the second of these cases, after restating the old practice of the judges of the Court of Appeal in Chancery to the effect that they would not allow an appeal unless they were satisfied that the judge in the lower court was wrong, Lord Esher MR said:

'That is the rule of conduct which we ought now to apply in this Court. The judge in the Court below may have heard witnesses; and if so the Court of Appeal would be more unwilling to set aside his judgment, especially if there was a conflict of evidence, than in a case tried on written evidence where the witnesses were not before the judge, because of the opportunity afforded of judging how far the witnesses were worthy of credit. Where witnesses are not examined before the judge, but the case is determined on evidence taken on affidavit, or examination not before the judge, or partly on one and partly on the other, the Court of Appeal is not hampered by the consideration that the judge in the Court below has seen the witnesses, whilst the Court of Appeal has not, and the rule of conduct would not apply so strongly, but still this Court would not reverse the judgment and give a different one, unless satisfied that the judge was wrong.'

This principle is still adopted today. Only in exceptional circumstances will an appeal court differ from a judge's decision in the lower court which is based on an assessment of the credibility and reliability of witnesses (see also *Akerhielm v De Mare*[4]).

1 See **para 2.23** above.
2 [1895] WN 109, CA, Lopes LJ.
3 [1896] 1 QB 38, CA at 39, per Lord Esher MR.
4 [1959] 3 All ER 485, PC and see the speech of Lord Jenkins at 503G.

The basis of the presumption

2.37 The basis of the presumption was that the judge in the lower court had had the advantage of seeing and hearing the witnesses. Whilst the appeal court can and should undertake:

'... the task of weighing conflicting evidence and drawing its own inferences and conclusions, it should always bear in mind that it has neither seen nor heard the witnesses, and should make due allowance in this respect.'[1]

1 *The Glannibanta* (1876) 1 PD 283, 287, CA. See also *Powell v Streatham Manor Nursing Home* [1935] AC 243, HL, per Viscount Sankey at 249–251.

2.38 In *Coghlan v Cumberland*[1] Lord Lindley MR said:

'Even where, as in this case, the appeal turns on a question of fact, the Court of Appeal has to bear in mind that its duty is to rehear the case, and the Court must reconsider the materials before the judge with such other materials as it may have decided to admit. The Court must then make up its own mind, not disregarding the judgment appealed from, but carefully weighing and considering it; and not shrinking from overruling it if on full consideration the Court comes to the conclusion that the judgment is wrong. When, as often happens, much turns on the relative credibility of witnesses who have been examined and cross-examined before the judge, the court is sensible of the great advantage he has had in seeing and hearing them. It is often very difficult to estimate correctly the relative credibility of witnesses from written depositions; and when the question arises which witness is to be believed rather than another, and that question turns on manner and demeanour, the Court of Appeal always is, and must be, guided by the impression made on the judge who saw the witnesses. But there may obviously be other circumstances, quite apart from manner and demeanour, which may show whether a statement is credible or not; and these circumstances may warrant the court in differing from the judge, even on a question of fact turning on the credibility of witnesses whom the court has not seen.'

Some of the circumstances to which Lord Lindley referred are identified in **paras 2.42–2.46** below.

1 (1898) 1 Ch 704, CA, per Lord Lindley MR at 704, 705.

2.39 In *SS Hontestroom v SS Sagaporack*[1], Lord Sumner said that:

'... not to have seen the witnesses puts appellate judges in a permanent position of disadvantage ...'

1 [1927] AC 37, 47, HL.

2.40 An appeal court will show the same deference to a lower court which has had the advantage (denied to it) of seeing and hearing expert witnesses. In *Wilsher v Essex Area Health Authority* Lord Bridge said[1]:

'Where expert witnesses are radically at issue about complex technical questions within their own field and are examined and cross-examined at length about their conflicting theories, I believe that the judge's advantage in seeing them and hearing them is scarcely less important than when he has to resolve some conflict of primary fact between lay witnesses in purely mundane matters.'

1 [1988] AC 1074, 1091, HL.

2.41 In *Eckersley v Binnie* Bingham LJ provided important guidance as to the appropriate judicial approach to the evidence of an expert witness, which has often been relied on in later cases[1]:

'In resolving conflicts of expert evidence, the judge remains the judge; he is not obliged to accept evidence simply because it comes from an illustrious source; he can take account of demonstrated partisanship and lack of objectivity. But, save where an expert is guilty of a deliberate attempt to mislead (as happens only very rarely), a coherent reasoned opinion expressed by a suitably qualified expert should be the subject of a coherent reasoned rebuttal, unless it can be discounted for other good reasons. The advantages enjoyed by the trial judge are great indeed, but they do not absolve the Court of Appeal from weighing, considering and comparing the evidence in the light of his findings, a task made longer but easier by possession of a verbatim transcript usually (as here) denied to the trial judge.'

1 (1988) 18 Con LR 1, 77–78.

Reasons for displacing the presumption: failure to take into account material matters

2.42 The appeal court will adjudge this presumption to be displaced in limited circumstances and only on compelling grounds. Where, for example, upon an issue depending upon oral evidence there is plainly perjury on the one side or the other, an appeal court ought to be greatly influenced by the opinion of the trial judge, who has seen and examined the witnesses, except where he has failed to take account of material circumstances or probabilities. In *Khoo Sit Hoh v Lim Thean Tong*[1] Lord Robson said:

> 'Of course, it may be that in deciding between witnesses he has clearly failed on some point to take account of particular circumstances or probabilities material to an estimate of the evidence, or has given credence to testimony, perhaps plausibly put forward, which turns out on more careful analysis to be substantially inconsistent with itself, or with indisputable fact, but except in are cases of that character, cases which are susceptible of being dealt with wholly by argument, a Court of Appeal will hesitate long before it disturbs the findings of a trial judge based on verbal testimony.'[2]

1 [1912] AC 323, PC.
2 [1912] AC 323 at 325.

2.43 An impression as to the demeanour of a witness ought not to be adopted by a judge without testing it against the whole of the evidence of the witness in question. It was open to an appeal court to find that the view of the judge as to the demeanour of the witness was ill-founded, although such interference would only be justified on the rarest occasions and where the appeal court was convinced that the trial judge had formed a wrong view (*Yuill v Yuill*[1]).

1 [1945] P 15; [1945] 1 All ER 183, CA. See Lord Greene MR at 188H.

2.44 The appeal court is free to reverse a judge's conclusions in respect of findings of fact if the grounds given by him are unsatisfactory by reason of material inconsistencies or inaccuracies, or if it appears unmistakably from the evidence that in reaching them he has not taken a proper advantage of having seen the witnesses, or has failed to appreciate the weight and bearing of the admitted or proven circumstances. In *Watt (Or Thomas) v Thomas*. Viscount Simon said[1]:

> 'Apart from the classes of case in which the powers of the Court of Appeal are limited to deciding a question of law (for example, on a case

stated or on an appeal under the County Courts Acts) an appellate court has, of course, jurisdiction to review the record of the evidence in order to determine whether the conclusion originally reached upon that evidence should stand; but this jurisdiction has to be exercised with caution. If there is no evidence to support a particular conclusion (and this is really a question of law), the appellate court will not hesitate so to decide. But if the evidence as a whole can reasonably be regarded as justifying the conclusion arrived at the trial, and especially if that conclusion has been arrived at on conflicting testimony by a tribunal which saw and heard the witnesses, the appellate court will bear in mind that it has not enjoyed this opportunity and that the view of the trial judge as to where credibility lies is entitled to great weight. This is not to say that the judge of first instance can be treated as infallible in determining which side is telling the truth or is refraining from exaggeration. Like other tribunals, he may go wrong on a question of fact, but it is a cogent circumstance that a judge of first instance, when estimating the value of verbal testimony, has the advantage (which is denied to courts of appeal) of having the witnesses before him and observing the manner in which their evidence is given ... Lord President Clyde, in *Dunn v Dunn's Trustees*, summarized the scope of appellate correction, with copious citation of earlier authority, and I agree with him that the true rule is that expounded by Lord President Inglis in *Kinnell v Peebles*, that a court of appeal should "attach the greatest weight to the opinion of the judge who saw the witnesses and heard their evidence" and consequently should not disturb a judgment of fact unless they are satisfied that it is unsound. It not infrequently happens that a preference for A's evidence over the contrasted evidence of B is due to inferences from other conclusions reached in the judge's mind, rather than from an unfavourable view of B's veracity as such: in such cases it is legitimate for an appellate tribunal to examine the grounds of these other conclusions and the inferences drawn from them, if the materials admit of this; and if the appellate tribunal is convinced that these inferences are erroneous, and that the rejection of B's evidence was due to the error, it will be justified in taking a different view of the value of B's evidence. I would only add that the decision of an appellate court whether or not to reverse conclusions of fact reached by the judge at the trial must naturally be affected by the nature and circumstances of the case under consideration.'

1   [1947] AC 484, HL at 486, 487.

2.45   An appeal court will not take the responsibility of reversing a lower court's conclusions on the facts merely on the basis of its own comparisons and criticisms of witnesses and of its own view of the probabilities of the case: *SS Hontestroom v SS Sagaporack*[1]. Valuable guidance was given in this context by Robert Goff LJ in *The Ocean Frost*[2], in which he said:

'Speaking from my own experience, I have found it essential in cases of fraud when considering the credibility of witnesses, always to test their veracity by reference to the objective facts proved independently of their testimony, in particular by reference to the documents in the case and also to pay particular regard to their motives and to the overall probabilities. It is frequently very difficult to tell whether a witness is telling the truth or not; and where there is a conflict of evidence such as there was in the present case, reference to the objective facts and documents, to the witnesses' motives, and to the overall probabilities, can be of very great assistance to a judge in ascertaining the truth.'

1   [1927] AC 37, 47 and 48.
2   [1985] 1 Lloyd's Rep 1, 57. His approach was adopted with approval by the Privy Council in *Grace Shipping Inc and Hai Nguan & Co v CF Sharp & Co (Malaya) Pte Ltd* [1987] 1 Lloyd's Rep 207, 215.

2.46 In *Gow v Harker*[1], a clinical negligence appeal in which the Court of Appeal reversed the decision of the trial judge on the facts and ordered a retrial, Brooke LJ said that trial judges would always do well to model their fact-finding technique, in a case as difficult as that one, on the approach advocated by Robert Goff LJ in *The Ocean Frost*. He added:'

'55. While spoken in the context of a fraud case, these words are equally apposite in a case like the present where the claimant's case is inherently improbable, where there is little or no objective evidence supporting her account of a radial nerve injury, and where they may be a risk that she may have persuaded herself over the months that followed the incident in the doctor's surgery of a history of that incident which materially departed from what actually occurred.

56. A judge who adopted conventional judicial techniques in a case as difficult as this would begin by considering the contemporary written evidence ...'

1   [2003] EWCA Civ 1160 at paras 54–56.

The distinction between primary facts and inferences from primary facts

2.47 CPR 15.11(4) provides that:

'The appeal court may draw any inference of fact which it considers justified on the evidence.'

2.48 Where there is no question before the court of the credibility of witnesses, but the sole question is the proper inference to be drawn from specific facts, an appeal court is in as good a position to evaluate the evidence as the trial judge and should form its own independent opinion, though it will give weight to the opinion of the trial judge. In *Montgomerie & Co v Wallace-James*[1], Lord Halsbury said:

> 'Where a question of fact has been decided by a tribunal which has seen and heard the witnesses, the greatest weight ought to be attached to the finding of such a tribunal. It has had the opportunity of observing the demeanour of the witnesses and judging of their veracity and accuracy in a way that no appellate tribunal can have. But where no question arises as to truthfulness, and where the question is as to the proper inferences to be drawn from the truthful evidence, then the original tribunal is in no better position to decide than the judges of the appellate court.'

1 [1904] AC 73, 75, HL, approved and applied in *Dominion Trust Co v New York Life Insurance Co* [1919] AC 254, PC. See Lord Dunedin at 257, 258.

2.49 This distinction was later considered in *Benmax v Austin Motor Co Ltd*[1]. Viscount Simonds said:

> 'This does not mean that an appellate court should lightly differ from the finding of a trial judge on a question of fact, and I would say that it would be difficult for it to do so where the finding turned solely on the credibility of a witness. But I cannot help thinking that some confusion may have arisen from failure to distinguish between the finding of a specific fact and a finding of fact which is really an inference from facts specifically found, or, as it has sometimes been said, between the perception and evaluation of facts. An example of this distinction may be seen in any case in which a plaintiff alleges negligence on the part of the defendant. Here, it must first be determined what the defendant, in fact, did, and secondly, whether what he did amounted in the circumstances (which must also, so far as relevant, be found as specific facts) to negligence. A jury finds that the defendant has been negligent and that is an end of the matter unless its verdict can be upset according to well-established rules. A judge sitting without a jury would fall short of his duty if he did not first find the facts and then draw from them the inference of fact whether or not the defendant had been negligent. This is a simple illustration of a process in which it may often be difficult to say what is simple fact and what is inference from fact, or, to repeat what I have said, what is perception, what evaluation. Nor is it of any importance to do so except to explain why, as I think, different views have been expressed as to the duty of an appellate tribunal in relation to a finding by a trial judge. For I have found on the one hand universal reluctance to reject a finding of specific fact, particularly where the finding could be founded on the credibility or bearing of a witness, and, on the other hand, no less a willingness to form an independent opinion about the proper

inference of fact, subject only to the weight which should, as a matter of course, be given to the opinion of the learned judge ...'

1   [1955] C 370, 373, HL; see also the speech of Lord Reid at 376; [1955] 1 All ER 326.

2.50   This well-known passage must now be read subject to the gloss placed on it by Lord Hoffmann in *Biogen Inc v Medeva plc*[1]. He said:

'The question of whether an invention was obvious had been called "a kind of jury question" (see Jenkins LJ in *Allmanna Svenska Elektriska A/B v The Burntisland Shipbuilding Co Ltd* (1952) 69 RPC 63, 70) and should be treated with appropriate respect by an appellate court. It is true that in *Benmax v Austin Motor Co Ltd* [1955] AC 370 (1955) 72 RPC 39, 42, this House decided that, while the judge's findings of primary fact, particularly if founded upon an assessment of the credibility of witnesses, were virtually unassailable, an appellate court would be more ready to differ from the judge's evaluation of those facts by reference to some legal standard such as negligence or obviousness. In drawing this distinction, however, Viscount Simonds went on to observe, at page 374, that it was "subject only to the weight which should, as a matter of course, be given to the opinion of the learned judge". The need for appellate caution in reversing the judge's evaluation of the facts is based upon much more solid grounds than professional courtesy. It is because specific findings of fact, even by the most meticulous judge, are inherently an incomplete statement of the impression which was made upon him by the primary evidence. His expressed findings are always surrounded by a penumbra of imprecision as to emphasis, relative weight, minor qualification and nuance (as Renan said, *la vérité est dans une nuance*), of which time and language do not permit exact expression, but which may play an important part in the judge's overall evaluation. It would in my view be wrong to treat *Benmax* as authorising or requiring an appellate court to undertake a *de novo* evaluation of the facts in all cases in which no question of the credibility of witnesses is involved. Where the application of a legal standard such as negligence or obviousness involves no question of principle but is simply a matter of degree, an appellate court should be very cautious in differing from the judge's evaluation.'

1   [1997] RPC 1, 45, HL.

2.51   In the earlier case of *In re Grayan Building Services Ltd*[1] Hoffmann LJ (as he then was) said:

'Once one is clear about the precise nature of the decision which the judge has to make, it is easier to decide how an appellate tribunal should approach an appeal against his decision. The judge is deciding a question of mixed fact and law in that he is applying the standard laid down by the courts (conduct appropriate to a person fit to be a director) to the facts of the case. It is in principle no different from the decision as to whether someone has been negligent or whether a patented invention was obvious: see *Benmax v Austin Motor Co Ltd* [1955] AC 370. On the other hand, the standards applied by the law in different contexts vary a great deal in precision and generally speaking, the vaguer the standard and the greater the number of factors which the court has to weigh up in deciding whether or not the standards have been met, the more reluctant an appellate court will be to interfere with the trial judge's decision. So in *George Mitchell (Chesterhall) Ltd v Finney Lock Seeds Ltd* [1983] 2 AC 803 Lord Bridge of Harwich was considering the application of the test of "fair and reasonable" in the Unfair Contract Terms Act 1977. He said, at pp. 815–816:

> "It would not be accurate to describe such a decision as an exercise of discretion. But [such] a decision under any of the provisions referred to will have this in common with the exercise of a discretion, that, in having regard to the various matters to which ... section 11 of the Act of 1977 direct[s] attention, the court must entertain a whole range of considerations, put them in the scales on one side or the other, and decide at the end of the day on which side the balance comes down. There will sometimes be room for a legitimate difference of judicial opinion as to what the answer should be, where it will be impossible to say that one view is demonstrably wrong and the other demonstrably right. It must follow, in my view, that, when asked to review such a decision on appeal, the appellate court should treat the original decision with the utmost respect and refrain from interference with it unless satisfied that it proceeded upon some erroneous principle or was plainly and obviously wrong."

Similar comments were made in this court in *In re Coventry, decd* [1980] Ch 461 about a decision as to whether a testator had made "reasonable financial provision" for a dependant for the purposes of the Inheritance (Provision for Family and Dependants) Act 1975. Buckley LJ, at pp 495–496, described such a decision as a "value judgment" which should not be disturbed unless the judge had made an error of principle.

These cases are at one end of a spectrum and decisions such as whether a motorist has driven with due care and attention are probably somewhere near the other end. Where lies the decision that a director's conduct fell below the appropriate standard? In my view, nearer to the negligence end than that represented by *Finney Lock* or *Coventry*. If [counsel] were right in saying that the judge was involved in a general inquiry about the defendant's current fitness to be a director, then I think he would probably also be right about the approach to an appeal from such a decision. But since I think that the true question is a much narrower one, namely whether specific conduct measures up to a standard of probity and competence fixed by the court, I agree with the way in which the matter was put in *In re Hitco 2000 Ltd* [1995] BCC 161. After citing a passage in *In re Sevenoaks Stationers (Retail) Ltd* [1991] Ch 164, 176 in which Dillon LJ referred to the question of unfitness as a "jury question," the deputy judge went on:

> "Plainly the appellate court would be very slow indeed to disturb such a conclusion as to fitness or unfitness. In many, perhaps most, cases, the conclusion will have been so very much assisted and influenced by the oral evidence and demeanour of the director and other witnesses that the appellate court would be in nowhere near as good a position to form a judgment as to fitness or unfitness than was the trial judge. But there may be cases where there is little or no dispute as to the primary facts and the appellate court is in as good a position as the trial judge to form a judgment as to fitness. In such cases the appellate court should not shrink from its responsibility to do so and, if satisfied that the trial judge was wrong, to say so." '

1   [1995] Ch 241, 254.

2.52   In *South Cone Inc v Bessant (t/a Reef)*[1] Robert Walker LJ said:

> '24. It is worth reflecting on what judges mean when they speak of "inferences" in this context. An inference from a number of primary facts may itself be a simple matter of fact. That is an inference from circumstantial evidence, or what might be called the "smoking gun" type of inference. (Inferences from a litigant's failure to call a particular witness are also akin to this category.) In the present context, however, the inference is not a simple matter of fact because it involves a process of evaluation. It was put very clearly by Viscount Simonds in *Benmax v Austin Motor Co Ltd* [1955] AC 370, 373 (a patent case on obviousness):
>
>> "I cannot help thinking that some confusion may have arisen from failure to distinguish between the finding of a specific fact and a finding of fact which is really an inference from facts specifically found or, as it has sometimes been said, between the perception and evaluation of facts."
>
> 25. A few months later in *Edwards v Bairstow* [1956] AC 14, 29 (a tax case about an "adventure in the nature of trade") Viscount Simonds referred to the "inference or conclusion" which the general commissioners had drawn from the primary facts. Similar statements of high authority can be traced through to the recent decisions of the House of Lords in *Designers Guild*[1] and *Biogen*.

26. How reluctant should an appellate court be to interfere with the trial judge's evaluation of, and conclusion on, the primary facts? As Hoffmann LJ made clear in *Grayan* there is no single standard which is appropriate to every case. The most important variables include the nature of the evaluation required, the standing and experience of the fact-finding judge or tribunal, and the extent to which the judge or tribunal had to assess oral evidence.

27. It is worth noting that *Biogen* was a case very close to the top end of the scale. It involved very complex biotechnology which was the subject of a lot of expert evidence given at a lengthy trial before a very experienced judge of the Patents Court. In the circumstances Lord Hoffmann's memorable reference to Renan was not (if I may respectfully say so) out of place. There are far fewer nuances to be picked up from a bundle of statutory declarations which contain a good deal of irrelevant or tendentious material and on which there is no cross-examination.

28. In this case the hearing officer had to make what he himself referred to as a multi-factorial comparison, evaluating similarity of marks, similarity of goods and other factors in order to reach conclusions about likelihood of confusion and the outcome of a notional passing-off claim. It is not suggested that he was not experienced in this field, and there is nothing in the Civil Procedure Rules to diminish the degree of respect which has traditionally been shown to a hearing officer's specialised experience. (It is interesting to compare the observations made by Lord Radcliffe in *Edwards v Bairstow* [1956] AC 14, 38–9, about the general commissioners, a tribunal with a specialised function but often little specialised training.) On the other hand the hearing officer did not hear any oral evidence. In such circumstances an appellate court should in my view show a real reluctance, but not the very highest degree of reluctance, to interfere in the absence of a distinct and material error of principle.'

1   [2002] EWCA Civ 763; [2002] All ER (D) 426 (May); [2003] RPC 101.
2   *Designers Guild (Textiles) Ltd v Russell Williams (Textiles) Ltd* [2000] 1 All ER 700; [2000] 1 WLR 2416, HL.

2.53 In *Assicurazioni-Generali SpA v Arab Insurance Group (BSC)*[1] Clarke LJ, after reviewing these authorities, said:

'...[T]he extent to which the findings of fact depend upon oral evidence or what Lord Hoffmann called the "penumbra of imprecision as to emphasis, relative weight, minor qualification and nuance" will vary from case to case. In the instant case, the judge had the considerable advantage of seeing the witnesses and of assessing their credibility, although, as ever, he did so against the documentary material that was available. In these circumstances we should, I think, take particular care before holding that his conclusions of fact were wrong, especially since (as appears below) some of his conclusions depended to a significant extent upon the view which he formed of the witnesses. On the other hand this is not a case in which the judge was concerned to weigh a number of factors such that the judgment which he was called upon to make was a matter of degree.'

1   [2002] EWCA Civ 1642; [2003] 1 WLR 577; [2003] 1 All ER (Comm) 140.

2.54 In **para 2.7** above there are long extracts from the judgment of May LJ in the *Dupont* case[1]: When he was describing the nature of the review conducted by an appeal court, May LJ referred to the 'spectrum of appropriate respect' which an appeal court will show to the decision of the lower court. He concluded this passage in these terms:

'94... It will accord appropriate respect to the decision of the lower court. Appropriate respect will be tempered by the nature of the lower court and its decision making process. There will also be a spectrum of appropriate respect depending on the nature of the decision of the lower court which is challenged. At one end of the spectrum will be decisions of primary fact reached after an evaluation of oral evidence where credibility is in issue and purely discretionary decisions. Further along the spectrum will be multi-factorial decisions often dependent on inferences and an analysis of documentary material. Rule 52.11(4) expressly empowers the court to draw inferences. As [counsel] correctly submitted, the varying standard of review is discussed in paragraphs 17–30 of the judgment of Robert Walker LJ in *Reef Trade Mark*...'

1   See **para 2.7** above.

A recent restatement of the relevant principles

2.55 In *Indrakumar v Secretary of State for the Home Department*[1] Hale LJ referred to a number of the principles set out in this chapter when she was considering the power of the Immigration Appeal Tribunal to interfere with a finding of fact by an adjudicator in an asylum appeal:

'There is, therefore, room for some debate about nuances of meaning between terms such as "wrong", "plainly wrong", "clearly wrong", or "unsustainable". But consideration of all of those cases and the principles which they adopt leads me to the following propositions:
(1)   The Immigration Appeal Tribunal is not different from this court or any other court with jurisdiction to hear appeals on fact as well as law ...
(2)   The Immigration Appeal Tribunal, like this court or any other court, can only interfere if there has been an error: that is, if, on

analysis, the adjudicator's decision was wrong. There is a useful analogy here with the Civil Procedure Rules, Rule 52.11(3) which says the same thing. It is not enough that the Tribunal might have reached a different conclusion itself.

(3) I, for my part, do not find adverbs such as "plainly" or "clearly" wrong helpful in the context of a fact-finding exercise. They have sometimes proved useful for appellate courts when reviewing the exercise of a discretion.

(4) The test is the same, whatever the nature of the error alleged, but its application will often depend on the type of evidence on which the finding of fact is based. One can distinguish at least four different types:

  (i) There are findings of fact based on oral evidence and the assessment of credibility. These can only very rarely be overturned by an appellate Tribunal.

  (ii) There are findings based on documentary evidence specific to the individual case. These can more readily be overturned because the appellate tribunal is in just as good a position to assess it. But even there there may be an important relationship between the assessment of the person involved and the assessment of those documents. If so, great caution once again will be required.

  (iii) There are findings as to the general conditions or the backdrop in the country concerned which will be based on the objective country evidence. The Immigration Appeal Tribunal will be at least as well placed to assess this as is the adjudicator. Although in our law the notion of a factual precedent is, as Laws LJ termed it in *S and Others v Secretary of State for the Home Department* [2002] INLR 416 at paragraph 28, "exotic", in this context he considered it to be "benign and practical". There will be no public interest and no legitimate individual interest in multiple examinations of the state of this backdrop at any particular time once that had been considered in detail and guidance is given by the Tribunal.

  (iv) There are findings as to the application of those general country conditions to the facts of the particular case. These will be an inference to be drawn by the adjudicator and then, if appropriate, by the Tribunal. The Tribunal will be entitled to draw its own inferences, just as is the appellate court under the CPR, once it has detected an error in the adjudicator's approach.'

---

1 [2003] EWCA 1677. Considered and applied in *Subesh and Ors v Secretary of State for the Home Department* [2004] EWCA Civ 56.

APPEALS IN RESPECT OF THE EXERCISE OF A DISCRETION

When an appeal court may interfere

2.56 Rules of procedure or statute law very frequently give the judge a discretion whether or not to make an order which is within his powers to make. Whether or not to grant a pre-trial injunction; to extend the time for taking a step in the action; or to strike an action out; are examples of decisions taken in the exercise of a judge's discretion. Appeal courts have always been very slow to interfere with such decisions. The reason for this reluctance was explained by James LJ in *Golding v The Wharton Saltworks Co*[1], the first occasion when the newly created Court of Appeal heard an appeal from such a decision made by a common law judge. He said:

> 'The Court of Appeal in Chancery has laid down over and over again that, on a question which depends on the discretion of the judge, the Court of Appeal does not in general interfere with that discretion. Not that the Court of Appeal has not complete jurisdiction over such cases, or that the decision of the Court below would not be overruled where serious injustice would result from that decision; but, as a general rule, the Court of Appeal declines to interfere. Now that there is an appeal to this Court from a Common Law Division, it is more than ever desirable that this rule should be adhered to. There may be, first, an application to the master, then before the judge in chambers, then an appeal to the Common Law Division, and then an appeal to the Court of Appeal. And, if upon every interlocutory application of this kind, all these appeals were to be made, actions could never be tried and the expense would be enormous.
>
> The rules (Order XXVII., Rule 1) say, that in order to prevent embarrassing pleas, the Court may order to be struck out any matter which may tend to prejudice, embarrass, or delay the fair trial of the action. But it is a question of discretion whether the pleading is embarrassing; and no doubt the Common Law Division will say that, except in an extreme case, they will not interfere with the discretion which the judge has exercised, and we, as the Court of Appeal, say the same thing with even more force.'

1 (1876) 1 QBD 374.

2.57 Judges have been striving over many decades to formulate the principles according to which their power to interfere should be exercised. In *Re Wray*[1] Cotton LJ suggested that an appeal court would only interfere in a case of gross miscarriage of justice; in *Mangan v Metropolitan Electric Supply Co*[2] Lindley LJ said that it would only interfere if there was likely to be a failure of justice if it did not; in *Maxwell v Keun*[3] Atkin LJ observed that it would have a duty to review an order if its effect was to defeat the rights of the applicant altogether and this would be an injustice to one or other of the parties. It is now unnecessary to revisit this old case-law. The modern approach is most vividly delineated in the judgment of Asquith LJ in *Bellenden v Satterthwaite*[4] and the speech of Lord Fraser of Tullybelton in *G v G*[5]. In the former Asquith LJ said:

'It is, of course, not enough for the wife to establish that this court might, or would, have made a different order. We are here concerned with a judicial discretion, and it is of the essence of such a discretion that on the same evidence two different minds might reach widely different decisions without either being appealable. It is only where the decision exceeds the generous ambit within which reasonable disagreement is possible, and is, in fact, plainly wrong, that an appellate body is entitled to interfere.'

The relevant extract from Lord Fraser's speech in *G v G* is set out in **para 2.13** above.

1   (1887) 36 Ch D 138, CA. A decision not to commit for contempt.
2   [1891] 2 Ch 551, CA. A decision to transfer an action for nuisance from the Chancery Division to Queen's Bench Division so that it could be tried with a jury.
3   [1928] 1 KB 645, CA. A decision to refuse an adjournment.
4   [1948] 1 All ER 343, CA; see Asquith LJ at 345B.
5   [1985] 2 All ER 225, [1985] 1 WLR 647, HL.

2.58 These dicta are concerned with the quality of the lower court's ultimate decision. An appeal court will also interfere if it appears that the judge has taken into consideration irrelevant matters or if he has omitted to consider relevant matters. In *Egerton v Jones*, Sir Wilfrid Greene MR said[1]:

'It has been contended that this is a case where the judge has exercised his discretion; and that this court should not interfere with that exercise except according to well-known principles, which, it is said, do not operate in the present case. It is quite certain, on the one hand, that the discretion of the court is not to be fettered by rules. The discretion is given by statute, and must be exercised according to the circumstances of each particular case. On the other hand, it is equally true that, when a matter involving discretion comes before a judge, there must be in every case a number of considerations which he ought to have in mind for the purpose of enabling him to exercise his discretion. If it appears that he has taken into consideration something which he ought not to have taken into consideration, or has omitted to take into consideration something which he ought to have taken into consideration, or if on all the facts this court is satisfied and convinced that the discretion has been wrongly exercised, it is the duty of this court to interfere.'

1   [1939] 3 All ER 889, CA at 891H. A case concerned with the discretionary grant of relief against forfeiture under the Law of Property Act 1925, s 146.

2.59 More recently Lord Woolf MR succinctly described the appellate function in these cases in the following way in *Phonographic Performance Ltd v AEI Rediffusion Music Ltd*[1]:

> 'Before the court can interfere it must be shown that the judge has either erred in principle in his approach or has left out of account or has taken into account some feature that he should, or should not, have considered, or that his decision was wholly wrong because the court is forced to the conclusion that he has not balanced the various factors fairly in the scale.'

1   [1999] 1 WLR 1507, 1523C–D; [1999] 2 All ER 299.

2.60 The new rule which expressly provides that an appeal court will only interfere if a decision was wrong, interpreted by reference to the overriding objective set out in CPR1.1, provides the authority for the courts to continue to adopt the same approach under the CPR regime.

When an appeal court may exercise a discretion itself

2.61 CPR 52.10(1) confers on an appeal court all the powers of the lower court. It is not, however, the function of the appeal court, when considering the exercise of a discretion by the lower court, to exercise a discretion of its own immediately. Instead, it must first consider whether it should set aside the exercise of the judge's discretion in the lower court. If it decides that it should, it is then and only then that it is entitled to exercise a discretion of its own. In *Hadmor Productions Ltd v Hamilton*[1] Lord Diplock said[2]:

> 'Before adverting to the evidence that was before the learned judge and the additional evidence that was before the Court of Appeal, it is I think appropriate to remind our Lordships of the limited function of an appellate court in an appeal of this kind. An interlocutory injunction is a discretionary relief and the discretion whether or not to grant it is vested in the High Court judge by whom the application for it is heard. Upon an appeal from the judge's grant or refusal of an interlocutory injunction the function of an appellate court, whether it be the Court of Appeal or your Lordships' House, is not to exercise an independent discretion of its own. It must defer to the judge's exercise of his discretion and must not interfere with it merely upon the ground that the members of the appellate court would have exercised the discretion differently. The function of the appellate court is initially one of review only ... It is only if and after the appellate court has reached the conclusion that the judge's exercise of his discretion must be set aside ... that it becomes entitled to exercise an original discretion of its own.'

1   [1983] 1 AC 191, HL; [1982] 1 All ER 1042. An appeal concerned with the grant of an interim injunction.

2   [1983] 1 AC 191, HL at 220. The passage omitted is reproduced in **para 2.14** above.

NEW EVIDENCE OR CHANGE OF CIRCUMSTANCES AS A GROUND OF APPEAL

Fresh evidence

2.62   CPR 52.11(2) provides that:

'Unless it orders otherwise, the appeal court will not receive—
(a)   oral evidence; or
(b)   evidence which was not before the lower court.'

2.63   Neither the Practice Direction nor the rule itself offered any guidance in relation to the circumstances in which new evidence would be admitted. The rule applies, on the face of it, to all appeals whether, for example, in respect of case management decisions or decisions made at the conclusion of a trial, but the court will necessarily take into account the nature of the issues it has to determine on the appeal, not least if its jurisdiction is limited to the consideration of issues of law.

2.64   Previous case law drew distinctions between the admission of fresh evidence in respect of final decisions (when it was generally not admitted) and interlocutory decisions (when the rules in relation to its admission were more relaxed).

2.65   The rules relating to the admission of fresh evidence in cases in the first category were set out by Denning LJ in *Ladd v Marshall*[1], when he said that where there had been a trial or hearing on the merits, the decision could only be overturned by the use of further evidence if it could be shown that:
(1)   the evidence could not with reasonable diligence have been obtained for use at the trial (or hearing);
(2)   the evidence must be such that, if given, it would probably have had an important influence on the result of the case (though it need not be decisive);
(3)   the evidence was apparently credible although it need not be incontrovertible.

This test was strictly applied. A summary judgment was a hearing on the merits for this purpose[2].

1   [1954] 3 All ER 745, 748, [1954] 1 WLR 1489, 1491, CA.
2   *Langdale v Danby* [1982] 3 All ER 129, [1982] 1 WLR 1123, HL.

2.66 The distinction between a hearing on the merits and a different type of hearing gave rise to disputes as to the appropriate categorisation of the decision under appeal. The pre-CPR position is usefully summarised in the judgment of Auld LJ in *Electra Private Equity Partners v KPMG Peat Marwick*[1] (see **para A2.7**). After explaining the nature of the problem, and recognising that there should be some control over attempts by disappointed litigants to retrieve lost ground in interlocutory appeals by relying upon evidence which they could and should have put before the court below, he favoured an approach whereby (i) the admission of further evidence would be 'a matter for the court's discretion to be exercised according to the nature of the interlocutory hearing and the individual circumstances of the case', and (2) the court might adopt a more relaxed approach in relation to applications at an early stage of the litigation where it might be unjust to expect a party (particularly a defendant) to have 'all his tackle in order'.

1 [1999] EWCA Civ 1247, [2001] 1 BCLC 589.

2.67 The former definitional difficulties have all been swept away by the broad language of the new rule. Although the previous case law is no longer directly applicable, the thought processes of previous decisions are not thrown overboard[1]. In *Banks v Cox*[2] Sir Andrew Morritt V-C commented in these terms on the language of the new rule:

> '40... This provides that on an appeal the Court will not consider evidence not before the Court below unless it has given permission for it to be used. Thus the permission of the Court is still required but it is no longer necessary to show "special grounds". The discretion of the Court under this rule also must also be exercised in accordance with the overriding objective.
>
> 41. In my view the principles reflected in the rules in *Ladd v Marshall* remain relevant to any application for permission to rely on further evidence, not as rules but as matters which must necessarily be considered in an exercise of the discretion whether or not to permit an appellant to rely on evidence not before the Court below. As May LJ, with whom Forbes J and I agreed, said in *Hickey v Marks* (Court of Appeal 6th July 2000) unreported:
>
>> "The principle for the future will be that, since the Civil Procedure Rules are a new procedural code, the former body of authority will not apply, although of course the intrinsic persuasiveness of all relevant considerations, including, if they arise, those which were considered persuasive under the former procedure, will be capable of contributing to a just result."

42. The contrary was not argued. For my part I would accept as apt the description of counsel ... that the principles remain the same but the Court is freed from the straitjacket of so-called rules, adopting this statement of principle.'

1   To borrow and paraphrase from the judgment of May LJ in *Purdy v Cambran* [1999] CPLR 843, CA when he was considering the effect of the CPR on the body of case law in respect of striking out an action.
2   17 July 2000, unreported, CA.

2.68   In *Hertfordshire Investments Ltd v Bubb*[1] (see **para A2.11**) Hale LJ made comments to very similar effect. She said:

'35. The position governing applications to adduce fresh evidence on appeal is now governed by the Civil Procedure Rules, rule 52.11(2). The court will not consider evidence which was not before the court below unless it has given permission for it to be used. It is no longer necessary to show "special grounds". The discretion must also be exercised in accordance with the overriding objective of doing justice.'

After referring to *Banks v Cox* she continued:

'37. It follows from all of this that it cannot be a simple balancing exercise as the judge in this case seemed to think. He had to approach it on the basis that strong grounds were required. The *Ladd v Marshall* criteria are principles rather than rules but, nevertheless, they should be looked at with considerable care and in this particular case, of course, the first of those principles was not fulfilled: The evidence could clearly have been available readily at trial.'

1   [2000] 1 WLR 2318 at 2325D–H.

2.69   This guidance was followed by the Court of Appeal in *Hamilton v Al Fayed (No 4)*[1] in which Lord Phillips MR stated:

'We consider that under the new, as under the old, procedure special grounds must be shown to justify the introduction of fresh evidence on appeal. In a case such as this, which is governed by the transitional provisions, we do not consider that we are placed in the straightjacket of previous authority when considering whether such special grounds have been demonstrated. That question must be considered in the light of the overriding objective of the new CPR. The old cases will, nonetheless, remain powerful persuasive authority, for they illustrate the attempts of the courts to strike a fair balance between the need for concluded litigation to be determinative of disputes and the desirability that the judicial process should achieve the right result. That task is one which accords with the overriding objective.

[The *Ladd v Marshall*] principles have been followed by the Court of Appeal for nearly half a century and are in no way in conflict with the overriding objective. In particular it will not normally be in the interests of justice to reopen a concluded trial in order to introduce fresh evidence unless that evidence will probably influence the result.

Often the fresh evidence relied upon demonstrates that perjured evidence was given at the trial. In such circumstances, provided that the requirements of *Ladd v Marshall* are satisfied, the practice of the Court of Appeal has been to order a new trial without resolving the issue of whether the alleged fraud in fact occurred. That issue is best resolved on the retrial.'

Lord Phillips MR continued that the 'test in *Ladd v Marshall* requires that, if fresh evidence is to justify a retrial, it must be such as would probably have an important influence on the result of a case. This will seldom be satisfied when the fresh evidence goes solely to credit.'

1 (2000) *Independent*, 21 December, [2001] EMLR 15.

2.70 In effect the practice of the Court of Appeal under the CPR appellate regime has run along the lines suggested in the first edition of this book:

i. in relation to an application to admit new evidence on an appeal against a decision made upon a full consideration of the case, the principles of *Ladd v Marshall* are still to be applied, but they are now subject to the overriding objective which permits a more flexible approach (if and where appropriate);

ii in relation to such an application on an appeal against an interim decision, the court broadly follows the approach favoured by Auld LJ in *Electra Private Equity Partners v KPMG Peat Marwick*[1] (see **para A2.7**), namely, that the admission of further evidence is a matter for the court's discretion to be exercised according to the nature of the interim hearing and the individual circumstances of the case.

1 [1999] EWCA Civ 1247.

2.71 In the *Dupont* case[1] May LJ summarised the current position in these terms:

'As to fresh evidence, under rule 52.11(2) on an appeal by way of review the court will not receive evidence which was not before the lower court unless it orders otherwise. There is an obligation on the parties to bring forward all the evidence on which they intend to rely before the lower court, and failure to do this does not normally result in indulgence by the appeal court. The principles on which the appeal court will admit fresh evidence under this provision are now well understood and do not require elaboration here. They may be found, for instance, in the judgment of

Hale LJ in *Hertfordshire Investments Limited v Bubb* [2000] 1 WLR 2318 at 2325D–H. Rule 52.11(2) also applies to appeals by way of rehearing under rule 52.11(1)(b), so that decisions on fresh evidence do not depend on whether the appeal is by way of review or rehearing.'

1   See **para 2.7** above.

2.72 The principle in *Ladd v Marshall*[1], as explained and adapted in the post CPR cases set out in the preceding paragraphs in this section, has recently been considered and applied in the context of a statutory appeal where the court was concerned with a mistake of fact giving rise to unfairness and, in order to demonstrate the mistake, the appellant applied to adduce fresh evidence. In *E v Secretary of State for the Home Department*[2], Carnwath LJ made it clear (at para 82) that *Ladd v Marshall* principles represented the starting point for considering whether to admit fresh evidence on appeal in public law cases, but added that there was a discretion to depart from them in exceptional circumstances. He restated this conclusion in his summary at para 91 of his judgment (for which see **para 2.34** above).

1   [1954] 3 All ER 745, 748, [1954] 1 WLR 1489, 1491, CA.
2   [2004] EWCA Civ 49, Lord Phillips MR, Mantell LJ and Carnwath LJ. See **paras 2.32–2.34** for a consideration of the scope and effect of the principle of 'incorrect basis of fact giving rise to unfairness' in the field of statutory appeals.

Change of circumstances

2.73 In the *Hadmor Productions* case[1] Lord Diplock referred in general terms to 'change of circumstances' as one of the situations in which an appeal court could properly interfere with the decision of a lower court. The language of CPR 52.10 and 52.11, so far as is relevant, is different in certain respects from the language of RSC Order 59 rule 10 and its predecessor and there does not appear to have been any authoritative examination of this matter under the CPR regime.

1   See **para 2.14** above.

2.74 The former rule explicitly recognised that matters which had occurred after the date of the trial or hearing might be admitted on the hearing of an appeal. Some of the governing principles were discussed by the House of Lords in *Murphy v Stone Wallwork (Charlton) Ltd*[1]. It is necessary first to set out the position as it was understood before the CPR, and then consider whether the CPR has produced any alterations.

1   [1969] 1 WLR 1023, 1027c–1028d, 1030f–1031e and 1034a–1036e; [1969] 2 All ER 949.

2.75 In cases decided under the pre-CPR regime it was recognised that changes of circumstance might involve either law or fact. As to changes of law, where there was a change in the understanding of the common law between the time of the decision of the lower court and the hearing of the appeal, the appeal court would apply the law as properly understood. Where there was a change in the law by means of a statute more difficult issues arose. Where the change related to the availability of a remedy then, subject to the statute having retrospective effect[1], the court was likely to apply any new remedy that it provided. Where the change affected the substantive law applied in the court below, careful consideration had to be given in each particular case to the effect of that change.

1   See *Quilter v Mapelson* (1882) 9 QBD 672.

2.76   The courts also recognised that in some cases an appeal would be determined on the state of the facts that obtained at the appeal, rather than upon the facts as they were before the trial court. Examples of this approach could be seen in the following situations:
- where there has been a change of circumstance after the granting of an interlocutory injunction such that, if it had been before the judge, it would have justified the variation of the injunction[1];
- more generally, where change of circumstances since the trial, have falsified the basis on which discretionary relief was granted[2];
- where the passage of time since the trial has falsified a conclusion of the trial court based on complaints of delay[3];
- more generally, on the basis that the court should not speculate where it knows[4], damages will be assessed on the facts as they appear at the date of the appeal hearing[5].

1   Per Lord Diplock in *Hadmoor v Hamilton* [1983] AC 191, 220D.
2   *A-G v Birmingham, Tame and Rea District Drainage Board* [1912] AC 788, 802.
3   Per Lord Scarman in *Engineers' and Managers' Association v Advisory, Conciliation and Arbitration Service (No 2)* [1980] 1 WLR 302, 320F.
4   Per Harman LJ in *Curwen v James* [1963] 1 WLR 748, 753.
5   See e.g. *Lim Poh Choo v Camden and Islington Area Health Authority* [1980] AC 174, 194E. This case seems to have resolved, even if only *sub silentio*, the point left open in *Curwen v James* as to whether changes of circumstance after the date for service of the notice of appeal could be taken into account.

2.77   The House of Lords, however, warned against too wide an extension of these principles. Thus:
- An attempt by Lord Denning MR in *Engineers' and Managers' Association v Advisory, Conciliation and Arbitration Service (No 2)*[1] to generalise the authorities into a principle that the court should always give judgment as if the case had come before the court of first instance on the date of the appellate hearing was specifically disapproved by Lord Scarman[2].
- In the same passage Lord Scarman emphasised that an appellate court could not reverse a judgment given for a defendant when there was no cause of action actual, imminent or threatened, when the writ was issued.

- The discretion to admit fresh evidence that shows the basis on which damages were assessed to have been false should be exercised very sparingly, in view of the importance of finality in litigation[3].

1 [1979] 1 WLR 1113, 1126E.
2 *EMA v ACAS* [1980] 1 WLR 302 at p 320G.
3 *Murphy v Stone Wallwork* [1969] 1 WLR 1023, e.g. per Lord Pearce at p 1028B and per Lord Upjohn at p 1031A.

2.78 These authorities must now be considered in the light of the changes in the appellate regime made by CPR 52.11. Those changes are that (i) appeals will normally be limited to a review of the decision of the lower court, and not be a rehearing; and (ii) an appeal will only be allowed where the decision of the lower court was 'wrong' (unless complaint is made of a serious procedural irregularity).

2.79 The importance of these changes is that many or all of the authorities referred to in **para 2.76** above involved rehearings in the Court of Appeal under the former appellate regime. If these authorities are to be applied under the CPR it would seem that the appellate court must first determine under CPR 52.11 (1)(b) that justice requires that a rehearing be held. There is also the point that, as a matter of language, it seems difficult to say that a decision of a lower court that was correct on the facts and law before it was nonetheless wrong. In *DEG-Deutsche Investitions v Koshy*[1] Robert Walker LJ, obiter, expressed 'considerable scepticism' about an argument that the requirement that the Court of Appeal should find the decision of the lower court to have been wrong had been intended to make any alteration as to the effect of change of circumstances. The precise mechanism by which the appeal court may be entitled to say that the judgment of the lower court was wrong in these circumstances has not yet been explained judicially.

1 [2001] EWCA Civ 79, at para 24.

2.80 These issues clearly still await full argument on an appropriate occasion. For the moment, therefore, the only useful guidance that can be given to practitioners who seek to base an appeal (or opposition to an appeal) on change of circumstance is that the case must be fully set out in their appeal documents, and they must be ready to argue the court's jurisdiction to entertain it.

SERIOUS PROCEDURAL OR OTHER IRREGULARITY RESULTING IN INJUSTICE

2.81 Rule 53.11(3)(b) provides that an appeal will be allowed where the decision of the lower court was 'unjust because of a serious procedural or other irregularity in the proceedings in the lower court'.

2.82 The case-law to which reference is made in **para 2.57** above shows that the Court of Appeal has always regarded itself as possessing the power to intervene where there has been a serious or other procedural irregularity which has caused injustice[1]. This power – to be read in conjunction with and subject to the overriding objective – has been refined in this rule. Its effect and limits were explained by Brooke LJ in *Tanfern Ltd v Cameron MacDonald*[2] (see **para A2.22**):

> 'So far as the second ground for interference is concerned, it must be noted that the appeal court only has power to interfere if the procedural or other irregularity which it has detected in the proceedings in the lower court was a serious one, and that this irregularity caused the decision of the lower court to be an unjust decision.'

1   In these cases injustice is identified as a ground for disturbing the exercise of a discretion of the lower court.
2   [2000] 2 All ER 801, [2000] 1 WLR 1311, CA.

2.83 It is probably best to categorise under this heading the cases which fall foul of Article 6(1) of the European Convention on Human Rights because, for example, the trial judge was or appeared to be biased, or because the trial was not conducted in public[1]. In *CG v United Kingdom*[2] there was a serious procedural irregularity in that the trial judge interrupted to an excessive degree during the cross-examination of the chief prosecution witness. The European Court of Human Rights, however, held that this did not amount to a breach of the right to a fair trial, because defence counsel had been able to make an adequate and uninterrupted closing speech and because the essence of the defence had been restated by the judge. In CPR terms, it might have been said that the irregularity did not cause the outcome to be unjust.

1   *Storer v British Gas plc* [2002] 2 All ER 440, [2000] 1 WLR 1237, CA.
2   (2002) 34 EHRR 1.

INFRINGEMENTS OF ART 6 OF SCH 1 TO THE HUMAN RIGHTS ACT 1998: 'RIGHT TO A FAIR TRIAL'

2.84 The European Convention on Human Rights is contained in Sch 1 to the Act. Article 6 provides as follows:

> 'In the determination of his civil rights and obligations ... everyone is entitled to a fair and public hearing within a reasonable time by an independent and impartial tribunal established by law. Judgment shall be pronounced publicly but the press and public may be excluded from all or part of the trial in the interest of morals, public order or national security in a democratic society, where the interests of juveniles or the protection

of the private life of parties so require, or to the extent strictly necessary in the opinion of the court in special circumstances where publicity would prejudice the interests of justice.'

2.85 It should be observed at the outset that companies have human rights. Article 1 of the Convention requires the parties to the Convention to secure Convention Rights to *'everyone within their jurisdiction'*. Under the case law and under the Convention itself there is no distinction drawn between a natural person and an artificial person.

2.86 Article 6(1) applies to rules of procedure and their application. It applies to time periods specified both in rules of procedure and in directions given by the court. It applies not only to the right of access to the court to bring a claim but to the court's conduct of a claim once decided – including the right to appeal and the regulation of that appeal[1].

1   Recourse should be had to a specialist publication for different examples of the effect of the Convention on civil procedure.

2.87 Speaking generally, the provisions of the CPR do themselves comply with Art 6. Where the Article may be infringed is by any rigorous and disproportionate application of the rules. If the overriding objective is observed and applied, then a challenge under Art 6 is unlikely to succeed.

2.88 More difficult considerations are likely to arise in relation not to Art 6 on its own but in relation to the interaction of Art 6 with other Articles such as Art 8 ('Right to respect for private and family life ... and correspondence') in relation to such matters as disclosure under Pt 31 and the use of covertly obtained video evidence. If the lower court's decision has the effect of violating a Convention right of one or other of the parties and the appeal court is able to put things right, then there will have been an error of law such that the decision of the lower court was wrong.

2.89 If, in any context, practitioners are minded to take a point under Art 6, then they should take heed of the warning by Lord Woolf MR in *Daniels v Walker*[1] that they should take a responsible attitude as to when it was right to raise a Human Rights Act point; and that, in relation to CPR matters, the court was already under a duty to deal with cases justly. The implication of this is that, if the overriding objective in CPR Pt 1 was correctly applied, then there would be no infringement of Art 6 and no scope for any argument that Art 6 had been infringed.

1   [2000] 1 WLR 1382, CA.

2.90 The courts have been careful in the application of the Human Rights Act 1998 both in relation to the substantive law and in relation to recourse to the Act by an appellant as a ground of appeal in respect of the conduct of the management of the claim or of the hearing which is the subject-matter of the appeal. A clear and useful indication of the value of the Act and of judicial thinking in relation to its application may be found in *Goode v Martin*[1] in which Brooke LJ explained the combined effect of the overriding objective and the Human Rights Act 1998:

> 'We now possess more tools for enabling us to do justice than were available before April 1999. Since then, the CPR and the provisions of the 1998 Act have come into force. By the former we must seek to give effect to the overriding objective of dealing with cases justly when we interpret any rule (see CPR 1.2(b)). By the latter we must read and give effect to subordinate legislation, so far as it is possible to do so, in a way which is compatible with the Convention rights set out in Schedule 1 to the Act (see s 3(1) of the 1998 Act).'[2]

1   [2001] EWCA Civ 1899, [2002] 1 WLR 1828, [2002] 1 All ER 620. *Goode v Martin* was a case concerned with an application by a claimant to amend her statement of case where the court departed from previous practice in order to ensure that her right to access to the court was not unjustifiably hampered by the natural interpretation of the relevant Rule.
2   See also *Cachia v Faluyi* [2001] EWCA Civ 998, [2001] 1 WLR 1966, [2002] 1 All ER 192.

CHAPTER 3

Routes of Appeal

Access to Justice Act 1999 (Destination of Appeals) Order 2000	3.1
Small claims	3.2
Fast track claims	3.8
Part 8 claims	3.13
Contempt of court and committal orders	3.17
Multi-track claims and specialist proceedings	3.20
Second appeals	3.26
Costs	3.31
Original or ancillary order	3.35
Assignment of appeals to the Court of Appeal	3.36
Family proceedings	3.39
Insolvency proceedings	3.43
Access to Justice Act 1999	3.45
Access to Justice Act 1999 (Destination of Appeals) Order 2000	3.53

ACCESS TO JUSTICE ACT 1999 (DESTINATION OF APPEALS) ORDER 2000

3.1 The Access to Justice Act 1999 (Destination of Appeals) Order 2000, SI 2000/1071, is made under s 56 of the Access to Justice Act 1999. That provision empowers the Lord Chancellor, after consulting the Heads of Divisions, to prescribe an alternative destination for appeals which would otherwise lie to a county court, the High Court or the Court of Appeal. Under the Order, the route of appeal depends on:

- the type of case and/or to which track a claim was allocated;
- the court from whose decision the appeal is brought ('the lower court');
- the level of judge[1] who made the decision being appealed;
- the nature of the decision being appealed.

The Order is subject to any enactment which provides a different route of appeal (art 1(4)(b)(i)) such as s 13 of the Administration of Justice Act 1960 and to any requirement to obtain permission to appeal (art 1(4)(b)(ii)) such as CPR 52.3 The text of the Order, as amended, is at **paras 3.53–3.60**.

1   A deputy circuit judge or a recorder who sits as a Judge for a county court district has the same powers as a circuit judge. See County Courts Act 1984, s 5; Courts Act 1971 s 24.

SMALL CLAIMS

3.2 The circuit judge is the appeal court where the decision being appealed was made by a district judge hearing a claim allocated to the small claims track[1]

1   Access to Justice Act 1999 (Destination of Appeals) Order 2000, SI 2000/1071, art 3(2).

3.3 Permission is required for these appeals, as CPR Pt 52 applies to small claims following the revocation of CPR 27.12 and 27.13 (appeals in small claims).

3.4 Special provision is made by the Practice Direction which supplements CPR Pt 52 for the documents to be filed where the appeal relates to a claim allocated to the small claims track[1]. This is to reduce costs in such cases.

1   CPR PD 52 para 5.8.

3.5 Where the circuit judge dismisses an appeal at a hearing, the Court of Appeal is the appeal court[1] but such an appeal is a second appeal[2] (see **paras 3.26, 3.27** below). If the circuit judge refuses permission to appeal without a hearing, a request may be made for an oral hearing[3]. If, at a hearing, the circuit judge refuses permission to appeal to himself, no further right of appeal exists[4]. See **para 3.35** below where an original order is made.

1   Access to Justice Act 1999 (Destination of Appeals) Order 2000, SI 2000/1071, art 5.
2   Access to Justice Act 1999, s 55.
3   CPR 52.3(4).
4   Access to Justice Act 1999, s 54(4).

3.6 Where, exceptionally, a circuit judge hears a claim allocated to the small claims track, a High Court judge is the appeal court[1].

1   Access to Justice Act 1999 (Destination of Appeals) Order 2000, SI 2000/1071, art 3(1).

3.7 Where a High Court judge hears a small claims appeal from a circuit judge, the Court of Appeal is the appeal court[1]. Permission to appeal is required for an appeal to the Court of Appeal (from the Court of Appeal itself) but such an appeal is a second appeal[2] and there is a stricter test to overcome (see **paras 3.26, 3.27** below).

1 Access to Justice Act 1999 (Destination of Appeals) Order 2000, SI 2000/1071, art 5.
2 Access to Justice Act 1999, s 55.

FAST TRACK CLAIMS

3.8 The circuit judge is the appeal court where the decision being appealed was made by a district judge hearing a claim allocated to the fast track[1]. Permission to appeal is required for such an appeal[2].

1 Access to Justice Act 1999 (Destination of Appeals) Order 2000, SI 2000/1071, art 3(2).
2 CPR 52.3.

3.9 Where the circuit judge dismisses an appeal at a hearing, the Court of Appeal is the appeal court but such an appeal is a second appeal[1]. If the circuit judge refuses permission to appeal without a hearing, a request may be made for an oral hearing[2]. If, at a hearing, the circuit judge refuses permission to appeal to himself, no further right of appeal exists[3]. See **para 3.35** below where an original order is made.

1 Access to Justice Act 1999 (Destination of Appeals) Order 2000, SI 2000/1071, art 5; see **paras 3.26, 2.27** below.
2 CPR 52.3(4); this is the only remedy which is available as there is no right of appeal: *Hyams v Plender* [2001] 1 WLR 32, [2001] 2 All ER 179, CA.
3 Access to Justice Act 1999, s 54(4).

3.10 Where a circuit judge hears a fast track appeal from a district judge, the Court of Appeal is the appeal court[1]. Permission to appeal is required for an appeal to the Court of Appeal but such an appeal is a second appeal[2] (see **paras 3.26, 3.27** below).

1 Access to Justice Act 1999 (Destination of Appeals) Order 2000, SI 2000/1071, art 5.
2 Ibid.

3.11 Where a circuit judge hears a claim allocated to the fast track, a High Court judge is the appeal court[1]. Permission to appeal is required for such an appeal[2]. If the High Court judge refuses permission without a hearing, a request may be made for an oral hearing[3]. If at a hearing the appeal court refuses permission to appeal, then no further right of appeal exists[4]. See **para 3.35** below where an original order is made.

1 Access to Justice Act 1999 (Destination of Appeals) Order 2000, SI 2000/1071, art 3(1).

2   CPR 52.3.
3   CPR 52.3(4); this is the only remedy which is available as there is no right of appeal: *Hyams v Plender* [2001] 1 WLR 32, [2001] 2 All ER 179, CA.
4   Access to Justice Act 1999, s 54(4).

3.12 Where a High Court judge hears a fast track appeal from a circuit judge, the Court of Appeal is the appeal court[1]. Permission to appeal is required for an appeal to the Court of Appeal but such an appeal is a second appeal[2] (see **paras 3.26, 3.27** below).

1   Access to Justice Act 1999 (Destination of Appeals) Order 2000, SI 2000/1071, art 5.
2   Access to Justice Act 1999, s 55.

PART 8 CLAIMS

3.13 This section applies where the claimant uses the Part 8 procedure and the Part 8 claim form, Form N208 (or another form listed in the Practice Direction supplementing CPR Pt 8 (PD 8B)). The Part 8 procedure is used for claims brought under certain Acts of Parliament, e.g. the Housing Act 1996, s 153 or for damages under the Protection from Harassment Act 1997.

Although Part 8 claims are treated as allocated to the multi-track under CPR 8.9(c), art 4 of the Access to Justice Act 1999 (Destination of Appeals) Order 2000 does not apply to them: it is only appeals from final decisions which are made in Part 7 claims which are allocated to the multi-track that are required by that article to be brought in the Court of Appeal.

3.14 The circuit judge is the appeal court where the decision being appealed was made by a district judge hearing a Part 8 claim[1]. Permission to appeal is required for such an appeal[2].

1   Access to Justice Act 1999 (Destination of Appeals) Order 2000, SI 2000/1071, art 3(2).
2   CPR 52.3.

3.15 Where the circuit judge dismisses an appeal from a district judge at a hearing, the Court of Appeal is the appeal court but such an appeal is a second appeal[1]. If the circuit judge refuses permission to appeal without a hearing, a request may be made for an oral hearing[2]. If, at a hearing, the circuit judge refuses permission to appeal to himself, no further right of appeal exists[3]. See **para 3.35** below where an original order is made.

1   Access to Justice Act 1999 (Destination of Appeals) Order 2000, SI 2000/1071, art 5; see **paras 2.26, 2.27** below.
2   CPR 52.3(4); this is the only remedy which is available as there is no right of appeal: *Hyams v Plender* [2001] 1 WLR 32, [2001] 2 All ER 179, CA.
3   Access to Justice Act 1999, s 54(4).

3.16 Where a circuit judge hears a Part 8 claim, a High Court judge is the appeal court[1]. Permission to appeal is required for such an appeal[2]. If the High Court judge refuses permission without a hearing, a request may be made for an oral hearing[3]. If at a hearing the appeal court refuses permission to appeal, then no further right of appeal exists[4]. See **para 3.35** below where an original order is made. Where a High Court judge hears a Part 8 appeal from a circuit judge, the Court of Appeal is the appeal court[5]. Permission to appeal is required for an appeal to the Court of Appeal but such an appeal is a second appeal[6] (see **paras 3.26, 3.27** below).

1 Access to Justice Act 1999 (Destination of Appeals) Order 2000, SI 2000/1071, art 3(1).
2 CPR 52.3.
3 CPR 52.3(4); this is the only remedy which is available as there is no right of appeal: *Hyams v Plender* [2001] 1 WLR 32, [2001] 2 All ER 179, CA.
4 Access to Justice Act 1999, s 54(4).
5 Access to Justice Act 1999 (Destination of Appeals) Order 2000, SI 2000/1071, art 5.
6 Access to Justice Act 1999, s 55.

CONTEMPT OF COURT AND COMMITTAL ORDERS

3.17 An appellant does not require permission to appeal against a committal order[1]. A 'committal order' is an order which commits a party to prison (see *Government of Sierra Leone v Davenport* [2002] EWCA Civ 230, [2002] All ER (D) 160 (Jan)). A suspended committal order is a 'committal order' and can be appealed without permission: *Wilkinson v S* [2003] 2 All ER 184, [2003] 1 WLR 1244. Any other order or decision made by a court in the exercise of jurisdiction to punish for contempt (such as the refusal to make an order except as to costs or an order for the adjournment of the whole or part of a committal application) comes within s 13 of the 1960 Act, but permission to appeal is required.

1 CPR 52.3(1).

3.18 The Access to Justice Act 1999 (Destination of Appeals) Order 2000, SI 2000/1071, is subject to any enactment that provides a different route of appeal (art 1(4)(b)(i)). Section 13 of the Administration of Justice Act 1960 provides an express right of appeal to the Court of Appeal in any case involving the jurisdiction to punish for contempt of court.

The Court of Appeal has given comprehensive guidance on the routes of appeal in committal proceedings in *Barnet London Borough Council v Hurst*[1]; *King v Read and Slack*[2]; *Hampshire County Council v Gillingham*[3].

1 [2002] EWCA Civ 1009, [2003] 1 WLR 722, [2002] 4 All ER 457.
2 [1999] 1 FLR 425, CA [2002] EWCA Civ 230, [2002] All ER (D) 160 (Jan).
3 Unreported, 22 June 2000, CA.

3.19

(1) An appeal from a committal order made by a circuit judge (or recorder) in a county court lies to the Court of Appeal as of right under s 13(2) of the 1960 Act.

(2) An appeal against any other decision of a circuit judge in a county court in the exercise of jurisdiction to punish for contempt lies to the Court of Appeal but permission to appeal is required.

(3) A first appeal from a committal order made by a district judge in a county court will ordinarily lie to a circuit judge in the county court. Exceptionally, it may lie to the Court of Appeal through the transfer mechanism contained in CPR 52.14 and the Access to Justice Act 1999, s 57.

(4) A first appeal from any order of a district judge in a county court in the exercise of jurisdiction to punish for contempt will follow the same routes as in (3) but permission to appeal will be required.

(5) Except where a committal order is made by the circuit judge on appeal or the circuit judge makes an original order on the appeal (e.g. for costs), CPR 52.13 will apply to an appeal against the circuit judge's order as a second appeal. Second appeals lie to the Court of Appeal and permission to appeal is always required. Even if there is a second appeal in relation to a committal order originally made by a district judge, the order appealed from is not itself a committal order within the meaning of CPR 52.3(1)(a).

MULTI-TRACK CLAIMS AND SPECIALIST PROCEEDINGS

3.20 Article 4 of Access to Justice Act 1999 (Destination of Appeals) Order 2000, SI 2000/1071, applies where a final decision is made in a Part 7 claim which has been allocated to the multi-track[1] or in proceedings under the Companies Act 1985 or the Companies Act 1989 or in proceedings to which Sections I, II or III of Part 57 or any of Parts 58–63 of the Civil Procedure Rules 1998 apply.

1   A claim must be allocated to the multi-track as the Court of Appeal does not have jurisdiction to hear an appeal from a final decision of a district judge in a claim which has not been allocated: *Jenkins v BP Oil UK Ltd* (1 September 2000) reported in *Clark v Perks* [2001] 1 WLR 17, 30; [2000] 4 All ER 1 (see **para A2.5**).

3.21 Where a district judge or circuit judge in a county court or a Master or a High Court judge in the High Court gives a final decision in a multi-track claim, the Court of Appeal is the appeal court[1]. A 'final decision' is one which finally determines (subject to any possible appeal or detailed assessment of costs) the entire proceedings 'whichever way the court decided the issues before it'[2]. A final decision includes a decision on liability, on limitation, the assessment of damages or any other final decision made at the conclusion of 'part of a hearing or trial which has been split into parts'; it does not include a decision only on costs[2]. The same route of appeal applies where a final decision is given in:

- admiralty claims under CPR Pt 61;
- arbitration claims under CPR Pt 62;
- commercial and mercantile claims under CPR Pt 58 or 59;
- patents and other intellectual property claims under CPR Pt 63;
- Technology and Construction Court claims under CPR Pt 60;
- proceedings under the Companies Acts 1985 and 1989; and
- contentious probate proceedings under CPR Pt 57[3].

Final decisions for the purposes of the Destination of Appeals Order should not be confused with decisions which, by statute, are declared to be final[4].

1   Access to Justice Act 1999 (Destination of Appeals) Order 2000, SI 2000/1071, art 4.
2   Access to Justice Act 1999 (Destination of Appeals) Order 2000, SI 2000/1071, art 1(2)(c), (3). See also CPR PD 52, paras 2A.1–2A.5.
3   Claims under the Inheritance (Provision for Family and Dependants) Act 1975 are governed by Section IV of Part 57 and are excluded from the 'specialist proceedings' regime.
4   See the note to CPR 52.1 and the restriction on appeals made by Supreme Court Act 1981, s 18(1)(c).

3.22 Permission to appeal is required for such appeals[1].

1   CPR 52.3, except where the appeal is against a committal order, a refusal of habeas corpus or a secure accommodation order made under s 25 of the Children Act 1989.

3.23 Where the decision given is not final or treated as final[1], e.g.:
- a case management decision;
- an order striking out the proceedings or a statement of case[2]; or
- an order giving summary judgment under CPR Pt 24[2],

the route of appeal depends on the level of judge who made the order being appealed.

Judge making order	Appeal Court	Second Appeal
District judge in county court	Circuit judge in county court	Court of Appeal
Circuit judge in county court	High Court judge	Court of Appeal
District judge in District Registry	High Court judge	Court of Appeal
High Court judge	Court of Appeal	House of Lords

1   Access to Justice Act 1999 (Destination of Appeals) Order 2000, SI 2000/1071, art 1(2)(c), (3).
2   These are not final decisions for the purposes of art 1(2)(c) because the result would not be the same 'whichever way the court decided the issues before it'.

3.24 Permission to appeal is required for such appeals[1].

1   CPR 52.3 except where the appeal is against a committal order, a refusal of habeas corpus or a secure accommodation order made under s 25 of the Children Act 1989.

3.25 If the appeal court refuses permission without a hearing, a request may be made for an oral hearing[1]. If at a hearing the appeal court refuses permission to appeal, then no further right of appeal exists[2]. Where the decision being appealed was itself made on appeal, permission to appeal is required for an appeal to the Court of Appeal (from the Court of Appeal itself[3]) and there is a stricter test to overcome, because such an appeal is a second appeal[4]. See **paras 3.26, 3.27** below.

1   CPR 52.3(4); this is the only remedy which is available as there is no right of appeal: *Hyams v Plender* [2001] 1 WLR 32, [2001] 2 All ER 179, CA.
2   Access to Justice Act 1999, s 54(4).
3   CPR 52.13.
4   Access to Justice Act 1999, s 55: no appeal may be made unless the Court of Appeal considers that the appeal would raise an important point of principle or practice or there is some other compelling reason for the Court of Appeal to hear it.

SECOND APPEALS

3.26 Section 55 of the Access to Justice Act 1999, art 5 of the Access to Justice Act 1999 (Destination of Appeals) Order 2000, SI 2000/1071, and CPR 52.13 apply where the decision being appealed was itself made on appeal. The section and art 5 of the Order refer to 'second appeals' but their wording is not restricted to second appeals and could apply to third appeals in the rare cases where such further right of appeal exists: see **para 3.34** below.

3.27 Where an appeal is made to a county court or to the High Court (apart from the decision of a court officer authorised to assess costs) and, **on hearing the appeal**, the court makes a decision, an appeal from that decision lies to the Court of Appeal and not to any other court[1]. A decision made during the hearing of an application for permission to appeal is not a decision made on hearing the appeal. See **para 3.35** for such orders. Permission to appeal from the Court of Appeal itself is required for a second appeal[2] and there is a stricter test to overcome, as this is a 'second appeal'[3]. Under the Access to Justice Act 1999, s 55, no appeal may be made unless the Court of Appeal considers that 'the appeal would raise an important point of principle or practice or there is some other compelling reason for the Court of Appeal to hear it'.

1   Access to Justice Act 1999 (Destination of Appeals) Order 2000, SI 2000/1071, art 5.
2   CPR 52.13. The Court of Appeal has no jurisdiction in relation to a purported challenge to a judgment in the High Court on an appeal under the Arbitration Act 1996, s 69 when the High Court had not granted leave to appeal pursuant to s 69(8): *Henry Boot Construction (UK) Ltd v Malmaison Hotel (Manchester) Ltd* [2001] QB 388, [2001] 1 All ER 257, CA.

3   Access to Justice Act 1999, s 55.

3.28   The Court of Appeal has now made it clear that, for the purposes of the Access to Justice Act 1999, s 55, the following appeals are to be treated as appeals to a county court or the High Court within the meaning of that section:
(a) an appeal to the High Court on a point of law pursuant to the Tribunals and Inquiries Act 1992, s 11, from a tribunal;
(b) any application to the High Court which can be categorised as an appeal by way of case stated;
(c) an appeal to a county court on a point of law from a decision of a local housing authority under the Housing Act 1996, s 204(1) or s 204A;
(d) any other appeal to the High Court or the county court from any tribunal or other body or person[1].

1   *McNicholas Construction Co Ltd v Customs and Excise Comrs, Clark v Perks* [2001] 1 WLR 17, [2000] 4 All ER 1 and *Azimi v London Borough of Newham* (26 July 2000, unreported), CA.

The appellate policy

3.29   This was explained by Brooke LJ as follows[1]:

'Parliament ... has now made it clear that it is only in an exceptional case that a second appeal may be sanctioned.'

Section 55 imposes a stricter test than that provided by the former Practice Direction for 'second tier appeals' as that provision related only to cases where a would-be appellant had already lost twice in the courts below[2]. Under s 55 the decision of the first appeal court 'is now to be given primacy unless the Court of Appeal itself considers that the appeal would raise an important point of principle or practice, or that there is some other compelling reason for it to hear this second appeal'.

The reason for this change in appellate policy is found in the 1997 Bowman review of the business of the Court of Appeal (Civil Division) which had recorded the substantial increase in the number of cases coming to the Court of Appeal. The authors of the report believed that if there had to be an appeal in a civil case this should normally be the end of the matter. This principle reflected the need for certainty, reasonable expense and proportionality, and they concluded that there must be special circumstances if there was to be more than one level of appeal. In *Tanfern* Brooke LJ went on to say that:

'It is clear that in the 1999 Act Parliament not only accepted the report's analysis of the problems confronting the Court of Appeal but that it also adopted even tougher measures than those recommended by the review to ensure that second appeals would in future become a rarity and that the judges of this court would be freed to devote more of their time and energy in hearing first appeals in more substantive matters which either their court or a lower court had assessed as having a realistic prospect of success.'

1   *Tanfern v Cameron-Macdonald* [2000] 2 All ER 801, [2000] 1 WLR 1311, CA (see **para A2.22**).
2   *Practice Direction (Court of Appeal: Procedure)* [1999] 2 All ER 490, [1999] 1 WLR 1027, CA, para 2.19.1.

3.30 Section 55 applies only to appeals from decisions made by a county court or the High Court. Nevertheless, the Court of Appeal applied the stricter test for permission imposed by s 55 in an appeal from an expert tribunal, a Social Security Commissioner, in *Cooke v Secretary of State for Social Security* ([2001] EWCA Civ 734, [2002] 3 All ER 279, CA, Clarke, Hale LJJ, Butterfield J). The *Cooke* approach has also been applied to appeals from decisions of the Competition Commission Appeal Tribunal: *Napp Pharmaceutical Holdings Ltd v Director General of Fair Trading* [2002] EWCA Civ 796, [2002] 4 All ER 376, [2002] All ER (D). The same reasoning was not, however, extended to appeals from the Immigration Appeal Tribunal by the Court of Appeal in *Koller v Secretary of State for the Home Department* [2001] EWCA Civ 1267 (Brooke, Tuckey, Laws LJJ) (see **para A2.15**).

COSTS

3.31 Where costs are summarily assessed by the judge as part of a final decision in a multi-track claim, then **para 3.21** above applies.

3.32 An appeal against a decision made by an authorised costs officer in detailed assessment proceedings (formerly called a taxation) is to a costs judge or a district judge of the High Court[1]; that judge re-hears the proceedings which gave rise to the decision being appealed[2]. Permission to appeal is not required, as CPR Pt 52 does not apply to appeals from costs officers[3].

1   CPR 47.21, as substituted by SI 2000/940.
2   CPR 47.23, as substituted by SI 2000/940.
3   CPR 52.1(2)(b).

3.33 An appeal from a costs judge or a district judge of the High Court lies to a High Court judge[1]. This is not a 'second appeal' within art 5 of the Access to Justice Act 1999 (Destination of Appeals) Order 2000, SI 2000/1071, and does not lie to the Court of Appeal, as appeals from costs officers are excluded by art 5(a). Permission to appeal is required as the exception in CPR 52.1(2)(b) applies only to appeals from costs officers and not to the higher level of appeal[2].

1   Access to Justice Act 1999 (Destination of Appeals) Order 2000, SI 2000/1071, art 2.

2   CPR 52.1(2)(b), *Tanfern v Cameron-Macdonald* [2000] 2 All ER 801, [2000] 1 WLR 1311, CA (see **para A2.22**).

3.34 Any appeal from the decision of the High Court judge would lie to the Court of Appeal[1]. The stricter test in s 55 of the Access to Justice Act 1999 would apply[2] and permission to appeal would have to be given by the Court of Appeal itself[3].

1   Access to Justice Act 1999 (Destination of Appeals) Order 2000, SI 2000/1071, art 5.
2   See **paras 3.26, 3.27** above.
3   CPR 52.13.

ORIGINAL OR ANCILLARY ORDERS

3.35 Where a circuit judge or a High Court judge refuses to extend time for an appeal from a district judge or a master, that order may be appealed[1]. An appeal from such an order is not, however, a second appeal as the 'matter' on which the judge gives judgment (i.e. whether to extend time to appeal) is different from the 'matter' on which the district judge or master gave his decision. In refusing to extend time to appeal, the judge is exercising his original jurisdiction to make an original or ancillary order. Where a circuit judge in a county court or a High Court judge makes an original or ancillary order at the same time as refusing permission to appeal from the lower court, then the original or ancillary order may be appealed although permission will rarely be granted[2]. Where such an order is made by a circuit judge in a county court, an appeal lies to the High Court and not the Court of Appeal as the appeal from the original or ancillary order is not a second appeal[3].

1   *Foenander v Bond Lewis & Co* [2001] EWCA Civ 759, [2002] 1 WLR 525, [2001] 2 All ER 1019 (see **para A2.8**). S 54(4) of the Access to Justice Act 1999 only precludes appeals from the refusal of permission to appeal.
2   *Riniker v University College London (Practice Note)* [2001] 1 WLR 13, CA.
3   *Jolly v Jay* [2002] EWCA Civ 277 (see **para A2.13**).

ASSIGNMENT OF APPEALS TO THE COURT OF APPEAL

3.36 Section 57 of the Access to Justice Act 1999 enables the Master of the Rolls or the court from which or to which an appeal is made, or from which permission to appeal is sought, to direct that the appeal should instead be heard by the Court of Appeal. The section only applies to proceedings in a county court or the High Court in which a person seeks to appeal to a court other than the Court of Appeal or the House of Lords[1]. By definition it does not apply to second appeals and only applies where a first appeal would lie to a court other than the Court of Appeal or the House of Lords.

1   Access to Justice Act 1999, s 57(1).

3.37 The power conferred by s 57 on the lower courts is subject to rules of court[1] and CPR 52.14 provides that an order transferring an appeal to a Court of Appeal may be made where the lower court considers that the appeal 'would raise an important point of principle or practice or there is some other compelling reason for the Court of Appeal to hear it'. Where such an order has been made by the lower court the Master of the Rolls or the Court of Appeal may remit the appeal to the court to which the original appeal would have been brought[2] where it is considered that the criteria for a reference under s 57 have not been satisfied.

1   Access to Justice Act 1999, s 57(2). The power conferred by CPR 52.14 on courts lower than the Court of Appeal should be sparingly used: *Jenkins v BP Oil UK Ltd*, CA (1 September 2000) reported in *Clark v Perks* [2001] 1 WLR 17; [2000] 4 All ER 1 (see **para A2.5**).
2   CPR 52.14(2).

3.38 Lord Woolf, when Master of the Rolls, established the following criteria to be applied in considering whether to make a direction:
(a) where there appear to be conflicting authorities requiring resolution by the Court of Appeal;
(b) in relation to points of practice or procedure where there is no guidance at present and the point is of significant importance for the practice or procedure of the courts;
(c) where the issue is one of general principle and importance in the development of the substantive law; or
(d) the issue is one where there are a number of appeals on similar points so as to suggest that a theme or trend is developing which the Court of Appeal needs to consider.

Unless the position is sufficiently clear, judges are encouraged to leave the making of any direction to the Master of the Rolls. Since judges (other than High Court judges) are to seek advice from the Designated Civil Judge and, if necessary, from the Presiding Judge, the announcement of whether a direction will be made may be deferred and made subsequent to the decision to grant permission[1].

Where a case has been identified as suitable for assignment the papers are sent to the Head of the Civil Appeals Office, Room E307, Royal Courts of Justice, Strand, London WC2A 2LL. Parties are expected to supply three bundles of documents with the necessary transcripts (in compliance with the Practice Direction supplementing CPR Pt 52[2]) so the matter may be listed without unnecessary delay.

1   An application for permission to appeal cannot be transferred. Permission to appeal must be granted: *Re Claims Direct Test Cases* [2002] EWCA Civ 428.

2   See CPR PD 52, para 5.6A; para 10.1 of the Practice Direction enables the court to give such directions as it considers appropriate

FAMILY PROCEEDINGS

3.39 The Access to Justice Act 1999 (Destination of Appeals) Order 2000, SI 2000/1071, does not apply to family proceedings[1] and appeals to the Court of Appeal will continue to lie to that Court as at present. CPR Pt 52 does not apply to family proceedings in the county courts and the High Court[2] but does apply to family proceedings in the Court of Appeal.

1   Access to Justice Act 1999 (Destination of Appeals) Order 2000, SI 2000/1071, art 1(4)(a).
2   CPR PD 52, para 2.2.

3.40 The Family Proceedings Rules 1991 continue to govern appeals in family proceedings in the county courts and the High Court and so there is no requirement to obtain permission to appeal. The circuit judge of a county court is the appeal court where the decision being appealed was made by a district judge sitting in a county court.

3.41 A High Court judge of the Family Division is the appeal court where the decision being appealed was made by a district judge sitting in the Principal Registry of the Family Division.

3.42 The Court of Appeal is the appeal court where the decision being appealed was made by:
- a circuit judge sitting in a county court or as a judge of the Family Division of the High Court;
- a High Court judge;
- a circuit judge or High Court judge on appeal from a district judge.

INSOLVENCY PROCEEDINGS

3.43 The Destination Order is subject to any enactment which provides a different route of appeal[1] and s 375 of the Insolvency Act 1986 (as amended) provides that an appeal from a decision made in exercise of bankruptcy or insolvency jurisdiction by:
(a)   a district judge or circuit judge in a county court; or
(b)   a registrar in bankruptcy of the High Court,

lies to a single judge of the High Court[2]; there is no requirement for permission to appeal. An appeal from the decision of the High Court judge on such an appeal lies, with permission of the Court of Appeal, to the Court of Appeal[3].

An appeal from the decision of a High Court judge in insolvency proceedings which is not made on appeal lies, with permission of the judge or the Court of Appeal, to the Court of Appeal[4].

1   Access to Justice Act 1999 (Destination of Appeals) Order 2000, SI 2000/1071, art 1(4)(b)(i).
2   Insolvency Act 1986, s 375(2) as amended by Access to Justice Act 1999, s 106 and Sch 15, Part III.
3   This is a second appeal and the stricter test for the grant of permission applies.
4   See Part 4 of the Practice Direction: Insolvency Proceedings, para 17.4 which provides that CPR Part 52 and its Practice Direction apply to appeals from a judge of the High Court only; paras 17.8–17.23 apply to 'first appeals' i.e. appeals from district judges and circuit judges and from registrars.

Original/ancillary orders

Multi-track and specialist

3.44

Non-final orders

	Hearing	*Appeal*	*Second appeal*
County court	District judge	Circuit judge	Court of Appeal
	Circuit judge	High Court judge	Court of Appeal
High Court	District judge/master	High Court judge	Court of Appeal
	High Court judge	Court of Appeal	House of Lords

Final decisions

	Hearing	*Appeal*
County court	District judge	Court of Appeal
	Circuit judge	Court of Appeal
High court	District judge/Master	Court of Appeal
	High Court judge	Court of Appeal

Family proceedings

	Hearing	*Appeal*	*Second appeal*
County court	District judge	Circuit judge	Court of Appeal
	Circuit judge	Court of Appeal	

	Hearing	Appeal	Second appeal
High court	District judge	High Court judge	Court of Appeal
	High Court judge	Court of Appeal	

ACCESS TO JUSTICE ACT 1999

PART IV
APPEALS, COURTS, JUDGES AND COURT PROCEEDINGS

Appeals

3.45

54. Permission to appeal

(1) Rules of court may provide that any right of appeal to-
(a) a county court,
(b) the High Court, or
(c) the Court of Appeal,
may be exercised only with permission.

(2) This section does not apply to a right of appeal in a criminal cause or matter.

(3) For the purposes of subsection (1) rules of court may make provision as to-
(a) the classes of case in which a right of appeal may be exercised only with permission,
(b) the court or courts which may give permission for the purposes of this section,
(c) any considerations to be taken into account in deciding whether permission should be given, and
(d) any requirements to be satisfied before permission may be given,
and may make different provision for different circumstances.

(4) No appeal may be made against a decision of a court under this section to give or refuse permission (but this subsection does not affect any right under rules of court to make a further application for permission to the same or another court).

(5) For the purposes of this section a right to make an application to have a case stated for the opinion of the High Court constitutes a right of appeal.

(6) For the purposes of this section a right of appeal to the Court of Appeal includes-

(a) the right to make an application for a new trial, and
(b) the right to make an application to set aside a verdict, finding or judgment in any cause or matter in the High Court which has been tried, or in which any issue has been tried, by a jury.

3.46

55. Second appeals

(1) Where an appeal is made to a county court or the High Court in relation to any matter, and on hearing the appeal the court makes a decision in relation to that matter, no appeal may be made to the Court of Appeal from that decision unless the Court of Appeal considers that–
   (a) the appeal would raise an important point of principle or practice, or
   (b) there is some other compelling reason for the Court of Appeal to hear it.

(2) This section does not apply in relation to an appeal in a criminal cause or matter.

3.47

56. Power to prescribe alternative destination of appeals

(1) The Lord Chancellor may by order provide that appeals which would otherwise lie to–
   (a) a county court,
   (b) the High Court, or
   (c) the Court of Appeal,
shall lie instead to another of those courts, as specified in the order.

(2) This section does not apply to an appeal in a criminal cause or matter.

(3) An order under subsection (1)–
   (a) may make different provision for different classes of proceedings or appeals, and
   (b) may contain consequential amendments or repeals of enactments.

(4) Before making an order under subsection (1) the Lord Chancellor shall consult–
   (a) the Lord Chief Justice,
   (b) the Master of the Rolls,
   (c) the President of the Family Division, and
   (d) the Vice-Chancellor.

(5) An order under subsection (1) shall be made by statutory instrument.

(6) No such order may be made unless a draft of it has been laid before and approved by resolution of each House of Parliament.

(7) For the purposes of this section an application to have a case stated for the opinion of the High Court constitutes an appeal.

3.48

57. Assignment of appeals to Court of Appeal

(1) Where in any proceedings in a county court or the High Court a person appeals, or seeks permission to appeal, to a court other than the Court of Appeal or the House of Lords–
  (a) the Master of the Rolls, or
  (b) the court from which or to which the appeal is made, or from which permission to appeal is sought,

may direct that the appeal shall be heard instead by the Court of Appeal.

(2) The power conferred by subsection (1)(b) shall be subject to rules of court.

3.49

58. Criminal appeals: minor amendments

(1) In section 40(6) of the Criminal Justice Act 1991 (order returning offender to prison for unserved portion of sentence to be treated for purposes of appeal provisions as sentence passed for original offence), for the words from 'any enactment' to 'made' substitute 'sections 9 and 10 of the Criminal Appeal Act 1968, any order made by the Crown Court under subsection (2) above, or made under subsection (3A) above'.

(2) In section 8(1B)(b) of the Criminal Appeal Act 1968 (power of Court to direct entry of judgment and verdict of acquittal on applications relating to order for retrial), after 'to' insert 'set aside the order for retrial and'.

(3) In section 9(2) of that Act (right of appeal against sentence for summary offence), insert at the end 'or sub-paragraph (4) of that paragraph.'

(4) Section 10 of that Act (appeal to Court of Appeal by person dealt with by Crown Court for offence of which he was not convicted on indictment) is amended in accordance with subsections (5) to (7).

(5) In subsection (2) (proceedings from which an appeal lies), insert at the end

'; or

  (c)   having been released under Part II of the Criminal Justice Act 1991 after serving part of a sentence of imprisonment or detention imposed for the offence, is ordered by the Crown Court to be returned to prison or detention.'

(6) In subsection (3) (cases where person may appeal), in paragraph (cc) (order under section 40(3A)), for '40(3A)' substitute '40(2) or (3A)'.

(7) In subsection (4) (calculation of length of term of imprisonment), after 'imprisonment' insert 'or detention'.

3.50

Civil division of Court of Appeal

59. Composition

In section 54 of the Supreme Court Act 1981 (composition of court of civil division of Court of Appeal), for subsections (2) to (4) (number of judges) substitute–

- '(2) Subject as follows, a court shall be duly constituted for the purpose of exercising any of its jurisdiction if it consists of one or more judges.
- (3) The Master of the Rolls may, with the concurrence of the Lord Chancellor, give (or vary or revoke) directions about the minimum number of judges of which a court must consist if it is to be duly constituted for the purpose of any description of proceedings.
- (4) The Master of the Rolls, or any Lord Justice of Appeal designated by him, may (subject to any directions under subsection (3)) determine the number of judges of which a court is to consist for the purpose of any particular proceedings.
- (4A) The Master of the Rolls may give directions as to what is to happen in any particular case where one or more members of a court which has partly heard proceedings are unable to continue.'

3.51

60. Calling into question of incidental decisions

For section 58 of the Supreme Court Act 1981 (exercise of incidental jurisdiction in civil division of Court of Appeal) substitute–

'**Calling into question of incidental decisions in civil division.**

58. – (1) Rules of court may provide that decisions of the Court of Appeal which–
- (a) are taken by a single judge or any officer or member of staff of that court in proceedings incidental to any cause or matter pending before the civil division of that court; and
- (b) do not involve the determination of an appeal or of an application for permission to appeal,

may be called into question in such manner as may be prescribed.

(2) No appeal shall lie to the House of Lords from a decision which may be called into question pursuant to rules under subsection (1).'

PART VII
SUPPLEMENTARY

3.52

110 Short Title

This Act may be cited as the Access to Justice Act 1999.

ACCESS TO JUSTICE ACT 1999 (DESTINATION OF APPEALS) ORDER 2000(SI 2000/1071)

3.53

1. Citation, commencement and interpretation

(1) This Order may be cited as the Access to Justice Act 1999 (Destination of Appeals) Order 2000 and shall come into force on 2nd May 2000.

(2) In this Order–
(a) 'decision' includes any judgment, order or direction of the High Court or a county court;
(b) 'family proceedings' means proceedings which are business of any description which in the High Court is for the time being assigned to the Family Division and to no other Division by or under section 61 of (and Schedule 1 to) the Supreme Court Act 1981; and
(c) 'final decision' means a decision of a court that would finally determine (subject to any possible appeal or detailed assessment of costs) the entire proceedings whichever way the court decided the issues before it.

(3) A decision of a court shall be treated as a final decision where it–
(a) is made at the conclusion of part of a hearing or trial which has been split into parts; and
(b) would, if made at the conclusion of that hearing or trial, be a final decision under paragraph (2)(c).

(4) Articles 2 to 6–
(a) do not apply to an appeal in family proceedings; and
(b) are subject to–
   (i) any enactment that provides a different route of appeal (other than section 16(1) of the Supreme Court Act 1981 or section 77(1) of the County Courts Act 1984); and
   (ii) any requirement to obtain permission to appeal.

3.54

2. Appeals from the High Court

Subject to articles 4 and 5, an appeal shall lie to a judge of the High Court where the decision to be appealed is made by–
- (a) a person holding an office referred to in Part II of Schedule 2 to the Supreme Court Act 1981;
- (b) a district judge of the High Court; or
- (c) a person appointed to act as a deputy for any person holding such an office as is referred to in sub-paragraphs (a) and (b) or to act as a temporary additional officer in any such office.

3.55

3. Appeals from a county court

(1) Subject to articles 4 and 5 and to paragraph (2), an appeal shall lie from a decision of a county court to the High Court.

(2) Subject to articles 4 and 5, where the decision to be appealed is made by a district judge or deputy district judge of a county court, an appeal shall lie to a judge of a county court.

3.56

4. Appeals in a claim allocated to the multi-track or in specialist proceedings

An appeal shall lie to the Court of Appeal where the decision to be appealed is a final decision—
- (a) in a claim made under Part 7 of the Civil Procedure Rules 1998 and allocated to the multi-track under those Rules; or
- (b) made in proceedings under the Companies Act 1985 or the Companies Act 1989 or to which sections I, II or III of Part 57 or any of Parts 58 to 63 of the Civil Procedure Rules 1998 apply.

3.57

5. Appeals where decision was itself made on appeal

Where–
- (a) an appeal is made to a county court or the High Court (other than from the decision of an officer of the court authorised to assess costs by the Lord Chancellor); and
- (b) on hearing the appeal the court makes a decision,

an appeal shall lie from that decision to the Court of Appeal and not to any other court.

3.58

6. Transitional provisions

Where a person has filed a notice of appeal or applied for permission to appeal before 2nd May 2000–
  (a) this Order shall not apply to the appeal to which that notice or application relates; and
  (b) that appeal shall lie to the court to which it would have lain before 2nd May 2000.

3.59

7. Consequential amendments

In section 16(1) of the Supreme Court Act 1981, before 'the Court of Appeal' the second time it appears, insert 'or as provided by any order made by the Lord Chancellor under section 56(1) of the Access to Justice Act 1999,'.

3.60

8. In section 77(1) of the County Courts Act 1984, after 'Act' insert 'and to any order made by the Lord Chancellor under section 56(1) of the Access to Justice Act 1999'.

CHAPTER 4

Procedure

Introduction	4.1
General rules about appeals	4.4
CPR 52.1 Scope and interpretation	4.4
CPR 52.2 Parties to comply with the practice direction	4.9
CPR 52.3 Permission	4.11
CPR 52.4 Appellant' notice	4.25
CPR 52.5 Respondent' notice	4.31
CPR 52.6 Variation of time	4.38
CPR 52.7 Stay	4.45
CPR 52.8 Amendment of appeal notice	4.50
CPR 52.9 Striking out appeal notices	4.55
CPR 52.10 Appeal court's powers	4.64
CPR 52.11 Hearing of appeals	4.69
CPR 52.12 Non-disclosure of Part 36 offers and payments	4.84
Special provisions applying to the Court of Appeal	4.88
CPR 52.13 Second appeals to the court	4.88
General notes on appeals and applications to the Court of Appeal	4.97
CPR 52.14 Assignment of appeals to the Court of Appeal	4.111
CPR 52.15 Judicial review appeals	4.113
CPR 52.16 Who may exercise the powers of the Court of Appeal	4.115

Provisions about reopening appeals	4.117
CPR 52.17 Reopening of final appeals	4.117
Practice Direction 52	4.122

INTRODUCTION

4.1 CPR Pt 52 complements the changes made to appeals by ss 54–57 of the Access to Justice Act 1999 (see **Chapter 3** for the text of the Act) and provides a uniform procedure for appeals in the county courts, the High Court and the Civil Division of the Court of Appeal.

Part 52 does not apply to:
(a) family proceedings in the High Court or the county courts but does apply to appeals to the Court of Appeal from decisions made in family proceedings;
(b) appeals in detailed assessment proceedings against the decision of an authorised court officer.

Preliminary

Order to be appealed

4.2 If, for any reason, the order being appealed is not yet available, an explanation has to be furnished when the appeal notice is filed. The status of the order and the date on which the decision was made must be clear from the order itself. Care should therefore[1] be taken when drafting orders to ensure that the necessary information appears on the face of the order itself[2]. The Court of Appeal has on more than one occasion expressed concern about the way orders are drawn in the High Court and the county courts (see *Bulled v Khayat* [2002] EWCA Civ 804 and *Southern & District Finance plc v Turner* [2003] EWCA Civ 1574 (see **para A2.21**)). Practitioners should ensure that the order is drawn accurately to avoid delay in issuing an appellant's notice in the Court of Appeal since, if the order is inaccurate, the appellant's solicitor will be expected to arrange for the lower court to correct it. The Court of Appeal will not accept a sealed copy of a judgment given by the lower court and practitioners should ensure that an order is drawn[3]. See **Chapter 2 paras 2.8–2.10**.

1 See also **Chapter 2, paras** 2.8–2.10 above.
2 If a court considers that an application or claim or statement of case is totally devoid of merit, it should say so and this should appear on the face of the order: *Bhamjee v Forsdick & Ors* [2003] EWCA Civ 1113, CA. An order of the lower appeal court which refuses an application for an adjournment could conveniently set out the reasons why the adjournment was refused: *Paulson v Bandegani* [2001] EWCA Civ 1274.

3   The failure to draw an order reflecting the outcome of a preliminary issue trial in care proceedings has also been criticised (see *B (children: non-accidental injury)* [2002] EWCA Civ 902, [2002] 2 FCR 654).

Status of order

4.3   The provision made by the Destination of Appeals Order (SI 2000/1071) (see **Chapter 3**) for specific routes of appeal in certain appeals from county courts makes it necessary for the status of the order being appealed to be completely clear on its face:

- an order must record the name and status of the judge[1] making the order; and the name and the precise level of the court in which the order was made;
- the order of a lower appeal court should make it clear whether the judge was dealing with an application for permission to appeal or, having granted that application, with an appeal.
- if permission to appeal is refused[2] but the judge makes an ancillary order (such as an order in respect of costs) that should be made clear.
- The order of an appeal court should make it clear on the face of an order for a rehearing whether it is ordering a rehearing at appeal court level (in which case any subsequent appeal would be a second appeal) or whether it is ordering a rehearing of the original application at first instance: *Fowler de Pledge v Smith* [2003] EWCA Civ 703, [2003] All ER (D) 261 (May), CA.

In view of the need for the Court of Appeal to be satisfied that it has jurisdiction to entertain an appeal from a county court, the Civil Appeals Office requires the production of a copy of the order specifically allocating the claim to the multi-track[3] as well as a copy of the order being appealed if that order does not show the track to which the claim was allocated.

1   A High Court judge should be referred to as 'the Honourable Mr [or Mrs] Justice X'; a Circuit Judge as 'His [or Her] Honour Judge Y' and a district judge as 'District Judge X'. A recorder (sitting as a deputy Circuit Judge) should be referred to as 'Mr/Mrs/Miss/Ms Recorder Y'
2   The correct terminology is to refer to an application for permission to appeal as being 'refused', not 'dismissed': *Plymouth City Council v Hoskin* [2002] EWCA Civ 684.
3   A claim must be allocated to the multi-track at the time the judgment or order under appeal is given or made: *Jenkins v BP Oil UK Ltd*, CA (1 September 2000) reported in *Clark v Perks* [2001] 1 WLR 17; [2000] 4 All ER 1 (see **para A2.5**); allocation after judgment is not sufficient: *Milward v Three Rivers District Council* (25 October 2000, unreported), CA (see **para A2.16**).

GENERAL RULES ABOUT APPEALS
CPR 52.1 SCOPE AND INTERPRETATION

4.4

'52.1 Scope and interpretation
  (1)   The rules in this Part apply to appeals to—

(a) the civil division of the Court of Appeal;
(b) the High Court; and
(c) a county court.
(2) This Part does not apply to an appeal in detailed assessment proceedings against a decision of an authorised court officer.
(Rules 47.21 to 47.26 deal with appeals against a decision of an authorised court officer in detailed assessment proceedings)
(3) In this Part—
(a) "appeal" includes an appeal by way of case stated;
(b) "appeal court" means the court to which an appeal is made;
(c) "lower court" means the court, tribunal or other person or body from whose decision an appeal is brought;
(d) "appellant" means a person who brings or seeks to bring an appeal;
(e) "respondent" means—
  (i) a person other than the appellant who was a party to the proceedings in the lower court and who is affected by the appeal; and
  (ii) a person who is permitted by the appeal court to be a party to the appeal; and
(f) "appeal notice" means an appellant's or respondent's notice.
(4) This Part is subject to any rule, enactment or practice direction which sets out special provisions with regard to any particular category of appeal.'

Special provisions for appeals in possession proceedings

4.5 See the County Courts Act 1984 s 77(6) which prohibits appeals in possession proceedings on questions of fact if by virtue of the statutory provisions set out in that sub-section the court can only grant possession on being satisfied that it is reasonable to do so.

Arbitration

4.6 Part 52 is subject to any enactment which sets out special provisions with regard to any category of appeal. Section 69(2) and (3) of the Arbitration Act 1996 regulate appeals in arbitral proceedings and the Court of Appeal has no jurisdiction on an appeal under s 69 of the Arbitration Act 1996 where the High Court had not granted leave to appeal under s 69(8) of that Act: *Henry Boot Construction (UK) Ltd v Malmaison Hotel (Manchester) Ltd* [2001] QB 388, [2001] 1 All ER 257, CA. Similarly, only the trial judge could grant permission to appeal against the decision of a court under s 67 of the 1996 Act.

Where permission to appeal had been granted by the Court of Appeal, that permission would be set aside for want of jurisdiction: *Athletic Union of Constantinople v National Basketball Association* [2002] EWCA Civ 830, [2002] 3 All ER 897. For the statutory criteria for permission to appeal and the procedure see *CMA CGM SA v Beteiligungs-Kommanditgesellschaft MS Northern Pioneer Schiffahrtgesellschaft mbH & Co* [2002] EWCA Civ 1878, [2003] 1 All ER (Comm) 204.

Appeals from orders which are final

4.7 No appeal lies to the Court of Appeal from any order, judgment or decision which, by statute, is declared final: Supreme Court Act 1981,s 18(1)(c). The Access to Justice Act 1999 and the Access to Justice Act 1999 (Destination of Appeals) Order 2000, SI 2000/1071 do not confer a right of appeal where none previously existed: *Westminster City Council v O'Reilly* [2003] EWCA Civ 1007, [2004] 1 WLR 195.

Committal proceedings

4.8 For appeals in committal proceedings see **Chapter 3** and CPR PD 52 para 21.4.

CPR 52.2 PARTIES TO COMPLY WITH THE PRACTICE DIRECTION

4.9

'**52.2 Parties to comply with the practice direction**

All parties to an appeal must comply with the relevant practice direction.'

Practice Direction

4.10 See CPR PD 52.

CPR 52.3 PERMISSION

4.11

'**52.3 Permission**
(1) An appellant or respondent requires permission to appeal—

(a) where the appeal is from a decision of a judge in a county court or the High Court, except where the appeal is against—
  (i) a committal order;
  (ii) a refusal to grant habeas corpus; or
  (iii) a secure accommodation order made under section 25 of the Children Act 1989; or
(b) as provided by the relevant practice direction.
(Other enactments may provide that permission is required for particular appeals.)

(2) An application for permission to appeal may be made—
  (a) to the lower court at the hearing at which the decision to be appealed was made; or
  (b) to the appeal court in an appeal notice.
(Rule 52.4 sets out the time limits for filing an appellant's notice at the appeal court. Rule 52.5 sets out the time limits for filing a respondent's notice at the appeal court. Any application for permission to appeal to the appeal court must be made in the appeal notice (see rules 52.4(1) and 52.5(3)).)
(Rule 52.13(1) provides that permission is required from the Court of Appeal for all appeals to that court from a decision of a county court or the High Court which was itself made on appeal.)

(3) Where the lower court refuses an application for permission to appeal, a further application for permission to appeal may be made to the appeal court.

(4) Where the appeal court, without a hearing, refuses permission to appeal, the person seeking permission may request the decision to be reconsidered at a hearing.

(5) A request under paragraph (4) must be filed within 7 days after service of the notice that permission has been refused.

(6) Permission to appeal will only be given where—
  (a) the court considers that the appeal would have a real prospect of success; or
  (b) there is some other compelling reason why the appeal should be heard.

(7) An order giving permission may—
  (a) limit the issues to be heard; and
  (b) be made subject to conditions.
(Rule 3.1(3) also provides that the court may make an order subject to conditions.)
(Rule 25.15 provides for the court to order security for costs of an appeal.)'

Practice Direction

4.12 See CPR PD 52, paras 4.1–4.21.

The requirement for permission to appeal

4.13 An application for permission to appeal should be made to the lower court at the hearing; if made subsequently, it should be made to the appeal court see CPR PD 52, paras 4.6, 4.7 and *Lloyd Jones & Ors v T Mobile (UK) Ltd* [2003] EWCA Civ 1162 (see **para A2.14**). If permission is not sought at the hearing at which the decision being appealed was made, the appellant should not seek a further hearing in the lower court. The Court of Appeal will not accept a sealed copy of a judgment given by a lower court and practitioners should ensure that an order is drawn. See also **para 4.2** above.

4.14 The principal criterion for the grant of permission to appeal is that the appeal would have a 'real prospect of success' (CPR 52.3(6)(a))[1]. This does not require amplification, elaboration or explanation see *Swain v Hillman* [2001] 1 All ER 91, CA and *Three Rivers District Council v Bank of England (No 3)* [2001] UKHL 16, [2003] 2 AC 1, [2001] 2 All ER 513 and CPR 24.2 where the same phrase is used. A stricter test for the grant of permission to appeal is imposed in second appeals. No appeal may be made to the Court of Appeal in a second appeal unless the Court of Appeal considers that the appeal raises an important point of principle or practice or there is some other compelling reason for the Court of Appeal to hear it: Access to Justice Act 1999 s 55, see CPR 52.13. The wording of CPR 52.3(1)(b) enables the practice direction to impose a requirement for permission for specific appeals but the mere application of Part 52 to statutory appeals by para 17.2 of the Practice Direction does not impose a requirement for permission to appeal where otherwise the right to appeal was unrestricted: *Colley v Council for Licensed Conveyancers* [2001] EWCA Civ 1137, [2001] 4 All ER 998.

1   Some statutes specify the criteria on which permission (or leave) to appeal is to be granted see, for example, s 69 Arbitration Act 1996 and **para 4.6** above.

Refusal of permission to appeal at an oral hearing/Failure to attend permission hearing

4.15 There is no appeal from the decision of the appeal court, made at an oral hearing, to allow or refuse permission to appeal to that court: s 54(4) of the Access to Justice Act 1999, CPR 52.3(3) and (4). Where such an order is made refusing permission to appeal, the Court of Appeal (and the House of Lords) has no jurisdiction at all and will not list an application. Any case of doubt will be referred to a supervising Lord Justice on paper: *Jolly v Jay* [2002] EWCA Civ 277, [2002] All ER (D) 104 (Mar) (see **para A2.13**); *Bulled v Khayat* [2002] EWCA Civ 804. Where an appellant fails to attend a hearing and asks for his application to be reinstated, he does not have a right to a further hearing: *R (Idubo) v Home Secretary* [2003] EWCA Civ 1203, in which Pumfrey J said:

> 'The court has a discretion to reinstate the application not because this is a decision of the single judge taken without a hearing, but because there is a general discretion under the Civil Procedure Rules, rule 23.11, to re-list an application on application made for that purpose which could be dealt with without a hearing if the court thinks it appropriate: see CPR 23.8. The discretion is a general one. The court will take into account ... the reasons advanced from non-appearance at the original hearing, any delay in making the application, but also the underlying merits. If the court did not have regard to the underlying merits then any application could be indefinitely continued by repeated applications to reinstate on which the applicant did not attend.'

Judicial review of the grant or refusal of permission to appeal

4.16 Section 54(4) of the Access to Justice Act 1999 has not removed the jurisdiction of the High Court to review decisions of inferior courts and the question whether an inferior court, such as a county court, has acted within or exceeded its jurisdiction. An application for judicial review of the refusal of permission to appeal will generally be misconceived and should be dismissed summarily since there is an adequate system for reviewing the merits of decisions made by district judges and it is not appropriate that there should be further review by the High Court: *R (Sivasubramaniam) v Wandsworth County Court (Lord Chancellor's Department Intervening)* [2002] EWCA Civ 1738, [2003] 1 WLR 475, [2003] 2 All ER 160, CA. In that decision Lord Phillips MR indicated that in exceptional cases a proper case for judicial review could be made out. 'The possibility remains that there may be very rare cases where a litigant challenges the jurisdiction of a circuit judge giving or refusing permission to appeal on the ground of jurisdictional error in the narrow, pre-Anisminic sense [clear want of jurisdiction] or procedural irregularity of such a kind as to constitute a denial of the applicant's right to a fair hearing'. Further guidance has been given on 'jurisdictional error' in *Gregory & Anor v Turner & Anor* [2003] EWCA Civ 183, [2003] 1 WLR 1149, [2003] 2 All ER 1114. The Court of Appeal indicated that judicial review would not lie in that case where a circuit judge had refused permission to appeal from the district judge despite the Court's concerns about the course of the proceedings before the district judge. Brooke LJ said that whatever criticisms 'may be made of [the circuit judge's] reasoning, it cannot be categorised as amounting to a complete disregard of his duties or fundamental departure from the rules of natural justice'.

Case management decisions

4.17 Additional considerations may be taken into account where an appellant seeks permission to appeal a case management decision, such as whether the issue is of sufficient significance to justify the costs of appeal: whether the procedural consequences of an appeal outweigh the significance of the decision; and whether it would be more convenient to determine the issue at or after trial: see para 4.5 of the Practice Direction at CPR PD 52. See *Calden v Nunn and Partners* [2003] EWCA Civ 200 where the Court of Appeal dismissed the defendants' appeal against an order fixing the trial window and refusing their application to rely on expert evidence. 'The authority of the designated civil judge in raising local standards and correcting sloppy practice is a very important feature of the new CPR dispensation, and this court should not lightly override it' per Brooke LJ.

New grounds/grounds of appeal

4.18 An application for permission to appeal on grounds which were not argued in the lower court is likely to be refused: *Australia and New Zealand Banking Group Ltd v Société Générale* [2000] 1 All ER (Comm) 682, CA. This is 'not merely a matter of efficiency, expediency and cost, but of substantial justice': *Jones v MBNA International Bank* (30 June 2000, unreported), CA, May LJ. See also *Miriki v General Council of the Bar* [2001] EWCA Civ 1973, [2001] All ER (D) 364 (Dec) (where an employment appeal tribunal had limited the grounds of appeal on the grounds that it would not normally permit the appellant to seek to widen the case before the tribunal; it would be wrong to widen the case before the Court of Appeal). An appeal lies against the order made by the judge, not against the reasons given for his decision: *Lake v Lake* [1955] P 336, [1955] 2 All ER 538, CA; *Re Mathew* [2001] BPIR 531, Lawrence Collins J. Where a party has been successful, he cannot appeal if he disagrees with the reasons given for the decision. The role of the Court of Appeal is to determine appeals from decisions of trial judges. It is not the Court of Appeal's function to set out the law in advance of a trial on an appeal from a case management conference: *Skrine & Co v Euromoney Publications plc* [2001] EWCA Civ 1479, [2001] All ER (D) 134 (Oct).

See CPR PD 52, para 3.2 and **Chapter 2**.

Extension of time for appealing

4.19 See CPR 52.6 for applications for extensions of time.

Request under CPR 52.3(4)

4.20 Where an appeal court refuses permission to appeal on paper, the appellant may request that the decision is reconsidered at a hearing under CPR 52.3(4). See **CPR PD 52** paras 4.11–4.14, 4.14A, and, for the duty to inform the Legal Services Commission, **CPR PD 52** para 4.17.

The time limit for making a request under CPR 52.3(4) may be extended: *Slot v Isaac* [2002] EWCA Civ 481, [2002] All ER (D) 197 (see **para A2.20**). Where a represented appellant makes a request for a decision to be reconsidered at an oral hearing, his advocate must, at least 4 days before the hearing, in a brief written statement:
(a) inform the court and the respondent of the points which he proposes to raise at the hearing;
(b) set out his reasons why permission should be granted notwithstanding the reasons given for the refusal of permission; and
(c) confirm, where applicable, that the requirements of paragraph 4.17 have been complied with: CPR PD 52, para 4.14A.

If the appellant is in receipt of services funded by the Legal Services Commission and permission to appeal has been refused by the appeal court without a hearing, CPR PD 52 para 4.17 requires the appellant to send a copy of the reasons the appeal court gave for refusing permission to the relevant office of the Legal Services Commission as soon as it has been received from the court.

The right to review the application at an oral hearing must not be abused: *J (a child)* [2001] EWCA Civ 1813 (if the member of the Bar has nothing to say that has not been considered in the reasoned refusal of permission, 'there is no discernible purpose in the renewed hearing': Thorpe LJ).

Where a single Lord Justice had refused permission to appeal on paper, he was not precluded from being a member of the court hearing the appeal: *Mahomed v Morris* [2000] 2 BCLC 536, CA. See also *Sengupta v Holmes* [2002] EWCA Civ 1104, (2002) Times, 19 August, CA (in the absence of special circumstances, there was no reason as a matter of principle to regard a judge who had refused permission to appeal on paper as being anything other than a proper and impartial member of the tribunal convened to hear the appeal).

Notice of the permission hearing

4.21 Notice of a permission hearing in the appeal court will be given to the respondent but he is not required to attend unless the court requests him to do so[1]. If the court requests the respondent's attendance at the permission hearing, the appellant must supply the respondent with a copy of the appeal bundle within seven days of being notified of the request, or such other period as the court may direct[2].

1   CPR PD 52, para 4.15.
2   CPR PD 52, para 4.16; the costs of providing that bundle are borne by the appellant initially, but will form part of the costs of the permission application.

Limited permission to appeal

4.22 An order granting permission to appeal may limit the issues to be heard. Where the lower court refuses permission or grants limited permission, that order may be revisited on a further application to the appeal court. Where limited permission to appeal is granted by the lower court and the appellant wishes to raise additional grounds, the appellant's notice should include an application for permission to appeal on the other grounds for which permission was not granted. Where the appeal court grants limited permission at an oral hearing and the appeal is heard by a different tribunal, the court hearing the appeal has no jurisdiction to consider issues above and beyond that for which permission had been given at the oral hearing: *Fieldman v Markovic* [2001] The Times July 4, Sir Andrew Morritt V-C. Where the appeal court grants permission to appeal on some issues only, it will (1) refuse permission on any remaining issues or (2) reserve the question of permission to appeal on any remaining issues to the court hearing the appeal: CPR PD 52 para 4.18. Where the question of permission to appeal on any remaining issues is reserved to the court hearing the appeal, an appellant must inform the appeal court and the respondent in writing whether he intends to pursue the reserved issues. See CPR PD 52, paras 4.19–4.21 for time estimate, reconsideration of a refusal of permission on remaining issues.

Conditional permission to appeal

4.23 The court may grant permission to appeal subject to conditions, e.g. by requiring a sum of money to be paid into court: *Hammond Suddard Solicitors v Agrichem International Holdings Ltd* [2001] EWCA Civ 2065, [2001] All ER (D) 258 (Dec) (see **para A2.10**). See also CPR 52.9 [4]. In *Lloyd Jones & Ors v T Mobile (UK) Ltd* [2003] EWCA Civ 1162 (see **para A2.14**) the Court of Appeal used its power under CPR 3.1(2)(a) to grant permission to appeal out of time to a defendant who sought to have determined a point of law of general importance to its business on condition that it could not recover the costs of an appeal if successful. In *Grant v Kent County Council* [2003] EWCA Civ 1917 and *Donaldson v Wilson* [2004] EWCA Civ 123 the Court of Appeal granted permission to appeal on terms that the appellant paid the respondent's costs of the appeal (and any cross-appeal) in any event in cases in which the appellants (or their insurers) wished to obtain clear Court of Appeal authority in relation to matters that were of importance to their businesses when the court might not otherwise have been disposed to grant permission to appeal at all.

CPR 52.4 APPELLANT'S NOTICE

4.24

'**52.4 Appellant's notice**
(1) Where the appellant seeks permission from the appeal court it must be requested in the appellant's notice.
(2) The appellant must file the appellant's notice at the appeal court within—
 (a) such period as may be directed by the lower court; or
 (b) where the court makes no such direction, 14 days after the date of the decision of the lower court that the appellant wishes to appeal.
(3) Unless the appeal court orders otherwise, an appeal notice must be served on each respondent—
 (a) as soon as practicable; and
 (b) in any event not later than 7 days,
 after it is filed.'

Practice Direction

4.25 See CPR PD 52, paras 5.1–5.25.

Filing and service of appellant's notice

4.26 The time limit for filing an appellant's notice is 14 days: CPR 52.4(2). The notice must be filed within 14 days after the date of the decision of the lower court. This is the date when the judge makes his decision and not the date when the order recording his decision is drawn up: *Sayers v Clarke Walker* [2002] EWCA Civ 645, [2002] 3 All ER 490, [2002] All ER (D) 189. Time for appealing runs from the time the judgment is handed down in public. The formality of handing down the judgment in open court cannot be dispensed with, although the parties' attendance may be excused: *Owusu v Jackson (t/a Villa Holidays Ball-Inn Villas)* [2002] EWCA Civ 877, [2002] All ER (D) 130 (see **para A2.17**). Until a judgment has been handed down or delivered, the judge is at liberty to alter it: *Robinson v Fernsby* [2003] EWCA Civ 1820, [2004] The Times, 20 January; but material alterations should be made only in "exceptional circumstances" or "for strong reasons". The Court of Appeal will not accept a sealed copy of a judgment given by a lower court and practitioners should ensure that an order is drawn. See also **para 4.2** above for orders. Where the lower court directs a different period under r 52.4(2)(a), that period should not normally exceed 28 days: CPR PD 52, para 5.19. The time limit provided by CPR 52.4(2) will not apply if a statutory provision makes a contrary provision: *Van Aken v Camden London Borough Council* [2002] EWCA Civ 1724 (appeals under s 204 of the Housing Act 1996 are subject to a 21-day time limit). See CPR 52.6 and CPR PD 52, paras 5.2–5.4 if an extension of time is needed. In an appeal from a county court, service on the district judge of an appellant's notice is no longer necessary (except where the appeal is from the grant of a decree nisi of divorce or nullity: CPR PD 52, para 21.1(3); in cases of contempt, the appellant's notice must also be served on the lower court: CPR PD 52, para 21.4).

4.27 Where a party is seeking a declaration of incompatibility under the Human Rights Act or acknowledges that such a declaration may be made, he should give as much informal notice to the Crown as practical of the proceedings and the issues involved: *Poplar Housing and Regeneration Community Association Ltd v Donoghue* [2001] EWCA Civ 595, [2002] QB 48, [2001] 4 All ER 604. The formal and informal notice to the Crown should be given to a person named in the list published under s 17 of the Crown Proceedings Act 1947; for the list of persons see Annex to **CPR PD 19** (see **para 6.3C**). At the same time as the party gives notice informally to the Crown, it should send a copy of such notice to the court so that the court is alerted to the fact that it will have to consider whether formal notice should be given. A copy of the notice should be sent to the other parties as well.

Contents of appeal notice and supporting documentation

4.28 Detailed requirements apply to a statement of case where a party seeks to rely on any provision of or right arising under the Human Rights Act 1998 or seeks a remedy available under that Act see CPR PD 16, para 15.1. These requirements also apply where an appellant seeks to rely on the Act for the first time in an appeal notice: CPR PD 52, para 5.1A. The appellant is expected to file with his notice the documents required by para 5.6 of the Practice Direction (CPR PD 52, para 5.6). For guidance on appeal documentation see **Chapter 6.**

Extension of time for appealing

4.29 See CPR 52.6 for applications for extensions of time.

Form

4.30 For the form of appellant's notice see Form N161 (**Appendix 1**).

CPR 52.5 RESPONDENT'S NOTICE

4.31

'**52.5 Respondent's notice**
(1) A respondent may file and serve a respondent's notice.
(2) A respondent who—
 (a) is seeking permission to appeal from the appeal court; or
 (b) wishes to ask the appeal court to uphold the order of the lower court for reasons different from or additional to those given by the lower court,
 must file a respondent's notice.
(3) Where the respondent seeks permission from the appeal court it must be requested in the respondent's notice.
(4) A respondent's notice must be filed within—
 (a) such period as may be directed by the lower court; or
 (b) where the court makes no such direction, 14 days after the date in paragraph (5).
(5) The date referred to in paragraph (4) is—
 (a) the date the respondent is served with the appellant's notice where—
  (i) permission to appeal was given by the lower court; or
  (ii) permission to appeal is not required;
 (b) the date the respondent is served with notification that the appeal court has given the appellant permission to appeal; or
 (c) the date the respondent is served with notification that the application for permission to appeal and the appeal itself are to be heard together.
(6) Unless the appeal court orders otherwise a respondent's notice must be served on the appellant and any other respondent—
 (a) as soon as practicable; and
 (b) in any event not later than 7 days,
 after it is filed.'

Practice Direction

4.32 See CPR PD 52, paras 7.1–7.13.

Role of respondent in applications for permission to appeal and respondent's costs

4.33 A respondent served with an appellant's notice need not take any action until such time as notification is given to him that permission to appeal has been given: CPR PD 52, para 5.22. Where the court does not request submissions from or attendance by a respondent, costs will not normally be allowed to a respondent who volunteers submissions or attendance: CPR PD 52 para 4.23. Where the court does request submissions from, or attendance by, the respondent, the respondent will normally be allowed his costs if permission is refused CPR PD para 4.24.

A respondent's submission at the permission stage should be addressed to the point that the relevant threshold test (in CPR 52.3(6) or CPR 52.13(2)) is not met or that there is an inaccuracy in the papers placed before the court which might reasonably be expected to lead the court to grant permission to appeal when it would not otherwise have done so: *Jolly v Jay* [2002] EWCA Civ 277, [2002] All ER (D) 104 (Mar) (see **para A2.13**). Where a respondent wishes to submit written submissions to a court which is considering whether to grant permission to appeal or wishes to appear at such a hearing, any skeleton argument should be filed and served within a reasonable time before the hearing: *Philosophy Inc v Ferretti Studio SRL* [2002] EWCA Civ 921, per Brooke LJ. In *Robert Horne Group plc v Ablett & Or* [2003] EWCA Civ 1310, the Court of Appeal declined to hear counsel for the respondent who turned up at the hearing of a renewed application for permission to appeal 'hoping to be heard' without filing a skeleton argument.

Respondent's notice in an appeal

4.34 The only obligation on a respondent to file a respondent's notice arises when a respondent seeks permission to appeal from the appeal court or wishes to ask the appeal court to uphold the order of the lower court for reasons different from or additional to those given by the lower court[1]. Where a respondent seeks permission to appeal from the appeal court it must be requested in his respondent's notice[2]. A respondent's notice must be filed within such period as may be directed by the lower court (which should not exceed 28 days) or within 14 days after:
(a) the date the respondent is served with the appellant's notice where

(i) permission to appeal was given by the lower court; or
(ii) permission to appeal is not required;
(b) the date the respondent is served with notification that the appeal court has given the appellant permission to appeal; or
(c) the date the respondent is served with notification that the application for permission to appeal and the appeal itself are to be heard together[3].

1 CPR 52.5(2).
2 CPR 52.5(3).
3 CPR 52.5(5).

4.35 A respondent's notice must be served on the appellant and any other respondent as soon as practicable and in any event not later than seven days after it is filed[1]. A respondent who wishes only to file a skeleton argument may include that argument in his respondent's notice and may file such a notice although not required so to do. A respondent who wishes only to request that the appeal court upholds the judgment or order of the lower court whether for the reasons given in the lower court or otherwise does not 'make an appeal' and does not therefore need permission to appeal in accordance with CPR 52.3(1)[2]. Such a respondent does not need to file a respondent's notice. He must, however, file a skeleton argument if he proposes to address arguments to the court[3]. If the respondent does not file a respondent's notice, he will not be entitled, except with the permission of the court, to rely on any reason not relied on in the lower court[4].

1 CPR 52.5(6).
2 CPR PD 52, para 7.2.
3 CPR PD 52, para 7.6.
4 CPR PD 52, para 7.3(2)

4.36 The principles which govern a respondent's notice are the same as those which apply to an appellant's notice. Where an extension of time is required, the extension must be requested in the respondent's notice and the reasons why the respondent failed to act within the specified time must be included[1]. The respondent must provide a skeleton argument in all cases where he proposes to address arguments to the court. The respondent's skeleton argument may be included within a respondent's notice but, where it is, it will not form part of the notice for the purposes of CPR 52.8 (with the result that it can be amended without permission of the court)[2]. Where the respondent does not file a respondent's notice, his skeleton argument must be filed and served at least seven days before the appeal hearing [3]. A respondent's skeleton argument should, where appropriate, answer the arguments set out in the appellant's skeleton argument[4].

A respondent must file with his respondent's notice the following documents:
(1) two additional copies of the respondent's notice for the appeal court;
(2) one copy each for the appellant and any other respondent;

(3) two copies of any skeleton argument[5].

1   CPR PD 52, para 7.5.
2   CPR PD 52, para 7.6.
3   CPR PD 52, para 7.7(2).
4   CPR PD 52, para 7.8. See **Chapter 6** for contents of respondent's skeleton argument.
5   CPR PD 52, para 7.10. See **Chapter 6** for documents on which a respondent wishes to rely.

Form

4.37 For the form of respondent's notice see Form N162 (**Appendix 1**).

CPR 52.6 VARIATION OF TIME

4.38

'**52.6 Variation of time**
(1)   An application to vary the time limit for filing an appeal notice must be made to the appeal court.
(2)   The parties may not agree to extend any date or time limit set by—
    (a)   these Rules;
    (b)   the relevant practice direction; or
    (c)   an order of the appeal court or the lower court.
(Rule 3.1(2)(a) provides that the court may extend or shorten the time for compliance with any rule, practice direction or court order (even if an application for extension is made after the time for compliance has expired).)
(Rule 3.1(2)(b) provides that the court may adjourn or bring forward a hearing.)'

Time limit for appealing

4.39 The appellant must file his appellant's notice at the appeal court within such period as may be directed by the lower court[1] or, where no such direction is made, within 14 days after the date of the decision of the lower court that the appellant wishes to appeal[2]. Where it is anticipated that there may be difficulty in obtaining the documents needed for the appeal bundle (e.g. the transcript), the lower court judge should be invited to extend the time for filing the appellant's notice. Alternatively, the appellant's notice (if filed in time) should be accompanied by a letter asking for an extension of time within which to file the appeal bundle.

1   CPR 52.4(2)(a); this period should not normally exceed 28 days: CPR PD 52, para 5.19.

2   CPR 52.4(2)(b). The time limit runs from the date of the decision, not the date the order is drawn.

4.40 Where it is not possible to file the appellant's notice in time, the appellant must include in Section 10 of the appellant's notice an application for an extension of time and provide evidence in support of that application, stating the reason for the delay and the steps taken prior to the application being made[1]. Where an appellant's notice includes an application for an extension of time and permission to appeal has been given or is not required, the respondent has the right to be heard on that application. He must be served with a copy of the appeal bundle. A respondent who unreasonably opposes an extension of time runs the risk of being ordered to pay the appellant's costs of that application[2]. (The time limit for providing the appeal bundle may be extended by the court[3].)

1   CPR PD 52, para 5.2; in an urgent case, the filing of an appellant's notice should not be delayed pending confirmation of public funding: see *Jordan v Jordan* [1993] 1 FLR 169, CA (service of notice of appeal against a committal order should not be deferred pending the further grant of legal aid).
2   CPR PD 52, para 5.3.
3   CPR 3.1(2)(a) and 52.6.

Applications for an extension of time

4.41 CPR 52.6 prevents the parties from agreeing to extend the time limit for filing an appellant's notice. The practice in the Court of Appeal is to advise the appellant to obtain the respondent's views on the application for an extension of time[1]. If no objections are raised, the application may be considered on paper without a hearing[2]. Where objections are raised, directions will be given for the proper disposal of the matter such as, for example, that the application for the extension of time is listed with the appeal to follow if the extension is granted.

1   CPR 52.6 requires an application to vary the time limit for filing an appeal notice to be made to the appeal court and prevents the parties from agreeing to extend time limits set by the rules, a practice direction or a court order.
2   In the Court of Appeal the application may be granted by a master or deputy master in these circumstances. See **CPR 52.16(2)**.

4.42 Applications for an extension of time are to be viewed by reference to the criterion of justice. In many cases a judge will be able to decide whether to grant an application to shorten or to extend time after considering the matters set out in CPR PD 52, para 5.2 (the reason for the delay and the steps taken prior to the application being made). The focus should be on the prejudice caused by the extension of time, not on any pre-existing prejudice: *Robert v Momentum Services Ltd* [2003] EWCA Civ 299, [2003] 1 WLR 1577, [2003]

2 All ER 74. If the extension of time is being sought after the time for appealing has expired, it is appropriate to have regard to the checklist in CPR 3.9 when considering whether to grant an extension of time for appealing in a case of any complexity: *Sayers v Clarke Walker* [2002] EWCA Civ 645, [2002] 1 WLR 3095, [2002] 3 All ER 490. In *Pridding v Secretary of State for Work & Pensions* [2002] EWCA Civ 306, [2002] All ER (D) 30 (Mar), the Court of Appeal granted an extension of time despite the Department's substantial delay since there was no prejudice to the respondent and the legal issue to be resolved was of clear public importance. Ward LJ, however, observed that 'Government Departments ... are expected to set the standards of good practice, not win prizes for incompetence'.

Appeals against the refusal to extend time for appealing

4.43 The refusal of an extension of time for appealing, without consideration of the merits of the appeal, may be appealed. Such an appeal is not a second appeal within s 55 of the Access to Justice Act 1999 because the 'matter' which is refused is different from the 'matter' on which the decision being appealed was made; the refusal is an original order of the appeal court: *Foenander v Bond Lewis & Co* [2001] EWCA Civ 759, [2002] 1 WLR 525, [2001] 2 All ER 1019 (see **para A2.8**). See **para 3.35** for the route of appeal where a circuit judge makes an original order.

Applications for an extension of time in family cases

4.44 Applications made to the Court of Appeal for an extension of time in family proceedings are referred to the Supervising Lord Justice for listing directions. This practice is adopted where the application is made in contempt proceedings in order that a decision can be made on the need for expedition. See the notes to CPR PD 52 para 21.4 for committal proceedings.

CPR 52.7 STAY

4.45

> **'52.7 Stay**
>
> Unless—
> (a) the appeal court or the lower court orders otherwise; or
> (b) the appeal is from the Immigration Appeal Tribunal,

an appeal shall not operate as a stay of any order or decision of the lower court.'

Stay of execution

4.46 An appeal or the filing of an appellant's notice does not operate automatically as a stay of execution. An application for a stay should be made at the conclusion of the trial or hearing to the judge who makes the decision sought to be appealed. Such an application should be made when the trial judge is asked to grant permission to appeal (as to which see CPR 52.3(2)(a)). If a stay is refused or not applied for in the lower court, a separate application for a stay, supported by evidence, may be made or included in an application for permission to appeal to the appeal court. Applications made after the filing of an appeal notice are made in accordance with CPR Part 23 (see **para 4.49** below and CPR PD 52, paras 5.5 and 11).

The court will not order a stay unless satisfied, by cogent, full and frank evidence, that there is a real risk of injustice: *Hammond Suddard Solicitors v Agrichem International Holdings Ltd* [2001] EWCA Civ 2065, [2001] All ER (D) 258 (see **para A2.10**).

Asylum and immigration cases

4.47 CPR 52.7(b) reflects the statutory bar on removal pending an appeal from the Immigration Appeal Tribunal which is contained in the Nationality and Immigration Act 2002, s 78. The former practice was that the filing of an appeal notice in the Court of Appeal in an immigration or asylum case challenging the refusal of the High Court to grant permission to apply for judicial review was interpreted as giving rise to an automatic stay of the deportation process. That practice is no longer continued, and if a stay is sought an express application must be made. That application will be placed before a lord justice for a ruling on paper. The Civil Appeals Office should be notified immediately if the deportation takes place after an appeal notice has been filed where no stay was sought or where a stay has been expressly refused: *R (Pharis) v Secretary of State for the Home Department* [2004] EWCA Civ 654, [2004] The Times, May 27.

Effect of stay in the lower court

4.48 A stay of the proceedings in the High Court has no effect on the proceedings in the Court of Appeal: *Aoun v Bahri* [2002] EWCA Civ 1141 (see **para A2.1**).

Applications to the appeal court

4.49 Notice of an application to be made to the appeal court for a remedy incidental to the appeal (e.g. a stay of execution, an interim remedy or an order for security) may be included in the appeal notice or in a Part 23 application notice[1]. The provisions of CPR Part 23 apply to such an application and the applicant must file with his notice:
(1) one additional copy of the application notice for the appeal court and one copy for each of the respondents;
(2) (where applicable) a sealed copy of the order which is the subject of the main appeal;
(3) a bundle of documents in support which includes:
   (a) the Part 23 application notice;
   (b) any witness statements or affidavits in support[2].

1   CPR PD 52, paras 5.5, 7.9.
2   See **Chapter 6**.

CPR 52.8 AMENDMENT OF APPEAL NOTICE

4.50

'**52.8 Amendment of appeal notice**

An appeal notice may not be amended without the permission of the appeal court.'

Practice Direction

4.51 See CPR PD 52, para 5.25.

Applications to amend an appeal notice

4.52 An appeal notice may be amended with permission. Where a skeleton argument is included in an appeal notice, it may be amended without permission: CPR PD 52, paras 5.9 and 7.6. An application to amend and any application in opposition will normally be dealt with at the hearing unless that course would cause unnecessary expense or delay, in which case a request should be made for the application to amend to be heard in advance[1]. Where an appellant's notice contains only an application for permission to appeal and the appellant wishes to amend the notice, the Court of Appeal does not require the making of a formal application. The appellant must nevertheless serve the amended appellant's notice on the respondent and confirm to the court that he has done so. The question whether or not permission to amend should be granted will be dealt with on paper by one of the deputy masters. It is good practice to include in red ink the amendments which are sought to be made to the appeal notice.

1   CPR PD 52, para 5.25.

4.53 Where permission to appeal has been given, or is not required, and the appellant wishes to amend the appellant's notice, a formal application to amend has to be made and a fee is then payable. The appellant must serve the amended appellant's notice on the respondent. Where the respondent indicates that there will be no opposition to the amendment, the court[1] may give its consent to the amendment.

1   In the Court of Appeal this includes the master and deputy masters: CPR 52.16.

4.54 Where an appellant wishes to include grounds of appeal for which permission has not been given, an application for permission to appeal has to be made. Such an application may be dealt with at the hearing of the appeal[1] unless the court otherwise directs. Where a respondent objects to the amendment, his views and those of the appellant will be considered before the court gives a decision and gives directions for the appeal. For example the court may direct that the application for permission to appeal should be heard immediately before the appeal. See **para 4.22** above for guidance when limited permission to appeal is given. Permission is required to rely on a matter not contained in an appeal notice: **CPR 52.11(5)**. Where a party wishes to change his grounds of appeal, he should inform the court and the respondent so directions can be given as to whether and how the appeal should proceed: *Shire v Secretary of State for Work and Pensions* [2003] EWCA Civ 1465, [2003] The Times, October 30 (see **para A2.19**). The permission of the appeal court is required to withdraw a concession or to take a point which was not argued in the lower court[2].

1   CPR PD 52, para 5.25.
2   *Jones v MBNA International Bank* (30 June 2000, unreported), CA; this general principle 'is not merely a matter of efficiency, expediency and cost, but of substantial justice' per May LJ.

CPR 52.9 STRIKING OUT APPEAL NOTICES

4.55

'52.9 Striking out appeal notices and setting aside or imposing conditions on permission to appeal
(1)   The appeal court may—

(a) strike out the whole or part of an appeal notice;
(b) set aside permission to appeal in whole or in part;
(c) impose or vary conditions upon which an appeal may be brought.

(2) The court will only exercise its powers under paragraph (1) where there is a compelling reason for doing so.

(3) Where a party was present at the hearing at which permission was given he may not subsequently apply for an order that the court exercise its powers under sub-paragraphs (1)(b) or (1)(c).'

Security for costs of an appeal

4.56 CPR Rule 25.15(1) provides that the court may order security for costs of an appeal against:

(a) an appellant or

(b) a respondent who also appeals

on the same grounds as it may order security for costs against a claimant under CPR Part 25. These grounds are set out in CPR 25.13. By CPR 25.15(2) the court may make a similar order where the appellant, or the respondent who appeals, is a limited company and there is reason to believe it will be unable to pay the costs of the other parties to the appeal should its appeal be unsuccessful. In *Nasser v United Bank of Kuwait* [2001] EWCA Civ 556, [2002] 1 WLR 1868, [2002] 1 All ER 401 Mance LJ said that the court has to decide, when considering an application for security for costs for an appeal, what is justifiable, non-discriminatory and a 'proportionate exercise of discretion'.

Setting aside the grant of permission

4.57 Permission to appeal will only be set aside where cogent reasons demonstrate that the appeal would have no prospect of success: *Hunt v Peasegood* (2000) Times, 20 October, CA (see **para A2.12**). In *Beedell v West Ferry Printers Ltd* [2001] EWCA Civ 400, [2001] ICR 962, [2001] All ER (D) 177 (see **para A2.3**), the Court of Appeal refused to set aside permission to appeal even though the appeal for which permission had been granted had to be dismissed, because to do so would create a decision which would be unappealable in an area recognised by the Court of Appeal to be the subject of controversy. If a respondent 'can show ... that the judge was misled by an appellant, not necessarily deliberately, into giving permission to appeal, that may well be a compelling reason within the Rule. It must ... involve showing (a) that the materials put before the judge were inaccurate or incomplete; (b) that these deficiencies had a bearing upon the grounds on which permission to appeal was given; and (c) very importantly, that but for them permission to appeal would not have been given': *Hertsmere Borough Council v Harty* [2001] EWCA Civ 1238 per Sedley LJ at para 2. See also *Nathan v Smilovitch* [2002] EWCA Civ 759, [2002] All ER (D) 573 ('unless the nature of the application shows that some decisive authority or decisive statutory provision has been overlooked by the Lord Justice granting permission to appeal, an applicant would normally have to show that the single Lord Justice had actually been misled in the course of the presentation of an application': per Longmore LJ). In *Barings plc & v Coopers & Lybrand* [2002] EWCA Civ 1155, [2002] All ER (D) 278 (see **para A2.2**), Jonathan Parker LJ (agreeing with Longmore LJ's observation in *Nathan*) said that 'compelling reason', in this context, connotes ... something which is sufficiently serious to be in the nature of an irregularity in the grant of permission'. The fact that the appeal was now relevant only on limited matters did not amount to a compelling reason. The power in CPR 52.9(1) was not a power to entertain an appeal against the grant of permission or to second guess the judge who granted permission and thereby generate satellite litigation. Its purpose was to enable the court to do justice where something in the nature of an irregularity occurred in the granting of permission. Practitioners should 'think twice before launching an application of this kind, in the knowledge that only in very limited circumstances will such an application be likely to succeed'. An application to set aside the grant of permission to appeal or to impose conditions on the grant of permission should be made promptly: *Okta Crude Oil Refinery AD v Moil-Coal Trading Co Ltd* [2003] EWCA Civ 617.

Striking out of appeal notice

4.58 The Court of Appeal has power of its own initiative to strike out a notice of appeal if it represents an abuse of its process (CPR 3.3(4); CPR 2.1; see *Bhamjee v Forsdick (No 2)* [2003] EWCA Civ 1113, [2004] 1 WLR 88). CPR 52.9(1)(a), on the other hand, is intended to discourage respondents from applying to strike out a notice of appeal after permission to appeal has been granted.

4.59 There is a compelling reason to strike out an appeal where the court regards the appeal as an abuse of process: *Turner v Haworth Associates* [2001] EWCA Civ 370, [2001] All ER (D) 309, Chadwick and Hale LJJ. Guidance on the power to strike out was given by Brooke LJ, V-P, in *R (on the application of Nine Nepalese Asylum Seekers) v Immigration Appeal Tribunal* [2003] EWCA Civ 1892 (see **para A2.18**): 'applications of this kind represent an abuse of the processes of this Court, which exists to resolve genuine points of law in judicial review cases, and is not a fourth tier appellate court of fact when the original tribunal of fact has disbelieved the applicant'. Where an application is totally devoid of merit, it 'would be appropriate for a judge ... to strike the matter out under CPR 3.3(4) and give the applicant ten days in which to make an application for a hearing, if so advised'.

4.60 After giving judgment in the Nine Nepalese Asylum Seekers case on 19 December 2003, Brooke LJ, V-P, struck out seven similar cases on paper as an abuse of process and gave directions that any application to set aside his order should be filed, 'setting out full written grounds', by 4 January 2004. No such application was, in the event, made.

Imposition of conditions on which appeal may be brought

4.61 Under CPR 52.9(1)(c) the court may impose or vary conditions upon which an appeal may be brought. In *Hammond Suddard Solicitors v Agrichem International Holdings Ltd* [2001] EWCA Civ 2065, [2001] All ER (D) 258 (see **para A2.10**), the court made the continued prosecution of the appeal conditional upon the payment into court of the judgment debt and costs. In paras 41–42 of Clarke LJ's judgment he set out the six factors adding up to 'a compelling reason' for making the order –

> '41. We turn to the question whether there is a compelling reason for making the appellant either pay the judgment debt or secure it as a condition of permitting it to proceed with the appeal. We have reached the conclusion that the answer to that question is yes. In our judgment, the facts which combine to constitute a compelling reason are the following:
> (1) The appellant is an entity against whom it will be difficult to exercise the normal mechanisms of enforcement. It is registered in the British Virgin Islands and has no assets in the United Kingdom. There is, accordingly, a very real risk that if the appeal fails, the respondents will be unable to recover the judgment debt and costs as ordered by Silber J. Given the attitude of the appellant to date, including that demonstrated on these applications, it is fanciful to think that the appellant will co-operate in the enforcement process.
> (2) The appellant plainly either has the resources or has access to resources which enable it both to instruct solicitors and leading and junior counsel to prosecute its appeal and make an application to the court for a stay of execution and to provide a substantial sum by way of security for costs.
> (3) There is no convincing evidence that the appellant does not either have the resources or have access to resources which would enable

(4) it to pay the judgment debt and costs as ordered. It has failed to do so. It is, accordingly, in breach of the orders made by Silber J on 12 July 2001.

(4) The discovery which the appellant has provided of its financial affairs is inadequate and gives the court no confidence that it has been shown anything near the truth. Moreover, as stated earlier, it has produced evidence (when it wanted to) that it was a thriving and profitable institution. It has wealthy owners and there is no evidence that, if they were minded to do so, they could not pay the judgment debt including the outstanding orders for costs.

(5) For the reasons we have already given we are not persuaded that this appeal will be stifled if we make the order sought.

(6) In these circumstances, we find it unacceptable that absent any other orders of the court the appellant is intending to prosecute the appeal (and is willing to put up security for costs in order to do so) whilst at the same time continuing to disobey the orders of the court to pay the judgment debt and costs, as well as seeking to persuade us that it cannot do so.

42. In our judgment, these six factors add up to a compelling reason to make the orders sought by the respondents. We think there is a real risk that, unless the orders sought are made, the respondents, if the appeal is dismissed, will be deprived of the fruits of the judgment, and will only be able to recover whatever sum is secured by way of costs. In our judgment, on the facts of this case, it is not just to allow the appellant to proceed with an appeal which is designed not only to reverse the judge's decision that it is liable to the respondent but also to obtain judgment on its counterclaim for a very substantial amount, especially in circumstances in which it appears that it is willing and able to use resources from others, including perhaps its owners, while being unwilling to seek and obtain resources to discharge the judgment debt.'

4.62 It should be noted that, in that case, the Court of Appeal:
(1) refused an application for a stay of execution save on terms that the appellant provided security for the judgment debt and costs;
(2) granted an application for security for costs of the appeal in the sum of £85,000; and
(3) imposed upon the permission to appeal the condition that the appellant paid into court or provided security for the judgment debt and costs together with the sum ordered as security for costs.

4.63 A respondent who is unable to argue that an appellant is *unable* to pay the costs of the appeal and thus obtain an order for security for costs under CPR 25.15 may be able to rely on the difficulties in enforcing the judgment to obtain an order under CPR 52.9 for security in respect of the judgment sum. In *Bell Electric Ltd v Aweco Appliance Systems GmbH & Co KG* [2002] EWCA Civ 1501, [2003] 1 All ER 344, [2002] The Times 20 November, Potter LJ said that the judgment in *Hammond Suddards* (above) did not assist in a situation where there was no reason to suppose that 'vigorously pursued steps by way of enforcement will *ultimately* prove fruitless if the appeal fails'. He saw no reason in principle why there might nonetheless be a 'compelling reason ... to make an order staying the appeal if the interim order is not complied with, or a payment into court made or other security provided in respect of the judgment sum ... in a case where (i) the appellant is in deliberate breach of the order to pay the judgment sum; (ii) he has applied for and been refused a stay; (iii) his failure or delay in payment is due not to any financial difficulty but is cynically based upon the practical difficulties for the respondent in seeking enforcement in a foreign jurisdiction'. See *Contract Facilities Ltd v Rees' Estate* [2003] EWCA Civ 1105 (see **para A2.6**) and **paras 4.67 and 4.68** below.

CPR 52.10 APPEAL COURT'S POWERS

4.64

'52.10 Appeal court's powers
(1) In relation to an appeal the appeal court has all the powers of the lower court.
(Rule 52.1(4) provides that this Part is subject to any enactment that sets out special provisions with regard to any particular category of appeal—where such an enactment gives a statutory power to a tribunal, person or other body it may be the case that the appeal court may not exercise that power on an appeal)
(2) The appeal court has power to—
  (a) affirm, set aside or vary any order or judgment made or given by the lower court;
  (b) refer any claim or issue for determination by the lower court;
  (c) order a new trial or hearing;
  (d) make orders for the payment of interest;
  (e) make a costs order.
(3) In an appeal from a claim tried with a jury the Court of Appeal may, instead of ordering a new trial—
  (a) make an order for damages; or
  (b) vary an award of damages made by the jury.
(4) The appeal court may exercise its powers in relation to the whole or part of an order of the lower court.
(Part 3 contains general rules about the court's case management powers.)'

Powers of the appeal court

4.65 The general rule is that the appeal court has all the powers of the lower court[1]. It also has power to affirm, set aside or vary any order or judgment made or given by the lower court; to refer any claim or issue for determination by the lower court; to order a new trial or hearing and to make orders for the payment of interest and a costs order[2]. It may exercise its powers in relation to the whole or part of an order of the lower court[3]. This means that every appeal court, whether a circuit judge or a High Court judge or the Court of Appeal, has been expressly given the same powers in relation to appeals governed by CPR Pt 52. The Court of Appeal also has special powers in an appeal from a claim tried by a jury[4]. The exception to this general rule is in relation to an appeal from a decision of an authorised costs officer[5].

1   CPR 52.10(1).
2   CPR 52.10(2).
3   CPR 52.10(4).
4   CPR 52.10(3).

Bail

4.66 The Court of Appeal has jurisdiction to grant bail in relation to a civil appeal in judicial review proceedings: *R (Sezek) v Secretary of State for the Home Department* [2001] EWCA Civ 795, [2001] The Times, 20 June.

See also the note to CPR PD 52 para 21.4, bail.

Case management powers of the Court of Appeal

4.67 The Court of Appeal has by virtue of CPR 2.1 the case management powers provided by CPR Pt 3. It thus has power to stay an application for permission to appeal until security for costs has been provided and until orders for costs have been complied with: *Great Future International Ltd v Sealand Housing Corpn* [2003] EWCA Civ 682 (see **para A2.7**).

Past costs

4.68 In *CIBC Mellon Trust Company v Mora Hotel Corporation NV and Chascona NV* [2002] EWCA Civ 1688 (see **para A2.4**), the Court of Appeal overturned the decision of the judge at first instance who had used case management powers to make it a condition of the pursuit of certain applications the payment into court of £1.6m which related to past costs. That case was said to be very different from *Contract Facilities Ltd v Rees' Estate* [2003] EWCA Civ 1105 (see **para A2.6**), where the Court of Appeal ordered the appellant company (which was being financed by an individual) to pay into court sums to satisfy past costs orders and the respondent's costs of the application to the Court of Appeal. If these costs were not paid, the appeal was to be struck out. The Court had jurisdiction to make such an order as it was being asked to exercise its case management powers during the currency of an appeal 'by reference to conduct while the appeal is pending'. This was because the individual had financed the trial and was financing the appeal and the application against him under s.51 of the Supreme Court Act 1981 stood a considerable prospect of success.

'[T]his is not a case where the respondents were simply seeking to inflate the pool against which they can later execute any judgment ... But if [Mr S] chooses to fund an appeal there is no reason why the Court should not say Contract can bring the appeal but only on terms.'

CPR 52.11 HEARING OF APPEALS

4.69

'**52.11 Hearing of appeals**
(1) Every appeal will be limited to a review of the decision of the lower court unless—
   (a) a practice direction makes different provision for a particular category of appeal; or
   (b) the court considers that in the circumstances of an individual appeal it would be in the interests of justice to hold a re-hearing.
(2) Unless it orders otherwise, the appeal court will not receive—
   (a) oral evidence; or
   (b) evidence which was not before the lower court.
(3) The appeal court will allow an appeal where the decision of the lower court was—
   (a) wrong; or
   (b) unjust because of a serious procedural or other irregularity in the proceedings in the lower court.
(4) The appeal court may draw any inference of fact which it considers justified on the evidence.
(5) At the hearing of the appeal a party may not rely on a matter not contained in his appeal notice unless the appeal court gives permission.'

Nature of appeal hearing

4.70 As a general rule, every appeal will be limited to a review of the decision of the lower court. This general rule is applied unless a practice direction makes different provision for a particular category of appeal, or the court considers that in the circumstances of an individual appeal it would be in the interests of justice to hold a rehearing[1]. The Practice Direction supplementing CPR Pt 52 provides that a rehearing will not be held unless it is required by any enactment or rule or the appeal is from the decision of a minister, person or other body whose decision was reached without a hearing or the hearing did not provide for the consideration of evidence[2]. The appeal court will only allow an appeal where the decision of the lower court was wrong, or where it was unjust because of a serious procedural or other irregularity in the proceedings in the lower court[3].

1 CPR 52.11(1). See, generally, **Chapter 2**.
2 CPR PD 52, para 9.1.
3 CPR 52.11(3).

4.71 As Brooke LJ explained in *Tanfern Ltd v Cameron-MacDonald* [2000] 1 WLR 1311 (see **para A2.22**), this:

'marks a significant change in practice, in relation to what used to be called 'interlocutory appeals' from district judges or masters. Under the old practice, the appeal to a judge was a rehearing in the fullest sense of the word, and the judge exercised his/her discretion afresh, while giving appropriate weight to the way the lower court had exercised its discretion in the matter. Under the new practice, the decision of the lower court will attract much greater significance. The appeal court's duty is now limited to a review of that decision, and it may only interfere in the quite limited circumstances set out in r 52.11(3).'

Rehearing

4.72 For the principles to be applied in deciding whether there should be a review or a rehearing, see *Asiansky Television plc v Bayer-Rosin* [2001] EWCA Civ 1792, [2001] All ER (D) 271. (There must be some feature of the case that unusually makes it unjust for the appeal to be limited to one of review. Where the decision of the lower court is adequately reasoned and there has been no serious procedural irregularity in the court below, it should usually be possible for the appeal court to determine the appeal by review and not rehearing: per Dyson LJ.)

4.73 When considering whether to reverse a factual decision of the lower court (as to which, see **para 4.75** below for the circumstances in which an appeal will be allowed) the approach of the court should be the same, whether conducting a review or a rehearing, as those expressions are used in CPR 52.11: *Assicurazioni Generali SpA v Arab Insurance Group (BSC)* [2002] EWCA Civ 1642, [2003] 1 WLR 577, [2003] 1 All ER (Comm) 140.

4.74 Article 6 of the European Convention on Human Rights did not require an appeal from an administrative decision or a decision made ex parte (without notice) or by an officer who was not independent to be by way of a rehearing: *Dyson Ltd v Registrar of Trademarks* (2003) Times, 23 May.

Circumstances in which an appeal will be allowed

4.75 In *Tanfern* Brooke LJ explained the governing principles of the new practice at paras 31–33:

> 'Under the new practice, the decision of the lower court will attract much greater significance. The appeal court's duty is now limited to a review of that decision, and it may only interfere in the quite limited circumstances set out in r 52.11(3).
>
> The first ground for interference speaks for itself. The epithet "wrong" is to be applied to the substance of the decision made by the lower court. If the appeal is against the exercise of a discretion by the lower court, the decision of the House of Lords in *G v G* [1985] 2 All ER 225, [1985] 1 WLR 647 warrants attention. In that case Lord Fraser of Tullybelton said:
>
>> "Certainly it would not be useful to inquire whether different shades of meaning are intended to be conveyed by words such as 'blatant error' used by Sir John Arnold P in the present case, and words such as 'clearly wrong', 'plainly wrong' or simply 'wrong' used by other judges in other cases. All these various expressions were used in order to emphasise the point that the appellate court should only interfere when it considers that the judge of first instance has not merely preferred an imperfect solution which is different from an alternative imperfect solution which the Court of Appeal might or would have adopted, but has exceeded the generous ambit within which a reasonable disagreement is possible." (See [1985] 2 All ER 225 at 229, [1985] 1 WLR 647 at 652.)
>
> So far as the second ground for interference is concerned, it must be noted that the appeal court only has power to interfere if the procedural or other irregularity which it has detected in the proceedings in the lower court was a serious one, and that this irregularity caused the decision of the lower court to be an unjust decision.'

Oral evidence

4.76 Unless it orders otherwise, the appeal court will not receive oral evidence[1]. As for applications to rely on evidence which was not before the lower court see **para 4.81**. Where such evidence is admitted it will invariably be given by affidavit or witness statement.

1   CPR 52.11(2)(a).

Failure to give reasons

4.77 For failure to give reasons, see **paras 4.78 and 4.79.**

Reasons for decision

4.78 The terms of a judgment should enable the parties and the appellate court to understand why the judge reached his decision. Not every factor which weighed with the judge in his appraisal of the evidence has to be identified and explained. But the issues the resolution of which were vital to the judge's conclusion should be identified and the manner in which he resolved them explained: *English v Emery Reimbold & Strick Ltd* [2002] EWCA Civ 605, [2002] 3 All ER 385, [2002] All ER (D) 302, CA. The appeal court may adjourn an application for permission to appeal to invite the trial judge to give additional reasons.

4.79 See also *South Cone Inc v Bessant* [2002] EWCA Civ 763, [2002] All ER (D) 426 (the appellate court should not treat a judgment or written decision as containing an error of principle simply because of its belief that the judgment or decision could have been better expressed: 'The duty to give reasons must not be turned into an intolerable burden', per Robert Walker LJ).

Disposing of applications and appeals by consent

4.80 See Practice Direction paras 12.1–13.5 at CPR PD 52, paras 12.1–13.5 and the forms of request for the dismissal of an appeal in the Appendix: Forms.

Fresh evidence

4.81 Unless it orders otherwise, the appeal court will not receive evidence which was not before the lower court[1]. An application to rely on evidence which was not before the lower court needs to be supported by an affidavit or witness statement. The application may be included at Section 10 of the appellant's notice[2].

1   CPR 52.11(2)(b). See **Chapter 2, paras 2.62–2.72** for the principles to be applied.
2   For applications to the appeal court e.g. to rely on fresh evidence see **para 4.49**.

Changing grounds of appeal

4.82 Permission is required to rely on a matter not contained in an appeal notice: CPR 52.11(5). Where a party wishes to change his grounds of appeal, he should inform the court and the respondent so directions can be given as to whether and how the appeal should proceed: *Shire v Secretary of State for Work and Pensions* [2003] EWCA Civ 1465, [2003] The Times, October 30 (see **para A2.19**). The permission of the appeal court is required to withdraw a concession or to take a point which was not argued in the lower court[1].

1   *Jones v MBNA International Bank* (30 June 2000, unreported), CA; this general principle 'is not merely a matter of efficiency, expediency and cost, but of substantial justice' per May LJ.

Judge who refused permission

4.83 The fact that a judge was minded to refuse permission to appeal does not disqualify him from hearing the appeal: *Mahomed v Morris* [2000] 2 BCLC 536, CA. See also *Sengupta v Holmes* [2002] EWCA Civ 1104, [2002] The Times, August 19 (in the absence of special circumstances, there was no reason as a matter of principle to regard a judge who had refused permission to appeal on paper as being anything other than a proper and impartial member of the tribunal convened to hear the appeal).

CPR 52.12 NON-DISCLOSURE OF PART 36 OFFERS AND PAYMENTS

4.84

> **'52.12 Non-disclosure of Part 36 offers and payments**
> (1)   The fact that a Part 36 offer or Part 36 payment has been made must not be disclosed to any judge of the appeal court who is to hear or determine
> (a) an application for permission to appeal; or
> (b) an appeal
> until all questions (other than costs) have been determined.
> (2)   Paragraph (1) does not apply if the Part 36 offer or Part 36 payment is relevant to the substance of the appeal.

(3) Paragraph (1) does not prevent disclosure in any application in the appeal proceedings if disclosure of the fact that a Part 36 offer or Part 36 payment has been made is properly relevant to the matter to be decided.'

Disclosure of Part 36 offers and payments

4.85 The fact that a Part 36 offer or a Part 36 payment has been made must not be disclosed to any judge of the appeal court who is to hear or determine an application for permission to appeal or an appeal until all questions (other than costs) have been determined[1]. This provision does not apply if the Part 36 offer or payment is relevant to the substance of the appeal and does not prevent disclosure in any application in the appeal proceedings if disclosure of the fact that an offer or payment has been made is properly relevant to the matter to be decided[2].

1 CPR 52.12.
2 CPR 52.12(2), (3).

Removal of references to Part 36 offers and payments

4.86 References to Part 36 offers or payments should be removed from documents in the bundle unless the fact that an offer or payment has been made is relevant. This applies whether the bundle is in support of an application for permission to appeal or an appeal. The Civil Appeals Office will ask practitioners to confirm that an offer or payment is relevant if any such references are to remain.

In *Garratt v Saxby* [2004] EWCA Civ 341 at paras 11 and 20, Dyson LJ gave guidance on references to Part 36 offers. He said:

> '11. It seems to me that if something is included in the documents placed before the appeal judge, then it is 'disclosed' to the judge within the meaning of Part 52.12(1)... [That] part of the transcript [which contains a record of the discussion after judgment and includes a reference to a Part 36 offer or payment] should be redacted from the document provided to the appeal judge so that the fact of the offer or payment is not disclosed to him or her. It is regrettable that this obvious step was not taken in the present case.
>
> 20. It is for the judge to decide in each case whether the disclosure of a Part 36 offer or payment makes a fair trial impossible and whether justice demands that he recuse himself. But judges should not be too ready to reach such a conclusion; the delay and extra cost occasioned by a recusal

may be very considerable. Moreover, when exercising their discretion, judges should remind themselves that they ought to have little difficulty in analysing and deciding the issues in the case on their merits without being influenced by their knowledge of the amount of the Part 36 offer or payment.'

Compromise of appeal

4.87 A claimant who wishes to protect himself as to the costs of an appeal must make a separate, further Part 36 offer in the appeal proceedings: *Utaniko Ltd v P & O Nedlloyd BV* [2003] EWCA Civ 174, [2003] 1 Lloyd's Rep 265, [2003] The Times, 21 February. A respondent should not be expected to make an offer based on giving up a substantial part of what it was currently entitled to, when the appeal turned on a pure point of construction to which there was only one answer: *CEL Group Ltd v Nedlloyd Lines UK Ltd* [2003] EWCA Civ 1871 [2004] The Times, January 2.

SPECIAL PROVISIONS APPLYING TO THE COURT OF APPEAL

CPR 52.13 SECOND APPEALS TO THE COURT

4.88

'**52.13 Second appeals to the court**
(1) Permission is required from the Court of Appeal for any appeal to that court from a decision of a county court or the High Court which was itself made on appeal.
(2) The Court of Appeal will not give permission unless it considers that—
 (a) the appeal would raise an important point of principle or practice; or
 (b) there is some other compelling reason for the Court of Appeal to hear it.'

Second appeals

4.89 Where the decision being appealed was itself made on appeal, an appeal from that decision is a second appeal within the meaning of s 55 of the Access to Justice Act 1999 (see **Chapter 3** for the text of the Act). By virtue of the Access to Justice Act 1999 (Destination of Appeals) Order 2000, SI 2000/1071 art 5 (see **Chapter 3** for the text of the Order) an appeal from the decision of a county court or of the High Court which was itself made on appeal, lies to the Court of Appeal. Where an appeal is a 'second appeal' within s 55 of the 1999 Act, it may be made to the Court of Appeal only if the Court of Appeal considers that the appeal raises an important point of principle or practice or there is some other compelling reason for the Court of Appeal to hear it. For guidance on the test imposed by s 55, see *Clark v Perks* [2001] 1 WLR 17, [2000] 4 All ER 1 paras 16–18 (see **para A2.5**); *Scott v Shipp* [2001] CPLR 5, CA; *Pepin v Watts* [2001] CPLR 9, CA. The Court of Appeal has now made it clear that, for the purposes of s 55, the following appeals are to be treated as appeals to a county court or the High Court within the meaning of that section:

(1) an appeal to the High Court on a point of law pursuant to s 11 of the Tribunals and Inquiries Act 1992 from a tribunal;
(2) any application to the High Court which can be categorised as an appeal by way of case stated;
(3) an appeal to a county court on a point of law from a decision of a local housing authority under s 204(1) [or s 204A] of the Housing Act 1996;
(4) any other appeal to the High Court or the county court from any tribunal or other body or person: *McNicholas Construction Co Ltd v Customs and Excise Comrs, Clark v Perks* [2001] 1 WLR 17, [2000] 4 All ER 1 (see **para A2.5**), and *Azimi v London Borough of Newham* (2001) 33 HLR 51, CA.

4.90 A decision made during the hearing of an application for permission to appeal is not a decision made on hearing the appeal. See further **Chapter 3**.

4.91 Section 55 applies only to appeals from decisions made by a county court or the High Court. Nevertheless, the Court of Appeal applied the stricter test for permission imposed by s 55 in an appeal from an expert tribunal, a Social Security Commissioner, in *Cooke v Secretary of State for Social Security* [2001] EWCA Civ 734, [2002] 3 All ER 279. The *Cooke* approach has also been applied to appeals from decisions of the Competition Commission Appeal Tribunal (see CPR PD 52, para 21.10): *Napp Pharmaceutical Holdings Ltd v Director General of Fair Trading* [2002] EWCA Civ 796, [2002] 4 All ER 376. The same reasoning was not, however, extended to appeals from the Immigration Appeal Tribunal by the Court of Appeal in *Koller v Secretary of State for the Home Department* [2001] EWCA Civ 1267 (see **para A2.15**) see further the note to CPR PD 52, para 21.7.

Second appeal or original order

4.92 An appeal is not a 'second appeal' if the 'matter' on which the judgment being appealed was given is different from the 'matter' on which the first decision was given. In other words to give rise to a second appeal, the subject matter of the first decision and of the first appeal must be the same. Thus an appeal against the refusal to extend the time for appealing is not a second appeal: *Foenander v Bond Lewis & Co* [2001] EWCA Civ 759, [2002] 1 WLR 525, [2001] 2 All ER 1019 (see **para A2.8**). Where an appeal court orders a rehearing at appeal court level, any subsequent appeal would be a second appeal: *Fowler de Pledge v Smith* [2003] EWCA Civ 703, [2003] All ER (D) 261, (2003) The Times, 27 May.

4.93 Where a circuit judge refuses permission to appeal from an order made by a district judge but makes an ancillary or original order (such as for costs or refusing an adjournment), any appeal against that order lies to a High Court Judge not the Court of Appeal: *Jolly v Jay* [2002] EWCA Civ 277 [2002] All ER (D) 104, [2002] The Times, 3 April (see **para A2.13**). This is because the circuit judge is not making a decision 'on hearing the appeal'.

Point of principle or practice or other compelling reason

4.94 For a discussion of a point of principle in an ancillary relief matter see *Madray v Madray* [2001] EWCA Civ 524 per Ward LJ:

> 'There is a difference between a point of principle, that means legal principle, and the weight to be given to the various factors. The principle is that you look to the contributions ... to the welfare of the family ... In assessing that it is an equal contribution, that is really giving weight to that factor, and weight is for the judges in the court below. The Court of Appeal does not interfere unless these have gone plainly wrong ... [W]here you are assessing the weight to be given to any factor or where you are exercising a discretion holding in balance this factor as having that weight, the other factor and the other scale having that weight, the balance to be struck can only be attacked if it is so outside the generous ambit within which people can reasonably disagree.'

4.95 In *Major v Lamyman* [2003] EWCA Civ 1701 the alternative basis for granting permission to appeal was said by Brooke LJ V-P to be 'another compelling reason':

> 'appellate judges must not reverse first instance decisions for reasons as thin as those given by Royce J, who did not expressly or impliedly refer to either of the grounds on which an appeal court can properly intervene.'

Practice Direction

4.96 For special provisions regarding appeals to the Court of Appeal see Practice Direction paras 15.1–15.21 at **CPR PD 52**.

GENERAL NOTES ON APPEALS AND APPLICATIONS TO THE COURT OF APPEAL

Appeals to the Court of Appeal

4.97 CPR Pt 52 and its Practice Direction apply to appeals to the Court of Appeal. The main features of appeals to the Court of Appeal are referred to below. The importance of complying with the provisions of the Practice Direction relating (in particular) to bundles and skeleton arguments cannot be over-emphasised. Failures to comply will be met with costs orders see CPR PD 52 paras 5.10(6), 15.4, 15.11B(2) and *Harvey Shop Fitters Ltd v ADI Ltd* [2003] EWCA Civ 1757, [2003] The Times, November 26, *Jennings & Anor v Cairns* [2003] EWCA Civ 1935, [2003] Times, November 26.

Practice Direction

4.98 There is no longer a separate Practice Direction for the Court of Appeal. CPR PD 52 applies to appeals to the Court of Appeal as well as to appeals to the High Court and county courts. There are special provisions at CPR PD 52, paras 10.1, 15.1–15.21, 21.1–21.11 which apply only to the Court of Appeal but reference has to be made to the Practice Direction as a whole.

Filing of documents – provision of orders

4.99 Since the Court of Appeal has to be satisfied that it has jurisdiction to entertain an appeal from a county court, the Civil Appeals Office requires the production of a copy of the order specifically allocating the claim to the multi-track as well as a copy of the order being appealed (*see* **para 4.3**) In a second appeal, the order which was the subject of the first appeal should also be provided. If, for any reason, the order being appealed is not yet available, an explanation has to be furnished when the appellant's notice is filed. Documents should be filed with the Civil Appeals Office Registry, Room E307, Royal Court of Justice, Strand, London WC2A 2LL, DX 44450 STRAND (telephone 020 7947 6409). For the fees payable see Supreme Court Fees Order, Fees 9.1, 9.2.

Bundles of documents

4.100 An appellant is expected to file with his appellant's notice his appeal bundle in support of his appeal: CPR PD 52, para 5.6. This means that a transcript of judgment should accompany the notice (see CPR PD 52, para 5.12). The Practice Direction reinforces the duty on solicitors and advocates in relation to transcripts and notes of judgment: see paras 5.12 and 5.14. See, for example, *Re D (Child)* FAFMF 99/1102, (8 November 1999, unreported), CA (when solicitors are instructed to pursue an appeal they are under a duty to obtain a copy of the transcript of the judgment from the court below). Where it is not possible to file the appeal bundle with the appellant's notice, a request for further time may be made by separate letter to the Civil Appeals Office. Proof that the transcript has been ordered and paid for should be provided. See further **Chapter 6**.

Amendment of appeal notices

4.101 Permission is needed to amend an appeal notice (except in relation to a skeleton argument included within the notice): CPR 52.8, CPR PD 52, paras 5.9, 5.25, 7.6.

Service

4.102 The Court of Appeal seals an appeal notice. Service on the respondent takes place after filing and must be effected by the appellant; the Court of Appeal does not serve documents: CPR PD 52, para 15.1(2). A respondent has to be served with an appellant's notice which seeks permission to appeal although he need take no action until such time as permission has been given: CPR PD 52, para 5.21–5.22. See further CPR 52.5

Applications and evidence in support of applications

4.103 For applications to the Court of Appeal see CPR PD 52, para 11.2. Where an appellant's notice includes an application for an extension of time (e.g. because it was not possible to file the notice within the 14-day time limit) or an application to rely on further evidence or for a stay of execution, the application must be supported by evidence. This may be provided either as part of the notice by completing the witness statement in Section 10 or by means of a separate witness statement or affidavit. Failure to file evidence in support will delay the issue of the appellant's notice. For further guidance see **paras 4.41–4.42.**

Transition to an appeal

4.104 The same reference number will be used for the appeal after permission has been given and it is not necessary to 'set down' the appeal. A fee is, however, payable on filing the appeal questionnaire: see the Supreme Court Fees Order, Fee 9.1(c). An appellant will be required to serve his appeal bundle on the respondent within seven days of receiving the order granting permission to appeal: CPR PD 52, para 6.2.

Appeal questionnaire

4.105 This must contain the time estimate and confirmation that the appeal bundle has been served on the respondent and that copies of the appeal bundle are being prepared and will be held ready for the court's use: CPR PD 52, para 6.5. For the fee payable see the Supreme Court Fees Order, Fee 9.1(c).

Respondent's notice etc

4.106 See CPR 52.5 and CPR PD 52, para 7. A respondent is required to notify the Civil Appeals Office whether he proposes to file a respondent's notice or whether he proposes to rely on the reasons given by the lower court: see CPR PD 52, para 15.6 and Chapter 6.

Composition of the Court of Appeal

4.107 A court is duly constituted if it consists of one or more judges: Supreme Court Act 1981 s 54 as amended. The significance of this amendment is that there is no longer an appeal to the full Court from an order made in open court by a single Lord Justice such as an order striking out an appeal or providing for security for costs: *Paragon Finance plc v Noueiri* [2001] EWCA 1114, Robert Walker, Tuckey LJJ). The Master of the Rolls is empowered by s 54(3) to give directions about the minimum number of judges of which a court is to consist for any particular proceedings but, as yet, no such directions have been given. Where the parties consider that issues of complexity or general importance arise such that a listing before a three-judge court is desirable, the master of civil appeals should be informed.

Hearings in the Court of Appeal: requests for expedition and settlements

4.108 For listing in the Court of Appeal see CPR PD 52, para 15.7–15.9. Where an expedited hearing is to be requested, the Civil Appeals Listing Office should be provided with a letter setting out the reasons why expedition is needed and a bundle of documents. See *Unilever plc v Chefaro Proprietaries Ltd (Practice Note)* [1995] 1 WLR 243 (see **para A2.23**). It is essential that a transcript (or note) of the judgment being appealed is provided: *Hertsmere Borough Council v Harty* [2001] EWCA Civ 1238 (the 'want of an adequate note is a breach of both counsel's and solicitor's obligations ... both counsel and solicitor ... have an obligation to take the fullest possible manuscript note of a judgment ... because of the possibility that a decent note of the judge's reasons will be required before the transcript can be provided' per Sedley LJ). Where an advocate is aware that an application or an appeal in which he is instructed is linked with another case, or raises issues similar to or connected with those raised in other applications or appeals, they should inform the master, by letter, as soon as practicable. Solicitors and, where appropriate counsel, have a duty to inform the Listing Office at the earliest opportunity if there is a settlement and an appeal may be compromised: *Tasyurdu v Secretary of State for the Home Dept* [2003] EWCA Civ 447, [2003] The Times, 16 April;

see CPR PD 52 paras 12, 13 and *HFC Bank plc v HSBC Bank plc, CA* (unreported10 February 2000). It is very important that the parties inform the Court of Appeal listing office if an appeal which has been listed may not proceed. There is a professional obligation to notify the court if there is a likelihood that judicial time will be wasted in preparing for an appeal which has settled or is subject to negotiations, if necessary through the 24-hour switchboard at the Royal Courts of Justice (020 7947 6000); *Yell Ltd v Garton* [2004] EWCA Civ 87, [2004] All ER (D) 80 (Feb). In the first instance, counsel or solicitors should ask to speak to one of the deputy masters in the Court of Appeal.

Hearings in the Court of Appeal are in public even in children cases.

Costs in the Court of Appeal

4.109 The Court of Appeal may assess the costs of an appeal summarily see CPR PD 52, para 14. Parties attending the hearing of an appeal which is listed for one day or less should be prepared to deal with the summary assessment. For costs in publicly funded cases *see R (on the application of Gunn) v Secretary of State for the Home Department* [2001] EWCA Civ 891, [2001] 1 WLR 1634, [2001] 3 All ER 481. As for the costs consequences of turning down alternative dispute resolution when suggested by the court, see **Chapter 7**.

Appeals in family proceedings

4.110 CPR Pt 52 applies to appeals to the Court of Appeal in family proceedings. Hearings in family proceedings in the Court of Appeal are in public.

CPR 52.14 ASSIGNMENT OF APPEALS TO THE COURT OF APPEAL

4.111

'**52.14 Assignment of appeals to the Court of Appeal**
(1) Where the court from or to which an appeal is made or from which permission to appeal is sought ('the relevant court') considers that—
    (a) an appeal which is to be heard by a county court or the High Court would raise an important point of principle or practice; or
    (b) there is some other compelling reason for the Court of Appeal to hear it,

the relevant court may order the appeal to be transferred to the Court of Appeal.

(The Master of the Rolls has the power to direct that an appeal which would be heard by a county court or the High Court should be heard instead by the Court of Appeal—see section 57 of the Access to Justice Act 1999)

(2) The Master of the Rolls or the Court of Appeal may remit an appeal to the court in which the original appeal was or would have been brought.'

4.112 Where an appeal would not normally lie to the Court of Appeal (as to which see **Chapter 2**: routes of appeal), s 57 of the Access to Justice Act 1999 provides a mechanism for the transfer of an appeal to the Court of Appeal. The power conferred on county courts and the High Court to direct the transfer of an appeal to the Court of Appeal is subject to CPR 52.14 which provides that an order transferring an appeal to the Court of Appeal may be made where the appeal 'would raise an important point of principle or practice or there is some other compelling reason for the Court of Appeal to hear it'. Guidance was given in a letter from Lord Woolf MR as to the criteria which are to be applied in considering whether to make a direction. These are:

(1) where there appear to be conflicting authorities requiring resolution by the Court of Appeal;
(2) in relation to points of practice or procedure where there is no guidance at present and the point is of significant importance for the practice or procedure of the courts;
(3) where the issue is one of general principle and importance in the development of the substantive law; or
(4) the issue is one where there are a number of appeals on similar points so as to suggest that a theme or trend is developing which the Court of Appeal needs to consider.

Where a case has been identified as suitable for assignment the papers are sent to the Head of the Civil Appeals Office at the Royal Courts of Justice, Strand, London WC2A 2LL and parties are expected to supply three bundles of documents with the necessary transcripts so the matter may be listed without unnecessary delay. The power of the courts below the Court of Appeal to transfer an appeal to the Court of Appeal should be sparingly used: *Jenkins v BP Oil Ltd* (1 September 2000), CA reported in *Clark v Perks* [2001] 1 WLR 17, [2000] 4 All ER 1, CA (see **para A2.13**). Even where an appeal is transferred to the Court of Appeal, it may be remitted back again. It should be noted that an application for permission to appeal cannot be transferred; permission to appeal must be granted: *Re Claims Direct Test Cases* [2002] EWCA Civ 428.

CPR 52.15 JUDICIAL REVIEW APPEALS

4.113

'52.15 Judicial review appeals
(1) Where permission to apply for judicial review has been refused at a hearing in the High Court, the person seeking that permission may apply to the Court of Appeal for permission to appeal.
(2) An application in accordance with paragraph (1) must be made within 7 days of the decision of the High Court to refuse to give permission to apply for judicial review.
(3) On an application under paragraph (1), the Court of Appeal may, instead of giving permission to appeal, give permission to apply for judicial review.
(4) Where the Court of Appeal gives permission to apply for judicial review in accordance with paragraph (3), the case will proceed in the High Court unless the Court of Appeal orders otherwise.'

Judicial review appeals

4.114 Applications which used to be called 'renewed applications for leave to move for judicial review' are, under CPR Pt 52, applications for permission to appeal against the refusal of the High Court to grant permission to apply for judicial review. Instead of granting permission to appeal, the Court of Appeal may give permission to apply for judicial review and the case then proceeds in the High Court. In some cases, however, the Court of Appeal may hear the substantive judicial review application itself. If the Court of Appeal considers that there is a real prospect of the appellant being able to show at a contested appeal hearing that the application is fit for consideration at a substantive judicial review hearing but it wishes to hear the respondent on the matter, 'it will probably adjourn the application to be heard on notice, with the appeal to follow if permission is granted. This will represent a speedier and more convenient way of dealing with the matter than merely granting permission to appeal there and then, and then holding things up until a substantive appeal hearing can be heard on the question whether the appeal should be allowed and permission to apply for judicial review granted': *R (on the application of Werner) v IRC & Ors* [2002] EWCA Civ 979 per Brooke LJ. If the Court of Appeal refuses permission there is no appeal to the House of Lords: *R v Secretary of State for Trade and Industry, ex p Eastaway* [2001] 1 All ER 27, [2000] 1 WLR 2222, HL. Where the Court of Appeal grants permission to appeal from a refusal to give permission to apply for judicial review and hears the appeal but dismisses it, there is potentially a right of appeal to the House of

Lords: *R (on the application of Burkett) v Hammersmith and Fulham London Borough Council* [2002] UKHL 23, [2002] 3 All ER 97, [2002] 1 WLR 1593.

CPR 52.16 WHO MAY EXERCISE THE POWERS OF THE COURT OF APPEAL

4.115

'**52.16 Who may exercise the powers of the Court of Appeal**
(1)   A court officer assigned to the Civil Appeals Office who is—
    (a)   a barrister; or
    (b)   a solicitor
may exercise the jurisdiction of the Court of Appeal with regard to the matters set out in paragraph (2) with the consent of the Master of the Rolls.
(2)   The matters referred to in paragraph (1) are—
    (a)   any matter incidental to any proceedings in the Court of Appeal;
    (b)   any other matter where there is no substantial dispute between the parties; and
    (c)   the dismissal of an appeal or application where a party has failed to comply with any order, rule or practice direction.
(3)   A court officer may not decide an application for—
    (a)   permission to appeal;
    (b)   bail pending an appeal;
    (c)   an injunction$^{(GL)}$;
    (d)   a stay$^{(GL)}$ of any proceedings, other than a temporary stay of any order or decision of the lower court over a period when the Court of Appeal is not sitting or cannot conveniently be convened.
(4)   Decisions of a court officer may be made without a hearing.
(5)   A party may request any decision of a court officer to be reviewed by the Court of Appeal.
(6)   At the request of a party, a hearing will be held to reconsider a decision of—
    (a)   a single judge; or
    (b)   a court officer
made without a hearing.
(6A) A request under paragraph (5) or (6) must be filed within 7 days after the party is served with notice of the decision.
(7)   A single judge may refer any matter for a decision by a court consisting of two or more judges.

(Section 54(6) of the Supreme Court Act 1981 provides that there is no appeal from the decision of a single judge on an application for permission to appeal.[1])

(Section 58(2) of the Supreme Court Act 1981 provides that there is no appeal to the House of Lords from decisions of the Court of Appeal that—
(a) are taken by a single judge or any officer or member of staff of that court in proceedings incidental to any cause or matter pending before the civil division of that court; and
(b) do not involve the determination of an appeal or of an application for permission to appeal,
and which may be called into question by rules of court. Rules 52.16(5) and (6) provide the procedure for the calling into question of such decisions.)'

1   Editorial note: the rule is incorrect: s 54(6) has been repealed by Access to Justice Act 1999.

Master

4.116 When the Head of the Civil Appeals Office acts in a judicial capacity pursuant to CPR 52.16, he is known as master. Other officers designated to exercise judicial authority are known as deputy masters[1]. See CPR PD 52, para 15.5.

The master and deputy masters may exercise the jurisdiction of the Court of Appeal with regard to any matter incidental to any proceedings, any other matter where there is no substantial dispute between the parties and the dismissal of an appeal or application for failure to comply with any order, rule or practice direction[2]. The master and his deputies may give directions in relation to applications and appeals or may refer a request for directions to one of the Supervising Lord Justices. A request for directions should be addressed to the Civil Appeals Office and not direct to a Lord Justice or to his clerk: CPR PD 52 para 15.10.

1   CPR PD 52, para 15.2.
2   CPR 52.16(2); see also CPR 52.16(3).

PROVISIONS ABOUT REOPENING APPEALS

CPR 52.17 REOPENING OF FINAL APPEALS

4.117

'52.17 Reopening of final appeals
(1)   The Court of Appeal or the High Court will not reopen a final determination of any appeal unless—

(a) it is necessary to do so in order to avoid real injustice;
(b) the circumstances are exceptional and make it appropriate to reopen the appeal; and
(c) there is no alternative effective remedy.
(2) In paragraphs (1), (3), (4) and (6), 'appeal' includes an application for permission to appeal.
(3) This rule does not apply to appeals to a county court.
(4) Permission is needed to make an application under this rule to reopen a final determination of an appeal even in cases where under rule 52.3(1) permission was not needed for the original appeal.
(5) There is no right to an oral hearing of an application for permission unless, exceptionally, the judge so directs.
(6) The judge will not grant permission without directing the application to be served on the other party to the original appeal and giving him an opportunity to make representations.
(7) There is no right of appeal or review from the decision of the judge on the application for permission, which is final.
(8) The procedure for making an application for permission is set out in the practice direction.'

Jurisdiction to reopen a decision of the Court of Appeal or of the High Court

4.118 CPR 52.17 was inserted by the Civil Procedure (Amendment No 4) Rules 2003, SI 2003/2113, to provide the procedure for reopening an appeal or an application for permission to appeal. The jurisdiction to reopen a final decision was established in *Taylor v Lawrence* where it was decided that the Court of Appeal possesses a residual jurisdiction inherent in its function as a court of justice, 'to avoid real injustice in exceptional circumstances': *Taylor v Lawrence* [2002] EWCA Civ 90, [2002] 2 All ER 353, [2002] 3 WLR 640, (2002) Times, Lord Woolf CJ. The High Court, as an appeal court, possesses a similar jurisdiction: *Seray-Wurie v Hackney London Borough Council* [2002] EWCA Civ 909, [2003] 1 WLR 257, [2002] 3 All ER 448.

4.119 The 'quite exceptional nature' of this jurisdiction has been emphasised on a number of occasions by the Court of Appeal see *Matlaszek v Bloom Camillion* [2003] EWCA Civ 154 ('The fact that the jurisdiction has been identified for the purposes of awarding significant injustice in extraordinary circumstances must not be shown as giving any form of green light to the kind of applications that we have received today, unless those making it are completely satisfied that it does indeed fall within this particular rubric' per Brooke LJ. In that case the Court of Appeal was satisfied that it had power, under the *Taylor v Lawrence* jurisdiction, to reopen an order dismissing an appeal with the parties' consent but refused to do so in the particular circumstances of the case.) There is no right of recourse to a further appeal court even where the lower appeal court made its refusal to re-open at an oral hearing: *Parker v Hutchings* [2004] EWCA Civ 254.

Reopening county court decisions

4.120 CPR 52.17 does not apply to appeals to a county court. For the limited circumstances in which judicial review may be available in respect of the refusal by a county court of permission to appeal see **para 4.15**.

It should be noted that the power to enable a county court judge to order a rehearing under CCR Order 37, rule 1 has now been revoked in relation to civil proceedings to which the CPR apply. That power is, however, still available in family proceedings: *H (Children) (application for rehearing), Re* [2003] EWCA Civ 345.

Practice Direction

4.121 See CPR PD 52 para 25.

PRACTICE DIRECTION 52

4.122

'1.1. This Practice Direction is divided into four sections:

Section I – General provisions about appeals

Section II – General provisions about statutory appeals and appeals by way of case stated

Section III – Provisions about specific appeals

Section IV – Provisions about reopening appeals

SECTION I – GENERAL PROVISIONS ABOUT APPEALS

2.1. This practice direction applies to all appeals to which Part 52 applies except where specific provision is made for appeals to the Court of Appeal.

2.2. For the purpose only of appeals to the Court of Appeal from cases in family proceedings this Practice Direction will apply with such modifications as may be required.

ROUTES OF APPEAL

2A.1. Subject to paragraph 2A.2, the following table sets out to which court or judge an appeal is to be made (subject to obtaining any necessary permission):

Decision of:	Appeal made to:
District judge of a county court	Circuit judge
Master or district judge of the High Court	High Court judge
Circuit judge	High Court judge
High Court judge	Court of Appeal

2A.2. Where the decision to be appealed is a final decision –
(1) in a Part 7 claim allocated to the multi-track; or
(2) made in specialist proceedings (under the Companies Acts 1985 or 1989 or to which Sections I, II or III of Part 57 or any of Parts 58 to 63 apply),
the appeal is to be made to the Court of Appeal (subject to obtaining any necessary permission).

2A.3. A "final decision" is a decision of a court that would finally determine (subject to any possible appeal or detailed assessment of costs) the entire proceedings whichever way the court decided the issues before it.

2A.4. A decision of a court is to be treated as a final decision for routes of appeal purposes where it:
(1) is made at the conclusion of part of a hearing or trial which has been split into parts; and
(2) would, if it had been made at the conclusion of that hearing or trial, have been a final decision.

2A.5. An order made:
(1) on a summary or detailed assessment of costs; or
(2) on an application to enforce a final decision,
is not a "final decision" and any appeal from such an order will follow the appeal routes set out in the table in paragraph 2A.1.

(Section 16(1) of the Supreme Court Act 1981 (as amended); section 77(1) of the County Courts Act 1984 (as amended); and the Access to Justice Act 1999 (Destination of Appeals) Order 2000 set out the provisions governing routes of appeal)

2A.6. (1) Where the decision to be appealed is a final decision in a Part 8 claim treated as allocated to the multi-track under rule 8.9(c), the court to which the permission application is made should, if permission is given, and unless the appeal would lie to the Court of Appeal in any event, consider whether to order the appeal to be transferred to the Court of Appeal under rule 52.14.

(2) An appeal against a final decision on a point of law in a case which did not involve any substantial dispute of fact would normally be a suitable appeal to be so transferred.
(See also paragraph 10.1)

GROUNDS FOR APPEAL

3.1. Rule 52.11(3) (a) and (b) sets out the circumstances in which the appeal court will allow an appeal.

3.2. The grounds of appeal should–
(1) set out clearly the reasons why rule 52.11(3)(a) or (b) is said to apply; and
(2) specify, in respect of each ground, whether the ground raises an appeal on a point of law or is an appeal against a finding of fact.

PERMISSION TO APPEAL

4.1. Rule 52.3 sets out the circumstances when permission to appeal is required.

4.2. The permission of–
(1) the Court of Appeal; or
(2) where the lower court's rules allow, the lower court,

is required for all appeals to the Court of Appeal except as provided for by statute or rule 52.3.

(The requirement of permission to appeal may be imposed by a practice direction – see rule 52.3(b).)

4.3. Where the lower court is not required to give permission to appeal, it may give an indication of its opinion as to whether permission should be given.

(Rule 52.1(3)(c) defines "lower court")

Appeals from case management decisions

4.4. Case management decisions include decisions made under rule 3.1(2) and decisions about:
(1) disclosure
(2) filing of witness statements or experts reports
(3) directions about the timetable of the claim
(4) adding a party to a claim

(5)   security for costs.

4.5. Where the application is for permission to appeal from a case management decision, the court dealing with the application may take into account whether:
(1)   the issue is of sufficient significance to justify the costs of an appeal;
(2)   the procedural consequences of an appeal (e.g. loss of trial date) outweigh the significance of the case management decision;
(3)   it would be more convenient to determine the issue at or after trial.

Court to which permission to appeal application should be made

4.6. An application for permission should be made orally at the hearing at which the decision to be appealed against is made.

4.7. Where:
(a)   no application for permission to appeal is made at the hearing; or
(b)   the lower court refuses permission to appeal,
an application for permission to appeal may be made to the appeal court in accordance with rules 52.3(2) and (3).

4.8. There is no appeal from a decision of the appeal court to allow or refuse permission to appeal to that court (although where the appeal court, without a hearing, refuses permission to appeal, the person seeking permission may request that decision to be reconsidered at a hearing). See section 54(4) of the Access to Justice Act and rule 52.3(2), (3), (4) and (5).

Second appeals

4.9. An application for permission to appeal from a decision of the High Court or a county court which was itself made on appeal must be made to the Court of Appeal.

4.10. If permission to appeal is granted the appeal will be heard by the Court of Appeal.

Consideration of Permission without a hearing

4.11. Applications for permission to appeal may be considered by the appeal court without a hearing.

4.12. If permission is granted without a hearing the parties will be notified of that decision and the procedure in paragraphs 6.1 to 6.6 will then apply.

4.13. If permission is refused without a hearing the parties will be notified of that decision with the reasons for it. The decision is subject to the appellant's right to have it reconsidered at an oral hearing. This may be before the same judge.

4.14. A request for the decision to be reconsidered at an oral hearing must be filed at the appeal court within 7 days after service of the notice that permission has been refused. A copy of the request must be served by the appellant on the respondent at the same time.

Permission hearing

4.14A. (1) This paragraph applies where an appellant, who is represented, makes a request for a decision to be reconsidered at an oral hearing.

(2) The appellant's advocate must, at least 4 days before the hearing, in a brief written statement–
   (a) inform the court and the respondent of the points which he proposes to raise at the hearing;
   (b) set out his reasons why permission should be granted notwithstanding the reasons given for the refusal of permission; and
   (c) confirm, where applicable, that the requirements of paragraph 4.17 have been complied with (appellant in receipt of services funded by the Legal Services Commission).

4.15. Notice of a permission hearing will be given to the respondent but he is not required to attend unless the court requests him to do so.

4.16. If the court requests the respondent's attendance at the permission hearing, the appellant must supply the respondent with a copy of the appeal bundle (see paragraph 5.6A) within 7 days of being notified of the request, or such other period as the court may direct. The costs of providing that bundle shall be borne by the appellant initially, but will form part of the costs of the permission application.

Appellants in receipt of services funded by the Legal Services Commission applying for permission to appeal

4.17. Where the appellant is in receipt of services funded by the Legal Services Commission (or legally aided) and permission to appeal has been refused by the appeal court without a hearing, the appellant must send a copy of the reasons the appeal court gave for refusing permission to the relevant office of the Legal Services Commission as soon as it has been received from the court. The court will require confirmation that this has been done if a hearing is requested to re-consider the question of permission.

Limited permission

4.18. Where a court under rule 52.3(7) gives permission to appeal on some issues only, it will–
(1)   refuse permission on any remaining issues; or

(2) reserve the question of permission to appeal on any remaining issues to the court hearing the appeal.

4.19. If the court reserves the question of permission under paragraph 4.18(2), the appellant must, within 14 days after service of the court's order, inform the appeal court and the respondent in writing whether he intends to pursue the reserved issues. If the appellant does intend to pursue the reserved issues, the parties must include in any time estimate for the appeal hearing, their time estimate for the reserved issues.

4.20. If the appeal court refuses permission to appeal on the remaining issues without a hearing and the applicant wishes to have that decision reconsidered at an oral hearing, the time limit in rule 52.3(5) shall apply. Any application for an extension of this time limit should be made promptly. The court hearing the appeal on the issues for which permission has been granted will not normally grant, at the appeal hearing, an application to extend the time limit in rule 52.3(5) for the remaining issues.

4.21. If the appeal court refuses permission to appeal on remaining issues at or after an oral hearing, the application for permission to appeal on those issues cannot be renewed at the appeal hearing. See section 54(4) of the Access to Justice Act 1999.

Respondents' costs of permission applications

4.22. In most cases, applications for permission to appeal will be determined without the court requesting–
(1) submissions from, or
(2) if there is an oral hearing, attendance by
the respondent.

4.23. Where the court does not request submissions from or attendance by the respondent, costs will not normally be allowed to a respondent who volunteers submissions or attendance.

4.24. Where the court does request–
(1) submissions from; or
(2) attendance by the respondent,
the court will normally allow the respondent his costs if permission is refused.

APPELLANT'S NOTICE

5.1. An appellant's notice must be filed and served in all cases. Where an application for permission to appeal is made to the appeal court it must be applied for in the appellant's notice.

Human Rights

5.1A. (1) This paragraph applies where the appellant seeks–
  (a) to rely on any issue under the Human Rights Act 1998; or
  (b) a remedy available under that Act,
  for the first time in an appeal.
  (2) The appellant must include in his appeal notice the information required by paragraph 15.1 of the practice direction supplementing Part 16.
  (3) Paragraph 15.2 of the practice direction supplementing Part 16 applies as if references to a statement of case were to the appeal notice.

5.1B. CPR rule 19.4A and the practice direction supplementing it shall apply as if references to the case management conference were to the application for permission to appeal.

(The practice direction to Part 19 provides for notice to be given and parties joined in certain circumstances to which this paragraph applies)

Extension of time for filing appellant's notice

5.2. If an appellant requires an extension of time for filing his notice the application must be made in the appellant's notice. The notice should state the reason for the delay and the steps taken prior to the application being made.

5.3. Where the appellant's notice includes an application for an extension of time and permission to appeal has been given or is not required the respondent has the right to be heard on that application. He must be served with a copy of the appeal bundle (see paragraph 5.6A). However, a respondent who unreasonably opposes an extension of time runs the risk of being ordered to pay the appellant's costs of that application.

5.4. If an extension of time is given following such an application the procedure at paragraphs 6.1 to 6.6 applies.

Applications

5.5. Notice of an application to be made to the appeal court for a remedy incidental to the appeal (e.g. an interim remedy under rule 25.1 or an order for security for costs) may be included in the appeal notice or in a Part 23 application notice.

(Rule 25.15 deals with security for costs of an appeal)

(Paragraph 11 of this practice direction contains other provisions relating to applications)

Documents

5.6. (1) This paragraph applies to every case except where the appeal –
   (a) relates to a claim allocated to the small claims track; and
   (b) is being heard in a county court or the High Court.
   (Paragraph 5.8 applies where this paragraph does not apply)

(2) The appellant must file the following documents together with an appeal bundle (see paragraph 5.6A) with his appellant's notice–
   (a) two additional copies of the appellant's notice for the appeal court; and
   (b) one copy of the appellant's notice for each of the respondents;
   (c) one copy of his skeleton argument for each copy of the appellant's notice that is filed (see paragraph 5.9);
   (d) a sealed copy of the order being appealed;
   (e) a copy of any order giving or refusing permission to appeal, together with a copy of the judge's reasons for allowing or refusing permission to appeal;
   (f) any witness statements or affidavits in support of any application included in the appellant's notice.

5.6A. (1) An appellant must include in his appeal bundle the following documents:
   (a) a sealed copy of the appellant's notice;
   (b) a sealed copy of the order being appealed;
   (c) a copy of any order giving or refusing permission to appeal, together with a copy of the judge's reasons for allowing or refusing permission to appeal;
   (d) any affidavit or witness statement filed in support of any application included in the appellant's notice;
   (e) a copy of his skeleton argument;
   (f) a transcript or note of judgment (see paragraph 5.12), and in cases where permission to appeal was given by the lower court or is not required those parts of any transcript of evidence which are directly relevant to any question at issue on the appeal;
   (g) the claim form and statements of case (where relevant to the subject of the appeal);
   (h) any application notice (or case management documentation) relevant to the subject of the appeal;
   (i) in cases where the decision appealed was itself made on appeal (eg from district judge to circuit judge), the first order, the reasons given and the appellant's notice used to appeal from that order;

(j) in the case of judicial review or a statutory appeal, the original decision which was the subject of the application to the lower court;

(k) in cases where the appeal is from a Tribunal, a copy of the Tribunal's reasons for the decision, a copy of the decision reviewed by the Tribunal and the reasons for the original decision and any document filed with the Tribunal setting out the grounds of appeal from that decision;

(l) any other documents which the appellant reasonably considers necessary to enable the appeal court to reach its decision on the hearing of the application or appeal; and

(m) such other documents as the court may direct.

(2) All documents that are extraneous to the issues to be considered on the application or the appeal must be excluded. The appeal bundle may include affidavits, witness statements, summaries, experts' reports and exhibits but only where these are directly relevant to the subject matter of the appeal.

(3) Where the appellant is represented, the appeal bundle must contain a certificate signed by his solicitor, counsel or other representative to the effect that he has read and understood paragraph (2) above and that the composition of the appeal bundle complies with it.

5.7. Where it is not possible to file all the above documents, the appellant must indicate which documents have not yet been filed and the reasons why they are not currently available. The appellant must then provide a reasonable estimate of when the missing document or documents can be filed and file them as soon as reasonably practicable.

Small claims

5.8. (1) This paragraph applies where–

(a) the appeal relates to a claim allocated to the small claims track; and

(b) the appeal is being heard in a county court or the High Court.

(2) The appellant must file the following documents with his appellant's notice –

(a) a sealed copy of the order being appealed; and

(b) any order giving or refusing permission to appeal, together with a copy of the reasons for that decision.

(3) The appellant may, if relevant to the issues to be determined on the appeal, file any other document listed in paragraph 5.6 or 5.6A in addition to the documents referred to in sub-paragraph (2).

(4) The appellant need not file a record of the reasons for judgment of the lower court with his appellant's notice unless sub-paragraph (5) applies.
(5) The court may order a suitable record of the reasons for judgment of the lower court (see paragraph 5.12) to be filed –
  (a) to enable it to decide if permission should be granted; or
  (b) if permission is granted to enable it to decide the appeal.

Skeleton arguments

5.9. (1) The appellant's notice must, subject to (2) and (3) below, be accompanied by a skeleton argument. Alternatively the skeleton argument may be included in the appellant's notice. Where the skeleton argument is so included it will not form part of the notice for the purposes of rule 52.8.
(2) Where it is impracticable for the appellant's skeleton argument to accompany the appellant's notice it must be filed and served on all respondents within 14 days of filing the notice.
(3) An appellant who is not represented need not file a skeleton argument but is encouraged to do so since this will be helpful to the court.

Content of skeleton arguments

5.10. (1) A skeleton argument must contain a numbered list of the points which the party wishes to make. These should both define and confine the areas of controversy. Each point should be stated as concisely as the nature of the case allows.
(2) A numbered point must be followed by a reference to any document on which the party wishes to rely.
(3) A skeleton argument must state, in respect of each authority cited–
  (a) the proposition of law that the authority demonstrates; and
  (b) the parts of the authority (identified by page or paragraph references) that support the proposition.
(4) If more than one authority is cited in support of a given proposition, the skeleton argument must briefly state the reason for taking that course.
(5) The statement referred to in sub-paragraph (4) should not materially add to the length of the skeleton argument but should be sufficient to demonstrate, in the context of the argument–
  (a) the relevance of the authority or authorities to that argument; and
  (b) that the citation is necessary for a proper presentation of that argument.
(6) The cost of preparing a skeleton argument which –
  (a) does not comply with the requirements set out in this paragraph; or

(b) was not filed within the time limits provided by this Practice Direction (or any further time granted by the court),

will not be allowed on assessment except to the extent that the court otherwise directs.

5.11. The appellant should consider what other information the appeal court will need. This may include a list of persons who feature in the case or glossaries of technical terms. A chronology of relevant events will be necessary in most appeals.

Suitable record of the judgment

5.12. Where the judgment to be appealed has been officially recorded by the court, an approved transcript of that record should accompany the appellant's notice. Photocopies will not be accepted for this purpose. However, where there is no officially recorded judgment, the following documents will be acceptable:

Written judgments

(1) Where the judgment was made in writing a copy of that judgment endorsed with the judge's signature.

Note of judgment

(2) When judgment was not officially recorded or made in writing a note of the judgment (agreed between the appellant's and respondent's advocates) should be submitted for approval to the judge whose decision is being appealed. If the parties cannot agree on a single note of the judgment, both versions should be provided to that judge with an explanatory letter. For the purpose of an application for permission to appeal the note need not be approved by the respondent or the lower court judge.

Advocates' notes of judgments where the appellant is unrepresented

(3) When the appellant was unrepresented in the lower court it is the duty of any advocate for the respondent to make his/her note of judgment promptly available, free of charge to the appellant where there is no officially recorded judgment or if the court so directs. Where the appellant was represented in the lower court it is the duty of his/her own former advocate to make his/her note available in these circumstances. The appellant should submit the note of judgment to the appeal court.

Reasons for Judgment in Tribunal cases

(4) A sealed copy of the Tribunal's reasons for the decision.

5.13. An appellant may not be able to obtain an official transcript or other suitable record of the lower court's decision within the time within which the appellant's notice must be filed. In such cases the appellant's notice must still be completed to the best of the appellant's ability on the basis of the documentation available. However it may be amended subsequently with the permission of the appeal court.

Advocates' notes of judgments

5.14. Advocates' brief (or, where appropriate, refresher) fee includes:
(1) remuneration for taking a note of the judgment of the court;
(2) having the note transcribed accurately;
(3) attempting to agree the note with the other side if represented;
(4) submitting the note to the judge for approval where appropriate;
(5) revising it if so requested by the judge,
(6) providing any copies required for the appeal court, instructing solicitors and lay client; and
(7) providing a copy of his note to an unrepresented appellant.

Transcripts or Notes of Evidence

5.15. When the evidence is relevant to the appeal an official transcript of the relevant evidence must be obtained. Transcripts or notes of evidence are generally not needed for the purpose of determining an application for permission to appeal.

Notes of evidence

5.16. If evidence relevant to the appeal was not officially recorded, a typed version of the judge's notes of evidence must be obtained.

Transcripts at public expense

5.17. Where the lower court or the appeal court is satisfied that an unrepresented appellant is in such poor financial circumstances that the cost of a transcript would be an excessive burden the court may certify that the cost of obtaining one official transcript should be borne at public expense.

5.18. In the case of a request for an official transcript of evidence or proceedings to be paid for at public expense, the court must also be satisfied that there are reasonable grounds for appeal. Whenever possible a request for a transcript at public expense should be made to the lower court when asking for permission to appeal.

Filing and service of appellant's notice

5.19. Rule 52.4 sets out the procedure and time limits for filing and serving an appellant's notice. The appellant must file the appellant's notice at the appeal court within such period as may be directed by the lower court which should not normally exceed 28 days or, where the lower court directs no such period, within 14 days of the date of the decision that the appellant wishes to appeal.

(Rule 52.15 sets out the time limit for filing an application for permission to appeal against the refusal of the High Court to grant permission to apply for judicial review)

5.20. Where the lower court judge announces his decision and reserves the reasons for his judgment or order until a later date, he should, in the exercise of powers under rule 52.4(2)(a), fix a period for filing the appellant's notice at the appeal court that takes this into account.

5.21. (1) Except where the appeal court orders otherwise a sealed copy of the appellant's notice, including any skeleton arguments must be served on all respondents in accordance with the timetable prescribed by rule 52.4(3) except where this requirement is modified by paragraph 5.9(2) in which case the skeleton argument should be served as soon as it is filed.

(2) The appellant must, as soon as practicable, file a certificate of service of the documents referred to in paragraph (1).

5.22. Unless the court otherwise directs a respondent need not take any action when served with an appellant's notice until such time as notification is given to him that permission to appeal has been given.

5.23. The court may dispense with the requirement for service of the notice on a respondent. Any application notice seeking an order under rule 6.9 to dispense with service should set out the reasons relied on and be verified by a statement of truth.

5.24. (1) Where the appellant is applying for permission to appeal in his appellant's notice, he must serve on the respondents his appellant's notice and skeleton argument (but not the appeal bundle), unless the appeal court directs otherwise.

(2) Where permission to appeal–
 (a) has been given by the lower court; or
 (b) is not required,
 the appellant must serve the appeal bundle on the respondents with the appellant's notice.

Amendment of Appeal Notice

5.25. An appeal notice may be amended with permission. Such an application to amend and any application in opposition will normally be dealt with at the hearing unless that course would cause unnecessary expense or delay in which case a request should be made for the application to amend to be heard in advance.

PROCEDURE AFTER PERMISSION IS OBTAINED

6.1. This paragraph sets out the procedure where:
(1) permission to appeal is given by the appeal court; or

(2) the appellant's notice is filed in the appeal court and–
  (a) permission was given by the lower court; or
  (b) permission is not required.

6.2. If the appeal court gives permission to appeal, the appeal bundle must be served on each of the respondents within 7 days of receiving the order giving permission to appeal.

(Part 6 (service of documents) provides rules on service)

6.3. The appeal court will send the parties–
(1) notification of–
  (a) the date of the hearing or the period of time (the "listing window") during which the appeal is likely to be heard; and
  (b) in the Court of Appeal, the date by which the appeal will be heard (the "hear by date");
(2) where permission is granted by the appeal court a copy of the order giving permission to appeal; and
(3) any other directions given by the court.

6.3A. (1) Where the appeal court grants permission to appeal, the appellant must add the following documents to the appeal bundle–
  (a) the respondent's notice and skeleton argument (if any);
  (b) those parts of the transcripts of evidence which are directly relevant to any question at issue on the appeal;
  (c) the order granting permission to appeal and, where permission to appeal was granted at an oral hearing, the transcript (or note) of any judgment which was given; and
  (d) any document which the appellant and respondent have agreed to add to the appeal bundle in accordance with paragraph 7.11.
(2) Where permission to appeal has been refused on a particular issue, the appellant must remove from the appeal bundle all documents that are relevant only to that issue.

Appeal Questionnaire in the Court of Appeal

6.4. The Court of Appeal will send an Appeal Questionnaire to the appellant when it notifies him of the matters referred to in paragraph 6.3.

6.5. The appellant must complete and file the Appeal Questionnaire within 14 days of the date of the letter of notification of the matters in paragraph 6.3. The Appeal Questionnaire must contain:
(1) if the appellant is legally represented, the advocate's time estimate for the hearing of the appeal;
(2) where a transcript of evidence is relevant to the appeal, confirmation as to what parts of a transcript of evidence have been ordered where this is not already in the bundle of documents;

(3) confirmation that copies of the appeal bundle are being prepared and will be held ready for the use of the Court of Appeal and an undertaking that they will be supplied to the court on request. For the purpose of these bundles photocopies of the transcripts will be accepted;
(4) confirmation that copies of the Appeal Questionnaire and the appeal bundle have been served on the respondents and the date of that service.

Time estimates

6.6. The time estimate included in an Appeal Questionnaire must be that of the advocate who will argue the appeal. It should exclude the time required by the court to give judgment. If the respondent disagrees with the time estimate, the respondent must inform the court within 7 days of receipt of the Appeal Questionnaire. In the absence of such notification the respondent will be deemed to have accepted the estimate proposed on behalf of the appellant.

RESPONDENT

7.1. A respondent who wishes to ask the appeal court to vary the order of the lower court in any way must appeal and permission will be required on the same basis as for an appellant.

(Paragraph 3.2 applies to grounds of appeal by a respondent.)

7.2. A respondent who wishes only to request that the appeal court upholds the judgment or order of the lower court whether for the reasons given in the lower court or otherwise does not make an appeal and does not therefore require permission to appeal in accordance with rule 52.3(1).

(Paragraph 7.6 requires a respondent to file a skeleton argument where he wishes to address the appeal court)

7.3. (1) A respondent who wishes to appeal or who wishes to ask the appeal court to uphold the order of the lower court for reasons different from or additional to those given by the lower court must file a respondent's notice.
(2) If the respondent does not file a respondent's notice, he will not be entitled, except with the permission of the court, to rely on any reason not relied on in the lower court.

7.3A. Paragraphs 5.1A, 5.1B and 5.2 of this practice direction (Human Rights and extension for time for filing appellant's notice) also apply to a respondent and a respondent's notice.

Time limits

7.4. The time limits for filing a respondent's notice are set out in rule 52.5 (4) and (5).

7.5. Where an extension of time is required the extension must be requested in the respondent's notice and the reasons why the respondent failed to act within the specified time must be included.

7.6. Except where paragraph 7.7A applies, the respondent must file a skeleton argument for the court in all cases where he proposes to address arguments to the court. The respondent's skeleton argument may be included within a respondent's notice. Where a skeleton argument is included within a respondent's notice it will not form part of the notice for the purposes of rule 52.8.

7.7. (1) A respondent who–
  (a) files a respondent's notice; but
  (b) does not include his skeleton argument within that notice,
  must file and serve his skeleton argument within 14 days of filing the notice.
(2) A respondent who does not file a respondent's notice but who files a skeleton argument must file and serve that skeleton argument at least 7 days before the appeal hearing.
(Rule 52.5(4) sets out the period for filing and serving a respondent's notice)

7.7A. (1) Where the appeal relates to a claim allocated to the small claims track and is being heard in a county court or the High Court, the respondent may file a skeleton argument but is not required to do so.
(2) A respondent who is not represented need not file a skeleton argument but is encouraged to do so in order to assist the court.

7.7B. The respondent must–
(1) serve his skeleton argument on –
  (a) the appellant; and
  (b) any other respondent,
  at the same time as he files it at the court; and
(2) file a certificate of service.

Content of skeleton arguments

7.8. A respondent's skeleton argument must conform to the directions at paragraphs 5.10 and 5.11 with any necessary modifications. It should, where appropriate, answer the arguments set out in the appellant's skeleton argument.

Applications within respondent's notices

7.9. A respondent may include an application within a respondent's notice in accordance with paragraph 5.5 above.

Filing respondent's notices and skeleton arguments

7.10. (1) The respondent must file the following documents with his respondent's notice in every case:
   (a) two additional copies of the respondent's notice for the appeal court; and
   (b) one copy each for the appellant and any other respondents.
(2) The respondent may file a skeleton argument with his respondent's notice and–
   (a) where he does so he must file two copies; and
   (b) where he does not do so he must comply with paragraph 7.7.

7.11. If the respondent wishes to rely on any documents which he reasonably considers necessary to enable the appeal court to reach its decision on the appeal in addition to those filed by the appellant, he must make every effort to agree amendments to the appeal bundle with the appellant.

7.12. (1) If the representatives for the parties are unable to reach agreement, the respondent may prepare a supplemental bundle.
(2) If the respondent prepares a supplemental bundle he must file it, together with the requisite number of copies for the appeal court, at the appeal court –
   (a) with the respondent's notice; or
   (b) if a respondent's notice is not filed, within 21 days after he is served with the appeal bundle.

7.13. The respondent must serve–
(1) the respondent's notice;
(2) his skeleton argument (if any); and
(3) the supplemental bundle (if any),

on–
(a) the appellant; and
(b) any other respondent,

at the same time as he files them at the court.

APPEALS TO THE HIGH COURT

Application

8.1. This paragraph applies where an appeal lies to a High Court judge from the decision of a county court or a district judge of the High Court.

8.2. The following table sets out the following venues for each circuit–

(a) Appeal centres – court centres where appeals to which this paragraph applies may be filed, managed and heard. Paragraphs 8.6 to 8.8 provide for special arrangements in relation to the South Eastern Circuit.

(b) Hearing only centres – court centres where appeals to which this paragraph applies may be heard by order made at an appeal centre (see paragraph 8.10).

Circuit	Appeal Centres	Hearing Only Centres
Midland Circuit	Birmingham	Lincoln
	Nottingham	Leicester
	Northampton	Stafford
North Eastern Circuit	Leeds	Teesside
	Newcastle	Sheffield
Northern Circuit	Manchester	Carlisle
	Liverpool	Preston
Wales and Chester Circuit	Cardiff	Swansea
	Chester	
Western Circuit	Bristol	Truro
	Exeter	Plymouth
	Winchester	
South Eastern Circuit	Royal Courts of Justice	Lewes
	Luton	Norwich
	Reading	Chelmsford
	St Albans	Maidstone
	Oxford	

Venue for appeals and filing of notices on circuits other than the South Eastern Circuit

8.3. Paragraphs 8.4 and 8.5 apply where the lower court is situated on a circuit other than the South Eastern Circuit.

8.4. The appellant's notice must be filed at an appeal centre on the circuit in which the lower court is situated. The appeal will be managed and heard at that appeal centre unless the appeal court orders otherwise.

8.5. A respondent's notice must be filed at the appeal centre where the appellant's notice was filed unless the appeal has been transferred to another appeal centre, in which case it must be filed at that appeal centre.

Venue for appeals and filing of notices on the South Eastern Circuit

8.6. Paragraphs 8.7 and 8.8 apply where the lower court is situated on the South Eastern Circuit.

8.7. The appellant's notice must be filed at an appeal centre on the South Eastern Circuit. The appeal will be managed and heard at the Royal Courts of Justice unless the appeal court orders otherwise. An order that an appeal is to be managed or heard at another appeal centre may not be made unless the consent of the Presiding Judge of the circuit in charge of civil matters has been obtained.

8.8. A respondent's notice must be filed at the Royal Courts of Justice unless the appeal has been transferred to another appeal centre, in which case it must be filed at that appeal centre.

General provisions

8.9. The appeal court may transfer an appeal to another appeal centre (whether or not on the same circuit). In deciding whether to do so the court will have regard to the criteria in rule 30.3 (criteria for a transfer order). The appeal court may do so either on application by a party or of its own initiative. Where an appeal is transferred under this paragraph, notice of transfer must be served on every person on whom the appellant's notice has been served. An appeal may not be transferred to an appeal centre on another circuit, either for management or hearing, unless the consent of the Presiding Judge of that circuit in charge of civil matters has been obtained.

8.10. Directions may be given for–
(a) an appeal to be heard at a hearing only centre; or
(b) an application in an appeal to be heard at any other venue,
instead of at the appeal centre managing the appeal.

8.11. Unless a direction has been made under 8.10, any application in the appeal must be made at the appeal centre where the appeal is being managed.

8.12. The appeal court may adopt all or any part of the procedure set out in paragraphs 6.4 to 6.6.

8.13. Where the lower court is a county court:
(1) appeals and applications for permission to appeal will be heard by

a High Court Judge or by a person authorised under paragraphs (1), (2) or (4) of the Table in section 9(1) of the Supreme Court Act 1981 to act as a judge of the High Court; and
(2) other applications in the appeal may be heard and directions in the appeal may be given either by a High Court Judge or by any person authorised under section 9 of the Supreme Court Act 1981 to act as a judge of the High Court.

8.14. In the case of appeals from Masters or district judges of the High Court, appeals, applications for permission and any other applications in the appeal may be heard and directions in the appeal may be given by a High Court Judge or by any person authorised under section 9 of the Supreme Court Act 1981 to act as a judge of the High Court.

Appeals to a judge of a county court from a district judge

8A.1. The Designated Civil Judge in consultation with his Presiding Judges has responsibility for allocating appeals from decisions of district judges to circuit judges.

Re-hearings

9.1. The hearing of an appeal will be a re-hearing (as opposed to a review of the decision of the lower court) if the appeal is from the decision of a minister, person or other body and the minister, person or other body–
(1) did not hold a hearing to come to that decision; or
(2) held a hearing to come to that decision, but the procedure adopted did not provide for the consideration of evidence.

Appeals Transferred to the Court of Appeal

10.1. Where an appeal is transferred to the Court of Appeal under rule 52.14 the Court of Appeal may give such additional directions as are considered appropriate.

Applications

11.1. Where a party to an appeal makes an application whether in an appeal notice or by Part 23 application notice, the provisions of Part 23 will apply.

11.2. The applicant must file the following documents with the notice
(1) one additional copy of the application notice for the appeal court and one copy for each of the respondents;
(2) where applicable a sealed copy of the order which is the subject of the main appeal;
(3) a bundle of documents in support which should include:
   (a) the Part 23 application notice; and

(b) any witness statements and affidavits filed in support of the application notice.

DISPOSING OF APPLICATIONS OR APPEALS BY CONSENT

Dismissal of applications or appeals by consent

12.1. These paragraphs do not apply where any party to the proceedings is a child or patient.

12.2. Where an appellant does not wish to pursue an application or an appeal, he may request the appeal court for an order that his application or appeal be dismissed. Such a request must contain a statement that the appellant is not a child or patient. If such a request is granted it will usually be on the basis that the appellant pays the costs of the application or appeal.

12.3. If the appellant wishes to have the application or appeal dismissed without costs, his request must be accompanied by a consent signed by the respondent or his legal representative stating that the respondent is not a child or patient and consents to the dismissal of the application or appeal without costs.

12.4. Where a settlement has been reached disposing of the application or appeal, the parties may make a joint request to the court stating that none of them is a child or patient, and asking that the application or appeal be dismissed by consent. If the request is granted the application or appeal will be dismissed.

Allowing unopposed appeals or applications on paper

13.1. The appeal court will not normally make an order allowing an appeal unless satisfied that the decision of the lower court was wrong, but the appeal court may set aside or vary the order of the lower court with consent and without determining the merits of the appeal, if it is satisfied that there are good and sufficient reasons for doing so. Where the appeal court is requested by all parties to allow an application or an appeal the court may consider the request on the papers. The request should state that none of the parties is a child or patient and set out the relevant history of the proceedings and the matters relied on as justifying the proposed order and be accompanied by a copy of the proposed order.

Procedure for structured settlements and consent orders involving a child or patient

13.2. Settlements relating to appeals and applications where one of the parties is a child or a patient; and structured settlements which are agreed upon at the appeal stage require the court's approval.

Child

13.3. In cases involving a child a copy of the proposed order signed by the parties' solicitors should be sent to the appeal court, together with an opinion from the advocate acting on behalf of the child.

Patient

13.4. Where a party is a patient the same procedure will be adopted, but the documents filed should also include any relevant reports prepared for the Court of Protection and a document evidencing formal approval by that court where required.

Structured settlements

13.5. Where a structured settlement has been negotiated in a case which is under appeal the documents filed should include those which would be required in the case of a structured settlement dealt with at first instance. Details can be found in the Practice Direction which supplements CPR Part 40.

SUMMARY ASSESSMENT OF COSTS

14.1. Costs are likely to be assessed by way of summary assessment at the following hearings:
(1) contested directions hearings;
(2) applications for permission to appeal at which the respondent is present;
(3) dismissal list hearings in the Court of Appeal at which the respondent is present;
(4) appeals from case management decisions; and
(5) appeals listed for one day or less.

14.2. Parties attending any of the hearings referred to in paragraph 14.1 should be prepared to deal with the summary assessment.

OTHER SPECIAL PROVISIONS REGARDING THE COURT OF APPEAL

Filing of Documents

15.1. (1) The documents relevant to proceedings in the Court of Appeal, Civil Division must be filed in the Civil Appeals Office Registry, Room E307, Royal Courts of Justice, Strand, London, WC2A 2LL.
(2) The Civil Appeals Office will not serve documents and where service is required by the CPR or this practice direction it must be effected by the parties.

Core Bundles

15.2. In cases where the appeal bundle comprises more than 500 pages, exclusive of transcripts, the appellant's solicitors must, after consultation with the respondent's solicitors, also prepare and file with the court, in addition to copies of the appeal bundle (as amended in accordance with paragraph 7.11) the requisite number of copies of a core bundle.

15.3. (1) The core bundle must be filed within 28 days of receipt of the order giving permission to appeal or, where permission to appeal was granted by the lower court or is not required, within 28 days of the date of service of the appellant's notice on the respondent.

(2) The core bundle–
  (a) must contain the documents which are central to the appeal; and
  (b) must not exceed 150 pages.

Preparation of bundles

15.4. The provisions of this paragraph apply to the preparation of appeal bundles, supplemental respondents' bundles where the parties are unable to agree amendments to the appeal bundle, and core bundles.

(1) **Rejection of bundles.** Where documents are copied unnecessarily or bundled incompletely, costs may be disallowed. Where the provisions of this Practice Direction as to the preparation or delivery of bundles are not followed the bundle may be rejected by the court or be made the subject of a special costs order.

(2) **Avoidance of duplication.** No more than one copy of any document should be included unless there is a good reason for doing otherwise (such as the use of a separate core bundle – see paragraph 15.2).

(3) **Pagination**
  (a) Bundles must be paginated, each page being numbered individually and consecutively. The pagination used at trial must also be indicated. Letters and other documents should normally be included in chronological order. (An exception to consecutive page numbering arises in the case of core bundles where it may be preferable to retain the original numbering).
  (b) Page numbers should be inserted in bold figures at the bottom of the page and in a form that can be clearly distinguished from any other pagination on the document.

(4) **Format and presentation**
  (a) Where possible the documents should be in A4 format. Where a document has to be read across rather than down

the page, it should be so placed in the bundle as to ensure that the text starts nearest the spine.
- (b) Where any marking or writing in colour on a document is important, the document must be copied in colour or marked up correctly in colour.
- (c) Documents which are not easily legible should be transcribed and the transcription marked and placed adjacent to the document transcribed.
- (d) Documents in a foreign language should be translated and the translation marked and placed adjacent to the document translated. The translation should be agreed or, if it cannot be agreed, each party's proposed translation should be included.
- (e) The size of any bundle should be tailored to its contents. A large lever arch file should not be used for just a few pages nor should files of whatever size be overloaded.
- (f) Where it will assist the Court of Appeal, different sections of the file may be separated by cardboard or other tabbed dividers so long as these are clearly indexed. Where, for example, a document is awaited when the appeal bundle is filed, a single sheet of paper can be inserted after a divider, indicating the nature of the document awaited. For example, "Transcript of evidence of Mr J Smith (to follow)".

(5) **Binding**
- (a) All documents, with the exception of transcripts, must be bound together. This may be in a lever arch file, ring binder or plastic folder. Plastic sleeves containing loose documents must not be used. Binders and files must be strong enough to withstand heavy use.
- (b) Large documents such as plans should be placed in an easily accessible file. Large documents which will need to be opened up frequently should be inserted in a file larger than A4 size.

(6) **Indices and labels**
- (a) An index must be included at the front of the bundle listing all the documents and providing the page references for each. In the case of documents such as letters, invoices or bank statements, they may be given a general description.
- (b) Where the bundles consist of more than one file, an index to all the files should be included in the first file and an index included for each file. Indices should, if possible, be on a single sheet. The full name of the case should not be inserted on the index if this would waste space. Documents should be identified briefly but properly.

(7) **Identification**
 (a) Every bundle must be clearly identified, on the spine and on the front cover, with the name of the case and the Court of Appeal's reference. Where the bundle consists of more than one file, each file must be numbered on the spine, the front cover and the inside of the front cover.
 (b) Outer labels should use large lettering e g "Appeal Bundle A" or "Core Bundle". The full title of the appeal and solicitors' names and addresses should be omitted. A label should be used on the front as well as on the spine.

(8) **Staples etc.** All staples, heavy metal clips etc, must be removed.

(9) **Statements of case**
 (a) Statements of case should be assembled in "chapter" form – i.e claim followed by particulars of claim, followed by further information, irrespective of date.
 (b) Redundant documents, e g particulars of claim overtaken by amendments, requests for further information recited in the answers given, should generally be excluded.

(10) **New Documents**
 (a) Before a new document is introduced into bundles which have already been delivered to the court, steps should be taken to ensure that it carries an appropriate bundle/page number so that it can be added to the court documents. It should not be stapled and it should be prepared with punch holes for immediate inclusion in the binders in use.
 (b) If it is expected that a large number of miscellaneous new documents will from time to time be introduced, there should be a special tabbed empty loose-leaf file for that purpose. An index should be produced for this file, updated as necessary.

(11) **Inter-solicitor correspondence.** Since inter-solicitor correspondence is unlikely to be required for the purposes of an appeal, only those letters which will need to be referred to should be copied.

(12) **Sanctions for non-compliance.** If the appellant fails to comply with the requirements as to the provision of bundles of documents, the application or appeal will be referred for consideration to be given as to why it should not be dismissed for failure to so comply.

Master in the Court of Appeal, Civil Division

15.5. When the Head of the Civil Appeals Office acts in a judicial capacity pursuant to rule 52.16, he shall be known as Master. Other eligible officers may also be designated by the Master of the Rolls to exercise judicial authority under rule 52.16 and shall then be known as Deputy Masters.

Respondent to notify Civil Appeals Office whether he intends to file respondent's notice

15.6. A respondent must, no later than 21 days after the date he is served with notification that–
(1) permission to appeal has been granted; or
(2) the application for permission to appeal and the appeal are to be heard together,

inform the Civil Appeals Office and the appellant in writing whether–
(a) he proposes to file a respondent's notice appealing the order or seeking to uphold the order for reasons different from, or additional to, those given by the lower court; or
(b) he proposes to rely on the reasons given by the lower court for its decision.

(Paragraph 15.11B requires all documents needed for an appeal hearing, including a respondent's skeleton argument, to be filed at least 7 days before the hearing)

Listing and hear-by dates

15.7. The management of the list will be dealt with by the listing officer under the direction of the Master.

15.8. The Civil Appeals List of the Court of Appeal is divided as follows:
- *The applications list* – applications for permission to appeal and other applications.
- *The appeals list* – appeals where permission to appeal has been given or where an appeal lies without permission being required where a hearing date is fixed in advance. (Appeals in this list which require special listing arrangements will be assigned to the special fixtures list)
- *The expedited list* – appeals or applications where the Court of Appeal has directed an expedited hearing. The current practice of the Court of Appeal is summarised in *Unilever plc v Chefaro Proprietaries Ltd (Practice Note)* [1995]1 W.L.R. 243 [see **para A2.23**].
- *The stand-out list* – Appeals or applications which, for good reason, are not at present ready to proceed and have been stood out by judicial direction.
- *The second fixtures list* – [see **para 15.9A(1)** below].
- *The second fixtures list* – if an appeal is designated as a "second fixture" it means that a hearing date is arranged in advance on the express basis that the list is fully booked for the period in question and therefore the case will be heard only if a suitable gap occurs in the list.

- *The short-warned list* – appeals which the court considers may be prepared for the hearing by an advocate other than the one originally instructed with a half day's notice, or such other period as the court may direct.

Special provisions relating to the short-warned list

15.9. (1) Where an appeal is assigned to the short-warned list, the Civil Appeals Office will notify the parties' solicitors in writing. The court may abridge the time for filing any outstanding bundles in an appeal assigned to this list.

(2) The solicitors for the parties must notify their advocate and their client as soon as the Civil Appeals Office notifies them that the appeal has been assigned to the short-warned list.

(3) The appellant may apply in writing for the appeal to be removed from the short-warned list within 14 days of notification of its assignment. The application will be decided by a Lord Justice, or the Master, and will only be granted for the most compelling reasons.

(4) The Civil Appeals Listing Officer may place an appeal from the short-warned list "on call" from a given date and will inform the parties' advocates accordingly.

(5) An appeal which is "on call" may be listed for hearing on half a day's notice or such longer period as the court may direct.

(6) Once an appeal is listed for hearing from the short warned list it becomes the immediate professional duty of the advocate instructed in the appeal, if he is unable to appear at the hearing, to take all practicable measures to ensure that his lay client is represented at the hearing by an advocate who is fully instructed and able to argue the appeal.

Special provisions relating to the special fixtures list

15.9A. (1) The special fixtures list is a sub-division of the appeals list and is used to deal with appeals that may require special listing arrangements, such as the need to list a number of cases before the same constitution, in a particular order, during a particular period or at a given location.

(2) The Civil Appeals Office will notify the parties' representatives, or the parties if acting in person, of the particular arrangements that will apply. The notice –
   (a) will give details of the specific period during which a case is scheduled to be heard; and
   (b) may give directions in relation to the filing of any outstanding documents.

(3) The listing officer will notify the parties' representatives of the

precise hearing date as soon as practicable. While every effort will be made to accommodate the availability of counsel, the requirements of the court will prevail.

Requests for directions

15.10. To ensure that all requests for directions are centrally monitored and correctly allocated, all requests for directions or rulings (whether relating to listing or any other matters) should be made to the Civil Appeals Office. Those seeking directions or rulings must not approach the supervising Lord Justice either directly, or via his or her clerk.

Bundles of authorities

15.11. (1) Once the parties have been notified of the date fixed for the hearing, the appellant's advocate must, after consultation with his opponent, file a bundle containing photocopies of the authorities upon which each side will rely at the hearing.
(2) The bundle of authorities should, in general–
 (a) have the relevant passages of the authorities marked;
 (b) not include authorities for propositions not in dispute; and
 (c) not contain more than 10 authorities unless the scale of the appeal warrants more extensive citation.
(3) The bundle of authorities must be filed–
 (a) at least 7 days before the hearing; or
 (b) where the period of notice of the hearing is less than 7 days, immediately.
(4) If, through some oversight, a party intends, during the hearing, to refer to other authorities the parties may agree a second agreed bundle. The appellant's advocate must file this bundle at least 48 hours before the hearing commences.
(5) A bundle of authorities must bear a certification by the advocates responsible for arguing the case that the requirements of sub-paragraphs (3) to (5) of paragraph 5.10 have been complied with in respect of each authority included.

Supplementary skeleton arguments

15.11A. (1) A supplementary skeleton argument on which the appellant wishes to rely must be filed at least 14 days before the hearing.
(2) A supplementary skeleton argument on which the respondent wishes to rely must be filed at least 7 days before the hearing.
(3) All supplementary skeleton arguments must comply with the requirements set out in paragraph 5.10.
(4) At the hearing the court may refuse to hear argument from a party not contained in a skeleton argument filed within the relevant time limit set out in this paragraph.

152 *Procedure*

Papers for the appeal hearing

15.11B. (1) All the documents which are needed for the appeal hearing must be filed at least 7 days before the hearing. Where a document has not been filed 10 days before the hearing a reminder will be sent by the Civil Appeals Office.

(2) Any party who fails to comply with the provisions of paragraph (1) may be required to attend before the Presiding Lord Justice to seek permission to proceed with, or to oppose, the appeal.

Disposal of bundles of documents

15.11C. (1) Where the court has determined a case, the official transcriber will retain one set of papers. The Civil Appeals Office will destroy any remaining sets of papers not collected within 21 days of–
   (a) where one or more parties attend the hearing, the date of the court's decision;
   (b) where there is no attendance, the date of the notification of court's decision.

(2) The parties should ensure that bundles of papers supplied to the court do not contain original documents (other than transcripts). The parties must ensure that they–
   (a) bring any necessary original documents to the hearing; and
   (b) retrieve any original documents handed up to the court before leaving the court.

(3) The court will retain application bundles where permission to appeal has been granted. Where permission is refused the arrangements in sub-paragraph (1) will apply.

(4) Where a single Lord Justice has refused permission to appeal on paper, application bundles will not be destroyed until after the time limit for seeking a hearing has expired.

Availability of Reserved judgments before hand down

15.12. This section applies where the presiding Lord Justice is satisfied that the result of the appeal will attract no special degree of confidentiality or sensitivity.

15.13. A copy of the written judgment will be made available to the parties' legal advisers by 4 p.m. on the second working day before judgment is due to be pronounced or such other period as the court may direct. This can be shown, in confidence, to the parties but only for the purpose of obtaining instructions and on the strict understanding that the judgment, or its effect, is not to be disclosed to any other person. A working day is any day on which the Civil Appeals Office is open for business.

15.14. The appeal will be listed for judgment in the cause list and the judgment handed down at the appropriate time.

Attendance of advocates on the handing down of a reserved judgment

15.15. Where any consequential orders are agreed, the parties' advocates need not attend on the handing down of a reserved judgment. Where an advocate does attend the court may, if it considers such attendance unnecessary, disallow the costs of the attendance. If the parties do not indicate that they intend to attend, the judgment may be handed down by a single member of the court.

Agreed orders following judgment

15.16. The parties must, in respect of any draft agreed orders–
(a) fax a copy to the clerk to the presiding Lord Justice; and
(b) file four copies in the Civil Appeals Office,

no later than 12 noon on the working day before the judgment is handed down.

15.17. A copy of a draft order must bear the Court of Appeal case reference, the date the judgment is to be handed down and the name of the presiding Lord Justice.

Corrections to the draft judgment

15.18. Any proposed correction to the draft judgment should be sent to the clerk to the judge who prepared the draft with a copy to any other party.

Application for leave to appeal

15.19. Where a party wishes to apply for leave to appeal to the House of Lords under section 1 of the Administration of Justice (Appeals) Act 1934 the court may deal with the application on the basis of written submissions.

15.20. A party must, in relation to his submission–
(a) fax a copy to the clerk to the presiding Lord Justice; and
(b) file four copies in the Civil Appeals Office,

no later than 12 noon on the working day before the judgment is handed down.

15.21. A copy of a submission must bear the Court of Appeal case reference, the date the judgment is to be handed down and the name of the presiding Lord Justice.

SECTION II – GENERAL PROVISIONS ABOUT STATUTORY APPEALS AND APPEALS BY WAY OF CASE STATED

16.1. This section of this practice direction contains general provisions about statutory appeals (paragraphs 17.1–17.6) and appeals by way of case stated (paragraphs 18.1–18.20).

16.2. Where any of the provisions in this section provide for documents to be filed at the appeal court, these documents are in addition to any documents required under Part 52 or section I of this practice direction.

STATUTORY APPEALS

17.1. This part of this section–
(1)   applies where under any enactment an appeal (other than by way of case stated) lies to the court from a Minister of State, government department, tribunal or other person ("statutory appeals"); and
(2)   is subject to any provision about a specific category of appeal in any enactment or Section III of this practice direction.

Part 52

17.2. Part 52 applies to statutory appeals with the following amendments:

Filing of appellant's notice

17.3. The appellant must file the appellant's notice at the appeal court within 28 days after the date of the decision of the lower court he wishes to appeal.

17.4. Where a statement of the reasons for a decision is given later than the notice of that decision, the period for filing the appellant's notice is calculated from the date on which the statement is received by the appellant.

Service of appellant's notice

17.5. In addition to the respondents to the appeal, the appellant must serve the appellant's notice in accordance with rule 52.4(3) on the chairman of the tribunal, Minister of State, government department or other person from whose decision the appeal is brought.

Right of Minister etc. to be heard on the appeal

17.6. Where the appeal is from an order or decision of a Minister of State or government department, the Minister or department, as the case may be, is entitled to attend the hearing and to make representations to the court.

APPEALS BY WAY OF CASE STATED

18.1. This part of this section–
(1)   applies where under any enactment–
      (a)   an appeal lies to the court by way of case stated; or

(b) a question of law may be referred to the court by way of case stated; and

(2) is subject to any provision about to a specific category of appeal in any enactment or Section III of this practice direction.

Part 52

18.2. Part 52 applies to appeals by way of case stated subject to the following amendments.

Case stated by Crown Court or Magistrates' Court

Application to state a case

18.3. The procedure for applying to the Crown Court or a Magistrates' Court to have a case stated for the opinion of the High Court is set out in the Crown Court Rules 1982 and the Magistrates' Courts Rules 1981 respectively.

Filing of appellant's notice

18.4. The appellant must file the appellant's notice at the appeal court within 10 days after he receives the stated case.

Documents to be lodged

18.5. The appellant must lodge the following documents with his appellant's notice:

(1) the stated case;
(2) a copy of the judgment, order or decision in respect of which the case has been stated; and
(3) where the judgment, order or decision in respect of which the case has been stated was itself given or made on appeal, a copy of the judgment, order or decision appealed from.

Service of appellant's notice

18.6. The appellant must serve the appellant's notice and accompanying documents on all respondents within 4 days after they are filed or lodged at the appeal court.

Case stated by Minister, government department, tribunal or other person

Application to state a case

18.7. The procedure for applying to a Minister, government department, tribunal or other person ("Minister or tribunal etc.") to have a case stated for the opinion of the court may be set out in–

(1) the enactment which provides for the right of appeal; or
(2) any rules of procedure relating to the Minister or tribunal etc.

Signing of stated case by Minister or tribunal etc.

18.8. A case stated by a tribunal must be signed by the chairman or president of the tribunal. A case stated by any other person must be signed by that person or by a person authorised to do so.

Service of stated case by Minister or tribunal etc.

18.9. The Minister or tribunal etc. must serve the stated case on–
(1) the party who requests the case to be stated; or
(2) the party as a result of whose application to the court, the case was stated.

18.10. Where an enactment provides that a Minister or tribunal etc. may state a case or refer a question of law to the court by way of case stated without a request being made, the Minister or tribunal etc. must–
(1) serve the stated case on those parties that the Minister or tribunal etc. considers appropriate; and
(2) give notice to every other party to the proceedings that the stated case has been served on the party named and on the date specified in the notice.

Filing and service of appellant's notice

18.11. The party on whom the stated case was served must file the appellant's notice and the stated case at the appeal court and serve copies of the notice and stated case on–
(1) the Minister or tribunal etc. who stated the case; and
(2) every party to the proceedings to which the stated case relates,
within 14 days after the stated case was served on him.

18.12. Where paragraph 18.10 applies the Minister or tribunal etc. must–
(1) file an appellant's notice and the stated case at the appeal court; and
(2) serve copies of those documents on the persons served under paragraph 18.10
within 14 days after stating the case.

18.13. Where–
(1) a stated case has been served by the Minister or tribunal etc. in accordance with paragraph 18.9; and
(2) the party on whom the stated case was served does not file an appellant's notice in accordance with paragraph 18.11,
any other party may file an appellant's notice with the stated case at the appeal court and serve a copy of the notice and the case on the persons listed in paragraph 18.11 within the period of time set out in paragraph 18.14.

18.14. The period of time referred to in paragraph 18.13 is 14 days from the last day on which the party on whom the stated case was served may file an appellant's notice in accordance with paragraph 18.11.

Amendment of stated case

18.15. The court may amend the stated case or order it to be returned to the Minister or tribunal etc. for amendment and may draw inferences of fact from the facts stated in the case.

Right of Minister etc. to be heard on the appeal

18.16. Where the case is stated by a Minister or government department, that Minister or department, as the case may be, is entitled to appear on the appeal and to make representations to the court.

Application for order to state a case

18.17. An application to the court for an order requiring a minister or tribunal etc. to state a case for the decision of the court, or to refer a question of law to the court by way of case stated must be made to the court which would be the appeal court if the case were stated.

18.18. An application to the court for an order directing a Minister or tribunal etc. to–
(1) state a case for determination by the court; or
(2) refer a question of law to the court by way of case stated, must be made in accordance with CPR Part 23

18.19. The application notice must contain–
(1) the grounds of the application;
(2) the question of law on which it is sought to have the case stated; and
(3) any reasons given by the minister or tribunal etc. for his or its refusal to state a case.

18.20. The application notice must be filed at the appeal court and served on–
(1) the minister, department, secretary of the tribunal or other person as the case may be; and
(2) every party to the proceedings to which the application relates,

within 14 days after the appellant receives notice of the refusal of his request to state a case.

SECTION III – PROVISIONS ABOUT SPECIFIC APPEALS

20.1. This section of this Practice Direction provides special provisions about the appeals to which the following table refers. This Section is not exhaustive and does not create, amend or remove any right of appeal.

20.2. Part 52 applies to all appeals to which this section applies subject to any special provisions set out in this section.

20.3. Where any of the provisions in this section provide for documents to be filed at the appeal court, these documents are in addition to any documents required under Part 52 or sections I or II of this practice direction.

APPEALS TO THE COURT OF APPEAL	Paragraph
Articles 81 and 82 of the EC Treaty and Chapters I and II of the Competition Act 1998	21.10A
Competition Appeal Tribunal	21.10
Contempt of Court	21.4
Decree nisi of divorce	21.1
Immigration Appeal Tribunal	21.7
Lands Tribunal	21.9
Nullity of marriage	21.1
Patents Court on appeal from Comptroller	21.3
Revocation of patent	21.2
Social Security Commissioners	21.5
Special Commissioner (where the appeal is direct to the Court of Appeal)	21.8
Value Added Tax and Duties Tribunals (where the appeal is direct to the Court of Appeal)	21.6
APPEALS TO THE HIGH COURT	
Agricultural Land Tribunal	22.7
Architects Act 1997, s. 22	22.3
Charities Act 1993	23.8A
Chiropractors Act 1994, s. 31	22.3
Clergy Pensions Measure 1961, s. 38(3)	23.2
Commons Registration Act 1965	23.9
Consumer Credit Act 1974	22.4
Dentists Act 1984, s. 20 or s. 44	22.3
Extradition Act 2003	22.6A
Friendly Societies Act 1974	23.7

APPEALS TO THE COURT OF APPEAL	Paragraph
Friendly Societies Act 1992	23.7
Industrial and Provident Societies Act 1965	23.2, 23.7
Industrial Assurance Act 1923	23.2, 23.7
Industrial Assurance Act 1923, s. 17	23.6
Inheritance Tax Act 1984, s. 222	23.3
Inheritance Tax Act 1984, s. 225	23.5
Inheritance Tax Act 1984, ss. 249(3) and 251	23.4
Land Registration Act 1925	23.2
Land Registration Act 2002	23.2, 23.8B
Law of Property Act 1922, para. 16 of Sched. 15	23.2
Medical Act 1983, s. 40	22.3
Medicines Act 1968, ss. 82(3) and 83	(2) 22.3
Mental Health Review Tribunal	22.8
Merchant Shipping Act 1995	22.2
Nurses, Midwives and Health Visitors Act 1997, s. 12	22.3
Opticians Act 1989, s. 23	22.3
Osteopaths Act 1993, s. 31	22.3
Pensions Act 1995, s. 97	23.2
Pension Schemes Act 1993, ss. 151 and 173	23.2
Pensions Appeal Tribunal Act 1943	22.5
Pharmacy Act 1954	22.3
Social Security Administration Act 1992	22.6
Stamp Duty Reserve Tax Regulations 1986, reg. 10	23.5
Taxes Management Act 1970, ss. 53 and 100C	(4) 23.4
Taxes Management Act 1970, s. 56A	23.5
Value Added Tax and Duties Tribunal	23.8

APPEALS TO THE COURT OF APPEAL	Paragraph
Water Resources Act 1991, s. 205	(4) 23.2

APPEALS TO THE COUNTY COURT	Paragraph
Local Government (Miscellaneous Provisions) Act 1976	24.1
Housing Act 1996, ss. 204 and 204A	24.2
Immigration and Asylum Act 1999, Part II	24.3

APPEALS TO THE COURT OF APPEAL

Appeal against decree nisi of divorce or nullity of marriage

21.1. (1) The appellant must file the appellant's notice at the Court of Appeal within 28 days after the date on which the decree was pronounced.

(2) The appellant must file the following documents with the appellant's notice–
   (a) the decree; and
   (b) a certificate of service of the appellant's notice.

(3) The appellant's notice must be served on the appropriate district judge (see sub-paragraph (6)) in addition to the persons to be served under rule 52.4(3) and in accordance with that rule.

(4) The lower court may not alter the time limits for filing of the appeal notices.

(5) Where an appellant intends to apply to the Court of Appeal for an extension of time for serving or filing the appellant's notice he must give notice of that intention to the appropriate district judge (see sub-paragraph 6) before the application is made.

(6) In this paragraph "the appropriate district judge" means, where the lower court is–
   (a) a county court, the district judge of that court;
   (b) a district registry, the district judge of that registry;
   (c) the Principal Registry of the Family Division, the senior district judge of that division.'

Editorial note

Appeals from divorce decrees

There is no appeal to the Court of Appeal from a decree absolute of divorce or nullity of marriage by a party who, having had the opportunity to appeal from the decree nisi, has not so appealed: Supreme Court Act 1981 s 18(1)) and *Lomas v Lomas* [2001] EWCA Civ 1891.

'Appeal against order for revocation of patent

21.2. (1) This paragraph applies where an appeal lies to the Court of Appeal from an order for the revocation of a patent.

(2) The appellant must serve the appellant's notice on the Comptroller-General of Patents, Designs and Trade Marks (the "Comptroller") in addition to the persons to be served under rule 52.4(3) and in accordance with that rule.

(3) Where, before the appeal hearing, the respondent decides not to oppose the appeal or not to attend the appeal hearing, he must immediately serve notice of that decision on–
   (a) the Comptroller; and
   (b) the appellant

(4) Where the respondent serves a notice in accordance with paragraph (3), he must also serve copies of the following documents on the Comptroller with that notice–
   (a) the petition;
   (b) any statements of claim;
   (c) any written evidence filed in the claim.

(5) Within 14 days after receiving the notice in accordance with paragraph (3), the Comptroller must serve on the appellant a notice stating whether or not he intends to attend the appeal hearing.

(6) The Comptroller may attend the appeal hearing and oppose the appeal–
   (a) in any case where he has given notice under paragraph (5) of his intention to attend; and
   (b) in any other case (including, in particular, a case where the respondent withdraws his opposition to the appeal during the hearing) if the Court of Appeal so directs or permits.

Appeal from Patents Court on appeal from Comptroller

21.3. Where the appeal is from a decision of the Patents Court which was itself made on an appeal from a decision of the Comptroller-General of Patents, Designs and Trade Marks, the appellant must serve the appellant's notice on the Comptroller in addition to the persons to be served under rule 52.4(3) and in accordance with that rule.

Appeals in cases of contempt of court

21.4. In an appeal under section 13 of the Administration of Justice Act 1960 (appeals in cases of contempt of court), the appellant must serve the appellant's notice on the court from whose order or decision the appeal is brought in addition to the persons to be served under rule 52.4(3) and in accordance with that rule.'

Editorial note

Service of appellant's notice

In an appeal in a contempt case the appellant must serve the appellant's notice on the court from whose order the appeal is brought, in addition to the persons required to be served under CPR 52.4(3).

Bail

Although RSC Order 109 rr 3 and 4 enable the High Court and the Court of Appeal to release an appellant on bail, bail applications are unusual in the Court of Appeal: the usual practice is to ensure that, where the appellant is in custody, the substantive appeal is listed to be heard as quickly as possible. The appellant's solicitors should file with the appellant's notice a transcript (or note) of the judgment being appealed in order that directions can be given on the need for an expedited hearing.

Powers of the Court of Appeal and sentence

The Court of Appeal is readier to allow the admission of further evidence in a contempt appeal than in an ordinary civil appeal: *Irtelli v Squatriti* [1993] QB 83, [1992] 3 All ER 294, CA. The Court of Appeal may allow a committal order to stand, despite procedural errors: *Butler v Butler* [1993] Fam 167, [1992] 4 All ER 833, CA. It also has power to order a retrial of the committal proceedings before another judge: *Duo v Duo* [1992] 3 All ER 121, sub nom *Duo v Osborne* [1992] 1 WLR 611, CA. The Court of Appeal has jurisdiction to hear an appeal by the applicant for committal and will exercise it if the sentence is wholly inadequate: *Wilson v Webster* [1998] 2 FCR 575, [1998] 1 FLR 1097, CA. It is a power to be exercised sparingly and only if the sentence is 'unduly lenient': *Lomas v Parle* [2003] EWCA Civ 1804, [2004] 1 FCR 97, (2004) Times, 13 January. A judge should bear in mind when considering the appropriate period of imprisonment to impose in respect of a contempt of court that any time spent on remand will not be deducted. Any time so spent should therefore be taken into account doubly: *McKnight v Northern* [2001] EWCA Civ 2028 and *Sevketoglu v Sevketoglu* [2003] EWCA Civ 1570, [2003] All ER (D) 111 (Aug).

'Appeals from Social Security or Child Support Commissioners
21.5. (1) This paragraph applies to appeals under section 25 of the Child

Support Act 1991, section 24 of the Social Security Administration Act 1992 and section 15 of the Social Security Act 1998 (appeals from the decision of a Commissioner on a question of law).

(2) The appellant must file the appellant's notice within 6 weeks after the date of the Commissioner's decision on permission to appeal to the Court of Appeal was given in writing to the appellant.

(3) The appellant must serve the appellant's notice on –
    (a) the Secretary of State; and
    (b) any person appointed by him to proceed with a claim
    in addition to the persons to be served under rule 52.4(3) and in accordance with that rule.'

Editorial note

Although an appeal from a Social Security Commissioner is not a 'second appeal' within s 55 of the Access to Justice Act 1999, the Court of Appeal applied the stricter test for permission imposed by s 55 in an appeal from a Social Security Commissioner in *Cooke v Secretary of State for Social Security* [2001] EWCA Civ 734, [2002] 3 All ER 279 (Clarke, Hale LJJ, Butterfield J).

'Appeals from Value Added Tax and Duties Tribunals

21.6. (1) An application to the Court of Appeal for permission to appeal from a value added tax and duties tribunal direct to that court must be made within 28 days after the date on which the tribunal certifies that its decision involves a point of law relating wholly or mainly to the construction of–
    (a) an enactment or of a statutory instrument; or
    (b) any of the Community Treaties or any Community Instrument,
    which has been fully argued before and fully considered by it.

(2) The application must be made by the parties jointly filing at the Court of Appeal an appellant's notice that–
    (a) contains a statement of the grounds for the application; and
    (b) is accompanied by a copy of the decision to be appealed, endorsed with the certificate of the tribunal.

(3) The court will notify the appellant of its decision and–
    (a) where permission to appeal to the Court of Appeal is given, the appellant must serve the appellant's notice on the chairman of the tribunal in addition to the persons to be served under rule 52.4(3) within 14 days after that notification.
    (b) where permission to appeal to the Court of Appeal is refused, the period for appealing to the High Court is to be calculated from the date of the notification of that refusal.

Appeals from Immigration Appeal Tribunal

21.7. (1) This paragraph applies to appeals under section 103(1) of the Nationality, Immigration and Asylum Act 2002 (appeal on a point of law from a determination of the Immigration Appeal Tribunal).

(2) The appellant's notice must be filed at the Court of Appeal within 14 days after the appellant is served in accordance with the Immigration and Asylum Appeals (Procedure) Rules 2003 with written notice of the Tribunal's decision to grant or refuse permission to appeal.

(3) The appellant must serve the appellant's notice in accordance with rule 52.4(3) on–
   (a) the persons to be served under that rule; and
   (b) the President of the Tribunal.'

Editorial note

The Court of Appeal declined to apply the stricter test for permission to appeal for 'second appeals' in an appeal from the IAT in *Koller v Secretary of State for the Home Department* [2001] EWCA Civ 1267 (Brooke, Tuckey, Laws LJJ) (see **para A2.15**). See, in particular the guidance given by Brooke LJ in paras 26 and 27 of his judgment:

> 'This court will be reluctant to permit a second appeal if the IAT set out the relevant principles of law correctly and set out the facts clearly ...If the IAT refuses permission on appeal and a single Lord Justice also refuses permission, the Legal Services Commission should be slow to grant a certificate granting an oral hearing.'

In order to minimise costs and to avoid being responsible for the applicant's costs, the Home Secretary should decide as soon as possible whether to oppose an appeal from the IAT: *Sengoz v Secretary of State for the Home Department* [2001] EWCA Civ 1135, (2001) Times, 13 August, CA.

'Appeal from Special Commissioners

21.8. (1) An application to the Court of Appeal for permission to appeal from the Special Commissioners direct to that court under section 56A of the Taxes Management Act 1970 must be made within 28 days after the date on which the Special Commissioners certify that their decision involves a point of law relating wholly or mainly to the construction of an enactment which has been fully argued before and fully considered before them.

(2) The application must be made by the parties jointly filing at the Court of Appeal an appellant's notice that–
   (a) contains a statement of the grounds for the application; and
   (b) is accompanied by a copy of the decision to be appealed, endorsed with the certificate of the tribunal.

(3) The court will notify the parties of its decision and—
   (a) where permission to appeal to the Court of Appeal is given, the appellant must serve the appellant's notice on the Clerk to the Special Commissioners in addition to the persons to be served under rule 52.4(3) within 14 days after that notification.
   (b) where permission to appeal to the Court of Appeal is refused, the period for appealing to the High Court is to be calculated from the date of the notification of that refusal.

Appeal from Lands Tribunal

21.9. The appellant must file the appellant's notice at the Court of Appeal within 28 days after the date of the decision of the tribunal.'

'Appeal from Competition Appeal Tribunal

21.10. (1) Where the appellant applies for permission to appeal at the hearing at which the decision is delivered by the tribunal and—
   (a) permission is given; or
   (b) permission is refused and the appellant wishes to make an application to the Court of Appeal for permission to appeal,
   the appellant's notice must be filed at the Court of Appeal within 14 days after the date of that hearing.
(2) Where the appellant applies in writing to the Registrar of the tribunal for permission to appeal and—
   (a) permission is given; or
   (b) permission is refused and the appellant wishes to make an application to the Court of Appeal for permission to appeal,
   the appellant's notice must be filed at the Court of Appeal within 14 days after the date of receipt of the tribunal's decision on permission.
(3) Where the appellant does not make an application to the tribunal for permission to appeal, but wishes to make an application to the Court of Appeal for permission, the appellant's notice must be filed at the Court of Appeal within 14 days after the end of the period within which he may make a written application to the Registrar of the tribunal.

Editorial note

The Court of Appeal applied the stricter test for permission to appeal for 'second appeals', second appeals) in an appeal from the decision of the Competition Commission Appeal Tribunal in *Napp Pharmaceutical Holdings Ltd v Director General of Fair Trading* [2002] EWCA Civ 796, [2002] 4 All ER 376, [2002] All ER (D) 31 (Jul).

Appeals relating to the application of Articles 81 and 82 of the EC Treaty and Chapters I and II of Part I of the Competition Act 1998

21.10A. (1) This paragraph applies to any appeal to the Court of Appeal relating to the application of–
- (a) Article 81 or Article 82 of the Treaty establishing the European Community; or
- (b) Chapter I or Chapter II of Part I of the Competition Act 1998.

(2) In this paragraph–
- (a) "the Act" means the Competition Act 1998;
- (b) "the Commission" means the European Commission;
- (c) "the Competition Regulation" means Council Regulation (EC) No. 1/2003 of 16 December 2002 on the implementation of the rules on competition laid down in Articles 81 and 82 of the Treaty;
- (d) "national competition authority" means–
  - (i) the Office of Fair Trading; and
  - (ii) any other person or body designated pursuant to Article 35 of the Competition Regulation as a national competition authority of the United Kingdom;
- (e) "the Treaty" means the Treaty establishing the European Community.

(3) Any party whose appeal notice raises an issue relating to the application of Article 81 or 82 of the Treaty, or Chapter I or II of Part I of the Act, must–
- (a) state that fact in his appeal notice; and
- (b) serve a copy of the appeal notice on the Office of Fair Trading at the same time as it is served on the other party to the appeal (addressed to the Director of Competition Policy Co-ordination, Office of Fair Trading, Fleetbank House, 2–6 Salisbury Square, London EC4Y 8JX).

(4) Attention is drawn to the provisions of article 15.3 of the Competition Regulation, which entitles competition authorities and the Commission to submit written observations to national courts on issues relating to the application of Article 81 or 82 and, with the permission of the court in question, to submit oral observations to the court.

(5) A national competition authority may also make written observations to the Court of Appeal, or apply for permission to make oral observations, on issues relating to the application of Chapter I or II.

(6) If a national competition authority or the Commission intends to

make written observations to the Court of Appeal, it must give notice of its intention to do so by letter to the Civil Appeals Office at the earliest opportunity.

(7) An application by a national competition authority or the Commission for permission to make oral representations at the hearing of an appeal must be made by letter to the Civil Appeals Office at the earliest opportunity, identifying the appeal and indicating why the applicant wishes to make oral representations.

(8) If a national competition authority or the Commission files a notice under sub-paragraph (6) or an application under sub-paragraph (7), it must at the same time serve a copy of the notice or application on every party to the appeal.

(9) Any request by a national competition authority or the Commission for the court to send it any documents relating to an appeal should be made at the same time as filing a notice under sub-paragraph (6) or an application under sub-paragraph (7).

(10) When the Court of Appeal receives a notice under sub-paragraph (6) it may give case management directions to the national competition authority or the Commission, including directions about the date by which any written observations are to be filed.

(11) The Court of Appeal will serve on every party to the appeal a copy of any directions given or order made–
   (a) on an application under sub-paragraph (7); or
   (b) under sub-paragraph (10).

(12) Every party to an appeal which raises an issue relating to the application of Article 81 or 82, and any national competition authority which has been served with a copy of a party's appeal notice, is under a duty to notify the Court of Appeal at any stage of the appeal if they are aware that–
   (a) the Commission has adopted, or is contemplating adopting, a decision in relation to proceedings which it has initiated; and
   (b) the decision referred to in (a) above has or would have legal effects in relation to the particular agreement, decision or practice in issue before the court.

(13) Where the Court of Appeal is aware that the Commission is contemplating adopting a decision as mentioned in sub-paragraph (12)(a), it shall consider whether to stay the appeal pending the Commission's decision.

(14) Where any judgment is given which decides on the application of Article 81 or 82, the court shall direct that a copy of the transcript of the judgment shall be sent to the Commission.

Appeal from Proscribed Organisations Appeal Commission

21.11. (1) The appellant's notice must be filed at the Court of Appeal within 14 days after the date when the Proscribed Organisations Appeal Commission–
- (a) granted; or
- (b) where section 6(2)(b) of the Terrorism Act 2000 applies, refused permission to appeal.

APPEALS TO THE HIGH COURT – QUEEN'S BENCH DIVISION

22.1. The following appeals are to be heard in the Queen's Bench Division.

Statutory Appeals

Appeals under the Merchant Shipping Act 1995

22.2. (1) This paragraph applies to appeals under the Merchant Shipping Act 1995 and for this purpose a re-hearing and an application under section 61 of the Merchant Shipping Act 1995 are treated as appeals.

(2) The appellant must file any report to the Secretary of State containing the decision from which the appeal is brought with the appellant's notice.

(3) Where a re-hearing by the High Court is ordered under sections 64 or 269 of the Merchant Shipping Act 1995, the Secretary of State must give reasonable notice to the parties whom he considers to be affected by the re-hearing.

Appeals against decisions affecting the registration of architects and health care professionals

22.3. (1) This paragraph applies to an appeal to the High Court under–
- (a) section 22 of the Architects Act 1997;
- (b) section 82(3) and 83(2) of the Medicines Act 1968;
- (c) section 12 of the Nurses, Midwives and Health Visitors Act 1997;
- (cc) article 38 of the Nursing and Midwifery Order 2001;
- (d) section 10 of the Pharmacy Act 1954;
- (e) section 40 of the Medical Act 1983;
- (f) section 29 or section 44 of the Dentists Act 1984;
- (g) sections 23 of the Opticians Act 1989;
- (h) section 31 of the Osteopaths Act 1993; and
- (i) section 31 of the Chiropractors Act 1994.

(2) Every appeal to which this paragraph applies must be supported by written evidence and, if the court so orders, oral evidence and will be by way of re-hearing.

(3) The appellant must file the appellant's notice within 28 days after the decision that the appellant wishes to appeal.

(4) In the case of an appeal under an enactment specified in column 1 of the following table, the persons to be made respondents are the persons specified in relation to that enactment in column 2 of the table and the person to be served with the appellant's notice is the person so specified in column 3.

1	2	3
Enactment	**Respondents**	**Person to be served**
Architects Act 1997, s. 22	The Architects' Registration Council of the United Kingdom	The registrar of the Council
Medicines Act 1968, s. 82(3) and s. 83(2)	The Pharmaceutical Society of Great Britain	The registrar of the Society
Nurses, Midwives and Health Visitors Act 1997, s. 12; Nursing and Midwifery Order 2001, art. 38	The Nursing and Midwifery Council	The Registrar of the Council
Pharmacy Act 1954, s. 10	The Royal Pharmaceutical Society of Great Britain	The registrar of the Society
Medical Act 1983, s. 40	The General Medical Council	The Registrar of the Council
Dentists Act 1984, s. 29 or s. 44	The General Dental Council	The Registrar of the Council
Opticians Act 1989, s. 23	The General Optical Council	The Registrar of the Council
Osteopaths Act 1993, s. 31	The General Osteopathic Council	The Registrar of the Council
Chiropractors Act 1994, s. 31	The General Chiropractic Council	The Registrar of the Council

Consumer Credit Act 1974: appeal from Secretary of State

22.4. (1) A person dissatisfied in point of law with a decision of the Secretary of State on an appeal under section 41 of the Consumer Credit Act 1974 from a determination of the Director General of

Fair Trading who had a right to appeal to the Secretary of State, whether or not he exercised that right, may appeal to the High Court.

(2) The appellant must serve the appellant's notice on–
   (a) the Secretary of State;
   (b) the original applicant, if any, where the appeal is by a licensee under a group licence against compulsory variation, suspension or revocation of that licence; and
   (c) any other person as directed by the court.

(3) The appeal court may remit the matter to the Secretary of State to the extent necessary to enable him to provide the court with such further information as the court may direct.

(4) If the appeal court allows the appeal, it shall not set aside or vary the decision but shall remit the matter to the Secretary of State with the opinion of the court for hearing and determination by him.

The Pensions Appeal Tribunal Act 1943

22.5. (1) In this paragraph "the judge" means the judge nominated by the Lord Chancellor under section 6(2) of the Pensions Appeal Tribunals Act 1943 ("the Act").

(2) An application to the judge for permission to appeal against a decision of a Pensions Appeal Tribunal–
   (a) may not be made unless an application was made to the tribunal and was refused; and
   (b) must be made within 28 days after the date of the tribunal's refusal.

(3) The appellant's notice seeking permission to appeal from the judge must contain–
   (a) the point of law as respects which the appellant alleges that the tribunal's decision was wrong; and
   (b) the date of the tribunal's decision refusing permission to appeal.

(4) The court officer shall request the chairman of the tribunal to give the judge a written statement of the reasons for the tribunal's decision to refuse permission to appeal, and within 7 days after receiving the request, the chairman must give the judge such a statement.

(5) Where permission to appeal was given by–
   (a) the tribunal, the appellant must file and serve the appellant's notice;
   (b) the judge, the appellant must serve the appellant's notice,
within 28 days after permission to appeal was given.

(6) Within 28 days after service of the notice of appeal on him, the chairman of the tribunal must–
  (a) state a case setting out the facts on which the decision appealed against was based;
  (b) file the case stated at the court; and
  (c) serve a copy of the case stated on the appellant and the respondent.
(7) A copy of the judge's order on the appeal must be sent by the court officer to the appellant, the respondent and the chairman of the tribunal.

The Social Security Administration Act 1992

22.6. (1) Any person who by virtue of section 18 or 58(8) of the Social Security Administration Act 1992 ("the Act") is entitled and wishes to appeal against a decision of the Secretary of State on a question of law must, within the prescribed period, or within such further time as the Secretary of State may allow, serve on the Secretary of State a notice requiring him to state a case setting out–
  (a) his decision; and
  (b) the facts on which his decision was based.
(2) Unless paragraph (3) applies the prescribed period is 28 days after receipt of the notice of the decision.
(3) Where, within 28 days after receipt of notice of the decision, a request is made to the Secretary of State in accordance with regulations made under the Act to furnish a statement of the grounds of the decision, the prescribed period is 28 days after receipt of that statement.
(4) Where under section 18 or section 58(8) of the Act, the Secretary of State refers a question of law to the court, he must state that question together with the relevant facts in a case.
(5) The appellant's notice and the case stated must be filed at the appeal court and a copy of the notice and the case stated served on–
  (a) the Secretary of State; and
  (b) every person as between whom and the Secretary of State the question has arisen,
  within 28 days after the case stated was served on the party at whose request, or as a result of whose application to the court, the case was stated.
(6) Unless the appeal court otherwise orders, the appeal or reference shall not be heard sooner than 28 days after service of the appellant's notice.

(7) The appeal court may order the case stated by the Secretary of State to be returned to the Secretary of State for him to hear further evidence.

Appeals under the Extradition Act 2003

22.6A. (1) In this paragraph, "the Act" means the Extradition Act 2003.

(2) Appeals to the High Court under the Act must be brought in the Administrative Court of the Queen's Bench Division.

(3) Where an appeal is brought under section 26 or 28 of the Act–
   (a) the appellant's notice must be filed and served before the expiry of 7 days, starting with the day on which the order is made;
   (b) the appellant must endorse the appellant's notice with the date of the person's arrest;
   (c) the High Court must begin to hear the substantive appeal within 40 days of the person's arrest; and
   (d) the appellant must serve a copy of the appellant's notice on the Crown Prosecution Service, if they are not a party to the appeal, in addition to the persons to be served under rule 52.4(3) and in accordance with that rule.

(4) The High Court may extend the period of 40 days under paragraph (3)(c) if it believes it to be in the interests of justice to do so.

(5) Where an appeal is brought under section 103 of the Act, the appellant's notice must be filed and served before the expiry of 14 days, starting with the day on which the Secretary of State informs the person under section 100(1) or (4) of the Act of the order he has made in respect of the person.

(6) Where an appeal is brought under section 105 of the Act, the appellant's notice must be filed and served before the expiry of 14 days, starting with the day on which the order for discharge is made.

(7) Where an appeal is brought under section 108 of the Act the appellant's notice must be filed and served before the expiry of 14 days, starting with the day on which the Secretary of State informs the person that he has ordered his extradition.

(8) Where an appeal is brought under section 110 of the Act the appellant's notice must be filed and served before the expiry of 14 days, starting with the day on which the Secretary of State informs the person acting on behalf of a category 2 territory, as defined in section 69 of the Act, of the order for discharge.
(Section 69 of the Act provides that a category 2 territory is that designated for the purposes of Part 2 of the Act).

(9) Subject to paragraph (10), where an appeal is brought under

section 103, 105, 108 or 110 of the Act, the High Court must begin to hear the substantive appeal within 76 days of the appellant's notice being filed.

(10) Where an appeal is brought under section 103 of the Act before the Secretary of State has decided whether the person is to be extradited–
(a) the period of 76 days does not start until the day on which the Secretary of State informs the person of his decision; and
(b) the Secretary of State must, as soon as practicable after he informs the person of his decision, inform the High Court–
   (i) of his decision; and
   (ii) of the date on which he informs the person of his decision.

(11) The High Court may extend the period of 76 days if it believes it to be in the interests of justice to do so.

(12) Where an appeal is brought under section 103, 105, 108 or 110 of the Act, the appellant must serve a copy of the appellant's notice on–
(a) the Crown Prosecution Service; and
(b) the Home Office,
if they are not a party to the appeal, in addition to the persons to be served under rule 52.4(3) and in accordance with that rule.

Appeals by way of case stated

Reference of question of law by Agriculture Land Tribunal

22.7. (1) A question of law referred to the High Court by an Agricultural Land Tribunal under section 6 of the Agriculture (Miscellaneous Provisions) Act 1954 shall be referred by way of case stated by the Tribunal.

(2) Where the proceedings before the tribunal arose on an application under section 11 of the Agricultural Holdings Act 1986, an–
(a) application notice for an order under section 6 that the tribunal refers a question of law to the court; and
(b) appellant's notice by which an appellant seeks the court's determination on a question of law,
must be served on the authority having power to enforce the statutory requirement specified in the notice in addition to every other party to those proceedings and on the secretary of the tribunal.

(3) Where, in accordance with paragraph (2), a notice is served on the authority mentioned in that paragraph, that authority may attend the appeal hearing and make representations to the court.

Case stated by Mental Health Review Tribunal

22.8. (1) In this paragraph "the Act" means the Mental Health Act 1983 and "party to proceedings" means–
   (a) the person who initiated the proceedings; and
   (b) any person to whom, in accordance with rules made under section 78 of the Act, the tribunal sent notice of the application or reference or a request instead notice of reference.

(2) A party to proceedings shall not be entitled to apply to the High Court for an order under section 78(8) of the Act directing the tribunal to state a case for determination by court unless–
   (a) within 21 days after the decision of the tribunal was communicated to him in accordance with rules made under section 78 of the Act he made a written request to the tribunal to state a case; and
   (b) either the tribunal
      (i) failed to comply with that request within 21 days after it was made; or
      (ii) refused to comply with it.

(3) The period for filing the application notice for an order under section 78(8) of the Act is–
   (a) where the tribunal failed to comply with the applicant's request to state a case within the period mentioned in paragraph 2(b)(i), 14 days after the expiration of that period;
   (b) where the tribunal refused that request, 14 days after receipt by the applicant of notice of the refusal of his request.

(4) A Mental Health Review Tribunal by whom a case is stated shall be entitled to attend the proceedings for the determination of the case and make representations to the court.

(5) If the court allows the appeal, it may give any direction which the tribunal ought to have given under Part V of the Act.

APPEALS TO THE HIGH COURT – CHANCERY DIVISION

23.1. The following appeals are to be heard in the Chancery Division.

Determination of appeal or case stated under various Acts

23.2. Any appeal to the High Court, and any case stated or question referred for the opinion of that court under any of the following enactments shall be heard in the Chancery Division–

(1) paragraph 16 of Schedule 15 to the Law of Property Act 1922;
(2) the Industrial Assurance Act 1923;
(3) the Land Registration Act 1925;
(4) section 205(4) of the Water Resources Act 1991;
(5) section 38(3) of the Clergy Pensions Measure 1961;

(6) the Industrial and Provident Societies Act 1965;
(7) section 151 of the Pension Schemes Act 1993;
(8) section 173 of the Pension Schemes Act 1993;
(9) section 97 of the Pensions Act 1995;
(10) The Charities Act 1993.
(11) section 13 and 13B of the Stamp Act 1891;
(12) section 705A of the Income and Corporation Taxes Act 1988;
(13) regulation 22 of the General Commissioners (Jurisdiction and Procedure) Regulations 1994;
(14) section 53, 56A or 100C(4) of the Taxes Management Act 1970;
(15) section 222(3), 225, 249(3) or 251 of the Inheritance Tax Act 1984;
(16) regulation 8(3) or 10 of the Stamp Duty Reserve Tax Regulations 1986;
(17) the Land Registration Act 2002.
(This list is not exhaustive)

Statutory Appeals

Appeal under section 222 of the Inheritance Tax Act 1984
23.3. (1) This paragraph applies to appeals to the High Court under section 222(3) of the Inheritance Tax Act 1984 (the "1984 Act") and regulation 8(3) of the Stamp Duty Reserve Tax Regulations 1986 (the "1986 Regulations").
(2) The appellant's notice must–
 (a) state the date on which the Commissioners of Inland Revenue (the "Board") gave notice to the appellant under section 221 of the 1984 Act or regulation 6 of the 1986 Regulations of the determination that is the subject of the appeal;
 (b) state the date on which the appellant gave to the Board notice of appeal under section 222(1) of the 1984 Act or regulation 8(1) of the 1986 Regulations and, if notice was not given within the time permitted, whether the Board or the Special Commissioners have given their consent to the appeal being brought out of time, and, if they have, the date they gave their consent; and
 (c) either state that the appellant and the Board have agreed that the appeal may be to the High Court or contain an application for permission to appeal to the High Court.
(3) The appellant must file the following documents with the appellant's notice–
 (a) 2 copies of the notice referred to in paragraph 2(a);
 (b) 2 copies of the notice of appeal (under section 222(1) of the 1984 Act or regulation 8(1) of the 1986 Regulations) referred to in paragraph 2(b); and

176 *Procedure*

        (c)   where the appellant's notice contains an application for permission to appeal, written evidence setting out the grounds on which it is alleged that the matters to be decided on the appeal are likely to be substantially confined to questions of law.

(4)   The appellant must–
- (a) file the appellant's notice at the court; and
- (b) serve the appellant's notice on the Board,

within 30 days of the date on which the appellant gave to the Board notice of appeal under section 222(1) of the 1984 Act or regulation 8(1) of the 1986 Regulations or, if the Board or the Special Commissioners have given consent to the appeal being brought out of time, within 30 days of the date on which such consent was given.

(5)   The court will set a date for the hearing of not less than 40 days from the date that the appellant's notice was filed.

(6)   Where the appellant's notice contains an application for permission to appeal–
- (a) a copy of the written evidence filed in accordance with paragraph (3)(c) must be served on the Board with the appellant's notice; and
- (b) the Board–
  - (i) may file written evidence; and
  - (ii) if it does so, must serve a copy of that evidence on the appellant, within 30 days after service of the written evidence under paragraph (6)(a).

(7)   The appellant may not rely on any grounds of appeal not specified in the notice referred to in paragraph (2)(b) on the hearing of the appeal without the permission of the court.

Appeals under section 53 and 100C(4) of the Taxes Management Act 1970 and section 249(3) or 251 of the Inheritance Tax Act 1984

23.4. (1) The appellant must serve the appellant's notice on–
- (a) the General or Special Commissioners against whose decision, award or determination the appeal is brought; and
- (b)
  - (i) in the case of an appeal brought under section 100C(4) of the Taxes Management Act 1970 or section 249(3) of the Inheritance Tax Act 1984 by any party other than the defendant in the proceedings before the Commissioners, that defendant; or
  - (ii) in any other case, the Commissioners of Inland Revenue.

(2) The appellant must file the appellant's notice at the court within 30 days after the date of the decision, award or determination against which the appeal is brought.
(3) Within 30 days of the service on them of the appellant's notice, the General or Special Commissioners, as the case may be, must–
    (a) file 2 copies of a note of their findings and of the reasons for their decision, award or determination at the court; and
    (b) serve a copy of the note on every other party to the appeal.
(4) Any document to be served on the General or Special Commissioners may be served by delivering or sending it to their clerk.

Appeals under section 56A of the Taxes Management Act 1970, section 225 of the Inheritance Tax Act 1984 and regulation 10 of the Stamp Duty Reserve Tax Regulations 1986

23.5. (1) The appellant must file the appellant's notice–
    (a) where the appeal is made following the refusal of the Special Commissioners to issue a certificate under section 56A(2)(b) of the Taxes Management Act 1970, within 28 days from the date of the release of the decision of the Special Commissioners containing the refusal;
    (b) where the appeal is made following the refusal of permission to appeal to the Court of Appeal under section 56A(2)(c) of that Act, within 28 days from the date when permission is refused; or
    (c) in all other cases within 56 days after the date of the decision or determination that the appellant wishes to appeal.

Appeal under section 17 of the Industrial Assurance Act 1923

23.6. The appellant must file the appellant's notice within 21 days after the date of the Commissioner's refusal or direction under section 17(3) of the Industrial Assurance Act 1923.

Appeals affecting industrial and provident societies etc.

23.7. (1) This paragraph applies to all appeals under–
    (a) the Friendly Societies Act 1974;
    (b) the Friendly Societies Act 1992;
    (c) the Industrial Assurance Act 1923; and
    (d) the Industrial and Provident Societies Act 1965
(2) At any stage on an appeal, the court may –
    (a) direct that the appellant's notice be served on any person;
    (b) direct that notice be given by advertisement or otherwise of –
        (i) the bringing of the appeal;
        (ii) the nature of the appeal; and
        (iii) the time when the appeal will or is likely to be heard; or

(c) give such other directions as it thinks proper to enable any person interested in–
   (i) the society, trade union, alleged trade union or industrial assurance company; or
   (ii) the subject matter of the appeal, to appear and be heard at the appeal hearing.

Appeal from Value Added Tax and Duties Tribunal
23.8. (1) A party to proceedings before a Value Added Tax and Duties Tribunal who is dissatisfied in point of law with a decision of the tribunal may appeal under section 11(1) of the Tribunals and Inquiries Act 1992 to the High Court.
(2) The appellant must file the appellant's notice–
   (a) where the appeal is made following the refusal of the Value Added Tax and Duties Tribunal to grant a certificate under article 2(b) of the Value Added Tax and Duties Tribunal Appeals Order 1986, within 28 days from the date of the release of the decision containing the refusal;
   (b) in all other cases within 56 days after the date of the decision or determination that the appellant wishes to appeal.

Appeal against an order or decision of the Charity Commissioners
23.8A. (1) In this paragraph–
"the Act" means the Charities Act 1993; and
"the Commissioners" means the Charity Commissioners for England and Wales.
(2) The Attorney-General, unless he is the appellant, must be made a respondent to the appeal.
(3) The appellant's notice must state the grounds of the appeal, and the appellant may not rely on any other grounds without the permission of the court.
(4) Sub-paragraphs (5) and (6) apply, in addition to the above provisions, where the appeal is made under section 16(12) of the Act.
(5) If the Commissioners have granted a certificate that it is a proper case for an appeal, a copy of the certificate must be filed with the appellant's notice.
(6) If the appellant applies in the appellant's notice for permission to appeal under section 16(13) of the Act–
   (a) the appellant's notice must state–
      (i) that the appellant has requested the Commissioners to grant a certificate that it is a proper case for an appeal, and they have refused to do so;
      (ii) the date of such refusal;
      (iii) the grounds on which the appellant alleges that it is a proper case for an appeal; and

(iv) if the application for permission to appeal is made with the consent of any other party to the proposed appeal, that fact;

(b) if the Commissioners have given reasons for refusing a certificate, a copy of the reasons must be attached to the appellant's notice;

(c) the court may, before determining the application, direct the Commissioners to file a written statement of their reasons for refusing a certificate;

(d) the court will serve on the appellant a copy of any statement filed under sub-paragraph (c).

Appeal against a decision of the adjudicator under section 111 of the Land Registration Act 2002

23.8B. (1) A person who is aggrieved by a decision of the adjudicator and who wishes to appeal that decision must obtain permission to appeal.

(2) The appellant must serve on the adjudicator a copy of the appeal court's decision on a request for permission to appeal as soon as reasonably practicable and in any event within 14 days of receipt by the appellant of the decision on permission.

(3) The appellant must serve on the adjudicator and the Chief Land Registrar a copy of any order by the appeal court to stay a decision of the adjudicator pending the outcome of the appeal as soon as reasonably practicable and in any event within 14 days of receipt by the appellant of the appeal court's order to stay.

(4) The appellant must serve on the adjudicator and the Chief Land Registrar a copy of the appeal court's decision on the appeal as soon as reasonably practicable and in any event within 14 days of receipt by the appellant of the appeal court's decision.

Appeals by way of case stated

Proceedings under the Commons Registration Act 1965

23.9. A person aggrieved by the decision of a Commons Commissioner who requires the Commissioner to state a case for the opinion of the High Court under section 18 of the Commons Registration Act 1965 must file the appellant's notice within 42 days from the date on which notice of the decision was sent to the aggrieved person.

APPEALS TO A COUNTY COURT

Local Government (Miscellaneous Provisions) Act 1976

24.1. Where one of the grounds upon which an appeal against a notice under sections 21, 23 or 35 of the Local Government (Miscellaneous Provisions) Act 1976 is brought is that–
(a) it would have been fairer to serve the notice on another person; or
(b) that it would be reasonable for the whole or part of the expenses to which the appeal relates to be paid by some other person,

that person must be made a respondent to the appeal, unless the court, on application of the appellant made without notice, otherwise directs.

Appeals under sections 204 and 204A of the Housing Act 1996

24.2. (1) An appellant should include appeals under section 204 and section 204A of the Housing Act 1996 in one appellant's notice.

(2) If it is not possible to do so (for example because an urgent application under section 204A is required) the appeals may be included in separate appellant's notices.

(3) An appeal under section 204A may include an application for an order under section 204A(4)(a) requiring the authority to secure that accommodation is available for the applicant's occupation.

(4) If, exceptionally, the court makes an order under section 204A(4)(a) without notice, the appellant's notice must be served on the authority together with the order. Such an order will normally require the authority to secure that accommodation is available until a hearing date when the authority can make representations as to whether the order under section 204A(4)(a) should be continued.

Appeal under Part II of the Immigration and Asylum Act 1999 (carriers" liability)

24.3. (1) A person appealing to a county court under section 35A or section 40B of the Immigration and Asylum Act 1999 ("the Act") against a decision by the Secretary of State to impose a penalty under section 32 or a charge under section 40 of the Act must, subject to paragraph (2), file the appellant's notice within 28 days after receiving the penalty notice or charge notice.

(2) Where the appellant has given notice of objection to the Secretary of State under section 35(4) or section 40A(3) of the Act within the time prescribed for doing so, he must file the appellant's notice within 28 days after receiving notice of the Secretary of State's decision in response to the notice of objection.

(3) Sections 35A and 40B of the Act provide that any appeal under

those sections shall be a re-hearing of the Secretary of State's decision to impose a penalty or charge, and therefore rule 52.11(1) does not apply.

SECTION IV – PROVISIONS ABOUT REOPENING APPEALS

REOPENING OF FINAL APPEALS

25.1. This paragraph applies to applications under rule 52.17 for permission to reopen a final determination of an appeal.

25.2. In this paragraph, "appeal" includes an application for permission to appeal.

25.3. Permission must be sought from the court whose decision the applicant wishes to reopen.

25.4. The application for permission must be made by application notice and supported by written evidence, verified by a statement of truth.

25.5. A copy of the application for permission must not be served on any other party to the original appeal unless the court so directs.

25.6. Where the court directs that the application for permission is to be served on another party, that party may within 14 days of the service on him of the copy of the application file and serve a written statement either supporting or opposing the application.

25.7. The application for permission, and any written statements supporting or opposing it, will be considered on paper by a single judge, and will be allowed to proceed only if the judge so directs.'

CHAPTER 5

Miscellaneous Points of Practice

Striking out of appeal notice: abuse of process	5.1
Change of solicitor	5.2
Discontinuance of proceedings in the lower court	5.4
Appeals against consent orders	5.5
Bankruptcy of appellant	5.6
Master in the Court of Appeal, Civil Division	5.7
Dismissal list hearings in the Court of Appeal	5.8
Enforcement of appeal order	5.9

STRIKING OUT OF APPEAL NOTICE: ABUSE OF PROCESS

5.1 The Court of Appeal has power of its own motion to strike out a notice of appeal if it represents an abuse of its process (CPR 3.3(4); CPR 2.1;see *Bhamjee v Forsdick (No 2)* [2003] EWCA Civ 1113, [2004] 1 WLR 88). There is a compelling reason to strike out an appeal where the court regards the appeal as an abuse of process: *Turner v Haworth Associates* [2001] EWCA Civ 370, [2001] All ER (D) 309, Chadwick and Hale LJJ. Guidance on the power to strike out in a judicial review context was given by Brooke LJ, V-P, in *R (on the application of Nine Nepalese Asylum Seekers) v Immigration Appeal Tribunal* [2003] EWCA Civ 1892 (see **para A2.18**): '... applications of this kind represent an abuse of the processes of this Court, which exists to resolve genuine points of law in judicial review cases, and is not a fourth tier appellate court of fact when the original tribunal of fact has disbelieved the applicant'. Where an application is totally devoid of merit, it 'would be appropriate for a judge ... to strike the matter out under CPR 3.3(4) and give the applicant ten days in which to make an application for a hearing, if so advised'.

After giving judgment in the *Nine Nepalese Asylum Seekers* case on 19 December 2003, Brooke LJ, V-P, struck out seven similar cases on paper as an abuse of process and gave directions that any application to set aside his order should be filed, 'setting out full written grounds', by 4 January 2004. No such application was, in the event, made.

See **Chapter 4** for setting aside the grant of permission to appeal, the imposition of conditions and the case management powers of the Court of Appeal in the notes to CPR 52.10

CHANGE OF SOLICITOR

5.2 The procedure for solicitors ceasing to act in appeals in the High Court and the county courts will not give rise to difficulty. This paragraph explains the practice where an appeal is made to the Court of Appeal. The Court of Appeal requires notice of change to be given, either in letter form or through the making of an order in the lower court.

Under the Rules of the Supreme Court, the Court of Appeal would require the making of an application to remove solicitors from the record where an application or appeal was pending in that court[1]. Since the introduction of the CPR, CPR Pt 42 simply refers to an application having to be made[2] and refers to CPR Pt 23 for the mode of application. Under CPR 23.2 the general rule is that an application must be made to the court where the claim was started and, if a claim has been transferred to another court since it was started, an application must be made to the court to which the claim has been transferred. It could be argued that a claim has been transferred when an application is made to the Court of Appeal and that the claim has been transferred there with the result that the application should be made to that court. Since the claim is still proceeding in the court below notwithstanding the making of an application to the Court of Appeal, a party has the option of making his application in either court. Where an application has been granted in the lower court, provided the parties notify the Court of Appeal of the result of that application, then the Court of Appeal will accept the order made by the lower court. Where a legal aid/pubic funding certificate is discharged, no application needs to be made for solicitors to come off the record since the effect of the discharge provides for the change to be effected[3].

1 See RSC Ord 67, r 6(2).
2 See CPR 42.3.
3 CPR 42.2(6).

5.3 Where an application has to be made in the Court of Appeal for solicitors to cease to act, the application may be listed before the master or a deputy master. The application may be dealt with without a hearing where the application is straightforward and all the necessary documentation has been provided: *Miller v Allied Sainiff (UK) Ltd* [2000] The Times, 31 October. Where the application is listed for hearing a short bundle of documents should be filed before the hearing (which usually take place on Wednesday mornings). The bundle should contain the application and the witness statement in support together with copies of the relevant documents e.g. letters to the client. Where the appeal is listed for hearing, the application should be made promptly as sufficient time must be allowed for the client to instruct new solicitors if the application is granted. It cannot be assumed that the hearing of the appeal will be adjourned. The costs of the application may be disallowed if the (deputy) master considers that the application should have been made earlier.

DISCONTINUANCE OF PROCEEDINGS IN THE LOWER COURT

5.4 Where a claim is discontinued in the lower court, any appeal which is made in that claim is vacated: the appeal comes to an end on the discontinuance[1]. The notice of discontinuance is sufficient and no further notice need be given in relation to the appeal. In practice the appeal court will draw an order striking out the appeal on paper[2]. Similarly where a claim is struck out in the lower court, the appeal will be struck out of the court's own initiative. An appeal will also be struck out where the reason for the appeal no longer exists, such as where extraneous events remove the need for the appeal to continue. In *R v Home Secretary ex p Saleh* [1999] AC 150 Lord Slynn restated the principles according to which the House of Lords is willing to continue to determine a point of public law even though the *lis* between the parties is no longer a live one.

1   Where the parties settle after reading the draft judgment, the judge has a discretion to hand down the judgment in open court even though the parties request him not so to do: *Prudential Assurance Co. Ltd. V McBains Cooper (a firm) & Ors* [2000] 1 WLR 2000.
2   This was the practice under the Rules of the Supreme Court (see *Conybeare v Lewis* (1880) 13 Ch D 469) but there seems no reason why it should not continue to apply under the CPR.

APPEALS AGAINST CONSENT ORDERS

5.5 The appeal court cannot entertain an appeal against a perfected and subsisting order by a party who is expressed to have consented to it[1]. The only remedy is to commence a fresh proceeding at first instance to have the order set aside. The reasons for this are that there is a judgment of record to which the party consented and which the party cannot go behind and there is no judgment against which there could be an appeal[2]. The Court of Appeal and the High Court have power, under the Taylor v Lawrence jurisdiction (see: [2002] EWCA Civ 90, [2002] 3 WLR 640) to reopen an order dismissing an appeal with the parties' consent: *Matlaszek v Bloom Camillion* [2003] EWCA Civ 154. See: CPR 52.17.

1 *Re F* [1992] 1 FCR 167, [1992] 1 FLR 561, CA.
2 *Gill v London Borough of Southwark* (8 May 2000, unreported) Aldous LJ.

BANKRUPTCY OF APPELLANT

5.6 Where an appellant is made bankrupt, his cause of action vests in his trustee in bankruptcy[1] unless the cause of action is personal to him, such as a claim for defamation or divorce proceedings. Unless the trustee elects to pursue the application or the appeal, it will be listed for dismissal; the bankrupt has no standing and is not entitled to pursue it himself[2]. In a claim for personal injuries, any damages awarded may have to be split between the trustee and the bankrupt with the result that the bankrupt retains the right to damages for pain and suffering and the right to damages for past and future earnings vests in the trustee[3]. In such cases the cause of action vests in the trustee and it is for him to prosecute the application or appeal; the trustee holds the right to recover personal damages on constructive trust for the bankrupt. For the position as to property acquired before and after the bankruptcy see *Mulkerrins v Price Waterhouse Coopers*[4].

1 *Heath v Tang* [1993] 4 All ER 694, [1993] 1 WLR 1421, CA.
2 The subsequent discharge of the bankruptcy makes no difference: *Barclays Bank plc v Henson* (2 February 1999, unreported), CA, although the bankrupt may be able to take steps under the insolvency legislation.
3 *Ord v Upton* [2000] 1 All ER 193, [2000] Ch 352, CA. See also *Khan v Trident Safeguards Ltd* [2004] EWCA Civ 624.
4 [2003] UKHL 41, [2003] 1 WLR 1937.

MASTER IN THE COURT OF APPEAL, CIVIL DIVISION

5.7 When the Head of the Civil Appeals Office acts in a judicial capacity pursuant to CPR 52.16, he is known as master. Other officers designated to exercise judicial authority are known as deputy masters[1]. The master and deputy masters may exercise the jurisdiction of the Court of Appeal with regard to any matter incidental to any proceedings, any other matter where there is no substantial dispute between the parties and the dismissal of an appeal or application for failure to comply with any order, rule or practice direction[2]. The master and his deputies may give directions in relation to applications and appeals or may refer a request for directions to one of the

Supervising Lord Justices. A request for directions should be addressed to the Civil Appeals Office and not direct to a Lord Justice or to his clerk[3].

1   CPR PD 52, para 15.5.
2   CPR 52.16(2); see also CPR 52.16(3).
3   CPR PD 52, para 15.10.

DISMISSAL LIST HEARINGS IN THE COURT OF APPEAL

5.8 The master and deputy masters consider matters for dismissal every week during term time. Where there is failure to prosecute an application or an appeal, such as the failure to provide bundles or skeleton arguments, it will be referred for consideration to be given for its dismissal. An order dismissing an appeal or an application may be made without a hearing. Such an order will, on request, be reconsidered at a hearing: CPR 52.16(6).

ENFORCEMENT OF APPEAL ORDER

5.9 An order made by the Court of Appeal can be enforced by the lower court[1]. This may be the most effective way of enforcement.

1   *Ager v Ager* [1998] 1 All ER 703, [1998] 1 WLR 1074, CA.

CHAPTER 6

Documents

The appellant's notice	6.1
Appellant's documents	6.7
Skeleton arguments	6.15
Transcripts of judgment	6.17
Service of the appellant's notice	6.18
Amendment of appeal notice	6.19
Applications for permission to appeal	6.20
Respondent's submissions on application for permission to appeal	6.23
Documents for the appeal hearing	6.24
Respondent's notices, skeleton arguments and documents	6.29
Summary assessment of costs	6.38
Appeal hearings in the Court of Appeal	6.39
Disposing of applications or appeals by consent	6.51

Most of the requirements relating to documents are in the Practice Direction to CPR Pt 52 itself. The text of this chapter contains a large number of extracts from that Practice Direction, which has been substantially revised with effect from 30 June 2004.

THE APPELLANT'S NOTICE

6.1 An appellant's notice in Form N161 must be filed and served in all cases and, where an application for permission to appeal is made to the appeal court, it must be applied for in the appellant's notice.

'5.1

An appellant's notice must be filed and served in all cases. Where an application for permission to appeal is made to the appeal court it must be applied for in the appellant's notice.'

Grounds of appeal

6.2 CPR 52.11(3) (a) and (b) set out the circumstances in which the appeal court will allow an appeal. The grounds of appeal should:
(a) clearly set out the reasons why rule 52.11(3)(a) or (b) is said to apply; and
(b) specify, in respect of each ground, whether the ground raises an appeal on a point of law or is an appeal against a finding of fact: CPR PD 52 para 3.2.

'3.1

Rule 52.11(3) (a) and (b) sets out the circumstances in which the appeal court will allow an appeal.

3.2

The grounds of appeal should–
(a) set out clearly the reasons why rule 52.11(3)(a) or (b) is said to apply; and
(b) specify, in respect of each ground, whether the ground raises an appeal on a point of law or is an appeal against a finding of fact.'

Human rights

6.3 Where an appellant relies on the Human Rights Act for the first time in an appeal, he must comply with paras 5.1A and 5.1B of the Practice Direction.

'5.1A (1)

This paragraph applies where the appellant seeks–
(a) to rely on any issue under the Human Rights Act 1998; or
(b) a remedy available under that Act,
for the first time in an appeal.

(2)

The appellant must include in his appeal notice the information required by paragraph 15.1 of the practice direction supplementing Part 16.

(3)

Paragraph 15.2 of the practice direction supplementing Part 16 applies as if references to a statement of case were to the appeal notice.

5.1B

CPR rule 19.4A and the practice direction supplementing it shall apply as if references to the case management conference were to the application for permission to appeal.

(The practice direction to Part 19 provides for notice to be given and parties joined in certain circumstances to which this paragraph applies).'

Practice Direction 16—Statement of Case

6.3A

'THIS PRACTICE DIRECTION SUPPLEMENTS CPR PART 16

HUMAN RIGHTS
15.1 A party who seeks to rely on any provision of or right arising under the Human Rights Act 1998 or seeks a remedy available under that Act—
(1) must state that fact in his statement of case; and
(2) must in his statement of case—
  (a) give precise details of the Convention right which it is alleged has been infringed and details of the alleged infringement;
  (b) specify the relief sought;
  (c) state if the relief sought includes— (i)a declaration of incompatibility in accordance with section 4 of that Act, or (ii)damages in respect of a judicial act to which section 9(3) of that Act applies;
  (d) where the relief sought includes a declaration of incompatibility in accordance with section 4 of that Act, give precise details of the legislative provision alleged to be incompatible and details of the alleged incompatibility;

(e) where the claim is founded on a finding of unlawfulness by another court or tribunal, give details of the finding; and
(f) where the claim is founded on a judicial act which is alleged to have infringed a Convention right of the party as provided by section 9 of the Human Rights Act 1998, the judicial act complained of and the court or tribunal which is alleged to have made it.

(The practice direction to Part 19 provides for notice to be given and parties joined in the circumstances referred to in (c), (d) and (f).)

15.2 A party who seeks to amend his statement of case to include the matters referred to in paragraph 15.1 must, unless the court orders otherwise, do so as soon as possible.

(Part 17 provides for the amendment of a statement of case.)'

Practice Direction 19A – Addition and substitution of parties

6.3B

'THIS PRACTICE DIRECTION SUPPLEMENTS CPR PART 19

A party applying for an amendment will usually be responsible for the costs of and arising from the amendment.

HUMAN RIGHTS, JOINING THE CROWN

Section 4 of the Human Rights Act 1998

6.1 Where a party has included in his statement of case–
(1) a claim for a declaration of incompatibility in accordance with section 4 of the Human Rights Act 1998, or
(2) an issue for the court to decide which may lead to the court considering making a declaration,

then the court may at any time consider whether notice should be given to the Crown as required by that Act and give directions for the content and service of the notice. The rule allows a period of 21 days before the court will make the declaration but the court may vary this period of time.

6.2 The court will normally consider the issues and give the directions referred to in paragraph 6.1 at the case management conference.

6.3 Where a party amends his statement of case to include any matter referred to in paragraph 6.1, then the court will consider whether notice should be given to the Crown and give directions for the content and service of the notice.

(The practice direction to CPR Part 16 requires a party to include issues under the Human Rights Act 1998 in his statement of case.)

6.4 The notice given under rule 19.4A must be served on the person named in the list published under section 17 of the Crown Proceedings Act 1947.

(The list, made by the Minister for the Civil Service, is annexed to this practice direction.)

The notice will be in the form directed by the court but will normally include the directions given by the court and all the statements of case in the claim. The notice will also be served on all the parties.

The court may require the parties to assist in the preparation of the notice.

In the circumstances described in the National Assembly for Wales (Transfer of Functions)(No. 2) Order 2000 the notice must also be served on the National Assembly for Wales.

(Section 5(3) of the Human Rights Act 1998 provides that the Crown may give notice that it intends to become a party at any stage in the proceedings once notice has been given.)

6.5 Unless the court orders otherwise, the Minister or other person permitted by the Human Rights Act 1998 to be joined as a party must, if he wishes to be joined, give notice of his intention to be joined as a party to the court and every other party. Where the Minister has nominated a person to be joined as a party the notice must be accompanied by the written nomination.

(Section 5(2)(a) of the Human Rights Act 1998 permits a person nominated by a Minister of the Crown to be joined as a party. The nomination may be signed on behalf of the Minister.)

Section 9 of the Human Rights Act 1998

6.6 The procedure in paragraphs 6.1 to 6.5 also applies where a claim is made under sections 7(1)(a) and 9(3) of the Human Rights Act 1998 for damages in respect of a judicial act.

Notice must be given to the Lord Chancellor and should be served on the Treasury Solicitor on his behalf, except where the judicial act is of a Court-Martial when the appropriate person is the Secretary of State for Defence and the notice must be served on the Treasury Solicitor on his behalf.

The notice will also give details of the judicial act, which is the subject of the claim for damages, and of the court or tribunal that made it.

(Section 9(4) of the Human Rights Act 1998 provides that no award of damages may be made against the Crown as provided for in section 9(3) unless the appropriate person is joined in the proceedings. The appropriate person is the Minister responsible for the court concerned or a person or department nominated by him (section 9(5) of the Act).)

Annex

List of Authorised Government Departments

6.3C

Authorised Government Departments
Solicitors and Addresses For Service
Advisory, Conciliation and Arbitration Service
Assets Recovery Agency
Board of Trade
Building Societies Commission
Cabinet Office
Central Office of Information
Crown Prosecution Service
Department for Constitutional Affairs
Department for Culture, Media and Sport
Department for Education and Skills
Department for International Development
Department for Transport
Department of Trade and Industry
Director General of Telecommunications
Export Credits Guarantee Department
Foreign and Commonwealth Office
Government Actuary's Department
Health and Safety Executive
Her Majesty's Chief Inspector of Schools in England
Her Majesty's Chief Inspector of Schools in Wales
Her Majesty's Treasury
Home Office
Lord Chancellor's Department
Ministry of Defence
National Savings and Investments
Northern Ireland Office
Office for National Statistics
Office of Fair Trading
Office of the Deputy Prime Minister
Ordnance Survey
Privy Council Office
Public Record Office

Public Works Loan Board
The Rail Regulator
Royal Mint
Serious Fraud Office
Wales Office (Office of the Secretary of State for Wales) (see Note (3))
The Treasury Solicitor, Queen Anne's Chambers, 28 Broadway, Westminster, London SW1H 9IS. (See Notes (1) and (2).)
Commissioners of Customs and Excise – The Solicitor for the Customs and Excise, New King's Beam House, 22 Upper Ground, London SE1 9PJ.
Commissioners of Inland Revenue – The Solicitor of Inland Revenue, Somerset House, The Strand, London WC2R 1LB.
Crown Estate Commissioners – The Solicitor to the Crown Estate Commissioners, Crown Estate Office, 16 Carlton House Terrace, London SW1Y 5AH.
Department for Environment, Food and Rural Affairs – (see Note (3)).
Forestry Commissioners.
The Solicitor to the Department for Environment, Food and Rural Affairs – Nobel House, 17 Smith Square, London SW1P 3IR.
Department of Health
Department for Work and Pensions.
Food Standards Agency.
The Solicitor to the Department for Work and Pensions and the Department of Health – New Court, 48 Carey Street, London WC2A 2LS.
Director General of Water Services.
Head of Legal Services.
The Office of Water Services – Centre City Tower, 7 Hill Street, Birmingham B5 4UA.
Gas and Electricity Markets Authority.
General Counsel – Office of Gas and Electricity Markets, 9 Millbank, London SW1P 3GE.
National Assembly for Wales.
The Counsel General to the National Assembly for Wales – Cathays Park, Cardiff CF10 3NG.
Postal Services Commission.
The Chief Legal Adviser – Postal Services Commission, Hercules House, 6 Hercules Road, London SE1 7DB.'

Extension of time for filing appellant's notice

6.4 Where it is not possible to file an appellant's notice in time then an application for an extension of time should be included in Section 10 of the appellant's notice. The time limit for filing an appellant's notice is 14 days

(CPR 52.4) except where the appellant is applying for permission to appeal against the refusal by the High Court to grant permission to apply for judicial review when the time limit is seven days (CPR 52.15). See CPR PD paras 5.19 and 5.20. The time limit of 14 days runs from the date of the decision of the lower court i.e. the date when the judge makes his decision and not the date when the order recording his decision is drawn up: *Sayers v Clarke Walker* [2002] EWCA Civ 645, [2002] 1 WLR 3095, [2002] 3 All ER 490. Time for appealing runs from the time the judgment is handed down in public. The formality of handing down the judgment in open court cannot be dispensed with, although the parties' attendance may be excused: *Owusu v Jackson (t/a Villa Holidays Ball-Inn Villas)* [2002] EWCA Civ 877, [2002] All ER (D) 130 (see **para A2.17**). The Court of Appeal will not accept a sealed copy of a judgment given by a lower court and practitioners should ensure that an order is drawn. See the notes in **para 4.3** of **Chapter 4** for orders.

Practice in Court of Appeal

6.5 Where permission to appeal has been granted or is not required but the appellant is unable to file his appellant's notice within the relevant time limit, the appellant should seek the respondent's views on the application for an extension of time. If the respondent has no objections to the application, the appellant should file a copy of the respondent's letter containing his views and the application may then be dealt with without a hearing by one of the deputy masters.

'5.19

Rule 52.4 sets out the procedure and time limits for filing and serving an appellant's notice. The appellant must file the appellant's notice at the appeal court within such period as may be directed by the lower court which should not normally exceed 28 days or, where the lower court directs no such period, within 14 days of the date of the decision that the appellant wishes to appeal.'

(Rule 52.15 sets out the time limit for filing an application for permission to appeal against the refusal of the High Court to grant permission to apply for judicial review.)

'5.20

Where the lower court judge announces his decision and reserves the reasons for his judgment or order until a later date, he should, in the exercise of powers under rule 52.4(2)(a), fix a period for filing the appellant's notice at the appeal court that takes this into account.

5.2

If an appellant requires an extension of time for filing his notice the application must be made in the appellant's notice. The notice should state the reason for the delay and the steps taken prior to the application being made.

5.3

Where the appellant's notice includes an application for an extension of time and permission to appeal has been given or is not required the respondent has the right to be heard on that application. He must be served with a copy of the appeal bundle (see paragraph 5.6A). However, a respondent who unreasonably opposes an extension of time runs the risk of being ordered to pay the appellant's costs of that application.

5.4

If an extension of time is given following such an application the procedure at paragraphs 6.1 to 6.6 applies.'

Applications

6.6 An application which the appellant wishes to make may be included in Section 10 of the appellant's notice or in a separate application notice in Form N244. Any application made should be fully supported by a witness statement or affidavit. Failure to do so may delay the issue of the appellant's notice.

'**5.5**

Notice of an application to be made to the appeal court for a remedy incidental to the appeal (e.g. an interim remedy under rule 25.1 or an order for security for costs) may be included in the appeal notice or in a Part 23 application notice.

(Rule 25.15 deals with security for costs of an appeal.)

(Paragraph 11 of this practice direction contains other provisions relating to applications.)

11.1

Where a party to an appeal makes an application whether in an appeal notice or by Part 23 application notice, the provisions of Part 23 will apply.

11.2

The applicant must file the following documents with the notice:
(1) one additional copy of the application notice for the appeal court and one copy for each of the respondents;
(2) where applicable a sealed copy of the order which is the subject of the main appeal;
(3) a bundle of documents in support which should include:
 (a) the Part 23 application notice; and
 (b) any witness statements and affidavits filed in support of the application notice.'

APPELLANT'S DOCUMENTS

Documents to be filed with the appellant's notice

6.7 Paragraphs 5.6 and 5.6A specify the documents which are to be filed with an appellant's notice. There are special provisions relating to the appeal bundle.

Court of Appeal

6.8 Paragraphs 5.6 and 5.6A apply where an appellant's notice is filed in the Court of Appeal but there are additional requirements where an appellant appeals to the Court of Appeal.
(1) Special provisions apply to the preparation of the appeal bundle, see para 15.4.
(2) The Civil Appeals Office will ask the appellant to provide a copy of the order allocating the claim to the multi track where the appellant asserts the Court of Appeal has jurisdiction to issue the appellant's notice on the basis that the order being appealed is a final decision in a claim allocated to the multi track. See **Chapter 3** for an explanation of the routes of appeal.
(3) The Court of Appeal does not serve documents. A party is required to effect service himself.

'**15.1(1)**

The documents relevant to proceedings in the Court of Appeal, Civil Division must be filed in the Civil Appeals Office Registry, Room E307, Royal Courts of Justice, Strand, London, WC2A 2LL.

(2)

The Civil Appeals Office will not serve documents and where service is required by the CPR or this practice direction it must be effected by the parties.'

Small claims

6.9 Special provisions also apply in order to reduce costs where the appeal relates to a claim allocated to the small claims track and is being heard in a county court or the High Court (see para 5.8). In all other cases the documents to be filed are specified in paragraph 5.6.

Orders

6.10 See the notes in **para 4.3** of **Chapter 4**.

References to Part 36 payments and offers

6.11 The fact that a Part 36 offer or a Part 36 payment has been made must not be disclosed to any judge of the appeal court which is to hear or determine an appeal or an application for permission to appeal until all questions (other than costs) have been determined: CPR 52.12. This provision does not apply if the Part 36 offer or payment is relevant to the substance of the appeal and does not prevent disclosure in any application in the appeal proceedings if disclosure of the fact that an offer or payment has been made is properly relevant to the matter to be decided. Care must, therefore, be taken to ensure that references to an offer or a payment are removed from the documents filed in support of an appellant's notice or in the appeal bundle.

The practice in the Court of Appeal is to require the solicitor to certify that the removal of references to Part 36 offers and payments is unnecessary because CPR 52.12(2) or (3) applies. See paras 11 and 20 of Dyson LJ's judgment in *Garratt v Saxby* [2004] EWCA Civ 341, 148 Sol Jo LB 237. See **Chapter 4 at para 4.86** for guidance where the disclosure of a Part 36 offer or payment makes a fair trial impossible and whether justice demands that the judge should recuse himself.

Documents to be filed

6.12

'5.6(1)

This paragraph applies to every case except where the appeal–

(a) relates to a claim allocated to the small claims track; and
(b) is being heard in a county court or the High Court.

(Paragraph 5.8 applies where this paragraph does not apply.)

(2)

The appellant must file the following documents together with an appeal bundle (see paragraph 5.6A) with his appellant's notice–
(a) two additional copies of the appellant's notice for the appeal court; and
(b) one copy of the appellant's notice for each of the respondents;
(c) one copy of his skeleton argument for each copy of the appellant's notice that is filed (see paragraph 5.9);
(d) a sealed copy of the order being appealed;
(e) a copy of any order giving or refusing permission to appeal, together with a copy of the judge's reasons for allowing or refusing permission to appeal;
(f) any witness statements or affidavits in support of any application included in the appellant's notice.'

The appeal bundle

6.13 The appeal bundle must include those documents which are necessary to enable the appeal court to decide whether to grant permission to appeal and to determine the appeal. Documents which are extraneous to the issues must be excluded and only those documents which are directly relevant to the subject matter of the appeal should be included. The appellant's legal representative must certify that these requirements have been satisfied. There are additional requirements for bundles in the Court of Appeal.

'5.6A(1)

An appellant must include in his appeal bundle the following documents:
(a) a sealed copy of the appellant's notice;
(b) a sealed copy of the order being appealed;
(c) a copy of any order giving or refusing permission to appeal, together with a copy of the judge's reasons for allowing or refusing permission to appeal;
(d) any affidavit or witness statement filed in support of any application included in the appellant's notice;
(e) a copy of his skeleton argument;
(f) a transcript or note of judgment (see paragraph 5.12), and in cases where permission to appeal was given by the lower court or is not

required those parts of any transcript of evidence which are directly relevant to any question at issue on the appeal;
(g) the claim form and statements of case (where relevant to the subject of the appeal);
(h) any application notice (or case management documentation) relevant to the subject of the appeal;
(i) in cases where the decision appealed was itself made on appeal (eg from district judge to circuit judge), the first order, the reasons given and the appellant's notice used to appeal from that order;
(j) in the case of judicial review or a statutory appeal, the original decision which was the subject of the application to the lower court;
(k) in cases where the appeal is from a Tribunal, a copy of the Tribunal's reasons for the decision, a copy of the decision reviewed by the Tribunal and the reasons for the original decision and any document filed with the Tribunal setting out the grounds of appeal from that decision;
(l) any other documents which the appellant reasonably considers necessary to enable the appeal court to reach its decision on the hearing of the application or appeal; and
(m) such other documents as the court may direct.

(2)

All documents that are extraneous to the issues to be considered on the application or the appeal must be excluded. The appeal bundle may include affidavits, witness statements, summaries, experts' reports and exhibits but only where these are directly relevant to the subject matter of the appeal.

(3)

Where the appellant is represented, the appeal bundle must contain a certificate signed by his solicitor, counsel or other representative to the effect that he has read and understood paragraph (2) above and that the composition of the appeal bundle complies with it.

5.7

Where it is not possible to file all the above documents, the appellant must indicate which documents have not yet been filed and the reasons why they are not currently available. The appellant must then provide a reasonable estimate of when the missing document or documents can be filed and file them as soon as reasonably practicable.

Special provisions relating to bundles for the Court of Appeal

15.4

The provisions of this paragraph apply to the preparation of appeal bundles, supplemental respondents' bundles where the parties are unable to agree amendments to the appeal bundle, and core bundles.

(1) **Rejection of bundles.**

Where documents are copied unnecessarily or bundled incompletely, costs may be disallowed. Where the provisions of this Practice Direction as to the preparation or delivery of bundles are not followed the bundle may be rejected by the court or be made the subject of a special costs order.

(2) **Avoidance of duplication.**

No more than one copy of any document should be included unless there is a good reason for doing otherwise (such as the use of a separate core bundle – see paragraph 15.2).

(3) **Pagination**
- (a) Bundles must be paginated, each page being numbered individually and consecutively. The pagination used at trial must also be indicated. Letters and other documents should normally be included in chronological order. (An exception to consecutive page numbering arises in the case of core bundles where it may be preferable to retain the original numbering).
- (b) Page numbers should be inserted in bold figures at the bottom of the page and in a form that can be clearly distinguished from any other pagination on the document.

(4) **Format and presentation**
- (a) Where possible the documents should be in A4 format. Where a document has be read across rather than down the page, it should be so placed in the bundle as to ensure that the text starts nearest the spine.
- (b) Where any marking or writing in colour on a document is important, the document must be copied in colour or marked up correctly in colour.
- (c) Documents which are not easily legible should be transcribed and the transcription marked and placed adjacent to the document transcribed.
- (d) Documents in a foreign language should be translated and the

(e) The size of any bundle should be tailored to its contents. A large lever arch file should not be used for just a few pages nor should files of whatever size be overloaded.

(f) Where it will assist the Court of Appeal, different sections of the file may be separated by cardboard or other tabbed dividers so long as these are clearly indexed. Where, for example, a document is awaited when the appeal bundle is filed, a single sheet of paper can be inserted after a divider, indicating the nature of the document awaited. For example, "Transcript of evidence of Mr J Smith (to follow)".

(5) **Binding**

(a) All documents, with the exception of transcripts, must be bound together. This may be in a lever arch file, ring binder or plastic folder. Plastic sleeves containing loose documents must not be used. Binders and files must be strong enough to withstand heavy use.

(b) Large documents such as plans should be placed in an easily accessible file. Large documents which will need to be opened up frequently should be inserted in a file larger than A4 size.

(6) **Indices and labels**

(a) An index must be included at the front of the bundle listing all the documents and providing the page references for each. In the case of documents such as letters, invoices or bank statements, they may be given a general description.

(b) Where the bundles consist of more than one file, an index to all the files should be included in the first file and an index included for each file. Indices should, if possible, be on a single sheet. The full name of the case should not be inserted on the index if this would waste space. Documents should be identified briefly but properly.

(7) **Identification**

(a) Every bundle must be clearly identified, on the spine and on the front cover, with the name of the case and the Court of Appeal's reference. Where the bundle consists of more than one file, each file must be numbered on the spine, the front cover and the inside of the front cover.

(b) Outer labels should use large lettering e g "Appeal Bundle A" or

"Core Bundle". The full title of the appeal and solicitors' names and addresses should be omitted. A label should be used on the front as well as on the spine.

(8) **Staples etc.**

All staples, heavy metal clips etc, must be removed.

(9) **Statements of case**
(a) Statements of case should be assembled in "chapter" form – ie claim followed by particulars of claim, followed by further information, irrespective of date.
(b) Redundant documents, eg particulars of claim overtaken by amendments, requests for further information recited in the answers given, should generally be excluded.

(10) **New documents**
(a) Before a new document is introduced into bundles which have already been delivered to the court, steps should be taken to ensure that it carries an appropriate bundle/page number so that it can be added to the court documents. It should not be stapled and it should be prepared with punch holes for immediate inclusion in the binders in use.
(b) If it is expected that a large number of miscellaneous new documents will from time to time be introduced, there should be a special tabbed empty loose-leaf file for that purpose. An index should be produced for this file, updated as necessary.

(11) **Inter-solicitor correspondence**

Since inter-solicitor correspondence is unlikely to be required for the purposes of an appeal, only those letters which will need to be referred to should be copied.

(12) **Sanctions for non-compliance**

If the appellant fails to comply with the requirements as to the provision of bundles of documents, the application or appeal will be referred for consideration to be given as to why it should not be dismissed for failure to so comply.'

Documents to be filed in small claims appeals heard in a county court or the High Court

6.14

'5.8(1)

This paragraph applies where–

(a) the appeal relates to a claim allocated to the small claims track; and
(b) the appeal is being heard in a county court or the High Court.

(2)

The appellant must file the following documents with his appellant's notice–
(a) a sealed copy of the order being appealed; and
(b) any order giving or refusing permission to appeal, together with a copy of the reasons for that decision.

(3)

The appellant may, if relevant to the issues to be determined on the appeal, file any other document listed in paragraph 5.6 or 5.6A in addition to the documents referred to in sub-paragraph (2).

(4)

The appellant need not file a record of the reasons for judgment of the lower court with his appellant's notice unless sub-paragraph (5) applies.

(5)

The court may order a suitable record of the reasons for judgment of the lower court (see paragraph 5.12) to be filed–
(a) to enable it to decide if permission should be granted; or
(b) if permission is granted to enable it to decide the appeal.'

SKELETON ARGUMENTS

6.15 An appellant is required to file a skeleton argument in support of his appellant's notice except where he is not represented. Specific provision is made for the content of skeleton arguments by CPR PD 52 para 5.10.

'**5.9(1)**

The appellant's notice must, subject to (2) and (3) below, be accompanied by a skeleton argument. Alternatively the skeleton argument may be included in the appellant's notice. Where the skeleton argument is so included it will not form part of the notice for the purposes of rule 52.8.

(2)

Where it is impracticable for the appellant's skeleton argument to accompany the appellant's notice it must be filed and served on all respondents within 14 days of filing the notice.

(3)

An appellant who is not represented need not file a skeleton argument but is encouraged to do so since this will be helpful to the court.'

Content of skeleton arguments

6.16

'5.10(1)

A skeleton argument must contain a numbered list of the points which the party wishes to make. These should both define and confine the areas of controversy. Each point should be stated as concisely as the nature of the case allows.

(2)

A numbered point must be followed by a reference to any document on which the party wishes to rely.

(3)

A skeleton argument must state, in respect of each authority cited–
(a)   the proposition of law that the authority demonstrates; and
(b)   the parts of the authority (identified by page or paragraph references) that support the proposition.

(4)

If more than one authority is cited in support of a given proposition, the skeleton argument must briefly state the reason for taking that course.

(5)

The statement referred to in sub-paragraph (4) should not materially add to the length of the skeleton argument but should be sufficient to demonstrate, in the context of the argument–
(a)   the relevance of the authority or authorities to that argument; and

(b) that the citation is necessary for a proper presentation of that argument.

(6)

The cost of preparing a skeleton argument which–
(a) does not comply with the requirements set out in this paragraph; or
(b) was not filed within the time limits provided by this Practice Direction (or any further time granted by the court),

will not be allowed on assessment except to the extent that the court otherwise directs.

5.11

The appellant should consider what other information the appeal court will need. This may include a list of persons who feature in the case or glossaries of technical terms. A chronology of relevant events will be necessary in most appeals.'

TRANSCRIPTS OF JUDGMENT

Suitable record of the judgment

6.17 The appeal bundle must include a suitable record of the reasons given for the order being appealed. An official copy of the transcript of judgment should be provided unless this is not possible. The importance of placing an early order for the transcript of judgment cannot be over-emphasised. Practitioners should also check in a lengthy trial that the proceedings are being recorded. In the county courts a request for a transcript should be made on Form Ex 107. In the Royal Courts of Justice requests should be made to the Mechanical Recording Department. Transcripts of evidence are generally not needed for the purpose of determining an application for permission to appeal: CPR PD 52 para 5.15.

'5.12

Where the judgment to be appealed has been officially recorded by the court, an approved transcript of that record should accompany the appellant's notice. Photocopies will not be accepted for this purpose. However, where there is no officially recorded judgment, the following documents will be acceptable:

Written judgments
(1) Where the judgment was made in writing a copy of that judgment endorsed with the judge's signature.

Note of judgment
(2) When judgment was not officially recorded or made in writing a note of the judgment (agreed between the appellant's and respondent's advocates) should be submitted for approval to the judge whose decision is being appealed. If the parties cannot agree on a single note of the judgment, both versions should be provided to that judge with an explanatory letter. For the purpose of an application for permission to appeal the note need not be approved by the respondent or the lower court judge.

Advocates' notes of judgments where the appellant is unrepresented
(3) When the appellant was unrepresented in the lower court it is the duty of any advocate for the respondent to make his/her note of judgment promptly available, free of charge to the appellant where there is no officially recorded judgment or if the court so directs. Where the appellant was represented in the lower court it is the duty of his/her own former advocate to make his/her note available in these circumstances. The appellant should submit the note of judgment to the appeal court.

Reasons for judgment in Tribunal cases
(4) A sealed copy of the Tribunal's reasons for the decision.

5.13
An appellant may not be able to obtain an official transcript or other suitable record of the lower court's decision within the time within which the appellant's notice must be filed. In such cases the appellant's notice must still be completed to the best of the appellant's ability on the basis of the documentation available. However it may be amended subsequently with the permission of the appeal court.

Advocates' notes of judgments

5.14
Advocates' brief (or, where appropriate, refresher) fee includes:
(1) remuneration for taking a note of the judgment of the court;
(2) having the note transcribed accurately;
(3) attempting to agree the note with the other side if represented;
(4) submitting the note to the judge for approval where appropriate;

(5) revising it if so requested by the judge;
(6) providing any copies required for the appeal court, instructing solicitors and lay client; and
(7) providing a copy of his note to an unrepresented appellant.

Transcripts or Notes of Evidence

5.15

When the evidence is relevant to the appeal an official transcript of the relevant evidence must be obtained. Transcripts or notes of evidence are generally not needed for the purpose of determining an application for permission to appeal.

Notes of evidence

5.16

If evidence relevant to the appeal was not officially recorded, a typed version of the judge's notes of evidence must be obtained.

Transcripts at public expense

5.17

Where the lower court or the appeal court is satisfied that an unrepresented appellant is in such poor financial circumstances that the cost of a transcript would be an excessive burden the court may certify that the cost of obtaining one official transcript should be borne at public expense.

5.18

In the case of a request for an official transcript of evidence or proceedings to be paid for at public expense, the court must also be satisfied that there are reasonable grounds for appeal. Whenever possible a request for a transcript at public expense should be made to the lower court when asking for permission to appeal.'

SERVICE OF THE APPELLANT'S NOTICE

6.18 The appellant's notice must be served on all the respondents in every case unless the appeal court dispenses with service. The appellant is required to file a certificate of service. It is not necessary to serve the appeal bundle when the appellant is applying only for permission to appeal.

'**5.21(1)**

Except where the appeal court orders otherwise a sealed copy of the appellant's notice, including any skeleton arguments must be served on all respondents in accordance with the timetable prescribed by rule 52.4(3) except where this requirement is modified by paragraph 5.9(2) in which case the skeleton argument should be served as soon as it is filed.

(2)

The appellant must, as soon as practicable, file a certificate of service of the documents referred to in paragraph (1).

5.22

Unless the court otherwise directs a respondent need not take any action when served with an appellant's notice until such time as notification is given to him that permission to appeal has been given.

5.23

The court may dispense with the requirement for service of the notice on a respondent. Any application notice seeking an order under rule 6.9 to dispense with service should set out the reasons relied on and be verified by a statement of truth.

5.24(1)

Where the appellant is applying for permission to appeal in his appellant's notice, he must serve on the respondents his appellant's notice and skeleton argument (but not the appeal bundle), unless the appeal court directs otherwise.

(2)

Where permission to appeal–
(a)   has been given by the lower court; or
(b)   is not required,

the appellant must serve the appeal bundle on the respondents with the appellant's notice.'

AMENDMENT OF APPEAL NOTICE

6.19 In the Court of Appeal a formal application in Form N244 is not required where an appellant seeks permission to amend an appellant's notice applying for permission to appeal. An unopposed application will be dealt with on paper by one of the deputy masters. An order will be drawn to record the fact that permission to amend has been granted. The amended appellant's notice will be sealed and the appellant will be instructed to serve the amended notice on the respondent.

'**5.25**

An appeal notice may be amended with permission. Such an application to amend and any application in opposition will normally be dealt with at the hearing unless that course would cause unnecessary expense or delay in which case a request should be made for the application to amend to be heard in advance.'

APPLICATIONS FOR PERMISSION TO APPEAL

Refusal of permission to appeal without a hearing

6.20 Where permission to appeal is refused without a hearing, the appellant may request that the decision is reconsidered at an oral hearing. The request must be filed within seven days after service of the notice (order) that permission has been refused and a copy of the request must be served on the respondent. When such a request is made, the appellant must file a brief statement dealing with the matters specified in para 4.14A. An appellant who is publicly funded must inform the Legal Services Commission of the reasons given for the refusal of permission and confirm that he has done so in the statement required by para 4.14A. The statement must be filed at least four days before the oral hearing and a copy should be served on the respondent.

'**4.11**

Applications for permission to appeal may be considered by the appeal court without a hearing.

4.12

If permission is granted without a hearing the parties will be notified of that decision and the procedure in paragraphs 6.1 to 6.6 will then apply.

4.13

If permission is refused without a hearing the parties will be notified of that decision with the reasons for it. The decision is subject to the appellant's right to have it reconsidered at an oral hearing. This may be before the same judge.

4.14

A request for the decision to be reconsidered at an oral hearing must be filed at the appeal court within 7 days after service of the notice that permission has been refused. A copy of the request must be served by the appellant on the respondent at the same time.

4.14A

(1)

This paragraph applies where an appellant, who is represented, makes a request for a decision to be reconsidered at an oral hearing.

(2)

The appellant's advocate must, at least 4 days before the hearing, in a brief written statement–
(a)   inform the court and the respondent of the points which he proposes to raise at the hearing;
(b)   set out his reasons why permission should be granted notwithstanding the reasons given for the refusal of permission; and
(c)   confirm, where applicable, that the requirements of paragraph 4.17 have been complied with (appellant in receipt of services funded by the Legal Services Commission).

4.15

Notice of a permission hearing will be given to the respondent but he is not required to attend unless the court requests him to do so..

4.16

If the court requests the respondent's attendance at the permission hearing the appellant must supply the respondent with a copy of the appeal bundle (see paragraph 5.6A) within 7 days of being notified of the request , or such other period as the court may direct. The costs of providing that bundle shall be borne by the appellant initially, but will form part of the costs of the permission application.'

Appellants in receipt of services funded by the Legal Services Commission applying for permission to appeal

6.21

'4.17

Where the appellant is in receipt of services funded by the Legal Services Commission (or legally aided) and permission to appeal has been refused by the appeal court without a hearing, the appellant must send a copy of the reasons the appeal court gave for refusing permission to the relevant office of the Legal Services Commission as soon as it has been received from the court. The court will require confirmation that this has been done if a hearing is requested to re-consider the question of permission.'

Limited permission

6.22 Permission to appeal may be limited to certain grounds or issues. Where the court reserves the question of permission on remaining issues (under paragraph 4.18(2)), the appellant must, within 14 days after service of the court's order, inform the appeal court and the respondent in writing whether he intends to pursue the reserved issues. Where reserved issues are to be pursued, the parties must include in any time estimate for the appeal hearing, their time estimate for the reserved issues. Where permission to appeal has been refused on a particular issue, the appellant must remove from the appeal bundle all documents that are relevant only to that issue: CPR PD 52 para 6.3A(2).

'**4.18**

Where a court under rule 52.3(7) gives permission to appeal on some issues only, it will–
(1) refuse permission on any remaining issues; or
(2) reserve the question of permission to appeal on any remaining issues to the court hearing the appeal.

4.19

If the court reserves the question of permission under paragraph 4.18(2), the appellant must, within 14 days after service of the court's order, inform the appeal court and the respondent in writing whether he intends to pursue the reserved issues. If the appellant does intend to pursue the reserved issues, the parties must include in any time estimate for the appeal hearing, their time estimate for the reserved issues.

4.20

If the appeal court refuses permission to appeal on the remaining issues without a hearing and the applicant wishes to have that decision reconsidered at an oral hearing, the time limit in rule 52.3(5) shall apply. Any application for an extension of this time limit should be made promptly. The court hearing the appeal on the issues for which permission has been granted will not normally grant, at the appeal hearing, an application to extend the time limit in rule 52.3(5) for the remaining issues.

4.21

If the appeal court refuses permission to appeal on remaining issues at or after an oral hearing, the application for permission to appeal on those issues cannot be renewed at the appeal hearing. See section 54(4) of the Access to Justice Act 1999.'

RESPONDENT'S SUBMISSIONS ON APPLICATION FOR PERMISSION TO APPEAL

Respondents' costs of permission applications

6.23 Although a respondent has to be served with an appellant's notice and skeleton argument when an appellant seeks permission to appeal, he is not required to take any action until he is notified that permission to appeal has been granted (see para 5.22). A respondent's submissions at the permission stage should be addressed to the point that the relevant threshold test (in CPR 52.3(6) or CPR 52.13(2)) is not met or that there is an inaccuracy in the papers placed before the court which might reasonably be expected to lead the court to grant permission to appeal when it would not otherwise have done so: *Jolly v Jay* [2002] EWCA Civ 277, (2002) The Times 3 April (see **para A2.13**) in the Appendix. Any submissions which the respondent volunteers should be served on the appellant.

'**4.22**

In most cases, applications for permission to appeal will be determined without the court requesting–
(1) submissions from, or
(2) if there is an oral hearing, attendance
by the respondent.

4.23

Where the court does not request submissions from or attendance by the respondent, costs will not normally be allowed to a respondent who volunteers submissions or attendance.

4.24

Where the court does request–
(1) submissions from; or
(2) attendance by the respondent,
the court will normally allow the respondent his costs if permission is refused.'

DOCUMENTS FOR THE APPEAL HEARING

6.24 Further steps are necessary to ensure that the appeal court has the necessary documents in order for it to determine the appeal.

Service of the appeal bundle

'6.2

If the appeal court gives permission to appeal, the appeal bundle must be served on each of the respondents within 7 days of receiving the order giving permission to appeal.

(Part 6 (service of documents) provides rules on service.)

6.3

The appeal court will send the parties–
(1) notification of–
 (a) the date of the hearing or the period of time (the "listing window") during which the appeal is likely to be heard; and
 (b) in the Court of Appeal, the date by which the appeal will be heard (the "hear by date");
(2) where permission is granted by the appeal court a copy of the order giving permission to appeal; and
(3) any other directions given by the court.'

Appeal Questionnaire in the Court of Appeal

6.25 In the Court of Appeal the appellant has to file an appeal questionnaire. It is on this document that the appeal fee will be paid.

'6.4

The Court of Appeal will send an Appeal Questionnaire to the appellant when it notifies him of the matters referred to in paragraph 6.3.

6.5

The appellant must complete and file the Appeal Questionnaire within 14 days of the date of the letter of notification of the matters in paragraph 6.3. The Appeal Questionnaire must contain:
(1) if the appellant is legally represented, the advocate's time estimate for the hearing of the appeal;

(2) where a transcript of evidence is relevant to the appeal, confirmation as to what parts of a transcript of evidence have been ordered where this is not already in the bundle of documents;
(3) confirmation that copies of the appeal bundle are being prepared and will be held ready for the use of the Court of Appeal and an undertaking that they will be supplied to the court on request. For the purpose of these bundles photocopies of the transcripts will be accepted;
(4) confirmation that copies of the Appeal Questionnaire and the appeal bundle have been served on the respondents and the date of that service.'

Time estimates

6.26

'6.6

The time estimate included in an Appeal Questionnaire must be that of the advocate who will argue the appeal. It should exclude the time required by the court to give judgment. If the respondent disagrees with the time estimate, the respondent must inform the court within 7 days of receipt of the Appeal Questionnaire. In the absence of such notification the respondent will be deemed to have accepted the estimate proposed on behalf of the appellant.'

Revision of the appeal bundle

6.27

In many cases the appeal bundle will have been prepared for the purpose of seeking permission to appeal. Once permission has been granted, additional documents will be required for the appeal hearing. The parties should make every attempt to agree the amendments which are required to the appeal bundle. Only if the parties are unable to agree should the respondent file a bundle of his own.

'6.3A(1)

Where the appeal court grants permission to appeal, the appellant must add the following documents to the appeal bundle–
(a) the respondent's notice and skeleton argument (if any);
(b) those parts of the transcripts of evidence which are directly relevant to any question at issue on the appeal;

(c) the order granting permission to appeal and, where permission to appeal was granted at an oral hearing, the transcript (or note) of any judgment which was given; and

(d) any document which the appellant and respondent have agreed to add to the appeal bundle in accordance with paragraph 7.11.

(2)

Where permission to appeal has been refused on a particular issue, the appellant must remove from the appeal bundle all documents that are relevant only to that issue.'

Core Bundles in the Court of Appeal

6.28 Where the appeal bundle for an appeal hearing in the Court of Appeal comprises more than 500 pages, a core bundle of the central documents must be prepared and filed.

'**15.2**

In cases where the appeal bundle comprises more than 500 pages, exclusive of transcripts, the appellant's solicitors must, after consultation with the respondent's solicitors, also prepare and file with the court, in addition to copies of the appeal bundle (as amended in accordance with paragraph 7.11) the requisite number of copies of a core bundle.

15.3
(1) The core bundle must be filed within 28 days of receipt of the order giving permission to appeal or, where permission to appeal was granted by the lower court or is not required, within 28 days of the date of service of the appellant's notice on the respondent.
(2) The core bundle–
 (a) must contain the documents which are central to the appeal; and
 (b) must not exceed 150 pages.'

RESPONDENT'S NOTICES, SKELETON ARGUMENTS AND DOCUMENTS

Respondent's notice

6.29 The provisions relating to a respondent's notice are contained in CPR 52.5. In certain cases the filing of a notice in Form N162 is mandatory. A respondent must file a skeleton argument for the court in all cases where he proposes to address arguments to the court. The provisions in para 5.10 relating to the content of skeleton arguments apply to respondents' skeletons. See below where a respondent to an appeal in the Court of Appeal is required to give notice of his intentions.

'7.1

A respondent who wishes to ask the appeal court to vary the order of the lower court in any way must appeal and permission will be required on the same basis as for an appellant.

(Paragraph 3.2 applies to grounds of appeal by a respondent.)

7.2

A respondent who wishes only to request that the appeal court upholds the judgment or order of the lower court whether for the reasons given in the lower court or otherwise does not make an appeal and does not therefore require permission to appeal in accordance with rule 52.3(1).

(Paragraph 7.6 requires a respondent to file a skeleton argument where he wishes to address the appeal court.)

7.3(1)

A respondent who wishes to appeal or who wishes to ask the appeal court to uphold the order of the lower court for reasons different from or additional to those given by the lower court must file a respondent's notice.

(2)

If the respondent does not file a respondent's notice, he will not be entitled, except with the permission of the court, to rely on any reason not relied on in the lower court.

7.3A

Paragraphs 5.1A, 5.1B and 5.2 of this practice direction (Human Rights and extension for time for filing appellant's notice) also apply to a respondent and a respondent's notice.'

Time limit for filing respondent's notice

6.30 Where it is not possible to file the notice in time the respondent should make an application for an extension of time in Section 9 of his respondent's notice. An extension of time cannot be granted prospectively.

Court of Appeal

6.31 A respondent should seek the appellant's views where he is unable to file his notice in time. If the appellant does not raise any objections to the late filing of the notice, the application for an extension of time may be dealt with without a hearing by one of the deputy masters.

'7.4

The time limits for filing a respondent's notice are set out in rule 52.5 (4) and (5).

7.5

Where an extension of time is required the extension must be requested in the respondent's notice and the reasons why the respondent failed to act within the specified time must be included.'

Skeleton arguments

6.32 The respondent may include his skeleton argument within his notice or it may be filed separately.

'7.6

Except where paragraph 7.7A applies, the respondent must file a skeleton argument for the court in all cases where he proposes to address arguments to the court. The respondent's skeleton argument may be included within a respondent's notice. Where a skeleton argument is included within a respondent's notice it will not form part of the notice for the purposes of rule 52.8.

7.7(1)

A respondent who–
(a)   files a respondent's notice; but
(b)   does not include his skeleton argument within that notice,

must file and serve his skeleton argument within 14 days of filing the notice.

(2)

A respondent who does not file a respondent's notice but who files a skeleton argument must file and serve that skeleton argument at least 7 days before the appeal hearing.

(Rule 52.5(4) sets out the period for filing and serving a respondent's notice.)

7.7A(1)

Where the appeal relates to a claim allocated to the small claims track and is being heard in a county court or the High Court, the respondent may file a skeleton argument but is not required to do so.

(2)

A respondent who is not represented need not file a skeleton argument but is encouraged to do so in order to assist the court.

7.7B

The respondent must–
(1)　serve his skeleton argument on–
　　(a)　the appellant; and
　　(b)　any other respondent,
　　at the same time as he files it at the court; and
(2)　file a certificate of service.'

Court of Appeal: Respondent to notify Civil Appeals Office whether he intends to file respondent's notice

6.33 A respondent to an appeal in the Court of Appeal is required to notify the Civil Appeals Office and the appellant of the course of action which he proposes to take. If he does not intend to file a respondent's notice and will file only a skeleton argument, he must file that document at least seven days before the appeal hearing.

'**15.6**

A respondent must, no later than 21 days after the date he is served with notification that–
(1)　permission to appeal has been granted; or
(2)　the application for permission to appeal and the appeal are to be heard together,
inform the Civil Appeals Office and the appellant in writing whether–
(a)　he proposes to file a respondent's notice appealing the order or seeking to uphold the order for reasons different from, or additional to, those given by the lower court; or
(b)　he proposes to rely on the reasons given by the lower court for its decision.

Respondent's notices, skeleton arguments and documents 219

(Paragraph 15.11B requires all documents needed for an appeal hearing, including a respondent's skeleton argument, to be filed at least 7 days before the hearing.)

Content of skeleton arguments

7.8

A respondent's skeleton argument must conform to the directions at paragraphs 5.10 and 5.11 with any necessary modifications. It should, where appropriate, answer the arguments set out in the appellant's skeleton argument.'

Applications within respondent's notices

6.34 The provisions of paras 5.5 and 11 apply to applications made by respondents.

'**7.9**

A respondent may include an application within a respondent's notice in accordance with paragraph 5.5 above.

11.1

Where a party to an appeal makes an application whether in an appeal notice or by Part 23 application notice, the provisions of Part 23 will apply.

11.2

The applicant must file the following documents with the notice–
(1)   one additional copy of the application notice for the appeal court and one copy for each of the respondents;
(2)   where applicable a sealed copy of the order which is the subject of the main appeal;
(3)   a bundle of documents in support which should include:
        (a)   the Part 23 application notice; and
        (b)   any witness statements and affidavits filed in support of the application notice.'

Documents to be filed with respondent's notices: skeleton arguments

6.35

'7.10(1)

The respondent must file the following documents with his respondent's notice in every case:
(a) two additional copies of the respondent's notice for the appeal court; and
(b) one copy each for the appellant and any other respondents.

(2)

The respondent may file a skeleton argument with his respondent's notice and–

(a) where he does so he must file two copies; and
(b) where he does not do so he must comply with paragraph 7.7.'

Respondent's supplemental bundle

6.36 Supplemental bundles are to be filed only if the parties are unable to agree amendments to the appeal bundle.

'7.11

If the respondent wishes to rely on any documents which he reasonably considers necessary to enable the appeal court to reach its decision on the appeal in addition to those filed by the appellant, he must make every effort to agree amendments to the appeal bundle with the appellant.

7.12
(1) If the representatives for the parties are unable to reach agreement, the respondent may prepare a supplemental bundle.
(2) If the respondent prepares a supplemental bundle he must file it, together with the requisite number of copies for the appeal court, at the appeal court–
  (a) with the respondent's notice; or
  (b) if a respondent's notice is not filed, within 21 days after he is served with the appeal bundle.'

Service of respondent's notice, skeleton argument and supplemental bundle

6.37

'7.13

The respondent must serve–
(1) the respondent's notice;
(2) his skeleton argument (if any); and
(3) the supplemental bundle (if any),

on–
(a) the appellant; and
(b) any other respondent,

at the same time as he files them at the court.'

SUMMARY ASSESSMENT OF COSTS

6.38 Costs may be assessed summarily in certain cases and the parties should submit schedules of costs in the usual way. See CPR Pt 44 and para 13 of the Practice Direction supplementing that Part.

'14.1

Costs are likely to be assessed by way of summary assessment at the following hearings:
(1) contested directions hearings;
(2) applications for permission to appeal at which the respondent is present;
(3) dismissal list hearings in the Court of Appeal at which the respondent is present;
(4) appeals from case management decisions; and
(5) appeals listed for one day or less.

14.2

Parties attending any of the hearings referred to in paragraph 14.1 should be prepared to deal with the summary assessment.'

APPEAL HEARINGS IN THE COURT OF APPEAL

Special provisions relating to the short-warned list

6.39 Where an appeal has been assigned to the short warned list, it may be called on for hearing at short notice. The court may abridge the time limits for providing additional bundles and the parties' solicitors must notify their advocate and their client that the appeal has been assigned to the list.

'**15.9**
(1) Where an appeal is assigned to the short-warned list, the Civil Appeals Office will notify the parties' solicitors in writing. The court may abridge the time for filing any outstanding bundles in an appeal assigned to this list.
(2) The solicitors for the parties must notify their advocate and their client as soon as the Civil Appeals Office notifies them that the appeal has been assigned to the short-warned list.
(3) The appellant may apply in writing for the appeal to be removed from the short-warned list within 14 days of notification of its assignment. The application will be decided by a Lord Justice, or the Master, and will only be granted for the most compelling reasons.
(4) The Civil Appeals Listing Officer may place an appeal from the short-warned list "on call" from a given date and will inform the parties' advocates accordingly.
(5) An appeal which is "on call" may be listed for hearing on half a day's notice or such longer period as the court may direct.
(6) Once an appeal is listed for hearing from the short-warned list it becomes the immediate professional duty of the advocate instructed in the appeal, if he is unable to appear at the hearing, to take all practicable measures to ensure that his lay client is represented at the hearing by an advocate who is fully instructed and able to argue the appeal.'

Special provisions relating to the special fixtures list

6.40 Where an appeal is assigned to the special fixtures list, special directions may be given about the documents to be provided.

'**15.9A**
(1) The special fixtures list is a sub-division of the appeals list and is used to deal with appeals that may require special listing arrangements, such as the need to list a number of cases before the same constitution, in a particular order, during a particular period or at a given location.
(2) The Civil Appeals Office will notify the parties' representatives, or the parties if acting in person, of the particular arrangements that will apply. The notice–

(a) will give details of the specific period during which a case is scheduled to be heard; and
(b) may give directions in relation to the filing of any outstanding documents.
(3) The listing officer will notify the parties' representatives of the precise hearing date as soon as practicable. While every effort will be made to accommodate the availability of counsel, the requirements of the court will prevail.'

Requests for directions

6.41 Requests for directions for appeal hearings in the Court of Appeal should not be sent directly to a member of the Court. Many directions will be given on paper to avoid the expense of a hearing. A formal application will seldom be required. Guidance should be sought from the relevant case management section.

'15.10

To ensure that all requests for directions are centrally monitored and correctly allocated, all requests for directions or rulings (whether relating to listing or any other matters) should be made to the Civil Appeals Office. Those seeking directions or rulings must not approach the supervising Lord Justice either directly, or via his or her clerk.'

Bundles of authorities for the Court of Appeal

6.42 Detailed guidance on bundles of authorities is provided by para 15.11. This provision includes part of the guidance given by the Practice Direction – Citation of Authorities [2001] 1 WLR 1002 but reference should be made to the PD where it is proposed to rely on authorities decided in other jurisdictions etc.

'15.11
(1) Once the parties have been notified of the date fixed for the hearing, the appellant's advocate must, after consultation with his opponent, file a bundle containing photocopies of the authorities upon which each side will rely at the hearing.
(2) The bundle of authorities should, in general–
  (a) have the relevant passages of the authorities marked;
  (b) not include authorities for propositions not in dispute; and
  (c) not contain more than 10 authorities unless the scale of the appeal warrants more extensive citation.

(3) The bundle of authorities must be filed–
  (a) at least 7 days before the hearing; or
  (b) where the period of notice of the hearing is less than 7 days, immediately.
(4) If, through some oversight, a party intends, during the hearing, to refer to other authorities the parties may agree a second agreed bundle. The appellant's advocate must file this bundle at least 48 hours before the hearing commences.
(5) A bundle of authorities must bear a certification by the advocates responsible for arguing the case that the requirements of sub-paragraphs (3) to (5) of paragraph 5.10 have been complied with in respect of each authority included.'

Supplementary skeleton arguments

6.43

'15.11A
(1) A supplementary skeleton argument on which the appellant wishes to rely must be filed at least 14 days before the hearing.
(2) A supplementary skeleton argument on which the respondent wishes to rely must be filed at least 7 days before the hearing.
(3) All supplementary skeleton arguments must comply with the requirements set out in paragraph 5.10.
(4) At the hearing the court may refuse to hear argument from a party not contained in a skeleton argument filed within the relevant time limit set out in this paragraph.'

Papers for the appeal hearing

6.44

'15.11B
(1) All the documents which are needed for the appeal hearing must be filed at least 7 days before the hearing. Where a document has not been filed 10 days before the hearing a reminder will be sent by the Civil Appeals Office.
(2) Any party who fails to comply with the provisions of paragraph (1) may be required to attend before the Presiding Lord Justice to seek permission to proceed with, or to oppose, the appeal.'

Availability of reserved judgments before hand down

6.45

'15.12

This section applies where the presiding Lord Justice is satisfied that the result of the appeal will attract no special degree of confidentiality or sensitivity.

15.13

A copy of the written judgment will be made available to the parties' legal advisers by 4 p.m. on the second working day before judgment is due to be pronounced or such other period as the court may direct. This can be shown, in confidence, to the parties but only for the purpose of obtaining instructions and on the strict understanding that the judgment, or its effect, is not to be disclosed to any other person. A working day is any day on which the Civil Appeals Office is open for business.

15.14

The appeal will be listed for judgment in the cause list and the judgment handed down at the appropriate time.'

Attendance of advocates on the handing down of a reserved judgment

6.46

'15.15

Where any consequential orders are agreed, the parties' advocates need not attend on the handing down of a reserved judgment. Where an advocate does attend the court may, if it considers such attendance unnecessary, disallow the costs of the attendance. If the parties do not indicate that they intend to attend, the judgment may be handed down by a single member of the court.'

Agreed orders following judgment

6.47

'15.16

The parties must, in respect of any draft agreed orders–

(a) fax a copy to the clerk to the presiding Lord Justice; and
(b) file four copies in the Civil Appeals Office,

no later than 12 noon on the working day before the judgment is handed down.

15.17

A copy of a draft order must bear the Court of Appeal case reference, the date the judgment is to be handed down and the name of the presiding Lord Justice.'

Corrections to the draft judgment

6.48

'15.18

Any proposed correction to the draft judgment should be sent to the clerk to the judge who prepared the draft with a copy to any other party.'

Application for leave to appeal

6.49

'15.19

Where a party wishes to apply for leave to appeal to the House of Lords under section 1 of the Administration of Justice (Appeals) Act 1934 the court may deal with the application on the basis of written submissions.

15.20

A party must, in relation to his submission–

(a) fax a copy to the clerk to the presiding Lord Justice; and
(b) file four copies in the Civil Appeals Office,

no later than 12 noon on the working day before the judgment is handed down.

15.21

A copy of a submission must bear the Court of Appeal case reference, the date the judgment is to be handed down and the name of the presiding Lord Justice.'

Disposal of bundles of documents

6.50

'15.11C
(1) Where the court has determined a case, the official transcriber will retain one set of papers. The Civil Appeals Office will destroy any remaining sets of papers not collected within 21 days of–
  (a) where one or more parties attend the hearing, the date of the court's decision;
  (b) where there is no attendance, the date of the notification of court's decision.
(2) The parties should ensure that bundles of papers supplied to the court do not contain original documents (other than transcripts). The parties must ensure that they–
  (a) bring any necessary original documents to the hearing; and
  (b) retrieve any original documents handed up to the court before leaving the court.
(3) The court will retain application bundles where permission to appeal has been granted. Where permission is refused the arrangements in sub-paragraph (1) will apply.
(4) Where a single Lord Justice has refused permission to appeal on paper, application bundles will not be destroyed until after the time limit for seeking a hearing has expired.'

DISPOSING OF APPLICATIONS OR APPEALS BY CONSENT

6.51 The documentation to be provided where the parties have reached a compromise depends on the nature of the matter before the appeal court and the consent order being requested. In the Court of Appeal standard forms are available for the dismissal of applications or appeals: see Forms 253, 254A and 254B in the Appendix. These forms may be adapted for use in the High Court and the county courts.

Where, however, the parties request that an appeal be allowed by consent, the requirements of para 13 must be satisfied.

In addition it is open to the parties to submit a Tomlin order for approval. Any such order submitted to the Court of Appeal should provide for any liberty to apply to be made to the court being appealed from.

The deputy masters in the Court of Appeal are empowered to approve consent orders by CPR 52.16.

Special provisions apply where one of the parties is a child or patient and to structured settlements.

Dismissal of applications or appeals by consent

6.52

'12.1

These paragraphs do not apply where any party to the proceedings is a child or patient.

12.2

Where an appellant does not wish to pursue an application or an appeal, he may request the appeal court for an order that his application or appeal be dismissed. Such a request must contain a statement that the appellant is not a child or patient. If such a request is granted it will usually be on the basis that the appellant pays the costs of the application or appeal.

12.3

If the appellant wishes to have the application or appeal dismissed without costs, his request must be accompanied by a consent signed by the respondent or his legal representative stating that the respondent is not a child or patient and consents to the dismissal of the application or appeal without costs.

12.4

Where a settlement has been reached disposing of the application or appeal, the parties may make a joint request to the court stating that none of them is a child or patient, and asking that the application or appeal be dismissed by consent. If the request is granted the application or appeal will be dismissed.'

Allowing unopposed appeals or applications on paper

6.53

'13.1

The appeal court will not normally make an order allowing an appeal unless satisfied that the decision of the lower court was wrong, but the appeal court may set aside or vary the order of the lower court with consent and without determining the merits of the appeal, if it is satisfied that there are good and sufficient reasons for doing so. Where the appeal court is requested by all parties to allow an application or an appeal the court may consider the request on the papers. The request should state that none of the parties is a child or patient and set out the relevant history of the proceedings and the matters relied on as justifying the proposed order and be accompanied by a copy of the proposed order.'

Procedure for structured settlements and consent orders involving a child or patient

6.54

'13.2

Settlements relating to appeals and applications where one of the parties is a child or a patient; and structured settlements which are agreed upon at the appeal stage require the court's approval.'

Child

6.55

'13.3

In cases involving a child a copy of the proposed order signed by the parties' solicitors should be sent to the appeal court, together with an opinion from the advocate acting on behalf of the child.'

Patient

6.56

'13.4

Where a party is a patient the same procedure will be adopted, but the documents filed should also include any relevant reports prepared for the Court of Protection and a document evidencing formal approval by that court where required.'

Structured settlements

6.57

> '13.5
>
> Where a structured settlement has been negotiated in a case which is under appeal the documents filed should include those which would be required in the case of a structured settlement dealt with at first instance. Details can be found in the Practice Direction which supplements CPR Part 40.'

CHAPTER 7

Alternative Dispute Resolution

Introduction: The CPR and ADR	7.1
Power of the court to compel the parties to participate in ADR	7.3
Sanctions for refusing to participate in ADR	7.4
The Court of Appeal scheme	7.5
Useful addresses	7.6

INTRODUCTION: THE CPR AND ADR

7.1 Part 1 of the Civil Procedure Rules contains the overriding objective of enabling the court to deal with cases 'justly'[1]. The court must further that objective by actively managing cases[2]. 'Active case management' includes:

> 'encouraging the parties to use an alternative dispute resolution procedure if it considers that appropriate, and facilitating the use of such a procedure.'[3]

The Court of Appeal has made it clear that fulfilment of the overriding objective is a duty on the parties as well as on the court[4]; it must follow that there is an equivalent obligation on the parties to use ADR when it is appropriate so to do

The encouragement to use alternative dispute resolution procedures is reinforced by CPR 44.5 (factors to be taken into account in deciding the amount of costs):

'CPR 44.5(3)

The court must also have regard to—
(a) the conduct of all the parties, including in particular—
  (i) conduct before, as well as during, the proceedings; and
  (ii) the efforts made, if any, before and during the proceedings in order to try to resolve the dispute;'

1   CPR 1.1 (1).
2   CPR 1.4(1).
3   CPR 1.4 (2)(e).
4   CPR 1.3 See Brooke LJ, *Dunnett v Railtrack plc (in railway administration)* [2002] EWCA Civ 303, [2002] 1 WLR 2434, [2002] 2 All ER 850, 853.

7.2 The virtues of mediation in suitable cases are further recognised in the Chancery Guide (paras 17.1 and 17.3), the Queen's Bench Guide (para 6.6), the Admiralty and Commercial Court Guide (para D8.8) and the Technology and Construction Court Guide (para 6.4). Judges in the Commercial Court routinely make 'ADR orders' in the form set out in Appendix 7 to the Admiralty and Commercial Court Guide[1].

In the CPR 'alternative dispute resolution' (ADR) means any 'method of resolving disputes otherwise than through the normal trial process'[2]. In practice, that is most likely to be mediation.

Mediation is a flexible procedure. As stated by Colman J in *Cable & Wireless plc v IBM United Kingdom Ltd*[3]:

> '[M]ediation as a tool for dispute resolution is not designed to achieve solutions which reflect the precise legal rights and obligations of the parties, but rather solutions which are mutually commercially acceptable at the time of the mediation.'

It is a procedure which is suitable not only for commercial disputes but for disputes between individuals and the Government and between individuals and statutory authorities. In 2001, the Lord Chancellor directed that Government Departments have recourse to ADR whenever the other party agrees[4]:

> 'In future, Government Departments will only go to court as a last resort. Instead, Government legal disputes will be settled by mediation or arbitration whenever possible.'[5]

Subsequently, in *R (Cowl and Others) v Plymouth City Council*[6], Lord Woolf CJ stressed the value of ADR, 'even in disputes between public authorities and the members of the public for whom they are responsible'.

1   Glossary, Civil Procedure Rules.
2   Glossary, Civil Procedure Rules.
3   [2002] EWHC 2059 (Comm), [2002] 2 All ER (Comm) 1041.

4   'ADR Pledge' issued by Lord Irvine LC, 23 March 2001; http://www.dca.gov.uk/civil/adr/adrmon.htm#part2.
5   Statement by Lord Irvine LC, 23 March 2001. In *Royal Bank of Canada v Secretary of State for Defence* [2003] EWHC 1841 (Ch) (Lewison J), the substantially successful defendant – a Government Department – was refused an order for costs in its favour where it had declined to accept the claimant's proposal for mediation. In *Halsey v Milton Keynes General NHS Trust* [2004] EWCA (Civ) 576, at paragraph 35 the Court of Appeal, however, disagreeing with the approach taken by Lewison J in that case commented that the 'Pledge' was no more than an undertaking, 'that ADR would be considered and used in all *suitable* cases' (Court's emphasis). *Halsey* is addressed in some detail below.
6   [2001] EWCA Civ 1935, [2002] 1 WLR 803.

POWER OF THE COURT TO COMPEL THE PARTIES TO PARTICIPATE IN ADR

7.3 Since the coming into effect of the CPR in April 1999 the courts have adopted a variety of stances towards ADR, ranging from more or less gentle persuasion, through the standard Admiralty and Commercial Court order, to the making of direct orders to the parties to submit to mediation[1].

The Court of Appeal, in *Halsey v Milton Keynes General NHS Trust*[2], however, has now stated its view that even if the court has a power to compel parties to participate in ADR, it should not exercise it[3]. Rather, the court should encourage the participation in ADR in appropriate cases and make clear the possible costs and consequences of refusal to participate in an appropriate case[4].

Dyson LJ, giving the judgment of the court, said:[5]:

'9. We heard argument on the question whether the court has power to order parties to submit their disputes to mediation against their will. It is one thing to encourage the parties to agree to mediation, even to encourage them in the strongest terms. It is another to order them to do so. It seems to us that to oblige truly unwilling parties to refer their disputes to mediation would be to impose an unacceptable obstruction on their right of access to the court. The court in Strasbourg has said in relation to article 6 of the European Convention on Human Rights that the right of access to a court may be waived, for example by means of an arbitration agreement, but such waiver should be subjected to "particularly careful review" to ensure that the claimant is not subject to "constraint": see *Deweer v Belgium* (1980) 2 EHRR 439, para 49. If that is the approach of the ECtHR to an *agreement* to arbitrate, it seems to us likely that *compulsion* of ADR would be regarded as an unacceptable constraint on the right of access to the court and, therefore, a violation of article 6. Even if (contrary to our view) the court does have jurisdiction to order unwilling parties to refer their disputes to mediation, we find it difficult to conceive of circumstances in which it would be appropriate to exercise it. We would adopt what the editors of Volume 1 of the White Book (2003) say at para 1.4.11:

> "The hallmark of ADR procedures, and perhaps the key to their effectiveness in individual cases, is that they are processes voluntarily entered into by the parties in dispute with outcomes, if the parties so wish, which are non-binding. Consequently the court cannot direct that such methods be used but may merely encourage and facilitate."

10. If the court were to compel parties to enter into a mediation to which they objected, that would achieve nothing except to add to the costs to be borne by the parties, possibly postpone the time when the court determines the dispute and damage the perceived effectiveness of the ADR process. If a judge takes the view that the case is suitable for ADR, then he or she is not, of course, obliged to take at face value the expressed opposition of the parties. In such a case, the judge should explore the reasons for any resistance to ADR. But if the parties (or at least one of them) remain intransigently opposed to ADR, then it would be wrong for the court to compel them to embrace it.

11. Parties sometimes need to be encouraged by the court to embark on an ADR. The need for such encouragement should diminish in time if the virtue of ADR in suitable cases is demonstrated even more convincingly than it has been thus far. The value and importance of ADR have been established within a remarkably short time. All members of the legal profession who conduct litigation should now routinely consider with their clients whether their disputes are suitable for ADR. But we reiterate that the court's role is to encourage, not to compel. The form of encouragement may be robust: see para 30 below.

...

29. So far we have been considering the question whether a successful party's refusal of ADR was unreasonable without regard to the impact of any encouragement that the court may have given in the particular case. Where a successful party refuses to agree to ADR despite the court's encouragement, that is a factor which the court will take into account when deciding whether his refusal was unreasonable. The court's encouragement may take different forms. The stronger the encouragement, the easier it will be for the unsuccessful party to discharge the burden of showing that the successful party's refusal was unreasonable.

30. An ADR order made in the Admiralty and Commercial Court in the form set out in Appendix 7 to the Guide is the strongest form of

encouragement. It requires the parties to exchange lists of neutral individuals who are available to conduct "ADR procedures", to endeavour in good faith to agree a neutral individual or panel and to take "such serious steps as they may be advised to resolve their disputes by ADR procedures before the neutral individual or panel so chosen". The order also provides that if the case is not settled, "the parties shall inform the court what steps towards ADR have been taken and (without prejudice to matters of privilege) why such steps have failed". It is to be noted, however, that this form of order stops short of actually compelling the parties to undertake an ADR.

31. Nevertheless, a party who, despite such an order, simply refuses to embark on the ADR process at all would run the risk that *for that reason alone* his refusal to agree to ADR would be held to have been unreasonable, and that he should therefore be penalised in costs. It is to be assumed that the court would not make such an order unless it was of the opinion that the dispute was suitable for ADR.

32. A less strong form of encouragement is mentioned in the other Court Guides to which we have referred at para 6 above. A particularly valuable example is the standard form of order now widely used in clinical negligence cases, and which was devised by Master Ungley. The material parts of this order provide:

"The parties shall by consider whether the case is capable of resolution by ADR. If any party considers that the case is unsuitable for resolution by ADR, that party shall be prepared to justify that decision at the conclusion of the trial, should the judge consider that such means of resolution were appropriate, when he is considering the appropriate costs order to make.

The party considering the case unsuitable for ADR shall, not less than 28 days before the commencement of the trial, file with the court a witness statement without prejudice save as to costs, giving reasons upon which they rely for saying that the case was unsuitable."

33. This form of order has the merit that (a) it recognises the importance of encouraging the parties to *consider* whether the case is suitable for ADR, and (b) it is calculated to bring home to them that, if they refuse even to consider that question, they may be at risk on costs even if they are ultimately held by the court to be the successful party. We can see no reason why such an order should not also routinely be made at least in general personal injury litigation, and perhaps in other litigation too. A party who refuses even to consider whether a case is suitable for ADR is always at risk of an adverse finding at the costs stage of litigation, and particularly so where the court has made an order requiring the parties to consider ADR.'

1   *Thompson v Metropolitan Police Comr* [1998] QB 498, Lord Woolf MR at p 519, [1997] 2 All ER 762; *Muman v Nagasena* [2000] 1 WLR 299, 305, Mummery LJ; *Guinle v Kirreh ('Kinstreet')* 3rd August 1999 Arden J; *Hurst v Leeming* [2002] EWHC 1051 (Ch), [2003] 1 Lloyd's Rep 279 Lightman J; *R (Cowl and Others) v Plymouth City Council* [2001] EWCA Civ 1935, [2002] 1 WLR 803; *Dunnett v Railtrack* [2002[EWCA Civ 303, [2002] 1 WLR 2434, [2002] 2 All ER 850; *Cable & Wireless plc v IBM United Kingdom Ltd* [2002] EWHC 2059 (Comm), [2002] 2 All ER (Comm) 1041 Colman J.
2   [2004] EWCA Civ 576.
3   *Halsey v Milton Keynes General NHS Trust* [2004] EWCA Civ 576 at para 9 of the judgment (see below).
4   See below.
5   [2004] EWCA Civ 576.

SANCTIONS FOR REFUSING TO PARTICIPATE IN ADR

7.4 It might be asked, what role do the threat of costs sanctions have in connection with the participation in a voluntary and confidential process? Moreover, how far is it appropriate to impose sanctions for refusing to participate in a process which as yet still has an uneven track record? Professor Hazel Genn's 2002 review of the Court of Appeal scheme[1], for example, revealed, albeit on a statistically small sample, an overall success rate then of only between 40% and 45%. CEDR, however, now reports a general success rate of around 75% in commercial disputes, and courts in this and in other jurisdictions have been sufficiently sure of its efficacy to believe that sanctions are appropriate. The case-law has demonstrated that the court is generally critical of a party declining to participate in ADR but there has not been uniformity of approach. This lack of consistency has now been remedied.

In *Halsey v Milton Keynes General NHS Trust*[2], the Court of Appeal has comprehensively considered the previous case-law on this issue and has laid down clear and detailed guidelines in respect of the appropriate approach to be adopted by the court where a party has refused to participate in ADR. Dyson LJ, giving the judgment of the court, said:

> **'The costs issue**
>
> 12. CPR 44.3(2) provides that "if the court decides to make an order about costs (a) the general rule is that the unsuccessful party will be ordered to pay the cost of the successful party; but (b) the court may make a different order". CPR 44.3(4) provides that "in deciding what order (if any) to make about costs, the court must have regard to all the circumstances, including– (a) the conduct of the parties". Rule 44.3(5) provides that the conduct of the parties includes "(a) conduct before, as well as during, the proceedings and in particular the extent to which the parties followed any relevant pre-action protocol."

13. In deciding whether to deprive a successful party of some or all of his costs on the grounds that he has refused to agree to ADR, it must be borne in mind that such an order is an exception to the general rule that costs should follow the event. In our view, the burden is on the unsuccessful party to show why there should be a departure from the general rule. The fundamental principle is that such departure is not justified unless it is shown (the burden being on the unsuccessful party) that the successful party acted unreasonably in refusing to agree to ADR. We shall endeavour in this judgment to provide some guidance as to the factors that should be considered by the court in deciding whether a refusal to agree to ADR is unreasonable.

14. We make it clear at the outset that it was common ground before us (and we accept) that parties are entitled in an ADR to adopt whatever position they wish, and if as a result the dispute is not settled, that is not a matter for the court. As is submitted by the Law Society, if the integrity and confidentiality of the process is to be respected, the court should not know, and therefore should not investigate, why the process did not result in agreement.

15. We recognise that mediation has a number of advantages over the court process. It is usually less expensive than litigation which goes all the way to judgment, although it should not be overlooked that most cases are settled by negotiation in the ordinary way. Mediation provides litigants with a wider range of solutions than those that are available in litigation: for example, an apology; an explanation; the continuation of an existing professional or business relationship perhaps on new terms; and an agreement by one party to do something without any existing legal obligation to do so. As Brooke LJ pointed out in *Dunnett* at para [14]:

> "Skilled mediators are now able to achieve results satisfactory to both parties in many cases which are quite beyond the power of lawyers and courts to achieve. This court has knowledge of cases where intense feelings have arisen, for instance in relation to clinical negligence claims. But when the parties are brought together on neutral soil with a skilled mediator to help them resolve their differences, it may very well be that the mediator is able to achieve a result by which the parties shake hands at the end and feel that they have gone away having settled the dispute on terms with which they are happy to live. A mediator may be able to provide solutions which are beyond the powers of the court to provide."

16. In deciding whether a party has acted unreasonably in refusing ADR, these considerations should be borne in mind. But we accept the submission made by the Law Society that mediation and other ADR processes do not offer a panacea, and can have disadvantages as well as advantages:

they are not appropriate for every case. We do not, therefore, accept the submission made on behalf of the Civil Mediation Council that there should be a presumption in favour of mediation. The question whether a party has acted unreasonably in refusing ADR must be determined having regard to all the circumstances of the particular case. We accept the submission of the Law Society that factors which may be relevant to the question whether a party has unreasonably refused ADR will include (but are not limited to) the following: (a) the nature of the dispute; (b) the merits of the case; (c) the extent to which other settlement methods have been attempted; (d) whether the costs of the ADR would be disproportionately high; (e) whether any delay in setting up and attending the ADR would have been prejudicial; and (f) whether the ADR had a reasonable prospect of success. We shall consider these in turn. We wish to emphasise that in many cases no single factor will be decisive, and that these factors should not be regarded as an exhaustive check-list.

17. (a) **The nature of the dispute**. Even the most ardent supporters of ADR acknowledge that the subject-matter of some disputes renders them intrinsically unsuitable for ADR. The Commercial Court Working Party on ADR stated in 1999:

> "The Working Party believes that there are many cases within the range of Commercial Court work which do not lend themselves to ADR procedures. The most obvious kind is where the parties wish the court to determine issues of law or construction which may be essential to the future trading relations of the parties, as under an on-going long term contract, or where the issues are generally important for those participating in a particular trade or market. There may also be issues which involve allegations of fraud or other commercially disreputable conduct against an individual or group which most probably could not be successfully mediated."

Other examples falling within this category are cases where a party wants the court to resolve a point of law which arises from time to time, and it is considered that a binding precedent would be useful; or cases where injunctive or other relief is essential to protect the position of a party. But in our view, most cases are not by their very nature unsuitable for ADR.

18. (b) **The merits of the case.** The fact that a party reasonably believes that he has a strong case is relevant to the question whether he has acted reasonably in refusing ADR. If the position were otherwise, there would be considerable scope for a claimant to use the threat of costs sanctions to extract a settlement from the defendant even where the claim is without merit. Courts should be particularly astute to this danger. Large organisations, especially public bodies, are vulnerable to pressure from claimants who, having weak cases, invite mediation as a tactical ploy. They calculate

that such a defendant may at least make a nuisance-value offer to buy off the cost of a mediation and the risk of being penalised in costs for refusing a mediation even if ultimately successful.

19. Some cases are clear-cut. A good example is where a party would have succeeded in an application for summary judgment pursuant to CPR 24.2, but for some reason he did not make such an application. Other cases are more border-line. In truly border-line cases, the fact that a party refused to agree to ADR because he thought that he would win should be given little or no weight by the court when considering whether the refusal to agree to ADR was reasonable. Border-line cases are likely to be suitable for ADR unless there are significant countervailing factors which tip the scales the other way. In *Hurst*, Lightman J said:

> "The fact that a party believes that he has a watertight case again is no justification for refusing mediation. That is the frame of mind of so many litigants."

In our judgment, this statement should be qualified. The fact that a party *unreasonably* believes that his case is watertight is no justification for refusing mediation. But the fact that a party *reasonably* believes that he has a watertight case may well be sufficient justification for a refusal to mediate.

20. **(c) Other settlement methods have been attempted.** The fact that settlement offers have already been made, but rejected, is a relevant factor. It may show that one party is making efforts to settle, and that the other party has unrealistic views of the merits of the case. But it is also right to point out that mediation often succeeds where previous attempts to settle have failed. Although the fact that settlement offers have already been made is potentially relevant to the question whether a refusal to mediate is unreasonable, on analysis it is in truth no more than an aspect of factor (f).

21. **(d) The costs of mediation would be disproportionately high.** This is a factor of particular importance where, on a realistic assessment, the sums at stake in the litigation are comparatively small. A mediation can sometimes be at least as expensive as a day in court. The parties will often have legal representation before the mediator, and the mediator's fees will usually be borne equally by the parties regardless of the outcome (although the costs of a mediation may be the subject of a costs order by the court after a trial). Since the prospects of a successful mediation cannot be predicted with confidence (see further para 27 below), the possibility of the ultimately successful party being required to incur the costs of an abortive mediation is a relevant factor that may be taken into account in deciding whether the successful party acted unreasonably in refusing to agree to ADR.

22. **(e) Delay.** If mediation is suggested late in the day, acceptance of it may have the effect of delaying the trial of the action. This is a factor which it may be relevant to take into account in deciding whether a refusal to agree to ADR was unreasonable.

23. **(f) Whether the mediation had a reasonable prospect of success.** In *Hurst*, Lightman J said that he considered that the "critical factor" in that case was whether "objectively viewed" a mediation had any real prospect of success. He continued (p 381):

> "If mediation can have no real prospect of success, a party may, with impunity, refuse to proceed to mediation on this ground. But refusal is a high risk course to take, for if the Court finds that there was a real prospect, the party refusing to proceed to mediation may, as I have said, be severely penalized. Further, the hurdle in the way of a party refusing to proceed to mediation on this ground is high, for in making this objective assessment of the prospects of mediation, the starting point must surely be the fact that the mediation process itself can and often does bring about a more sensible and more conciliatory attitude on the part of the parties than might otherwise be expected to prevail before the mediation, and may produce a recognition of the strengths and weaknesses by each party of his own case and of that of his opponent, and a willingness to accept the give and take essential to a successful mediation. What appears to be incapable of mediation before the mediation process begins often proves capable of satisfactory resolution later."

24. Consistently with the view expressed in this passage, Lightman J said that on the facts of that case he was persuaded that "quite exceptionally" the successful party was justified in taking the view that mediation was not appropriate because it had no realistic prospects of success.

25. In our view, the question whether the mediation had a reasonable prospect of success will often be relevant to the reasonableness of A's refusal to accept B's invitation to agree to it. But it is not necessarily determinative of the fundamental question, which is whether the successful party acted unreasonably in refusing to agree to mediation. This can be illustrated by a consideration of two cases. In a situation where B has adopted a position of intransigence, A may reasonably take the view that a mediation has no reasonable prospect of success because B is most unlikely to accept a reasonable compromise. That would be a proper basis for concluding that a mediation would have no reasonable prospect of success, and that for this reason A's refusal to mediate was reasonable.

26. On the other hand, if *A* has been unreasonably obdurate, the court might well decide, on that account, that a mediation would have had no

reasonable prospect of success. But obviously this would not be a proper reason for concluding that A's refusal to mediate was reasonable. A successful party cannot rely on his own unreasonableness in such circumstances. We do not, therefore, accept that, as suggested by Lightman J, it is appropriate for the court to confine itself to a consideration of whether, viewed objectively, a mediation would have had a reasonable prospect of success. That is an unduly narrow approach: it focuses on the nature of the dispute, and leaves out of account the parties' willingness to compromise and the reasonableness of their attitudes.

27. Nor should it be overlooked that the potential success of a mediation may not only depend on the willingness of the parties to compromise. Some disputes are inherently more intractable than others. Some mediators are more skilled than others. It may therefore, sometimes be difficult for the court to decide whether the mediation would have had a reasonable prospect of success.

28. The burden should not be on the refusing party to satisfy the court that mediation had no reasonable prospect of success. As we have already stated, the fundamental question is whether it has been shown by the unsuccessful party that the successful party unreasonably refused to agree to mediation. The question whether there was a reasonable prospect that a mediation would have been successful is but one of a number of potentially relevant factors which may need to be considered in determining the answer to that fundamental question. Since the burden of proving an unreasonable refusal is on the unsuccessful party, we see no reason why the burden of proof should lie on the successful party to show that mediation did not have any reasonable prospect of success. In most cases it would not be possible for the successful party to prove that a mediation had no reasonable prospect of success. In our judgment, it would not be right to stigmatise as unreasonable a refusal by the successful party to agree to a mediation unless he showed that a mediation had no reasonable prospect of success. That would be to tip the scales too heavily against the right of a successful party to refuse a mediation and insist on an adjudication of the dispute by the court. It seems to us that a fairer balance is struck if the burden is placed on the unsuccessful party to show that there was a reasonable prospect that mediation would have been successful. This is not an unduly onerous burden to discharge: he does not have to prove that a mediation would *in fact* have succeeded. It is significantly easier for the unsuccessful party to prove that there was a reasonable prospect that a mediation would have succeeded than for the successful party to prove the contrary[3].

...

Public bodies

34. Another issue that has arisen is whether the court should be particularly disposed to make an adverse costs order against a successful public body on the grounds that it refused to agree to ADR. We can see no basis for the court discriminating against successful public bodies when deciding whether a refusal to agree to ADR should result in a costs penalty. The only reason for doing so that was suggested to us in the course of argument was that Government departments and agencies (including the NHSLA) should be held to the ADR pledge (see para 7 above). We need, therefore, to consider whether the ADR pledge has any special significance. In *Royal Bank of Canada v Secretary of State for Defence* [2003] EWHC 1841 (Ch) the main issue was the true interpretation of a lease. Lewison J said that, although it concerned a question of law, this dispute was suitable for ADR. He considered that the ADR pledge given by Government was something to which he ought to attach "great weight". At para 12 of his judgment he said:

> "As I have said, however, the most important feature to my mind is the formal pledge given on behalf of the government and its various departments to use ADR in appropriate cases. The government did not abide by that pledge in this case. I am not in a position to form any real view of whether a mediation would or would not have succeeded. It may well have done, but in my judgment a failure to abide by the formal pledge given on the part of government, coupled with the fact that ..., justifies a decision that the defendant should not recover any further costs from the claimant."

35. In our judgment, the judge was wrong to attach such weight to the ADR pledge. The pledge was no more than an undertaking that ADR would be considered and used in all *suitable* cases. If a case is suitable for ADR, then it is likely that a party refusing to agree to it will be acting unreasonably, whether or not it is a public body to which the ADR pledge applies. If the case is not suitable for ADR, then a refusal to agree to ADR does not breach the pledge. It is, therefore, difficult to see in what circumstances it would be right to give great weight to the ADR pledge.'

1 *Court-Based ADR Initiatives for Non-Family Civil Disputes* Lord Chancellor's Department Research Series No 1/02. Summary at www.dca.gov.uk/research/2002/1-02es.htm.
2 *Halsey v Milton Keynes General NHS Trust* [2004] EWCA Civ 576.
3 Paras 29–33 of Dyson LJ's judgment are set out in para 7.3 above. In these paragraphs he considered the different ways in which the court might encourage the parties to agree to ADR. The stronger the encouragement, the easier it will be for the unsuccessful party to discharge the requisite burden.

THE COURT OF APPEAL SCHEME

7.5 Following a Practice Statement in 1993[1] by the Judge in charge of the Commercial List encouraging parties to consider the use of ADR, and a Practice Direction in 1995[2] issued by the then Lord Chief Justice containing provisions to a similar effect, the then Master of the Rolls, Sir Thomas Bingham, said in a Practice Statement[3] that: 'The [Court of Appeal] hopes that it may be possible to identify cases which might be susceptible to settlement by mediation.' He noted, however, that 'it is not thought likely that mediation will be fruitful in a majority of appeals'.

Initially, the Court of Appeal's scheme was largely dependent on a general invocation to consider ADR rather than anything more selective. In the light of Professor Genn's recommendations[4], that has changed. Now the Lord Justice considering an application for permission to appeal is expressly required to consider whether the matter is suitable for mediation. If so, an invitation is sent to the appellant and the respondent urging them, 'seriously to consider the possibility of mediation', and to notify the Civil Appeals Office within 14 days whether they agree to that course. Also, the Court itself may propose mediation where there are outstanding issues and a possibility of further litigation[5].

Whilst parties are, of course, free to make their own arrangements, the Court of Appeal has a scheme for the provision of ADR, administered on its behalf by 'CEDR Solve'[6]. CEDR Solve is responsible for nominating mediators suitable for each case, preparing a mediation agreement, and liaising with the parties over administrative arrangements. The Court remains responsible for the composition of the panel of mediators and for any adjustments to the fees payable. A mediator should be agreed upon within seven days of a case being referred to CEDR, and CEDR's target thereafter is to fix a mediation appointment for within six weeks of that agreement.

In all but family matters there is a fixed fee, at present £850 plus VAT, for each party. That covers nine hours of the mediator's time, including preparation time, and the administration. Each party bears its own costs of the mediation. If a party has Legal Services Commission funding, that will cover the associated legal costs. It might also cover the mediation fee.

Family mediations, however, are not within the CEDR scheme, the administration being undertaken by the Civil Appeals Office, which draws on a panel of mediators from the UK College of Family Mediators. In family matters, parties may either opt for the fixed fee family scheme, or they may opt for an hourly rate, presently £170 plus VAT, and an administration fee of £350 plus VAT per party[7].

Where a party is unable to afford the mediation fee, it may apply to the court for a waiver.

244 Alternative Dispute Resolution

During the first year of its operation, from May 2003, the scheme achieved a settlement rate at mediation of 68%.

1 *Practice Statement (Commercial Court) (Alternative Dispute resolution)* [1994] 1 WLR 14, [1994] 1 All ER 34.. See also a second statement at [1996] 1 WLR 1024, [1996] 3 All ER 383.
2 *Practice Direction (Civil Litigation: Case Management)* [1995] 1 WLR 262, [1995] 1 All ER 385.
3 *Practice Direction (Court of Appeal: Procedure)* [1995] 1 WLR 1191, [1995] 3 All ER 850..
4 *Court-Based ADR Initiatives for Non-Family Civil Disputes* Lord Chancellor's Department Research Series No 1/02. Summary at www.dca.gov.uk/research/2002/1-02es.htm.
5 See, for example, *Michael v Miller* [2004] EWCA Civ.282: 'In my judgment, it would be wholly disproportionate for the parties to proceed to a full-scale inquiry involving issues of liability relating to the lavender plants. I strongly urge them to have recourse to mediation in the hope of disposing of the issue speedily and economically, without the need for further, possibly substantial, litigation' (per Jonathan Parker LJ).
6 CEDR Solve is the service arm of CEDR, the Centre for Effective Dispute Resolution.
7 The scale of fees is subject to confirmation.

USEFUL ADDRESSES

7.6 CEDR Solve, International Dispute Resolution Centre, 70 Fleet Street, London EC4Y 1EU.

The Court Manager, Civil Appeals Office, Royal Courts of Justice, Strand, London WC2A 2LL.

CHAPTER 8

Appeals to the House of Lords

Introduction	8.1
Leave to appeal	8.5
Appeals	8.29
Procedural table	8.84

INTRODUCTION

8.1 This chapter describes the procedures that apply to appeals to the House of Lords from the Court of Appeal in England and Wales and in Northern Ireland, from the High Court in England and Wales and in Northern Ireland under the 'leapfrog procedure', and from the Court of Session in Scotland.

8.2 The procedures of the House of Lords when sitting in its judicial capacity are governed by standing orders of the House regulating judicial business and by Practice Directions[1]. Copies of these and other documents may be obtained free of charge from the Judicial Office of the House of Lords or downloaded from the Internet[2].

1 The orders are made pursuant to the Appellate Jurisdiction Act 1876, s 11. The current edition of the *House of Lords Practice Directions and Standing Orders applicable to Civil Appeals* (*2003*) is dated November 2003. All references to Directions in this chapter are to the November 2003 edition.
2 Postcode of the office is SW1A 0PW; telephone number is 020 7219 3111; fax number is 020 7219 2476. All House of Lords judicial material is available on the Internet at www.parliament.uk.

8.3 Applications for leave to appeal to the House of Lords are considered by an Appeal Committee consisting of three Lords of Appeal. Most applications are decided on the papers alone, without a hearing. Appeals to the House are heard by an Appellate Committee consisting usually of five Lords of Appeal but sometimes seven or nine. Appeals are usually heard in Committee Room 1 on the Committee Corridor of the Palace of Westminster but from time to time are heard in the Chamber of the House of Lords. The Human Rights Act 1998 applies to the House of Lords in its judicial capacity.

8.4 Paragraphs 8.5–8.83 below describe the main procedures involved in applications for leave to appeal and in appeals to the House of Lords. Steps 1 to 133 of the Procedural Table in **para 8.84** complete the picture and give more detail about what is required of parties to an appeal and of the practice at the various stages of the appeals process.

LEAVE TO APPEAL

Appeals from the Court of Appeal to the House of Lords

8.5 An appeal to the House of Lords from any order or judgment of the Court of Appeal may only be brought with the leave of the Court of Appeal or the House of Lords itself[1]. In certain cases, only the Court of Appeal may grant leave to appeal, for example, if the appeal relates to certain compulsory purchase orders[2].

1 Administration of Justice (Appeals) Act 1934, s 1(1); Judicature (Northern Ireland) Act 1978, s 42.
No appeal lies to House of Lords from an order of the Court of Appeal in exercise of its discretion to grant or refuse leave to appeal under the Arbitration Act 1996, s 69(8).
No appeal lies to the House of Lords from a decision of the Court of Appeal to refuse leave to appeal to that Court: Access to Justice Act 1999, s 54; *Lane v Esdaile* [1891] AC 210.
2 Housing Act 1985.

8.6 An application for leave to appeal must be made first to the Court of Appeal and only if that Court refuses leave may application be made to the House of Lords[1]. Application to the Court of Appeal should be made at the hearing before the Court of Appeal. If the application is not made at the hearing, it may be made by written application to the Master of the Court of Appeal, who refers it to the Lords Justices who heard the appeal[2].

1 Direction 1.2.
2 Procedural table at **para 8.84**, steps 1–6.

8.7 If the Court of Appeal refuses leave to appeal, an application may then be made to the House of Lords. This is done by presenting a petition for leave to appeal[1]. Presentation of a petition for leave to appeal (or of a petition of appeal – see **para 8.29**) does not operate as a stay of execution of any order or decision of the lower court. Moreover, it is not the practice of the House to grant a stay of execution of legal proceedings[2]. A party seeking a stay must apply to the court appealed from.

1   Appellate Jurisdiction Act 1876, s 4; Administration of Justice (Appeals) Act 1934, s 1(2) proviso. For form of petition see *Practice Directions*, Appendix A.
2   So far as regards interlocutors of the Court of Session in Scotland, the practice of the House has been placed on a statutory basis: s 41(2) of the Court of Session Act 1988 (c 36).

8.8   The granting of leave to appeal to an appellant does not entitle a respondent to present a cross-appeal. So a respondent to an appeal who wishes to reverse or vary an order of the Court of Appeal must also first obtain leave from that court or, if leave is refused, apply to the House for leave to cross-appeal[1].

1   Direction 1.7.

Appeals direct from High Court to House of Lords ('leapfrog' appeals)

8.9   In certain cases, and subject to certain conditions, an appeal lies direct from the High Court in England and Wales or in Northern Ireland to the House of Lords. A certificate of the High Court must be obtained and the leave of the House of Lords given before the appeal may proceed[1].

1   Administration of Justice Act 1969 ss 12–15.

8.10   An application for a certificate may be made by any of the parties to any civil proceedings in the High Court before a single judge or before a Divisional Court. The application must be made immediately after the trial judge gives judgment in the proceedings or, if no such application is made, within 14 days from the date on which judgment was given. The procedure to be followed is set out in the procedural table at **para 8.84**[1].

1   Steps 28–42.

8.11   The judge may grant a certificate under s 12 of the Administration of Justice Act 1969 if he is satisfied (a) that the relevant conditions are fulfilled; (b) that a sufficient case has been made to justify taking to the House of Lords an application for leave; and (c) that all the parties to the proceedings consent to the grant of a certificate. The relevant conditions are that a point of law of general public importance is involved in the judge's decision, and that that point of law either (a) relates wholly or mainly to the construction of an enactment or of a statutory instrument and has been fully argued in the proceedings and fully considered in the judgment of the judge in the proceedings[1], or (b) is one in respect of which the judge is bound by a decision of the

Court of Appeal or House of Lords in previous proceedings and was fully considered in the judgments of the Court of Appeal or House of Lords in those previous proceedings[2].

1 Administration of Justice Act 1969, s 12(3)(a).
2 Administration of Justice Act 1969, s 12(3)(b).

8.12 The judge may not grant a certificate in cases where no appeal would lie (with or without leave) from the judge's decision to the Court of Appeal, apart from the provisions of the Administration of Justice Act 1969. Similarly, a certificate may not be granted where no appeal would lie (with or without leave) from the Court of Appeal on an appeal from the judge's decision. Where no appeal would lie from the judge's decision to the Court of Appeal except with the leave of the judge or the Court of Appeal, no certificate may be granted unless it appears to the judge that it would be a proper case for granting such leave. No certificate may be given where the judge's decision concerns punishment for contempt of court.

8.13 At any time within one month from the date on which the judge grants the certificate, or such extended time as the House of Lords may allow[1], any of the parties may apply to the House of Lords for leave to appeal[2]. Application is made by petition. The petition should indicate whether the certificate was granted under s 12(3)(a) or s 12(3)(b) of the Administration of Justice Act 1969. The House of Lords may grant leave for an appeal to be brought directly from the High Court if it appears to be expedient to do so. Applications for such leave are determined by an Appeal Committee without a hearing.

1 For applications to extend time see Procedural Table, steps 38–40.
2 Administration of Justice Act 1969, s 13(1).

8.14 If the House of Lords grants leave to appeal direct from the High Court, no appeal from the decision of the judge lies to the Court of Appeal but only to the House of Lords. Such an appeal is brought by petition and the usual requirements apply[1]. However, an appeal does lie to the Court of Appeal from the judge's decision after the time within which an application may be made for leave to the House of Lords has expired and where leave to appeal direct to the House has been refused by the House of Lords.

1 Procedural Table, steps 41 onwards.

8.15 In proceedings for a writ of habeas corpus, an appeal lies from the Queen's Bench Divisional Court to the House of Lords at the instance of the defendant or prosecutor with the leave of the Divisional Court or the House of Lords. No certificate involving a point of law of general public importance is required[1].

1   Administration of Justice Act 1969, ss 1, 15(3); Judicature (Northern Ireland) Act 1978, s 45(3).

Appeals from the Court of Session (Scotland) to the House of Lords

8.16 An appeal lies to the House of Lords from an interlocutor of the Court of Session and leave to appeal is not required except in certain cases[1]. There is no appeal to the House of Lords against a decision of the High Court of Justiciary in Scotland.

1   Appellate Jurisdiction Act 1876, s 3(2). Leave to appeal from the Court of Session to the House of Lords may be required under the Building (Scotland) Act 1959, s 16(3), the Caravan Sites and Control of Development Act 1960, s 32(2)(b), the Aircraft and Shipbuilding Industries Act 1977, Sch 7, para 9(2), the Estate Agents Act 1979, s 7(6), the Transport Act 1985, s 9(9), the Banking Act 1987, s 31(4), the Court of Session Act 1988, s 40(1)(b), and the Tribunals and Inquiries Act 1992, s 11(7)(d): see Direction 1.3.

Procedures applicable to all petitions for leave to appeal

General

8.17 A petition for leave to appeal to the House of Lords is required to be lodged in the Judicial Office within one month from the date of the order appealed from[1]. However, petitions for leave to appeal out of time are admissible[2]. A petition for leave to appeal lodged outside the one month period laid down by Standing Order II is accepted by the Judicial Office provided that (a) it has been drafted in the style required for such petitions and seeks leave to appeal out of time; (b) it sets out in the first paragraph the reason(s) why it was not lodged within the time limit; and (c) it is in order in all other respects. The reasons should not normally exceed one paragraph in length. In considering the petition for leave, the Appeal Committee may reject it on the sole ground that it is out of time; but usually the Appeal Committee grants an extension of time and decides the application for leave on the merits. However, a petition for leave to appeal lodged more than three months after the date of the order appealed from (i.e. more than two months out of time) is allowed only in exceptional circumstances.

1   Direction 2.1 and Standing Order II; for admissibility of petitions for leave, see Direction 1.6. If a petitioner has applied for public funding, the period is extended to one month after decision whether funding should be granted. Judicial Office must be informed in writing within the one month period that public funding has been applied for: Direction 1.8.
2   Directions 2.3–2.5.

8.18 As for all formal documents to the House of Lords, the petition for leave should be produced on good quality A4 paper, bound on the left like a book and using both sides of the paper. It should be word-processed rather than printed. The petition should set forth briefly the facts and points of law, and conclude with a summary of reasons for leave being granted[1]. The case title is that used in the courts below except that the parties are described as petitioners and respondents[2]. The petition must be signed by the petitioners or their agents. It must be served, together with a copy, on the respondents or their agents[3]. A certificate of service must be endorsed on the original petition lodged in the Judicial Office[4]. One copy of the order of the Court of Appeal complained of must be lodged with the petition. The number and type of other documents required for the use of the Appeal Committee is set out in **para 8.84**[5]. Supporting documents are not usually required or accepted[6].

1 Direction 3.1–3.2.
2 The names of parties to the original action who are not parties in the petition to the House are still included in the title; the identity of children is protected by use of the form *In re A*.
3 Direction 3.4.
4 See *Practice Directions*, Appendix A for form of endorsement of service.
5 Steps 13–14.
6 Directions 3.1, 4.2.

Appearance

8.19 Respondents or their agents should enter an appearance to a petition for leave as soon as they have received service, but no appearance should be entered in connection with petitions for leave to appeal direct from the High Court. The respondents or their agents enter an appearance by attending at the Judicial Office to enter their name and address or that of their firm and paying the fee. Communications from the Judicial Office are sent only to those who have entered an appearance. Respondents who do not intend to take part in the proceedings need not enter an appearance[1].

1 Direction 3.8.

Public funding/legal aid

8.20 The House of Lords does not provide public funding or legal aid. Application must be made in England and Wales to the Legal Services Commission, in Scotland to the Scottish Legal Aid Board and in Northern Ireland to the Legal Aid Committee. Deadlines for the deposit of documents are extended while public funding or legal aid is being sought, provided the Judicial Office and the other parties have been notified in writing[1]. A party to whom a legal aid certificate has been issued must lodge a copy in the Judicial Office[2].

1 Directions 1.8, 41.
2 Direction 41.2.

Appeal Committee

8.21 A petition for leave to appeal to the House of Lords is referred to an Appeal Committee consisting of three Lords of Appeal who consider whether the petition should be dismissed, allowed or referred for an oral hearing[1]. In deciding whether or not to allow a petition for leave, the Appeal Committee consider whether the petition raises an arguable point of law of general public importance that ought to be considered by the House at that time, bearing in mind that the matter will already have been reviewed on appeal. The Appeal Committee give brief reasons for refusing leave but do not otherwise give reasons for their decisions[2].

1   Procedural table, steps 17–20. For requests for expedited consideration of petition for leave see Direction 4.18.
2   Appeal Committee, 38th Report (2002–03): *Petitions for leave to appeal: reasons for the refusal of leave* (HL Paper 89).

Petition dismissed

8.22 If the Appeal Committee are unanimous that a petition should be refused, the parties are notified that the petition is dismissed[1].

1   Direction 4.6; Procedural table, step 17.

Petition allowed

8.23 If the Appeal Committee are unanimous that a petition should be allowed without further proceedings, the House grants leave outright (without inviting respondents' objections).

8.24 If the Appeal Committee decide that leave should be given on terms, the Committee suggest the terms and require the parties to lodge observations on them within two weeks.

Respondents' objections

8.25 The Appeal Committee may invite the respondents to lodge objections to the petition. Such objections should set out briefly the reasons why the petition should be refused or make submissions as to the terms on which the petition should be allowed (for example, as to costs). A copy of the objections should be sent to the agents for the other parties. In certain circumstances the Appeal Committee may invite further submissions from the petitioners in the light of the respondents' objections but petitioners have no right to comment on respondents' objections. The Appeal Committee will not accept objections or submissions from respondents before they are invited, and parties must not anticipate the Committee's decision in this regard. If, having considered the respondents' objections, the Appeal Committee are unanimously of the opinion that leave to appeal should be given, the parties are informed that the petition is allowed and are told of any terms on which leave to appeal has been given[1].

1   Procedural Table, step 19.

Petition referred for hearing

8.26 In all cases where the members of the Appeal Committee are not unanimous, a petition for leave to appeal is referred for hearing[1]. In that event, the petitioner's agents and the agents for all respondents who have entered appearance are given notice of the meeting of the Appeal Committee before whom all parties are directed to attend. Agents or counsel may be heard, but only one agent or counsel may appear on each side and only a junior counsel's fee is allowed on taxation[2]. If counsel is briefed, agents should ensure that the Judicial Office is informed of his name.

1   Direction 4.10. Procedural Table, step 20.
2   Directions 4.13–4.14.

Costs in petitions for leave

8.27 If leave is granted, the costs of the petition for leave become costs in the appeal. If leave is refused without a hearing, an order is automatically made that the respondents are at liberty to apply for their costs. If leave is refused after an oral hearing, the respondents' counsel or agent must apply to the Appeal Committee at the end of the hearing immediately after the Committee's decision is announced.

Expedition

8.28 The procedures described above are normally completed within eight sitting weeks from the day of the presentation of the petition for leave. However in cases involving liberty of the subject, urgent medical intervention or the well-being of children, application for expedition may be made in writing to the Clerk of the Judicial Office.

APPEALS

Petition of appeal

8.29 The contents and style of a petition of appeal are prescribed[1]. Petitions of appeal (and all other formal documents to the House of Lords) should be produced on good quality A4 paper, bound on the left like a book and using both sides of the paper. The petition of appeal must contain a schedule setting out the whole of the relevant order of the court below and the part or parts complained of must be underlined. If leave to appeal was granted by a later order, that order must also be set out in the schedule. Where leave to appeal has been obtained, it is enough for the petition to be signed by the appellants or their agents. In appeals where leave to appeal was not required (for example, in most Scottish appeals) the petition of appeal must be certified as reasonable by two counsel and signed by them[2]. In Scottish appeals, a certificate of difference of opinion must also be included where appropriate[3]. Case titles in the House of Lords are those used in the courts below but the parties are described as appellants and respondents[4].

1   For form of petition of appeal, see *Practice Directions*, Appendix C.
2   Direction 9.2 and Standing Order IV.
3   Standing Order XI.
4   The names of parties to the original action who are not parties in the appeal to the House are still included in the title; the identity of children is protected by use of the form *In re A*.

8.30 A copy of the petition of appeal must be served on the respondents or their agents, either by delivery in person or first-class post, before lodgment in the Judicial Office. A certificate of such service must be endorsed on the back of the original petition[1]. The petition of appeal, together with seven copies, must be lodged in the Judicial Office within three months from the date of the last order or interlocutor appealed from, unless other time limits apply[2]. In a case involving a child, where delay might affect the facts of the case or the interests of the child, parties should draw these facts to the attention of the Clerk of the Judicial Office not later than the day of presentation of the petition of appeal[3].

1   Direction 9.7.
2   For example, limits imposed by the Appeal Committee when granting leave to appeal.
3   Direction 9.11.

Appearance for respondents

8.31 Respondents or their agents should enter an appearance on behalf of their clients to an appeal as soon as they have received service. The respondents or their agents enter an appearance by attending at the Judicial Office to enter their name and address or that of their firm and paying the fee. Communications from the Judicial Office are sent only to those who have entered an appearance. Respondents who do not intend to take part in the appeal need not enter an appearance[1].

1   Direction 9.10.

Security for costs

8.32 Appellants must give security for costs in the sum fixed by the House unless the House orders otherwise or they have been granted public funding or are a government minister or department[1]. A cheque for this sum, payable to the House of Lords Security Fund Account, must be paid within one week of the presentation of the appeal[2]. Failure to do so will result in the appeal being dismissed by default. Appellants may lodge a consent form signed by all the respondents agreeing that security for costs should be waived. The consent must be lodged with the appropriate fee within one week of the presentation of the appeal; the House will then make an order absolving the appellants from giving security[3].

1 Directions 10.1 and 10.4 and Standing Order V(1); Procedural Table, step 55.
2 Direction 10.1.
3 Direction 10.3. A consent form may be obtained from the Judicial Office.

Public funding/legal aid

8.33 The House of Lords does not provide public funding or legal aid. Application must be made in England and Wales to the Legal Services Commission, in Scotland to the Legal Aid Board and in Northern Ireland to the Legal Aid Committee. Deadlines for the deposit of documents are extended while public funding or legal aid is being sought, provided that the other parties and the Judicial Office have been notified in writing[1]. A party to whom a legal aid certificate has been issued must lodge a copy in the Judicial Office[2]. An appellant to whom a certificate is granted is free of the requirement to give security for costs and no waiver is necessary[3].

1 Directions 1.8, 41.
2 Direction 41.2.
3 Direction 10.4.

Human Rights Act 1998

8.34 Appellants must notify the Judicial Office in writing when:
(a) the House is to be asked to consider whether to make, uphold or reverse a declaration that a provision of primary or subordinate legislation is incompatible with a European Human Rights Convention right or is to be asked to consider any issue which may lead the House to make such a declaration, or where such an issue may be raised in respect of a judicial act;
(b) a party seeks to challenge an act of a public authority under the Human Rights Act 1998; or

(c) a party relies in whole or in part on the provisions of the Human Rights Act 1998.

Appellants should indicate whether notification is made under (a), (b) or (c) above; they should set out briefly the arguments involved; and state whether the point was taken in the courts below. In appeals in which (a) above is an issue, the Crown has a right to be joined as a party to the appeal.

Preparation of Statement of Facts and Issues

8.35 Appellants must lodge a Statement of Facts and Issues and an Appendix containing documents used in evidence or recording proceedings in the courts below[1]. This must be done within six weeks of the presentation of the petition of appeal, or longer period approved by the House[2]. The Statement should be a succinct account of the main facts of the case, including an account of judicial proceedings up to that point and an account of the issues raised by the appeal. The appellants are responsible for drawing up the Statement in draft and they must submit it to the respondents for discussion and agreement. The Statement lodged must be a single document agreed between the parties. In the event of disagreement, disputed material should be removed from the draft Statement and included instead in each party's case (see **para 8.45**). The Statement must be signed on behalf of each party by at least one counsel who appeared in the court below or who will appear at the hearing before the House.

1   Directions 11, 12 and 13, Standing Order VI(1); Procedural Table, steps 62–69.
2   Granted on a petition for extension of time: see **para 8.67**.

8.36 Appellants must lodge eight copies of the Statement, eight copies of part I of the Appendix, and 15 copies of each subsequent part of the Appendix. Statements must be reproduced on A4 paper with letters down the margin and references in the margin to the relevant pages of the Appendix or additional documents[1]. The reference of every law report of the cause in the courts below, together with the catchword summary of one of the reports, should be shown on the front cover of the statement; a headnote summary should be given, whether the cause has been reported or not.

1   Direction 30.

Preparation of Appendix

8.37 It is the Appellants' responsibility, in consultation with the respondents, to prepare and lodge an Appendix of documents used in evidence or recording proceedings in the courts below. As soon as possible after the presentation of the appeal, the appellants' agents should submit to the respondents' agents a list of documents considered necessary for the appeal. The list must include all the documents in evidence referred to in the judgments of the courts below. The list should be divided into (a) documents to be lodged as the Appendix, and (b) documents (if any) to be held in readiness and produced at the hearing if required. The appellants bear the costs of reproduction of the documents, although these costs are ultimately subject to the decision of the House as to the costs of the appeal[1].

1   Direction 12.2.

8.38   The Appendix should contain only documents or extracts from documents that are clearly necessary to support and understand the argument when the appeal is heard by the Appellate Committee. No document which was not used in evidence or which does not record proceedings relevant to the action in the courts below may be included. Transcripts of arguments in the courts below may not be included unless remarks by a judge are relied on by any party or the arguments refer to facts which are admitted by all parties and as to which no evidence was called.

8.39   The Appendix consists of one or more parts. Part 1 must contain:
(1)   formal originating documents;
(2)   case stated (if any);
(3)   judgments and orders relating to the decisions at first instance and on appeal[1];
(4)   the relevant statutory provisions, including provisions of statutory instruments[2];
(5)   any crucial document on which the action is founded, for example, a will, contract, map, plan etc, or the relevant extract from such document.

Published documents under (2), (3) and (4) above should so far as is practicable be placed in a pocket attached to the inside of the back cover of the Appendix.

Other documents should be included in Part 2 of the Appendix and, if the bulk of the documents makes it necessary, in Parts 3, 4 etc.

1   For judgments that have been published, unbound parts of the relevant Law Reports or the Weekly Law Reports should be used if available; in other cases, the All England Reports, Tax Cases, Simon's Tax Cases, Reports of Patent Cases or Lloyd's List Reports may be used. In Scottish appeals, Session Cases and Scots Law Times may be used. If any judgment is not fully set out in the reports, a copy of it must be included.
2   If the printed Act or set of regulations is conveniently small, it should be used; if the provisions are bulky or numerous, the relevant provisions should be copied.

8.40   The Appendix must be bound with a plastic comb binding and blue card covers (blue indicating a civil appeal). All documents must be numbered, and each part of the Appendix must include a list of its contents. Documents must be reproduced on A4 paper in a form approved by the Judicial Office; by agreement between the parties documents may be printed. Documents of an unsuitable size or form for binding with the other documents, for example, booklets or charts, should be included in a pocket attached to the appropriate part of the Appendix[1].

1   Direction 30.10–30.13

8.41   Agents may submit their lists to the Judicial Office for inspection before documents are sent to press and also proofs before final copies are made.

8.42   The Appendix is for the use of all parties and the contents of the Appendix must be agreed by appellants and respondents. As soon as proofs are available they should be examined against the originals by all parties, if possible at one joint examination. Disputed documents should not be included in the Appendix but held in readiness at the hearing and, subject to the Appellate Committee giving leave, they may be introduced at an appropriate moment. Documents to be held in readiness at the hearing should be reproduced in a form approved by the Judicial Office. Fifteen copies are required. All documents are subject to previous examination by the other parties. Where the appellants decline to include in the Appendix any documents that the respondents consider necessary, respondents must prepare and reproduce them at their own expense (subject to the final order on costs).

As soon as practicable after the examination, a final proof of the Appendix must be supplied to each party[1].

1   Direction 12.10.

Lodgment of Statement and Appendix and setting down appeal for hearing

8.43   The appellants must lodge the Statement and Appendix within six weeks of the presentation of the appeal. But if this time limit expires during a parliamentary recess, it is automatically extended to the third next sitting day of the House of Lords; and if an application has been made for legal service funding/legal aid, the time limit is automatically extended to one month after notification of the result of the funding decision, provided that the Judicial Office has been informed of the application[1]. Appellants who are unable to complete preparation of the Statement and Appendix within the six weeks may apply by petition for an extension of time[2].

1   Direction 41.3.
2   For petitions for extension of time, see **para 8.67**. Up to three extensions are normally granted: Direction 13.5.

8.44 Eight copies of the Statement, eight copies of Part 1 of the Appendix and 15 copies of Parts 2 etc (if any) must be lodged in the Judicial Office with the appropriate fee. When the appellants lodge the required number of copies of the Statement and Appendix, they must apply at the same time to set down the cause for hearing[1].

1   Direction 14.1.

Appellants' and respondents' cases

8.45 The case is the statement of a party's argument in the appeal. It should be confined to the heads of argument that counsel propose to submit at the hearing and omit material contained in the Statement of Facts and Issues[1]. A party's case should make particular mention if they are abandoning any point taken below, or if they are inviting the House to depart from one of its own decisions. Cases must conclude with a numbered summary of the reasons upon which the argument is founded and be signed by at least one counsel who appeared in the court below or who will appear before the Appellate Committee. Lodgment of a case entitles a party to be heard by two counsel, one of whom may be a leading counsel. The fees of two counsel only for any party are allowed on taxation unless the Appellate Committee orders otherwise on application at the hearing[2].

1   See Lord Diplock's speech in *MV Yorke Motors v Edwards*, [1982] 1 WLR 444, [1982] 1 All ER, 1024.
2   Direction 15.8.

Separate and joint cases

8.46 All the appellants must join in one case. All the respondents must also join in one case, unless it can be shown that the interests of one or more of the respondents are distinct from those of the rest[1]. If the respondents' interests are distinct, the agents who first lodge their case must certify that they have offered to join in a case with the other respondents whose interests are similar, or certify that their interests are distinct.

1   Direction 15.9.

8.47 When one of the certificates has been given, all remaining respondents wishing to lodge a case must respectively petition to do so in respect of each of their separate cases. Each such petition must set out the reasons for separate lodgement and must be consented to by the appellants. Parties whose interests in the appeal are passive, for example, trustees and executors, are not required to lodge a separate case, but they should ensure that their position is explained in one of the cases lodged.

8.48 In certain circumstances, a joint case may be lodged on behalf of both appellants and respondents.

Lodgment and exchange of cases

8.49 At least five weeks before the expected date of the hearing, the appellants must lodge eight copies of their case in the Judicial Office, and serve it on the respondents. At least three weeks before the expected date of the hearing, the respondents must lodge eight copies of their case and serve it on the appellants[1].

1   Direction 15.13.

Consolidation and conjoinder of appeals

8.50 Where the issues in two or more appeals are similar, it may be appropriate for them to be consolidated or conjoined.

8.51 Consolidation results in the appeals being conducted as a single cause, with one set of counsel and one case only on each side and with a single Appendix of documents.

8.52 Conjoinder is a looser linking of two or more appeals and a number of variations is possible, for example, that the appellants lodge separate cases but be represented by one leader and two juniors, and that the respondents lodge separate cases and be separately represented.

8.53 Applications to consolidate or conjoin appeals are made by petition which must be consented to by all the parties that have entered appearance. If any party refuses consent, the petition is referred to an Appeal Committee and may be determined after a hearing.

Cross-appeals

8.54 Presentation of an appeal does not carry the right for the respondents to present a cross-appeal. The respondents must first apply to the Court of Appeal for leave to cross-appeal and, if leave is refused, then to apply to the House[1]. The petition for leave and the petition to cross-appeal take the same form as an ordinary petition for leave and petition of appeal[2]. Petitions of cross-appeal must be presented within six weeks of presentation of the original appeal[3]. Each party should include in their case for the original appeal argument in respect of a cross-appeal[4]. Such an inclusive case must clearly state that it is lodged in respect of both the original and cross-appeals. The documents in respect of both the original and cross-appeal should be included in the one Appendix[5].

1   Direction 26.
2   See *Practice Directions*, Appendices A and B.
3   Standing Orders VI(1), VIII.
4   Direction 26.3.
5   Direction 26.4.

Bound volumes

8.55 As soon as all cases have been exchanged, and no later than two weeks before the proposed date of the hearing, the appellants must lodge (in addition to the documents already lodged on setting down) 15 bound volumes, each containing:
(1)   petition of appeal;
(2)   petition of cross-appeal (if any);
(3)   Statement of Facts and Issues;
(4)   appellants' and respondents' cases;
(5)   case of the amicus curiae or intervener (if any);
(6)   Part 1 of the Appendix;
(7)   index to the authorities volumes.

8.56 The bound volumes should be bound in the same manner as the Appendix, with plastic comb binding and blue card covers. They must include cut-out indices for each of the documents set out in **para 8.55**, tabbed with the name of the document on the front sheet of each. The front cover should show a list of the contents and the names of the agents for all parties. The volume number and the short title of the appeal should be indicated on a sticker attached to the plastic spine.

8.57 To enable the appellants to produce the bound volumes, the respondents must provide the appellants' agents with a further 15 copies of the respondents' case in addition to the cases already exchanged[1].

1   Direction 16.3.

Authorities volumes

8.58 Ten copies of all authorities that may be needed during the hearing must be lodged at the same time as the bound volumes. The authorities volumes should be comb bound with green card covers. The appellants are responsible for producing the green authorities volumes. The respondents should therefore provide the appellants with ten copies of any authorities that they need but which the appellants do not need. The costs of producing the authorities volumes are costs in the appeal.

Notice of hearing

8.59 The Judicial Office lists appeals to meet the convenience of all the parties. The Judicial Office agrees provisional dates with the parties well in advance of the hearing and makes every effort to keep to these dates. Counsel, agents and parties are however advised to hold themselves in readiness during the week before and the week following the provisional date given. Agents receive formal notification shortly before the hearing.

Allocation of time

8.60 Within seven days of the setting down of the appeal, each party must notify the Judicial Office of the number of hours that their counsel consider necessary for each of them to address the Appellate Committee[1]. Subject to any directions given before or at the hearing, counsel are expected to confine their submissions to the time indicated in their estimates.

1   Direction 14.3.

Scottish appeals

8.61 In general, the procedures described in this chapter apply to appeals to the House of Lords from Scotland. Certain variations or additional procedures also apply to Scottish appeals.

8.62 In most Scottish appeals leave to appeal is not required and in all such cases the petition of appeal must be certified as reasonable by two counsel and signed by them[1].

1   Direction 9.2 and Standing Order IV.

8.63 When any petition of appeal is presented from any interlocutory judgment of either division of the Court of Session, the counsel signing the petition, or two of the counsel who represented the appellant to the House of Lords in the court below, must sign a certificate or declaration stating either that leave to present the appeal was given by the judges pronouncing the interlocutory judgment or that there was a difference of opinion among the judges[1].

1   Standing Order XI.

8.64 In all Scottish appeals the appellants are required to include in Part 1 of the Appendix:
(1) a copy of the Record as authenticated by the Deputy Principal Clerk of Session or a Clerk of Session delegated by him;
(2) a supplement containing an account, without argument or statement of other facts, of the further steps which have been taken in the appeal since the Record was completed;
(3) copies of the interlocutors (or parts of interlocutors) complained of.

8.65 Each party must include in their case to the House a copy of the case presented by them to the Court of Session, with a short summary of any additional reasons on which they propose to insist. If no case was presented to the Court of Session, each party must set forth in their case as shortly and succinctly as possible the reasons upon which they found their argument[1].

1   Standing Order VI(2).

Numbers of documents normally required for hearing of appeal[1]

1   This table is adapted from the *Practice Directions*. The actual requirements must be subject to agreement, to the number of parties, counsel and agents concerned and to the special circumstances of each appeal.

8.66 The appellants must provide:

	For Judicial Office	For other side	For themselves
Petition of Appeal	Original and seven on lodgement; 15 in bound volumes	One on service	As required
Statement of Facts and Issues	Eight on setting down; 15 in bound volumes	As arranged	As required
Appendix Part 1	Eight on setting down; 15 in bound volumes	One in advance; otherwise as arranged	As required

	For Judicial Office	For other side	For themselves
Appendix Part 2 and any subsequent Parts	15 on setting down	One in advance; otherwise as arranged	As required
Case	Eight no later than five weeks before hearing; 15 in bound volumes	As arranged on exchange	As required
Bound Volumes	15 no later than two weeks before hearing	As arranged	As required
Authorities volumes	Ten at least two weeks before hearing	As arranged	As required
Documents held in readiness at hearing (if any)	15	At least three	As required

The respondents must provide:

	For Judicial Office	For other side	For themselves
Case	Eight no later than three weeks before hearing	As arranged on exchange; 15 for bound volumes	As required
Documents in readiness at hearing (if any)	15	At least three	As required

Petitions for extension of time and incidental petitions

8.67 Appellants who are unable to complete preparation of the Statement and Appendix within the six weeks' period may apply by petition for an extension of time[1]. The petition should be produced in the form common to all formal documents to the House[2]. It should explain briefly why the Statement and Appendix cannot be lodged within the time allowed, and ask for an extension to a particular date (usually six weeks from the original expiry date). Up to three extensions are normally granted. The procedure is described more fully in **para 8.84**, steps 70–76.

1   Direction 13.2. A petition for restoration of appeal must be presented if time for lodging Statement of Facts and Issues has expired.
2   See **para 8.18, 8.29**.

8.68 There are various other types of incidental petition, for example, petitions to intervene, petitions to consolidate or conjoin appeals, petitions to withdraw an appeal, petitions to revive an appeal after the death of a party, petitions to render an appeal effective following bankruptcy. The procedure for incidental petitions broadly follows that for petitions for an extension of time. If an incidental petition is opposed, it may be referred to an Appeal Committee[1]. Eight copies of any incidental petition must be lodged and the original must bear a certificate of service on the agents for the opposing parties.

1   Direction 39.1.

Appeal withdrawn

8.69 If an appeal has not been set down for hearing, it can be withdrawn by written notification to the Judicial Office, who should be informed of the nature of the agreements between the parties as to the costs of the appeal. Written notification must also be given to the respondents, who must notify the Judicial Office of their agreement to the withdrawal and confirm that costs have been agreed[1]. If an appeal has already been set down for hearing, it may only be withdrawn by order of the House of Lords on petition[2].

1   Direction 45.
2   Direction 45.3.

Death

8.70 If a party to an appeal dies before the hearing, the appeal abates. So immediate notice of the death must be given by that party's agent in writing to the Judicial Office and to the other parties. The addition of a new party to represent the deceased person's interest cannot proceed until a petition for reviving the appeal has been agreed to by the House[1]. The petition for reviving must be lodged within three months of the date of notice of death and it must be accompanied by an affidavit explaining the circumstances in which it is being lodged. If abatement takes place after the case for the deceased person has been lodged but before the appeal has been heard, the appellant must lodge a supplemental case in which are set out the orders of the House on reviving the appeal and information about the newly-added parties.

1 Procedural table, step 90.

Bankruptcy

8.71 If a party is adjudicated bankrupt, their agent must give immediate notice in writing to the other parties and to the Judicial Office, who must also be provided with a certified copy of the bankruptcy order. The bankrupt party must lodge a petition to render the appeal effective within three months of the date of the notice[1].

1 Procedural table, steps 93–94. In appeals to the House of Lords, bankruptcy does not normally terminate a bankrupt's locus standi; this differs from the position in the courts below, see *Heath v Tang* [1993] 4 All ER 694; [1993] 1 WLR 1491.

Submissions on costs

8.72 If counsel seek an order other than that costs should be awarded to the successful party, they should make submissions on costs at the conclusion of the argument before the Appellate Committee[1]. Oral submissions should be followed up by written submissions within 14 days. In appeals involving legal service funding, a successful unassisted party who wishes to apply for costs against the Community Legal Service under s 11 of the Access to Justice Act 1999 should make the application at the conclusion of the hearing and also in writing within 14 days.

1 Submissions whether or not made at the hearing should also be made in writing no more than 14 days after the conclusion of the hearing: Direction19.1.

Judgment

8.73 At the conclusion of the hearing by the Appellate Committee, the Lord in the chair announces that the Committee will take time to consider their decision and will report to the House in due course. Judgment takes the form of a set of opinions by the law lords on the Appellate Committee collected into a report from the Appellate Committee to the House, and is the judgment of the House. It is given in the Chamber of the House on a date notified to all the parties. Counsel receive in advance in the strictest confidence copies of the judgment and of the orders that the House proposes to make to dispose of the appeal. Counsel should satisfy themselves that the proposed orders are consistent with the judgment. Submissions on costs should wherever possible be made first in writing, but submissions may be made at the judgment provided the Judicial Office has been given two days' notice.

8.74 After the House has given judgment, drafts of the final order disposing of the appeal are sent to all parties who lodged a case. The drafts, either approved or with suggested amendments, must be returned to the Judicial Office within one week of the date of receipt. If substantial amendments are proposed, these must be submitted to the agents for the other parties, who should indicate their approval or disagreement, both to the agents submitting the proposals and to the Judicial Office. A final order signed by the Clerk of the Parliaments (who is registrar of the court) is issued to the agents for the successful party. Prints of the order are sent free of charge to the agents for all parties who have entered appearance.

Bills of costs and disposal of money in Security Fund

8.75 The following paragraphs apply when the parties cannot agree their costs and a taxation (assessment of costs) is carried out by the House's Taxing Officer[1].

1   See *Practice Directions applicable to judicial taxations* (2003), available free of charge from Judicial Office.

8.76 Bills of costs for taxation must be lodged within three months of either:
(a) the date on which the final judgment in the appeal is delivered; or
(b) the date on which a petition for leave to appeal is dismissed by an Appeal Committee; or
(c) the date on which a petition for leave or a petition of appeal is withdrawn[1].

1   Taxation Direction 5.1.

8.77 Applications for extensions of time are also entertained if made after the expiry of the three-month period. In deciding whether to grant an application the Taxing Officer takes into account all the circumstances, including:
(a) the interests of the administration of justice;
(b) whether the failure to lodge in time was intentional;
(c) whether there is a good explanation for the failure to lodge in time;
(d) the effect which the delay has had on each party; and
(e) the effect which the granting of an extension of time would have on each party[1].

1   Taxation Directions 6.1–6.2.

8.78 If the appellants are ordered to pay the costs of the appeal, the respondents' costs are met, either in whole or in part, by direct payment to them from the money deposited in the Security Fund. If the total amount of the respondents' costs as allowed on taxation can be so met, any balance of the money in the Security Fund is returned to the party who paid it in. If the respondents' costs are in part satisfied by such payment, the certificate of taxation that is forwarded to the respondents takes account of the amount so paid.

8.79 In appeals where the appellants must pay more than one bill of respondents costs, and the money deposited as security is insufficient to meet all the bills, the money paid out is divided between the bills in proportion to their amounts on taxation.

8.80 If the appellants are not ordered to pay the costs of an appeal, money paid into the Security Fund is returned to them when the final judgment has been issued.

8.81 If an appeal is withdrawn before setting down, or is dismissed for want of prosecution, or if the respondents fail to lodge a bill of costs within three months, the appellants may apply in writing for the return of the money deposited by them in the security fund. Such an application must be accompanied by the written consent of all the respondents who have entered appearance. If any respondent refuses consent, the appellants can send them a written demand to lodge a bill of costs within four weeks from the date of notice. If the Clerk of the Parliaments is satisfied that such a written demand was duly sent and if the respondent fails to lodge a bill of costs within the time specified, the money in the security fund is returned to the appellants.

Enforcement of Judgment Order

8.82 The House of Lords has no machinery to enforce its orders, and so orders of the House may be made orders of the High Court. If the House affirms the order appealed against, it is not necessary for the order to be made an order of the High Court. In all other instances it is necessary to make the order of the House an order of the High Court so that the High Court has a record of the reversal or variation. Application may be made in accordance with CPR Pt 23[1]. The application is made to the procedural judge of the Division, District Registry or court in which the proceedings are taking place and may be made without notice unless the court directs otherwise.

1   CPR 40BPD.13.

8.83 The application must be supported by the following:
(1) details of the order appealed against;
(2) details of the House's order with a copy annexed;
(3) a copy annexed of the certificate of the Clerk of the Parliaments (as registrar of the court) of the assessment of the costs of the appeal.

PROCEDURAL TABLE

8.84 Contents:
- Leave to appeal (steps 1–40)
- Presentation of appeal, service and appearance (steps 41–50)
- Patent appeal from High Court (steps 51–54)
- Security for costs (steps 55–57)
- Public funding and legal aid (steps 58–60)
- Human Rights Act 1998 (step 61)
- Preparation of Statement of Facts and Issues and Appendix of documents (steps 62–68)
- Setting down for hearing (steps 69, 78–79)
- Extensions of time to lodge Statement and Appendix (steps 70–77)
- Petitions to intervene by outside party (steps 80–81)
- Lodgment of cases (steps 82–85)
- Conjoinder and consolidation (step 86)
- Exchange of cases and lodgment of Bound Volumes (steps 87–88)
- Death of party and petition for reviving appeal (steps 89–92)
- Bankruptcy of party (steps 93–94)
- Withdrawal of appeal (steps 95–99)
- Specialist advisers (step 100)
- Nautical appeals (step 101)
- Preparation for hearing (steps 102–104)
- Authorities for hearing (step 105)
- Hearing of appeal (step 106)
- Judgment and order for costs (steps 107–111)
- Draft Judgment Order (steps 112–115)
- Repayment of security for costs (step 116)
- References to European Court of Justice (steps 117–118)
- Costs and taxation (steps 119–133)

Steps to be taken	Para no of text	HL Standing Order No.	HL PD No.
If Applicant wishes to appeal to House of Lords from order of Court of Appeal:			
Either			
1. Applicant applies at hearing in Court of Appeal for leave to appeal to House of Lords.	8.5–8.8		Dir 1.2
2. Court of Appeal considers application and may: 1. grant leave to appeal to House of Lords (step 41 follows): or 2. refuse leave to appeal (step 7 follows).			
Or, if application has not been made at Court of Appeal hearing:			
3. Applicant applies by letter to the Lords Justices who heard the case. The letter should be send to the Associate's Office, c/o Civil Appeals Office, Room E330 Royal Courts of Justice, Strand, London WC2 2LL. The letter should state the title of the action, the name of the applicant, the date of the order against which leave to appeal is sought, and a brief statement of the grounds on which leave to appeal is sought.			
4. Court of Appeal considers the application and may:			

Steps to be taken	Para no of text	HL Standing Order No.	HL PD No.
1. grant leave to appeal (step 41 follows); 2. refuse leave to appeal (step 7 follows); 3. direct an oral hearing of the application (step 5 follows).			
If oral hearing is directed:			
5. Applicant follows the steps laid down in the directions for the oral hearing and, if required, serves notice on the other parties. Time: within the time laid down in the directions.			
6. Parties attend hearing of application on appointed day when Court of Appeal may:. 1. grant leave to appeal to House of Lords (step 41 follows); or 2. refuse leave to appeal (step 7 follows)			
Then, *if Court of Appeal refuses application for leave to appeal:*			
7. Applicant ('petitioner') prepares petition for leave to appeal to House of Lords.	8.17	SO II	
8. A petition for leave to appeal is not admissible if: 1. it is a petition for leave to appeal to the House of Lords against the Court of Appeal's refusal to grant leave to appeal from a judgment of a lower court;			Dir 1.6

Procedural table 271

Steps to be taken		Para no of text	HL Standing Order No.	HL PD No.
	2. the Court of Appeal has not given leave to appeal in a housing appeal relating to a rehabilitation order or compulsory purchase order;			
	3. the High Court has not given leave to proceed to a vexatious litigant;			
	4. it is a petition for leave to appeal from the Court of Appeal from a county court in any probate proceedings;			
	5. it is a petition for leave to appeal from a decision of the High Court on a question of law under Part III of the Representation of the People Act 1983.			
9.	The original petition for leave should be produced on good-quality A4 paper, bound on the left like a book and using both sides of the paper. It should be word-processed rather than printed. The petition should set forth briefly the facts and points of law, and conclude with a summary of reasons for leave being granted.	8.18		Dir 3.1–3.2
10.	A petitioner who (i) invites the House to depart from one of its own decisions or (ii) relies on the Human Rights Act 1998 or (iii) seeks a reference to the European Court of Justice, must make that clear in the petition.			Dir 3.1

Steps to be taken	Para no of text	HL Standing Order No.	HL PD No.
11. Petitioner serves on respondents or their agents a copy of the petition for leave.			Dir 3.4; Appx A
12. Petitioner endorses original petition for leave with certificate of service on respondents.			
13. Petitioner lodges in Judicial Office of House of Lords:	8.18		Dir 3.6
(i) two copies of original petition for leave endorsed with certificate of service on respondents;			
(ii) one copy of order of Court of Appeal appealed from;			
(iii) if separate from (ii), one copy of the order of the Court of Appeal refusing leave. Fee on presentation of petition for leave: £570.			
Time: Within one month from date of order appealed from.			Dir 2.1
14. Petitioner also lodges in Judicial Office:			Dir 4.2
(i) four additional copies of petition for leave;			
(ii) four additional copies of order appealed from;			
(iii) four copies of order of court below refusing leave to appeal, if a separate order;			
(iv) five copies of transcript of judgment of court below;			
(v) five copies of order of court of first instance;			

Steps to be taken		Para no of text	HL Standing Order No.	HL PD No.
	(vi) five copies of transcript of judgment of court of first instance, or, in the case of a county court, of judge's notes			
	Time: If possible, at same time as lodgment of petition, but not later than one week after lodgment.			
	Copies of documents must be clearly legible; copies deemed illegible by the Judicial Office will not be accepted.			Dir 4.3
15.	Petition is referred to Appeal Committee and recorded in the Minutes of Proceedings of the House.			Dir 3.7
16.	Respondents or their agents enter appearance by attending at Judicial Office to record their name and address or that of their firm, and pay fee. Time: As soon as they have received service. Fee on entering appearance: £115.	8.19		Dir 3.8
	Respondents who intend to take no part in the appeal need not enter appearance. Respondents who have not entered appearance are not sent communications by the Judicial Office.			
17.	*If Appeal Committee consider unanimously that leave should be refused:* Judicial Office notifies parties that petition is dismissed.	8.22		Dir 4.6

Steps to be taken		Para no of text	HL Standing Order No.	HL PD No.
18.	*If Appeal Committee consider that leave should be given outright*: House grants leave with or without terms.	8.23		Dir 4.6
19.	*If Appeal Committee requires further submissions before deciding whether leave should be given:* respondents are invited to lodge objections if they wish setting out reasons why leave should not be given or making submissions as to terms on which leave should be given. Seven copies of any respondents' objections must be lodged in Judicial Office; a copy must be served on other parties. Time: Usually within 14 days of invitation to lodge respondents' objections.	8.25		Dir 4.6
20.	*In all cases where Appeal Committee are not unanimous:* petition is referred for hearing.	8.26		Dir 4.10
21.	Judicial Office gives notice of date and time of hearing before Appeal Committee to petitioner's agents and respondents' agents who have entered appearance.			

Steps to be taken	Para no of text	HL Standing Order No.	HL PD No.
22. Agents or counsel may be heard before the Appeal Committee; only one counsel on each side is heard. Queen's Counsel may appear at the hearing but only a junior's fee is allowed on taxation of petitions for leave even when a public funding certificate authorises briefing of a QC.			Dir 4.13–4.14; 1.9
23. Parties notify the Judicial Office of the name of counsel to appear on their behalf.			
24. Parties or their agents or counsel attend meeting of Appeal Committee. If petition is refused, no further action may be taken. If petition is allowed, the appeal proceeds (*step 41 follows*).			

Public funding

25. The House of Lords does not receive applications for public funding. Application should be made to the Legal Services Commission or in Scotland and Northern Ireland to relevant legal aid committee. Time limits are suspended pending decision on public funding, provided Judicial Office has been informed of application (see also steps 58–60).	8.20	SO IX	Dir 1.8

Steps to be taken	Para no of text	HL Standing Order No.	HL PD No.
Costs of petitions for leave are awarded as follows:			
26. If a petition for leave is allowed, costs become costs in the appeal. If petition refused without a hearing, an order is automatically made that respondents are at liberty to apply for costs. If petition refused at hearing, application for costs must be made at end of hearing.	8.27		Dir 5
27. At whatever stage of above process Appeal Committee determines a petition for leave. Committee's decision is recorded formally in Minutes of Proceedings of the House and copies of Minutes sent to the parties. *If leave has been granted the next step is 41. If applicant wishes to apply for leave to appeal direct from High Court to House of Lords, steps 26–40 apply:*			
Either			
28. Applicant applies to trial judge or Divisional Court at hearing for certificate for leave to appeal direct to House of Lords. Time: immediately after judgment has been given on the proceedings.	8.9–8.15	SO III	Dir 6

Steps to be taken	Para no of text	HL Standing Order No.	HL PD No.
Or, *if applicant does not apply for certificate at hearing:*			
29. Applicant enters motion in Crown Office, Royal Courts of Justice, by lodging: (i) notice of motion for certificate to be issued; (ii) three copies of notice for judges' use; (iii) affidavit explaining delay. Time: Within 14 days from date on which judgment was given including day on which judgment was given. In practice, where the appeal is from a single Chancery or Queen's Bench judge the judge's clerk would put the matter in the list for the application to be made without a formal motion.			
30. Applicant serves notice of motion on respondents. Time: At least two clear days before day named in notice for hearing.			
31. Parties attend on appointed day for hearing of motion.			

Steps to be taken	Para no of text	HL Standing Order No.	HL PD No.
Then:			
32. *If judge is satisfied that the relevant conditions are fulfilled, that sufficient case to justify application for leave to bring such appeal has been made out and that all parties consent to grant of certificate:* Judge may grant certificate. If judge grants a certificate, then any of the parties to the proceedings may apply for leave to appeal.			
33. No appeal lies against the grant or refusal of a certificate, although, if a certificate is refused, the applicant may appeal to the Court of Appeal from the High Court's decision in the normal way, once the time for applying for a certificate has expired. The relevant conditions are that a point of law of general public importance is involved: 1. which relates wholly or mainly to the construction of an Act or statutory instrument; and 2. which has been fully argued in the proceedings; and 3. which has been fully considered in the judgment of the judge in the proceedings; or			

Steps to be taken	Para no of text	HL Standing Order No.	HL PD No.
4 in respect of which the judge is bound by a decision of the Court of Appeal or House of Lords in previous proceedings; and which was fully considered by the Court of Appeal or House of Lords in the previous proceedings.			
34. Party applying for leave to appeal prepares petition as in steps 7–10. Time: Within one month from date when certificate was granted			
35. Applicant ('Petitioner') serves petition on other parties and endorses certificate of service on petition as in steps 11–12.			
36. Petitioner lodges petition by lodging in Judicial Office, House of Lords: (i) original petition endorsed with certificate of service; (ii) one copy of High Court's certificate. Time: Within one month from date on which certificate was granted by High Court, unless time is extended (for extensions of time, see steps 71–74). Fee on lodging petition: £570.			

Steps to be taken	Para no of text	HL Standing Order No.	HL PD No.
37. Petitioner also lodges in Judicial Office: (i) four additional copies of petition; (ii) five copies of order of High Court; (iii) four additional copies of High Court's certificate, if not contained in the order; (iv) five copies of transcript of judgment of High Court; Time: At same time as or within 1 week of lodgment of petition. *If petitioner cannot lodge petition within one month from date on which certificate was granted:* **38.** Petitioner lodges in Judicial Office: (i) request for extension of time to lodge petition; (ii) three copies of transcript of High Court judgment. Time: Within one month from date on which certificate was granted. The request must state the reasons why time should be extended. The request is referred to Appeal Committee and determined without a hearing. **39.** Judicial Office notifies petitioner of decision of Appeal Committee.			

Steps to be taken	Para no of text	HL Standing Order No.	HL PD No.
If extension of time is granted:			
40. Petitioner lodges petition as in steps 43–48.			
As soon as petition of appeal has been lodged:			
41. Petition is referred to Appeal Committee. Appeal Committee consider and determine petition without a hearing.			
42. Appeal Committee decision is recorded in House of Lords Minutes of Proceedings. Judicial Office sends copies of Minutes recording the decision to parties.			
Then, *if leave to appeal is granted:*			
43. Appellants prepare petition of appeal.	8.29	SO I	Dir 9.1; 30, App C
44. An original petition and at least seven copies should be prepared. The original petition should be produced on good quality A4 paper, bound on the left like a book and using both sides of the paper. It should be word-processed rather than printed.			

Steps to be taken		Para no of text	HL Standing Order No.	HL PD No.
	When leave to appeal has been given by the Court of Appeal or the House of Lords (i.e. the vast majority of appeals), the petition of appeal should be signed by the appellants or their agents. In all other cases, except where leave has been given under any Act of Parliament, the petition must be signed by two counsel who must certify that the appeal is reasonable. These signatures are mandatory even if the appellants have previously conducted the litigation themselves or propose to conduct the appeal in person.		SO IV	Dir 9.2
45.	A special certificate is required in the case of Scottish appeals.	8.29	SO IX	Dir 9.2
46.	Appellants serve on respondents or their agents copy of petition of appeal.	8.30		Dir 9.7
47.	Appellants endorse certificate of service on original petition of appeal.			
48.	Appellants lodge in Judicial Office: (i) original petition of appeal endorsed with certificate of service; (ii) seven copies of petition; (iii) if possible, at time of lodgment, if not, within one week: security for costs (see step 55).	8.30		Dir 9.8

Procedural table 283

Steps to be taken		Para no of text	HL Standing Order No.	HL PD No.
	Time: Within three months of date of last order appealed from, unless other time limits apply. Fee on lodgment of petition of appeal following successful petition for leave: £570. Fee on lodgment of petition of appeal if leave granted by the lower court: £1140.		SO I	
49.	The petition is presented to the House and the presentation is recorded in the Minutes of Proceedings of the House. Time: On same day as lodgment if House is sitting; if not, on next sitting day.			
50.	Respondents or their agents enter appearance by attending at Judicial Office and recording their name and address or that of their firm, and pay fee. Time: As soon as they have received service. Fee on entering appearance: £230.	8.31		Dir 9.10
If appeal is direct from High Court against revocation of a patent or on a counterclaim for revocation of a patent:				Dir 40
51.	If respondents decide not to appear or not to oppose appeal: respondents serve:			

Steps to be taken	Para no of text	HL Standing Order No.	HL PD No.
1. on Comptroller-General of Patents, Designs and Trade Marks: (i) notice of his decision not to appear or oppose appeal; (ii) copy of petition or of pleadings and affidavits filed in the action; 2. on appellants: notice of decision not to appear or oppose appeal. Time: At any time before the appeal begins in the Appellate Committee.			
52. Comptroller then: 1. serves on appellants a notice stating whether or not he intends to appear in the appeal. 2. lodges such notice in Judicial Office. Time: Within 14 days after receiving notice of respondents' decision.			
53. Comptroller may appear and be heard in opposition to the appeal if he has given notice of his intention to do so or if House so directs.			
If Comptroller has given notice of his intention to appear or in any case where the House so directs:			
54. Comptroller enters appearance as in step 50.			

Steps to be taken	Para no of text	HL Standing Order No.	HL PD No.
In all appeals, unless the House has ordered otherwise or appellants have been granted legal aid or security for costs has been waived, appellants must give security for costs in the sum of £25,000:			
55. Appellants gives security by paying £25,000 into Security Fund Account of House of Lords. Time: Within one week of presentation of appeal. Drafts and cheques must be made payable to 'House of Lords Security Fund Account'.	**8.32**	SO V	Dir 10
56. Certain classes of appellant are not required to give security for costs. If appellants who are not exempt fail to give security for costs, the appeal stands dismissed.			Dir 10.4
57. If all respondents agree to waive security for costs: Appellants' agents lodge form of consent to waive security signed by all respondents' agents. Time: Within one week of presentation of appeal. Fee on lodging form of consent of waiver: £115. An order is then made by the House absolving the appellants from giving security.			
In any appeal where public funding is required:			
58. Party desiring public funding:			

Steps to be taken	Para no of text	HL Standing Order No.	HL PD No.
1. applies: (a) in England, to a Funding Review Committee; (b) in Scotland, to the Scottish Legal Aid Board; (c) in Northern Ireland, to the Legal Aid Committee; 2. gives notice in writing of application to other parties to appeal and to Judicial Office.	8.33		Dir 41
59. Time limits for the following stages are extended so as to expire one month after determination of the funding application provided notice of the application has been given to Judicial Office: 1. petitioning for leave to appeal (step 13); 2. presenting a petition of appeal (step 48); 3. giving security for costs (step 55). Where respondents have applied for public funding, the time for lodging Statement and Appendix is extended to six weeks after determination of the application.			

If public funding is granted:

60. Party obtaining public funding lodges copy of certificate in Judicial Office.			

Steps to be taken	Para no of text	HL Standing Order No.	HL PD No.
In all appeals to the House of Lords:			
61. Human Rights Act 1998: Appellants must notify the Judicial Office in writing when:	**8.34**		Dir 9.6
(a) the House is to be asked to consider whether to make, uphold or reverse a declaration that a provision of primary or subordinate legislation is incompatible with a European Human Rights Convention right or is to be asked to consider any issue which may lead the House to make such a declaration, or where such an issue may be raised in respect of a judicial act;			
(b) a party seeks to challenge an act of a public authority under the Human Rights Act 1998; or			
(c) a party relies in whole or in part on the provisions of the Human Rights Act 1998.			
Appellants should indicate whether notification is made under (a), (b) or (c) above; they should set out briefly the arguments involved; and state whether the point was taken in the courts below. In appeals in which (a) above is an issue, the Crown has a right to be joined as a party to the appeal.			
62. Appellants prepare a Statement of Facts and Issues and Appendix of documents.	**8.35–8.42**		Dir 11; 12

Steps to be taken		Para no of text	HL Standing Order No.	HL PD No.
	Appellants draw up Statement and submit it to respondents for agreement. Statement should be a succinct account of the facts of the case and of the issues involved in the appeal. Statement must be a single document agreed between the parties and any disputed material removed and included instead in a party's case (step 82). Time: Within six weeks of presentation of appeal.			
63.	Appellants prepare Appendix. Appendix contains documents used in evidence or recording proceedings in courts below. Preparation of Appendix should be done in consultation with respondents and contents must be agreed between parties.			
	Appendix should contain only documents necessary to support and understand the argument when the appeal is heard.			
64.	Appendix may consist of one or more parts. Part 1 should contain:			

Steps to be taken	Para no of text	HL Standing Order No.	HL PD No.
1. formal originating documents; 2. case stated (if any); 3. judgments and orders relating to decisions at first instance and on appeal; 4. relevant statutory provisions; 5. any crucial documents on which action is founded; Other documents should be included in Part 2 of Appendix and subsequent parts if necessary. Any documents disputed between the parties and any documents not included in the Appendix which may be required at the hearing should be held in readiness and subject to leave being given may be introduced at appropriate moment. 15 copies should be prepared and other parties must be given notice of any documents to be held in readiness.			
65. Cost of preparing Statement and Appendix is borne in the first instance by appellants but is subject to decision of the House as to costs of appeal.			

Steps to be taken	Para no of text	HL Standing Order No.	HL PD No.
Where appellants decline to include in the Appendix any documents which the respondents consider necessary, respondents must prepare and reproduce them at their own expense.			
In Scottish appeals only:			
66. Appellants must include in Part 1 of the Appendix: the Record, an account of steps taken since the Record was completed, and interlocutors complained of.	8.61–8.65	SO VI (2)	Dir 12.11
In all appeals:			
67. As soon as a proof of the Appendix is available it should be examined and approved by all parties.			
68. Appellants must then lodge in Judicial Office: (i) eight copies of Statement (ii) eight copies of Part 1 of Appendix; (iii) 15 copies of each subsequent part of Appendix.	8.43		Dir 13.6
Time: Within six weeks of date of presentation of appeal. If this time expires during a recess of the House, it is extended to the third next sitting day.		SO VI (1)	Dir 13.1

Procedural table 291

Steps to be taken	Para no of text	HL Standing Order No.	HL PD No.
69. When appellants lodge the required number of Statements and Appendix, they must apply at same time to set down appeal for hearing. The necessary form is available from the Judicial Office			
Time: At time of lodgment of Statement and Appendix. Fee on lodging Statement and Appendix and setting down: £3,420.			
If appellants are unable to complete preparation of Statement and Appendix within six weeks:			
70. Appellants must lodge within the six weeks' period a petition for an extension of time to lodge Statement and Appendix.	8.67		Dir 13.2
71. Applications for extensions of time are normally made for periods of six weeks, and up to three extensions are usually granted, if necessary. The petition must specify the date to which further time is asked.			
72. If the date specified is likely to fall in a parliamentary recess, the Judicial Office may advise that the petition ask for an extension until the third sitting day of the next ensuing meeting of the House.			

Steps to be taken	Para no of text	HL Standing Order No.	HL PD No.
73. Appellants must submit petition for extension to agents for all respondents for their consent and petitions must be endorsed with the respondents' consent. It is expected that respondents will not unreasonably withhold their consent.			Dir 13.3–13.4
74. If respondents consent to petition for extension, it is presented to the House, which makes an order for extension of time.			
75. If appellants fail to lodge petition for extension of time within the time allowed, the appeal stands dismissed. It may then only be restored if the House agrees to a petition to restore appeal.			
Time for lodging petition for extension of time: Before six weeks' period allowed for lodgment of Statement runs out. Fee on lodging petition for extension of time: £230.			Dir 13.2
If respondents refuse consent to petition for extension of time or restoration of appeal:			
76. Appellants' agents lodge petition and six copies. It is then referred to the Appeal Committee and may be decided after an oral hearing. Fee on lodging petition: £570.			Dir 13.4

Steps to be taken	Para no of text	HL Standing Order No.	HL PD No.
When extended period for lodging Statement and Appendix expires:			
77. Steps 68–69 apply (appellants lodge required number of Statements and Appendix, and must apply at same time to set down appeal for hearing on form available from Judicial Office). Fee on lodging Statement and Appendix and setting down: £3,420.			
As soon as appellants have lodged Statement and Appendix.			
78. House orders appeal to be set down for hearing			
79. Judicial Office informs parties of likely date of hearing of appeal.			
If any outside party wishes to intervene and take part in an appeal:			
80. Special application must be made to intervene in an appeal to the House of Lords even if the proposed intervener was heard on the matter in the courts below.			Dir 36

Steps to be taken	Para no of text	HL Standing Order No.	HL PD No.
Applications for leave to intervene must be made by petition at any time after the petition of appeal has been presented to the House. The petition to intervene must indicate whether leave is sought for written intervention only or for both written intervention and oral intervention at the hearing of the appeal. The petition must be endorsed with a certificate of service on the parties and also, if the parties agree to the intervention, a certificate of the parties' consent. All petitions to intervene whether consented to or not are referred to the Appeal Committee.			
81. Party petitions for leave to intervene (petition modelled on step 70).			
In all appeals:			
82. Parties must lodge cases. Time: Appellants must lodge their case at least five weeks before date of hearing and respondents at least three weeks before. The case should be a succinct statement of party's argument in appeal and omit material contained in Statement of Facts and Issues.	8.45–8.47		Dir 15

Steps to be taken	Para no of text	HL Standing Order No.	HL PD No.
If either party is abandoning any point taken below, this should be made plain in the case. If they intend to apply for leave to introduce a new point not taken below, this too should be indicated in the case and the Judicial Office informed.			
If either party intends to invite the House to depart from one of its own decisions, this intention must be clearly stated in a separate paragraph of the case to which special attention must be drawn.			
All cases must conclude with numbered summary of reasons upon which argument is founded and must bear signature of at least one counsel who appeared in courts below or who will appear before Appellate Committee.			
Eight copies of the case must be lodged.			
Separate cases			
83. In every appeal, all the appellants must join in one case; and all respondents must also join in one case unless it can be shown that the interests of one or more respondents are distinct from those of the rest.			Dir 15.9

Steps to be taken	Para no of text	HL Standing Order No.	HL PD No.
In the latter event the respondents' agents who first lodge their case must certify that they have offered to join in a case with the other respondents whose interests are similar, or certify that their interests are distinct.			
84. Parties with passive interests in an appeal are not required to lodge a separate case.			
85. Argument in respect of a cross-appeal must be included in the case and the case must state clearly that it is lodged in respect of both the original and the cross-appeal.	8.54		Dir 26
Consolidation and conjoinder			
86. Consolidation or conjoinder may be appropriate when the issues in two or more appeals are similar. The parties may join in a single case on each side and a single set of counsel, or other variations to save time and costs.	8.50–8.53		Dir 25
In all appeals:			
87. Parties exchange cases by arrangement between the respective agents. Time: As soon as the cases are ready and at least five weeks before the expected date of hearing, the appellants must lodge eight copies of their case in the Judicial Office, and serve it on the respondents.	8.49		Dir 15.13

Steps to be taken		Para no of text	HL Standing Order No.	HL PD No.
	At least three weeks before the expected date of hearing, the respondents must lodge eight copies of their case and serve it on the appellants.			
88.	Appellants lodge in Judicial Office 15 bound volumes each containing copies of: 1. petition of appeal; 2. petition of cross-appeal (if any); 3. Statement of Facts and Issues; 4. Appellants' and respondents' cases: 5. Part 1 of Appendix; 6. index to the authorities' volumes. Time: Not later than two weeks before the proposed date of hearing.	**8.55**		Dir 16 Dir 16.1
If a party to appeal dies before hearing:		**8.70**	SO X	Dir 27
89.	Agents give notice of death in writing, and appeal abates. Time: Immediately on death of party.			
90.	Abated appeals cannot proceed until petition for reviving appeal is presented.			

Steps to be taken	Para no of text	HL Standing Order No.	HL PD No.
91. Appellants' agents: 1. lodge draft petition for reviving appeal in Judicial Office; 2. serve petition on respondents' agents; 3. endorse certificate of service on petition; 4. lodge petition in Judicial Office; 5. lodge affidavit explaining circumstances in which petition is being lodged. Time for lodging petition and affidavit: Within three months of notification of death. Fee on lodging petition: £230.			
If appeal abates after case for deceased person has been lodged:			
92. Appellants lodge supplemental case giving: 1. order of House on reviving appeal; and 2. information about newly-added parties. Copies of supplemental case required to be lodged: eight.			
If a party is adjudicated bankrupt:	8.71	SO X	Dir 24
93. Party's agents give to Judicial Office: 1. notice in writing of bankruptcy; 2. certified copy of bankruptcy order. Time: Immediately upon adjudication.			

Steps to be taken	Para no of text	HL Standing Order No.	HL PD No.
94. Bankrupt party lodges petition to render appeal effective. Time: Within three months of date of adjudication.			
If appellants wish to withdraw appeal: **Either**, *if appeal has not yet been set down for hearing*:	**8.69**		Dir 45
95. Appellants: 1. request all respondents' agents who have entered appearance to give written consent to withdrawal of appeal. 2. reach agreement with other parties as to costs.			
96. Appellants notify Judicial Office: 1. that they wish to withdraw appeal; 2. that parties have reached agreement on costs and indicate nature of agreement.			
97. Appeal is then withdrawn.			
Or, *if appeal has already been set down for hearing, it can only be withdrawn by order of the House:*			
98. Appellants: 1. prepare draft petition for withdrawal; 2. submit draft petition for consent of respondents' agents who have entered appearance;			

Steps to be taken	Para no of text	HL Standing Order No.	HL PD No.
3. submit draft petition to Judicial Office for approval. The petition should include information on costs and where appropriate indicate how the money paid into the Security Fund is to be disposed of. 4. then lodge agreed formal petition for withdrawal. Fee on lodging petition: £230.			
When an appeal has been withdrawn or dismissed for want of prosecution or if respondents fail to lodge a bill of costs within three months of date of final judgment:			
99. Money in Security Fund is repaid, provided appellants' agents send to Judicial Office: 1. written application for return to them of money deposited in Security Fund; 2. written consent of respondents' agents.			Dir 23.6
In all appeals:			
100. Any party may apply for specialist advisers to attend the hearing.		SO XIV	Dir 42
In nautical appeals:			
101. Any party to an appeal in Admiralty or maritime causes may apply in writing for attendance of Nautical Assessors.		SO XIV	Dir 42

Procedural table 301

Steps to be taken	Para no of text	HL Standing Order No.	HL PD No.
In all appeals:			
102. Agents keep themselves informed of expected date of hearing by inquiry at Judicial Office. Time: From time to time after appeal has been set down.			
103. Judicial Office sends provisional notice to agents of expected date of hearing. Time: Before beginning of each Law Term.			
104. Judicial Office formally notifies agents of date of hearing. Time: Shortly before hearing.			
105. Appellants lodge ten copies of all authorities which may be needed during the hearing bound together in green folders. To enable appellants to do this respondents must provide ten copies of any authorities which they require but appellants do not. Time: At the same time as Bound Volumes (step 88).			Dir 17
106. Counsel and agents and parties attend hearing before Appellate Committee.			

Steps to be taken	Para no of text	HL Standing Order No.	HL PD No.
At conclusion of hearing counsel should make any submissions they have on costs, if they seek any order other than that costs should follow the event. They should in addition set out such submissions in writing within 14 days of end of the hearing. Judgment is usually given some weeks after the end of the hearing.			Dir 19.1
If necessary, a further opportunity for submissions on costs arises when judgment is delivered (step 110) but it is more convenient if issues relating to costs are raised before the judgment stage.			Dir 19.4
107. Judicial Office notifies parties of date of judgment.			
108. Counsel receive in advance in the strictest confidence copies of judgment and orders that House proposes to make to dispose of appeal. Counsel should satisfy themselves that the proposed orders are consistent with the judgment.			Dir 20.2

Steps to be taken	Para no of text	HL Standing Order No.	HL PD No.
109. One counsel for each party to the appeal is required to attend judgment. Leading counsel or junior counsel may attend, but only a junior's fee is allowed on taxation. By convention (because judgment is given in the chamber of the House of Lords) Queen's Counsel wear full-bottomed wigs at judgment.			Dir 20.1
If parties wish to make submissions on costs at judgment:			
110. Submissions on costs should wherever possible be made at the hearing of the appeal and then in writing, but submissions may be made at judgment provided the Judicial Office has been given two clear days' notice and both the Judicial Office and the other parties to the appeal have been sent an outline of the submissions and an indication of the nature of the Order sought.			
111. A series of questions is proposed from the Woolsack to dispose of the appeal.			
112. Judicial Office sends to all parties who lodged a case drafts of the Judgment Order for checking and approval.			
Time for return of draft Judgment Order: one week from date of receipt, either approved or with amendments.			Dir 21.1

Steps to be taken	Para no of text	HL Standing Order No.	HL PD No.
If substantial amendments are proposed to Judgment Order:			
113. They must be submitted to the other parties for approval.			
114. Formal Judgment Order of the House signed by the Clerk of the Parliaments (as registrar of the court) is sent free of charge to the agents for the successful party.			
115. Prints of final Judgment Order are sent free of charge to all parties who entered appearance.			
If appellants are not ordered to pay costs of appeal:			
116. Money paid into Security Fund Account is returned to appellants. Time: after final Judgment Order has been issued.			
References to European Court of Justice			
117. The House may order a reference to the European Court of Justice before granting leave to appeal or after a petition of appeal has been lodged. In the latter event it may be convenient for the Court of Justice if the Statement of Facts and Issues is prepared as usual. Where the Statement has already been prepared before the issue of a reference arises it may be necessary to prepare a further Statement.			Dir 32

Steps to be taken	Para no of text	HL Standing Order No.	HL PD No.
118. When the House intends to make a reference, the hearing is adjourned and the parties invited to submit an agreed draft of the questions to be referred. The draft may be considered at a further brief hearing before the reference is made.			
Steps 119–133 apply when the costs of a successful party are required to be taxed by the House's Taxing Officer:			
119. The Practice Directions applicable to judicial taxations in the House of Lords (2003) may be obtained free of charge from the Judicial Office.			
120. The receiving party (whose bill of costs is to be taxed) sends a copy of bill to agents for other parties entitled to be represented at taxation and then lodges in Judicial Office: (i) bill of costs plus one copy; (ii) counsel's fee notes; (iii) written evidence of any other disbursement claimed which exceeds £250. Time: within three months from date of issue of judgment (but application may be made for bills to be taxed out of time).			Tax Dir 8.1, 9.1 Tax Dir 5.1 Tax Dir 6

Steps to be taken		Para no of text	HL Standing Order No.	HL PD No.
121.	Within 21 days after service of bill on them, paying parties may lodge points of dispute. They must serve these on receiving party. Where paying party does not lodge points of dispute and fails to attend a taxation, the Taxing Officers generally allow the bill as drawn.			Tax Dir 14.1
122.	There are two Taxing Officers of the House of Lords, namely, the Clerk of the Judicial Office and the Senior Costs Judge of the Supreme Court of England and Wales (or any costs judge nominated by him).			
123.	The Taxing Officers sit as a court of two, in public, usually in Committee Room 2 on the Committee Corridor of the Palace of Westminster.			
124.	Costs in the House of Lords are ordered to be taxed on the standard basis or indemnity basis in accordance with Part 44.4 of the Civil Procedure Rules or the equivalent bases in Scotland and Northern Ireland.			Tax Dir 10.1
125.	A provisional taxation procedure exists for the taxation of costs involving public funding. If the result of the provisional taxation proves unsatisfactory to the parties, the Taxing Officer appoints a date for a hearing.			Tax Dir 13

Steps to be taken		Para no of text	HL Standing Order No.	HL PD No.
126.	Bills to be taxed between the parties and large or complex bills are dealt with only at a hearing before the Taxing Officers.			Tax Dir 13.2
127.	The Taxing Officers give at least 21 days' notice of the day and time appointed for the taxation to all those entitled to be heard at the taxation.			
128.	The receiving party or their agent must attend the taxation.			
129.	The Taxing Officers have discretion as to the amount they allow. In exercising this discretion they bear in mind the terms 'unreasonably incurred' and 'unreasonable in amount' in CPR 44.4, or in Scotland the provisions of Rule 42.10 of the Rules of the Court of Session 1994.			Tax Dir 14.4
130.	There is an appeals procedure against the decisions of the Taxing Officers but an appeal is admissible only on a question of principle and not in respect of any quantum allowed on any item.			Tax Dir 17
131.	Fees are payable on taxation: (1) on bills where the amount allowed does not exceed £500, a flat rate of £50; (2) on bills where the amount allowed exceeds £500, for every £1 or fraction of £1 an amount of 5p;			

Steps to be taken		Para no of text	HL Standing Order No.	HL PD No.
	(3) on the withdrawal of a bill of costs within 21 days of the day appointed for taxation: 1 per cent of the agreed sum or £50, whichever is larger; (4) On the withdrawal of a bill of costs within seven days of the day appointed for taxation: 2 per cent of the agreed sum or £50, whichever is larger.			
	The fee on taxation is added to the taxed bill of costs. A form of allocatur can be obtained at the taxation hearing. Vouchers for disbursements (except court fees) must be produced on completion of the bill.			
132.	Agents then attend Judicial Office with: (1) Completed bill to pay taxing fee (2) Allocatur signed by all agents who attended taxation. Time: within one month of taxation.			
133.	Taxing Officer issues certificate of taxation for costs as allowed and sends it to agents who lodged bill, except to respondents whose costs can be met totally from the Security Fund. Time: when taxing fee has been paid.			

CHAPTER 9

Applications to the ECtHR and ECJ

Introduction	9.1
The European Court of Human Rights	9.5
Court of Justice of the European Communities	9.9

INTRODUCTION

9.1 There are at least three systems of law governing activity within England and Wales: domestic law, the law of the European Union, and the European Convention on Human Rights. In an ideal world these three systems should blend together seamlessly, but they do not. The President of the European Court of Human Rights[1] illustrated this 'complementarity', or its lack, with the following example:

> 'The case of *Koua Poirrez v France*[2] looked fairly run-of-the-mill but provides a very good summary of the state of relations between the [European Convention on Human Rights] and the law of the European Union and their consequences, in terms of the law as it is and the law as it should be. Here was a physically disabled applicant, a national of Ivory Coast, who had been adopted as an adult by a French citizen although he did not thereby acquire French nationality. He applied for an adult disability allowance but his application was turned down on the ground of his Ivory Coast nationality. The court hearing his appeal decided to ask the Court of Justice of the European Communities for a preliminary ruling on the compatibility between the relevant French law and Community law, on the basis that the applicant was a direct descendant of a

citizen of the European Union. The Court of Justice found that Community law did not apply to the facts of the case: although the applicant's adoptive father was indeed a national of a Member State of the European Communities, he did not qualify as a migrant worker since he had always lived and worked in France. On the strength of this Luxemburg judgment, all the French courts which successively dealt with the appeal rejected the applicant's request for a disability allowance He then applied to [the European Court of Human Rights] which, in a judgment of 30 September 2003, ie more than 13 years after he had originally applied, found that the applicant had been the victim of discrimination based on nationality, contrary to Article 14 of the Convention taken together with Article 1 of Protocol No 1, and, ruling on an equitable basis, awarded him €20,000 for the damage he had suffered.'[3]

1 Luzius Wildhaber.
2 40892/98, 30 September 2003.
3 Solemn hearing of the European Court of Human Rights on the occasion of the opening of the judicial year, 22 January 2004.

9.2 Recourse neither to the European Court of Human Rights nor to the European (EU) Court of Justice is an 'appeal' from the national court. In the case of the Court of Human Rights it is essentially a fresh action; and in the case of the European Court of Justice, for the cases with which we are concerned here, those involving individual or corporate parties as opposed to actions between member states or between a Community institution and a member state, it is a subsidiary action the outcome of which might have a determinative effect on the national proceedings.

9.3 Sadly these two courts are often confused, even by those who should know better. The European Court of Human Rights has nothing to do with the European Community: it is a creature of the older Council of Europe, of which the United Kingdom was a founder member in 1949, and which now has 45 member states, including all the present EU member states and many of the transition countries of central and eastern Europe. It is the practice that members of the Council of Europe should ratify the human rights convention.

9.4 Since the coming into effect of the Human Rights Act 1998, the rights enshrined in the European Convention are now a part of domestic law, to be had regard to by national courts almost in the way that European Community law has been for the past three decades[1].

1 Although, by s 2(1) Human Rights Act 1998, a court or tribunal determining a question which has arisen in connexion with a Convention right is only enjoined to 'take into account' any judgment, decision, declaration or advisory opinion of the European Court of Human Rights 'so far as it is relevant to the proceedings in which that question has arisen'. This reflects the 'margin of appreciation' allowed to member states by the European Court of Human Rights:

see, for example, *Elsholz v Germany* (25735/94, 13 July 2000). Under s 3(1) European Communities Act 1972, however, any question as to the meaning or effect of any of those Treaties shall be 'determined in accordance with' the principles laid down by the Court of Justice.

THE EUROPEAN COURT OF HUMAN RIGHTS

9.5 Section I of the European Convention on Human Rights sets out the rights and freedoms which are at its heart. Section II[1] contains the provisions relating to the establishment[2] of the European Court of Human Rights[3], its jurisdiction, the admissibility of applications and its procedures. It is for the Court to interpret the Convention. In essence it is open to any individual, group or non-governmental organisation which is the victim of a violation of a Convention right by one of the member states to lodge a claim once all national remedies have been exhausted. The member states undertake to abide by the final judgment of the Court in any case to which they are parties[4].

1 As amended by Protocol No. 11, which entered into force on 1 November 1998.
2 Art 19.
3 http://www.echr.coe.int/
4 Art 46 (1).

9.6

'Article 32 – Jurisdiction of the Court
1 The jurisdiction of the Court shall extend to all matters concerning the interpretation and application of the Convention and the protocols thereto which are referred to it as provided in Articles 33, 34 and 47[1].
2 In the event of dispute as to whether the Court has jurisdiction, the Court shall decide.

Article 34 – Individual applications

The Court may receive applications from any person, non-governmental organisation or group of individuals claiming to be the victim of a violation by one of the High Contracting Parties of the rights set forth in the Convention or the protocols thereto. The High Contracting Parties undertake not to hinder in any way the effective exercise of this right.

Article 35 – Admissibility criteria
1 The Court may only deal with the matter after all domestic remedies have been exhausted, according to the generally recognised rules of international law, and within a period of six months from the date on which the final decision was taken.

2   The Court shall not deal with any application submitted under Article 34 that
   a   is anonymous; or
   b   is substantially the same as a matter that has already been examined by the Court or has already been submitted to another procedure of international investigation or settlement and contains no relevant new information.
3   The Court shall declare inadmissible any individual application submitted under Article 34 which it considers incompatible with the provisions of the Convention or the protocols thereto, manifestly ill-founded, or an abuse of the right of application.
4   The Court shall reject any application which it considers inadmissible under this Article. It may do so at any stage of the proceedings.'

First, the applicant must claim to be a victim of a violation of a Convention right by one of the signatory states. Whether the applicant meets that test is not always straightforward. In *Posokhov v Russia*[2], the applicant, who had been charged with smuggling vodka, challenged his conviction on the basis that the appointment of one of the lay judges was flawed in breach of Art 6(1)[3]. Ultimately the Rostov Regional Court quashed the conviction as being time barred, but no decision of the domestic courts had touched on the issue of the lay judge or contained any acknowledgement of the violation alleged. The Court of Human Rights held that, 'a decision or measure favourable to the applicant is not in principle sufficient to deprive him of his status as a "victim" unless the national authorities have acknowledged, either expressly or in substance, and then afforded redress for, the breach of the Convention'.

1   Art 47 deals with advisory opinions.
2   No 63486/2000.
3   'In the determination of his civil rights and obligations or of any criminal charge against him, everyone is entitled to a fair and public hearing within a reasonable time by an independent and impartial tribunal established by law.'

9.7 The exhaustion precondition is applied with some discretion. In *JL v Finland*[1], the Court said:

'Normal recourse should be had by an applicant to remedies which are available and sufficient to afford redress in respect of the breaches alleged. The existence of the remedies in question must be sufficiently certain not only in theory but also in practice, failing which they will lack the requisite accessibility and effectiveness. The exhaustion rule must be applied with some degree of flexibility and without excessive formalism. It is neither absolute nor capable of being applied automatically, since in reviewing whether it has been observed it is essential to have regard to the particular circumstances of each individual case. This means amongst other things that the Court must take realistic account not only of the existence of formal remedies in the legal system of the Contracting Party concerned but also of the general legal and political context in which they operate as well as the personal circumstances of the applicant.'

As to the procedure to be followed, rule 45 of the Rules of Court[2] requires that all applications are signed by the applicant or his representative, and rule 47 sets out the contents of an individual application:

'1. Any application under Article 34 of the Convention shall be made on the application form provided by the Registry, unless the President of the Section concerned decides otherwise. It shall set out
    (a) the name, date of birth, nationality, sex, occupation and address of the applicant;
    (b) the name, occupation and address of the representative, if any;
    (c) the name of the Contracting Party or Parties against which the application is made;
    (d) a succinct statement of the facts;
    (e) a succinct statement of the alleged violation(s) of the Convention and the relevant arguments;
    (f) a succinct statement on the applicant's compliance with the admissibility criteria (exhaustion of domestic remedies and the six-month rule) laid down in Article 35 § 1 of the Convention; and
    (g) the object of the application; and be accompanied by
    (h) copies of any relevant documents and in particular the decisions, whether judicial or not, relating to the object of the application.

2. Applicants shall furthermore
    (a) provide information, notably the documents and decisions referred to in paragraph 1 (h) of this Rule, enabling it to be shown that the admissibility criteria (exhaustion of domestic remedies and the six-month rule) laid down in Article 35 § 1 of the Convention have been satisfied; and
    (b) indicate whether they have submitted their complaints to any other procedure of international investigation or settlement.

3. Applicants who do not wish their identity to be disclosed to the public shall so indicate and shall submit a statement of the reasons justifying such a departure from the normal rule of public access to information in proceedings before the Court. The President of the Chamber may authorise anonymity in exceptional and duly justified cases.

4. Failure to comply with the requirements set out in paragraphs 1 and 2 of this Rule may result in the application not being examined by the Court.
5. The date of introduction of the application shall as a general rule be considered to be the date of the first communication from the applicant setting out, even summarily, the object of the application. The Court may for good cause nevertheless decide that a different date shall be considered to be the date of introduction.
6. Applicants shall keep the Court informed of any change of address and of all circumstances relevant to the application.'

1   No 32526/1996.
2   Which entered into force on 1 November 2003.

9.8 The Court's Practice Direction[1] on the Institution of Proceedings in respect of individual applications, supplements rules 45 and 47 of the Rules of Court, above, and sets out the general requirements in straightforward terms.

The Rules also provide that, whilst an application may be presented by the applicant or applicants themselves, once the respondent contracting state has been notified of the application, the applicant must be represented by an advocate authorised to practise in any of the contracting states and resident in one of them[2]. The President of the Chamber does have power to waive or alter this requirement.

Once a case is found admissible, the emphasis is then on effecting a settlement. Only if that fails, will the formal proceedings resume. The framework set out in the Convention is:

> '**Article 38 – Examination of the case and friendly settlement proceedings**
> 1   If the Court declares the application admissible, it shall
>   a   pursue the examination of the case, together with the representatives of the parties, and if need be, undertake an investigation, for the effective conduct of which the States concerned shall furnish all necessary facilities;
>   b   place itself at the disposal of the parties concerned with a view to securing a friendly settlement of the matter on the basis of respect for human rights as defined in the Convention and the protocols thereto.
> 2   Proceedings conducted under paragraph 1.b shall be confidential.
>
> **Article 39 – Finding of a friendly settlement**
>
> If a friendly settlement is effected, the Court shall strike the case out of its list by means of a decision which shall be confined to a brief statement of the facts and of the solution reached.

Article 45 – Reasons for judgments and decisions
1   Reasons shall be given for judgments as well as for decisions declaring applications admissible or inadmissible.
2   If a judgment does not represent, in whole or in part, the unanimous opinion of the judges, any judge shall be entitled to deliver a separate opinion.

Article 46 – Binding force and execution of judgments
1   The High Contracting Parties undertake to abide by the final judgment of the Court in any case to which they are parties.
2   The final judgment of the Court shall be transmitted to the Committee of Ministers, which shall supervise its execution.'

By Art 36 of the Convention, and rule 44, a third-party contracting state may submit written comments or take part in a hearing.

1   Issued by the President of the Court on 1 November 2003.
2   Rule 36.

COURT OF JUSTICE OF THE EUROPEAN COMMUNITIES

9.9 Article 220 of the present text of the Treaty Establishing the European Community provides, simply enough, that:

'The Court of Justice shall ensure that in the interpretation and application of this Treaty the law is observed.'

However, that obligation is really only effective if decisions of the Court of Justice[1] are applicable throughout the Community. Moreover, its decisions must have precedence over those of national courts.

In the legislation giving effect to our accession to the Community, there is a provision reflecting this[2]:

'For the purposes of all legal proceedings, any question as to the meaning or effect of any of the Treaties or of any Community instrument, shall, if not referred to the Court of Justice, be determined in accordance with the principles laid down by, and any relevant decision of, the Court of Justice.'

So UK courts are *required*[3] to follow Luxembourg precedent. And the same is true in the other member states.

1   http://www.curia.eu.int
2   European Communities Act 1972, s 3(1).
3   Cf the position under s 2(1) Human Rights Act 1998, in respect of the jurisprudence of the European Court of Human Rights.

9.10 However, the single most important provision in the EC Treaty in ensuring the consistent application of Community law is Art 234, which derives from a provision in the German constitution of 1949. Art 234 EC provides:

> 'The Court of Justice shall have jurisdiction to give preliminary rulings concerning the interpretation of this Treaty. Where such a question is raised before any court of a Member State, that court may, if it considers that a decision on the question is necessary to enable it to give judgment, request the Court of Justice to give a ruling thereon.'

It remains for the domestic court to apply the European Court's ruling, on the law, to the facts in the particular case, although in many instances that is little more than a formality. Where such a question arises before the national court of *final* instance, that court *must* bring the matter before the Court of Justice[1]. However, no doubt in deference to national sensitivities, there is no power for the Court of Justice to 'call in' questions of Community law arising in litigation before a national court. That surprises American lawyers, and is seen by some as a weakness in the Community regime.

1   There are three so-called exceptions, although they are really self-evident: where the issue of Community law is not relevant, where the question has already been decided by the European Court, and finally where there is already clear jurisprudence on the point (the *acte clair* doctrine).

9.11 Nonetheless, the Art 234 reference procedure is a wonderfully simple, and amazingly effective, mechanism for ensuring consistency in the interpretation of Community legislation across 25 jurisdictions with widely differing legal traditions and cultures. Since 1974 there have been 374 references by UK courts[1], running at about 20 each year over the past ten years.

The procedure[2], so far as our courts are concerned, is set out in CPR Pt 68. Rule 68.2 provides that:

'(1)   An order may be made at any stage of the proceedings –
    (a)   by the court of its own initiative; or
    (b)   on an application by a party in accordance with Part 23.
(2)   An order may not be made –
    (a)   in the High Court, by a Master or district judge;
    (b)   in a county court, by a district judge.
(3)   The request to the European Court for a preliminary ruling must be set out in a schedule to the order, and the court may give directions on the preparation of the schedule.'

The order will be transmitted to the Registrar of the European Court by the Senior Master.

1   To the end of 2003.
2   We are here concerned only with Art 234 EC references.

9.12 The Practice Direction to CPR Part 68 indicates that where the court intends to refer a question to the European Court it will welcome suggestions from the parties for the wording of the reference. However the responsibility for settling the terms of the reference lies with the court and not with the parties. The reference should identify as clearly and succinctly as possible the question on which the court seeks the ruling of the European Court. Moreover, in choosing the wording of the reference, it should be remembered that it will need to be translated into the other 19 Union languages, and the problems are not just linguistic: common law concepts often have no precise counterpart in the civil law.

9.13 Title III of the Protocol on the Statute of the Court of Justice sets out the procedures of the European Court. By Art 20:

'The procedure before the Court shall consist of two parts: written and oral.

The written procedure shall consist of the communication to the parties and to the institutions of the Communities whose decisions are in dispute, of applications, statements of case, defences and observations, and of replies, if any, as well as of all papers and documents in support or of certified copies of them.

Communications shall be made by the Registrar in the order and within the time laid down in the Rules of Procedure.

The oral procedure shall consist of the reading of the report presented by a Judge acting as Rapporteur, the hearing by the Court of agents, advisers and lawyers and of the submissions of the Advocate-General, as well as the hearing, if any, of witnesses and experts.

Where it considers that the case raises no new point of law, the Court may decide, after hearing the Advocate-General, that the case shall be determined without a submission from the Advocate-General.'

Article 23 is the counterpart to CPR Pt 68.

Article 26 provides that witnesses may be heard on the terms set out in Arts 27–30, for example that evidence may be taken on oath.

By Art 38, the Court shall adjudicate on costs.

And Art 40 provides for intervention in cases before the Court by member states and institutions of the Community, or by 'any other person establishing an interest in the result of any case'. An application to intervene shall be limited to supporting the form of order sought by one of the parties.

9.14 These procedures are further elaborated in Title II of Rules of Procedure of the Court of Justice; and Chapter 9 of Title III deals specifically with references for interpretation. A consolidated edition of the Rules may be found on the Court's website[1].

1 http://www.curia.eu.int/en/instit/txtdocfr/txtsenvigueur/txt5.pdf

9.15 Article 55 of the Rules of Procedure provides that, in the normal course of events, the Court will hear cases in strict order. However, Art 55(2) gives the President power, 'in special circumstances', to order that the oral proceedings in a particular case be given priority. And Art 104a(1) allows for the adoption of a generally accelerated procedure for a reference for a preliminary ruling:

> 'At the request of the national court, the President may exceptionally decide, on a proposal from the Judge-Rapporteur and after hearing the Advocate General, to apply an accelerated procedure derogating from the provisions of these Rules, where the circumstances referred to establish that a ruling on the question put to the Court is a matter of exceptional urgency.'

The 'exceptional urgency' test, however, is not easy to satisfy. The Court of Appeal made a request for the procedure to be accelerated in *Owusu v Jackson*[1] (see **para A2.17**), where the claimant had been grievously injured in an accident, and the Court believed that, 'it is in the interests of justice for the jurisdictional issues in this case to be resolved without unreasonable delay'. This request was not acceded to.

The normal procedure can be slow. A reference made to the European Court of Justice on 22 February 2001, for example, resulted in a preliminary ruling on 29 April 2004[2].

1 [2002] EWCA Civ 877, a reference under the Protocol concerning the interpretation by the Court of Justice of the Convention of 27 September 1968 on jurisdiction and the enforcement of judgments in civil and commercial matters, signed at Luxembourg on 3 June 1971.
2 *Novartis Pharmaceuticals v Medicines Control Agency* C106/01.

APPENDIX 1

Forms

Appellant's notice (N161)	A1.1
Guidance notes on completing the appellant's notice (N161A)	A1.2
Respondent's notice (N162)	A1.3
Request for dismissal of an appellant's notice (253)	A1.4
Request for dismissal of an appellant's notice (254A)	A1.5
General form of request for dismissal of an application (254B)	A1.6

320 *Forms*

APPELLANT'S NOTICE (N161)

A1.1

Appellant's Notice

In the [   ]

Notes for guidance are available which will help you complete this form. Please read them carefully before you complete each section.

Seal

For Court use only	
Appeal Court Reference No.	
Date filed	

Section 1 Details of the claim or case

Name of court [   ]   Case or claim number [   ]

Names of claimants/ applicants/ petitioner

Names of defendants/ respondents

In the case or claim, were you the
(tick appropriate box)

☐ claimant   ☐ applicant   ☐ petitioner
☐ defendant   ☐ respondent   ☐ other *(please specify)* _____

Section 2 Your (appellant's) name and address

Your (appellant's) name _____

Your solicitor's name _____ *(if you are legally represented)*

Your (your solicitor's) address

reference or contact name [   ]

contact telephone number [   ]

DX number [   ]

N161 Appellant's Notice (10.00)

Appellant's notice (N161) 321

Section 3	Respondent's name and address

Respondent's name _____

Solicitor's name _____ *(if the respondent is legally represented)*

Respondent's (solicitor's) contact address

	reference or contact name	
	contact telephone number	
	DX number	

Details of other respondents are attached ☐ Yes ☐ No

Section 4	Time estimate for appeal hearing

Do not complete if appealing to the Court of Appeal

How long do you estimate it will take to put your appeal to the appeal court at the hearing?

Days ☐ Hours ☐ Minutes ☐

Who will represent you at the appeal hearing? ☐ Yourself ☐ Solicitor ☐ Counsel

Section 5	Details of the order(s) or part(s) of order(s) you want to appeal

Was the order you are appealing made as the result of a previous appeal? Yes ☐ No ☐

Name of Judge _____

Date of order(s) _____

If only part of an order is appealed, write out that part (or those parts)

Was the case allocated to a track? ☐ Yes ☐ No

If Yes, which track was the case allocated to? ☐ small claims track ☐ fast track ☐ multi-track

Is the order you are appealing a case management order? ☐ Yes ☐ No

2

322 *Forms*

Section 6 — Permission to Appeal

Has permission to appeal been granted?

Yes ☐ complete box **A**   No ☐ complete box **B**
if you are asking for permission or it is not required

A
Date of order granting permission _____
Name of Judge _____
Name of Court _____

B
☐ I do not need permission
☐ I _____ appellant('s solicitor) seek permission to appeal the order(s) at **section 5** above.

Are you making any other applications?   Yes ☐   No ☐
If Yes, complete section 10

Is the appellant in receipt of legal aid certificate or a community legal service fund (CLSF) certificate?   Yes ☐   No ☐

Does your appeal include any issues arising from the Human Rights Act 1998?   Yes ☐   No ☐

Section 7 — Grounds for appeal

I (the appellant) appeal(s) the order(s) at **section 5** because:

Appellant's notice (N161) 323

| Section 8 | Arguments in support of grounds |

My skeleton argument is:-

☐ set out below ☐ attached ☐ will follow within 14 days of filing this notice

I (the appellant) will rely on the following arguments at the hearing of the appeal:-

Section 9 — What decision are you asking the appeal court to make?

I (the Appellant) am (is) asking that:-

(tick appropriate box)

☐ the order(s) at **section 5** be set aside

☐ the order(s) at **section 5** be varied and the following order(s) substituted :-

☐ a new trial be ordered

☐ the appeal court makes the following additional orders :-

Appellant's notice (N161) 325

| Section 10 | Other applications |

I wish to make an application for additional orders
☐ in this section
☐ in the Part 23 application form (N244) attached

Part A
I apply (the appellant applies) for an order (a draft of which is attached) that :-

because :-

Part B
I (we) wish to rely on:

☐ evidence in Part C
☐ witness statement (affidavit)

Part C
I (we) wish to rely on the following evidence in support of this application:-

Statement of Truth

I believe (the appellant believes) that the facts stated in Section 10 are true.

Full name _____

Name of appellant's solicitor's firm _____

signed _____ position or office held _____
Appellant ('s solicitor)   (if signing on behalf of firm or company)

Appellant's notice (N161) 327

Section 11	Supporting documents

If you do not yet have a document that you intend to use to support your appeal, identify it, give the date when you expect it to be available and give the reasons why it is not currently available in the box below.

Please tick the papers you are filing with this notice and any you will be filing later.
- [ ] Your skeleton argument (*if separate*)
- [ ] A copy of the order being appealed
- [ ] A copy of any order giving or refusing permission to appeal together with a copy of the reasons for that decision
- [ ] Any witness statements or affidavits in support of any application included in this appellant's notice
- [ ] A copy of the legal aid or CLSF certificate (*if legally represented*)
- [ ] A bundle of documents for the appeal hearing containing copies of your appellant's notice and all the papers listed above and the following :-
    - [ ] a suitable record of the reasons for the judgment of the lower court;
    - [ ] any statements of case;
    - [ ] any other affidavit or witness statement filed in support of your appeal;
    - [ ] any relevant transcript or note of evidence;
    - [ ] any relevant application notices or case management documents;
    - [ ] any skeleton arguments relied on by the lower court;
    relevant affidavits, witness statements, summaries, experts' reports and exhibits;
    - [ ] any other documents ordered by the court; (give details)

    _____

    - [ ] in a second appeal, the original order appealed, the reasons given for making that order and the appellant's notice appealing that original (first) order
    - [ ] if the appeal is from a decision of a Tribunal, the Tribunal's reasons for that decision, the original decision reviewed by the Tribunal and the reasons for that original decision

Reasons why you have not supplied a document and date when you expect it to be available:-

Signed _____ Appellant ('s Solicitor)

GUIDANCE NOTES ON COMPLETING THE APPELLANT'S NOTICE (N161A)

A1.2

Guidance notes on completing the appellant's notice

A free leaflet *I want to appeal* giving information about making an appeal in or to the High Court or a county court is available from any county court or the Clerk of the lists General Office/ Appeals Office at the Royal Courts of Justice, Strand, London WC2A 2LL. The leaflet will also explain the meaning of some of the terms and expressions used in this guidance.

Information is available about making an appeal to the Court of Appeal, from the Civil Appeals Office Registry, Room E307, Royal Courts of Justice, Strand, London WC2A 2LL

- Court staff can help you complete the appellant's notice and tell you about procedure. But they cannot give legal advice, for example, whether you should appeal or whether your appeal will be successful.
- If you need legal advice about bringing your appeal, you should contact a solicitor or a Citizens Advice Bureau immediately.
- If you are legally represented, your solicitor should complete this form on your behalf

Important - time limits for issuing (filing) your appeal.

You have only a limited time in which to file your appellant's notice at the appeal court, so you must act quickly.

> The leaflet *I want to appeal* will tell you which is the appropriate appeal court in your case.

You must file your appellant's notice:-

- within the time limit set by the judge whose order you are appealing against; or
- where that judge set no time limit, within **14 days** after the date of the decision you wish to appeal against was made.

General notes on completing the notice

Set out below are notes to help you fill in the form. You should read the notes to each section carefully before you begin to complete that particular section.

Use a separate sheet if you need more space for your answers, marking clearly which section the information refers to. Write the claim or case number on it and attach it securely to the notice.

If you do not have all the documents or information you need for your appeal, you must **not** allow this to delay sending or taking the form to the appeal court within the correct time. Complete the form as fully as possible and provide what documents you have. The notes to Section 11 will explain more about what you have to do in these circumstances.

Section 1

Details of the claim or case

Give the name of the court or tribunal whose order you are appealing against, the number of the case or claim in that court or tribunal, and the full names of all parties. You can take these details from the order or decision you are appealing against.

Indicate, by ticking the appropriate box, which party you were in those proceedings.

Section 2

Your (appellant's) name and address

Give your full name and an address to which all documents relating to the appeal are to be sent. Include contact information, e.g. telephone, and any other reference numbers.

Section 3

Respondent's name and address

Give the respondent's full name, address and contact details. The court will need this information to be able to send correspondence and other papers to the respondent. If the respondent has a solicitor, give the solicitor's address and contact details.

If there is more than one respondent, list their names, addresses and contact details on a separate sheet of paper. Write the claim number on it and attach it securely to your notice.

Tick the appropriate box to let the court know if separate details are attached.

Section 4

Time estimate for the appeal hearing

> You do not need to complete this section if your appeal is being made to the Court of Appeal in London.

Please give an estimate of how long you believe it will take you to present your case to the court at the appeal hearing. The court needs this information to assess how much of a judge's time to allow.

Section 5

Details of order you are seeking to appeal

> If you have already appealed **unsuccessfully** against the order in a county court or the High Court and wish to appeal that decision (make a second appeal) you should enter details of the first appeal in this section. Your appellant's notice appealing the original order should be included in your bundle of documents *(see notes to section 11)*.

If you are appealing only part of an order or tribunal decision, you must write out that part (or parts) of the order in the box provided.

You should give the full title and name of the judge, e.g. 'His Honour Judge Jones' or 'District Judge Smith', and the date of the order or decision being appealed.

If the order being appealed was made in the High Court or a county court, and did not relate to a family matter, it may have been allocated to the fast track or multi-track for the purpose of preparation of evidence and trial. If it was allocated to a track, you should tick the appropriate box to show which. (The notice of allocation or other order should give this information.)

You should also tick the appropriate box if the order you are appealing against was a case management decision. Case management decisions include orders relating to:
- the timetable for trial;
- the filing and exchange of information (of witnesses and experts);
- disclosure of documents (papers the court said you must make available to the other parties); or
- adding a party to a claim.

Section 6

Permission to appeal

You will usually need permission to appeal the decision of a judge of the High Court or a county court. If you are appealing the decision of a tribunal, you should check with that tribunal whether you need permission to appeal and, if so, whether you need to ask for that permission from the tribunal, or from the appeal court.

> If you wish to make a **second appeal** against the same order, you can only do so if the Court of Appeal in London gives you permission. You must make your application for permission to that court – permission for a second appeal will only be given exceptionally.

You should note that permission will only be given where the court considers that your appeal has a real prospect of success. Where your appeal is against a case management decision, the court will also consider :-

- whether the issue is significant enough to justify the costs of an appeal;
- the overall effect on the case management timetable, e.g. whether the loss of the trial date is more significant than the procedural point you wish to appeal; and
- whether it would be more convenient to deal with your point at the trial.

> You **do not** need permission if the order you are appealing against is one of the following:
> - a committal order;
> - an order refusing the grant of habeus corpus;
> - a secure accommodation order under Section 25 of the Children Act 1989.

You need only request permission in this notice if :-
- you did not ask for permission to appeal at the hearing at which the decision you are appealing against was made; or

- you asked for permission, but it was refused, and you wish the appeal court to reconsider your request.

> The court when giving permission to appeal may, **exceptionally**, direct that your appeal be referred to the Court of Appeal if it considers that it raises an important point of principle or practice or there is some other important reason for the Court of Appeal to hear it. Where the court gives this direction, it will be shown on Form N460 *Reasons for allowing or refusing permission to appeal (including referral to the Court of Appeal)* which the court will send you.

If you need more time than is allowed for filing your appellant's notice, you must make an application in the notice itself. *(See the notes to Section 10)*

Section 7

Grounds for appeal

An appeal must be based on relevant 'grounds' (reasons for appealing). An appeal court will only allow an appeal against a decision that was either:-
- wrong; or
- unjust because of a serious procedural or other irregularity in the lower court proceedings.

> The appeal court will be unlikely to overturn a decision where no real difference would be made to the outcome of the case; or the appeal would involve re-examining the factual investigation undertaken by the lower court.

Set out briefly your reasons why you think the judge's decision was wrong or unjust. If possible, list your reasons in short separately numbered paragraphs.

Remember that you **must not** include any grounds for appealing which rely on new evidence, that is evidence that has become available since the order was made. You may not produce new evidence in your appeal without first obtaining the permission of the appeal court. (*See the notes to Section 10*)

Section 8

Arguments in support of grounds

Your arguments (referred to as a 'skeleton argument') may be set out in this section of the notice, or in a separate document attached to the notice.

> Any separate skeleton argument has to be filed and served on the respondent with your completed notice or, if you are unable to complete your skeleton argument in time, no later then 14 days after filing your notice.

Skeleton arguments should contain a numbered list of points that you intend to argue at the hearing. Each point should be stated in no more than a few sentences. Refer at each point to any documents you are filing with your appellant's notice which supports that argument *(see Section 11 on documents)*.

Other useful information

Try to consider what other information the appeal court might find useful. For example, the court may find it helpful to have a list of people who feature in the case, an explanation of technical terms used in the papers, or a list of events in date order (a chronology). If you are providing any of these, they should be on a separate piece of paper attached to your notice marked with the case or claim number and names of the parties.

Section 9

What decision are you asking the court to make

Set out the order or orders that you want the appeal court to make.

Section 10

Other applications

Any application for an extension of time for appealing must be made in the notice itself. You should state the reason for the delay and the steps taken up to the time of filing the notice.

You may wish to make additional applications to the appeal court in connection with your appeal. Any other applications may be made either in the notice, or in a separate application notice (Form N244). This form can be obtained from the court. You may have to pay additional fees if it is filed at a later date than your appellant's notice. The type of application you might want to make will include:-

- asking for permission to amend (make changes to) your appellant's notice after it has been filed at court. But note that you can amend your skeleton argument (even if it is set out in part 8 of your notice) without making an application;
- asking the appeal court to issue a stay on executing the order being appealed or suspend any action in the case pending the outcome of your appeal. (You do not need to do this if you have already obtained a stay from the lower court or your appeal is from the Immigration Appeal Tribunal.)
- producing new evidence in your appeal or asking for permission to produce oral evidence at the appeal hearing. You will need to give reasons why the new evidence was not before the original court and, where oral evidence is requested, the reasons why you think it is necessary.

Section 11

Supporting documents

> **Do not delay filing your appellant's notice at the appeal court.** If you have not been able to obtain any of the documents listed below within the time allowed, complete the notice as best you can and ensure the notice is filed on time. Set out the reasons why you have been unable to obtain any of the information or documents and give the date when you expect them to be available.

Whenever possible, the following documents **must** be filed with your appellant's notice:-

> If your appeal relates to a claim in the small claims track, you **must** file the documents marked with an asterisk * below. You **may** file any of the other documents listed, if you wish, **except** the record of reasons for the judgment of the lower court. The appeal court will decide if a record of reasons is necessary. You will be told if one is needed.

*1) a sealed copy of the order you are appealing against;

*2) any order giving or refusing permission to appeal, together with a copy of the form giving the judge's reasons for giving or refusing permission (Form N460);

3) any witness statements or affidavits in support of any application included in Sections 6 or 10 of your notice or in a separate application notice (Form N244); and

4) your bundle of documents in support which should include copies of:

- your appellant's notice and any skeleton argument (if separate);
- a sealed copy of the order you are appealing;
- the documents at 2 and 3 above (if appropriate);
- any other affidavit or witness statement filed in support of the appeal;
- a suitable record of the reasons for the judgment of the lower court *(see note on page 10)*;

9

Guidance notes on completing the appellant's notice (N161A)

- any statements of case (that is, the particulars of claim, defence);
- any relevant transcript or note of evidence;

- any application notice or case management documentation relevant to the decision being appealed;
- if appropriate, any skeleton arguments relied on by the lower court; and
- relevant affidavits, witness statements, summaries, experts' reports and exhibits
- any other documents directed by the court to be filed in the appeal
- in a second appeal, the original order appealed, the reasons given for making that order and the appellant's notice appealing that original (first) order
- if the appeal is from a decision of a Tribunal, the Tribunal's reasons for that decision, the original decision reviewed by the Tribunal and the reasons for that original decision

A record of the judgment may be either
- an approved transcript of the judgment where the hearing was recorded; or
- a copy of the written judgment (endorsed with the judge's signature); or
- a note of the judgment. If you were not legally represented in the lower court but the respondent was, the respondent's advocate should make their note of the judgment available to you free of charge.

> You should remember that if you file any of the documents at a later date, you must check whether or not the information you are providing alters any of the details already given in your appellant's notice. If it does, you will need to apply to the court for permission to amend the notice. The court can tell you how to do this.

What happens next?

Filing your completed notice and documents

Copy
- your completed notice;
- any separate skeleton argument;
- any supporting documents *(see the notes to Section 11)*; and
- your bundle of documents *(the notes to Section 11 tell you what should be included in your bundle).*

so that you have one copy for yourself, one copy for the court, and one copy for each respondent. Send or take the notice and copies of all the other documents to the appeal court office with the appropriate fee. The court can tell you how much this is. The court will stamp the notice with the court seal.

Serving the respondent

The court will serve your appellant's notice, your skeleton argument and any other documents on the respondent unless you tell the court that you wish to serve them yourself.

The respondent must be served with -
- **a sealed copy of your appellant's notice** as soon as practicable but no later than 7 days after it is filed at the court
- **any separate skeleton argument** *(see the notes to Section 8)* at the same time as the notice. If you have been unable to complete your skeleton argument in time, it must be served no later than 14 days after filing your notice at the court
- **your bundle of documents**
    - if you have already obtained permission to appeal or do not need permission, the bundle must be served at the same time as your notice; **or**

- if you have asked for permission to appeal in your notice and permission has been granted without a hearing, the bundle must be served within 7 days of receiving notice that permission has been given; **or**
- if you have asked for permission to appeal in your notice which is to be considered at a hearing, the bundle must be served within 7 days of receiving notice of that hearing.

340 *Forms*

RESPONDENT'S NOTICE (N162)

A1.3

Respondent's Notice

In the

Appeal Court Reference No.

Notes for guidance are available which will help you complete this form. Please read them carefully before you complete each section.

For Court use only	
Date filed	

Seal

Section 1 — Details of the claim or case

Name of court _____   Case or claim number _____

Name or title of case or claim _____

In the case or claim, were you the
(tick appropriate box)

☐ claimant   ☐ applicant   ☐ petitioner

☐ defendant   ☐ respondent   ☐ other *(please specify)* _____

Section 2 — Your (respondent's) name and address

Your (respondent's) name _____

Your solicitor's name _____ *(if you are legally represented)*

Your (your solicitor's) address

Your reference or contact name _____

Your contact telephone number _____

DX number _____

Details of other respondents are attached ☐ Yes ☐ No

Section 3 — Time estimate for appeal hearing

Do not complete if appealing to the Court of Appeal

	Days	Hours	Minutes
How long do you estimate it will take to put your case to the appeal court at the hearing?			

Who will represent you at the appeal hearing?   ☐ Yourself   ☐ Solicitor   ☐ Counsel

N162 Respondent's Notice (10.00)   Printed on behalf of The Court Service

Respondent's notice (N162) 341

| Section 4 | Details of the order(s) or part(s) of order(s) you want to appeal |

Name of Judge

Date of order(s)

If only part of an order is appealed, write out that part (or those parts)

| Section 5 | Permission to file a respondent's notice |

Has permission to appeal been granted?

Yes ☐ complete box **A**   No ☐ complete box **B**
if you are asking for permission or it is not required

A

Date of order granting permission _____

Name of judge _____

Name of court _____

B

☐ I do not need permission

☐ I _____
respondent('s solicitor) seek permission to appeal the order(s) at **section 4** above.

Are you making any other applications?   Yes ☐   No ☐
If Yes, complete section 9

Is the respondent in receipt of legal aid certificate or a community legal service fund (CLSF) certificate?   Yes ☐   No ☐

Does your appeal include any issues arising from the Human Rights Act 1998?   Yes ☐   No ☐

| Section 6 | Grounds for appeal or for upholding the order |

I (the respondent)

☐ appeal(s) the order   ☐ wish(es) the appeal court to uphold the order on different or additional grounds

because:-

Section 7 — Arguments in support of grounds

My skeleton argument is:-

☐ set out below   ☐ attached   ☐ will follow within 21 days of receiving the appellant's skeleton arguments

I (the respondent) will rely on the following arguments at the hearing of the appeal:-

344 *Forms*

| Section 8 | What decision are you asking the appeal court to make? |

I (the respondent) am (is) asking that:-

(tick appropriate box)

☐ the order(s) at **section 4** be set aside

☐ the order(s) at **section 4** be varied and the following order(s) substituted :-

[ ]

☐ a new trial be ordered

☐ the appeal court makes the following additional orders :-

[ ]

☐ the appeal court upholds the order but for the following different or additional reasons

[ ]

Respondent's notice (N162) 345

Section 9	Other applications

I wish to make an application for additional orders ☐ in this section

☐ in the Part 23 application form (N244) attached

Part A
I apply (the respondent applies) for an order (a draft of which is attached) that :-

because :-

Part B
I (the respondent) wish(es) to rely on :

☐ evidence in Part C
☐ witness statement (affidavit)

Part C
I (the respondent) wish(es) to rely on the following evidence in support of this application:-

---

Statement of Truth

I believe (the respondent believes) that the facts stated in Section 9 are true.

Full name _____

Name of respondent's solicitor's firm _____

signed _____ position or office held _____
Respondent ('s solicitor) (if signing on behalf of firm or company)

Respondent's notice (N162) 347

| Section 10 | Supporting documents |

Please tick the papers you are filing in your bundle:-

☐ your respondent's notice and any skeleton arguments (if separate);
☐ any witness statements or affidavits in support of any application included in section 5 or 9 of your notice or in a separate Part 23 application notice;
☐ any other affidavit or witness statement filed in support of your arguments;
☐ a copy of the legal aid or CLSF certificate (if legally represented); and
☐ any other documents directed by the court to be filed in your appeal *(give details)*.

Reasons why you have not supplied a document and date when you expect it to be available:-

Signed _____ Respondent/'s Solicitor

REQUEST FOR DISMISSAL OF AN APPELLANT'S NOTICE (253)

A1.4

Notice of Amount Allowed on Provisional Assessment

To [Claimant][Defendant]['s Solicitor]

In the	
Claim No.	
Claimant (including Ref.)	
Defendant (including Ref.)	
Date	

Take notice that the [claimant's][defendant's][receiver's] bill of costs has been provisionally assessed and is returned with this notice

If you wish to be heard on the assessment, you must, within 14 days of the receipt of this notice inform the court in writing and return the bill of costs to the court. A date for assessment will then be fixed.

If you accept the provisional assessment as final, please complete and return the bill together with the balance of the assessment fee.

Note: In Legal aid only/LSC only cases
1) Within 7 days of receipt of the notice the solicitor must notify counsel in writing where the fees claimed on counsel's behalf have been provisionally reduced or disallowed.
2) The solicitor should not accept the provisional assessment as final without first enquiring whether any counsel whose fees have been provisionally reduced or disallowed has also accepted it.
3) Attention is drawn to the need to endorse on the bill a certificate in the form of precedent F(4) before returning the bill to the court.

The court office at

is open between 10 am and 4 pm Monday to Friday. Address all communications to the Court Manager quoting the claim number
N253 Notice of amount allowed on provisional assessment (7.00)

REQUEST FOR DISMISSAL OF AN APPELLANT'S NOTICE (254A)

A1.5

FORM 254A   REQUEST FOR DISMISSAL OF AN APPELLANT'S NOTICE

[Permission   WHICH HAS BEEN SERVED ONLY FOR INFORMATION

Without Notice]   AND ON WHICH THE RESPONDENT(S) IS/ARE NOT EXPECTED TO HAVE TAKEN ANY ACTION

FOR USE WHERE PERMISSION TO APPEAL IS REQUIRED AND HAS NOT YET BEEN OBTAINED

USING THIS FORM WILL HAVE THE EFFECT OF DISMISSING THE ENTIRE PROCEEDINGS IN THE APPEAL COURT

IN THE COURT OF APPEAL   **Court of Appeal Ref.****

ON APPEAL FROM

BETWEEN:

Claimant
(Plaintiff)/Appellant
Petitioner/Respondent

and

Defendant/Appellant
Respondent/Respondent

WE, the solicitors* for the above-named Appellant, who is not a child or a patient

(1) CERTIFY that the appellant's notice seeking permission to appeal has been served on the Respondent(s) solely in compliance with rule 52.4 of the Civil Procedure Rules and that the Court has not directed service of any other document and no such service has been effected.

(2) REQUEST the dismissal of the said appellant's notice [and the applications contained within it] with no order for costs.

DATED this   day of   20

(Signed) _____

* (Solicitor for the Appellant)

*   If any party is acting in person, please modify the wording as appropriate.

**   Please list the full reference including any relevant suffix.

GENERAL FORM OF REQUEST FOR DISMISSAL OF AN APPLICATION (254B)

A1.6

FORM 254B   GENERAL FORM OF REQUEST FOR DISMISSAL OF AN APPLICATION

[*Applications* Within Appellant's Notice   MADE WITHIN AN APPELLANT'S NOTICE WHERE THAT NOTICE IS NOT BEING DISMISSED

for Ancillary Applications]   OR SEPARATELY AS AN ANCILLARY RELIEF APPLICATION

SECTION A IS TO BE COMPLETED WHERE THE APPLICATION IS BEING DISMISSED WITH COSTS: IN THAT CASE, ONLY THE APPLICANT'S SOLICITOR (OR THE APPLICANT, IF ACTING IN PERSON) NEED SIGN

IN ALL OTHER CASES SECTION B MUST BE COMPLETED AND IT MUST BE SIGNED BY THE SOLICITORS FOR ALL PARTIES (AND BY ANY PARTY ACTING IN PERSON)

IN THE COURT OF APPEAL   **Court of Appeal Ref.**† _____

ON APPEAL FROM

BETWEEN:

Claimant
(Plaintiff)/Appellant
Petitioner/Respondent

and

Defendant/Appellant
Respondent/Respondent

Section A

WE, the solicitors* for the above-named Applicant, who is not a child or a patient, REQUEST the dismissal of the application(s) for** in the above matter with costs.

DATED this   day of   20

(Signed)
* (Solicitor for the Appellant)

Section B

WE, the solicitors* for the above-named Respondent and Applicant, who are not children or patients, REQUEST the dismissal of the application(s) for in the above matter with no order as to costs *(or specify other costs order required)*.

DATED this   day of   20

(Signed) _____
*(Solicitor for the Appellant)
(Signed) _____
*(Solicitor for the Respondent)

†   Please list the full reference for any application to which this applies including any relevant suffix.
*   If any party is acting in person, please modify the wording as appropriate.
**   Please specify in detail the application(s) you are seeking to be dismissed.

APPENDIX 2

Case Law

Aoun v Bahri and Angelou	A2.1
Barings plc (in liquidation) and another v Coopers & Lybrand (a firm) and others	A2.2
Beedell v West Ferry Printers Ltd	A2.3
CIBC Mellon Trust Co and others v Mora Hotel Corp NV and another	A2.4
Clark (Inspector of Taxes) v Perks and other applications	A2.5
Contract Facilities Ltd v Rees' Estate	A2.6
Electra Private Equity Partners and others v KPMG Peat Marwick (a firm) and others	A2.7
Foenander v Bond Lewis & Co	A2.8
Great Future International Limited and others v Sealand Housing Corporation and others	A2.9
Hammond Suddards Solicitors v Agrichem International Holdings Ltd	A2.10
Hertfordshire Investments Ltd v Bubb and another	A2.11
Hunt v Peasegood	A2.12
Jolly v Jay	A2.13
Sarah Lloyd Jones and others v T Mobile (UK) Ltd	A2.14
Koller v Secretary of State for the Home Department	A2.15
Milward v Three Rivers District Council	A2.16
Owusu v Jackson and others	A2.17

R (on the application of Nine Nepalese Asylum Seekers) v Immigration Appeal Tribunal — A2.18

Shire v Secretary of State for Work and Pensions — A2.19

Slot and another v Isaac — A2.20

Southern & District Finance Plc v Turner — A2.21

Tanfern Ltd v Cameron-MacDonald and another — A2.22

Unilever plc v Chefaro Proprietaries Ltd and other appeals — A2.23

AOUN V BAHRI AND ANGELOU

A2.1

[2002] EWCA Civ 1141

COURT OF APPEAL (CIVIL DIVISION)

BROOKE LJ and WALL J

31 JULY 2002

JUDGMENT: APPROVED BY THE COURT FOR HANDING DOWN (SUBJECT TO EDITORIAL CORRECTIONS)

Lord Justice Brooke:

This is the judgment of the court.

1. On 19th February 2002 Moore-Bick J, sitting in the Commercial Court, made an order requiring the claimant Mohamad Ali Aoun to provide security for the costs of the two defendants Hassan Bahri and Costas Angelou in the sums of £200,000 and £175,000 respectively. This order was expressed to cover their costs up to and including the conclusion of any alternative dispute resolution proceedings. The judge directed that the action should be stayed if this security was not provided by 4.30pm on 12 March 2002. He also ordered Mr Aoun to pay the defendants £35,000 and £25,000 respectively on account of their costs of the application within 28 days. The judge made his order pursuant to the provisions of CPR 25.12 and CPR 25.13(2)(g), having been satisfied that Mr Aoun had taken steps in relation to his assets that would make it difficult to enforce an order for costs against him.

2. Mr Aoun now appeals to this court against this order pursuant to permission granted by Mance LJ on 28 March 2002. Both defendants have filed and served respondent's notices whereby they seek to uphold the judge's orders on additional grounds. The appeal is now pending, but the defendants now seek orders

from this court providing for security for their costs of the appeal and also providing that permission to appeal should be set aside unless Mr Aoun complies with the judge's order to provide security and to pay the costs ordered to be paid on account within 14 days of the date of the order the defendants are now seeking from this court. The first of these applications was made under CPR 25.15(1) and the second under CPR 52.9(1). The first defendant sought security for their costs of the appeal in the sum of £41,759.50 and the second defendant in the sum of £26,520. Agreement was reached just before the hearing as to the amount of the security for the costs of the appeal which Mr Aoun should provide for each defendant. He was also in the process of paying the costs ordered by the judge to be paid on account. The only unresolved issue arose out of the defendants' application under CPR 52.9(1). We said at the end of the hearing that we were dismissing this application, and we are giving our reasons for doing so in this judgment.

3. Before considering the issues raised on that application it is necessary to say a little about the evidence in the court below and the judge's findings on the evidence, following the cross-examination of Mr Aoun.

4. It was not in dispute that until some time after October 2000, when the defendants first sought orders for security for their costs of the action, Mr Aoun had no connection of any kind with this country. The evidence showed that he had a peripatetic lifestyle, living variously in Switzerland, Australia, Greece, Dubai and elsewhere in the Middle East, and spending a great deal of time in other places such as Pakistan. He lived away from his wife and children for long periods. His business, personal and family connections were all with the Middle East and Australia. In particular he was born in Lebanon, and his family and his wife are Lebanese. He used a Lebanese passport and has addresses in Lebanon. He also had long term residence in Dubai. So far as his Australian connections are concerned, his parents and his wife's family and brother live there, and his children attended school there. He has Australian joint nationality.

5. The judge found that Mr Aoun's evidence was unsatisfactory and contradictory and shot through with inconsistencies and discrepancies. We were told, for instance, that in November 2000 his solicitors told the defendants' solicitors that their client lived in Greece. In December 2000 Mr Aoun told a Greek court that he had no assets in Greece and that he and his family were permanently in Australia. In the spring of 2001 he told the Commercial Court that he had been living with his family in England since the previous December. In November 2001 he never answered a question put to him in cross-examination as to the date when he had formed an intention to move to England.

6. In about July 2001 Mr Aoun mentioned for the first time that he had placed his house on the market in Australia. A little later he told the Commercial Court that he intended to use £50,000 from the sale proceeds (supplemented by

a £300,000 loan) for the purpose of acquiring a property in England. In November 2001 he represented to UK immigration officials that he was a resident of Australia. He failed to comply with an order made by the Commercial Court in July 2001 that he should produce his passport and the passports of the other members of his family, averring that he had left his own Lebanese passport in Greece and that five of his family's Australian passports had been destroyed on an aeroplane following an incident when baby's milk had been spilt over them. In July 2001 he also asserted that he had applied to the UK authorities for status as a long-term resident. He later admitted that this was untrue and that he made such an application for the first time the day before the hearing on 15 November 2001 when he was to be cross-examined.

7. The judge concluded that there were solid grounds for thinking that if Mr Aoun was unsuccessful in the litigation it would be difficult to enforce any order for costs that was made against him. He also said he was unable to find that an order for security would have the effect of stifling Mr Aoun's claim. In the exercise of his discretion he decided that it would be just to make an order for security in favour of both defendants.

8. Factors he took into account in the exercise of his discretion included Mr Aoun's lack of significant or permanent assets located within the jurisdiction or within the territories covered by the Brussels and Lugano Conventions, his conclusion that the London house represented inadequate and uncertain security, Mr Aoun's propensity to move countries, and the size of the defendants' costs. The defendants will argue on the appeal that there were other matters which would have justified the judge in making the order he did, namely Mr Aoun's lack of probity and the misleading evidence he gave, the fact that he had no substantial connection with this jurisdiction, and the size of his own legal costs. As to the first of these matters the judge concluded that Mr Aoun was not a witness whose evidence could be relied upon with any great degree of confidence, although he thought that this was due as much to his willingness to make ill-considered statements as to any desire to mislead. A little later he said that many of the inconsistencies and discrepancies with which Mr Aoun's evidence was 'shot through' seemed to reflect an exceptionally casual attitude to giving evidence rather than a deliberate intention to mislead. Others, however, were less easily explained.

9. It was in these circumstances that the judge made the order whose main effect we have summarised in paragraph 1 above. Mr Aoun appealed against that order, and Mance LJ has granted permission to appeal. The appeal raises a point of law on the proper construction of CPR 25.13(2)(g) and also a challenge to the exercise of the judge's discretion on the facts.

10. The defendants make their present application under CPR 52.9 which provides that:

'(1) The appeal court may:

(a) strike out the whole or part of an appeal notice,
(b) set aside permission to appeal in whole or in part,
(c) impose or vary conditions upon which an appeal may be brought.
(2) The court will only exercise its powers under paragraph (1) where there is a compelling reason to do so.'

11. The strong wording of this rule reflects the strict tests the Court of Appeal used to apply under the old procedural regime in order to discourage applications of this type (see note 59/14/27 to RSC O59 R14 in the 1999 edition of the White Book).

12. The defendants argue that because Mr Aoun did not furnish the requisite security or pay the costs ordered by the judge to be paid on account within the time prescribed by the judge's order, and because he has not applied to any court for what is described as a stay of execution of that order, the court should set aside this appeal unless he now complies with the judge's requirements in full within a short period. They speak of a wholesale disregard for the judge's order on Mr Aoun's part, and of their concern that the policy behind CPR 52.7 will be frustrated if Mr Aoun is now permitted to continue with his appeal without applying for and being granted a stay of the judge's order.

13. Mr Aoun for his part has now filed a witness statement in which he has explained the problems he faced in raising the money ordered by the judge. It is not necessary to go into this matter in any detail. It is sufficient to say that he has now raised sufficient funds to pay, albeit late, the defendants the costs the judge ordered him to pay on account and also to provide an agreed sum by way of security for their costs of the appeal.

14. The effect of the defendants' application was to require Mr Aoun to pay the sums which the judge had ordered to be paid by way of security for the costs of the action before the appeal could be allowed to proceed. This seemed on the face of it odd, because Mr Aoun has been given permission to appeal against that order, and if he succeeds in his appeal the order is likely to be set aside or reduced in amount.

15. The defendants argued that the action was now stayed, with effect from 12 March 2002, because Mr Aoun did not furnish the ordered security by that date. They said there was no dispute about the fact that:
(i) he had not complied with the order;
(ii) he had made no application for any variation of, or any time extension for compliance with, the order;
(iii) he had made no application for any stay of execution of the order;
(iv) he had offered no explanation for his conduct except in the witness statement filed just before the start of the hearing in this court;
(v) he had offered no apology for his conduct; and

(vi) as a result of his conduct, the action was now stayed.

16. Mr Graham Dunning QC, who appeared for Mr Bahri, submitted that if Mr Aoun's appeal was allowed to proceed even though he had not complied with the judge's order for security of the costs of the action, his wholesale disregard for the judge's order would remain unmarked. Furthermore, he said that the policy behind CPR 52.7 (whereby an appeal does not automatically operate as a stay of any order of the lower court) would be completely frustrated, because Mr Aoun would achieve the same result without complying with the requirements made by the judge or applying to this court or to the judge for a stay of the judge's order pending the appeal. Mr Dunning submitted that Mr Aoun had thus far evaded his liabilities and flouted the authority of the court, and that his conduct should be checked immediately. He said that the order sought by his client clearly represented a fair and proportionate response to Mr Aoun's behaviour. He added that his client had already incurred significant costs, which were covered by the order for security in the High Court, and that he should be protected from having to incur any further costs until the money ordered by the judge to be paid by way of security for his costs was forthcoming.

17. Mr Huw Davies, for Mr Angelou, made submissions to similar effect. He observed that the judge had decided that Mr Aoun's claim would not be stifled by having to put up substantial security (and pay the interim costs orders) and that Mr Aoun had not appealed against this finding of fact.

18. It appears to us that the defendants' submissions were based on a fundamental misunderstanding of the nature of the order made by the judge. The judge did not order Mr Aoun to do anything in relation to the order for security for costs (other than to pay the costs of the defendants' application, including the sums ordered to be paid on account). His order, rather, had the negative effect that if Mr Aoun did not provide the ordered security by 12 March 2002, all further proceedings in his action in the High Court would be stayed. That order remains in effect, and it will remain in effect unless and until it is altered or discharged by an appeal court or varied or discharged by the judge himself. In due course, after the action remained stayed for an appropriate period of time, it would be open to the defendants to apply to have it dismissed. Incidentally, the judge's order was not drawn up on this occasion in the way suggested by paragraph 6 of Appendix 16 to the Commercial Court Guide.

19. It follows that Mr Aoun should not be regarded as showing a wholesale disregard for the judge's order simply because he chose not to provide the ordered security within the time set by the judge. He was entitled to seek permission to appeal against it. He filed his appellant's notice on 4 March 2002, and by granting permission to appeal Mance LJ has indicated that he considered that the appeal would have a real prospect of success.

20. Although there appears to be no authority directly in point, we are satisfied that the stay of the action in the High Court which took effect from 12 March 2002 had no effect on the proceedings in this court. It is certainly the case that with effect from 13 March 2002 the High Court was in effect declining to exercise its jurisdiction over the action. In *Ministry of Foreign Affairs, Trade and Industry v Vehicles and Supplies Ltd* [1991] 1 WLR 550 Lord Oliver said at p 556:

> 'A stay of proceedings is an order which puts a stop to the further conduct of proceedings in court before a tribunal at the stage which they have reached, the object being to avoid the hearing or trial taking place.
>
> It simply means that the relevant court or tribunal cannot, whilst the stay endures, effectively entertain any further proceedings except for the purpose of lifting the stay.'

21. The fact that the Court of Appeal and the High Court are two different courts, each possessing their own inherent power to take steps to prevent the process in their court from being abused is evident, if further confirmation was needed, from the language of section 49(3) of the Supreme Court Act 1981:

> 'Nothing in this Act shall affect the power of the Court of Appeal or the High Court to stay any proceedings before it, where it thinks fit to do so.'

22. *Taylor v Lawrence* [2002] EWCA Civ 90, [2002] 2 All ER 353 and *Seray-Wurie v Hackney London Borough* [2002] EWCA Civ 909, [2002] 3 All ER 448 provide two recent examples of the way in which the jurisdiction of the Court of Appeal and the jurisdiction of the High Court, being two separate courts, are separately regulated.

23. There are plenty of examples in the books of this court entertaining appeals against orders staying proceedings in the lower courts without any hint of a suggestion that the order in the court below had the effect of staying proceedings in the Court of Appeal as well. Section 16(1) of the Supreme Court Act 1981 gives this court jurisdiction to hear and determine appeals from any judgment or order of the High Court, and once this court is seized of an appeal it has both jurisdiction and a duty to entertain it (at any rate until the permission stage is reached) unless and until a stay is placed on proceedings in the Court of Appeal.

24. It follows that unless there were any special features of this case which would constitute a compelling reason (see CPR 52.9(2)) for placing onerous conditions on permitting the future progress of an appeal for which a lord justice has granted permission we should decline to give the defendants the relief they sought. Although the defendants made strong submissions about Mr Aoun's lack of credibility and untrustworthiness, Mance LJ did not see fit to place any conditions under CPR 52.3(7)(b) on Mr Aoun being granted

permission to appeal, and we saw no reason why we should impose any such conditions so long as he provided the agreed security for the costs of the appeal itself and paid the defendants the sums by way of costs which the judge ordered him to pay on account.

25. It was for these reasons that we dismissed the defendants' application.

BARINGS PLC (IN LIQUIDATION) AND ANOTHER V COOPERS & LYBRAND (A FIRM) AND OTHERS

A2.2

[2002] EWCA Civ 1155

COURT OF APPEAL (CIVIL DIVISION)

LAWS and PARKER LJJ

18 JULY 2002

Appeal – Permission to appeal – Application to set aside permission to appeal – Whether grant of permission should be set aside – CPR 52.9

(*Transcript: Smith Bernal*)

Lord Justice Laws: **[1]** I will ask Lord Justice Jonathan Parker to give the first judgment.

Lord Justice Parker

[2] This is an application to set aside a grant of permission to appeal. The application is made by the second and third Defendants in an action in which the Claimants (to whom the permission to appeal was granted) are Barings Plc (in liquidation) ('PLC') and Bishopscourt (BS) Ltd (also in liquidation), formerly Barings Securities Ltd ('BSL'). BSL was at the time an indirect subsidiary of PLC. I will refer to the action as 'the PLC action'. The Applicants are sued in their capacity as partners at the material time in the accountancy firm of Deloitte & Touche (Singapore), and I will refer to them as 'D&T'. Also joined as a Defendant in the PLC action is the accountancy firm Coopers & Lybrand ('C&L').

[3] D&T applies to set aside a grant by Robert Walker LJ, made on the papers on 5 February 2002, of permission for PLC and BSL, as Claimants in the PLC action, to appeal against an order made by Evans-Lombe J on 5 December 2001 striking out the PLC action as against D&T.

[4] The background to the application is somewhat complex, but I shall attempt to summarise it as shortly as I can.

[5] The PLC action is one of two actions being heard together by Evans-Lombe J arising out of the collapse of Barings Bank in February 1995 as a result of the fraudulent activities of Nicholas Leeson in trading on the Singapore International Monetary Exchange (otherwise known as SIMEX). Leeson was general manager of Barings Futures Singapore Pte Ltd ('BFS') from 1992 until he went missing shortly before the collapse. BFS was an indirect subsidiary of BSL and hence of PLC.

[6] The other action is brought by BFS as Claimant against D&T and C&L I will refer to it as 'the BFS action'.

[7] In each action, the respective Claimants claim damages against D&T for negligence in acting as auditors of BFS, on the footing (expressing it broadly) that had D&T carried out its duties properly Leeson's activities would have been discovered earlier and their catastrophic consequences would have been avoided. The BFS action is based specifically on the local statutory reports made by D&T in respect of BFS' accounts.

[8] In the PLC action, essentially three different heads of claim are pleaded.

[9] Firstly, BSL claims damages in respect of very substantial sums advanced by it to BFS by way of dollar funding, which were then lost by BFS. By way of defence to this claim, D&T contends, among other things, that this a loss which would be made good if BFS were to succeed in achieving full recovery in the BFS action, and that BSL, as the parent company of BFS, has no direct claim against D&T as auditors of BFS. This defence is based upon the decision of the House of Lords in the case of *Johnson v Gore Wood* [2001] 1 All ER 481, [2001] 2 WLR 72. D&T also contends that the claim fails the 'purpose test', in that there is no pleaded allegation that the loss was caused by BSL entering into transactions of which D&T were aware at the time and for the purposes of which D&T provided its services.

[10] Secondly, PLC and BSL claim damages representing the loss in value of their respective groups, which were rendered insolvent as a consequence of Leeson's unauthorised activities. By way of defence to this claim, D&T repeat the contention that the claim as pleaded does not meet the 'purpose test'.

[11] Thirdly, PLC claims damages in respect of bonuses alleged to have been paid out by PLC on the basis of profits of BFS as shown in its 1993 accounts, which were audited by D&T and in respect of which D&T reported direct to PLC. As to that claim, D&T raises (among other things) a defence based on *Johnson v Gore Wood*. D&T further contends that the loss arising from paying the bonuses was in fact borne not by PLC but by BSL, and that accordingly the claim as pleaded must fail.

[12] The trial of the two actions began in June 2001 but was halted after a short time because settlement negotiations were taking place between the respective

Claimants on the one hand and C&L on the other. The trial resumed on 2 October 2001. Shortly before its resumption, on 28 September 2001, D&T applied to strike out the PLC action. It also applied for a direction for the hearing of a preliminary issue, the nature of which I shall indicate in a moment.

[13] As I say, the trial resumed on 2 October 2001. Six days later, on 8 October, settlement agreements were concluded with C&L between the Claimants and C&L, conditional on the approval of creditors and of the courts both in England and in Singapore. The agreements became unconditional, as I understand it, in the course of January 2002.

[14] Prior to the resumption of the hearing in October 2001, and in anticipation of a binding compromise being reached with C&L, PLC and BSL had informed D&T that in that event they would limit their claims against D&T in the PLC action to damage suffered prior to 31 December 1994, and they further proposed that (and I quote from a letter dated 9 October 2001 from Ashurst Morris Crisp to Clifford Chance (D&T's solicitors)):

> ' the PLC action against your clients should be stayed on terms that such a stay will only be lifted in the event that the Court finds your clients to have been negligent but they avoid any damages award in favour of BFS on grounds which would not be a bar to a claim by PLC/BSL.'

[15] In effect, PLC and BSL took the position (which they have since maintained) that, assuming a binding settlement was reached with C&L, they would be content to leave it to BFS to prosecute its claims against D&T, provided that this did not lead to D&T escaping liability by reason of a defence which it could not have run as against them.

[16] By that stage, the only defence which might have fallen into that category was D&T's pleaded defence in the BFS action that two representation letters written to D&T by Mr Jones, the finance director of BFS, were written dishonestly and/or recklessly. This defence, if made good, would entitle D&T to a cross-claim against BFS which would serve to extinguish any claim by BFS; but it could not be run as against PLC or BSL. D&T had earlier applied for a direction that the issue whether this defence was a good defence as against BFS be tried as a preliminary issue (this being the application to which I referred a moment ago). In the event, the judge made the direction sought.

[17] The judge then heard argument as to whether it was appropriate that he should hear and determine the strike-out application in advance of the hearing of the preliminary issue. PLC and BSL submitted that there was no point in dealing with the strike-out application at that stage since under the proposals made in Ashursts' letter of 9 October 2001 the court was unlikely to have to consider any substantive issues which were peculiar to the PLC action. D&T, on the other hand, submitted (through Mr Gaisman QC) that the judge should go ahead and determine the strike-out application, in advance of the hearing of

the preliminary issue. In this context Mr Gaisman identified costs as being, as he put it, 'a serious consideration'. His oral submission continued, according to the transcript:

> 'It would be a highly material consideration, to put it no higher, on the question of costs if I were able to demonstrate that this claim was always doomed to failure.'

[18] In the event the judge decided that it was appropriate to hear the strike-out application in advance of the preliminary issue.

[19] The judge then proceeded to hear the strike-out application. The hearing of that application began on 23 October 2001. In a lengthy and detailed judgment which he handed down in draft on 21 November and which was released to the public on 23 November, the judge concluded that the first head of claim (dollar funding) failed on *Johnson v Gore Wood* grounds and also because it failed the 'purpose test'. As to the second head of claim (value of the groups), he held that it too failed the 'purpose test'. As to the third head of claim (PLC's claim in respect of bonuses), he held that it failed on *Johnson v Gore Wood* grounds and because the uncontroverted evidence established that the loss claimed was not in fact suffered by PLC but by BSL.

[20] Consequential matters arising out of his judgment were dealt with at a further hearing which took place on 5 December 2001. In the course of that hearing counsel for PLC applied for leave to amend its pleading in relation to the third head of claim so as to change its case from one of overpayment by the parent company to one of a loss suffered by the parent company as a result of an overpayment by its subsidiary, BSL. The judge refused permission to amend, on the ground that the application had come too late. In this connection, it is to be noted that in paras 144 and 145 of his substantive judgment the judge recorded that in the course of the hearing an amendment to the same effect had been (as he put it) tabled, but that no formal application had been made to make it. The judge went on to say (in para 145) that he would in any event have refused such an application as being embarrassing to D&T.

[21] The judge also refused permission to appeal.

[22] PLC and BSL applied to the court for permission to appeal against the strike out. The grounds of appeal annexed to the Appellants' notice extended to 35 paragraphs and cover each of the three heads of claim which I identified earlier. Paragraphs 30 to 34 inclusive of the grounds of appeal were devoted exclusively to the third head of claim (bonuses).

[23] As I recounted earlier, on 5 February 2002 permission was granted by Robert Walker LJ on the papers. He expressed his reasons for granting permission as follows:

'It will not be easy to overturn the judge's careful and thorough judgment. Nevertheless the grounds of appeal are arguable, and the issues are important both to the parties and generally.'

[24] Since the grant of permission, the preliminary issue in the BFS action has been heard by the judge, and determined in favour of BFS. In other words, the judge has concluded that the defence based on the representation letters is not a good defence to BFS' claims. That in turn means that, as PLC and BSL accept, under the proposals to which I referred earlier, the first and second heads of claim against D&T in the PLC action are stayed. As a matter of analysis, the third head of claim (bonuses) remains as a live issue on the appeal, but PLC and BSL have confirmed that the appeal is now relevant only in relation to costs. As one may expect, the costs of the PLC action are likely to be very substantial. According to a witness statement of Mr Grandison, of Slaughter & May, D&T's costs of the PLC action have been estimated at £3 million.

[25] D&T has announced that it does not propose to seek permission to appeal against the judge's decision on the preliminary issue.

[26] It is against that somewhat complex procedural background that D&T now applies to set aside the grant of permission to appeal by Robert Walker LJ.

[27] At this point I turn to the relevant provisions of the 1998 Civil Procedure Rules, which are to be found in CPR 52.9. Paragraph (1) of the rule gives an appeal court power to set aside permission to appeal in whole or in part. Paragraph (2) of the rule provides that the court will only exercise its powers under para (1) 'where there is a compelling reason for doing so'.

[28] So what is relied on by D&T as providing such a 'compelling reason'?

[29] Mr Christopher Butcher QC, for D&T, submits that the permission should be set aside primarily because of developments which have occurred since the permission was granted, to which I have referred, in consequence of which the appeal is now only relevant to the issue of costs. He further submits that it is highly unlikely that if Robert Walker LJ had been asked to grant permission in respect of the bonuses issue alone, he would have done so, since an appeal on that issue would (Mr Butcher submits) have no real prospect of success. Indeed, he submits that it would be bound to fail. Mr Butcher also submits that in applying for permission to appeal, PLC and BSL 'failed properly to disclose the relevant facts relating to the bonuses claim and in particular those relating to the proposed amendment' (I quote from para 12(c) of D&T's initial written skeleton argument in support of the present application). The suggestion is that neither the grounds of appeal nor the skeleton argument makes it sufficiently clear that the formal application to amend the pleadings in relation to the bonuses issue was made after judgment had been handed down, the inference (I take it) being that if that had been made clear to Robert Walker LJ he would inevitably have refused permission on the bonuses issue.

[30] Mr Butcher also points out that PLC and BSL have not sought to appeal against the judge's refusal to allow the amendment, and he submits that in any event the bonuses issue does not give rise to any point of general importance such as might otherwise justify a grant of permission to appeal in respect of that issue.

[31] In the first place, I reject straightaway the submission (which is implicit if not explicit in Mr Butcher's submissions) that PLC and BSL misled the court on the question of the application for permission to amend the pleading in relation to the bonuses issue. Paragraph 72 of their skeleton argument in support of their application for permission to appeal is in the following terms:

> 'The learned Judge gave a written judgment ... which was released in final form on 23 November 2001 and formally handed down on 27 November 2001 (when it was indicated for PLC and BSL that consideration was being given to the possibility of putting forward amendments). Consequential matters were then dealt with on 5 December 2001 ... *On that occasion* PLC and BSL put forward draft amendments on the duty of care point and the bonuses point, which they sought leave to make if the Judge considered that they would remedy the deficiencies which he saw in the Statement of Claim ... D&T submitted that such amendments were too late (relying on *Stewart v Engel* [2001] 1 WLR 2268, CA) and, in any event, that they added nothing new. The learned Judge refused the application on the ground it was made too late.' (Original emphasis)

[32] I cannot for my part see anything remotely misleading in that paragraph. On the contrary, as I read it, it makes it clear that the formal application to amend was made at the hearing on 5 December 2001 when 'consequential matters' were being considered.

[33] So what is left? In my judgment, the remaining factors relied on by Mr Butcher do not amount, singly or collectively, to anything which even begins to resemble 'a compelling reason' for setting aside the grant of permission.

[34] 'Compelling reason', in this context, connotes, in my judgment, something which is sufficiently serious to be in the nature of an irregularity in the grant of permission. In *Nathan v Smilovitch* [2002] EWCA Civ 759 Longmore LJ said, at paragraph 9, referring to an application to set aside a grant of permission to appeal:

> 'For my part, unless the nature of the application shows that some decisive authority or decisive statutory provision has been overlooked by the Lord Justice granting permission to appeal, an Applicant would normally have to show that the single Lord Justice had actually been misled in the course of the presentation of an application.'

[35] I respectfully agree.

[36] The fact that the appeal is now relevant on costs only is a matter which can (and no doubt will) be brought to the attention of the court hearing the substantive appeal, and the court will give that factor such weight as it sees fit in disposing of the appeal. But it cannot in my judgment amount to a compelling reason for setting aside the grant of permission.

[37] In my judgment the power conferred by para (1) of r 52.9 is emphatically not a power to, in effect, entertain an appeal against the grant of permission. Yet that, in substance, is what Mr Butcher has invited this court to do in relation to the bonuses issue. In my judgment the power to set aside a grant of permission to appeal is not available for the purpose of second-guessing the single judge who granted the permission and thereby generating satellite litigation: rather, its purpose is to enable the court to do justice in those rare cases where something in the nature of an irregularity has occurred in the granting of permission, whether by reason of the single judge having been misled or for some other like reason.

[38] It follows that in so far as D&T seek to rely on the fact that the only issue remaining in the appeal is the issue of costs I regard this application as wholly misconceived; and that in so far as D&T seek to assert that Robert Walker LJ was misled, I consider that there is no substance whatever in that assertion. Indeed, I regard it as regrettable that it was ever made.

[39] I would accordingly dismiss this application, and in doing so I would express the hope that in future practitioners will think twice before launching an application of this kind, in the knowledge that only in very limited circumstances will such an application be likely to succeed.

[40] That leaves one outstanding matter. PLC and BSL have proposed in correspondence, and they have repeated this proposal on this application, that given that the appeal is now relevant only as to costs, the hearing of the appeal should be deferred until after the conclusion of the BFS action.

[41] Mr Butcher has indicated that D&T are willing to concur in that proposal, on the footing that it is a sensible way of managing the case in this respect. I agree that the proposal seems a thoroughly sensible one and I would make a direction accordingly.

Lord Justice Laws: [42] I agree that this application should be refused for the reasons given by my Lord. I agree also that the direction proposed by Mr Davies QC should be made.

[43] I add only this. It seems to me to be of the highest importance that the court should very firmly discourage the bringing of satellite litigation under the guise of an application under CPR Pt 52.9. The rule is there to cater for the rare case in which the Lord Justice granting permission to appeal has actually been

misled. If he has, the court's process has been abused and that is of course a special situation. There may also be cases where, as Longmore LJ indicated in *Nathan v Smilovitch* [2002] EWCA Civ 759, some decisive authority or statute has been overlooked by the Lord Justice granting permission. But where such a state of affairs is asserted, the learning in question must in my view be plainly and unarguably decisive of the issue. If there is anything to argue about, an application to set aside the grant of permission will be misconceived.

[44] This application should not have been made.

Application refused.

BEEDELL V WEST FERRY PRINTERS LTD

A2.3

[2001] EWCA Civ 400

COURT OF APPEAL (CIVIL DIVISION)

ALDOUS, MAY and MUMMERY LJJ

15 MARCH 2001

Court of Appeal – Permission to appeal – Application to set aside permission to appeal – Applicant obtaining permission to appeal without single lord justice having the benefit of a recent Court of Appeal decision – Whether grant of permission to appeal should be set aside – CPR Pt 52.9.

Lord Justice Aldous:

[1] I will ask Mummery LJ to give the first judgment.

Lord Justice Mummery

[2] There are before the court, first, an application to set aside permission to appeal to this court granted by May LJ on 15 September 2000; and, second, the appeal brought with that permission, being an appeal by Mr Beedell against the decision of the Employment Appeal Tribunal on 7 July 2000 dismissing the appeal against the decision of the Employment Tribunal. The Employment Tribunal on 14 December 1999 dismissed Mr Beedell's complaints of unfair dismissal and dismissal for trade union activities. The finding of the Employment Tribunal in his favour on an issue of wrongful dismissal was reversed by the Employment Appeal Tribunal, allowing a cross-appeal by his former employers, West Ferry Printers Ltd.

[3] The background to the claims can be very shortly stated. West Ferry Printers carry on the business of providing printing services. Mr Beedell was an

employee. He was dismissed from their employment on 29 September 1998 with effect from 5 October following a violent incident.

[4] The question for decision today is in essence a procedural one following on the decision of this court in *Foley* on 31 July 2000; i.e. after the decision of the Employment Appeal Tribunal, but before the application for permission to appeal against the decision of the Employment Appeal Tribunal was considered on paper by May LJ.

[5] In deciding Mr Beedell's claim the Employment Tribunal explained in their extended reasons of 14 December 1999 that, applying the conventional range of reasonable responses test West Ferry Printers had acted reasonably in accordance with equity and the substantial merits of the case in dismissing Mr Beedell. As explained in para 51 of the extended reasons:

> 'In so doing, we also concluded (to adopt the words of Dillon LJ in *Gilham & Others v Kent County Council (No 2)* [1985] ICR 233) "What the employer did is not what we ourselves would have done, but we cannot say that it was unreasonable".'

[6] The Tribunal went on say at paragraph 52 that:

> '... this is one of the "marginal cases" referred to by Morison J in *Haddon v van den Bergh Foods Ltd* [1999] IRLR 672 "where a decision not to dismiss would be reasonable and a decision to dismiss would also be reasonable".'

[7] What happened in *Foley* was that a challenge was mounted to the conventional range of reasonable responses approach. The history of the controversy is set out in the judgment given on 31 July 2000 in the cases of *Foley v Post Office* and *HSBC Bank Plc (formerly Midland Bank Plc) v Madden* [2000] ICR 1283. The effect of that unanimous decision of the Court of Appeal was that, as far as the Court of Appeal and all lower courts and tribunals are concerned, the range of reasonable responses test is the subject of binding authority. The application of a different test by the Employment Appeal Tribunal in the case of *Haddon v van den Bergh Foods Ltd* [1999] ICR 1150, [1999] IRLR 672, was disapproved.

[8] The decision in *Foley* was not drawn to the attention of May LJ when the application for permission was made. He granted permission to appeal unaware of the decision. That led Mr Swift, who appears for West Ferry Printers Ltd, to launch an application to set aside the grant of permission to appeal. Such an application can be made under the Civil Procedure Rules 1998 Pt 52.9, which provides:

> '(1)   The appeal court may:
> (a)   ...
> (b)   set aside permission to appeal in whole or in part;

(c) ...
(2) The court will only exercise its powers under paragraph (1) where there is a compelling reason for doing so.'

[9] Mr Swift submits that there is a compelling reason for setting aside the permission to appeal. Whichever test is applied, the case of *Haddon* or the case of *Foley*, the result will be the same. The appeal will fail. So, he says, as the appeal cannot possibly succeed, it should never have been allowed to be brought. We should set aside the permission.

[10] The effect of the court adopting that approach is that Mr Beedell would not be entitled to make any application either to this court or to the House of Lords for permission to appeal. The effect of s 54(4) of the Access to Justice Act 1998 is that it is not possible to appeal against a refusal of permission to appeal.

[11] Mr Swift submits that that should be so here, because there is a possible prejudice to his clients, if what his clients regard as a hopeless case is taken either with the permission of this court or with the permission of the House of Lords to the House of Lords. His clients would be exposed to a risk as to costs in arguing a case which has wider implications, perhaps, than are the concern of his clients in their particular case. He contends that whatever is decided by the House of Lords, whether *Foley* is right or whether *Haddon* is right, the result will be the same. So why should his clients be exposed to further litigation and further expense?

[12] A direction was given by me for the appeal to come on at the same time as this application. In dealing with the discretion under CPR Pt 52.9 the court must bear in mind the overriding objective in CPR Pt 1.1 which provides:

'(1) These Rules are a new procedural code with the overriding objective of enabling the court to deal with cases justly.

1.2. The court must seek to give effect to the overriding objective when it:
(a) exercises any power given to it by the Rules.'

[13] So the critical question for the court on Mr Swift's application is whether this court would be dealing with this appeal justly if it exercised its power to set aside the permission to appeal, rather than letting the permission to appeal stand and dismissing the appeal, which Mr Millar QC, on behalf of Mr Beedell, accepts is the inevitable consequence of this appeal being heard.

[14] I have no doubt that the correct approach to the exercise of our discretion – bearing in mind the overriding objective – is to refuse to set aside the permission to appeal. If we followed the course which Mr Swift invites us to follow, the consequence would be, in effect, that this court would be making an

unappealable decision in an area recognised by the Court of Appeal in its judgments in *Foley* to be the subject of considerable controversy in unfair dismissal cases.

[15] That would not be a just result. If we take the alternative course which Mr Millar accepts is inevitable of dismissing this appeal, we will be able to entertain an application for permission to appeal; and if we refuse that, it will be open to Mr Beedell to petition the appellate committee for permission to appeal. It will be a matter of discretion for the court which hears the application for permission to appeal to decide, if it grants permission, what conditions, if any, should be attached to that permission. That is not a matter which, in my view, should concern us at this stage. We are deciding simply whether to set aside the permission, or to refuse to set aside the permission and dismiss the appeal in consequence of the concession which has been made.

[16] I would refuse the application to set aside the permission. On Mr Millar's concession, I would dismiss this appeal.

Lord Justice May

[17] I agree.

Lord Justice Aldous

[18] I also agree.

Application refused; appeal dismissed.

(*Transcript: Smith Bernal*)

CIBC MELLON TRUST CO AND OTHERS V MORA HOTEL CORP NV AND ANOTHER

A2.4

[2003] 1 All ER 564

[2002] EWCA Civ 1688

COURT OF APPEAL, CIVIL DIVISION

GIBSON, MANCE and HALE LJJ

8 OCTOBER 2002, 19 NOVEMBER 2002

Costs – Security for costs – Past costs orders – Judge ordering defendant companies to pay money into court in respect of past costs orders as condition for proceeding with application to set aside default judgment – Order retrospectively

improving claimants' position by increasing pools of assets from which to recoup past costs orders – Whether judge erring.

In the course of protracted proceedings, the claimant trustees obtained default judgments, costs orders and a post-judgment freezing order against the defendant companies. Subsequently, the companies applied to have the default judgments set aside. That application was funded by the companies' controlling shareholder. He was not a party to the litigation, and had only become involved in it after the trustees had obtained the default judgments and costs orders against the companies. There was therefore no basis for ordering him, under s 51 of the Supreme Court Act 1981, to pay the past costs orders, and the trustees had not sought any such order. Instead, they obtained an order requiring the companies to pay £1.6m into court – £100,000 as security for the costs of the application to set aside and £1.5m in respect of the past costs orders – as a condition for their being allowed to pursue the application. In making that order, and in refusing to vary the freezing order so as to allow the companies to make the payment out of their frozen assets, the judge concluded that the shareholder, who was the only person able to provide the necessary funds, should do so since the application to set aside was being brought to protect his investment. The judge did not, however, bear in mind that his order would have the effect of retrospectively improving the trustees' position by enlarging the pool of assets from which they could recoup the past costs if the application to set aside failed. On the companies' appeal, the Court of Appeal considered, inter alia, whether the judge should have taken that into account in the exercise of his discretion.

Held – Where (i) a claimant sought an order requiring a defendant to pay money into court in respect of past costs orders against the defendant as a condition of allowing him to proceed with an application to set aside default judgments, and (ii) such an order would retrospectively improve the claimant's position in relation to those costs orders, the retrospective improvement was a relevant factor for the court to take into account in the exercise of its discretion. There could be injustice in making such an order when the court knew that the defendant could not make such payment out of his own resources and that the only source of funding to make the payment was a third party against whom no order for costs had been sought, under s 51 of the 1981 Act, in respect of those costs, and there was little reason to think that a s 51 order could be made. In that context, it had to be a relevant consideration that requiring such payment would, if the application to set aside judgment failed, have the effect of giving the claimant the ability to recoup part of what he was owed from additional assets which would not have been available to him if the application had not been made. It followed in the instant case that, while there was no basis for interfering with the judge's exercise of discretion to grant security for the costs of the application to set aside, he had erred in failing to consider, and giving no weight to, the fact that the proposed order would retrospectively improve the trustees' position in relation to the past costs orders. He had also erred in treating the shareholder's controlling interest in the companies as a sufficient reason for making an order that in reality was directed at him when no s 51 order had been, or could be, made against him in respect of past costs. It was not an appropriate case for imposing on the companies a requirement to make any payment into court in respect of any past costs, knowing that a third party would have to fund the payment, unless the trustees were to agree to a variation of the freezing order to allow such payment out of the frozen assets. Accordingly, the appeal would be allowed to the extent indicated (see [31]–[34], [37], [41]–[46], [53]–[56], below).

Atlas Maritime Co SA v Avalon Maritime Ltd, The Coral Rose (No 3) [1991] 4 All ER 783 and *Hammond Suddards Solicitors v Agrichem International Holdings Ltd* [2001] All ER (D) 258 (Dec) distinguished.

Notes

For security for costs generally, see 37 *Halsbury's Laws* (4th ed reissue) para 834.

Cases referred to in judgments

Atlas Maritime Co SA v Avalon Maritime Ltd, The Coral Rose (No3) [1991] 4 All ER 783, [1991] 1 WLR 917, CA.

Canada Trust Co v Stolzenberg (No 2) [2000] 4 All ER 481, [2002] 1 AC 1, [2000] 3 WLR 1376, HL.

Graham v Sutton Carden & Co [1897] 2 Ch 367, CA.

Hammond Suddards Solicitors v Agrichem International Holdings Ltd [2001] EWCA Civ 2065, [2001] All ER (D) 258 (Dec).

Keary Developments Ltd v Tarmac Construction Ltd [1995] 3 All ER 534, CA.

MV Yorke Motors (a firm) v Edwards [1982] 1 All ER 1024, [1982] 1 WLR 444, HL.

Olatawura v Abiloye [2002] EWCA Civ 998, [2002] 4 All ER 903.

Reed v Oury [2002] EWHC 369 (Ch), [2002] All ER (D) 218 (Mar).

Taylor v Pace Developments Ltd [1991] BCC 406, CA.

Appeal

Mora Hotel Corp NV and Chascona NV, the tenth and thirty-eighth defendants to proceedings brought by the claimants, CIBC Mellon Trust Co, appealed with permission of Arden LJ from the order of Jacob J on 13 May 2002 requiring the appellants to pay £1.6m into court by 10 June 2002 as a condition of their being allowed to pursue applications to set aside default judgments that had been entered against them. The facts are set out in the judgment of Peter Gibson LJ.

Cur adv vult

19 November 2002. The following judgments were delivered.

Lord Justice Gibson

[1] This is an appeal by the tenth defendant, Mora Hotel Corp NV (Mora), and the thirty-eighth defendant, Chascona NV (Chascona), from the order made by Jacob J on 13 May 2002, whereby (1) he ordered that, as a condition of the appellants being allowed to pursue applications to set aside default judgments entered against them, they should pay £1.6m into court by 10 June 2002 and (2) he refused to vary a freezing order earlier made against them in favour of the claimants to enable the appellants to make the required payment out of frozen assets. Of the sum of £1.6m, £1.5m was in respect of costs orders already made but unpaid and £100,000 was security for the claimants' costs of the applications to set aside. The appeal is brought with the permission of the single Lord Justice, Arden LJ.

[2] The dispute arises in litigation brought by the claimants as trustees of certain pension and other benefit funds established by DaimlerChrysler Canada Inc for its employees. The claimants made substantial loans to and investments in an international group of finance and investment companies known as the Castor Group. The Castor Group collapsed and it was discovered that a major fraud had been perpetrated. The loans were irrecoverable and the investments virtually worthless. The claimants alleged that four individual defendants, including a Swiss lawyer, Marco Gambazzi, instigated or participated in the fraud, and did so through many of the corporate defendants.

[3] The appellants are companies incorporated in the Netherlands Antilles. They operate and own the Gorham Hotel in New York. The claimants alleged that Mr Gambazzi owned and controlled the appellants. The appellants on 23 November 2001 asserted for the first time that Paolo Cavazza is the owner of 75% of the shares in the appellants, having acquired 50% in 1994 and a further 25% in 1995. No imputations are made by the claimants against Mr Cavazza, who is a wealthy Italian businessman and who, on his evidence, procured in 1994 the provision of a $US10.3m deposit for the benefit of the appellants and in 1995 paid $US5m for shares in the appellants.

[4] Mora was a party to the proceedings from the outset and a proprietary tracing claim was made against it as the recipient of moneys derived from the Castor Group. On 4 June 1996 after a nine-day hearing, a worldwide freezing order was made by Rimer J against it, amongst other defendants. Mora was one of several defendants who applied to set aside service of the writ on them

on the ground of lack of jurisdiction. That application was dismissed with costs by Rattee J and, on appeal, by this court and on 12 October 2000 by the House of Lords (see *Canada Trust Co v Stolzenberg (No 2)* [2000] 4 All ER 481, [2002] 1 AC 1). When Chascona was joined as a defendant it too challenged the jurisdiction, but abandoned its application following the decision of the House of Lords.

[5] The freezing order made by Rimer J was accompanied by disclosure orders. Mora, with certain other defendants, did not comply with the orders and applied to Rattee J for the discharge of the entire freezing order. But the application was rejected on 10 July 1998, and unless an order was made against Mora. That order was not obeyed. On 4 February 1999 a default judgment was entered against Mora in the sums of $Can357,738.21 and $US386,687.95 in respect of the tracing claim against it.

[6] On 11 January 1999 a claim of conspiracy with other defendants to defraud the claimants was added against Mora, and Chascona was joined as a co-conspirator. A further worldwide freezing order with orders for disclosure was made by Rattee J on 3 March 1999 against Mora and one other defendant. On 23 July 1999 another worldwide freezing order with orders for disclosure was made by Lightman J against, amongst others, the appellants. Other obligations were imposed on Mora including the immediate opening of a bank account in this jurisdiction into which it was to direct any payment received in certain Canadian proceedings. Unless orders were made on 4 October 1999 but not complied with and on 21 October 1999, default judgments were entered against the appellants, amongst others, for damages to be assessed. On 7 December 1999 they were assessed in the sums of $Can245,701,477.70 and $US134,315,511.10 against Mora and slightly larger sums against Chascona.

[7] On 8 May 2000 a post-judgment worldwide freezing order was made against, amongst others, the appellants by Evans-Lombe J. This contained the standard exception allowing the appellants to spend reasonable sums on legal advice and representation.

[8] On 18 May 2000 the claimants applied to the New York court for recognition and enforcement of the English judgment obtained against the appellants, and an attachment order was made in respect of their assets in New York and a temporary special fiscal monitor and a receiver were appointed. The claimants then applied to the New York court for summary judgment. The appellants instructed attorneys to oppose the application, asking for a full hearing of the action on the merits. But the judge of the New York Supreme Court was not persuaded by the appellants and made an order for summary judgment as requested by the claimants. An order for the sale of the Gorham Hotel has subsequently been made. The appellants' appeal was dismissed by the New York Appeal Court on 28 May 2002. A further appeal is now being sought.

[9] The claimants also sought and obtained an order in the New York court on 7 February 2001 that the appellants pay $US2m to the claimants out of the frozen assets to cover the costs of the enforcement proceedings in New York. In return the claimants were required to put up a bond as security.

[10] Other successful proceedings have been brought in Ontario and the Netherlands Antilles for the recognition and enforcement of the English judgment. However no sums have yet been realised.

[11] It is apparent from the appellants' own evidence that it was a tactical decision on their part to dispute the English proceedings on jurisdictional grounds, and not to take active steps to resist the tracing claim and the claim in conspiracy against them. They themselves appear to have no connection with England. They may have expected to be able to establish their case on the merits in the proceedings in New York, which is where what they say is their only asset, the Gorham Hotel, is situate. Those tactics have failed. We are told by Mr Wardell QC for the appellants that Mr Cavazza only became involved in the litigation in August 2001. Prior to that, Mr Gambazzi appears to have been the prime mover in the appellants. Mr Cavazza's company, Chinablue Investment SA (Chinablue), was involved in the provision of a deposit of $US10.3m to secure loans to the appellants, as the claimants discovered. They joined Chinablue as the fifty-fifth defendant and obtained a freezing order from Jacob J against it. As I understand the position, the judge has since discharged that order, accepting that there was no evidence that Mr Cavazza was party to any fraud on the claimants. It was with funding from Mr Cavazza that the appellants instructed attorneys in New York in the proceedings there. It is with his funding that the appellants applied on 5 December 2001 to set aside the judgment dated 21 October 1999 and the order dated 7 December 1999 for the assessment of damages. Application was also made by Mora on 30 April 2002 to set aside the judgment dated 4 February 1999.

[12] On 27 February 2002 the claimants applied for an order that the appellants' application of 5 December 2001 be stayed and that the appellants only be permitted to proceed with that application upon the satisfaction of certain conditions: (1) the payment by Mora of (a) £525,570.30, being costs already ordered to be paid by it and assessed, and (b) an interim payment of £4,050,000 in relation to other outstanding costs orders; (2) the payment by Mora of the sums ordered to be paid by the judgment of 4 February 1999; (3) the payment by Chascona of (a) £3,199.48, being costs already ordered to be paid by it and assessed, and (b) an interim payment of £3.8m in relation to other outstanding costs orders; (4) compliance by the appellants with the terms of certain specified orders requiring disclosure. The claimants also sought an inquiry into expenses incurred by the claimants in reliance on the judgment and payment of the amount so found.

[13] These applications came before JacobJ on 13 May 2002. In the course of the argument before him, Mr Philip Marshall for the claimants modified the conditions which they were asking the court to impose on the appellants. In view of objections raised by the judge to the inclusion of costs of some £7m incurred in respect of the initial hearing before Rimer J, Mr Marshall was content to seek payment of £500,000 in respect of assessed costs and £1m in respect of costs after the initial application plus the estimated costs of the claimants on the application to set aside which he put at £300,000. Mr Wardell conceded that Mr Cavazza could afford to pay £1.5m, but objected in principle to a third party being made to pay past costs orders made against a defendant, thereby improving a claimant's position. It was argued that there was no jurisdiction, alternatively, if there was jurisdiction, that it would be wrong to exercise the court's discretion, to make such an order.

[14] The judge then gave judgment. He dealt together with both the application for £1.5m for past costs and £300,000 as security for the application to be set aside. He found that the court had jurisdiction under CPR 3.1(2)(f), 3.1(3) and 3.1(5). He then turned to the question whether he should make the (modified) order requested by the claimants. He said:

> '[28] I have come to the firm conclusion that it is appropriate that there be sums paid into court on behalf of the companies both to cover the past unpaid costs and towards the costs of this application to set aside the judgments, if it turns out that that application is unsuccessful. The fact that the money has to come from the man behind the companies rather than the companies themselves worries me not a jot. It may be he is the unfortunate victim of his own lawyer, but it is his investment that is sought to be protected by these proceedings. The fact that he is a third party and that the companies themselves are unable to provide the money is irrelevant.
>
> [29] There are clear analogies here with security for costs applications. The court is, of course, anxious to prevent any stifling of a claim, but it has never accepted the proposition from a party who is urging stifling that the party's own impecuniosity is enough. The court has always looked at the real position: if a company with no assets has rich backers it has always said that it does not regard the absence of money in the company itself to be a sufficient reason for refusing the security. The court has looked at the commercial reality.
>
> [30] The commercial reality here is that Mr Cavazza is seeking, in these proceedings, to protect his investment. They are his companies which allowed the costs to run up, albeit through the activities of the dishonest lawyer. He must take responsibility for what happened in the past. If he wishes the companies to proceed with this application he must be the source of the money for security and for the almost inevitable conditions

relevant if the companies are successful. I do not, of course, actually make an order against Mr Cavazza—the order is against the companies.'

[15] In the discussion after judgment the judge limited the sum to be provided as security for the costs of the applications to set aside to £100,000. The judge was asked to vary the freezing order so that the amount ordered by him to be paid could be paid out of the frozen assets of the appellants. But the judge refused saying that he had made his judgment clear: 'it is the backer who has to pay ... it is his investment that is being protected by these proceedings.' He went on to say that it was inappropriate to vary the freezing order being one granted post-judgment covering assets to meet the judgment.

[16] Mr Cavazza provided the appellants with £1.6m which was paid into court in compliance with the judge's order.

[17] In this court the appellants, although formally challenging the whole of the order of Jacob J including the ordering of security for costs in the sum of £100,000 in respect of the applications to set aside the judgments, concentrated on that part of the order which required the payment of £1.5m in respect of past costs. Mr Wardell submitted that the court cannot, alternatively should not, use its powers under the CPR to make an order requiring payment into court of past costs. Of the two alternative ways in which that submission is put, one based on jurisdiction and the other on the appropriate exercise of discretion, he concentrated on the latter.

[18] I shall consider the question of jurisdiction first. Mr Marshall submitted, and the judge accepted that the court had jurisdiction under CPR 3.1(2)(f), 3.1(3)(a) and 3.1(5) to make the order which the judge made. Those provisions are in the following form:

'3.1(2) Except where these Rules provide otherwise, the court may— ...
  (f)   stay the whole or part of any proceedings either generally or until a specified date or event ...
(3)   When the court makes an order, it may—
  (a)   make it subject to conditions, including a condition to pay a sum of money into court ...
(5)   The court may order a party to pay a sum of money into court if that party has, without good reason, failed to comply with a rule, practice direction or a relevant pre-action protocol.'

[19] Mr Wardell submitted that a stay under r 3.1(2)(f) would be justified only in the event of the party against whom the stay is ordered being guilty of conduct that is oppressive or vexatious or is tantamount to an abuse of process. That submission was based on the unreported decision of Field J in *Reed v Oury* [2002] EWHC 369 (Ch), [2002] All ER (D) 218 (Mar) where that judge was considering an application to strike out or stay a counterclaim in the light of the defendant's conduct of the litigation. He said (at [34]):

'... the conduct in question must be looked at in the round and, even if it cannot be shown that there has been bad faith, if in respect of a particular incident or having regard to a course of conduct overall, a party has acted oppressively or very unreasonably, it may still be appropriate to stay his claim conditionally or unconditionally or strike it out or order a payment into court.'

[20] Mr Wardell acknowledged that that case went more to the question how the court's discretion should be exercised than to the question of jurisdiction. In my judgment the court has the power under the general wording of r 3.1(2)(f) to grant a stay in any appropriate case.

[21] Mr Wardell then submitted that r 3.1(3)(a) does not empower the court to impose preconditions before an application can be made. However, again the wording is quite general. I see nothing in the rule to prevent the court, when ordering a stay, making the stay subject to conditions including a condition to pay a sum into court.

[22] In view of that conclusion it is unnecessary to consider r 3.1(5) which in any event, was primarily relied on by Mr Marshall in respect of that part of the £1.6m which related to assessed costs, there having been a failure to comply with r 44.8, providing for payment of assessed costs within 14 days.

[23] The substantial issue on this appeal relates to the appropriateness of the order for a payment into court in respect of past costs. Mr Wardell submits that implicit in the judge's decision were two novel propositions: (1) the court can, in advance of hearing an application to set aside a default judgment, impose a condition that a corporate defendant must, by raising money from its shareholders, enlarge the pool of available assets with which to meet the judgment in the event of the application failing; (2) the court can and should, in the exercise of its discretion, refuse to vary a freezing order to allow the appellants to pay a debt to the claimants.

[24] Mr Wardell relies on the following matters: (1) the claimants have security for costs already incurred by virtue of the existing judgment which had given it control of the Gorham Hotel having a net equity of $US27m including cash reserves of $US7m; (2) the appellants cannot comply with the judge's order because its assets are frozen by a court order; (3) the court refuses to vary the freezing order to enable such payment to be made; (4) to the court's knowledge the only person who will be able to comply with the order is a shareholder who is not a party to the proceedings; (5) any application for an order against that person under s 51 of the Supreme Court Act 1981 to pay the outstanding costs orders would fail; (6) if the shareholder declines to put up the funds, the application to set aside the judgments will be defeated without it being given the opportunity of being heard; (7) if the shareholder puts up the funds, but the applications are unsuccessful, the claimants will have a windfall.

[25] Mr Marshall supports the judge's decision. He submits that it is well established that the court can take account of all potential sources of funding available to a party when considering whether to require payment into court as a condition of granting leave to defend or the provision of security (*MV Yorke Motors (a firm) v Edwards* [1982] 1 All ER 1024, [1982] 1 WLR 444, *Keary Developments Ltd v Tarmac Construction Ltd* [1995] 3 All ER 534), and it is for the party asserting inability to meet such a requirement to demonstrate that inability by proper evidence. Similar principles, he says, have been applied when a party has sought a variation of a freezing injunction to make some desired payment out of frozen assets (*Atlas Maritime Co SA v Avalon Maritime Ltd, The Coral Rose (No 3)* [1991] 4 All ER 783, [1991] 1 WLR 917). He points out that all such payments by a third party may be said to constitute a windfall, but that has not deterred the court from requiring such payments in full knowledge that the party to the proceedings cannot or may not be able to pay out of his own resources.

[26] Mr Marshall relies on the following factors: (1) the appellants are applying to set aside judgments entered years earlier in consequence of their deliberate failure to comply with unless orders, and there is a long history of failure by the appellants to comply with court orders; (2) the appellants will need to apply for relief under CPR 3.8, and the circumstances which the court is required to consider under CPR 3.9 include several which are likely to tell against the granting of relief, such as the lateness of the application, the intentional failure to comply with rules and court orders consequent on the tactical decision taken by the appellants, and the long delay, if there is to be a trial, since the relevant events occurred; (3) in addition to the costs already assessed, the unassessed costs which the appellants have been ordered to pay exceed £8m; (4) there is no prospect of the appellants meeting any of the claimants' costs if the applications to set aside fail unless the order made by the judge of payment into court stands; (5) the value of the appellants' assets subject to the freezing order is a fraction of what is owed under the orders made against the appellants, so that the claimants do not have security for their costs; (6) Mr Cavazza is the person instigating the applications and, through his interest in the appellants, he will be the primary beneficiary if the applications succeed.

[27] Mr Marshall placed particular reliance on the decision of this court in *Hammond Suddards Solicitors v Agrichem International Holdings Ltd* [2001] EWCA Civ 2065, [2001] All ER (D) 258 (Dec). In that case the claimants had recovered judgment in a sum with costs. The defendant obtained permission to appeal from this court and sought a stay of the orders made by the trial judge. The claimants applied for an order that the appeal be struck out unless by a specified date the defendant paid or secured the judgment debt, paid the costs awarded below and provided security for the costs of the appeal as a condition of the appeal being entertained. The defendant resisted that application on the grounds that it had insufficient assets and could not comply with the order so

that the appeal would be stifled. It argued that it was irrelevant that funding from a third party was available. Clarke LJ, delivering the judgment of the court (consisting of himself and Wall J) rejected the defendant's submissions and made the order requested. He referred to the evidence which the defendant had adduced of its impecuniosity and said it was wholly insufficient to show any risk of the appeal being stifled without a stay, and said that there was a compelling reason (for the purposes of CPR 52.9) for making the defendant pay or secure the judgment debt as a condition of permitting it to proceed with the appeal.

[28] Clarke LJ referred to six facts combining to produce such compelling reason: (1) the defendant was a foreign company with no assets in the UK and there was a real risk that if the appeal failed the respondents would not recover the judgment and costs; (2) the defendant had the resources, or access to resources, to enable it to instruct solicitors and counsel and to provide security for costs; (3) there was no convincing evidence that the defendant did not have the resources or access to resources which would enable it to pay the judgment debt and costs orders of which it was in breach; (4) the defendant provided inadequate evidence of its financial affairs; (5) the defendant's appeal would not be stifled by making the order for payment; (6) it was unacceptable for the defendant to intend to prosecute the appeal while disobeying the orders of the court.

[29] Mr Marshall says that similar factors are present in this case. He submits that just as this court in the *Hammond Suddards* case saw nothing unjust or inconsistent with the overriding objective in CPR 1.1 in requiring the defendant to obey the court's orders as a condition of being permitted to continue to prosecute its appeal or in putting the owner of the defendant to the choice of providing the payment of the costs orders or of seeing the appeal struck out, so it was not unjust or inconsistent to put Mr Cavazza to a similar choice.

[30] As the judge had a discretion whether to require a payment into court, the first question that arises is whether this court can interfere with the exercise of his discretion. The judge has expressed his reasoning with economy and it is not entirely easy to be sure of all the considerations which he took into account in reaching his conclusion. It would appear that in his reasoning he did not make much differentiation between the application for payment into court of security for the costs of the application to set aside and the application for payment of past costs. He applied the principle established in security for costs applications, viz that the court can take into account not only what a party possesses but also what he might raise from other sources, to the whole of the application made to him.

[31] With respect to the judge, whilst in an appropriate case that may be a determinative consideration in respect of both types of application (for example, where the applicant has not satisfied the court that he has disclosed his full

assets but has asserted his impecuniosity), other differentiating factors may be crucial to the proper exercise of discretion. There is no injustice in requiring an applicant, asserting impecuniosity, to provide security for the respondent's future costs of the application, provided that thereby the application is not stifled. Nor is there injustice in requiring an applicant, who does not assert impecuniosity but has repeatedly failed to pay past costs orders, to pay what is already due to the other side if he is to be allowed to make a further application (see *Graham v Sutton Carden & Co* [1897] 2 Ch 367 at 371 per Chitty LJ). There may be injustice in requiring an applicant to set aside a judgment to make a payment into court in respect of past costs as a condition of being allowed to proceed with such application when the court knows that the applicant cannot make such payment out of his own resources, and that the only source of funding to make such payment is a third party against whom no order for costs under s 51 of the 1981 Act has been sought in respect of those costs, and little reason to think that such an order could be made. In this context it must be a relevant consideration that the effect of requiring such payment is, if the application fails, to give the respondent the ability to recoup part of what he is owed from additional assets which, had the application not been made, would not have been available to him.

[32] It is not apparent that the judge took into consideration this last point. In the discussion with counsel before judgment the judge asked Mr Wardell:

'Suppose I come to the conclusion that I cannot conceive any basis whereby Mora and Chascona would be allowed to have the judgment set aside without being made to pay the considerable costs which they allow to be incurred when they did not challenge the merits earlier?'

That point is referred to again (at [15]):

'One can postulate an application to set aside a judgment obtained in default, where one can really see in advance that, if the application is to be successful, conditions will be imposed as to the payment of costs.'

And again (at [30]):

'If [Mr Cavazza] wishes the companies to proceed with this application he must be the source of the money for security and for the almost inevitable conditions relevant if the companies are unsuccessful.'

[33] If, as it would appear, that was part of the thinking of the judge, then I am afraid that I cannot accept that it provides justification for the order to make a payment in respect of past costs, because it ignores the possibility that the application to set aside will fail. In that event the payment into court will have enlarged the pool of assets available to the other party from which it can recoup the past costs. The claimants have been allowed by the judge to improve their position against the appellants in respect of the past costs orders by taking advantage of the appellants' applications, even though those applications are not said to be frivolous or vexatious. Mr Wardell does not dispute that if the applications succeed, the court is likely to require the appellants to pay past costs and that Mr Cavazza is likely to be the source of moneys to comply with such order, but that does not meet the objection that the application may fail.

[34] The judge robustly stated his complete lack of concern that Mr Cavazza had to make the payment required of the appellants and that it was irrelevant that he was a third party. For my part I cannot see how that fact can be of no relevance to the exercise of discretion. Dealing with a case justly must require the court to have regard to the substantive effect of the order being made and to the justice of, in reality, requiring the third party to make payment. In fact the judge did have regard to Mr Cavazza's position. The judge rightly identifies the commercial reality as being that Mr Cavazza was seeking by the application to protect his investment in the appellants. That provides good justification for making an order for security for the costs of the applications even though the appellants could not pay. But the point in issue is whether that is sufficient to enable the court to require the payment into court in respect of the past costs when Mr Cavazza would have to fund such payment. The judge said that Mr Cavazza must take responsibility for what happened in the past. I presume that the judge is there adverting to the fact that Mr Cavazza has had 75% of the shares since 1995 and so he could have exercised his majority control earlier to prevent the appellants conducting the proceedings in such a way as to cause the judgments in default to be entered and the costs orders to be made against the appellants. But the court does not normally punish the person having share control of a litigant company against which a costs order is made by an order against that person under s 51 (see, for example, *Taylor v Pace Developments Ltd* [1991] BCC 406). The position might be different if there was evidence that Mr Cavazza had funded the appellants before August 2001, for example in the jurisdiction proceedings, or was actively involved in the litigation at that earlier time. But there is no such evidence and no s 51 application against Mr Cavazza.

[35] Mr Marshall sought to rely on other matters, not referred to by the judge in his judgment. Mr Marshall complained of defaults by the appellants in complying with disclosure and other orders. He also alleged conduct on behalf of Mr Cavazza in breach of the freezing order. In particular he referred us to the first affidavit of Andrew Ford, a solicitor for the appellants, said to show the extraction by Mr Gambazzi of US$600,000 from Mora, Mr Ford explaining that Mr Gambazzi acquired the previous shareholder's interest (including deposits advanced to the Gorham Hotel) on behalf of Mr Cavazza. Mr Wardell complained of being ambushed by Mr Marshall in this court with evidence not shown to the judge and arguments not advanced to the judge. It appears from the transcript of the hearing before the judge that when Mr Marshall was making his submissions the judge referred to what he called 'a number of minor

points: alleged breach of court order and so on', and the judge commented: 'All by the way really.' The judge asked if he had to go through the breaches alleged by the claimants, and Mr Marshall said that that could be dealt with on the hearing of the applications to set aside. It is apparent from the transcript that Mr Marshall was content not to argue the question of whether the appellants were in default of court orders and to argue the case on the two points taken by Mr Wardell – no jurisdiction, and, if there was, it was inappropriate to exercise the discretion by ordering payment. Further there is no respondent's notice. I therefore ignore such other matters, which are in any event, controversial.

[36] I can deal with other points raised more shortly. I do not accept Mr Wardell's point that the claimants have security for costs already incurred in the form of the Gorham Hotel. That asset covers only a fraction of what is owed to them under the existing judgments. However I do accept that that asset is safeguarded for them, through the receiver in New York who has complete control of the hotel, and just as they caused $US2m to be withdrawn to pay for the enforcement costs, so there seems no reason why they could not arrange for the £1,500,000 in respect of past costs to be paid from the same source if the English court varied the freezing order to permit such payment to the claimants. Normally there is no difficulty in obtaining such a variation of a freezing order to enable a debtor to pay the creditor in whose favour the freezing order was made. It is only because the claimants want other funds to be made available that they have not sought to recoup their debt out of the frozen assets and that they oppose the appellants' application that they should do so.

[37] None of the authorities to which we were referred seems to me to be precisely on all fours with the present case. It is a truism that each case falls to be decided on its own facts. In no other case is there the combination of features distinctive of the present case, viz that the appellants were ordered to pay into court sums in respect of past costs which, but for the freezing order, they could pay the claimants out of the appellants' own assets, but which by reason of that freezing order and the refusal of the court to vary it, they cannot pay, and that the third party who in reality would be the only person capable of providing the monies for that payment is not a person who has been or could be ordered to pay those past costs under s 51. This is not a case like the *Hammond Suddards* case where the court concluded that it had not been told all that it should be told in connection with the defendant's allegation of impecuniosity and suspected that the defendant had resources. Nor is it like the *Atlas Maritime* case where the court refused to vary a freezing order to enable a defendant to pay legal expenses in circumstances where the parent company of the defendant exercised financial control over the defendant and had chosen to operate the defendant's affairs in such a way as to leave it with no assets apart from the frozen fund.

[38] In *Olatawura v Abiloye* [2002] EWCA Civ 998, [2002] 4 All ER 903 Simon Brown LJ (with whom Dyson LJ agreed) confirmed that there was jurisdiction under the CPR to make orders tantamount to orders for security for costs outside the provisions of Pt 25, and suggested (at [25]) that a party only becomes amenable to an adverse order for security, in that case under r 3.1(5) –

> 'once he can be seen either to be regularly flouting proper court procedures (which must inevitably inflate the costs of the proceedings) or otherwise to be demonstrating a want of good faith – good faith for this purpose consisting of a will to litigate a genuine claim or defence as economically and expeditiously as reasonably possible according with the overriding objective.'

This authority, coupled with *Reed v Oury* [2002] All ER (D) 218 (Mar), suggests that it is only appropriate for the court to exercise its power under Pt 3 to require a payment into court in limited circumstances and should not do so in the absence of a want of good faith on the part of the party against whom the order is sought. That consideration is reinforced by the greater significance, since the Human Rights Act 1998 came into force, which the court attaches to not impeding access to justice.

[39] In the present case I accept that the appellants can be criticised for their tactical decision which led to failures to comply with unless orders and to the default judgments. Nevertheless I doubt if in the circumstances there was an absence of a want of good faith in the sense given by Simon Brown LJ. The question of jurisdiction was a serious one to pursue, even if ultimately unsuccessful, as can be seen from the fact that the House of Lords entertained the appeal. By the time the costs in the House of Lords, which form the greater part of the assessed costs, were assessed, the appellants' only assets were out of their control and the claimants could have sought and probably would have obtained an order that the freezing order be lifted to the extent needed to pay the assessed costs. The applications to set aside the default judgments are, it appears, proper applications.

[40] We have not been addressed by either counsel on the merits of the applications to set aside, although, as I have noted, Mr Marshall has drawn our attention to the difficulties facing the appellants in seeking relief from sanction under r 3.8 by reason of r 3.9. It will be for the judge at the hearing in December of the applications to set aside to determine whether on the merits the appellants have a good case and if so whether the factors referred to in r 3.9 on which Mr Marshall relies would nevertheless prevail.

[41] I return to the question whether this court can interfere with the judge's exercise of discretion. I have reached the conclusion that the judge did err in failing to consider, and giving no weight to, the consequence of the order he was minded to make that he was retrospectively improving the position of the claimants in relation to the past costs orders. Further the judge was, in my view, wrong to treat the fact that Mr Cavazza had a controlling interest in the appellants as a sufficient reason for making an order that in reality was directed at him, when no s 51 order was or could be made against him in respect of past costs. But the judge's exercise of discretion to grant security for the costs of the application to set aside cannot, in my judgment, be impugned. It was well within the proper ambit of his discretion to require such payment, even though it would have to be made by the backer of the applications to set aside, and there is no question of stifling those applications.

[42] If these views are shared by the other members this court, the question then arises whether this court should exercise the discretion afresh to make any order requiring payment in respect of past costs. In my judgment it should not. For the reasons given I do not see this as an appropriate case for imposing on the appellants a requirement to make any payment into court in respect of any past costs, knowing that a third party would have to fund the payment, unless the claimants were to agree to a variation of the freezing order to allow such payment out of the assets in New York.

[43] I would allow the appeal to the extent indicated.

Lord Justice Mance

[44] I have read in draft and agree with the judgment given by Peter Gibson LJ.

[45] There is a relevant difference between an application to obtain security in advance for costs being or about to be incurred and a retrospective attempt to improve the position with regard to past costs orders. The difference is not one of jurisdiction. As Peter Gibson LJ has demonstrated, there is clear jurisdiction to make an order in respect of both categories of costs. But the difference may go importantly to the exercise of discretion. In the present case, the judge failed both in argument and in his judgment to give any real consideration to the distinction or its implications.

[46] On the contrary, the judge attached much weight to his immediate impression that the appellants' applications dated 5 December 2001 to set aside two judgments against them (one dated 21 October 1999 for damages to be assessed and the other on 7 December 1999 assessing such damages in the sums of $Can245,701,477.70 and $US134,315,511.10) and dated 30 April 2002 to set aside a prior default judgment, dated 4 February 1999, against Mora Hotel Corp NV (Mora) for $Can357,738.21 and $US386,687.95 would, if they succeeded at all, only be allowed subject to conditions requiring payment or security for payment of a number of other past costs orders. So he thought that, by his actual order, he was merely anticipating an order which would anyway be made. As Peter Gibson LJ has shown, this overlooked the effect of his order if the applications failed, in increasing the pool of assets available to the claimants to meet the judgments.

[47] It was, I consider, also based on a misapprehension of the position if the applications succeeded. In that event, the judgments dated 4 February 1999, 21 October and 7 December 2001 would be set aside, both in this country and presumably also in New York, where they were (subject to a possible appeal) recognised by order of the New York Supreme Court (Index No 00/602149; IAS Pt 27 Case No 15979), dated 16 January 2001. Under the New York court's order, the claimants further obtained the appointment of a receiver to 'take title possession, custody and control' of the appellants' assets and to remit the proceeds of the hotel, when sold to the appellants. The claimants assert, and I am quite prepared to accept that this amounts or is to be regarded as analogous to a form of execution in respect of all three judgments. If the present applications to set aside were to succeed, the New York order would, so far as it recognised the judgments dated 4 February 1999, 21 October 1999 and 7 December 2001, presumably also be set aside; in that case, although the assets would remain frozen, it would be possible for either side to apply for their use to meet the outstanding costs orders. So there would be unlikely to be any call or basis to require Mr Cavazza or any third party to put further funds into the appellants in that situation. As it is, the judge made an order which would have the acknowledged effect of forcing Mr Cavazza to inject further funds, if the appellants were to be permitted to pursue their applications. Far from anticipating an inevitable order, he was making an order with different implications.

[48] It therefore falls for us to re-exercise the discretion. In this context, subject to the issue of jurisdiction, it was not really in issue before us that the appellants should be required to put up security for the costs of their current applications. The issue for determination is whether they should put up security for the past costs, excluding those incurred in obtaining the original freezing order in 1996 (apparently put at the extraordinary sum of £5.5m), but including assessed costs of some £500,000 and an estimated £1m of costs ordered to be paid, but as yet unassessed.

[49] The assessed costs include £121,668 taxed on 11 March 1999 and ordered to be paid by Mora in relation to an unsuccessful application on 10 July 1998 to discharge or vary the freezing order against it, £15,229 taxed on 24 May 1999 and ordered to be paid by Mora on 12 October 1998 on a successful application by the claimants for an order that Mora comply with its disclosure obligations and £299,956 assessed on 28 March 2001 and ordered to be paid by Mora in respect of its unsuccessful appeal on 12 October 2000 to the House of Lords on jurisdiction. Costs were also assessed against both Mora and Chascona NV (Chascona, which was only joined as a defendant on 11 January 1999) in the sum of £2,814 by the judge on the claimants' application for post-judgment injunctive relief on 8 May 2000. In Mora's skeleton before the judge, the total costs assessed against Mora were put at £441,167.21 and against Chascona at

£2,814. With interest at the judgment rate, these figures became respectively £525,570.80 and £3,199.48. The judge took £500,000 for the purposes of his judgment.

[50] As regards the unassessed costs, estimated at £1m, these included as against Mora, costs (estimated at £517,000) of Mora's challenge to the jurisdiction in courts below the House of Lords and costs (estimated at £3,583) of taking an account under the order dated 4 February 1999 in respect of the tracing claims. As against Mora and Chascona they included £98,177.50 plus indemnity costs relating to the entry of judgment on 21 October 1999. How the remainder of the £1m figure was made up is not clear to me.

[51] No-one seems to have drawn any distinction between Mora and Chascona before the judge, although the former is said to lease the Gorham Hotel from the latter, and the judge's order simply stays both the appellants' applications pending payment of £1.6m into court, of which £1.5m is to stand as security for the past costs orders, without distinguishing between costs orders made against Mora, and others made against both Mora and Chascona.

[52] Each appellant was in breach of the rules of the court in failing to pay the costs assessed as against it (see now CPR 44.8), though not the costs which, for whatever reason, the claimants had failed to have assessed. Before Jacob J the question whether the appellants were, in mid-2002, in continuing or outstanding breach of any (other) court orders was put on one side; it was left for consideration, if relevant, on the substantive applications to set aside the judgments. But there was never any doubt that the appellants had in the past breached other orders, notably for disclosure, since this was the basis for the unless orders made and judgments entered against them, particularly the judgment in default entered against them on 21 October 1999 for breach of a disclosure order made by Rattee J on 12 October 1998. So, if they had themselves had the assets available to meet the past costs, there could have been a case for requiring them to do so as a condition of pursuing the present applications (cf *Graham v Sutton Carden & Co* [1897] 2 Ch 367 at 370).

[53] But the present case falls into a different category. First, the appellants' substantial assets were from 1996 injuncted by the freezing orders made by this court, to preserve them in the light of the claimants' claims and latterly in the light of the English judgments. Secondly, not only did the claimants at no stage make any contemporaneous application for security for costs (quite likely for the very reason that they had the benefit of the freezing orders), but, even after costs had been assessed in their favour on 11 March 1999 and 24 May 1999 in the sums of £121,668 and £15,229, they made no application to execute against the appellants' assets the subject of the freezing orders. Thirdly, having obtained judgments against the appellants on 21 October and 7 December 1999 for damages far in excess of the appellants' frozen assets, the claimants took steps to execute such judgments (and the earlier tracing judgment against

Mora), rather than any of the past costs orders, against the frozen assets in New York by obtaining the order of the New York Supreme Court dated 16 January 2001. Fourthly, as a result the appellants now no longer have any assets available to meet the past costs orders. Fifthly, Jacob J's order was made in the knowledge and on the avowed basis that it would oblige the appellants' 'backer', Mr Cavazza, to provide the £1.6m, if the appellants were to pursue their applications to set aside the judgments against them. When a suggestion was made before Jacob J on 13 May 2002 that the English freezing order should be varied, to permit use of part of the frozen assets to discharge the past costs (although any actual use for this purpose would also have required a variation of the terms of the New York receivership), the claimants successfully resisted the suggestion. Sixthly, no basis has been shown for treating Mr Cavazza as a third party against whom it would be proper to make any order in respect of such past costs under s 51 of the 1981 Act.

[54] None of the steps taken by the claimants as recounted in the previous paragraph was anything other than perfectly legitimate, and one can understand their wish to increase the sums now available to meet the judgments and other orders which they have obtained. It is also true that the appellants themselves did not take any positive step to try to meet the outstanding past costs orders against them out of their frozen assets prior to 16 January 2001. But the simple and more important circumstances are that, until 16 January 2001, the appellants had assets against which the claimants could, if they had wished, have taken such steps, that, on 16 January 2001, the claimants preferred to utilise such assets to secure or pay judgment debts (which they had, of course, no basis for requiring Mr Cavazza to meet) and that, since then, as a result, the appellants have not had any assets available to them to meet the past costs orders. In these circumstances, I see no basis in principle for requiring Mr Cavazza now to inject further funds into the appellants in respect of past costs as a condition of the appellants being permitted to pursue the applications to set aside.

[55] For these reasons and those given by Peter Gibson LJ, I consider that it was inappropriate to make an order requiring security in respect of past costs as a condition of allowing the appellants to pursue their applications, and that the appeal should to that extent be allowed accordingly. No real criticism was directed by counsel at the judge's decision to require security for the estimated costs (put at £100,000) of the current applications to set aside, even though this would have to come from Mr Cavazza, and, like Peter Gibson LJ, I see no basis for interfering with that aspect of the judge's exercise of his discretion.

Lord Justice Hale

[56] I agree.

Appeal allowed as specified. Permission to appeal refused.

Kate O'Hanlon Barrister.

CLARK (INSPECTOR OF TAXES) V PERKS AND OTHER APPLICATIONS

A2.5

[2000] 4 All ER 1

COURT OF APPEAL, CIVIL DIVISION

GIBSON, BROOKE and WALKER LJJ

31 AUGUST, 1 SEPTEMBER 2000

Practice – Appeal – New provisions on second appeals from county court or High Court – Scope and effect – Access to Justice Act 1999, ss 54, 55 – CPR Pt 52.

(1) Where an appeal is made to a county court or to the High Court in relation to any matter, and on hearing that matter the court makes a decision in relation to it, s 55(1) of the Access to Justice Act 1999 prohibits an appeal from that decision to the Court of Appeal unless the latter considers that such an appeal will raise an important point of principle or practice or there is some other compelling reason for the Court of Appeal to hear it. That provision applies to (i) an appeal to the High Court on a point of law pursuant to s 11 of the Tribunal and Inquiries Act 1992 from a tribunal specified in the paragraphs of Sch 1 of that Act mentioned in that section; (ii) any application to the High Court which can colloquially be categorised as an appeal by way of case stated; (iii) an appeal to a county court on a point of law from a decision of a local housing authority under s 204(1) of the Housing Act 1996; and (iv) any other appeal to the High Court or the county court from any tribunal or other body or other person. It follows that an appeal from a decision of the High Court or of a county court in any of those cases is to be treated as a second appeal for the purposes of s 55 of the 1999 Act. Moreover, by virtue of CPR 52.13(1), only the Court of Appeal can give permission for a such an appeal, and it may do so only if it is satisfied that one or other of the tests mentioned in s 55 has been met. Thus if a judge in the lower court, whether the county court or the High Court, purports to grant permission for a second appeal, that grant of permission is a nullity.

(2) By virtue of s 54(4) of the 1999 Act, no appeal can be made against a decision to give or refuse permission to appeal. The Court of Appeal, whose jurisdiction is wholly statutory, has no inherent jurisdiction to hear an appeal against such a decision, unless it can be truly said that there has been no decision at all. On the other hand, if on such an occasion the appeal court (ie the court to which an appeal is made) makes a further order, such as a costs order or an order refusing adjournment, an appeal does in theory lie to the Court of Appeal with permission. However, it is likely to be a very rare case in which such permission will be granted.

(3) Neither the CPR themselves, nor the Practice Direction supplementing CPR Pt 26 (case management—preliminary stage: allocation and re-allocation), give any particularly useful guidance about the allocation of an assessment of damages or the purpose of any allocation. It therefore appears that it would be desirable for the appropriate authorities to reconsider that Practice Direction in order to give procedural judges more guidance about the mode of 'trial' of the assessment, the level of judge who should conduct the 'trial' in complex disputed cases and the principles to be followed when deciding whether to allocate an assessment of damages to a track and, if so, to which track. In potentially heavy assessments, it is desirable to postpone a final direction as to the mode of 'trial' and the level of the judge conducting the 'trial' until the evidence is complete and it is possible to see clearly what is in dispute and what is not.

(4) The exceptional power created by CPR 52.14, which enables a court lower than the Court of Appeal to transfer a first appeal to the latter if the specified tests are satisfied, ought to be used sparingly. In any case of doubt, the matter ought to be referred for consideration to the Master of the Rolls since an identical power is conferred on him by s 57 of the 1999 Act.

Cases referred to in judgment

Azimi v Newham LBC [2000] CA Transcript 1883.
Daisystar Ltd v Town and Country Building Society [1992] 2 All ER 321, [1992] 1 WLR 390, CA.
Greig Middleton & Co Ltd v Denderowicz [1997] 4 All ER 181, [1998] 1 WLR 1164, CA.
Henry Boot Construction (UK) Ltd v Malmaison Hotel (Manchester) Ltd (2000) Times, 31 August, CA.
Plender v Hyams (1 September 2000, unreported), CA.
Riniker v University College London (31 August 2000, unreported), CA.
Sandry v Jones (2000) Times, 3 August, [2000] CA Transcript 1343.
Scott v Shipp (31 August 2000, unreported), CA.
Tanfern Ltd v Cameron-MacDonald [2000] 2 All ER 801, [2000] 1 WLR 1311, CA.

Applications for permission to appeal

Clark (Inspector of Taxes) v Perks; *Macleod (Inspector of Taxes) v Perks*; *Guild (Inspector of Taxes) v Newrick and anr*

The appellant taxpayers, James Edward Perks, David Alan Newrick and James Granger, applied for permission to appeal from the order of Ferris J ([2000] STC 428) on 19 April 2000 directing, upon three cases stated by general commissioners of income tax in relation to appeals against assessments to income tax, that (i) the determination of the commissioners that the taxpayers were entitled to foreign earnings deduction for the relevant years be reversed, and (ii) that the assessment be confirmed in a given sum for taxable emoluments. The facts are set out in the judgment of the court.

McNicholas Construction Co Ltd v Customs and Excise Comrs

The appellants, McNicholas Construction Co Ltd, applied for permission to appeal from the decision of Dyson J ([2000] STC 553) on 16 June 2000 dismissing their appeal from a determination of a value added tax (VAT) tribunal sitting at the London Tribunal Centre on 12 January 2000 dismissing in part their appeals against certain VAT assessments made by the respondent, the Commissioners of Customs and Excise, on 21 March 1997. The facts are set out in the judgment of the court.

Jenkins v BP Oil UK Ltd and anr

The defendants, BP Oil UK Ltd and Wincanton Transport Ltd, applied for permission to appeal from the order of District Judge Batcup made in the Neath and Port Talbot County Court on 12 June 2000 awarding the respondent claimant, Royston Jenkins, £125,694.53 damages and interest in respect of injuries sustained and loss caused by an accident on 10 July 1996. The facts are set out in the judgment of the court.

Arshad Ghaffer (instructed by *Andrew M Jackson & Co*, Hull) for the appellant taxpayers in the first application.

Timothy Brennan and *Alison Padfield* (instructed by the *Solicitor for the Inland Revenue*) for the respondents in the first application.

The parties in the second application were excused attendance.

Gabriel Farmer (instructed by *Morgan Cole*, Swansea) for the appellants in the third application.

The respondent in the third application did not appear.

Lord Justice Brooke

1. This is the judgment of the court.

2. On 2 May 2000 new provisions governing civil appeals were introduced in England and Wales. The experience of the lawyers and staff in the Civil Appeals Office during the first week of May revealed that there was a good deal of confusion about the effect of the new rules. A three-judge court was therefore convened on 12 May to give guidance on their effect. Although the issue before that court (of which Peter Gibson LJ and Brooke LJ were members) related to a difficulty which had arisen before the new regime came into effect, the court took the opportunity to explain a number of features of the new regime which we knew to be causing uncertainties in the minds of practitioners. Brooke LJ therefore set out this guidance under a number of

different heads in paras 15 to 50 of his judgment in *Tanfern Ltd v Cameron-MacDonald* [2000] 2 All ER 801, [2000] 1 WLR 1311, with which Lord Woolf MR and Peter Gibson LJ agreed.

3. In para 14 ([2000] 2 All ER 801 at 805, [2000] 1 WLR 1311 at 1314) of that judgment he made it clear that he was concerned only with appeals in civil proceedings in private law matters, and not with appeals in public law cases or with appeals in family proceedings. The first of these exceptions arose out of the fact that no problems had been identified at that early stage in relation to public law appeals in civil cases, and it therefore appeared to be premature in those circumstances to give any guidance in that respect. The second exception arose from the fact that the Practice Direction which supplemented CPR Pt 52 stated that for the purposes of appeals to the Court of Appeal from cases in family proceedings the Practice Direction would apply with such modifications as might be required. It therefore seemed inappropriate to give dogmatic guidance in circumstances in which a new Practice Direction might render such guidance quickly incorrect or obsolete, particularly as no judge with specialist knowledge of family proceedings was sitting as a member of the court.

4. The judgment in the *Tanfern Ltd* case appears to have resolved a great many of the points of difficulty which had arisen at that early stage. Inevitably, however, a number of other difficulties and uncertainties have arisen on points which were not covered by that judgment. Sir Andrew Morritt V-C, sitting with May LJ and Forbes J in *Azimi v Newham LBC* [2000] CA Transcript 1883, has now clarified the situation in relation to appeals from decisions by judges in the county court on appeals from decisions of a local housing authority brought under s 204 of the Housing Act 1996. Six further applications, each raising a different issue under the new procedural scheme, were listed for hearing before this division of the court on 31 August 2000. We decided to hear three of these applications in two-judge divisions of the court, with a different constitution for the third application, and to hear the other three applications, which appeared to raise issues of general importance, in a three-judge division of the court. Brooke LJ was a member of the court on each occasion. In the event, ex tempore judgments were delivered in two of these cases on 31 August (*Scott v Shipp* (31 August 2000, unreported) and *Riniker v University College London* (31 August 2000, unreported)) and Peter Gibson and Brooke LJJ will give judgment in the third case (*Plender v Hyams* (1 September 2000, unreported)) immediately after this judgment has been delivered.

5. This judgment, therefore, relates directly to the three applications which we heard as a three-judge division of the court. As a convenience to practitioners we are also including references to the effect of our decisions on the three two-judge applications, as well as the effect of the decision of the Vice-Chancellor in *Azimi's* case, so that the effect of all these rulings can be seen in a single judgment, which we hope may be reported quite soon. Although the

scope of this judgment has been necessarily expanded to include issues which have arisen in connection with public law appeals, we believe it will be helpful if we deal with each issue against the background of the relevant passage in the *Tanfern Ltd* judgment. We will not be repeating, except so far as is necessary, what has already been said there. In this respect we are following the practice adopted by another division of this court in relation to cases under the former CCR Ord 17, r 11 in *Greig Middleton & Co Ltd v Denderowicz* [1997] 4 All ER 181, [1998] 1 WLR 1164.

6. Under the two relevant passages in the *Tanfern Ltd* judgment we will set out the principles to be followed, and we will then apply them to the three applications we have to decide before showing how they were (or will be) applied in two of the other cases (including *Azimi*'s case) to which we have referred. There is also a new point on s 54(4) of the Access to Justice Act 1999 which arose in *Riniker's* case (Brooke and Robert Walker LJJ), and in *Plender's* case which requires separate mention.

Appeals to the next level in the judicial hierarchy—the exceptions

Tanfern Ltd v Cameron-MacDonald [2000] 2 All ER 801 at 806, [2000] 1 WLR 1311 at 1315 (paras 16 to 19)

7. The Court of Appeal, which is a creature of statute, does not possess any jurisdiction to hear an appeal from a final decision of a district judge which has not been allocated by a court to the multi-track under CPR 12.7, 14.8 or 26.5. This is the case even if the district judge feels that he would have allocated the case to the multi-track if he had thought that there was any need for him to do so.

8. In the passage of this judgment which is concerned with the application in *Jenkins*'s case we have suggested that in the light of our decisions in that case and the recent decision of another division of this court in *Sandry v Jones* [2000] CA Transcript 1343 the appropriate authorities should reconsider the terms of the Practice Direction supplementing CPR Pt 26, so that procedural judges giving case-management directions in substantial cases involving the assessment of damages can be provided with appropriate guidance about the mode of 'trial' of the assessment, the level of judge who should conduct the 'trial', and the relevance of allocating a non-allocated action to a track following a default judgment under Pt 12 or a judgment on an admission under Pt 14.

9. We have also drawn attention to the exceptional power created by CPR 52.14 for a court lower than the Court of Appeal to transfer a first appeal to this court if the tests set out in that rule are satisfied. We have suggested, however, that this power should be sparingly used and that in any case of doubt the

matter should be referred to the Master of the Rolls for consideration, since s 57 of the 1999 Act has conferred an identical power on him.

Second appeals

Tanfern Ltd v Cameron-MacDonald [2000] 2 All ER 801 at 810–811, [2000] 1 WLR 1311 at 1319–1320 (paras 41 to 45)

10. Section 55(1) of the 1999 Act provides that:

> 'Where an appeal is made to a county court or the High Court in relation to any matter, and on hearing the appeal the court makes a decision in relation to that matter, no appeal may be made to the Court of Appeal from that decision unless the Court of Appeal considers that—(a) the appeal would raise an important point of principle or practice, or (b) there is some other compelling reason for the Court of Appeal to hear it.'

11. The rules in CPR Pt 52 apply to appeals to the civil division of the Court of Appeal, the High Court and a county court, subject to the exceptions mentioned in CPR 52.1(2). Section I of that part sets out general rules about appeals, and s II contains special provisions applying to the Court of Appeal. Throughout the part the words 'appeal court' mean 'the court to which an appeal is made', and the words 'lower court' mean 'the court, tribunal or other person or body from whose decision an appeal is brought' (see CPR 52.1(3)(b) and (c)).

12. It follows that the new procedural regime applies as much in relation to the handling of appeals to the courts from tribunals or other persons or bodies, as it does in relation to appeals from a lower court or a high court in the ordinary sense of those words. Furthermore, throughout the part the word 'appeal' included an appeal by way of case stated.

13. For the purposes of s 55 of the 1999 Act, the following appeals are to be treated as appeals to a county court or the High Court within the meaning of that section.

(i) An appeal to the High Court on a point of law pursuant to s 11 of the Tribunals and Inquiries Act 1992 from a tribunal specified in the paragraphs of Sch 1 of that Act mentioned in that section.

(ii) Any application to the High Court which can be colloquially categorised as an appeal by way of case stated.

(iii) An appeal to a county court on a point of law from a decision of a local housing authority pursuant to s 204(1) of the Housing Act 1996.

(iv) Any other appeal to the High Court or the county court from any tribunal or other body or person.

14. The first three of these propositions flow from our decisions in this judgment in the cases of *McNicholas Construction Co Ltd v Comrs of Customs*

& *Excise* and *Perks v Clark* and the judgment of the Vice-Chancellor in *Azimi's* case, and the fourth is the logical consequence of the Vice-Chancellor's judgment.

15. It follows that an appeal from a decision of the High Court or of a county court in any of these cases is to be treated as a second appeal for the purposes of s 55 of the 1999 Act. By CPR 52.13(1) only the Court of Appeal can give permission for a second appeal, and before it can do so, it must be satisfied that one or other of the tests mentioned in s 55 have been met (see CPR 52.13(2)). If a judge in the lower court, whether the county court or the High Court, purports to grant permission for a second appeal, that grant of permission is a nullity.

16. Despite the warning given by this court in the *Tanfern Ltd* case [2000] 2 All ER 801 at 811, [2000] 1 WLR 1311 at 1319 (para 43) about the likely fate of many applications for permission to make a second appeal and despite the clear warnings given by the Civil Appeals Office in the helpful written guidance they have issued to would-be appellants since the new appellate regime came into force, in *Scott v Shipp* (31 August 2000, unreported) (Peter Gibson and Brooke LJJ) two members of this court encountered a litigant in person who had paid his fee of £100 at a time when he told the court he had no idea of the very tough new hurdles confronting would-be appellants in second appeals. We hope that even more thought can be given to publicising the existence of this new rule so that if possible no litigant in person can fail to be aware of it before paying the fee of £100 for making the application.

17. At the same time we hope that thought can be given by the appropriate authorities to the position of litigants who are granted a remission of court fees and who are now lodging applications for permission to make a second appeal with no financial disincentives and no requirement to show any merits justifying a second appeal before being granted a fee remission. Current experience is showing that the staff and lawyers of the Civil Appeals Office and the judges of this court (who must under the present rules give the applicant a hearing in court before dismissing their applications, however hopeless they may be) are devoting a disproportionate amount of their time to such applications at a time when the whole thrust of the new appellate reforms, following the report of the *Review of the Court of Appeal (Civil Division)* (1997) (the Bowman report) and in anticipation of the implementation of the Human Rights Act 1998, is to use the time and resources of the judges of the Court of Appeal, and of the lawyers and staff who support them, on matters which really merit the attention of a court of this stature in the judicial hierarchy.

18. In *Scott's* case the application for permission to make a second appeal in a boundary dispute which turned on simple issues of fact was dismissed by Peter

Gibson LJ in a very short judgment, as envisaged in the *Tanfern Ltd* case [2000] 2 All ER 801 at 811, [2000] 1 WLR 1311 at 1319 (para 43). Other judgments of this type may be even shorter in future.

No power to appeal against a decision of a court to give or refuse permission to appeal

19. Section 54(4) of the 1999 Act provides that:

> 'No appeal may be made against a decision of a court under this section to give or refuse permission (but this subsection does not affect any right under rules of court to make a further application for permission to the same or another court).'

20. These words mean what they say. In his judgment in *Riniker's* case, with which Brooke LJ agreed, Robert Walker LJ explained that this court, whose jurisdiction is wholly statutory, has no inherent jurisdiction to hear an appeal against such a decision (unless it can be truly said that there was no decision at all, for which see *Daisystar Ltd v Town and Country Building Society* [1992] 2 All ER 321 at 324, [1992] 1 WLR 390 at 394). On the other hand, if on such an occasion, the appeal court makes a further order, such as a costs order or an order refusing an adjournment, an appeal does in theory lie to this court, with permission, although it is likely to be a very rare case in which such permission would be granted.

21. If a judge in an appeal court lower than the Court of Appeal has refused permission to appeal on the papers, there is no right of appeal against that refusal. The only remedy available to an aggrieved appellant is to make a request for that decision to be reconsidered at a hearing in that appeal court pursuant to CPR 52.3(4). This was the problem which arose in *Plender's* case, in which Peter Gibson and Brooke LJ will give judgment immediately after this judgment has been delivered. That judgment contains a great deal of practical guidance about the way in which appeals from a circuit judge to the High Court should and should not be handled administratively under these new appellate procedures. It is apparent that there have understandably been teething difficulties with the new procedures, not all of which have yet been satisfactorily resolved.

22. We would also in this context draw attention to the recent decision of another division of this court in *Henry Boot Construction (UK) Ltd v Malmaison Hotel (Manchester) Ltd* (2000) Times, 31 August, (Swinton Thomas and Waller LJJ and Arden J) in which this court held that it had no jurisdiction in relation to a purported challenge to a judgment in the High Court on an appeal under s 69 of the Arbitration Act 1996 when the High Court had not granted leave to appeal pursuant to s 69(8) of that Act.

Clark v Perks

23. In this appeal the appellants seek to appeal against a judgment of Ferris J ([2000] STC 428) on 19 April 2000 in respect of three cases stated by general commissioners of income tax in relation to appeals against assessments to income tax. The issue at the heart of the appeals relates to the allowability of foreign earnings deductions claimed by crew members who work on offshore structures known as jack-up drilling rigs.

24. The procedure before the judge is familiarly described as an appeal by way of case stated. It was referred to as an appeal by the Solicitor for Inland Revenue in a notice served in the High Court in connection with that hearing, and the judge started his judgment by referring to 'these three appeals from decisions of General Commissioners'. He ended it by saying that 'the result of this judgment is that I allow these appeals'. The order of the court in each case refers to the inspector of taxes as the appellant, although it otherwise makes no reference to the appeal being allowed: it merely directs that the determination of the commissioners that the taxpayer was entitled to foreign earnings deduction for the relevant year should be reversed, and that the assessment be confirmed in a given sum for taxable emoluments. The question we have to determine is whether an appeal from such an order is a second appeal for the purposes of s 55 of the 1999 Act and CPR 52.13.

25. The case stated procedure used in these matters is set out in regs 20 to 22 of the General Commissioners (Jurisdiction and Procedure) Regulations 1994, SI 1994/1812. Regulation 20 provides that within 30 days after the final determination of an appeal to the General Commissioners under the Taxes Acts (or any proceedings before them which are to be heard and determined in the same way as such an appeal), or after the other decisions by General Commissioners mentioned in that regulation:

> 'any party to the proceedings, if dissatisfied with the determination or decision as being erroneous in point of law, may by notice served on the Clerk require the [relevant panel of Commissioners] to state and sign a case for the opinion of the High Court.'

26. Section 56(6) of the Taxes Management Act 1970 gives the High Court its familiar powers to hear and determine any question or questions of law arising on such a case stated and to reverse, affirm or amend the determination in respect of which the case has been stated or to take one of the other courses mentioned in that section. The General Commissioners (Jurisdiction and Procedure) Regulations 1994 formed part of the scheme of reorganising the procedure for High Court challenges to decisions by General Commissioners or Special Commissioners which was permitted by the insertion of a new s 56B into the 1970 Act (see Finance (No 2) Act 1992, Sch 16, paras 1 and 4). Once the reorganisation was complete, the case stated procedure for challenging

decisions by Special Commissioners was replaced by an appeal on a point of law (see s 56A of the 1970 Act as substituted by reg 2(1) and Sch 1, paras 1 and 11 of the General and Special Commissioners (Amendment of Enactments) Regulations 1994, SI 1994/1813), while it was retained and reformulated in relation to challenges to decisions by General Commissioners in the part of the General Commissioners (Jurisdiction and Procedure) Regulations 1994 to which we have referred above.

27. In former times the case stated procedure was often provided by Parliament for challenges to the High Court on those occasions when a point of law had arisen in front of a lay tribunal charged with the responsibility of deciding cases concerned with people's rights. A convenient list of statutes creating 'case stated' procedures can be found in Annex 2 of the Law Commission's consultation paper *Judicial Review and Statutory Appeals* (Law Com No 126) (1993). Modern examples can be found in s 137 of the Water Industry Act 1991, s 65(1) of the Planning (Listed Buildings and Conservation Areas) Act 1990, s 289(1) of the Town and Country Planning Act 1990, s 84(4) of the Building Societies Act 1986, s 42(3) of the Building Act 1984, s 146 of the Representation of the People Act 1983 and s 78(8) of the Mental Health Act 1983. The usual form of the procedure is that adopted in the present model. Strictly it does not take the form of an appeal, although everyone tends colloquially to describe it as an appeal.

28. So far as Crown Office practice is concerned, the most familiar provisions in matters characterised as civil proceedings relate to proceedings by way of case stated in relation to decisions by magistrates' courts and the Crown Court in civil matters. These, no doubt, were what the authors of the Bowman report had in mind in paras 60 to 62 of chapter four of their report when in a passage headed 'Appeals by way of Case Stated' they equated these so-called appeals with a large number of other appeals, properly so called. The mischief they identified in that passage of their report was the fact that the time and resources of the Court of Appeal were being taken up in hearing second appeals in matters which had already been heard twice before courts, tribunals or other bodies performing quasi-judicial functions below the level of the Court of Appeal. Their recommendation no 32 'An appeal by way of case stated in a civil case should generally go no further than the Divisional Court or the nominated High Court judge' was based on this analysis.

29. They were in good company when they described these applications as appeals, because this description was used not only by the Law Commission in its consultation paper and its report *Administrative Law: Judicial Review and Statutory Appeals* (Law Com No 226) (1994) but also by the parliamentary draftsman in s 28(3)(a) of the Supreme Court Act 1981. As a matter of

historical curiosity the language of s 28(3)(a) can be contrasted with the language of s 25(1) of the Supreme Court of Judicature (Consolidation) Act 1925:

> 'Every case stated by a court of quarter sessions otherwise than under the Crown Cases Act, 1848, or the Quarter Sessions Act, 1849, for the consideration of the High Court shall be deemed to be an appeal, and shall be heard and determined accordingly.'

30. It is to be noted that ss 54(6) and 56(7) of the 1999 Act contain express provisions for the purposes of those sections which appear to assimilate case stated procedure with appeal procedure, and that no such assimilation is included either in s 55 or in s 61 (which enacts cl 2 of the draft bill included in the Law Commission report, and has a quite different origin from the Bowman report). It is difficult to understand, however, why in a group of sections concerned with streamlining and rationalising the civil appeal process, appeals from decisions of the High Court on applications by way of case stated should be categorised in a different manner for the purposes of s 55 from the way in which applications by way of case stated are categorised for the purposes of ss 54 and 56. If any ambiguity exists, it will be immediately resolved, as counsel for the appellants readily conceded, when recourse is had to the Bowman report.

31. He argued strenuously, however, that no ambiguity did exist, so that it was not legitimate for us to look for assistance from external sources. We asked him whether, if s 55 had not been included in the 1999 Act, the Civil Procedure Rules Committee would nevertheless have had power to restrict access to the Court of Appeal in these cases under its powers contained in s 54(3)(c) of the Act. He conceded that they would. This made his technical arguments, based on what he contended was the true status of the case stated procedure, even more unappealing, but this did not divert him from continuing to advance them. When we pointed out to him that it appeared strange that Parliament should have contemplated a restriction on a second appeal from a decision of the High Court on appeal from the Special Commissioners, but no such restriction in relation to a challenge to a High Court decision on a case stated by General Commissioners, when it was often a mere matter of chance (or tactics) which body entertained the taxpayer's challenge to an assessment, he was unmoved by this peculiar consequence of his submissions.

32. Counsel for the inspector of taxes reminded us that s 13 of the Stamp Act 1891 and s 28(3)(a) of the Supreme Court Act 1981 (which are both still on the statute book) each contained express recognition that a case stated procedure can amount to an appeal (or be subsumed within an appeal) in the eyes of a parliamentary draftsman. He submitted that to say in the other contexts in which the procedure is available that there is 'no such thing' as an appeal by way of case stated' would be to elevate label over substance. He contended that there was no aspect of a hearing on a case stated which was inherently incompatible

with such a hearing constituting an appeal. In this context he was referring to a case which was stated following a final decision of the relevant tribunal or other decision-making body, whether or not that decision was on a point which left other points still to be determined.

33. We are bound to say that we do not entirely understand why the draftsman of ss 54–57 of the 1999 Act adopted the techniques he chose to adopt. The language of ss 54(5) and 56(7) is itself rather dense. The first provision appears to envisage the control of the right to apply to the High Court to have a case stated for its opinion (which sounds like mandamus proceedings under Ord 53 when the inferior court, tribunal or other body has refused to state a case), and the latter to envisage the transfer of such an application to the Court of Appeal or to the county court. What was surely Parliament's intention was the control of the right to demand the hearing by the High Court of a case stated or the transfer of that hearing to a different court from the High Court. However that may be, we are satisfied that there is sufficient ambiguity about Parliament's intention in s 55 to entitle us to look at the Bowman report as an aid to interpretation. Once we have done that then it is quite clear that Parliament intended in s 55 to include challenges to decisions of the High Court on case stated among those challenges for which the stricter entry conditions imposed by s 55 were intended.

34. Given that this is a second appeal, we have to consider whether it satisfies the criteria for second appeals set out in CPR 52.13(2). When he granted permission to appeal (under the mistaken impression that he had jurisdiction to do so) Ferris J said:

> 'The point which arises in this case is one on which the opposite conclusion to that which I have reached is, I think, one which the Court of Appeal might conceivably prefer. These are tax cases of some general importance. £100 million of tax is said to depend on their outcome.'

35. We were told that in another case Special Commissioners had reached a conclusion diametrically opposite to that of Ferris J (before his decision in the present case), and that their decision is now under challenge in the High Court. Although counsel for the inspector of taxes placed before us a photograph of the structure at the heart of these appeals in an effort to beguile us into concluding that it could not by any stretch of the imagination be described as a ship (a result which would be necessary if these appeals were to succeed) it appears to us that the conclusion is not necessarily so clear-cut, and that the proposed appeal does satisfy the requirements of CPR 52.13(2). We therefore grant permission to appeal.

McNicholas Construction Co Ltd v HM Customs & Excise

36. In this matter the appellants sought to appeal from a judgment of Dyson J ([2000] STC 553) on 16 June 2000 whereby he dismissed their appeal, save in

certain minor respects, from a determination of a VAT tribunal sitting at the London Tribunal Centre dated 12 January 2000 which had allowed in part and dismissed in part their appeals against certain VAT assessments made by the Commissioners of Customs and Excise on 21 March 1997.

37. The appeal to the High Court lay pursuant to s 11 and para 44 of Sch 1 of the Tribunals and Inquiries Act 1992. A further appeal to this court would therefore be governed by s 55 of the 1999 Act and the procedure for granting permission to appeal governed by CPR 52.13. Although Dyson J purported to give permission to appeal, his grant of permission was a nullity because only the Court of Appeal can give permission for second appeals.

38. When Dyson J purported to grant permission to appeal he said: 'I have given permission to appeal because the attribution point is arguable. Absent that point, I would have refused permission.'

39. In those circumstances it appears that if he had in fact possessed jurisdiction to grant permission, he should have limited the issues to be heard on the appeal pursuant to his powers under CPR 52.3(7).

40. The appellants originally sought to reopen on their appeal to this court all the issues which had been litigated unsuccessfully on their appeal to Dyson J. Now that their attention has been drawn to the fact that this is a second appeal and that the order of Dyson J is a nullity, they have agreed to limit their proposed grounds of appeal to what has been called the attribution point. The commissioners, for their part, have been willing to concede that a second appeal should be permitted on this point, and we share the view of the parties that an appeal on the attribution point raises an important point of principle.

41. We therefore told the parties that although the application would be listed for hearing we would excuse their attendance, make an order granting permission to appeal on this limited basis, and give a short judgment to illustrate the fact that appeals from High Court decisions on appeals pursuant to s 11 of the Tribunals and Inquiries Act 1992 are second appeals for the purposes of CPR Pt 52.

Jenkins v BP Oil UK Ltd
42. This action was commenced in the Neath and Port Talbot County Court in August 1998. It relates to an accident the claimant sustained on 10 July 1996 at the Queen's Dock depot in Swansea when he was engaged in his work as a tanker operator. He was then aged 49. He was employed by the second defendants, and the depot, where he was loading up petrol, was operated by the first defendants. By his particulars of claim dated 9 August 1998 he claimed damages for negligence and/or breach of statutory duty limited to £50,000 against both defendants.

43. It appears that the defendants did not serve a defence. On 28 February 2000 District Judge Batcup directed that judgment be entered for the claimant against both defendants for damages to be assessed. His order set out a timetable for such steps as the service of an updated schedule of special damages and a counter-schedule in reply, and the exchange of witness statements and experts' reports, and directed that the hearing of the action be adjourned to 12 June 2000 before a district judge for disposal, estimated time 3 hours. He did not allocate the case to any particular track. The defendants were jointly represented at the hearing on 28 February.

44. Despite the limitation in the particulars of claim, which was never amended, the sums claimed in the schedule of special damages amounted to £182,853.75. In their counter-schedule the defendants averred that the claimant was fit and able to return to work in September 1998 and that if he was unfit to work thereafter this was due to psychological factors which had nothing to do with this incident.

45. The order dated 28 February 2000 directed that the expert evidence on the issue of psychiatric injuries should be limited to a single expert, and that the experts (sic) reports should be filed and served by 4 April 2000. It was not clear whether the district judge intended this to refer to a joint report or reports. In the event the claimant's psychiatric expert delivered two reports (dated October 1998 and March 2000 respectively) and the defendants did not instruct a psychiatrist themselves. Instead, they availed themselves of the facility to ask questions about these reports, as was allowed for in the district judge's order. It followed that the sole psychiatric evidence before the district judge in June was to the effect that Mr Jenkins was suffering from a chronic reactive anxiety disorder (connected with the injury to his shoulder) which in all probability precluded him from any form of remunerative employment in the future.

46. So far as the orthopaedic evidence was concerned, the two orthopaedic consultants prepared a joint statement which disclosed a quite substantial measure of agreement. The only area of disagreement was that the claimant's expert believed that the claimant would have worked for a further seven to eight years before experiencing constitutional symptoms in his right shoulder if he had not sustained his accident, whereas the defendant's expert was of the opinion that the onset of symptoms had been accelerated by the accident by a period of two to three years. Although the claimant's orthopaedic expert attended the hearing on 12 June, no application had been made on behalf of either party for permission to adduce oral evidence, and the district judge therefore declined to allow the expert to supplement his written evidence. It is not easy to understand how the district judge found himself able in these circumstances to resolve judicially the critical difference of opinion between the two experts in a case in which he was to award damages at the rate of £260.72 a week for a number of years on the basis only of their untested written evidence.

47. In his judgment District Judge Batcup preferred the conclusions of the claimant's expert without explaining why he did so. He awarded £15,000 general damages, £56,228.18 for loss of earnings to date, £54,229.76 for four years' future loss of earnings and £236.39 for miscellaneous items of special damage, making a total of £125,694.53, subject to a CRU claw-back of £10,470.72. Interest brought the total award up to £135,097.18.

48. The defendants seek permission to appeal against this award on three grounds. It is sufficient for present purposes to say that if this court had jurisdiction to hear the appeal, we would be disposed to grant permission to appeal on all three grounds. The issue we have to decide is whether this court has jurisdiction to hear the appeal at all.

49. The notice of appeal is dated 26 July 2000, and the appeal is therefore governed by the new procedural regime. Since this was a judgment of a district judge in a county court, an appeal would normally lie to a circuit judge in the county court (see the *Tanfern Ltd* case [2000] 2 All ER 801 at 805, [2000] 1 WLR 1311 at 1314 (para 15) and see now the helpful table contained in para 2A.1 of the Practice Direction to CPR Pt 52). The claim had never been allocated to the multi-track under rr 12.7, 14.8 or 26.5, so that the exception mentioned in the *Tanfern Ltd* case [2000] 2 All ER 801 at 806, [2000] 1 WLR 1311 at 1315 (para 16) and para 2A.2 of the Practice Direction (which allows for an appeal to the Court of Appeal against a final decision in a claim allocated to the multi-track) does not apply.

50. We have been told by the appellants' solicitor that she has spoken to District Judge Batcup, and that he has told her that the designated civil judge for his area had indicated that he did not wish district judges to allocate pre-26 April 1999 cases to a track. The district judge has also apparently told her that if the case had been allocated, it would have been a multi-track case. He has apparently expressed his willingness to confirm this information direct to a deputy master at the Civil Appeals Office, but there seemed to be no need to put him to the trouble of doing so. We were told by counsel, on instructions, that at one point the district judge said that he had been sitting as a district judge in the High Court, but the defendants' solicitors are not aware that any order for transfer has ever been made, and all the orders in the lower court are county court orders.

51. For the sake of completeness, it should be noted that when a court enters a default judgment for an amount to be decided under CPR Pt 12 or a judgment on an admission of liability for an amount to be decided under CPR 14.6 or 14.7, it will allocate the case to a track only if it considers it appropriate to do so (see CPR 12.7(2)(b) and CPR 14.8(1)(b)). Section 12 of the Practice Direction which supplements CPR Pt 26 deals with issues connected with allocation and case management in the assessment of damages and allied proceedings. It contains the following relevant provisions:

'12.3 *Allocation*—Where a claim has not been allocated to a track at the time a relevant order [for which see para 12.1] is made, the court will not normally consider it to be appropriate to allocate it to a track (other than the small claims track) unless the amount payable appears to be genuinely disputed on grounds which appear to be substantial. It may instead direct that a disposal hearing (referred to in paragraph 12.8) be listed ...

12.8 *Disposal hearings—*
(1)   At a disposal hearing the court may give directions or decide the amount payable in accordance with this sub-paragraph
...
(3)   If the court does not give directions and does not allocate the claim to the small claims track, it may nonetheless order that the amount payable is to be decided there and then without allocating the claim to another track.
(4)   Rule 32.6 applies to evidence at a disposal hearing unless the court otherwise directs °

12.10 *Jurisdiction of Masters and district judges*—Unless the court otherwise directs, a Master or a district judge may decide the amount payable under a relevant order irrespective of the financial value of the claim and the track to which the claim may have been allocated.'

52. Rule 32.6(1) provides, so far as is material, that the general rule is that evidence at hearings other than the trial is to be by witness statement unless the court, a practice direction, or any other enactment requires otherwise.

53. The Civil Procedure Rules which came into effect on 26 April 1999, and the Practice Directions which accompanied them, predated the new procedural regime for appeals which followed a year later, with which we are now concerned. Between 26 April 1999 and 2 May 2000 the former appellate regime was still in place. If an action was proceeding in the High Court, the appeal against an order made on an assessment of damages lay to this court, whether the order was made by a district judge or master on the one hand, or by a High Court judge on the other. If the action was proceeding in the county court, the *Tanfern Ltd* case is authority for the proposition that an appeal from an order of a district judge on an assessment of damages lay to a circuit judge, with scope for a second appeal in an appropriate case to this court. The track to which a case was allocated did not matter at that time, so far as the destination of an appeal was concerned. In relation to appeals in such cases from district judges, what was important was whether the proceedings were being conducted in the county court or in a district registry of the High Court.

54. Under the new appellate regime, the different routes of appeal are now clearly set out in para 2A.1 of the Practice Direction which supplements Pt 52. It does not now matter whether a decision by a district judge on an assessment

of damages was made in the county court or in the High Court. Appeal against such a decision will lie to a circuit judge unless the case was allocated to the multi-track in which case it will lie to this court. This case was not allocated to the multi-track, and this court therefore has no jurisdiction unless some special order is made. The difficult task of the staff in the Civil Appeals Office would be rendered quite impossible if they had to cope with arguments to the effect that the lower court would have allocated the case to a track if it had thought that this mattered. If the matter has not been allocated to the multi-track in the court below, the Court of Appeal, which is a creature of statute, has no jurisdiction to entertain an appeal.

55. It appears to us that it would be desirable if the appropriate authorities were to reconsider the terms of the Practice Direction supplementing CPR Pt 26 in the light of our judgment and of the judgment of another division of this court in *Sandry's* case. In the present case we can see no reason why a district judge should not have conducted the assessment of damages provided that he was considered to have appropriate experience in this type of litigation, once it had become clear that there were no really difficult issues to be decided which warranted the assignment of a judge at a higher level of the judiciary to conduct the assessment. The difficulty highlighted by this case is that neither the rules nor this Practice Direction give any particularly useful guidance about the allocation of an assessment of damages, or indeed, in the light of para 12.10 of the Practice Direction, the purpose of any allocation. CPR Pts 28 and 29 show that allocation to track is a concept designed for the pre-trial management of cases where liability is in issue, and they do not cast much light on the purpose of allocation to track when all that is in issue is the amount to be paid under a judgment which has already been entered.

56. *Sandry's* case was a quite different case. There were heavily contested medical and accountancy issues in connection with a claim for over £200,000, which continued to be in issue at the hearing. Swinton Thomas LJ (para 3) and Brooke LJ (paras 65 to 67), in ex tempore judgments with which Hale LJ agreed, expressed their views about the appropriate level of the judiciary at which assessments of that complexity should be conducted, barring special circumstances. It would in our judgment be desirable if the relevant Practice Direction could be revised so that procedural judges may be given more guidance as to the level of the judiciary by which assessments of damages should be conducted in complex disputed cases, and as to the principles they should follow when deciding whether to allocate an assessment of damages to a track, and if so to which track. Both this case and *Sandry's* case illustrate the desirability in potentially heavy assessments of postponing a final direction as to the mode of 'trial' and the level of judge conducting the 'trial' until the evidence is complete and it is possible to see clearly what is in dispute and what is not.

57. Counsel told us that he could not put forward with any degree of conviction any submissions to the effect that this was a case in which we might encourage the Master of the Rolls or a judge at either level in the county court to exercise their powers under s 57 of the 1999 Act and CPR 52.14(1) to transfer this appeal to this court on the grounds that it satisfied one of the tests which would justify such a transfer. The power conferred by CPR 52.14(1) on courts lower than the Court of Appeal is available to be used if one of the criteria mentioned in the rule are satisfied, but it should be used sparingly. It would always be open to such a court to refer the matter to the Master of the Rolls if it is in any doubt whether the point is important enough to justify a transfer.

58. For these reasons we ruled that this court had no jurisdiction to hear this application. Application should be made to the appropriate circuit judge in the local county court, and we hope that he will be able to extend time for appealing and grant permission to appeal reasonably quickly, so that the appeal may be pursued without being unduly prejudiced by the delay caused by the procedural uncertainty about its proper venue. We have directed that the costs of this application should be costs in the appeal.

First and second applications granted. Third application outside court's jurisdiction.

Gillian Crew Barrister.

CONTRACT FACILITIES LTD V REES' ESTATE

A2.6

[2003] EWCA Civ 1105

COURT OF APPEAL, CIVIL DIVISION

WALLER and HALE LJJ

24 JULY 2003

JUDGMENT: APPROVED BY THE COURT FOR HANDING DOWN (SUBJECT TO EDITORIAL CORRECTIONS)

Lord Justice Waller:

This is the judgment of the court.

1. On 6th December 2002 His Honour Judge Weeks QC dismissed a claim by the appellant company (Contract). Contract were claiming specific performance or damages by reference to a contract for the purchase of shares. Contract had however been struck off the register. It had by the time it commenced proceedings been restored to the register with retrospective effect. The issues

that the judge had to resolve related to the effect of that retrospective restoration in holding that that restoration did not prevent the company being in repudiation of the contract during the period when it was struck off the register. Contract's claim was thus dismissed with costs. The judge refused an application to assess costs on an issue basis taking the view that that question was essentially an academic one having regard to the fact that the company had no assets. He thus ordered an interim payment of £15,000 being the sum which Contract had been ordered to put up as security for costs.

2. Contract put in a notice of appeal on 20th December 2002. By that notice an application was made for a stay of execution in relation to the order for costs made in favour of the defendants.

3. As already indicated Contract has no assets. The action had been funded by certain individuals including a Mr Shuck. The defendants have at all times been concerned to see whether they can make the individuals who funded the action responsible for the costs.

4. It was in that context that the defendants made an application to the judge that he should reconsider the permission to appeal in the light of new evidence and make permission to appeal conditional on the payment of the defendants' costs in the sum of £100,000. The argument of the defendants involved submitting to the judge that when the matter got to the court of appeal the court of appeal would not have the power to impose such a condition and thus that it was a matter for the judge. The judge refused to impose any conditions. In addition the defendants made an application that the individuals who funded the application should be liable for the costs under section 51 of the Supreme Court Act 1981. The judge has refused to hear that application pending the appeal.

5. So far as the court of appeal is concerned an application for a stay in relation to the order for costs was made and dealt with by Waller LJ on 24 March 2003. He refused that application. At the same time there was an application by the respondents for security for costs for the appeal and an agreed order for that security in the sum of £20,000 was made. That security was to be supplied by 4.00pm, on 7 April 2003.

6. In considering whether to grant a stay the main issue was whether unless a stay were granted the appeal would be stifled. Waller LJ took the view that there was no cogent evidence of the appeal being stifled on the basis that Mr Shuck who had financed the action below and was financing the appeal had not demonstrated that he could not pay such liability for costs as there might be. However Waller LJ was concerned to relieve Contract or those funding Contract from incurring the costs of a detailed assessment and made an order that if the sum of £50,000 was paid into the court there would be a stay of execution. That sum has however never been paid into court.

7. Indeed what has happened is that those acting for Contract have done all they can to postpone the assessment of costs so that if possible the appeal would come on before the respondents have a sum in relation to which they can execute against Contract.

8. The solicitors for Contract appear to have been put in funds to make such applications as they have deemed necessary to support the stalling tactics or to resist the respondents' attempt to get the order they need. That seems to indicate that funds are available through Mr Shuck. He is content to fund his solicitors but determined the respondents do not get any money from him. Mr Shuck's aim is clearly to try and win the appeal in which event the costs order will be reversed, Contract will survive and he will benefit from that survival. We assume that he through Contract would have every intention of seeking an order for costs against the respondents which he would have no compunction in enforcing. But if the appeal is lost Contract will have no assets and go into liquidation. Mr Shuck will then fight tooth and nail to prevent any individuals who backed the original action and who backed the appeal being liable for costs.

9. The order to supply security for costs for the appeal was not in fact complied with. The sum was provided ten minutes late. As Waller LJ indicated in relieving Contract from sanctions that conduct by Mr Shuck was very close to being deliberate. Indeed his conduct was such that it was a close run thing as to whether Contract should be relieved from sanctions and have their appeal dismissed.

10. The attempts however to prevent the respondents obtaining an enforceable order have continued. The details appear in Mr Davies' seventh statement. Despite the efforts of those representing Contract the respondents have now obtained an interim costs certificate for £37,000 although the money is to be paid into court and not to the respondents personally. But the effect of the delaying tactics of those representing Contract is that that order was not obtained until 6 June 2003.

11. On 4 June 2003 the appellants had issued an application returnable before His Honour Judge Weeks QC asking him to vary the order made on 6 December 2002 to make the costs order issue based. This application appears to have been made to support an argument before Master Wright at the hearing on 6 June 2003 that an interim costs certificate was premature since the matter was going back in front of the trial judge. Master Wright as already indicated did issue a certificate of £37,000 payable within 14 days. However he ordered that the money be paid into court rather than to the respondents.

12. The application before His Honour Judge Weeks QC was heard on 24 June 2003. It was dismissed on the grounds that the judge had no jurisdiction to vary

his previous order and on the further basis that Contract had already informally made the same application at the hearing before His Honour Judge Weeks QC on 21 February 2003.

13. In addition to the interim costs order of £37,000, the respondents now also have an order for the payment of costs in relation to the hearing before Master Wright in the sum of £2,000. They have a further order from His Honour Judge Weeks QC in relation to the hearing before him in the sum of £4,791. Although those costs should have been paid within 14 days they have not been paid. Furthermore the sum of £37,000 has not been paid into court. It is obviously the aim of Contract to have the appeal heard before they actually pay those sums so that if the appeal is lost execution against Contract will achieve nothing.

14. When Waller LJ dealt with Contract's application for a stay on 24 March 2003 he held that the evidence that any appeal would be stifled was exceedingly weak. It is now clear both from a statement put before His Honour Judge Weeks QC by Mr Tasselli and from the concession made by Mr Reeve on behalf of Contract before us that there is no question of there being any stifling of the appeal if the above sums were ordered to be paid. Mr Shuck would find it inconvenient to pay those monies but he would be able to do so if it was made a condition of Contract being entitled to pursue their appeal that those orders should be met.

15. The application made by the respondents was to obtain either a dismissal of the appeal by reference to Contract's conduct or [more realistically] an order that those costs be paid within a short time or the appeal be dismissed or in the further alternative that the appeal be taken out of the list and adjourned until the costs were paid.

16. At the conclusion of the hearing before us we made the order that unless by 4.00pm on Friday 18 July 2003 Contract paid the sum of £37,000 into court and the sums of £2,000 and £4,792 to the respondents the appeal be struck out. We further ordered Contract to pay the respondents' costs of this application and ordered that sum also to be paid by 4.00pm 18 July 2003 and that the appeal would be struck out if the costs were not paid. We are now giving our reasons for making that order.

Jurisdiction

17. Mr Reeve submitted that there was no jurisdiction in the court of appeal to make the order sought. His submission was that CPR 52 laid down the powers of the court of appeal. In particular he submitted that CPR 52.9 identified the situations in which the court was empowered to impose conditions upon which an appeal might be brought. CPR 52.9 provides as follows:

'(1) The appeal court may–

(a) strike out the whole or part of an appeal notice;
(b) set aside permission to appeal in whole or in part;
(c) impose or vary conditions upon which an appeal may be brought.

(2) The court will only exercise its powers under paragraph (1) where there is a compelling reason for doing so.

(3) Where a party was present at the hearing at which permission was given he may not subsequently apply for an order that the court exercise its powers under sub-paragraphs (1)(b) or (1)(c).'

18. Mr Reeve has two prongs to his attack by reference to CPR 52.9. First he says that permission to appeal was granted by the judge at a time when the respondents were present. That was on 6 December 2002. Thus he argues CPR 52.9(3) prevents an application to impose conditions upon which an appeal may be brought. Second and additionally the respondents had made an attempt to persuade the judge to vary the order he had made for permission to appeal. They sought to persuade him to order that permission to appeal should be made conditional on a payment into court in respect of both costs orders made on 28 November 2002 and 6 December 2002 alternatively the provision of appropriate security in relation to the same. They made that application on the basis that there had been a change of circumstances since the judge had made his first order granting permission to appeal. The judge rejected that application. Mr Reeve relies again on CPR 52.9(3) but in addition suggests that even if CPR 52.9 does not apply on its true construction to prevent conditions now being imposed on permission to appeal, it would be wrong for the court of appeal to entertain what is in effect the same application already rejected by the judge.

19. In *Societe Eran Shipping* [2001] EWCACiv568 at para 18 Rix LJ was inclined to the view that CPR 52.9(3) was applicable only to applications for permission before the court of appeal. It was not he was inclined to the view applicable to applications to the trial judge. His reasoning was that parties would always be present at hearings at first instance. Further CPR 52.9(1)(c) relates to varying conditions which seems to indicate an application to the court of appeal to vary conditions made in the court below. We see the force of Rix LJ's reasoning but it is not necessary for the disposal of these applications to rule finally on that aspect.

20. There is an answer to Mr Reeve's objections to jurisdiction by reference to entirely different provisions of the CPR. These provisions also deal with his point that this court should not be entertaining a similar application to that which has already been made before His Honour Judge Weeks.

21. The court of appeal has the power to manage its own cases. It would be very strange if CPR 52.9 prevented the court of appeal imposing conditions under its case management powers where circumstances during the currency of the

appeal made it appropriate either to stay the appeal or stay the appeal subject to conditions. This matter was dealt with in *Great Future International Limited v Sealand Housing Corporation* [2003] EWCACiv682 where the court was concerned with its jurisdiction to impose a condition on the appellants' application for permission to appeal. Arguments were run in that case that the power to impose conditions came from CPR 52.10 but Waller LJ doubted whether that was the provision that provided the requisite powers. Waller LJ said this:

'8. The provisions on which Mr Kosmin relies are CPR 3.1. He suggested in his submissions that the Court of Appeal had the power to exercise the powers provided by CPR 3.1 by virtue of CPR 52.10, which provides for the Court of Appeal having the powers of the court below in relation to any appeal. For my part I am doubtful whether it is CPR 52.10 which provides the Court of Appeal with any of the requisite powers. It seems to me that it is CPR 2.1 which gives the Court of Appeal case management powers, which are the powers provided for by CPR 3 to which I will turn in a moment. CPR 2.1 provides that:

Subject to paragraph (2), these Rules apply to all proceedings in ...

(a) county courts;
(b) the High Court; and
(c) the Civil Division of the Court of Appeal.'

And the case management powers are clearly case management powers both in relation to the Court of Appeal and the other courts there referred to. The important parts of CPR 3.1 are 3.1(2), which provides:

'Except where these Rules provide otherwise, the court may ...

(f) stay the whole or part of any proceedings either generally or until a specified date or event; ...
(m) take any other step or make any other order for the purpose of managing the case and furthering the overriding objective'

and 3.1(3), which provides:

'When the court makes an order it may

(a) make it subject to conditions, including a condition to pay a sum of money into court; and
(b) specify the consequence of failure to comply with the order or a condition.

It is unnecessary to quote other aspects of 3.1, although they all provide support for the court having the power to make the form of order that Mr Kosmin seeks in this case.

9. The argument put forward by Mr Connerty for suggesting that 3.1 does not provide the requisite power rests essentially on the opening words of 3.1(2), which provide "Except where these Rules provide otherwise, the court may".

What he suggests is because there is CPR 25, dealing with security for costs, including CPR 25.15 dealing expressly with security for costs on an appeal, and CPR 52, dealing with what happens in relation to appeals and applications for permission "these Rules provide otherwise".

10. As my Lord, Lord Justice Kay pointed out during the argument, the truth is that the Rules are silent in relation to the situation that actually exists in this particular case. There is no provision of the Rules which deals with what should happen where an application for permission has been adjourned to an oral hearing and where the appeal is to follow. Furthermore, it seems to me that the argument put forward by Mr Connerty comes up against one of the authorities to which we were referred, which is *Olatawura v Abiloye* [2002] CP Reports 73, where Simon Brown LJ approved the use of CPR 3.1 in the context of a summary judgment application. What is referred to by 3.1(2) is something that expressly prohibits or expressly deals with the particular matter which might otherwise be dealt with under 3.1(2). In my view the jurisdiction is there.'

22. It seems clear that the court of appeal has case management powers in addition to those that it may have under CPR 52. Furthermore it seems to us that the application that is now before us is an application made during the currency of an appeal where the court is being asked to consider whether to exercise its case management powers by reference to conduct while the appeal is pending. That is totally different from the application before His Honour Judge Weeks. In our view the court of appeal has jurisdiction to deal with this application and it is not inappropriate to consider the making of the order asked even though the respondents did seek to impose conditions on the permission to appeal before His Honour Judge Weeks.

23. Mr Reeve's next point was to suggest that the costs order is flawed. His argument was that the original costs order should have been issue based. Although the judge has refused to make an issue based order that was at first because he thought it was academic and later because he did not think he had any jurisdiction to do so. It will be contended on the appeal that even if Contract lose, the costs order made by the judge should be reversed and an issue based costs order be made. So it is submitted by Mr Reeve that the liability for the costs may not be as high as the £37,000 certified by the costs judge. It would thus he submits be prejudicial to order the payment of £37,000 into court in those circumstances.

24. We do not think there will be any prejudice. Even if the costs order was varied to an issue based order, and a lower sum than the £37,000 was ordered to be paid, since this sum is in court any surplus would be ordered to be repaid to Contract.

25. The main point taken by Mr Reeve is that the respondents are attempting to prejudge the question whether Mr Shuck should be personally liable for the costs of the trial below. It is in this context that it is right to consider the authorities cited to us. We were referred to *Hammond Suddard v Agrichem International Holdings Limited* [2001] EWCACiv2065 and to *CIBC Mellon Trust Company v Mora Hotel Corporation NV and Chascona NV* [2002] EWCACiv1688.

26. *CIBC* was a case in which the judge at first instance had used case management powers to make it a condition of the pursuit of certain applications the payment into court of £1,600,000 which related to past costs. The circumstances of the case were that an individual shareholder had come in to finance later aspects of litigation and the order for the putting up of past costs was made on the basis that that individual could afford to put those costs up. A lengthy citation from the judgment of Lord Justice Peter Gibson will demonstrate both the points at issue in that case and the distinction between that case and the *Hammond Suddard* case. He dealt first with jurisdiction and having held there was jurisdiction said this:

'23. The substantial issue on this appeal relates to the appropriateness of the order for a payment into court in respect of past costs. Mr. Wardell submits that implicit in the judge's decision were two novel propositions:
(1) the court can in advance of hearing an application to set aside a default judgment impose a condition that a corporate defendant must, by raising money from its shareholders, enlarge the pool of available assets with which to meet the judgment in the event of the application failing;
(2) the court can and should in the exercise of its discretion refuse to vary a freezing order to allow the Appellants to pay a debt to the Claimants.

24. Mr. Wardell relies on the following matters:
(1) the Claimants have security for costs already incurred by virtue of the existing judgment which had given it control of the Gorham Hotel having a net equity of US $27 million including cash reserves of US $7 million;
(2) the Appellants cannot comply with the judge's order because its assets are frozen by a court order;
(3) the court refuses to vary the freezing order to enable such payment to be made;

(4) to the court's knowledge the only person who will be able to comply with the order is a shareholder who is not a party to the proceedings;
(5) any application for an order against that person under s 51 Supreme Court Act 1981 to pay the outstanding costs orders would fail;
(6) if the shareholder declines to put up the funds, the application to set aside the judgments will be defeated without it being given the opportunity of being heard;
(7) if the shareholder puts up the funds, but the applications are unsuccessful, the claimants will have a windfall.

25. Mr. Marshall supports the judge's decision. He submits that it is well established that the court can take account of all potential sources of funding available to a party when considering whether to require payment into court as a condition of granting leave to defend or the provision of security (*Yorke Motors v Edwards* [1982] 1 WLR 444, *Keary Developments Ltd. v Tarmac Construction Ltd.* [1995] 3 All E.R. 534), and it is for the party asserting inability to meet such a requirement to demonstrate that inability by proper evidence. Similar principles, he says, have been applied when a party has sought a variation of a freezing injunction to make some desired payment out of frozen assets (*Atlas Maritime Co. SA v Avalon Maritime Ltd* [1991] 1 WLR 917). He points out that all such payments by a third party may be said to constitute a windfall, but that has not deterred the court from requiring such payments in full knowledge that the party to the proceedings cannot or may not be able to pay out of his own resources.

26. Mr. Marshall relies on the following factors:
(1) the Appellants are applying to set aside judgments entered years earlier in consequence of their deliberate failure to comply with unless orders, and there is a long history of failure by the Appellants to comply with court orders;
(2) the Appellants will need to apply for relief under CPR 3.8, and the circumstances which the court is required to consider under r. 3.9 include several which are likely to tell against the granting of relief, such as the lateness of the application, the intentional failure to comply with rules and court orders consequent on the tactical decision taken by the Appellants, and the long delay, if there is to be a trial, since the relevant events occurred;
(3) in addition to the costs already assessed, the unassessed costs which the Appellants have been ordered to pay exceed £8 million;
(4) there is no prospect of the Appellants meeting any of the Claimants' costs if the applications to set aside fail unless the order made by the judge of payment into court stands;

(5) the value of the Appellants' assets subject to the freezing order is a fraction of what is owed under the orders made against the Appellants, so that the Claimants do not have security for their costs;

(6) Mr. Cavazza is the person instigating the applications and, through his interest in the Appellants, he will be the primary beneficiary if the applications succeed.

27. Mr. Marshall placed particular reliance on the decision of this court in *Hammond Suddard v Agrichem International Holdings Ltd.* [2001] EWCA Civ 2065. In that case the Claimants had recovered judgment in a sum with costs. The defendant obtained permission to appeal from this court and sought a stay of the orders made by the trial judge. The claimants applied for an order that the appeal be struck out unless by a specified date the defendant paid or secured the judgment debt, paid the costs awarded below and provided security for the costs of the appeal as a condition of the appeal being entertained. The defendant resisted that application on the grounds that it had insufficient assets and could not comply with the order so that the appeal would be stifled. It argued that it was irrelevant that funding from a third party was available. Clarke L.J., delivering the judgment of the court (consisting of himself and Wall J.) rejected the defendant's submissions and made the order requested. He referred to the evidence which the defendant had adduced of its impecuniosity and said it was wholly insufficient to show any risk of the appeal being stifled without a stay, and said that there was a compelling reason (for the purposes of CPR 52.9) for making the defendant pay or secure the judgment debt as a condition of permitting it to proceed with the appeal.

28. Clarke L.J. referred to six facts combining to produce such compelling reason:

(1) the defendant was a foreign company with no assets in the UK and there was a real risk that if the appeal failed the respondents would not recover the judgment and costs;

(2) the defendant had the resources, or access to resources, to enable it to instruct solicitors and counsel and to provide security for costs;

(3) there was no convincing evidence that the defendant did not have the resources or access to resources which would enable it to pay the judgment debt and costs orders of which it was in breach;

(4) the defendant provided inadequate evidence of its financial affairs;

(5) the defendant's appeal would not be stifled by making the order for payment;

(6) it was unacceptable for the defendant to intend to prosecute the appeal while disobeying the orders of the court.

29. Mr. Marshall says that similar factors are present in this case. He submits that just as this court in the *Hammond Suddard* case saw nothing unjust or inconsistent with the overriding objective in CPR 1.1 in requiring the defendant to obey the court's orders as a condition of being permitted to continue to prosecute its appeal or in putting the owner of the defendant to the choice of providing the payment of the costs orders or of seeing the appeal struck out, so it was not unjust or inconsistent to put Mr. Cavazza to a similar choice.

30. As the judge had a discretion whether to require a payment into court, the first question that arises is whether this court can interfere with the exercise of his discretion. The judge has expressed his reasoning with economy and it is not entirely easy to be sure of all the considerations which he took into account in reaching his conclusion. It would appear that in his reasoning he did not make much differentiation between the application for payment into court of security for the costs of the application to set aside and the application for payment of past costs. He applied the principle established in security for costs applications, viz. that the court can take into account not only what a party possesses but also what he might raise from other sources, to the whole of the application made to him.

31. With respect to the judge, whilst in an appropriate case that may be a determinative consideration in respect of both types of application (for example, where the applicant has not satisfied the court that he has disclosed his full assets but has asserted his impecuniosity), other differentiating factors may be crucial to the proper exercise of discretion. There is no injustice in requiring an applicant, asserting impecuniosity, to provide security for the respondent's future costs of the application, provided that thereby the application is not stifled. Nor is there injustice in requiring an applicant, who does not assert impecuniosity but has repeatedly failed to pay past costs orders, to pay what is already due to the other side if he is to be allowed to make a further application (see *Graham v Sutton Carden & Co.* [1897] 2 Ch. 367 at 371 per Chitty L.J.). There may be injustice in requiring an applicant to set aside a judgment to make a payment into court in respect of past costs as a condition of being allowed to proceed with such application when the court knows that the applicant cannot make such payment out of his own resources and that the only source of funding to make such payment is a third party against whom no order for costs under s 51 has been sought in respect of those costs and little reason to think that such an order could be made. In this context it must be a relevant consideration that the effect of requiring such payment is, if the application fails, to give the respondent the ability to recoup part of what he is owed from additional assets which, had the application not been made, would not have been available to him.

...

34. The judge robustly stated his complete lack of concern that Mr. Cavazza had to make the payment required of the Appellants and that it was irrelevant that he was a third party. For my part I cannot see how that fact can be of no relevance to the exercise of discretion. Dealing with a case justly must require the court to have regard to the substantive effect of the order being made and to the justice of, in reality, requiring the third party to make payment. In fact the judge did have regard to Mr. Cavazza's position. The judge rightly identifies the commercial reality as being that Mr. Cavazza was seeking by the application to protect his investment in the Appellants. That provides good justification for making an order for security for the costs of the applications even though the Appellants could not pay. But the point in issue is whether that is sufficient to enable the court to require the payment into court in respect of the past costs when Mr. Cavazza would have to fund such payment. The judge said that Mr. Cavazza must take responsibility for what happened in the past. I presume that the judge is there adverting to the fact that Mr. Cavazza has had 75% of the shares since 1995 and so he could have exercised his majority control earlier to prevent the Appellants conducting the proceedings in such a way as to cause the judgments in default to be entered and the costs orders to be made against the Appellants. But the court does not normally punish the person having share control of a litigant company against which a costs order is made by an order against that person under s 51 (see, for example, *Taylor v Pace Developments Ltd.* [1991] BCC 406). The position might be different if there was evidence that Mr. Cavazza had funded the Appellants before August 2001, for example in the jurisdiction proceedings, or was actively involved in the litigation at that earlier time. But there is no such evidence and no s 51 application against Mr. Cavazza.'

27. The instant case is very different from the CIBC case. First Mr Shuck had financed the whole of the trial process or been a party to the financing. Second this is a case in which a section 51 application must stand a considerable prospect of success. Third it is an appeal and that places the case management powers in a very different context. Fourth this is not a case where the respondents are simply seeking to inflate the pool against which they can later execute any judgment. Their position is that when Mr Shuck has financed the trial and is financing the appeal, there is no reason why he should be allowed to conduct that appeal on a heads he wins and a tails they lose basis.

28. It is not in our view to prejudge the question whether the individuals should be liable for the costs of the trial to make the orders that the respondents now seek. Contract can abandon the appeal and Mr Shuck can fight the question of personal liability for costs. But if Mr Shuck chooses to fund an appeal there is no reason why the court should not say Contract can bring the appeal but only on terms.

29. For these reasons we made the order that we did.

ELECTRA PRIVATE EQUITY PARTNERS AND OTHERS V KPMG PEAT MARWICK (A FIRM) AND OTHERS

A2.7

COURT OF APPEAL (CIVIL DIVISION)

AULD, CHADWICK and CLARKE LJJ

23 APRIL 1999

Lord Justice Auld

Further evidence [extract only]

As I have said, the Court have given Electra leave to adduce this further evidence in support of its appeal. As the question of its entitlement to do so was fully argued, I should set out the parties' rival submissions on the matter and my reasoning for joining in that decision.

Mr Aldous submitted that if the *Ladd v Marshall* test governs the matter, those documents clearly met the second and third conditions for admission of the evidence. They would have had an important influence on the result of the hearing on the issue of SKC's knowledge and intent, and they were undoubtedly credible. As to the first condition, he maintained that the documents could not have been obtained with reasonable diligence for use at the trial. He referred to KPMG's and SKC's failure to comply with their obligations under the RSC by respectively giving discovery and producing documents for inspection under Ord.24, r.10(2) in time for the hearing before Carnwath J.

Mr Aldous submitted in the alternative that the *Ladd v Marshall* rules do not apply to the admission of further evidence on an appeal against a strike-out order before discovery, or do not apply with the same rigour as they do to an appeal from a final 'judgment after trial or hearing of any cause or matter on the merit', to which RSC Ord.59 r.10(2) applies. He submitted that Carnwath J's judgment was not after such a hearing on the merits, since, albeit with the encouragement of the parties, he had approached the matter by testing the strength of Electra's then evidence in support of its pleaded claim, wrongly confining himself to what, in his view, it established, rather than considering what Electra might be able to prove, after discovery, at trial.

Mr Gross submitted: first, that Carnwath's strike-out decision was a judgment after a hearing on the merits and that there is no justification for relaxing the *Ladd v Marshall* rules in a case of this sort, particularly where, as here, the plaintiff has taken its stand on certain evidence; second, that, in any event Electra had not acted with reasonable diligence, having already had some of the critical documents in its possession and having allowed a year to elapse before seeking to inspect SKC's documents under RSC Ord.24, r.10, and not having sought an adjournment of the hearing before Carnwath J; and, third, that the documents were irrelevant to the duty of care pleaded against SKC, namely one arising out of its direct relationship with Electra, not through KPMG as an intermediary.

Taking the second and third *Ladd v Marshall* conditions first, the further documents, as I have said, could well have influenced Carnwath J's decision the other way, especially if he had applied the correct test of assumption of responsibility. They are, in particular, relevant to two of the important factors going to establish a direct assumption of responsibility by SKC to Electra for the accuracy of its accounts, namely: 1) SKC's knowledge that Electra was relying on its audit and the final report on it in making its decision whether to make the investment in Cambridge; and 2) the extent to which Electra would be relying on its, SKC's audit figures and not on independent verification of them by KPMG.

For example, on the question of the first *Ladd v Marshall* condition, reasonable diligence, I should start by saying that I am not convinced that Carnwath J's judgment was after a hearing on the merits. It is important to note the wording of the test in RSC Ord.59, r.10(2); it is the hearing, not the judgment, which has to be on the merits. This distinction is not so silly as it may at first sound when it is appreciated that in non-procedural interlocutory decisions courts appear to regard as critical the effect of the judgment rather than the nature of the hearing giving rise to it. Thus, if the outcome is that there will be no further hearing of the action on its merits, the *Ladd v Marshall* rules apply, but if the outcome is that there will be such a hearing, they don't. On that basis the following have been held to be judgments made after a hearing on the merits: a summary judgment – *Langdale v Danby* [1982] 3 All ER 129, [1982] 1 WLR 1123, CA and *K/S A/S Oil Transport v Saudi Research and Development Corporation Ltd (The 'Gudermes')* [1984] 1 Lloyd's Rep 5, CA; a decision striking out a defence because it discloses no triable issue – *Scotlife Home Loans (No 2) Ltd v Hedworth & Hedworth*, 15 May 1995, CA (unreported). On the other hand, decisions on interlocutory hearings which have been held not to be hearings on the merits are: an order setting aside a default judgment, albeit that the merits had been taken into account in the decision to set aside – *Weller v Dunbar*, 27 January 1984 CA; a refusal of defendants' application to set aside service on them out of the jurisdiction – *Canada Trust Co v Stolzenberg* [1998] CLC 1171 (for the same reason the editors of the White Book, at para 59/10/12, suggest that an order refusing summary judgment or granting conditional leave to defend should be treated in the same way).

The difficulty of this line of thinking is that it may be concentrating on the wrong 'cause or matter' the merits of which are the subject of the hearing, namely the issue as aired in the interlocutory hearing rather than the issue as it might be aired on a full hearing at trial. On the present approach of the courts, if the decision had gone the other way here, it would have been 'a' hearing on 'its' merits, but not a hearing on the merits with which RSC Ord.59 r.19(2) is concerned, because that was yet to come. Why should a hearing on application for summary judgment, as in *Langdale v Danby* or, as here strike-out, be characterized as a hearing on the merits or not, according to which way the decision has gone? It is no answer to say that it all depends on whether, as a result of it, a hearing on the merits yet to come, since the validity of the decision and hence the characterisation of the hearing giving rise to it may properly depend on the further evidence.

The dilemma is well illustrated by two recent cases. The first is *Williams v Attridge Solicitors (a firm)*, 8 July 1997, CA (unreported) a strike-out, seemingly not on the pleading of the claim, but on its hopelessness on the facts. The Court did not regard it as a decision on the merits. Brooke LJ, giving the judgment of the Court, consisting of himself and Potter LJ, said:

> 'On the face of it, there is no detectable difference in the present context between an interlocutory decision to strike an action out pursuant to Order 18 Rule 19 or under the inherent jurisdiction of the court. In neither case has there been a judgment on the merits.'

The second is *Rudra v Abbey National plc* (1998) 76 P&CR 537, in which Robert Walker LJ, with whom Schiemann LJ agreed, accepted and rationalised, obiter, the outcome in *Williams v Attridge*, as follows:

> '... it seems that the solicitor-defendants must have applied to strike out the Statement of Claim, not on the basis that it disclosed no reasonable cause of action, but on the basis that, although unimpeachable as a pleading, it was in all the circumstances a claim so obviously hopeless that it should be struck out on the threshold.
>
> In that case, therefore, the solicitor-defendants were seeking to prove a negative and to show at the very outset of the proceedings that the claim should be struck out without the need for any further inquiry. On a completely logical approach, the difference between that situation and the situation described by Lord Bridge ... in *Langdale v Danby* is not perhaps crystal clear.
>
> Nevertheless, it seems that the essential distinction between the two cases is that an application to strike out proceedings as an abuse of process is an even more summary procedure involving less consideration of the merits, although inevitably involving some consideration of the merits, than summary judgment given under Order 14 or Order 86.'

This attempt to rationalise the two different approaches according to the nature of the interlocutory process underlines the true difficulty of the *Langdale v Danby* ruling, namely that, it is illogical, before final judgment, to maintain that there has been a hearing on the merits in the context of an application to adduce evidence which it is maintained will show that there has not been such a hearing. This flaw was quickly recognised in the following editorial case note on the ruling in (1983) 99 LQR, at page 4 for reasons which, in my view, are as applicable to summary strike-outs on the basis that the claim is evidentially hopeless as on summary judgment:

'It is suggested, with all respect, that this is too restrictive an interpretation of the rule. In other contexts the trial or hearing of an action, cause or matter do not include a summary judgment: see Legal Aid (General) Regulations 1962, r.18(5) as interpreted in *Cope v United Dairies (London) Ltd* [1963] 2 QB 33, 40. Further, 'on the merits' has been held to mean a situation where the dispute is really fought out: *Reed v Nutt* (1890) 24 QBD 669, 673. In cases of summary judgment the defendant is often in a difficulty: there has been no discovery and time may be pressing ...'

The proper question, it seems to me, is whether, regardless of the form of the proceeding, there has been a judgment after a hearing in which the issues for determination in the cause of action have been considered and determined on their merits in the decision challenged. That is not to say that there should be no restriction on the introduction of further evidence on appeal from interlocutory orders where the hearings on which they are based were not hearings on the merits. If they are to remain a valuable tool for early and final disposal of actions that should not reach trial, there should be some control over attempts by disappointed litigants to retrieve lost ground in interlocutory appeals by relying on evidence which they could and should have put before the court below. It should be a matter for the court's discretion, according to the nature of the interlocutory hearing and the individual circumstances of the case; see *Star News Shops Ltd v Stafford Refrigeration Ltd* [1998] 4 All ER 408, [1998] 1 WLR 536, CA, per Otton LJ at G-H; and *Canada Trust Co v Stolzenberg* [1998] CLC 1171, CA, per Waller LJ at 1173B-1174A.

Even where the *Ladd v Marshall* conditions have been applied to interlocutory hearings, there are signs that the courts have recognised the need for some relaxation of the reasonable diligence condition where at an early stage of the litigation it is unjust to expect a party to have all his tackle in order. See e.g. *Langdale v Danby* [1982] 1 WLR 1123, HL, per Lord Bridge at 1133D-F; *The 'Gudermes'* [1984] 1 Lloyd's Rep 5, CA, per Ackner LJ at 10; *Canada Trust Co v Stolzenberg*, per Waller LJ at 1173. Such relaxation is especially justified where the battle ground or its timing were not of the appellant's choice, as in the case of a defendant facing an application for summary judgment or, as here, a plaintiff facing a strike-out application on the ground that his claim is bound to fail.

If, notwithstanding my reservations, Carnwath J's judgment was after a hearing on the merits, I would not, in the circumstances condemn Electra for lack of reasonable diligence because it could have pressed SKC and KPMG harder to comply with their respective obligations under the RSC to produce the documents in time for the hearing or in not seeking an adjournment until their production. In any event, I would regard it as highly unjust to apply the full rigour of the *Ladd v Marshall* first condition in this case. Electra was faced with an application in which, on the basis of the judge's approach, it was at risk of being struck out unless it deployed before him, in advance of discovery and without a full trial, all the material evidence it had in support of its pleaded claim. I find unattractive Mr Gross's submission that it is now too late for Electra to be allowed to rely on the further material when it was SKC's and KPMG's unjustifiable conduct which had the effect of keeping it from the judge.

Lord Justice Chadwick

I agree that these appeals should be allowed for the reasons given by Auld LJ. The only matter on which I think it necessary to add any observations of my own is the decision, in the course of the hearing of the appeals, to allow Electra to adduce evidence which had not been adduced before the judge.

In giving leave to adduce the new evidence, I shared the view, now expressed by Auld LJ in his judgment, that this was a case in which the three conditions prescribed in *Ladd v Marshall* [1954] 3 All ER 745, [1954] 1 WLR 1489 were satisfied. In particular, I was (and remain) satisfied that it does not lie in the mouth of SKC to assert that the documents in question could, with reasonable diligence, have been obtained by Electra prior to the hearing before the judge in the circumstances that both SKC and KPMG had failed (albeit inadvertently) to comply with their respective obligations to make discovery of those documents under the Rules of Court.

I share, also, the concern expressed by Auld LJ, and by Clarke LJ (whose judgment I have had the opportunity to read in draft), that, on the question whether an interlocutory hearing of an application to strike out proceedings on the basis that the claim is bound to fail is a hearing 'on the merits" for the purposes of Ord.59 r.10(2) RSC, the present state of the authorities is less than satisfactory. It is unnecessary for me to add to the observations made by this Court in *Pearce v Ove Arup Partnership Ltd* [1999] 1 All ER 769, 780g–781b, to which Clarke LJ will refer. Like him, I take the view that it would not be appropriate to attempt to resolve the problem posed by apparently conflicting authorities in a case where it is not necessary to do so.

Lord Justice Clarke

1. I agree with Auld LJ that both appeals should be allowed.

Further evidence

7. As Auld LJ has explained, a good deal of new evidence has become available to the plaintiffs since the hearing before the judge. There was much argument as to the circumstances in which this court should admit fresh evidence on an appeal of this kind. The relevant rule is at present RSC Ord.59 r.10(2), which provides so far as relevant as follows:

> '(2) The Court of Appeal shall have power to receive further evidence on questions of fact ... but in the case of an appeal from a judgment after trial or hearing of any cause or matter on the merits, no such further evidence (other than evidence as to matters which have occurred after the date of the trial or hearing) shall be admitted except on special grounds.'

It is common ground that the authorities show that in order to establish special grounds within the meaning of the rule it is necessary to satisfy the three conditions identified by Denning LJ in *Ladd v Marshall* [1954] 1 WLR 1489: see e.g. *Langdale v Danby* [1982] 1 WLR 1123, per Lord Bridge at p.1133.

8. I agree with Auld LJ for the reasons which he has given that Electra has satisfied those conditions on the facts of this case and it was on that basis that I agreed that the evidence should be admitted on this appeal. Moreover it seems to me that the conditions are satisfied without the need for any relaxation of the application of the conditions referred to by Auld LJ. It follows that neither the question what, if any, relaxation of the conditions is permissible, nor the question whether the order of the judge is a 'judgment after trial or hearing of any cause or matter on the merits'strictly arises for determination on this appeal.

9. In these circumstances I only wish to add this. Assuming that the order of the judge is such a judgment, it does seem to me that the question whether the first of Denning LJ's conditions is satisfied, namely whether the evidence could have been obtained with reasonable diligence for use before the judge, must depend upon all the circumstances of the case and that one of those circumstances must be the nature of the application. Thus in *Langdale v Danby* itself Lord Bridge said at p.1133 that he could see no injustice in requiring a party to use such diligence as is reasonable in the circumstances. As I see it, what will amount to reasonable diligence will depend upon all the circumstances of the case, which will include the nature of the application and the state of the proceedings at the time the particular application is made. There is nothing in *The 'Gudermes'* [1984] 1 Lloyd's Rep 5 to suggest the contrary. This approach does not involve a relaxation of the principles so much as an application of them.

10. As to the question whether the order of the judge was a judgment after a hearing on the merits, the cases referred to by Auld LJ seem to me to disclose a

somewhat unsatisfactory state of affairs. The problem has recently been discussed by this court in *Pearce v Ove Arup Partnership Ltd* [1999] 1 All ER 769, which was decided on 21 January 1999, after the oral hearing of this appeal had been concluded. It had there been submitted that *Williams v Attridge* (unreported), which decided on 8 July 1997 that an order striking out an action under one of the limbs of RSC Ord.18 r.19 or the inherent jurisdiction of the court was not a judgment after a hearing on the merits, was wrongly decided. It was presumably also argued that Robert Walker LJ's reconciliation in *Ramanthan Rudra v Abbey National Plc* (unreported 26 February 1998) of the reasoning in *Williams v Attridge* and that in *Langdale v Danby* is unsound.

11. In *Pearce v Ove Arup Partnership Ltd* Roch LJ, giving the judgment of the court which also comprised Chadwick and May LJJ, said this (at pp.780–1):

> 'In our judgment, it is not necessary to reach a conclusion on these submissions in this case and we do not do so. We only observe that, whichever submission on the question before us may be correct, it seems unsatisfactory if the criteria for admitting fresh evidence in the Court of Appeal in matters such as this differs upon the same subject matter depending on the outcome in the court below. For summary judgment applications, this appears to be so (see *Woodhouse v Consolidated Property Corporation Ltd* [1993] 1 EGLR 174 at 176D where Lord Justice Glidewell agreed with a passage in the Supreme Court Practice suggesting that an order refusing summary judgment or granting conditional leave to defend is not an order made after a hearing on the merits and that therefore the *Ladd v Marshall* conditions do not apply). In *Rudra v Abbey National* (unreported 26 February 1998) this Court held that the *Ladd v Marshall* conditions applied where a claim had been struck out after a ruling on a preliminary issue under RSC Ord.14A, this being closer to an application for summary judgment than to a strike out application. It appears from page 9 of the transcript that Lord Justice Robert Walker saw some logical difficulty in distinguishing between the situation in *Langdale v Danby* and that in *Williams v Attridge*. It is, we think, quixotic if a party against whom a summary order has been made, bringing to an end his ability to deploy his case in court, has less opportunity to rely on further evidence in the Court of Appeal than the other party would have had, if the summary order had not been made. In the first case, the appellant has lost his case: in the second case, he has not lost his case and retains the opportunity to rely on additional evidence at a later stage.'

I respectfully agree with those sentiments. In these circumstances it does not seem to me to be appropriate to try to resolve the problem in a case in which it is not necessary to do so, although I must say that there is in my opinion much to be said for the view that an order of this kind is not a judgment after a hearing on the merits. In any event *Limb v Union Jack Removals Ltd (in liquidation*) [1998] 2 All ER 513, [1998] 1 WLR 1354 is authority for the proposition that a decision of a two judge Court of Appeal on a substantive appeal (as opposed to an application for leave) has the same authority as a decision of a three or five judge court: see per Brooke LJ, giving the judgment of the court at p.1364:

12. However that may be, there is I think a further reason why it is not appropriate to reach a final conclusion in a case in which it is not necessary to do so. That is that the new Civil Procedure Rules come into force on 26 April and, as I understand it, consideration is at present being given to what if any changes should be made to RSC Ord.59. The problems identified by Auld LJ here and by Roch LJ in the passage just quoted will no doubt be considered in the context of such a change. I would only add that, having listened to the submissions in this case, it seems to me that there is much to be said for the view that the discretion of the court should not be fettered in a case of this kind. It seems to me to be desirable that the court should have what Otton LJ described in *Star News Shops Ltd v Stafford Refrigeration Ltd* [1998] 1 WLR 536 at 541 as a general discretion. In *Canada Trust Co v Stolzenberg* [1998] CLC 1171 Waller LJ considered the meaning of a general discretion. He said at p.1173:

> 'What I suggest is meant by "general discretion" is that circumstances differ greatly so far as interlocutory matters are concerned, and rigid conditions for the exercise of the discretion applicable to all interlocutory appeals are inapposite. The nature of the interlocutory application, the reason why the evidence was not adduced in the court below, the opportunity provided for putting in evidence in the court below, and the nature of the evidence sought to be put in will all be factors.'

I respectfully agree with that approach, which the argument in the instant case has persuaded me would be appropriate in a future case of this kind.

Appeals allowed.

(*Transcript: Smith Bernal*)

FOENANDER V BOND LEWIS & CO

A2.8

[2001] 2 All ER 1019

[2001] EWCA Civ 759

COURT OF APPEAL, CIVIL DIVISION

BROOKE, SEDLEY and DYSON LJJ

23 MAY 2001

Practice – Appeal – New provisions governing civil appeals in private law matters – Refusal by High Court judge to grant extension of time to appeal from decision of lower court – Whether refusal appealable to Court of Appeal – Access to Justice Act 1999, s 54(4).

Section 54(4)[a] of the Access to Justice Act 1999, which prohibits an appeal against a decision of a court under that section to refuse permission to appeal, is based on the principle that if both a lower court and an appeal court at a lower level of the judicial hierarchy have decided that a proposed appeal has no real prospect of success, and there is no other compelling reason why the appeal should be heard, that must be the end of the matter, and the issue cannot be relitigated higher up the judicial chain. That principle does not, however, apply to the order of a High Court judge refusing an application to extend time for an appeal from a decision of a lower court. Such an order can, with permission, be appealed to the Court of Appeal as can any other order made by a High Court judge. If a circuit judge or a High Court judge sitting in an appeal court has the choice of disposing of a belated and unmeritorious appeal either by refusing to extend time for appealing or by refusing permission to appeal, he should bear in mind that taking the latter course will bring the appellate proceedings to an end. The adoption of the former course, on the other hand, may entail further expense and delay while a challenge is launched at a higher appeal court against the decision not to extend time for appealing (see [16], [18], [19], [22], [23], post).

[a] Section 54, so far as material, provides: '(4) No appeal may be made against a decision of a court under this section to give or refuse permission …'.

Per curiam. Under the CPR appellate regime, an appeal from a district judge on an assessment of damages in the High Court will ordinarily lie to a High Court judge, not a circuit judge (see [20]–[23], post); dictum of Brooke LJ in *Clark (Inspector of Taxes) v Perks* [2000] 4 All ER 1 at 13 (para 54) corrected.

Cases referred to in judgments

Bokhari v Mahmood (1988) Times, 26 April, [1988] CA Transcript 323.

Clark (Inspector of Taxes) v Perks [2000] 4 All ER 1, [2001] 1 WLR 17, CA.

Lane v Esdaile [1891] AC 210, HL.

Podbery v Peak [1981] 1 All ER 699, [1981] Ch 344, [1981] 2 WLR 686, CA.

R v Secretary of State for Trade and Industry, ex p Eastaway [2001] 1 All ER 27, [2000] 1 WLR 2222, HL.

Rickards v Rickards [1989] 3 All ER 193, [1990] Fam 194, [1989] 3 WLR 748, CA.

Tanfern Ltd v Cameron-MacDonald [2000] 2 All ER 801, [2000] 1 WLR 1311, CA.

Application

On an application by Johan Michael Richard Foenander, the Court of Appeal was required to determine whether it had jurisdiction under the CPR to entertain an appeal by him against the order of Astill J on 11 November 1999 refusing his application for permission to appeal out of time against the decision of Deputy Master Chism on 1 October 1999 striking out his action for professional negligence against the respondent, Bond Lewis & Co. The facts are set out in the judgment of Brooke LJ.

Lord Justice Brooke

[1] This application by a litigant in person raises an issue of general importance in relation to the new CPR appeals regime.

[2] In January 1995 MrFoenander issued a writ against Bond Lewis & Co, who are a firm of solicitors, and against Mr Florence O'Donaghue of counsel, alleging professional negligence in the conduct of the matrimonial proceedings which followed the breakdown of his marriage. The action against the second defendant was dismissed in April 1995 on the grounds of forensic immunity. On 1 October 1999 Deputy Master Chism struck out the claim against the first defendant (the Chism order).

[3] Under the former appeals regime MrFoenander could appeal to a judge against a master's order as of right provided his notice of appeal was given and served within five days (RSC Ord 58, r 1). In the event he delayed for about two weeks, and on 11 November 1999 Astill J refused to make an order extending his time for appealing (the Astill order). Mr Foenander then had the right to seek permission to appeal to this court against the Astill order, provided that this application was made within four weeks (RSC Ord 58, r 4). He did not exercise that right.

[4] On 2 May 2000 the new CPR appeals regime was introduced. This court has explained various aspects of the new regime on a number of occasions, and in particular in my judgments in *Tanfern Ltd v Cameron-MacDonald* [2000] 2 All ER 801, [2000] 1 WLR 1311 and *Clark (Inspector of Taxes) v Perks* [2000] 4 All ER 1, [2001] 1 WLR 17. The new appeals regime applies to all applications lodged at the appeal court on and after 2 May 2000 (see the *Tanfern* case [2000] 2 All ER 801 at 812, [2000] 1 WLR 1311 at 1320 (para 47)). Under the new regime there is no appeal as of right against a master's order (CPR 52.3(1)(a): for the definition of the word 'judge' see CPR 2.3(1)).

[5] On 14 February 2000 the first defendants sent Mr Foenander their bill relating to the costs payable to them pursuant to the Chism order and the Astill order. On 31 October 2000 they obtained a default costs certificate in the sum of £9,713.77, and on 7 December 2000 Deputy Costs Judge Thum made an order refusing to set aside this certificate (the Thum order). Mr Foenander's application for permission to appeal against the Thum order was dismissed on paper by McKinnon J on 11 January 2001 and in court by Owen J on 14 February 2001. Although he has sought to challenge the Thum order by a further application to this court, this court clearly has no jurisdiction to entertain this application under the new CPR appellate regime (s 54(4) of the Access to Justice Act 1999). On 6 March 2001 Deputy Master Joseph ruled, correctly, that there was no further right of appeal to the Court of Appeal against the Thum order because Owen J had refused permission to appeal.

[6] Within his notice of appeal against the Thum order Mr Foenander also sought an extension of time to lodge an application for permission to appeal out of time against the Chism order and the Astill order. The notice stated, among other things, that someone had impersonated Deputy Master Chism on 1 October 1999. Owen J rejected this allegation after seeing the original order which had been initialled that day, and after taking judicial notice of the practice whereby a master's signature is compared with the stock signatures held in the central office before the order is stamped.

[7] McKinnon J dismissed this application on paper on the grounds that Mr Foenander had not sent out any explanation as to why he was now so many months out of time for appealing. On 19 January 2001 Mr Foenander purported to remedy this defect by swearing a long affidavit in which he described various features of the case going back to its inception. He attributed his failure to appeal against Astill J's order to the misconduct of solicitors he instructed 'to appeal this case' on 15 October, nearly a month before Astill J made his order. On 14 February 2001 Owen J dismissed the application for an extension of time on the same grounds as McKinnon J, namely that there were no proper grounds on which an extension could be granted. He went on to say that he had no power to grant permission to appeal against his order because the practice direction to CPR Pt 52 states (at para 4.8) that there is no appeal from a

decision of an appeal court, made at an oral hearing, to allow or refuse permission to appeal to that court. This rule is of course derived from s 54(4) of the 1999 Act.

[8] Owen J's order, which was sealed on 20 February 2001, provides:
'1. The application for permission to appeal from the Order of Deputy Costs Judge Thum dated 7 December 2000 be and hereby is refused;
2. The application for an extension of time to appeal from: (1) the order of Deputy Master Chism dated 1 October 1999 and (2) the order of Mr Justice Astill dated 11 November 1999 be and hereby is refused.'

[9] I am not surprised that the proceedings in the court below took a peculiar course, because as a lay litigant Mr Foenander had difficulty in identifying the appropriate procedure for the challenges he wished to make, but in fact neither McKinnon J nor Owen J had any power to extend the time for appealing against the Astill order. CPR 52.6(1) provides unequivocally that 'An application to vary the time limit for filing an appeal notice must be made to the appeal court'. Needless to say, the attempt by Mr Foenander to obtain an extension of time for appealing against the Chism order was doomed because he had already sought and been refused this relief by Astill J.

[10] On 28 February 2001 Mr Foenander lodged with this court a notice of appeal against the order of Owen J. He maintained on the face of the notice that he did not need permission to appeal against para 2 of that order, and he set out his grounds for appealing against para 1. The first of these contentions was clearly wrong (see CPR 52.3(1) which makes it obligatory to obtain permission to appeal against all decisions of a judge in the High Court, subject to exceptions which are irrelevant in the present case). I have already explained why this court would have no jurisdiction to entertain Mr Foenander's proposed challenge to para 1 of Owen J's order (see [5] above).

[11] In these circumstances the Civil Appeals Office notified Mr Foenander that it accepted his notice of appeal in so far as it related to the Astill order on the basis that the court might need to consider whether it had jurisdiction to entertain this appeal as a preliminary issue. In due course I directed that his application should be heard in court. I gave him notice that the court would wish to consider the status of this application under the new CPR appeals regime. Since the jurisdictional point was an important one, I elicited the assistance of a lawyer in the Civil Appeals Office who kindly prepared for Mr Foenander and for the court a bench memorandum explaining the legal issue we had to decide. We adopted the same technique in the *Tanfern* case (see [2000] 2 All ER 801 at 803, [2000] 1 WLR 1311 at 1312–1313 (para 4)). At the hearing today we also heard brief submissions from Mr Craig on behalf of the respondents.

[12] The short issue we have to decide is this. If Astill J had refused Mr Foenander permission to appeal against the Chism order, this court would have no jurisdiction to entertain an appeal against that refusal (s 54(4) of the 1999 Act). Is the position different because he decided to refuse an extension of time for appealing, so that he did not consider the application for permission to appeal against the Chism order on the merits?

[13] In the pre-CPR regime the answer to this question would have been very straightforward. In *Rickards v Rickards* [1989] 3 All ER 193, [1990] Fam 194 a party to matrimonial proceedings in a county court failed to file his notice of appeal from a decision of a registrar within the prescribed time limit. A circuit judge refused his application for leave to appeal out of time, but granted him leave to appeal to this court from his order refusing an extension of time. This court had held in the earlier case of *Podbery v Peak* [1981] 1 All ER 699, [1981] Ch 344 that it had no jurisdiction to entertain an appeal from a refusal to extend time for appealing. The court now held that that earlier decision had been made per incuriam. We are not concerned on this occasion with the reasons it gave for deciding that it was entitled not to follow the earlier case.

[14] Lord Donaldson of Lymington MR ([1989] 3 All ER 193 at 196–197, [1990] Fam 194 at 199–201) considered the effect of the decision of the House of Lords in *Lane v Esdaile* [1891] AC 210 on which the earlier decision has been based. He then said:

> 'In my judgment what *Lane v Esdaile* decided, and all that it decided, was that where it is provided that an appeal shall lie *by leave* of a particular court or courts neither the grant or refusal of leave is an appealable decision. Although the statute contained time limits, 21 days in the case of interlocutory orders and 12 months in the case of other orders, no court had any power to extend them, or, of course, was asked to do so. The effect of the expiry of those time limits was simply to attract a requirement for special leave to appeal. The grant or refusal of an application for leave to appeal is one thing. The grant or refusal of an application to extend the time limited for taking a step in proceedings, including but not limited to giving notice of appeal, is quite another. It arises in a multitude of contexts, none of which have even been held to be inherently unappealable, with the sole exception of an extension of time for appealing in *Podbery v Peak* ([1981] 1 All ER 699, [1981] Ch 344) and, following that decision, in *Bokhari v Mahmood* ((1988) Times, 26 April). Whilst it is true that a right of appeal may be barred either by a refusal of an extension of time or by a refusal of leave, the routes by which this result is achieved and the underlying concepts are essentially different. The husband did not need leave to appeal to the county court judge. He needed an extension of time. He did not need an extension of time for appealing to this court. He

needed, and obtained, leave to appeal.' (See [1989] 3 All ER 193 at 197, [1990] Fam 194 at 201; Lord Donaldson MR's emphasis.)

[15] Lord Donaldson MR was making a distinction between the grant or refusal of an application for leave to appeal on the one hand and the grant or refusal of an application to extend the time limited for taking a step in proceedings on the other. The former, he said, was governed by *Lane v Esdaile*: the latter was as appealable (subject to the necessity of obtaining permission to appeal) as any other decision made by a judge.

[16] The question we have to decide is whether this position has been affected by the introduction of the CPR regime. As I have already observed, s 54(4) of the 1999 Act prescribes that no appeal may be made against a decision of a court under that section to give or refuse permission, but it is silent in relation to decisions of the kind with which we are concerned in the present case. Prima facie (subject to the need to obtain leave to appeal) an appeal lies to this court pursuant to s 16(1) of the Supreme Court Act 1981 (as amended) which provides:

'Subject as otherwise provided by this or any other Act ... or as provided by any order made by the Lord Chancellor under section 56(1) of the Access to Justice Act 1999, the Court of Appeal shall have jurisdiction to hear and determine appeals from any judgment or order of the High Court.'

[17] Under the CPR appellate regime, an appeal from a decision of a High Court judge lies to this court, as I explained in para 15 of my judgment in the *Tanfern* case [2000] 2 All ER 801 at 805–806, [2000] 1 WLR 1311 at 1314–1315. The position is now set out clearly in para 2A.1 of the practice direction to CPR Pt 52. This is not a second appeal within the meaning of s 55(1) of the 1999 Act because the 'matter' on which Astill J gave judgment (viz whether to extend time for an appeal against the Chism order) is different from the 'matter' on which Deputy Master Chism made his ruling (viz whether the action against the second defendants should be struck out).

[18] The principle which underlies the rule in *Lane v Esdaile* (which was recently reaffirmed by the House of Lords in *R v Secretary of State for Trade and Industry, ex p Eastaway* [2001] 1 All ER 27, [2000] 1 WLR 2222) and in s 54(4) of the 1999 Act (in so far as it refers to the refusal of leave to appeal) is that if both a lower court and an appeal court at a lower level of the judicial hierarchy have decided that a proposed appeal has no real prospect of success, and that there is no other compelling reason why the appeal should be heard (see CPR 52.3(6)), that must be the end of the matter, and this issue cannot be relitigated higher up the judicial chain. This principle does not, however, in my judgment apply to an order of the type made by Astill J on 11 November 1999. He decided, in the exercise of his discretion, not to extend time for an appeal

from the deputy master's decision. Nobody else had considered, or had the power to consider (see CPR 52.6(1)) this exercise of discretion, and in those circumstances, provided that permission to appeal is granted, Astill J's order is as appealable to this court as any other order made by a High Court judge.

[19] The logic of this decision is that if a circuit judge or a High Court judge sitting in an appeal court has the choice of disposing of a belated and unmeritorious appeal either by refusing to extend time for appealing or by refusing permission to appeal, he/she should bear in mind that taking the latter course will bring the appellate proceedings to an end. The adoption of the former course, on the other hand, may entail further expense and delay while a challenge is launched at a higher appeal court against the decision not to extend time for appealing.

[20] Before I end this judgment, I would like to correct an error I made when describing the destination of appeals under the CPR appellate regime in para 54 of my judgment in *Clark (Inspector of Taxes) v Perks* [2000] 4 All ER 1 at 13, [2001] 1 WLR 17 at 30. I said:

> 'It does not now matter whether a decision by a district judge on an assessment of damages was made in the county court or in the High Court. Appeal against such a decision will lie to a circuit judge unless the case was allocated to the multi-track in which case it will lie to this court.'

[21] It has been pointed out to me, correctly, that an appeal from a district judge on an assessment of damages in the High Court will ordinarily lie to a High Court judge, not a circuit judge. Paragraph 54 of that judgment must now be read subject to this gloss.

Lord Justice Sedley

[22] I agree.

Lord Justice Dyson

[23] I agree.

Order accordingly.

Kate O'Hanlon Barrister.

GREAT FUTURE INTERNATIONAL LIMITED AND OTHERS V SEALAND HOUSING CORPORATION AND OTHERS

A2.9

[2003] EWCA Civ 682

COURT OF APPEAL (CIVIL DIVISION)

WALLER and KAY LJJ

1 MAY 2003

Practice and procedure – Court of Appeal – Jurisdiction – Jurisdiction on application for permission to appeal to make orders for security for costs or impose conditions before application for permission to come on – CPR 2.1 and 3.1.

Lord Justice Waller

[1] Aldous LJ adjourned an application for permission to appeal to an oral hearing with appeal to follow and that hearing will come on in July 2003. At that hearing in July, accordingly, the potential respondents will have to be represented and prepared to deal with the would-be appellants' arguments in case permission is granted. I shall from now on call the would-be appellants 'the Hansens' and the potential respondents 'Great Future' for convenience.

[2] It is common ground that Civil Procedure Rule r 25.15 is not applicable as a basis for ordering security for costs. The logic of a decision under the former rules in *Faryab v Philip Ross* (unreported), of which we have a transcript dated 20 November 1998, supports that view. Furthermore, there is no provision of CPR 52 which provides jurisdiction either to order security for costs or to order a stay of an application for permission subject to certain payments being made or security for costs being supplied. However, Mr Kosmin QC, acting for Great Future, has argued that under the CPR there are other provisions which enable the court to make orders effectively for security for costs or to make orders that certain costs orders be complied with before the application for permission and possible appeal hearing comes on. Indeed, he suggests that those provisions enable the court to stay the application for permission until security for costs has been provided and until certain orders for costs have been complied with.

[3] I can say straight away that I accept that the court does have that power. I will come back to the provisions to explain how that is, but first let me briefly set out the facts and circumstances of the case because, of course, the context in relation to the exercise of such a power is important.

[4] The Hansens were found liable to Great Future and other claimants for fraudulent representation at a trial on liability between June and October 2001.

A costs order was made in the sum of £1,023,500. Part of that sum (£27,000) was recovered by execution but subject to that the whole of the first costs order remains unpaid. Permission to appeal the judgment on liability was refused by the trial judge and then by the Court of Appeal, following a number of applications and an oral hearing.

[5] An inquiry as to damages was then heard between June and November 2002. Lightman J, by a judgment delivered on 3 December 2002, awarded interest and damages in the sum of $65m against the Hansens. He made an interim award of costs in the sum of £500,000. He then increased his order in relation to costs to £1m by an order dated 18 December 2002 and payment of costs was due by 2 January 2003. During that period also freezing orders were made and orders for disclosure of assets. The history of that in brief was that initially both freezing orders and orders to provide affidavits of means were made on 3 December, and those orders were then made again on 18 December 2002. By that date certain of those orders in relation to the swearing of affidavits ought in fact to have been complied with. Barry Hansen had had until 16 December to swear his affidavit. Stuart Hansen had until 20 December. In the event the order was repeated on 18 December and there has been no compliance with the order to provide affidavits. Lightman J refused permission to appeal the judgment in relation to the inquiry but, as indicated, Aldous LJ on 7 March directed there to be an oral hearing with appeal to follow if permission granted. That hearing has been listed for 14 or 15 July with an estimate of two days. He refused a stay pending the appeal.

[6] There are other costs orders outstanding as against the Hansens. The judge appended to his judgment a list of orders which had been made against the Hansens and which they had failed to pay. The total of those sums is some £2,053,600. It is also right to say that the conduct of the Hansens has been the subject of serious criticism by the judge. In the first witness statement of Mark Davenport at para 14, Mr Davenport sets out certain quotations from the judgment of the judge in relation to the conduct of the Hansens. The judge makes clear that in his view the Hansens have constantly flouted orders of the English court. In relation to other proceedings which have taken place in the Turks and Caicos Islands it appears that the view formed by the judge is that there has been a fairly constant flouting of the orders of that court too.

[7] It is in those circumstances that Great Future seek a stay of the application for permission until there has been a payment into court, first of the £1m ordered to be paid in respect of the trial on liability and secondly of the £1m ordered to be paid in respect of the costs of the inquiry; and until a sum of £80,000 has been put up as security for the costs of the respondents. They further seek an order that if those payments are not made by 4 o'clock on Friday 30 May, the appellants' application for permission to appeal should stand dismissed.

[8] The provisions on which Mr Kosmin relies are CPR 3.1. He suggested in his submissions that the Court of Appeal had the power to exercise the powers provided by CPR 3.1 by virtue of CPR 52.10, which provides for the Court of Appeal having the powers of the court below in relation to any appeal. For my part I am doubtful whether it is CPR 52.10 which provides the Court of Appeal with any of the requisite powers. It seems to me that it is CPR 2.1 which gives the Court of Appeal case management powers, which are the powers provided for by CPR 3 to which I will turn in a moment. CPR 2.1 provides that:

'Subject to paragraph (2), these Rules apply to all proceedings in–
(a) county courts;
(b) the High Court; and
(c) the Civil Division of the Court of Appeal.'

And the case management powers are clearly case management powers both in relation to the Court of Appeal and the other courts there referred to. The important parts of CPR 3.1 are 3.1(2), which provides:

'Except where these Rules provide otherwise, the court may–
(f) stay the whole or part of any proceedings either generally or until a specified date or event;
...
(m) take any other step or make any other order for the purpose of managing the case and furthering the overriding objective'

and 3.1(3), which provides:

'When the court makes an order it may
(a) make it subject to conditions, including a condition to pay a sum of money into court; and
(b) specify the consequence of failure to comply with the order or a condition.'

It is unnecessary to quote other aspects of 3.1, although they all provide support for the court having the power to make the form of order that Mr Kosmin seeks in this case.

[9] The argument put forward by Mr Connerty for suggesting that 3.1 does not provide the requisite power rests essentially on the opening words of 3.1(2), which provide 'Except where these Rules provide otherwise, the court may'. What he suggests is because there is CPR 25, dealing with security for costs, including CPR 25.15 dealing expressly with security for costs on an appeal, and CPR 52, dealing with what happens in relation to appeals and applications for permission, 'these Rules provide otherwise'.

[10] As my Lord, Kay LJ pointed out during the argument, the truth is that the Rules are silent in relation to the situation that actually exists in this particular case. There is no provision of the Rules which deals with what should happen

where an application for permission has been adjourned to an oral hearing and where the appeal is to follow. Furthermore, it seems to me that the argument put forward by Mr Connerty comes up against one of the authorities to which we were referred, which is *Olatawura v Abiloye* [2002] CP Reports 73, where Simon Brown LJ approved the use of CPR 3.1 in the context of a summary judgment application. What is referred to by 3.1(2) is something that expressly prohibits or expressly deals with the particular matter which might otherwise be dealt with under 3.1(2). In my view the jurisdiction is there.

[11] The question that then arises is whether this is an appropriate case for the exercise of that jurisdiction. The context, of course, in this case is that there is a permission to appeal outstanding and that has not yet been resolved, so the merits of an appeal have not been considered. On the other hand, if permission were given, the appeal will be heard and substantial costs will be incurred. Indeed substantial costs will be incurred attending the application for permission. As far as the particular facts of this case are concerned, there is a background of failure to pay costs, there is a background of flouting orders of the court and the Hansens are out of the jurisdiction. Thus this would appear to be pre-eminently a case where the respondents should have some form of protection.

[12] The question is how far should that protection go? Should there be an order that the costs orders should be complied with before the permission application comes on? Should there be some provision for security for costs? The cases to which we have been referred support the power of the court, and indeed the attitude of the court, in relation to both the supply of security and, in certain cases – usually, one would have to say, extreme cases – making compliance with orders a condition of being entitled to continue with an appeal. There is no reason why those principles should not apply to the circumstances of this case when the court is considering the powers to be exercised under CPR 3.1. Perhaps the most extreme case is *Hammond Suddards Solicitors v Agrichem International Holdings Ltd* [2001] EWCA 1915 where the court did impose conditions of having to pay sums which were the subject of a judgment as a condition of being able to appeal at all. So there are circumstances in which the court will go so far as not only to order security but to see that orders of the court are complied with. But there is one overriding aspect where the context is an appeal (or, I would add, an application for permission to appeal) and that is that the court should not stifle the appeal by the making of any order. *Hammond Suddards* is an example – and there are other cases – of this principle being applied. That case also illustrates two factors. The first is that once there is a basis on which the court will prima facie consider it right to impose a condition of going on with an appeal, that orders should be complied with or security for costs should be given, then the onus is on the person against whom that order would be made to satisfy the court, by evidence, that the effect of making such an order will be to stifle the appeal. The second factor is that it

is not only the means of the person against whom that order might be made which is relevant, but the possibility that third parties might be available to support the litigation is also relevant.

[13] When one looks at the evidence in this case, there are the following features. As already indicated, there has been a constant flouting of court orders. The Hansens have been ordered to put in affidavits of means and they have never done so. They were originally meant to be put in December 2002 and have not been produced, and the only reference to the non-production in the evidence they have put in on this application is para 87 in a witness statement of Mr Stuart Hansen, which reads as follows:

> 'We acknowledge that we have 2 outstanding statements that have been ordered. Although we have filed earlier affidavits on these matters, once the Claimants commenced contempt proceedings, we recall being advised by previous senior counsel that we should not be compelled to provide statements in the face of a contempt hearing. We have not had funds to engage specialist counsel to advise, and so have been afraid to say anything without advise in the face of possible imprisonment. We apologize, and do not mean to disrespect any court order.'

The only contempt proceedings were against Mr Barry Hansen, so there is absolutely no excuse so far as Mr Stuart Hansen is concerned. The contempt proceedings related to the sale of land, and thus it is impossible to see how there was any basis for suggesting that they were being asked to give information which would have been disadvantageous so far as their contempt proceedings were concerned.

[14] In the result there has been absolutely no disclosure of the means of the Hansens. Secondly, the Hansens have paid out in legal costs something over $1m. That is relevant to two aspects: (a) they have managed to pay their own lawyers and (b), the money has been got out of China where they now are. Thirdly, loans have been made from a company, SHTI. The total value of the loans, as I understand it, are in the region of $10m. They have been paid to the Hansens personally and no explanation has been given as to where that money has gone. Fourthly, so far as the costs of the liability hearing is concerned, that, of course, is an order which they are not challenging and cannot challenge on the present appeal. Furthermore, that is money which in the past they have said they have actually got. If one goes to para 49 of Mr Davenport's affidavit, there is a quotation of an explanation given by Mr Barry Hansen suggesting that the money was available, and that is supported by a letter at page 297 of the bundle in which again they were suggesting that they had that money available.

[15] In the circumstances of this case, as it seems to me, the Hansens have not demonstrated that this application for permission would be stifled if they were ordered to pay some form of security for the costs of the respondents and,

indeed, some part of the costs orders outstanding against them. There is some force in Mr Connerty's argument so far as the costs of the damages hearing is concerned. That is an order for costs which could be challenged on the appeal if permission to appeal was given. But there can be no argument about the costs which the Hansens have been ordered to pay on the liability hearing. That is a sum which has been due for some time and, as indicated, a sum which indeed they have said they had the money to pay. As it seems to me, there can be no reason why they should not pay that sum in order to be able to continue with their litigation here.

[16] One point that I made to Mr Kosmin during the hearing was to question whether it was right that the respondents should be placed in a better position than if an application for permission to appeal had not been made. It seems to me that the answer to that point is that this court does have an interest in seeing that its orders are complied with, and that the only real question here should be whether the appeal would be stifled if conditions were imposed on the Hansens. Once the court forms a view that the application would not be stifled, then there is no reason why that condition should not be imposed.

[17] I should deal with Mr Connerty's final point. He suggests that another basis on which no order should be made here is that there is already in the hands of Great Future and the other respondents security for the sums held at the moment to be due to Great Future. He took us to various documents indicating that offers at some stage had been made of $70m. Those offers appear to relate to the shareholding of Great Future, about which this litigation is being fought. He also took us to some documents seeking to show that certain houses are being sold, but those houses are the assets of a company SLEC. As it seems to me, Mr Connerty has failed to show that Great Future are in some way secured in relation to the orders outstanding against them.

[18] In the result, it seems to me that, exercising the court's powers under CPR 3.1, it is right to make an order that until there is paid into court the sum of £1m ordered to be paid in respect of the costs for trial on liability, and until there is paid into court the sum of £80,000 as security for the respondents' costs of the application for permission to appeal, and if permission is granted the appeal itself, this application for permission to appeal by the Hansens should be stayed. We can hear argument about the second paragraph of the draft order but it seems to me that it would be right to place a time limit on compliance with those conditions, subject to which, if those conditions have not been complied, with the permission to appeal application should stand dismissed. The timing of that we can hear counsel on but that is the order that I would propose to make.

Lord Justice Kay:

[19] I agree.

Appeal dismissed.

(*Transcript: Smith Bernal*)

HAMMOND SUDDARDS SOLICITORS V AGRICHEM INTERNATIONAL HOLDINGS LTD.

A2.10

[2001] EWCA Civ 2065

COURT OF APPEAL (CIVIL DIVISION)

CLARKE LJ and WALL J

18 DECEMBER 2001

JUDGMENT: APPROVED BY THE COURT FOR HANDING DOWN (SUBJECT TO EDITORIAL CORRECTIONS)

Lord Justice Clarke:

This is the judgment of the court, to which each of its members has contributed.

Introduction

1. The applications before the court in this case are at first sight straightforward. Pending the hearing of the substantive appeal, the appellant seeks a stay of orders made by the judge for the payment of the judgment debt and costs. The respondents make a cross-application for security for their costs of the appeal.

2. Two factors, however, make the case unusual. The first is that the appellant is a limited liability company registered in the British Virgin Islands, with a PO box address in Jersey, and with no assets within the United Kingdom (or, as it would have us believe, anywhere else). The second is that the respondents seek not only to oppose the appellant's application for a stay, but also ask for an order that the appeal be struck out unless, by a given date, the appellant pays or secures the full amount of both the judgment debt and the specific orders for costs made by the judge, as well as providing security for costs in whatever sum the court determines.

3. The application to strike out gives rise to two points point of principle. The first is whether it is a permissible exercise of the court's powers, either when granting permission to appeal or subsequently, to make the prosecution of the appeal conditional upon the payment of the judgment debt and costs. The second is, if so, whether it is appropriate to do so in a case where, as here, the appellant might have to obtain the funds to meet the various orders from a

third party. There appears to be little authority on these questions, which seem to us as potentially of some considerable practical importance. It was for this reason that, having heard full argument, we reserved judgment.

The Facts

...

Renewed Application for a Stay

...

Security for Costs

25. Under CPR rule 25.15, the court is given jurisdiction to order security for the costs of an appeal against an appellant on the same grounds as it may order security for costs against a claimant under Part 25. It follows that the criteria in rule 25.13 must be satisfied. Thus the court must be satisfied, having regard to all the circumstances of the case, that it is just to make such an order (rule 25.13(1)) and if one or more of a number of conditions apply. The relevant conditions in this case are contained in rules 25.13(2)(b) and (c), namely:

'(b) The [appellant] is a company or other incorporated body
  (i) which is ordinarily resident out of the jurisdiction; and
  (ii) is not a body against whom a claim can be enforced under the Brussels Conventions or the Lugano Convention.
(c) The [appellant] is a company or other body (whether incorporated inside or outside Great Britain and there is reason to believe that it will be unable to pay the [respondents'] costs if ordered to do so.'

26. It is not in dispute that the court has jurisdiction to make such an order under rules 25.13(2)(b) and 25.15(1). It is also conceded that it is appropriate for the court to make an order on the facts of this case. It follows that it is not necessary to consider the principles applicable to security for costs which are discussed in detail in the unreported decision of this court in *Amy Nasser v United Bank of Kuwait* [2001] EWCA Civ 556. In the instant case the only issues between the parties under this head are in what amount security should be ordered and when.

27. In the context of the above discussion as to whether a stay should be granted, it is of interest to note that it was not argued on behalf of the appellant that security for costs should not be ordered on the ground that to do so would stifle the appeal. That can only have been because it was recognised (in our view correctly) that the appellant could not satisfy the principles set out in the judgment of Peter Gibson LJ in *Keary Developments Ltd v Tarmac Construction Ltd* [1995] 3 All ER 534, 539h to 542g. We simply note in passing

that, in our judgment, although that case was decided before the advent of the CPR, the principles in it are relevant to the determination of any case in which the appellant asserts that an order for security for costs (or an order for security for costs above a certain amount) will stifle an appeal, or indeed where it is said that a refusal of a stay of execution will have that effect.

28. In this regard Peter Gibson LJ said at p 540j:

'However, the court should consider not only whether the plaintiff company can provide security out of its own resources to continue the litigation, but also whether it can raise the amount needed from its directors, shareholders or other backers or interested persons. As all this is likely to be peculiarly within the knowledge of the plaintiff company, it is for the plaintiff company to satisfy the court that it would be prevented by an order for security from continuing the litigation ...'

As already indicated, the appellant does not seek to satisfy that burden in order to resist the respondents' application for security for costs.

29. There are, accordingly, two issues for us to decide, namely: (1) How much? and (2) When? There was a third question, namely: How? But, as we understand it, the parties are content that security for costs should be provided by bank guarantee, as was done in the proceedings below.

30. We turn to quantum. The respondents have estimated their costs at £111,855. This is based on a schedule prepared by the respondents' solicitors' costs department. This in turn is based on a five day hearing, with charging rates for partners at £330 per hour, solicitors at £270 and £180 per hour based on seniority and experience, £195 per hour for the costs manager and £75 per hour for a paralegal. The brief for leading counsel is put in at £25,000 with four refreshers of £3,000 making £12,000. Junior counsel's fees are half those of leading counsel. The fees for the preparation of the skeleton argument and respondent's notice come to £7,000.

31. The appellant argues that this is excessive, and says that a reasonable estimate on the indemnity basis would be in the order of £60,000 to £65,000. It is, however, argued that any figure for security should be substantially less than that. Mr. Fenwick makes a number of points in relation to the respondents' figures. He says that Mance W's estimate when giving permission to appeal was three to four days and that the costs should be based on a four day hearing, not five. He argues that any security should take account of the fact that part of the hearing will be taken up by the respondent's notice, for which security is not appropriate. He also argues that the charging rates are higher than can be justified, and points out that the respondents appear to have given themselves an unwarranted pay rise since the hearing before the judge. Mr. Cullen counters by arguing that the appellant has calculated its figures on outdated rates which have been subsequently superseded.

32. It does not seem to us that there is any particular science in the exercise of the court's discretion in this respect. There are only two certainties. The first is that neither the respondents' nor the appellant's figures will prove correct and the second is that the respondents' figure is likely to be too high and the appellant's figure is likely to be too low. We are, however, of the view that the case should be assessed on a four day basis and that the rates advanced are somewhat too high. On the other hand, this is not a case in which the respondents are cross-appealing and it seems to us that the costs of and incidental to the respondents' notice should fairly regarded as part of the costs of the appeal. This is not an exact science and, doing the best we can, we require the appellant to give security for the respondents' costs of the appeal in the sum of £85,000.

33. There was some debate as to when the security should be provided. We have reached the conclusion that the appellants should be permitted a reasonable time in which to do so and that the security must be provided in the form of a payment into court or of an irrevocable bank guarantee in a form which is to the reasonable satisfaction of the respondents' solicitors on or before 1 March 2002, failing which the appeal to stand struck out without further order of the court. There will be liberty to apply as to the form of the guarantee if agreement cannot be reached, but any such application must be heard and determined before 1 March 2002.

Payment of or Security for the Judgment Debt

34. The respondent seeks an order that unless the appellant either pays or gives security for the whole of the judgment debt, including the amounts which the judge ordered should be paid on account of costs, it should not be permitted to proceed with the appeal. The appellant argues that such an order is contrary to principle and misconceived. There is no justification, it says, for linking the appellant's right to appeal to satisfying the order being appealed against. Mr. Fenwick submits that it is a fundamental requirement of a fair legal system that a party should be able to challenge an adverse order, provided the other party is not unfairly prejudiced. That balance, he says, is achieved by giving a party a right to appeal if he has a real prospect of success or other compelling reason to appeal, and the appeal is not otherwise an abuse of the legal process, while at the same time providing protection for a respondent to any such appeal by way of the requirement to obtain permission to appeal, an order for security for costs (where appropriate) and, absent a stay, by the normal processes of enforcement. If the appellant's application for a stay is unsuccessful, Mr. Fenwick argues, the appellant is vulnerable to enforcement by the respondents, but it does not lose its right of appeal. The order sought by the respondents, he argues, will deprive the appellant of its right to appeal, as it does not have the funds to satisfy the 12 July 2001 order. Mr. Fenwick submits that striking the balance between an appellant and a respondent does not require that the

respondent should be given the further protection of making an appellant first satisfy the order which he wishes to challenge. Still less does it mean, he argues, that an appellant should be required to seek funds from a third party to meet the Judgment as the price of appealing.

35. In the instant case, the respondents accept that the order they seek would not be just if to impose the condition would stifle the appeal. Thus, if the appellant does not have, and is unable to obtain, sufficient assets to pay the judgment debt and proceed with the appeal, no such condition should be imposed. However, if the appellant has and or can obtain sufficient assets to discharge the judgment debt and proceed with the appeal, Mr Cullen submits that justice requires that it should be required to pay or secure the judgment debt before being permitted to proceed.

36. The first logical question is whether the court has jurisdiction to make the order sought. CPR rule 52.9 provides:

'(1) The appeal court may–
 (a) strike out the whole or any part of an appeal notice;
 (b) set aside permission to appeal in whole or in part;
 (c) impose or vary conditions upon which an appeal may be brought.
(2) The court will only exercise its powers under paragraph (1) where there is a compelling reason for doing so.
(3) Where the party was present at the hearing at which permission was given he may not subsequently apply for an order that the court exercise its powers under sub-paragraphs (1) (b) or (1) (c).'

37. Rule 52.9 must be considered in the context of rule 52.3, which provides by rule 52.3(1) that permission to appeal is required in a case like this and which expressly provides by rule 52.3(7) that an order giving permission may be made subject to conditions. Immediately after paragraph (7) the CPR notes in brackets that rule 3.1(3) also provides that the court may make an order subject to conditions and rule 3.1(3) provides:

'(3) When the court makes an order, it may–
 (a) make it subject to conditions, including a condition to pay a sum of money into court; and
 (b) specify the consequence of failure to comply with the order or a condition.'

38. It is important to note that, contrary to the underlying basis of some of the submissions advanced by Mr Fenwick, a party who has lost at first instance in a case of this kind does not now have a right of appeal but must obtain permission. Moreover, the court has power to grant permission to appeal subject to conditions and it is plain from rules 52.3(7) and 3.1(3) that the CPR contemplate that one of those conditions may be that a sum of money is paid into court. It is thus clear that either the judge or a single lord justice

considering whether to grant permission to appeal has power to give permission subject to the applicant paying the judgment debt (or part of it) into court.

39. Where, as here, the judge has refused permission to appeal and permission has been granted by the single lord justice, as will ordinarily be the case without imposing conditions, the court has express power under rule 52.9(1)(c) to impose or vary conditions upon which the appeal may be brought, although by rule 52.9(2) it will only exercise such powers where there is a compelling reason to do so. We note in passing that the requirement that there must be a 'compelling reason' is curious if it is intended to create a higher threshold than would have been applicable to the exercise of the discretion of a judge considering the matter on an application on notice or of a lord justice considering the matter on an application without notice whether or not to impose a condition.

40. However that may be, the provisions of CPR 52.9 seem to us to be clear. Rule 52.9(3) does not apply in this case. Logically there are two questions posed by rule 52.9(1)(c) and (2). The first is whether there is in the instant case a compelling reason for making the continued prosecution of the appellant's appeal conditional upon the payment into court of the judgment debt and costs (or those debts being secured in some satisfactory way within the United Kingdom) and the second is whether the court should exercise its discretion to make the order.

41. We turn to the question whether there is a compelling reason for making the appellant either pay the judgment debt or secure it as a condition of permitting it to proceed with the appeal. We have reached the conclusion that the answer to that question is yes. In our judgment, the facts which combine to constitute a compelling reason are the following:
(1) The appellant is an entity against whom it will be difficult to exercise the normal mechanisms of enforcement. It is registered in the British Virgin Islands and has no assets in the United Kingdom. There is, accordingly, a very real risk that if the appeal fails, the respondents will be unable to recover the judgment debts and costs as ordered by Silber J. Given the attitude of the appellant to date, including that demonstrated on these applications, it is fanciful to think that the appellant will co-operate in the enforcement process.
(2) The appellant plainly either has the resources or has access to resources which enable it both to instruct solicitors and leading and junior counsel to prosecute its appeal and make an application to the court for a stay of execution and to provide a substantial sum by way of security for costs.
(3) There is no convincing evidence that the appellant does not either have the resources or have access to resources which would enable it to pay the judgment debt and costs as ordered. It has failed to do so. It is, accordingly, in breach of the orders made by Silber J on 12 July 2001.

(4) The discovery which the appellant has provided of its financial affairs is inadequate and gives the court no confidence that it has been shown anything near the truth. Moreover, as stated earlier, it has produced evidence (when it wanted to) that it was a thriving and profitable institution. It has wealthy owners and there is no evidence that, if they were minded to do so, they could not pay the judgment debt including the outstanding orders for costs.

(5) For the reasons we have already given we are not persuaded that this appeal will be stifled if we make the order sought.

(6) In these circumstances, we find it unacceptable that absent any other orders of the court the appellant is intending to prosecute the appeal (and is willing to put up security for costs in order to do so) whilst at the same time continuing to disobey the orders of the court to pay the judgment debt and costs, as well as seeking to persuade us that it cannot do so.

42. In our judgment, these six factors add up to a compelling reason to make the orders sought by the respondents. We think there is a real risk that, unless the orders sought are made, the respondents, if the appeal is dismissed, will be deprived of the fruits of the judgment, and will only be able to recover whatever sum is secured by way of costs. In our judgment, on the facts of this case, it is not just to allow the appellant to proceed with an appeal which is designed not only to reverse the judge's decision that it is liable to the respondent but also to obtain judgment on its counterclaim for a very substantial amount, especially in circumstances in which it appears that it is willing and able to use resources from others, including perhaps its owners, while being unwilling to seek and obtain resources to discharge the judgment debt.

43. Once it is concluded that there is a compelling reason to make the order sought, there can really be no doubt as to how the second question identified above, namely whether the court should exercise its discretion to make the order, should be answered. In short, it would be just, and in accordance with the overriding objective to make the order. We do not think that such a solution is in any way disproportionate. The appellant has been ordered to pay the judgment debt and costs after a trial, and should do so as a condition of the court giving it permission to challenge the order, provided only that it can raise the money. We see nothing unjust or inconsistent with the overriding objective in requiring such a company to obey the court's orders as a condition of being permitted to continue to prosecute its appeal. Thus we see nothing unjust in providing the trust which owns the appellant with a choice. If it is in the interests of the appellant for the appeal to continue, the trust must procure the payment of the current orders. If it does, the appeal will proceed. If it does not, the appeal will be struck out.

44. In these circumstances we have reached the firm view that the appellant should pay or secure both the judgment debt including existing orders for costs

and the appellant's costs of the appeal before being allowed to proceed with the appeal. In this way, if the appeal fails the appellant will have to pay the judgment debt and the respondents' costs of the appeal, while, if the appeal succeeds it will recover its costs of the appeal and the amount of any judgment given on the counterclaim. We would add that, in order that the appellant should be fully protected in case its appeal succeeds, the reasonable costs of putting up the security should be treated as the costs of the appeal. We shall therefore require the respondents to agree that such costs should be so treated as a condition of making the order sought.

45. We would also add that the position would be very different if the appellant were able to produce convincing evidence that the appeal would be stifled if it were required to take these steps. If it were able to produce evidence of the kind identified by Peter Gibson LJ in the passage from Keary quoted above, the position might well be different because it may well be that in that event justice would require that the appeal be allowed to continue. We should add in this regard that we are very conscious of the danger that orders such as those which we propose to make in this case could have the effect of deterring genuine appellants from prosecuting an appeal. Nothing we have said in this judgment is intended to have that effect. The key point here is that the evidence put before the court does not show that these orders will stifle the appeal.

46. We have reached the above conclusions by applying the CPR to the evidence before us. We are not aware of any case which requires us to reach any other conclusion. The only case to which we were referred is an unreported decision of Rix LJ given on 6 April 2001 in *Societe Eram Shipping Co. Ltd v Compagnie Internationale de Navigation & Others* [2001] EWCA Civ 568. In that case, a judgment creditor had obtained a garnishee order against a bank, which the judge had discharged. He gave the judgment creditor permission to appeal, but also made an immediate costs order summarily assessed against the judgment creditor for the payment of some £14,000 costs, to be paid in 14 days. When the money was not paid, the bank applied to the court for security for costs of the appeal and for a stay of the appeal pending payment of the costs ordered by the judge. The judgment creditor did not make the payment or offer an explanation as to why it had not paid. However, it cross-applied for discovery of the bank's documents in case it might emerge that the bank was entitled to an indemnity for its costs from its customer, the judgment debtor.

47. Rix LJ made an order for security for costs, but declined to order a stay of the appeal pending payment of the costs ordered by the judge. He commented that:

> 'interestingly enough, no example of a case in which a stay of an appeal has been ordered for non-payment of costs has been brought to my attention. There is not even a case in which the matter has been considered, let alone ordered.'

In the course of an analysis of CPR 52.9, Rix LJ said:

> 'the fact that conditions may only be imposed by an appeal court on appeal when there is "compelling reason to do so" does again suggest a very cautious approach to the question of a stay for non-payment. If I had found any encouragement either in specific provisions of the current rule or in authority for ordering a stay for non-payment of costs, I can well see that this case might well be considered to be a suitable case for the exercise of such a discretion. Not because of any doubt about the legitimacy of the appeal, but because of the complete absence of any explanation for non-payment and also because there is still some considerable time until the appeal takes place. It can be said that if the sanction of stay did not exist, then subject to all the difficulties of seeking to enforce the order in foreign jurisdictions and I bear in mind that the jurisdiction with which I am here concerned, Romania, is not one within the Brussels or European Conventions, then it is not clear to me what sanction there is to support the very desirable new provisions for summary assessment and the need for payment of costs.
>
> I am not saying there is no jurisdiction to order a stay for mere non-payment of costs. Nevertheless, I am not sure that I would be able to say that there was here a compelling reason for making such an order ...
>
> Ultimately, in the face of an absence of explanation for the non-payment of costs by the appellant, I am left with the choice of an inference between "cannot pay" or "will not pay". I have already given my reasons for preferring the inference of "cannot pay". If that is the correct inference to make in all the circumstances, then the inability to pay is not, it seems to me, a proper ground on which to deprive an appellant who has permission to appeal from pursuing his appeal.'

48. We note that Rix LJ expressly recognised the court's jurisdiction to make the order. We do not disagree with Rix LA 'cautious' approach to CPR rule 52.9. Nor do we disagree with the final extract from his judgment set out above, since each case of course depends upon its own facts. We do, however, take the view that the new regime of the CPR, with its emphasis on the timely payment of costs, and the use of costs as a sanction, warrants a robust approach to appellants who fail to obey orders for the payment of a judgment debt and costs when they can afford to pay them either themselves or through others.

49. We note that Rix LJ was not considering a case like this, where the evidence of the appellant's financial position is far from clear and where it is able to pursue its appeal with solicitors and counsel and there is no evidence that the appellant could not raise the money to pay or security the judgment debt, its own costs and the respondents costs.

Conclusion

50. For the reasons we have given we refuse the appellant's application of a stay of execution, save on terms that it pays into court or provides security for the judgment debt, including the orders for costs. We grant the application for security for costs of the appeal in the sum of £85,000. We further grant the respondents' application that a term be imposed upon the permission to appeal granted to the appellant, namely that it only be permitted to appeal if it pays into court or provides security for the judgment debt (including the orders for costs) and the above sum in respect of security for the respondents' costs of the appeal. The security is to be in a form to the reasonable satisfaction of the respondents' solicitors, failing which there be liberty to apply to the court. Any such application to be heard and determined before 1 March 2002. The reasonable costs of putting up such security are to be costs in the appeal and the respondents must agree to their being so treated as a condition of the order. If the appellant fails to pay or provide security for the above sums on or before 1 March 2002, the appeal is to stand struck out without further order.

HERTFORDSHIRE INVESTMENTS LTD V BUBB AND ANOTHER

A2.11 COURT OF APPEAL (CIVIL DIVISION)

SWINTON THOMAS, SEDLEY and HALE LJJ

25 JULY 2000

Evidence – Fresh Evidence – Appeal – Claimant producing new evidence – Judge allowing rehearing in county court – Judge allowing application for extension of time – Whether judge should have allowed appeal – Whether judge in error – County Court Rules Ord 37, r 1.

Lord Justice Hale

[1] This is an appeal from an order of HHJ Riddell in the Edmonton County Court made on 2 July 1999.

[2] The claimant company is a moneylender. On 31 January 1994 it entered into a loan agreement regulated under the Consumer Credit Act 1974 with the defendants who are husband and wife, although now estranged. It lent them a principal sum of £9012 secured by a first charge on their matrimonial home, 27 Nursery Street, Tottenham, London N17. After various deductions they received only £6,300-odd. The loan was repayable by 120 monthly instalments. The contractual instalment sum was £210.28 per month, representing an annual percentage rate of 32.74 per cent, but a side letter allowed instalments of £172.73, representing a rate of 24.67 per cent, provided that payments were received before the end of each month. The defendants fell into arrears but

never by a very great sum until after the end of November 1996 when the instalments were increased to the higher figure. Notice of default was given on 18 November 1997. A possession action was brought on 29 May 1998. At that time the arrears were £685.03.

[3] Various defences were raised against the claim. Paragraph 2 of the amended defence and counterclaim, which is dated 20 July 1998, alleged that Home Counties Finance Limited acted as the credit broker. The claimant was put to strict proof as to whether they were licensed as such. The defence and counterclaim also claimed relief under ss 129 and 136 of the Consumer Credit Act 1974.

[4] There were two affidavits filed on behalf of the claimant by a Mr Stern. The first dated 3 July 1998, before the amended defence, produced the claimant's own licence under the 1974 Act. The second dated 28 September 1998, after the amended defence, stated in para 5 that he was producing the licence issued to Home Counties Finance Limited, but he actually exhibited a licence for Home Counties Credit Limited with a place of business in Barkingside and a registered office in Finchley. The trial took place before DJ Morley on 30 September 1998. He dismissed the action. It had not been shown that the broker was licensed. It is common ground that in that event the agreement is unenforceable by virtue of s 149 of the 1974 Act. It appears that the claimant did not apply for an adjournment or to be nonsuited.

[5] On 25 November 1998 the claimant applied for the district judge's order to be set aside and the case set down for rehearing. There was an affidavit dated 26 November 1998 from a solicitor, Mr Levy, who now produced a licence for Home County Finance Limited, with a totally different place of business in Wembley and a registered office in Golders Green. By this time the arrears had mounted to £861.43.

[6] The application was made under Ord 37, r 1, of the County Court Rules 1981 which reads:

'In any proceedings tried without a jury the judge shall have power on application to order a rehearing where no error of the court at the hearing is alleged.'

[7] The time limit is provided under subrule 5:

'Any application for a rehearing under this rule shall be made on notice stating the grounds of the application and the notice shall be served on the opposite party not more than 14 days after the day of the trial and not less than 7 days before the day fixed for the hearing of the application.'

[8] The application was, therefore, made approximately six weeks late but there was then no application made to extend the time for making it.

[9] On 24 February 1999 it came before DJ Rose. Only then was an application made to extend time to apply, and we have seen no evidence giving an explanation for the delay on that occasion. The district judge dismissed the application. According to the later judgment of HHJ Riddell he held, firstly, that the fresh evidence did not fulfill the requirements of *Ladd v Marshall* [1954] 3 All ER 745, [1954] 1 WLR 1489: it could have been obtained with reasonable diligence at the trial; and, secondly, that there was no reason to extend time: time limits were there to be obeyed.

[10] The claimant appealed against that order. There was an affidavit from another solicitor, Mr Buchalter, dated 25 June 1999. It simply says in para 4:

> 'This delay was caused by my firm's failure to address the County Court Rules in relation to time limits for the making of such an application. I was unaware until shortly before issuing the application on behalf of the claimant that the application had to be issued within a period of time or that delay would prejudice the claimant's case.'

[11] The arrears had now claimed to over £1800. He continued to assert that there was no prejudice to the defendants from this delay.

[12] On 2nd July 1999 HHJ Riddell allowed the claimant's appeal. He did order the claimants to pay the costs but he imposed no other penalty, for example in relation to interest. He dealt first with the exercise of the discretion to order a rehearing. He referred to an argument raised by Mr Griffiths on behalf of the defendants that if there was no rehearing and the claimant tried to start new proceedings, these would be met with an argument that the issue of the enforceability of the contract was now res judicata. The judge did not decide that point but he did comment that:

> 'Here the position is that the consequences to the claimant of not allowing a rehearing would be disastrous if Mr Griffiths' res judicata argument were to be valid. There would, therefore, be very considerable prejudice to the claimant in those circumstances.'

[13] He summed up his reasons for allowing the appeal on this point at pages 17 to 18 of his judgment thus:

> 'The relevant factors are, it seems to me, the importance of the new evidence – that evidence, as I have said, is obviously important; the reliability of the new evidence – there is no question as to that; whether the new evidence could have been obtained with reasonable diligence – it clearly could have been; why that evidence was not adduced at the first hearing – it was a mistake, a mistake mitigated as regards culpability by the similarity of the name, so to that extent understandable. Another factor is, of course, the consequences to the parties of the case being reopened or not being reopened, a risk of considerable detriment to the

claimant if the case is not reheard. There is no prejudice to the defendant by granting the application for a rehearing, other than to deprive him of the fruits of his victory before the District Judge, a victory which on that issue was the result of a fortuitous development.

The defendant can, of course, be compensated in costs for all that has occurred, at any rate up to the launching of this appeal. A factor, though, to be taken into account is the continuing strain and worry to him, but if the application for a rehearing was to be refused by me he would, I am afraid, still be faced with that anxiety because fresh proceedings would be launched – inevitably as the arrears are accumulating.

As I have said, weighing up those factors, applying the over-riding objective, having regard to what is just and fair in these circumstances, I consider that the appellant succeeds on that issue.'

[14] It is noteworthy that the judge decided, as was clear, that the evidence could have been produced with reasonable diligence at the trial.

[15] The judge dealt next with the extension of time. He referred to the cases *of Mortgage Corporation v Sandoes* (1996) 141 SJ LB 30, *Costellow v Somerset County Council* [1993] 1 All ER 952, [1993] 1 WLR 256 and *Finnegan v Parkside Health Authority* [1998] 1 All ER 595, [1998] 1 WLR 411, the last two emphasising that it could rarely be appropriate to deny an extension of time because of a procedural default which, even if unjustified, had caused the defendant no prejudice for which he could not be compensated by an award for costs.

[16] The judge considered the factors laid down in the Civil Procedure Rules 1998, r 3.9, relevant to deciding whether or not to grant relief from sanctions. He concluded at page 22 of his judgment that the vital factor which caused him also to decide this point in favour of the claimant was the effect of the claimant's not being allowed a rehearing in the circumstances of the case. The first defendant now appeals from that order with the permission of Brooke LJ.

[17] Mr Crane QC, who appears for the appellant, emphasises that this case concerns events after a final judgment had been given following a trial on the merits at which both parties were present and represented. This has an important bearing, both on the application for a rehearing and on the application to extend time. As Leggatt LJ said in the case of *Shocked v Goldschmidt* [1998] 1 All ER 372 at page 382c:

'To equate judgments by default with judgments given after trial is heretical.'

[18] That is an important distinction between this case and the case of *Vann v Awford* (1986) 130 SJ LB 682, to which the learned judge had referred.

[19] Mr Crane argues that the principles applicable to the power to order a rehearing under Ord 37 r 1 of the County Court Rules on the ground of fresh evidence should be the same as those applicable to the power of the Court of Appeal to order a rehearing on appeal from the High Court.

[20] The history of the relevant provisions is conveniently set out by Ward J, as he then was, in the case of *B-T v B-T* [1990] 2 FLR 1, [1990] FCR 654. Before the Judicature Act 1873 there was a variety of powers in the courts of Chancery, common law and matrimonial causes to order a review or retrial of their own decisions. The 1873 Act set up the Court of Appeal which was given those powers. The relevant provision is now contained in s 17 of the Supreme Court Act 1981. Subsection (1) provides:

> 'Where any cause or matter or any issue in any cause or matter has been tried in the High Court any application for a new trial thereof or to set aside a verdict, finding or judgment therein shall be heard and determined by the Court of Appeal except where rules of court provide otherwise.'

[21] Sub-section 2 provides:

> 'As regards cases where the trial was by a judge alone and no error of the court at the trial was alleged or any prescribed class in such cases, rules of court may provide that any such application as is mentioned in sub-s (1) shall be heard and determined by the High Court.'

[22] No such rules have been made for the High Court, apart from what used to be the Matrimonial Causes Rules 1977, r 54, and is now contained in the Family Proceedings Rules 1991, r 2.42: an application for a rehearing of a matrimonial cause tried by a judge alone (whether in the High Court or a divorce County Court) where no error of the court at the hearing is alleged, shall be made to a judge.

[23] This means that anyone wishing a rehearing after a final order in the High Court, save in a matrimonial cause, has to come to the Court of Appeal. Where the ground alleged is fresh evidence, the matter was governed until this year by the rules of the Supreme Court Order 59, r 10 (2), subrule 2, the relevant part of which provides that:

> 'No such further evidence (other than evidence as to matters which have occurred after the date of the trial or hearing) shall be admitted except on special grounds.'

[24] Special grounds, as we all know, meant that the fresh evidence satisfied the principles in *Ladd v Marshall* [1954] 3 All ER 745, [1954] 1 WLR 1489: i.e. that it could not have been obtained with reasonable diligence for use at trial; if given it would probably have had an important influence on the result of the

case; and it is apparently credible although not incontrovertible; although there are exceptional cases in which those principles do not apply, for example those involving the welfare of children.

[25] There are, of course, strong reasons for this approach which has a long pedigree. It is in the interests of every litigant and the system as a whole that there should be an end to litigation. People should put their full case before the court at trial and should not be allowed to have a second bite at the cherry without a very good reason indeed.

[26] The procedural position in county courts was different. The forerunner rule to Ord 37 r 1 of the County Court Rules reproduced s 93 of the County Courts Act 1888. This allowed the judge:

'... if he thinks just, to order a new trial to be heard on such terms as he shall think reasonable.'

[27] Despite those very wide terms, that discretion had to be exercised judicially on the same principles as would apply to the High Court. Those principles were laid down in the case of *Brown v Dean* [1910] AC 373 by the House of Lords, and it is noteworthy that *Ladd v Marshall* was itself adopting and applying those principles when it laid down the rules which have governed matters since then.

[28] The procedure under Ord 37 r 1 was the proper procedure for applying to introduce new evidence in the county courts at that time. This was because under the county courts' legislation, until more recently, the rights of appeal to the Court of Appeal were limited. It was not possible to appeal to seek a rehearing on the grounds of fresh evidence. The reason was that the county courts were then designed as small claims courts. As Fletcher Moulton LJ had observed in the Court of Appeal in *Brown v Dean* [1909] 2 KB 573:

'The necessities of the case have led the legislature to restrict the guarantees against possible judicial error in view of the more practical advantage of rendering the procedure simple, speedy and cheap.'

[29] That gap was filled to some extent by the power to order a rehearing. Nevertheless it does not follow from that that the principles applicable to any such power are any different from those applicable in the Court of Appeal. Indeed, Fletcher Moulton LJ's suggestions that they might be wider were specifically rejected by the majority in the Court of Appeal and the House of Lords.

[30] Since then, the County Courts Act 1984, in s 77(1), has given broader rights to appeal to any party dissatisfied with the determination of the judge in a County Court. Hence this court, in *O'Connor v Diu* [1997] 1 FLR 226, [1997] Fam Law 244 decided that a party who wishes to adduce fresh evidence after the trial has two routes: either to appeal to this court or to apply for a

rehearing, although it was stressed in that case that an application for a rehearing was the preferable route especially where the evidence was likely to be disputed.

[31] Meanwhile, the wording of the relevant rule changed in the County Court Rules 1981 to its present form. This brought the wording into line with what had been envisaged might be done in the Supreme Court by s 17(2) of the Supreme Court Act but has in fact only been done in matrimonial causes.

[32] Mr Warwick for the claimant argues that the change in the wording imports a wider flexibility than had previously been the case. There is nothing at all in the case of *B-T* itself to suggest this. There is nothing in the commentary on the relevant rule in the last edition of the County Court Practice in 1998 to suggest this.

[33] The rule is now incorporated into schedule 2 of the Civil Procedure Rules. The commentators suggest in the White Book at page 1205 that:

> 'It must be anticipated that an order for a rehearing will be exceptional, on strong grounds and on terms as to costs.'

[34] In the light of that history, the reasons for the procedural difference between the High Court and the County Court, the fact that there is now a choice of remedies between an appeal and an application for a rehearing in the County Court, and the underlying principle of the Civil Procedure Rules that the rules or principles should be the same whatever the court in which the proceedings are brought, it must be correct, as Mr Crane argues, that the principles governing the exercise of the power to reopen a case after final judgment because of fresh evidence should be the same whatever the procedural route adopted. It would be most unjust if a party to County Court proceedings could reopen matters when a party to High Court proceedings could not.

[35] The position governing applications to adduce fresh evidence on appeal is now governed by the Civil Procedure Rules, r 52.11(2). The court will not consider evidence which was not before the court below unless it has given permission for it to be used. It is no longer necessary to show 'special grounds'. The discretion must also be exercised in accordance with the overriding objective of doing justice. However, in the very recent case of *Banks v Cox*, decided on 17 July 2000, for which we have the benefit of an, as yet, unpublished transcript, Morritt LJ said this:

> 'In my view, the principles reflected in the rules in *Ladd v Marshall* remain relevant to any application for permission to rely on further evidence, not as rules but as matters which must necessarily be considered in an exercise of the discretion whether or not to permit an appellant to rely on evidence not before the court below.'

[36] He referred to another decision of this court, *Hickey v Marks*, on 6 July 2000 to that effect. He then went on to consider each of the requirements in *Ladd v Marshall* in that case. He found that they had all been satisfied and he then went on to consider whether it was just to order a retrial and did so.

[37] It follows from all of this that it cannot be a simple balancing exercise as the judge in this case seemed to think. He had to approach it on the basis that strong grounds were required. The *Ladd v Marshall* criteria are principles rather than rules but, nevertheless, they should be looked at with considerable care and in this particular case, of course, the first of those principles was not fulfilled: The evidence could clearly have been available readily at trial.

[38] A similar difficulty arises in relation to the application to extend time. The time limit under r 37(5) is a strict one: the application must not only be made but served within 14 days of the order which it is desired to have set aside.

[39] The judge referred to cases on pre-trial delay or default in the timetable. He did not address his mind to the position after trial. In *Regalbourne Ltd v East Lindsay District Council* [1994] RA 1, [1994] 58 LGLR 81, page 85 of the latter report, the Master of the Rolls made it clear that what he had said in Costellow was not applicable to an application for permission to appeal out of time.

[40] The judge in this case went carefully through the factors set out in the Civil Procedure Rules, r 3.9 on relief from sanctions. But these are, clearly, mainly directed towards pre-trial defaults; they would not otherwise include as factor (g) the extent to which the trial date has been put in jeopardy. The Civil Procedure Rules do not otherwise deal expressly with a power to extend time under r 37.(1).

[41] They do deal with applications to set aside small claims and other judgments obtained in the absence of the party concerned. Both allow setting aside only if certain conditions are fulfilled. Rule 27.11(3) allows setting aside small claims judgments only if there was a good reason for not attending or being represented at the hearing and the case has a reasonable prospect of success. R 39.3(5) allows setting aside of other judgments obtained in the absence of a party only if the party acted promptly when he found out, had good reason for not attending and has a reasonable prospect of success. Both of those are more stringent than the comparable Rules of the Supreme Court, Ord 35 r 2, and the County Court Rules which they replace. These give strong support for the proposition that the position after trial is different from the position before and there must normally be a good reason for the delay if one is to extend time.

[42] What then is the conclusion of all of this? This was, of course, an exercise of discretion by the trial judge. But in my view he was unduly affected by the potential prejudice to the claimant. He did not properly address his mind to the fact that this was a final judgment obtained after trial at which both parties had

been represented. He did not consider the public policy in there being an end to litigation. In this particular case there was no excuse at all for not producing the proper evidence at the trial: it could have been obtained. There is also no excuse at all for the delay in applying to set aside the order: solicitors should know the rules. It is simply not good enough for professional litigators with legal representation to ask for a double indulgence when there has been no excuse for either default. If this was granted in this case, it is difficult to see a case in which it would not be granted. For those reasons, therefore, I would allow this appeal.

Lord Justice Sedley

[43] I agree.

Lord Justice Swinton Thomas

[44] I also agree.

Appeal allowed with costs.

(*Transcript:* Smith Bernal)

HUNT V PEASEGOOD

A2.12 COURT OF APPEAL (CIVIL DIVISION)

OTTON, WARD and MUMMERY LJJ

13 OCTOBER 2000

Insolvency – Appeal – Locus standi –Bankrupt challenging taxation order on which bankruptcy based – Whether bankrupt had locus standi

Lord Justice Otton

[1] I shall invite Lord Justice Mummery to give the first judgment.

Lord Justice Mummery

[2] This is an appeal by Mr Edwin Hunt as the trustee in bankruptcy of Mr James Peasegood. The appellant is represented by Mr Stephen Davies QC. The respondent to the appeal is the former wife of Mr James Peasegood, Mrs Hannah Peasegood. She appears in person.

[3] The order under appeal was made on an application by Mrs Peasegood issued in the Birmingham District Registry on 4 February 2000. Mrs Peasegood applied for orders that the bankruptcy order made against her in the Stoke-On-Trent County Court on 16 March 1998 be quashed. She also applied for an order that the statutory demand dated 22 May 1997, on which the bankruptcy order was made, should be set aside. She sought consequential orders quashing the bankruptcy order and dismissing the statutory demand.

[4] The application did not identify the jurisdiction being invoked by Mrs Peasegood. There is no reference to s.375 of the Insolvency Act 1986, under which the court has the power to review, rescind or vary any order made by the exercise of the jurisdiction under the relevant parts of the 1986 Act. Nor is there any reference to s.282 of the 1986 Act under which the court has power to annul a bankruptcy order if it at any time appears to the court (a) that on any grounds existing at the time the order was made, the order ought not to have been made or (b) that to the extent required by the rules the bankruptcy debts and expenses of the bankruptcy have since the making of the order been either paid or secured or to the satisfaction of the court.

[5] Mrs Peasegood submitted that she was invoking the inherent jurisdiction of the court to set aside orders which have been made without jurisdiction. There is no reference to the statutory provisions in the judgment given by His Honour Judge Boggis in justification of the order which he made on 10 February.

[6] Judge Boggis sitting as a judge of the High Court at Birmingham District Registry, made an order on Mrs Peasegood's application that:

'1. The bankruptcy order made against the respondent in Stoke-on-Trent County Court on 16 March 1998 be quashed.
2. The statutory demand issued 22 May 1997 be set aside.
3. All further proceedings concerning the taxation of costs in No 82 of 1989 are to be transferred to Birmingham District Registry to be heard by a Full District Judge sitting in Birmingham.
4. The order to pay dated 24 February 1997 is set aside.'

[7] Under that order made on 24 February 1997, the court notified the amount of taxed costs in relation to earlier proceedings, (which I shall describe in more detail later), that the costs had been taxed and allowed in the sums of £6,068 and £4,307.47. The notification was that the amount of those two sums was to be paid to the plaintiff, Mr Edwin Hunt, within 14 days from the date of that notification. Those sums have not been paid (nor have any part of them been paid) by Mrs Peasegood.

[8] Judge Boggis gave written reasons for his order in his judgment on 15 February. He held was that the order of 24 February 1997 was a nullity and should be set aside. If that order was set aside, there was no liquidated debt which could be the subject of a valid statutory demand. If there was no valid statutory demand, there was no basis on which a valid bankruptcy order could be made. He said:

'If an order ought not to have been made, it must be set aside. The Trustee is not entitled to proceed to bankruptcy on the basis of a taxation which has never been properly concluded.'

[9] In holding that the taxation of 24 February 1997 had not been properly concluded, Judge Boggis accepted as correct Mrs Peasegood's criticisms of the

taxation order. In essence her criticisms were that the trustee had failed in the taxation to take steps which had to be taken before a receiving party could obtain an order to pay. These arguments were based on the fact that the taxation had not been properly completed. There had been disbursements which had not been vouched. There had not been the necessary signature to the requisite documents. Therefore, Judge Boggis concluded, the order to pay had been wrongly issued, and it could not form the basis of the bankruptcy proceedings against Mrs Peasegood. So he should quash the bankruptcy order and set aside the order to pay.

[10] On 2 May, Aldous LJ granted permission to appeal. The grounds on which he granted permission were that it was probably arguable that the issues raised by Mrs Peasegood before Judge Boggis in February were res judicata and that her attacks on the order to pay in order to rid herself of the bankruptcy proceedings amounted to an abuse. The Lord Justice also stated as a further ground that, if the judge was exercising discretion under s.382 of the 1986 Act, there was a reasonable argument that he failed to exercise his discretion taking into account the history of the case. Matters did not proceed smoothly to the hearing of this appeal because Mrs Peasegood launched an application to set aside the grant of permission. That was rejected by this court on 26 July.

[11] Before I come to the points which have been made by Mr Davies in criticism of the judge's order and by Mrs Peasegood in defence of it, I should fill out more of the background history. It goes back many years. It has already been fully set out in two judgments of this court, one given on 1 May 1997 and another on 9 June 1999. Rather than simply referring to those judgments I shall, in an attempt to make this self-contained and coherent as a judgment, refer to such earlier events as are necessary to explain the submissions to this court.

[12] It all goes back to proceedings heard between Mr Hunt and Mrs Peasegood in the Stoke-on-Trent County Court in November 1995. There was a dispute as to whether certain assets were assets in the bankruptcy of Mr James Peasegood or not. Those assets included the proceeds of some property. The upshot of those proceedings was that an order for costs was made against Mrs Peasegood. There was an appeal by Mrs Peasegood against the decision of His Honour Judge Harold in the Stoke-on-Trent County Court. That was dismissed by Chadwick J on 1 March 1996. The taxation proceeded. There were various hearings which were adjourned in the autumn of 1996 and at the beginning of 1997. The taxation resulted in the order to pay dated 24 February 1997. There were further appeals against that order to Chadwick J in March 1997. An attempt was made by Mrs Peasegood to obtain permission to appeal from this court. That was rejected for the reasons given in the judgment on 1 May 1997.

[13] Following those hearings the statutory demand was served on 22 May 1997. The demand, which was in the prescribed form, stated that Mrs Peasegood owed the sum of £10,375.47 and that that sum was immediately payable. It referred to the order of the Stoke-on-Trent County Court in proceedings No 82 of 1989 in which Mrs Peasegood was ordered to pay him that sum by way of costs. Reference was made in the section of the statutory demand for particulars of debt to the order for payment of costs made on 2 November 1995 and the order of 24 February 1997 taxing those costs. The total of £10,375.47 was the addition of the two sums already mentioned, which sums were to be paid within 14 days.

[14] That demand was followed by litigious activity on the part of Mrs Peasegood attacking the statutory demand. Her application to District Judge Jack in December 1997 to set aside the statutory demand was unsuccessful. At the Stoke-on-Trent County Court District Judge Rowley made a bankruptcy order on 16 March 1998 based on that unsatisfied demand. Mrs Peasegood sought to have that bankruptcy order reviewed or rescinded or annulled. That was dismissed by District Judge Schroeder on 7 July 1998. She made an application to set aside the taxation order in conjunction with the bankruptcy order. That was unsuccessful, as were her attempts to obtain permission to appeal against those orders. The reasons for refusing permission to appeal against orders refusing to review, rescind or annul a bankruptcy order were given in the judgment of this court on 9 June 1999.

[15] One approaches the judgment and order of Judge Boggis with some surprise in view of all the previous unsuccessful attempts of Mrs Peasegood to attack the steps and orders taken in these bankruptcy proceedings. Judge Boggis appears to have justified his orders on the basis that, in her attack on the taxation order, Mrs Peasegood was relying on new points. These points demonstrated to the judge's satisfaction that the taxation process had not been complete, as the disbursements had not been vouched for and the taxing officer had not certified the taxed sum by an appropriate signing order. The result was a nullity. Everything done on the basis of that order was also a nullity. The judge does not appear to have addressed himself to the question as to what jurisdiction he was exercising, or to the relevant principles of law relevant to the exercise of his jurisdiction.

[16] Mr Davies cited a number of decisions which he submits place insuperably obstacles in the way of the exercise on which the judge had embarked. First, he relies on decisions of this court that a person against whom a bankruptcy order has been made has no locus standi to appeal against or attack the judgment of the court on the basis of which the bankruptcy order has been made. The fundamental principle is that when a person is adjudicated bankrupt he is divested of all interest in his property and liability for his debts. He has no right to challenge the judgments. That right vests in the trustee in bankruptcy.

[17] This is made clear by the decision of the Court of Appeal in *Heath v Tang* [1993] 4 All ER 694, [1993] 1 WLR 1421 at 1426C, 1426H and 1427B of the latter report. Hoffmann LJ, with whose judgment the other members of the court agreed, referred to the general principle that a bankrupt does not have the locus standi to appeal against the judgment on which the bankruptcy proceedings are based. He said at 1427B that:

'... the principle that the bankrupt is divested of an interest in his property and liability for his debts remains fundamental in the new code. The consequences for the bankrupt's right to litigate do not seem to us inconvenient or productive of injustice. The bankruptcy court acts as a screen which both prevents the bankrupt's substance from being wasted in hopeless appeals and protects creditors from vexatious challenges to their claims.'

[18] That decision was followed by another decision of this court in *Royal Bank of Scotland v Farley* [1996] BPIR 638. Hoffmann LJ, in his judgment (and two other members of the court agreed) said at 640H:

'The bankrupt had in fact no locus standi to make the application to set aside the default judgment in the first place.'

[19] That was a case not of an appeal but of an application to set aside a judgment. He continued:

'That, in my view, appears from the decision of this court in *Heath v Tang* [1993] 1 WLR 1421. The essence of that decision is that a bankruptcy order divests the bankrupt of any further interest in what debts he owes because it provides that he shall no longer be under any personal liability. An appeal from the judgment against him or an application to set aside the judgment against him is therefore a matter for his trustee, but does not concern the bankrupt.'

[20] I would also refer to what was said by Sir Thomas Bingham in *Wordsworth v Dixon* [1997] BPIR 337 at 338 where, having cited *Heath v Tang*, he said that that case:

'... clearly establishes that on the vesting of a bankrupt's estate in the trustee, the right to challenge a judgment which would take effect against the estate vests in the trustee.'

[21] The more recent decision of this court in *Ord v Upton* [2000] 1 All ER 193, [2000] 2 WLR 755 applies the same principle in respect of the vesting of causes of action in the trustee in bankruptcy.

[22] So the first point made by Mr Davies is that Judge Boggis ought never to have entertained the application made by Mrs Peasegood, because she was a bankrupt. She had no right, following the bankruptcy order, to challenge the

order for the payment of tax costs on 24 February 1997. That is all that needs to be said. Judge Boggis embarked on an exercise which Mrs Peasegood had no right to initiate.

[23] There are, however, other principles well settled by authority which would apply, if this were an application made by a debtor who did have a right to make it. It is well settled that the discretion of the court under s.375, that I may call the review discretion, and the discretion under s 282, which is the annulment discretion, are to be exercised in accordance with principles which the judge did not address. So far as I can see, he was not aware that any discretionary jurisdiction under these sections was being invoked. But assuming that it was, the position is that the review discretion under s 375 must be exercised judicially, having regard to costs and to the public policy of finality of decisions. It has been held that it is not to be used as a gateway for making late appeals. It should only be entertained, if a compelling fresh case is made out and a manifest injustice would be suffered if the power were not exercised. That is the effect of the decision of Lindsay J in *Re Debtors (Nos VA7 & and VA8), ex parte Stevens* [1996] BPIR 101.

[24] In *Commissioners of Inland Revenue v Robinson* [1999] BPIR 329 Mr Peter Whiteman QC, sitting as a deputy judge of the High Court, emphasised that the power to review or rescind bankruptcy orders should be sparingly used. It should be confined to cases whether there are exceptional circumstances, such as compelling new evidence. As far as the annulment power under s 282 is concerned, it is also settled that the doctrines of res judicata and abuse of process apply to the exercise of that discretion. So, for example, if an application to set aside a statutory demand has failed, the unsuccessful applicant should not be entitled to re-run the same arguments, which have failed on that application, in opposition to the making of the bankruptcy order on the petition. What is needed is some change of circumstances which would justify the debtor making a further attempt to question the basis of the bankruptcy proceedings.

[25] This is made clear by two cases. I refer to *Brillouet v Hachette Magazines Ltd* [1996] BPIR 518, a decision of Vinelot J against which permission to appeal was refused by Leggatt LJ. A decision to the same effect was given by this court earlier this year in *Turner v Royal Bank of Scotland*, which is so far unreported. The relevant passages are to be found in paras 47 to 49 of the judgment given by Chadwick LJ. He referred, as earlier judges have, to the policy consideration in discouraging the waste of court time and the waste of party money and to the obvious purpose of the statutory scheme of bankruptcy proceeding through statutory demands to the making of a bankruptcy order. Those are the principles which should be borne in mind in considering the reasons given by Judge Boggis for granting Mrs Peasegood the orders which he did.

[26] Mrs Peasegood has, in courteous and helpful submissions, both in writing and orally, sought to defend the judge's decision. She says this appeal should not be allowed. The position quite simply was that she was not applying to Judge Boggis to annul a bankruptcy order under s 282 nor, as I understand her, was she applying to review or rescind the order under s 375. She contends that she made her application under the inherent jurisdiction of the court, not to have the order annulled or reviewed or rescinded, but to have it quashed. She says that the courts have an inherent jurisdiction to quash orders made without jurisdiction. The order of 24 February 1997, which was the foundation of the bankruptcy proceedings against her, was made without jurisdiction, because the whole of the taxation process had not been lawfully completed to produce a valid order. She said it was a basic requirement for a statutory demand on which a petition is based that there should be a liquidated sum. There is no liquidated debt in this case. That could only be produced by a valid taxation. This taxation order was a nullity.

[27] She went on to explain that she had not raised this point earlier in many of her earlier applications attacking the demand and the petition, because she had not been aware of it. They were, as stated by Judge Boggis, new points. She should be entitled to raise them. These points had only been recently picked up. She did not deny that she was under a potential liability to pay because of the order for costs, but until there is a proper taxation she owes nothing. She cannot be made bankrupt. These matters are spelt out in more detail in her skeleton argument.

[28] I am unable to accept those submissions. This order ought never to have been made. I would allow this appeal for these reasons: First, Mrs Peasegood was not entitled to make the application on which the judge made the order. Any right she had to challenge the taxation order of 24 February 1997 was vested in the trustee in bankruptcy. Mrs Peasegood had no locus to appeal that order or to have it set aside or to have it quashed. It was a valid order, so far as she was concerned. She had no right to attack it.

[29] Secondly, insofar as the judge was exercising a discretion, whether derived from statute or from some inherent jurisdiction, which I have been unable to identify, he did not exercise that discretion in a judicial manner. He failed to have regard to the principles laid down in the cases relating to res judicata and abuse of process. Mrs Peasegood not only had the opportunity but took the opportunity at every stage to challenge the taxation order, to challenge the statutory demand based upon it and to challenge the bankruptcy order based on the statutory demand. She ventilated her arguments at every level that was open to her, without success. It was wrong for the judge to exercise any discretion that he may have had to entertain this matter without reference to the long history of this matter in which arguments had been fully presented by

Mrs Peasegood and entertained by the courts, including this court on two occasions on her applications for permission to appeal.

[30] For these reasons I would allow the appeal, set aside the order made by the judge on 10 of February and restore the order of 24 February 1997 and the bankruptcy order of 16 March 1998.

Lord Justice Ward

[31] The order from which these proceedings flow was made by Judge Orrell nearly five years ago. There have, on my count, been thirteen occasions since that Mrs Peasegood battled with her former husband in bankruptry before the courts. I hope this is the last. For the reasons my Lord has given I, too, would restore the bankruptcy order and allow the appeal.

[32] I should like to add that when the matter was before me in May of 1997 I expressed the fact that I felt sorry for Mrs Peasegood. I still feel sorry for her but she must now begin to realise that she is bankrupt and will remain bankrupt and there is nothing more she can do about it. I would allow the appeal.

Lord Justice Otton

[33] I agree.

Appeal allowed.

(*Transcript: Smith Bernal*)

JOLLY V JAY

A2.13

[2002] EWCA Civ 277

COURT OF APPEAL (CIVIL DIVISION)

BROOKE, SEDLEY and ARDEN LJJ

7 MARCH 2002

JUDGMENT: APPROVED BY THE COURT FOR HANDING DOWN (SUBJECT TO EDITORIAL CORRECTIONS)

Lord Justice Brooke:

This is the judgment of the court, to which all its members have contributed.

1. This application for permission to appeal was listed before us in order that the court could have the opportunity of considering the circumstances in which

a respondent may be awarded costs after he has resisted successfully an application for permission to appeal. In the event the issues between the parties were for all practical purposes resolved on the day before the hearing, so that there was virtually nothing left for us to decide, so far as issues of costs were concerned. The listing of the application, however, coupled with the assistance we received from counsel, alerted us to a number of inconsistencies and uncertainties about the early stages of the new regime under CPR Part 52, so far as they relate to the position of respondents. The resolution of these problems is clearly one for those who are concerned with the preparation of the rules and practice directions under the CPR regime. We believe, however, that it would be useful for us to draw attention to them in this judgment, and to explain the reasons why respondents are now served with certain documents (such as the appeal notice and the appellant's request for the reconsideration of a decision to refuse permission) in advance of an appeal court's decision to grant permission to appeal.

2. The reason why the present application was of interest to the court was that in the judgment under challenge, a decision of Neuberger J dated 19th October 2001, the judge when refusing the claimant permission to appeal against a decision by a High Court master had made an order for costs in favour of the defendant who had appeared by counsel to resist the application, even though there is no procedure set out in CPR Part 52 or its Practice Direction which envisages that a respondent will appear on such an application (unless the court so directs: see the Practice Direction to CPR Part 52 ('CPR 52 PD') para 4.15).

3. Although Mr Jolly did not take specific issue in his Notice of Appeal with Neuberger J's order that he pay £350 plus VAT (which he has already paid), the Civil Appeal Office formally notified the parties on 30 January 2002 that the court wished both parties to appear at the hearing:

> 'because the Court wishes to consider the proper approach for an appeal Judge to take when a Respondent applies for costs at an oral hearing of an application for permission to appeal following the refusal of permission to appeal on paper.'

The letter continued:

> 'Lord Justice Brooke has asked me to write to you ... to inform you of the question with which the Court will be concerned since the existence of the Judge's order might affect any order for costs made at the hearing on 7th February if Mr Jolly is not successful.'

4. These, then, were the circumstances in which the application came before the court for hearing. Mr Jolly, who has appeared before the courts many times in the last few years, appeared in person. Ms Cheryl Jones, who also appeared at

the hearing before the judge, appeared for Mr and Mrs Jay. The application was formally listed as an application for permission to appeal (with appeal to follow if permission is given).

5. Mr Jolly is the claimant in an action for rectification of the register pursuant to section 82 of the Land Registration Act 1925 against Mr and Mrs Jay. The action concerns Mr Jolly's former matrimonial home, Inglewood, Virginia Water, Surrey ('the property') which was sold to a Mr and Mrs White and then on 4 December 1996 to Mr and Mrs Jay. These transactions have been the subject of a considerable amount of litigation as a result of Mr Jolly's desire to recover title to the property. We need not summarise all the litigation that has taken place but only some of the salient events.

6. The sale of the property to the Whites was made tinder an order of the Staines County Court made in December 1994. The details of what then happened do not matter for the purposes of this judgment. Mr Jolly took proceedings for possession under RSC Ord 113, first against persons unknown, and then against the Whites, which were struck out with costs. Mr Jolly then made an application for rectification of the register, which was refused on 14 November 1996. The Whites had been registered as proprietors with effect from 29 May 1996. Meanwhile Mr Jolly sought permission to appeal against an order dismissing a claim he had made in relation to the prior sale of the property to the Whites' predecessors. The appeal was heard by the Court of Appeal on 29 January 1997 and dismissed.

7. In earlier proceedings between Mr and Mrs Jolly, the court declared that the property was held on 50/50 shares by Mr and Mrs Jolly. Mr Jolly appealed against that order but his appeal was unsuccessful. Mr Jolly also pursued other claims in connection with the sale of the property. He claimed damages against his former wife's solicitors for failing to pass over the full sum of monies due to him with some success, but some of his other claims have been struck out. He has received monies from the sale of the property but claims that not all of his share has been paid to him.

8. On 18th June 2001 Master Bragge made an order striking out Mr Jolly's claim in the present proceedings and ordered Mr Jolly to pay Mr and Mrs Jay their costs. These costs have now been paid. Mr Jolly filed a notice of appeal at the High Court against that order, which he duly served on Mr and Mrs Jay's solicitors pursuant to CPR 52.4(3).

9. The matter then came before Neuberger J for permission to appeal. Neuberger J refused permission to appeal on paper on 25 September 2001, giving reasons. On 3 October Mr Jolly made a request for this decision to be reconsidered at an oral hearing and served a copy of his request on Mr and Mrs Jay's solicitors at the same time (see CPR 52 PD para 4.14).

10. The High Court informed the parties on 4 October of the date fixed for the renewed application (19 October) in the following terms:

'The attendance of the appellant is required.

The respondent(s) may attend or submit written representations before the hearing but will not usually be awarded the costs of doing so.

If a respondent submits written representations or other written material it must be served on the applicant (or his/her solicitor if any) at least two clear days before the hearing.'

11. There is no provision in CPR Part 52 or its practice direction for a notice of this kind to be sent to respondents. CPR 52 PD para 4.15 provides:

'Notice of the hearing need not be given to the respondent unless the court so directs. The appeal court will usually so direct if the appellant is asking for a remedy against the respondent pending the appeal.'

12. The only other provision of CPR Part 52 or its Practice Direction which touches on the possibility that the needs of the respondent are to be accommodated at a renewed hearing of an application for permission to appeal is paragraph 4.16 of the Practice Direction which provides:

'If notice of the hearing is to be given to the respondent, the appellant must supply the respondent with a copy of the bundle (see paragraph 5.16) within 7 days of being notified, or such other period as the court may direct. The costs of providing that bundle shall be borne by the appellant initially, but will form part of the costs of the permission application.'

13. On 16 October (that is to say, on the final day allowed by the High Court's letter) Mr and Mrs Jay served a skeleton argument, settled by counsel, and they were represented by counsel at the hearing before Neuberger J three days later. The skeleton argument ended in the following terms:

'In the event that permission to appeal is not granted, [the defendants] ask the Court to award their costs of attending in that this is necessary to ensure that the Court receives an accurate picture of the matter.'

14. Neuberger J gave a short reasoned judgment dismissing the application. During the course of it he said:

'His application is opposed by Mr and Mrs Jay, who appear through counsel, Ms Cheryl Jones, who has provided me with a skeleton argument, as has Mr Jolly. The position of a respondent to an application for permission to appeal, particularly when that application, having been dismissed, is renewed orally, is somewhat unclear and has not been worked out by the courts. Mr Jolly suggests that it was inappropriate for Mr and Mrs Jay to be represented on this application and to make submissions to me. I do not think those criticisms are justified. The position of a respondent on an application of which he or she has notice, such as the present, namely a renewed application for permission to appeal, is difficult. Some respondents let matters take their course. Some respondents think it right that they should be there with a view to knocking out the appeal if they can. The problem is particularly acute where the applicant is a litigant in person, even a litigant – or perhaps I should say especially a litigant – as persistent and as expert as Mr Jolly. In some cases the court thinks the respondent's appearance is unhelpful; in other cases it thinks it is helpful; in other cases it thinks it is necessary. In the present case I have certainly found Ms Jones' skeleton helpful, and I think that any criticism (and to be fair it was not a very strong or bitter criticism, but criticism there has been) of Mr and Mrs Jay's legal advisers in representing them today, is misconceived.'

After judgment was delivered, the respondents asked for their costs.

15. Although they had not served a schedule of costs, they limited their application to the sum of £350 plus VAT, being counsel's fee for settling the skeleton argument and appearing at the hearing. We do not have a transcript of the judge's reasons for making his order for costs in this sum, but no doubt he followed the line of thought evidenced in the passage from his judgment which we have quoted.

16. It is now settled that this court has no jurisdiction to entertain an application for permission to appeal from a decision of an appeal court (see CPR 52(3)(b) for the meaning of this phrase) refusing permission to appeal (*Riniker v University College London* [2001] 1 WLR 13, a decision founded on the clear language of section 54(4) of the Access to Justice Act 1999). When Mr Jolly filed his notice of appeal Mr Jolly was told by the staff of the Civil Appeals Office that in their view the Court of Appeal had no jurisdiction to entertain his appeal, but he insisted that his notice of appeal should be set down. He repeated this stance when he was told formally by letter a little later that the court had no jurisdiction. In this letter specific reference was made to section 54(4) of the 1999 Act.

17. When we asked Mr Jolly to explain why he had persisted in requiring his application to be heard by the court, he referred us to CPR 52.13(2), which permits this court to give permission to appeal if it considers that the appeal would raise an important point of principle or practice. He said that at least some of the issues determined by Master Bragge and Neuberger J could be so categorised. In making this submission, Mr Jolly had overlooked the concluding words of CPR 52.1 (1), which reads:

'Permission is required from the Court of Appeal for any appeal from that court from a decision of a county court or the High Court which was *itself made on appeal.*' (Emphasis added).

18. These words, which allow for the possibility of a second appeal to this court from a decision of an appeal court on a substantive appeal, are to be contrasted with the clear language of CPR 52 PD para 4.8:

> 'There is no appeal from a decision of the appeal court, made at an oral hearing, to allow or refuse permission to appeal to that court. See section 54(4) of the Access to Justice Act 1999 and rule 52.3(3) and (4).'

19. We are told by the Civil Appeals Office that Mr Jolly is by no means the only litigant in person who has insisted in recent months in pursuing such an application to an oral hearing in this court notwithstanding that the court manifestly has no jurisdiction to entertain it. In future the Civil Appeals Office should not list such applications, which represent a complete waste of the resources of the court (see CPR 1.1(2)(e)). Any case of doubt should be referred on paper to one of the lords justices who supervise the administrative business of the court.

20. When Mr Jolly was given notice on 30 January 2002 of Lord Justice Brooke's directions for the hearing (see paras 3 and 4 above) he was once again told that the court had no jurisdiction to entertain an application for permission to appeal the substantive part of the judge's order. He was told, however, that the court did have power to deal with the judge's order for costs (see *Riniker v University College London (Practice Note)* [2001] 1 WLR 13, 16 at para 13). On 4 February he decided to 'withdraw' his notice of appeal. He therefore sent a draft consent order to Mr and Mrs Jay's solicitors (who had by now incurred costs by briefing counsel for the hearing) to the effect that his notice of appeal should be dismissed with no order as to costs. They told him that they would not consent unless provision was made for their costs, which they estimated at £2,000 (including the costs of the hearing). Mr Jolly told them that this figure was 'disproportionate to the issue directed to be heard'. He then offered to alter the consent form so that it would read 'ordinary costs to be taxed if not agreed'.

21. He discussed this matter with them over the telephone at about 11.30am on 6 February, the day before the hearing. They refused to agree to his offer (although they appreciated that their clients would be at risk of any costs incurred subsequent to this conversation). They had already briefed counsel for the hearing and they wished to use the opportunity afforded by the hearing to canvas with the court the possibility of their clients obtaining some form of relief from Mr Jolly, so that they could pursue the sale of their house free from the expense and trouble previously inflicted on them by Mr Jolly in connection with its purchase. They therefore required Mr Jolly to agree that he would not bring any further claims against Mr and Mrs Jay or their successors in title in connection with the property. Alternatively, they hoped that the court would impress finality on Mr Jolly.

22. Since the notice of appeal was not dismissed by consent, the application had to come before the court. Mr Jolly stood by his offer. At the sitting of the court the respondents, for their part, served on him a document described as a 'request' addressed to the court to make what they called an 'extended' *Grepe v Loam* order (see *Ebert v Venvil* [2000] Ch 484) against Mr Jolly.

23. Since the application was listed before us in order that we could consider the appropriateness of the costs order made by the judge (see para 3 above) we heard submissions from the parties on this question, notwithstanding the fact that Mr Jolly had never challenged that costs order as such and was standing by his offer to pay the respondents' standard costs of this appeal, in so far as they had been incurred prior to 11.30am on 6 February.

24. Ms Jones told us in this context that the notice of appeal filed in the High Court had contained significant inaccuracies. The court was led to believe, contrary to the fact, that the claimant's notice of rectification may still have been entered on the title at the date of the purchase. In fact, although it was present on the title when contracts were exchanged, it had been removed by a direction of the assistant land registrar before the purchase was completed. The notice also suggested incorrectly that the Staines County Court had found that the original purchasers failed to complete and had not acquired title or possession.

25. Mr Jolly refuted any suggestion that he intended to mislead the court by any inaccuracies in his appellant's notice in the High Court. If there were inaccuracies, the reason for them was, in part at least, that the respondents had failed to produce the relevant documents to him. Moreover, the respondents could have minimised costs simply by writing to the court to correct his errors. They did not need to attend by counsel. He also complained that they had lodged a bundle of documents with the court without giving him a copy or telling him what the bundle contained, although it later transpired that the bundle did not contain any documents which were not familiar to him, being the bundle used by Mr and Mrs Jay at the hearing before the Master.

26. Ms Jones argued that her clients were entitled to attend the hearing before the judge in order to prevent the litigation progressing any further. Their attendance was justified as the matter was of exceptional concern to them (it involved the potential loss of their home), and because of the inaccuracies in the appellant's notice and the fact that Mr Jolly acted in person. She reminded us that in his judgment the judge had said that he found counsel's skeleton argument helpful and that any criticism of Mr and Mrs Jay's legal advisers was misconceived.

27. She submitted that the judge was entitled to make the costs order which he did. Mr Jolly's application was unjustified and was wholly unsuccessful. By seeking an oral hearing he took the risk of an adverse costs order. She accepted

that where a respondent was entitled to attend a hearing but not required to do so, the general rule that costs should follow the event would not apply with the same force.

28. As we have already said (see paras 16 and 20 above), this court has no jurisdiction to entertain an appeal against the judge's refusal of permission to appeal, but there is jurisdiction to entertain an application for permission to appeal against the order for costs made by the judge on the hearing for permission. A judge may make an order of this kind because the respondent has been given notice of the application pursuant to a specific direction by the court, or, as in this case, because the court has sent him, as a matter of routine, notice of the time, date and venue of the hearing. Alternatively, the respondent may appear on the application simply as a result of learning that an application is to be heard at that time or watching the court lists.

29. There were at least two existing models on which the draftsmen of CPR Part 52 and its practice direction might have drawn when making provision for the participation of the respondent, if any, in an appeal court's consideration of the now almost universal requirement of permission to appeal.

30. They could have drawn on the model afforded by RSC Order 73 rule 2(1)(d) in arbitration proceedings when a would-be appellant seeks leave to appeal to the High Court from an award by arbitrators pursuant to section 1(2) of the Arbitration Act 1979. In such cases the rule prescribes that the application must be made by originating motion to a single judge in court. In *The Oinoussian Virtue* [1981] 2 All ER 887 Robert Goff J said at p 896 that as a matter of principle if leave to appeal was refused the normal order would be that the applicants should pay the costs.

31. Another model was afforded by the rules made under section 289 of the Town and Country Planning Act 1990 (as amended) which introduced for the first time a rule that the leave of the High Court was required before a challenge could be made to a decision dismissing an appeal against an enforcement notice under the planning laws. RSC Order 94 rule 12(2) required the application, with supporting documents, to be served on certain persons (such as the Secretary of State) identified in rule 13(5). Rule 12(3) provides:

> 'Any person served with the application shall be entitled to appear and be heard.'

In *R v Secretary of State for Wales ex p Rozhon* [1993] CAT 27th April 1993 (summarised in [1994] COD 111) this court held, as a general rule, that the costs of an application under O94 r 12 should follow the event.

32. It is noteworthy that Rose LJ contrasted that procedure (transcript p 10) with the procedure then prescribed by RSC O 53. After saying that applications

for leave to apply for judicial review were commonly dealt with on paper without any oral hearing, he continued:

> 'Furthermore, Order 53 applications are made ex parte and *a respondent is in general unaware* that such an application has been made unless and until leave is granted. He has no right under the rules either to appear on the application or to serve evidence.' (Emphasis added)

33. This citation gives a hint of the mischief which CPR 52.4(3) and CPR 52 PD para 4.14 were introduced to cure. After the requirement for permission to appeal had been extended, and before the reforms to the appeals procedures that took effect in May 2000, respondents to appeals often had no idea that a favourable judgment had been appealed until they were served with the notice of appeal some months later. This defect was identified in the Review of the Court of Appeal (Civil Division) ('the Bowman Review'), September 1997, Chapter 7, paras 11–13, where the authors expressed the opinion that the position was unfair to respondents. They did not, however, suggest that respondents should take part in the processes leading up to the grant of refusal of permission to appeal apart from advancing the idea (Chapter 7, para 27 and recommendation 79) that respondents should be allowed seven days in which they might submit any reasons why leave should not be granted. They said:

> 'Such submissions should not be required, the respondent being entitled to rely on the decision in the lower court and the judgment as his or her submission. If he or she does make a submission, the costs should not be recoverable. It seems illogical, however, to prohibit such a submission, especially as respondents already have the right to apply to have leave to appeal rescinded, where leave to appeal has been granted ex parte (i.e. in the absence of the respondents).'

34. This recommendation was not accepted, and it may be that the appropriate authorities will wish to revisit this topic in the light of experience accumulated since the new procedural regime was introduced. In this context, although we appreciate that the judicial review regime is different in significant respects, it is noteworthy that CPR 54.8(4) and 54.12(5), and CPR 54 PD paras 8.5 and 8.6, introduced a year later, contain provisions that do address this question directly.

35. Given that the aim of the new procedure appears to be to ensure that the respondent is informed of any landmarks in the appeal process (such as the filing of the notice of appeal, or the filing of a request to reconsider a refusal of permission) but is not entitled to take part in the process by which the appellant seeks permission to appeal (unless there is a specific direction of the court to that effect) we believe that it would be helpful at this stage of our judgment to set out the whole of the statutory scheme with this point in mind.

36. Appeals in civil cases to the county court, the High Court and the Court of Appeal are now governed by a single rule, CPR 52, and the practice direction

supplementing that rule. CPR Part 52 provides for respondents to be notified of applications for permission to appeal. By CPR 52.4(3) an appeal notice is to be served on each respondent not later than seven days after it is filed, unless the court orders otherwise. CPR 52 PD para 5.21 specifies that a sealed copy of the appellant's notice is to be served including any skeleton argument.

37. CPR 52 PD para 5.22 explains the role of the respondent, when served, in the following terms:

> 'Unless the Court otherwise directs a respondent need not take any action when served with an appellant's notice until such time as notification is given to him that permission to appeal has been given.'

38. Where an appellant first applies for permission to appeal, he is not required to serve copies of his bundles on the respondent: CPR 52 PD para 5.24.

39. Paragraphs 4.11 to 4.14 of CPR 52 PD deal with the consideration of permission to appeal without a hearing and require the parties to be notified of the decision given on paper. Paragraphs 4.13 and 4.14 are in the following terms:

> '4.13 If permission is refused without a hearing the parties will be notified of that decision with the reasons for it. The decision is subject to the appellant's right to have it reconsidered at an oral hearing. This may be before the same judge.
>
> 4.14 A request for the decision to be reconsidered at an oral hearing must be filed at the appeal court within 7 days after service of the notice that permission has been refused. A copy of the request must be served by the appellant on the respondent at the same time ...'

Paragraphs 4.15 and 4.16 apply to the permission hearing. We have set out their provisions in paragraphs 10 and 11 above and need not repeat them here. CPR 52 PD does not deal specifically with the costs of the permission hearing.

40. This practice direction, however, does envisage that an order for costs may be made at the hearing of an application for permission to appeal, since paragraph 14.1 makes provision for the summary assessment of the costs of a hearing of an application for permission to appeal at which the respondent is present. CPR 52 PD para 14.2 requires the parties attending such a hearing to be prepared to deal with the summary assessment.

41. Reverting to CPR 52 PD para 4.15, research carried out by the staff of the Civil Appeals Office shows that there is no uniform practice of notifying a respondent of the time fixed for any hearing in open court for permission to appeal. While the High Court in London gives notice to respondents (in the absence of any special direction by the court) in the terms in which Mr and Mrs Jay were notified, as set out in paragraph 10 above, other courts do not provide this information to respondents, or they provide it to respondents only

if, for example, a stay of the order of the lower court is sought. While, of course. individual cases may require to be deal with in some different way, we consider that civil courts should at least have the same starting point. Otherwise more favourable treatment may be given to respondents in some parts of the country than in others. We invite the appropriate authorities to consider whether the practice should be made uniform, and if so what the common starting point should be.

42. Against this background of the rules and the practice direction, it appears to us to be desirable that we should explain the nature of the respondent's potential involvement in the preliminary stages of the new appeals process, because this has given rise to a good many misunderstandings in the past.

43. At the permission stage, CPR Part 52 provides that, except in the case of second appeals, the court should give permission to appeal if (but only if) it considers that there is a real prospect of success on the appeal. or that there is some other reason for the appeal to be heard (CPR 52.3)(6)). In the case of a second appeal to the Court of Appeal, the appeal must raise an important point of principle or practice, or there must be some other compelling reason for the Court of Appeal to hear it (CPR 52.13).

44. Accordingly, a respondent should only file submissions at this early stage if they are addressed to the point that the appeal would not meet the relevant threshold test or tests, or if there is some material inaccuracy in the papers placed before the court. By this phrase we mean an inaccuracy which might reasonably be expected to lead the court to grant permission when it would not have done so if it had received correct information on the point.

45. If, on the other hand, the respondent wishes to advance submissions on the merits of the appeal (as opposed to the question whether it will pass the relatively low threshold tests for permission) the appropriate time for him to do so is at the appeal itself, if the matter gets that far. In general it is not desirable that respondents should make submissions on the merits at the permission stage, because this may well lead to delay in dealing with the permission application and take up the resources of the appeal court unnecessarily.

46. Respondents will not be prejudiced at the appeal itself by having refrained from filing or making submissions at the permission stage, since this is essentially a 'without notice' procedure. Attention should be paid, however, in this context to CPR 52.9(3): where a party was present at a hearing at which permission to appeal was granted, he may not subsequently apply for an order that the court should exercise any of its powers under sub-paragraphs (1)(b) or (1)(c) of that rule.

47. Where an application for permission is to be determined on paper, any submission from the respondent must be in writing. Even in the event of an oral hearing a respondent should consider whether he can make his submission

equally well in writing, particularly as he may not be allowed the costs of his attendance at the hearing. In very many cases a written submission will be sufficient, given the preliminary nature of the application and the fact that the respondent has no entitlement to address the court unless the court has made a specific written direction that he may do so, or grants him such permission at the hearing.

48. If a respondent applies for an order for costs in his favour, it is against this background, pending any further assistance that may be given in a Practice Direction, that the court should determine whether any such order should be made at all, and if an order is made, whether it should cover the costs of attending the hearing (as opposed to the costs which would be appropriate to cover a concise written submission). On every occasion, of course, the award of costs will be a matter for the discretion of the individual judge.

49. So far as the present application to this court is concerned, no particular difficulty arises because the respondents prepared their representations following a specific direction of this court. Once Mr Jolly decided to withdraw his application and offered to pay the respondents' costs on a standard basis, his liability to pay their costs terminated. The respondents were not then entitled at his expense to insist on the matter being heard in open court, or to require him to undertake or agree not to bring any further claim against them or their successors in title as owners of the property. They should therefore pay Mr Jolly's costs after that time. For this reason we announced at the end of the hearing that the application was dismissed on terms that the appellant should pay the respondents' costs of the application down to 12.00 noon on 6 February 2002, and that the respondent should pay the appellant's costs incurred thereafter.

50. So far as the respondents' request for a *Grepe v Loam* order was concerned, we directed that (if so advised) they should be at liberty in these proceedings to issue an application for such an order in the Chancery Division.

51. Finally, we have been invited by the Civil Appeal Office to clarify one further matter which is giving rise to difficulties in practice. As we have already said, if a lower appeal court refuses permission to appeal, there is no right of appeal against its ruling. There is, however, a right to appeal against any order for costs (or some other ancillary order, such as an order refusing an adjournment) made on that occasion. The question has arisen whether an appeal against such an order, when made by a circuit judge, lies to a High Court judge or to the Court of Appeal.

52. Such an appeal lies to a High Court judge as a 'first appeal' (see the Access to Justice Act 1999 (Destination of Appeals) Order 2000, article 2). It is not excluded from the ordinary appeal route by Article 4 (which is concerned with appeals against final decisions, an expression which does not embrace an order

made at a permission hearing) nor by Article 5 (which is entitled 'appeals where decision itself was made on appeal'). In the circumstances we are now considering, the circuit judge is not making a decision 'on hearing the appeal' (being the language of Article 5 (b) of the Order). He is making a decision in the course of refusing to hear an appeal.

SARAH LLOYD JONES AND OTHERS V T MOBILE (UK) LTD.

A2.14

[2003] EWCA Civ 1162

COURT OF APPEAL, CIVIL DIVISION

KENNEDY and BROOKE LJJ and HOLMAN J

31 JULY 2003

REASONS FOR JUDGMENT: APPROVED BY THE COURT FOR HANDING DOWN (SUBJECT TO EDITORIAL CORRECTIONS)

Lord Justice Kennedy

1. This is a defendant's appeal from a decision of Judge Morgan sitting at Kingston County Court who on 10 January 2003 resolved the preliminary issue in favour of the claimants.

Irregular Appeal

2. Unfortunately, after judgment was given in the County Court the matter did not proceed as it should have done. The parties, and in particular the present appellant, clearly recognised that permission to appeal was required, but it does not seem to have been appreciated that:

(1) an application for permission to appeal can only be made to the lower court at the hearing at which the decision to be appealed was made, or to the Appeal Court (CPR 52.3(2)).

(2) an Appellant's Notice must be filed within (a) such period as may be directed by the lower court, or (b) where the court makes no such direction, 14 days after the date of the decision of the lower court that the appellant wishes to appeal (CPR 52.4(2)).

(3) where a final order is made in relation to a preliminary issue in a case assigned to the multi-track the Court of Appeal has sole appellate jurisdiction (see Access to Justice Act 1999 (Destination of Appeals)

Order 2000 SI 4/1071 (as amended) Articles (1) (2) and (3)a and the judgment of Brooke LJ in *Tanfern Ltd v Cameron-MacDonald* [2001] 1 WLR 1131 at paragraph 17).

3. On 10 January 2003 Judge Morgan adjourned the question of permission to appeal to the 4 February. The appellant's solicitors then wrote to the judge's clerk on 14 January to clarify whether the next hearing would be 'the hearing' for the purposes of CPR 52.3(2) and were informed, following consultation with the judge, that it would be. On 4 February 2003 Judge Morgan granted permission to appeal, but, as he was never asked for any extension of time in which to serve the Appellant's Notice, the grant of permission was of no real value.

4. On 18 February 2003 the appellant's solicitors attempted to file the Appellant's Notice at the Court of Appeal Office, and were rightly told that it was out of time, it should have been filed by 24 January 2003 (i.e. within 14 days of the decision which the appellant wanted to appeal). An ineffective attempt was then made to proceed as though this were an appeal to the High Court, and on 26 March 2003 Aikens J at Reading made an order which on the face of it granted permission to appeal and referred the matter to this court pursuant to CPR 52.14. As I have indicated, he had no jurisdiction to act in this case because the Court of Appeal had sole appellate jurisdiction.

5. Thus, when the matter was listed before us there was no effective appeal in existence, but two judges had identified a point of law they considered to be worthy of the attention of this court, and both sides had prepared in the usual way for a contested hearing. We had before us what purported to be an Appellant's Notice, a Respondent's Notice, skeleton arguments and so forth. If the appeal could not proceed the Respondents could hold on to the advantages of having succeeded in the lower court, but otherwise they were not going to be prejudiced if we made such orders as were necessary to ensure that the appeal was properly before us. Mr Humphreys, for the appellants, urged us to adopt that course, and we agreed to do so on condition that so far as the appellants are concerned the costs of the appeal should be regarded as irrecoverable. Mr Hall-Taylor rightly pointed out that in order to obtain permission to appeal from this court the appellants need an extension of time, and the application for permission must be made in the Appellant's Notice. In order to enable the Appellant's Notice to be put into proper form we extended the time for filing it to close of business on Monday 21 July 2003. Meanwhile we granted permission to appeal, made all necessary abridgements of time, and on the basis of the existing documents proceeded to hear the appeal.

Facts

...

Law

…

Grounds of appeal

…

Respondent's notice

…

Conclusion

…

Lord Justice Brooke:

18. I am only adding this short judgment of my own because it is clear that difficulties are still arising in relation to the destination of appeals three years after the new regime in CPR Part 52 came into force, and because there are features of the conditional order we made when we granted permission to appeal out of time to which I wish to draw attention.

19. On 25 June 2002 District Judge Letts, sitting in the Epsom County Court, allocated this action to the multi-track pursuant to CPR 26.5 and ordered the trial of three preliminary issues, as Kennedy LJ explains in paragraph 6 of his judgment, which I have read in draft. The district judge set a procedural timetable leading up to that trial, and ordered that directions for the conduct of the remaining issues be considered upon the determination of the preliminary issues by the trial judge. This was the trial which Judge Morgan conducted on 9 December 2002, and it is his order on one of those preliminary issues which is the subject of this appeal. The question then arises: does the appeal lie to a High Court judge or to the Court of Appeal?

20. The answer to this question lies in the Access to Justice Act 1999 (Destination of Appeals) Order 2000, the general effect of which is reproduced in paras 2A. 1–2A.6 of the Practice Direction to CPR Part 52. Anyone who studies these provisions with care will see that a decision of a county court will lie to the High Court unless articles 3(2), 4 or 5 of the order apply. In this case the relevant provision is article 4 which states:

> '4. An appeal shall lie to the Court of Appeal where the decision to be appealed is a final decision–
> (a) in a claim allocated to the multi-track under rule … 26.5 of the Civil Procedure Rules 1998.'

21. Article 1 provides, so far as material:

> '1(2)(c) "final decision" means a decision of a county court that would

finally determine (subject to any possible appeal ...) the entire proceedings whichever way the court decided the issues before it.

(3) A decision of a court shall be treated as a final decision where it–
  (a) is made at the conclusion of part of ... a trial which had been split into parts; and
  (b) would, if made at the conclusion of that ... trial, be a final decision under paragraph (2)(c).'

22. In *Tanfern Ltd v Cameron-MacDonald (Practice Note)* [2000] 1 WLR 1311, 1315, I explained the effect of article 1(3) in these terms (at para 17):

'... This means that if a judge makes a final decision on any aspect of a claim, such as limitation, or on part of a claim which has been directed to be heard separately, this is a final decision within the meaning of this provision. [Counsel] told us that there was concern in some quarters that parts of a final decision might be subjected to one avenue of appeal and other parts might have a different avenue of appeal, but the language of article 1(3) appears to preclude this.'

23. In paragraph 18 of that judgment I went on to distinguish between decisions on issues in a trial which have been directed to be heard separately, and decisions on strike-out or summary judgment applications:

'Orders striking out the proceedings or a statement of case and orders giving summary judgment under CPR 24 are not final decisions because they are not decisions that would finally determine the entire proceedings whichever way the court decided the issues before it.'

24. Practitioners who rely only on the White Book for their procedural law will not have obtained the full flavour of what I said in my judgment in *Tanfern*. An abbreviated summary of this passage is given in the third main paragraph on page 1256 of Part 1 of the 2003 Edition. This is why I am returning to this topic now. There is a rather fuller treatment of the topic in Volume 1 of the Civil Court Practice 2002 (the Green Book) at pp 907–8.

25. For the purposes of article 1(2)(c) and article 1(3) the relevant proceedings are the proceedings which relate to the issue whether notice of objection was served by the claimants within three months of completion of the installation of the apparatus. In the event Judge Morgan decided that issue in favour of the claimants, and he determined it finally in the sense that the defendants could not have reopened it when the eventual trial on the merits took place. If he had decided it in favour of the defendants, that would be the end of the action. In either case the dissatisfied party's only method of redress was by way of appeal.

26. The other matter to which I wish to refer is the direction we made to the effect that the appellants might be permitted to appeal (with an extension of time of five months being granted for this purpose) on condition that they

should not be entitled to the costs of the appeal even if they succeeded. One of the reasons which prompted us to make this order was that the defendants (who were at mercy) are a very large corporation who regarded a decision of the Court of Appeal on this issue as so important to their business that their solicitors incurred costs of nearly £50,000 in prosecuting this relatively straightforward one day appeal, whereas the claimants were a group of individual objectors to the installation at Kingswood who had succeeded on a preliminary issue and still had to face the costs of the main trial.

27. This is the third occasion within four weeks on which this court has used its power under CPR 3.1(2)(a) to make an order subject to conditions in a manner that is out of the ordinary. In *Price v Price* [2003] EWCA Civ 888 a claimant was permitted to serve particulars of claim 17 months out of time on condition that he limited his case to the evidence that was available to him at the time he should have served the particulars. In *Beck v Ministry of Defence* [2003] EWCA Civ 1043 a defendant was permitted to rely on a second, substituted, expert in a personal injuries action on condition that he disclosed the report he had obtained from the first expert (on which the claimant would be entitled to rely if he wished: see CPR 35.11). And now we have granted permission to appeal out of time to a defendant who wished us to determine a point of law of general importance to its business on condition that it cannot recover the costs of the appeal if successful.

28. I mention these matters because this new power to make conditional orders gives a court a greater flexibility to make orders that are both proportionate and just than used to be the case when the court's powers were limited to saying 'yes' or 'no' in response to applications of this kind. As I said in *Price v Price*, an earlier example of the same trend is the decision of this court in *Walsh v Misseldine* [2000] CPLR 201 in which Stuart-Smith LJ and I declined to strike out a claim which had been subject to considerable delay on condition that the claimant was limited to prosecuting his claim on the basis of his case as it stood before the long period of delay commenced. This unconventional use of the court's powers to make a conditional order in the early days of the Civil Procedure Rules escaped the notice of the editors of the White Book and the Green Book. This is the reason why I am drawing attention now to the valuable weapon that CPR 3.1(2)(a) has added to the court's armoury of powers.

29. As to the main substance of the defendants' appeal, I agree with Kennedy LJ, and there is nothing I wish to add.

Mr Justice Holman:

...

41. For these reasons, and those given by my Lord, I would allow this appeal and answer no to preliminary issue 3(b) in the order of District Judge Letts of 25 June 2002.

KOLLER V SECRETARY OF STATE FOR THE HOME DEPARTMENT

A2.15

[2001] EWCA Civ 1267

COURT OF APPEAL (CIVIL DIVISION)

BROOKE, TUCKEY and LAWS LJJ

26 JULY 2001

Immigration - Asylum - Racial discrimination - Fear of persecution - Sufficiency of protection - Skinheads effecting acts of violence towards applicant and family - Applicant claiming fear of persecution - Immigration Appeal Tribunal finding country of origin able to provide sufficient protection if applicant and dependents returned to country - Whether IAT in error.

Lord Justice Brooke

[1] This is an application by Josef Koller for permission to appeal against a determination of the Immigration Appeal Tribunal ('the IAT') dated 5 February 2001, whereby it dismissed his appeal against a decision of a Special Adjudicator dated 9 October 2000, who had dismissed his appeal against a refusal by the Secretary of State in a letter dated 15 February 2000 of his application for asylum, which he made on 16 October 1998 when he arrived in this country from Calais accompanied by four dependants.

[2] The order of the Immigration Appeal Tribunal refusing permission to appeal was received by those representing the appellant on 18 April 2001. This appeal was not filed in the Court of Appeal office until 25 May 2001. We are told that the reason was that counsel was instructed to prepare the grounds of appeal on 26 April 2001 but he delayed until 24 May 2001 before the grounds were sent to those who have the carriage of the appeal.

[3] If the applicant were to be granted permission to appeal this would be his third appeal. The application has been listed before a three-judge court this morning in order that we can consider in the context of immigration appeals certain observations recently made by Hale LJ, with whom Clarke LJ and Butterfield J agreed, in *Cooke v Secretary of State for Social Security* [2001] EWCA Civ 734 about the criteria for the grant of permission to appeal to this court from decisions taken by appeal tribunals in specialist fields of law.

[4] It is first necessary to say something about the facts of the case ...

...

[24] I turn, therefore, to a matter of more general interest. In *Cooke v Secretary of State for Social Security* [2001] EWCA Civ 734. Hale LJ, with whom

Clarke LJ and Butterfield J agreed, set out certain principles in relation to appeals from expert tribunals which themselves represented a second layer of appeal in a specialist tribunal structure. At para 15, referring to social security law, she said:

'Firstly, this is a highly specialized area of laws which many lawyers – indeed, I would suspect most lawyers – rarely encounter in practice. Secondly, there is an independent two-tier appellate structure ... After the initial decision there is a fresh hearing before a specialist tribunal which is chaired by a lawyer and has an appropriate balance of experience and expertise amongst its members. After that there is an appeal on a point of law to a highly expert and specialized legally qualified body, the Social Security Commissioners. Thirdly, it is essential that the tribunal structure is sufficiently expert to be able to take an independent and robust view, particularly in cases where the government agency has gone wrong. It must be in a position to see through what the relevant sponsoring department is saying when he is arguing the case.'

[25] In those circumstances, she said, the Court of Appeal should be slow to grant permission for further appeal from the commissioners. She added:

'The point is also relevant for other similar appeal structures, such as those of the Employment Tribunals and Employment Appeal Tribunal, those of the Adjudicators and Immigration Appeal Tribunals, those of the Leasehold Valuation Tribunals and the Lands Tribunal. However, there are significant differences between this system and those which may affect matters,'

and, she continued:

'I would therefore confine my views ... to this particular tribunal structure, while expecting that similar arguments may be appropriate if they arise elsewhere.'

[26] I do not consider that the IAT is comparable in this context to the Social Security Commissioners. Appeals to the IAT often raise complex issues of fact as well as difficult questions of law. The law is still developing, as is evidenced by the number of major appeals coming to this court and to the House of Lords in recent years. The IAT has a complement of 16 full-time legal chairmen, and 20 part-time chairmen also assist in its work, quite apart from the lay members. It has been the experience of this court that the determination of some panels of the IAT must be of uncertain quality.

[27] The most in my judgment that can be said is that:
(1) Properly reasoned well-structured judgments of the IAT will normally mark the end of the road unless there is some uncertainty about the applicable law.

(2) This court will be reluctant to permit a second appeal if the IAT set out the relevant principles of law correctly and set out the facts clearly before applying the law to the facts.

(3) If the IAT refuses permission on appeal and a single Lord Justice also refuses permission, the Legal Services Commission should be slow to grant a certificate granting an oral hearing, representing a third attempt.

(4) It would be helpful if both the IAT and immigration adjudicators took care in the way they structured their judgments, so that a prospective appellate court or tribunal can see swiftly whether there is an issue or issues which wanted an appeal. The determinations should not be over-long, and it should not be felt to be necessary to cover every single argument or issue, however minor, in a determination. What is important is that the applicant should feel that proper attention has been paid to the main points he wishes to raise, and that an appellate court should be able to understand the reasoning process and should have little difficulty in satisfying itself that the correct principles of law have been applied (if they have).

(5) In all this, I have not forgotten the words of Lord Bridge in *Bugdaycay v Secretary of State for the Home Department* [1987] AC 514, [1987] 1 All ER 940, to the effect that, in cases touching on fundamental rights, courts and tribunals should apply 'the most anxious scrutiny'.

[28] So far as the delay is concerned, Mr Jorro did not attempt to justify the delay, but he urged us to consider that the appeal had sufficient merit to warrant an extension of time. In my judgment this proposed appeal does not have the merits which are contended for, and it would be wrong to extend time.

[29] This application is therefore dismissed.

Lord Justice Tuckey

[30] I agree.

Lord Justice Laws

[31] I also agree.

Application dismissed.

(*Transcript: Smith Bernal*)

MILWARD V THREE RIVERS DISTRICT COUNCIL

A2.16

COURT OF APPEAL (CIVIL DIVISION)

HENRY LJ

25 OCTOBER 2000

Civil Procedure – Application for permission to appeal out of time – Whether extension of time can be granted to take advantage of change in law – Whether delay in application justified – Chances of appeal succeeding if permission given – Appeal would be prejudicial to Respondent.

Lord Justice Henry

[1] This is an application for permission to appeal out of time against a finding made by His Honour Judge Simpson at the Mayor's and City of London Court on 9 August 1999 in the liability part of a split trial that the Three Rivers District Council had been negligent and were consequently liable for the damage sustained by the claimant, Mrs Milward, on 4 March 1995. The nature of their negligence was in not gritting an icy road which the highway authority, the county council, had instructed them to grit.

[2] The reason for the application is that on 15 June this year the House of Lords in a case called *Goodes v East Sussex County Council* [2000] 3 All ER 603, [2000] 1 WLR 1356 reversed three Court of Appeal authorities, including the Court of Appeal in that case, to hold that a highway authority's absolute duty to maintain the highway under s 41(1) of the Highways Act 1980 did not (and I quote from the headnote):

> '... include a duty to prevent the formation of ice or remove the accumulation of snow on the road.'

[3] The application for permission to appeal out of time is presumably based on the District Council's hope of reversing the finding of negligence and of liability against them.

[4] The dates of the various relevant decisions are as follows. On 21 December 1998 the Court of Appeal in the case of *Goodes* granted permission to appeal their decision to the House of Lords. On 9 August 1999 Mrs Milward obtained judgment on liability. On 15 June 2000 the appeal in *Goodes* was allowed by the House of Lords. On 17 July 2000 the defendant borough council, served their application for an extension of time and permission to appeal Mrs Milward's judgment on liability at the court. This application was made nearly a year out of time taking time as running from the date of the judgment in Mrs Milward's favour.

[5] Before coming to the facts, I must deal with one procedural matter. The decision appealed against was a decision on liability after a split trial. That decision is clearly a final decision within the meaning of the Access to Justice Act 1999 (Destination of Appeals) Order 2000. Under Article 3 of the 2000 Order, an appeal from a county court, where this judgment was given, lies to the High Court subject to certain exceptions. The only relevant exception here, as contained in Article 4, reads:

> 'An appeal shall lie to the Court of Appeal where the decision to be appealed is a final decision–
> (a)   in a claim allocated by a court to the multi-track under rules 12.7, 14.8 or 26.5 of the Civil Procedure Rules 1998.'

[6] At the time of the decision in this case, Mrs Milward's claim had not been allocated to the multi track. It was not allocated to the multi-track until 30 June 2000. It is clear that, unless the claim has actually been allocated to the multi-track when the judgment or order under appeal is given or made, the appeal lies to the High Court even though the case would have been allocated to the multi-track in time had everyone addressed their minds to the problem.

[7] In those circumstances, counsel for the respondent, seeing that the appeal which was then in place (an appeal to the Court of Appeal) lacked jurisdiction, sensibly drew it to the attention of this court. At the time judgment was given, the appeal had not been allocated to any track, therefore it is clear that the appeal should have gone to the High Court. That procedural matter was dealt with the agreement of the parties, by me sitting as a High Court judge under the discretion which lies with the Master of the Rolls. The parties raise no formal points on the state of the documents or pleadings. The only effect of my order was that I heard the application as a High Court judge as the jurisdictional rules require.

[8] Mrs Milward was a postman. On 4 March 1995, in very bad weather conditions with snow and ice under foot, she was riding her bicycle and delivering the Royal Mail in a road called Long Lane in Chorley Wood. The county council was the highway authority responsible for that road. They had instructed the Three Rivers District Council to carry out certain of their highway functions for them. Long Lane was a high priority road for clearance and gritting. It had been agreed between the parties that the highway authority had instructed the district council to grit Long Lane on 3 March. This was to be done at 7pm the night before. In contravention of that instruction, only part of Long Lane was gritted and the place where Mrs Milward's bicycle skidded was on the ice at a place where Long Lane should have been gritted had the defendant body performed their duties properly. Mrs Milward fell, striking her head on the pavement, sustaining serious personal injuries to her right shoulder and neck. She sued the Three Rivers District Council and a split trial was ordered.

[9] On 9 August 1999 Mrs Milward succeeded on liability before His Honour Judge Simpson in the Mayors and City of London Court. The case had been considerably refined in preparation and there was a single issue. The judge dealt with that issue in his short judgment as follows:

'It is common ground between the parties that instructions had been given to grit the roads in the area at seven o'clock the previous evening; Long Lane is a priority road for this purpose.

There is ample evidence that such instructions were given and the only point in that case for me to decide is whether those instructions were carried out the previous evening; in other words was Long Lane gritted? Did that happen? If it did not happen, then there is plainly negligence on the part of Three Rivers District Council. I should mention at this stage that a point was taken on the pleadings that the District Council is not the Highway Authority, Hertfordshire County Council is, but there is an agreement between the two Authorities relating to such matters; the District Council carries out its duties on behalf of the County Council and no point turns upon it.'

[10] Mrs Milward and two witnesses, one of them being her husband, gave evidence that that part of Long Lane where she fell had not been gritted. The local authority simply gave evidence of their system but did not call their gritting crew. The judge concluded that the gritting which should have taken place according to the instructions given the previous evening had not taken place and, accordingly, Mrs Milward succeeded in her claim which, as put at trial, was based on negligence in failing to grit a road which they had contracted to grit.

[11] The accident was a great misfortune to Mrs Milward who was about 50 at the time. As a result of the accident, she never worked again. Her special damages, largely loss of earnings until 60, are calculated at just over £90,000, with pain and suffering and loss of amenity calculated as possibly adding up to £10,000, as well as general damages, leaving a claim on the claimant's behalf valued at roughly £100,000.

[12] The defence, for their part, hoped to reduce that sum on the trial of quantum by alleging that the injuries she suffered merely accelerated a pre-existing medical condition which itself was a potential source of incapacity. But, whatever the sum was, her damages action was her only way of filling the financial gap caused by her inability to work again.

[13] She obtained judgment. The defendants now submit that the case of *Goodes* represented a change in the law, as indeed it did, and that they should be granted an extension of time to take advantage of that change. This is a matter of judicial discretion and I identify the four factors normally taken into account as (a) to (d):

(A) THE LENGTH OF THE DELAY

[14] Permission to seek leave to appeal out of time was made roughly eleven months out of time. It was made just one month after the decision was known but, as the case attracted a lot of professional attention, a precautionary extension of time could have been applied for the moment the decision was given in this case on 9 August 1999.

(B) THE REASONS FOR THE APPLICANT'S DELAY

[15] These remain totally unexplained by the applicant. No affidavit has been filed and s 8 on the application form 'Arguments in Support of Grounds', which has doubled as a skeleton on this application, says nothing as to the reasons for delay.

(C) THE CHANCES OF THE APPEAL SUCCEEDING IF THE PERMISSION IS GIVEN

[16] This is a difficult area. In the case of *Goodes*, the highway authority, under their statutory liability under s.41(1) of the Highways Act 1980, failed in the House of Lords with three Court of Appeal decisions being over-ruled. But the action in this case was not brought against the highway authority, it was brought against the District Council who had been instructed to do the work by the highway authority. The claim, as mounted at the trial, was negligence (misfeasance in failing to clear all of Long Lane) and not for any statutory liability – for the good reason that the District Council owed none. Additionally, the issue turned on the way that the parties had refined the evidence. Therefore the claimant contends that the issues here were defined in a way which made any change in the statutory duty owed by the highway authority under s 41 irrelevant. Those submissions of the claimant in this case, they might be right and they might be wrong, but they at least in my judgment, entitle the claimant to say that it is not a foregone conclusion that the appeal would succeed if the permission to appeal out of time was given. The highway authority instructed the defendants to grit Long Lane; they negligently did not grit all of Long Lane; that failure was arguably a breach of the duty in negligence that they owed to all users of Long Lane on that night.

(D) WHAT PREJUDICE WAS SUFFERED BY THE CLAIMANT?

[17] She had gone to court and obtained her judgment and damages to compensate her for the loss of the rest of her working life. She had enjoyed the security of the award of what would be, under our law, proper compensation for an accident, which was not her fault, for some eleven months without hearing that it was in any way threatened. The defendants could have told her when she got her judgment that they were intending to appeal subject to a

favourable decision in *Goodes*, but they did not. The first she knew that her entitlement to such damages was in danger was eleven months after the award.

[18] I remind myself that whenever an application such as this is made, if the application succeeds, there is at least the risk that the judgment will be set aside. I would still regard the loss of this judgment on its facts as being more than usually prejudicial to Mrs Milward.

[19] Against this, the defendants argue that, as damages have yet to be assessed, there is no prejudice to the claimant. For the reasons given above I do not accept that once the claimant has established her entitlement for judgment with damages to be assessed, that her chances of retaining that sum should be more precarious simply because the loss has not been quantified. Basically, as was said in *Greig Middleton & Co Ltd v Denderowicz* [1997] 4 All ER 181, [1998] 1 WLR 1164, at page 1175 of the latter report:

'... the longer time goes by, particularly if the defendant has been told, or reasonably assumes, that no appeal will be pursued, the greater the weight that will be attached to this factor.'

[20] I also remind myself of what Roskill LJ said in *Property and Reversionary Investment Corporation Ltd v Templar* [1978] 2 All ER 433, [1977] 1 WLR 1223, at page 1225 of the latter report:

'It is therefore plain that it is not enough for [counsel] to say that recent decisions of the House of Lords clearly show that [their] decision was wrong. He must show that there are special reasons why he should be allowed to argue that the judgment should not stand.'

[21] In my judgment, taking into account all the circumstances of the accident and all the circumstances of the application to set the judgment aside, in my judgment the right answer is that Mrs Milward should keep her judgment. I therefore dismiss this application.

Application dismissed.

(*Transcript: Smith Bernal*)

OWUSU V JACKSON AND OTHERS

A2.17

[2002] EWCA Civ 877

COURT OF APPEAL (CIVIL DIVISION)

BROOKE and LATHAM LJJ and HART J

19 JUNE 2002

JUDGMENT: APPROVED BY THE COURT FOR HANDING DOWN (SUBJECT TO EDITORIAL CORRECTIONS)

Lord Justice Brooke:

This is the judgment of the court.

1. Introductory

1. This is an appeal by the first, third, fourth and sixth defendants (whom we will call D1, D3, D4 and D6) against an order of Judge Bentley QC sitting as a deputy high court judge at Sheffield on 16 October 2001 whereby he dismissed D1's application for a stay of the action, D3's application for an order that the court should not exercise its jurisdiction to grant permission to serve these proceedings outside the jurisdiction of the English court, and the application by D4 and D6 (who are jointly represented) contesting the jurisdiction of the court under CPR Part 11. D2 and D5 have not been served with the proceedings.

...

(II) THE DELIVERY OF THE JUDGMENT AT SHEFFIELD

24. The next problem, on which we are not required to make a ruling, arose because the judge used an unorthodox method of delivering his reserved judgment. The hearing ended on 11 October 2001 and the judge initialled and dated his reserved judgment on 16 October. He then passed it to the officers of the court so that they could draw up and seal his order, which was perfected on 19 October. The judgment and order were then posted to the parties' solicitors, who received it on 24 October.

25. It is hardly surprising that this procedure caused difficulties in relation to the computation of time for appealing. CPR 52.4(2) prescribes that where the lower court makes no relevant order, the appellant must file the appellant's notice within 14 days after the date of the decision of the lower court that the appellant wishes to appeal. This means the date when the judge makes his decision, and not the date when the order reflecting his decision is drawn up. See *Sayers v Clarke Walker* [2002] EWCA Civ 645 at [5].

26. The judge was sitting in public, and it was his duty to give judgment and make his judgment available to the parties in public. Time for appealing will then run from the time he communicates his decision to the parties (other than in draft form, following the modem procedure discussed in *Prudential Assurance Co Ltd v McBains Cooper (A Firm)* [2000] 1 WLR 2000). If he sends his written judgment to the parties in draft, and they are able to agree the

consequential orders, he may be able to excuse their attendance when he delivers the judgment formally in court, thereby making it available to the public and the media (if interested), but he cannot dispense completely with the formality of handing down his judgment in open court. Time for appealing will then start to run.

27. We believe that it would be helpful if a Practice Direction were made which formalises this procedure, particularly in relation to part-time judges. Until such a Practice Direction is prepared and issued, it will be sufficient for us to indicate that if a part-time judge has sent a reserved written judgment to the parties in draft, and they have agreed upon any necessary consequential orders and filed them at the relevant court office, so that he is satisfied that nobody need attend when the judgment is formally handed down in court, he may make arrangements with another judge of the same court to hand the judgment down if it is inconvenient for him to return to the court for that purpose. Needless to say, a full-time judge may make similar arrangements if he is unavoidably absent from his court for any reason and he cannot hand down his judgment elsewhere.

28. On the present occasion, time for appealing was formally extended, so that we were not obliged to make a ruling on the point.

R (ON THE APPLICATION OF NINE NEPALESE ASYLUM SEEKERS) V IMMIGRATION APPEAL TRIBUNAL

A2.18

[2003] EWCA Civ 1892

COURT OF APPEAL (CIVIL DIVISION)

BROOKE LJ

19 DECEMBER 2003

Practice and procedure – Abuse of process – Striking out of action – Asylum claims – Adjudicator disbelieving claimants' evidence – Appeal tribunal refusing leave to appeal – Permission to seek judicial review being refused – Applications for permission to appeal against refusal of leave to seek judicial review – Applications an abuse of process.

Lord Justice Brooke:

[1] This judgment is concerned with issues of general importance and is released from the usual restrictions on citation.

[2] Nine applications for permission to appeal were listed before me today. All were made by asylum-seekers from Nepal: one of them is a citizen of Bhutan but has lived for many years in Nepal. In each case an Adjudicator dismissed their appeal from a decision by the Secretary of State to refuse them asylum. In each case the Adjudicator did not believe significant parts of the applicant's evidence. In seven of these cases the asylum-seeker sought permission to appeal from the Immigration Appeal Tribunal ('IAT'). Permission was not surprisingly refused since the appeal had turned on the credibility of the applicant. In the other two cases the applicant did not seek permission to appeal within the limited time prescribed by Parliament. Instead, an application was made much later for judicial review of the Adjudicator's decision. Those two applications should have been struck out soon after they were filed in the Administrative Court. In the other seven cases an application was made for permission to apply for judicial review of the IAT's refusal of permission.

[3] In all nine cases the application was refused on the papers by a judge of the Administrative Court. In each case the application was renewed for a hearing in court, when it was again dismissed by a judge of that court. In each case the applicant then sought permission to appeal to the Court of Appeal from the judgment in the Administrative Court.

[4] The grounds of appeal bear a very striking similarity. I will refer to the applicants by their case numbers. The standard form of words is:
'(i)   All my documentary evidence are not properly considered;
(ii)   My humanitarian grounds are not taken into account;
(iii) Relevant laws and country information are not properly considered;
(iv)   The correct standard of proof is not applied.'

[5] Sometimes the reference in (ii) is to 'my human rights claims'. Sometimes the reference in (iii) is to 'my country situation'. There also appear the rubrics 'Decision is not consistent with other cases' (once) and 'Relevant laws are not according to the Asylum laws and Human Rights Act' (once). Each Notice of Appeal is accompanied by a skeleton argument that has clearly been prepared by the same person. All draw attention to the distressing state of affairs in Nepal, and they variously complain that if the judge in the Administrative Court (who is described as 'Mr Justice' in eight of these skeleton arguments) had considered the documentary evidence with appropriate care, he would have granted permission to apply for judicial review. None of them address the point that the Adjudicator did not believe their evidence in material respects.

[6] Each of these appeals represents an abuse of the processes of this court. The Practice Direction to CPR Pt 52 refers to CPR52.11(3)(a) and (b), and prescribes that the grounds of appeal should set out clearly the reasons why one or other of these rules is said to apply. Since no complaint is made of any serious procedural or other irregularity in the proceedings in the lower court,

the only viable ground of appeal is that the judge in the Administrative Court was wrong. To show why he was wrong, it is insufficient to recite the generalised forms of words I have quoted in paragraph (iv) above, or to refer generally to the distressing situation in Nepal or to rely on the evidence the applicant gave to the Adjudicator which the Adjudicator did not believe.

[7] I have referred to the striking similarities between the nine grounds of appeal and the nine skeleton arguments. There are similar striking similarities between the Grounds for Judicial Review which were prepared in eight of these cases. In five of them it is said that these grounds were prepared with the help of Citizen's Advice Bureaux: in Aldershot (1663, 1790, 2183), Abbey Wood (1966) and Reading (2228). Another striking similarity is that although each applicant in the Administrative Court asked for an oral hearing after their application was refused on paper, none of them in fact attended before the judge at the oral hearing. In the same way, during the last 24 hours this court has received notification that none of the nine are going to attend court today.

[8] So far as the facts of the nine cases are concerned, No 1663 arrived here in May 2002. He said he was indirectly associated with Maoists and that he faced persecution by the Government. The Adjudicator did not believe him. No 1749 arrived here in 1999. She said that she was a member of the Maoist party and faced persecution. The Adjudicator rejected her evidence. No appeal was lodged with the IAT, and 20 months elapsed between the Adjudicator's decision and the application for judicial review. No 1790 arrived here in 1998. Her application was made on similar grounds. The Adjudicator said that her evidence was particularly unreliable, and that although she was arrested once in 1996, the police released her the next day and had no further interest in her.

[9] No 1966 arrived here in July 2001. He claimed to be a member of the Nepalese Congress Party and he said that he was threatened by members of the Maoist Party. The Adjudicator made adverse findings about his credibility. No 1984 arrived here in August 2001. He claimed that he was accused by the Nepalese authorities of being a member of the Maoist Party, whereas in fact he was a member of the Nepalese Communist party. The Adjudicator accepted that he had been arrested and badly treated in February 199, but he had been released after one week, and he rejected the applicant's evidence about further police interest in him. No 2156 arrived here in January 2001. He claimed that he was a member of the Maoist party, which he had left after his brother was killed in an operation, and he then went into hiding, fearing the party's reaction. The Adjudicator did not believe him, and said that a certificate he produced was manifestly false. The IAT said that it was quite untrue that his solicitor had failed him as he had alleged, and explained why.

[10] No 2182 arrived here in March 2002. He claimed to be a member of the National Democratic Party, and that he had been caught in the cross-fire between the authorities and the Maoists after a series of events which also

involved members of the Communist party He feared that the Maoists might kill him, and thought that he could not stay in Nepal. The Adjudicator did not believe him. He said that an internal flight alternative was available to him in any event. No 2183 is a citizen of Bhutan who has lived in Nepal for most of her life. She arrived here in March 2002. She said she feared persecution from the Nepalese authorities and the Maoist party. The Adjudicator said that she had been captured by the Maoists because she was a nurse. She had then been arrested by the police in a round-up of Maoists, but was released on proof that she was a local nurse. There was no evidence that nurses as a group were being targeted. The Adjudicator did not accept her reason for moving to Kathmandu, and said it was highly unlikely she would have been recognised there. No 2228 arrived here in June 2001. She said she feared persecution for her political opinions and her membership of the Maoist party. The Adjudicator did not believe her evidence.

[11] In each of these cases the applicants have stayed in this country long after their asylum appeals were determined by the Immigration Appellate Authority by making these unmeritorious applications for judicial review after being disbelieved by an Adjudicator. Judicial review lies to correct errors of law on well recognised grounds. It does not provide an appeal mechanism in cases where an applicant complains that the Adjudicator, who is the tribunal of fact, ought to have believed him/her, but did not. It is of course essential that there should be some appellate system in place to look out for clear cases in which it might be appropriate for an appellate court to intervene (for instance, where there were clearly problems with an interpreter, or clear signs that the Adjudicator did not understand critical evidence), but if the IAT, which is the specialist appellate tribunal, declines to grant permission to appeal, that should almost invariably be the end of the matter.

[12] The reasons why these appellants have decided not to attend the hearing today also bear striking similarities. In general they refer to the political situation in Nepal, and to the concerns they originally expressed to the Adjudicator. Two of them refer to health matters, without sending a medical certificate to the court. No 1790 says that she is totally ill. If there are compassionate grounds why she should not be returned to Nepal, she should make appropriate representations to the Home Office. There are certainly no legal grounds to challenge the IAT's decision. No 2183, the nurse from Bhutan, gave birth to a child on 13 November 2003, but there is no reason why she could not have sent a representative to court to argue her case. Mr Nicholas Blake QC, sitting as a deputy high court judge, considered a comparable application for an adjournment from her on 3 October on the grounds of her approaching confinement. He rejected it on the grounds that there were no prospects of a successful challenge to the Tribunal's decision, and there was no merit in her application for permission. This was obviously correct, and in the

exercise of my discretion I refuse her application for an adjournment on the grounds that her underlying appeal represents an abuse of the processes of this court and is totally devoid of merit.

[13] Since these applications have never possessed any merit at all, I dismiss them all today. There simply never have been any viable grounds for judicial review in these cases, and two experienced judges in the Administrative Court have already made this clear in each case.

[14] As I have said, applications of this kind represent an abuse of the processes of this court, which exists to resolve genuine points of law in judicial review cases, and is not a fourth tier appellate court of fact when the original tribunal of fact has disbelieved an applicant. By virtue of the operation of s 101(3) of the Nationality, Immigration and Asylum Act 2002, which is now in force, there are now very few of these applications still awaiting determination in the Court of Appeal, and I have given a direction to the court staff to bring them all to my attention today, so that I may consider whether they should be struck out as an abuse of the process of the court.

[15] The courts are receiving an increasing number of applications in these cases that are totally devoid of merit, and judges must be readier than ever to use their powers to strike out cases of their own initiative pursuant to CPR 3.3. If they are as devoid of merit as these nine appeals, it would be appropriate for a judge in the first instance to strike the matter out under CPR 3.3(4) and give the applicant ten days in which to make an application for a hearing, if so advised. If a hearing is then sought, it should be speedily arranged. Taking this course in clear cases will save the massive amount of time now taken up by the administrative processing of a case before it is listed for a hearing in the ordinary way.

[16] I have referred to the fact that these appellants all decided not to attend the hearing in the Administrative Court, and all decided not to attend the hearing arranged for today. Since they all clearly received notice of the hearing, no difficulty arises. It sometimes happens that an unmeritorious applicant does not attend a hearing and then complains that he/she did not receive notice of it and asks for the matter to be reinstated. Although a hearing will ordinarily be arranged, this does not follow as a matter of right in all circumstances. The decision of this court in *R (on the application of Idubo) v Home Secretary* [2003] EWCA Civ 1203 makes this clear. In that case Pumfrey J, with whom Judge LJ agreed, said at paras 5–9:

> '5. In his letter to the court and again in a skeleton argument which was provided to us today and which we have read during an adjournment for the purpose, Mr Idubo sets out again his reasons for challenging the decision of the Adjudicator. These are what Moses J described as an

attack on the merits. They do not advance a ground for review of the decision. To that extent the position remains as it was in front of Moses J.

6. The application for judicial review was renewed before Buxton LJ in the Court of Appeal. On 22 April 2002 the application was called on in court. Mr Idubo was not present and the application was struck out. The present application is dated 4 February 2003. In it Mr Idubo says that he never received any notice about his hearing before Buxton LJ. However he did in fact appear on 22 April 2002, a quarter of an hour after Buxton LJ had dismissed his application. He was told to put his application in writing; that he did. He explained that his bus had been late. The Civil Appeals Office wrote to him on 26 April 2002, that is four days after the hearing before Buxton LJ, enclosing an application and a fee exemption form, but he never replied. He was living at the same address, or at least his post was being sent to the same address throughout this period. It was still his address when he had written to the court in connection with the present application.

7. The contents of the application notice are, it seems to us, plainly untrue. The reason for this delay advanced by Mr Idubo is connected with the problems which he has had since the application before Buxton LJ, and in particular in his failure to obtain support from a firm of solicitors specialising in immigration matters in connection it would seem with his detention both at Hatfield and at Orpington. Be that as it may, the fact remains that the application is made to the court on a false basis. Two questions in these circumstances arise. The first is the nature of this application. Once an application has been called on in court there is a hearing. If the applicant does not turn up then the application is struck out or dismissed, which is what happened in this case. The court has a discretion to reinstate the application not because this is a decision of the single judge taken without a hearing, but because there is a general discretion under the Civil Procedure Rules, r 23.11, to re-list an application on application made for that purpose which could be dealt with without a hearing if the court thinks it appropriate: see CPR 23.8. The discretion is a general one. The court will take into account no doubt the reasons advanced from non-appearance at the original hearing, any delay in making the application, but also the underlying merits. If the court did not have regard to the underlying merits then any application could be indefinitely continued by repeated applications to reinstate on which the applicant did not attend.

8. The second question is what is to be done in Mr Idubo's case. In our view nothing has been advanced which can affect Moses J's assessment of the merits of the underlying application. It has none. The delay from the hearing before Buxton LJ in April 2002 was substantial; and no efforts were made to explain it. We understand today that in part Mr Idubo has

been in custody, but the court's invitation to reinstate made immediately after the hearing before Buxton LJ appears to have been turned down. The application notice itself is, for the reasons I have given, untrue.

9. It seems to us that in all the circumstances, the lack of merits in the underlying application are crucial, and for this reason, taken with the delay in the making of the application, and with the untruthfulness of the contents of the application, we take the view that there is no grounds shown for reinstating the application which has been dismissed by Buxton LJ and we refuse to do so.'

[17] Courts should be ready to follow this example, again only in very clear cases. If an application is totally devoid of merit, it is abusing the processes of the court and can be handled accordingly.

Judgment accordingly.

(*Transcript: Smith Bernal*)

SHIRE V SECRETARY OF STATE FOR WORK AND PENSIONS

A2.19

[2003] EWCA Civ 1465

COURT OF APPEAL (CIVIL DIVISION)

LORD WOOLF CJ, CHADWICK and BUXTON LJJ

13 OCTOBER 2003

Social security – Income support – Entitlement – Urgent cases – Asylum seeker – Claimant not having claimed asylum 'on arrival' in United Kingdom – Income Support (General) Regulations 1987 (SI 1987/1967), regs 21, 70

Lord Woolf CJ:

[1] This is an appeal with the permission of the Social Security Commissioner against a decision which he gave on 10 October 2002. On that occasion he dismissed the appeal of an Income Support Appeal Tribunal made on 19 January 2000 that the Claimant was not entitled to urgent case payment of income support because she was a person who arrived in this country from abroad and had not claimed political asylum on arrival in the United Kingdom.

[2] Put very shortly, her case was that she had been told by the agent who was responsible for managing her entry into this country not to make a claim and she did not do so.

[3] Before developing the appeal further in relation to the facts of this particular case it is desirable that I say something about the procedure which has occurred in relation to this appeal.

THE PROCEDURAL POINT

[4] The Appellant identified three grounds of appeal, which are set out in her Notice of Appeal to this court. The precise terms are not important, but, having obtained from the Commissioner permission to appeal on the basis of those three grounds, the Appellant (who was represented by junior counsel at that time) in due course had prepared on her behalf a skeleton argument which as far as the court is aware was served in accordance with the relevant Practice Direction. If there had been no further changes made in respect of that skeleton argument it would not be necessary for me to make the remarks that I now make. However, there came a stage where Mr Blake QC was instructed on the Appellant's behalf. As I understand the position, Mr Blake was only instructed at the end of last term. He was then not available in August. He returned in September and there came a stage when he was able to give attention to this case. In consequence on 26 September a fresh skeleton argument was delivered direct to counsel appearing on behalf of the Secretary of State, and presumably about the same time the fresh skeleton argument was sent to the court. By then the date of hearing was rapidly approaching.

[5] In the fresh skeleton argument the nature of the Appellant's case changed significantly. The previous grounds had depended partly on art 31 of the Geneva Convention and partly upon provisions of the European Convention on Human Rights. Finally, there was a reliance on guidance issued by the Department. No attempt was made to file amended grounds of appeal to cover the new argument which, as will appear hereafter, was, by contrast, a short point of interpretation. Instead, if the court had not intervened, Mr Blake would have developed the argument to which I will in due course turn when opening the appeal.

[6] It seems to me that this is an unfortunate way to go about the processing of an appeal where it is decided that the case which should be presented at the hearing of the appeal will differ radically from the case which had previously been intended to be presented, where that case is the one upon which permission to appeal had been given. In a situation of that nature it is highly desirable that those who act on behalf of the Appellant should write to the court and to the other party indicating the proposed nature of the changed case which is to be advanced, seeking the directions of the court as to whether the matter should be dealt with at the beginning of the hearing of the appeal or by directions being given by the court prior to the hearing of the appeal.

[7] If, as should happen, the Respondent is informed of the change in the nature of the case, the Respondent if he wishes can raise objection to the change in nature of the case. The court should be informed of the attitude of the Respondent. If this is done the court can decide whether the case is one which can be disposed of summarily because there is no merit in the new grounds. The court can also decide, that in the interests of justice, it is not right that the Appellant should not be allowed to change the grounds at a very late stage, as occurred in this case. Where the new grounds may have merit the course to which I have referred will also give the court the opportunity to consider the most appropriate way in which to dispose of the appeal if it is to proceed. It is to be hoped that action indicated will be taken in future where there is a change of the sort that I have indicated in the way the appeal is to be presented.

[8] In the present case the court was satisfied that it was appropriate to hear the appeal, notwithstanding the change in the nature of the arguments relied on which it was proposed would take place. That being so, I turn to consider the merits of the Appellant's argument.

...

The Merits

[17]... I would accordingly dismiss this appeal.

Lord Justice Chadwick:

[18] I agree.

Lord Justice Buxton:

[19] I also agree.

Appeal dismissed.

(*Transcript: Smith Bernal*)

SLOT AND ANOTHER V ISAAC

A2.20

[2002] EWCA Civ 481

CIVIL PROCEDURE

COURT OF APPEAL (CIVIL DIVISION)

BROOKE, LAWS and KEENE LJJ

12 APRIL 2002

Practice – Appeal – Application for permission to appeal – Whether party entitled to appeal to High Court against refusal of circuit judge for permission to appeal against decision of district judge – Access to Justice Act 1999, s 54 – CPR 52.1(3)(b), CPR 52.3(3)–(5).

Lord Justice Brooke

[1] This is an application by the claimants Robert Slot and Anne Slot for permission to appeal against an order of Jack J made on paper on 7 November 2001 whereby he decided he had no jurisdiction to hear their application for permission to appeal against an order of Judge Parry made on paper in the Guildford County Court on 30 April 2001. By that order Judge Parry refused the claimants permission to appeal against part of an order of District Judge Enser made in the same court at a hearing for case management directions on 8 March 2001.

[2] After Judge Parry made his order on 30 April, the claimants did not exercise their right to request him to reconsider his decision at an oral hearing. Instead, they sought to appeal to a High Court judge. On 16 July Judge Caitlin directed that their application for permission should be listed for an oral hearing before Judge Parry on 9 August. On 23 July the claimants told the court that they did not wish to return to Judge Parry. Instead, they wished their application to be heard by a High Court judge. Eventually, after an abortive visit to this court, their application was placed before Jack J on 7 November.

[3] In addition to holding that he had no jurisdiction to hear an application for permission to appeal against Judge Parry's order, Jack J refused permission to appeal against Judge Caitlin's order dated 16 July. He said that it was an order which was entirely appropriate in the circumstances. He ended his short written judgment by saying:

> 'The applicants are the authors of their own difficulties, for they have refused to use the procedure provided by the CPR, namely for a hearing of an application for permission to appeal, which may be before the same judge who has refused permission without a hearing. After this long hiatus the action should now proceed.'

[4] By their grounds of appeal to this court the claimants explained that they did not wish to be heard by Judge Parry at county court level because they knew it would be hopeless after they had been turned down on paper. They continued:

> 'We have asked Reading District Registry by appeal two times now, can we take the route as the booklets state, and we have done before in another case of ours. We explained that our appeal came after seven days (the time limit) after Judge Parry and his order was final as within the rules. An appeal from this lies with permission from a High Court judge.

We are not being allowed this route of appeal. As said although we have done so before (*sic*). We wish for the matter to be heard at High Court level.'

[5] The claimants have shown us papers relating to the other matter to which they have referred. This was a county court action they had brought against the Hampshire County Council who obtained an order from District Judge Hervey on 2 June 2000 whereby he struck out their action pursuant to CPR Pt 24 on the ground that they had no real prospect of success. On 19 June Judge Parry refused permission to appeal.

[6] On 18 September 2000 Rimer J made an order which, as drawn up and sealed by the court, granted the claimants permission to appeal from the order dated 2 June (being the order made by the district judge). We have been shown, however, the transcript of his judgment, whereby it appears he seems to have thought that the claimants were seeking to appeal against a substantive order by Judge Parry granting summary judgment. If that had indeed been the case, no difficulties about jurisdiction would have arisen. The true position seems to have been ascertained when the time came to draw up Rimer J's order. There is no evidence before us that any point on jurisdiction was taken by the county council before Laddie J.

[7] However that may be, what happened on another occasion cannot give a court jurisdiction which it does not in fact possess. On 30 April Judge Parry represented the 'appeal court' within the meaning of CPR 52.1(3)(b) for the purpose of the claimants' proposed appeal from the order of District Judge Enser, and he refused permission to appeal. By s 54(4) of the Access to Justice Act 1999, Parliament has expressly provided that: 'No appeal may be made against a decision of a court under this section to give or refuse permission.' In other words, it is not open to a dissatisfied litigant to seek permission from a High Court judge to appeal against a decision of a circuit judge to refuse permission to appeal from a decision of a district judge.

[8] In bracketed words at the end of s 54(4) Parliament explained that:

'this subsection does not affect any right under rules of court to make a further application for permission to the same or another court.'

These rights were conferred by CPR 52.3(3)–(5) which provide that:

'(3) Where the lower court refuses an application for permission to appeal, a further application for permission to appeal may be made to the appeal court.

(4) Where the appeal court, without a hearing, refuses permission to appeal, the person seeking permission may request the decision to be reconsidered at a hearing.

(5) A request under paragraph (4) must be filed within 7 days after service of the notice that permission has been refused.'

[9] The combined effect of these provisions is that after a lower court makes a decision with which a litigant is dissatisfied and itself refuses an application for permission to appeal, the litigant:

(i) May make a new application for permission to appeal against the original decision (and not against the decision to refuse permission to appeal against that decision) to the appropriate appeal court (in this case a circuit judge);

(ii) May, if the circuit judge refuses permission to appeal without a hearing, request his decision to be reconsidered at a hearing;

(iii) May not appeal to a further appeal court against the circuit judge's refusal of permission to appeal against the decision of the district judge.'

[10] The effect of these provisions are succinctly set out in paras 14 and 18 of the leaflet called 'Routes of Appeal', issued by the Civil Appeals Office, each of which explains that:

'If the circuit judge refuses permission to appeal without a hearing, a request may be made for an oral hearing. If, at a hearing, the circuit judge refuses permission to appeal to himself, no further right of appeal exists.'

[11] I also explained the effect of these provisions in my judgment in *Tanfern Ltd v Cameron-Macdonald* [2000] 2 All ER 801; [2000] 1 WLR 1311 at para 20 where I set out the procedure which might lead up to an oral hearing at the 'appeal court' and then said:

'If at that hearing the appeal court refuses permission to appeal, then no further right of appeal exists and that is the end of the matter: s 54(4) of the Access to Justice Act 1999; PD 52, para 4.8.'

[12] The present claimants did not understand that the new CPR appeals procedure limited their rights of appeal in this way. Instead, they believed that if a judge at one level made a decision with which they were dissatisfied, then whatever the content of that decision they were entitled to seek permission to appeal against it from a superior appeal court. Their grounds of appeal show that they were bolstered in that belief by the terms of the Court Service guide entitled 'I want to appeal – The High Court or a county court', which refers at p 8 to:

'appealing against a decision made by a Circuit Judge in a county court matter, other than a final decision in a multi-track claim, your appeal will be dealt with by a High Court Judge'

[13] The Practice Direction to CPR 52 ('CPR 52PD') contains some possible sources of confusion for non-lawyers who do not look beyond it to the primary or secondary legislation which contain the sources of the court's jurisdiction in any particular matter. CPR 52PD paras 4.6–4.8 appear under the heading

'Court to which permission to appeal application should be made'. Paragraphs 4.6 and 4.7 contain no difficulty, but the draftsman of the practice direction then decided to omit any express reference to the power to request an appeal court to reconsider its decision to refuse permission to appeal at an oral hearing. Instead, he moved directly to the effect of a further refusal of permission at the oral hearing and explained (in para 4.8) that:

> 'There is no appeal from a decision of the appeal court, made at an oral hearing, to allow or refuse permission to appeal to that court. See s 54(4) of the Access to Justice Act 1999 and r 52.3(3) and (4).'

[14] This language led the claimants mistakenly to believe that there was a right of appeal from the decision of an appeal court to refuse permission to appeal if it had been made on paper and not at an oral hearing. Their confusion seems to have been compounded by CPR 52PD para 4.14 which summarises the effect of CPR 52.3 (4) and (5) and also prescribes that the request for reconsideration of the decision must also be served on the respondent within the 7-day period prescribed by CPR 52.3(5). The following words are then added:

> 'If no request is made for the decision to be reconsidered, it will become final after the time limit for making the request has expired.'

[15] I imagine that this language was used because until the seven-day period expired, the refusal of permission to appeal on paper had the effect of what used to be called an order *nisi*, because it would have no effect at all if a request for reconsideration was made within the seven-day period. Unfortunately it seems to have been misunderstood by the claimants as meaning that they were not entitled to seek an extension of time (pursuant to CPR 3.1(2)(a)) for making a request for the reconsideration of Judge Parry's order on paper. There is nothing in the rules to deny them that right. The effect of the Practice Direction is also set out on p 12 of the guide I have mentioned in para 12 above. It, too, does not make it completely clear that there can be no further appeal (as opposed to a request for reconsideration) against the refusal by an appeal court of permission to appeal on paper.

[16] It follows that Jack J was correct in holding that he had no jurisdiction in the matter, so far as the proposed appeal against the district judge's order was concerned. This application should therefore be dismissed.

[17] In future, if an application for permission to appeal is lodged at the High Court in circumstances where it is quite obvious that a High Court judge has no jurisdiction, it should be rejected quite summarily, by reference to this judgment. Since its rejection will in essence be an administrative act (because the court has no jurisdiction) there will be no necessity for any kind of reasoned judgment, even if a judge is consulted by the staff of the court to confirm their view of the matter. Compare *Jolly v Jay* [2002] EWCA Civ 277 at [19].

Lord Justice Laws

[18] I agree.

Lord Justice Keene

[19] I also agree.

Application dismissed.

(*Transcript: Smith Bernal*)

SOUTHERN & DISTRICT FINANCE PLC V TURNER

A2.21

[2003] EWCA Civ 1574

COURT OF APPEAL, CIVIL DIVISION

BROOKE and LONGMORE LJJ and SIR MARTIN NOURSE

7 NOVEMBER 2003

JUDGMENT: APPROVED BY THE COURT FOR HANDING DOWN (SUBJECT TO EDITORIAL CORRECTIONS)

Lord Justice Brooke:

This is the judgment of the court.

1. This matter has a convoluted procedural history. It is best to set out the history of the litigation first before we describe the route by which it has come to this court, and the matters we have to decide.

2. On 3 June 1992 the claimants Southern & District Finance Ltd made a loan to the defendant Mrs Elizabeth Mary Turner. The loan was secured on her property in Formby Road, Lytham St Anne's. Mrs Turner fell into arrears, and on 21st May 1993 District Judge Woods made a suspended possession order. In due course a warrant for possession was issued, but this was suspended on terms in August 1993, these terms being later varied in April 1995.

3. On 22 January 2001 the defendant issued a notice by which she sought permission to counterclaim for a declaration as to the enforceability of the original loan agreement on the grounds that it had not been properly executed in accordance with the requirements of sections 60 to 65 of the Consumer Credit Act 1974 ('the 1974 Act') and the regulations made thereunder. She also sought to re-open the loan as an extortionate credit bargain pursuant to section 139 of the 1974 Act. At the same time she sought an order that the original possession order dated 21 May 1993 should be set aside.

4. On 16 March 2001 District Judge Bryce dismissed the application to set aside the 1993 order. He granted permission to counterclaim on a limited basis, however, and gave appropriate case management directions. The trial of the counterclaim was fixed to take place on 23 November 2001. The district judge directed that any order made on the counterclaim should be limited to relieving the defendant in whole or in part from any further obligations under the credit agreement; recovering payments she had made to the claimants on or [after] 22 January 1995 (save as to payments made pursuant to paragraph (2)(a) of the order dated 21 May 1993); and any consequential orders as to costs. This order is said to have meant that although the defendant could maintain her contention that there was an extortionate credit bargain, she was not allowed to contend that the agreement had been improperly executed.

5. On 15 November 2001 the defendant's solicitors told the claimants that they wanted the trial adjourned because they wished to appeal the March 2001 order. They knew they were out of time for appealing the order. On 22 November an order was made that the trial be vacated on the defendant's undertaking to file an application for permission to appeal out of time by 4pm on 30 November 2001.

6. The appeal notice was filed on 29 November 2001. It made no mention of an application for an extension of time. In due course Judge Appleton refused permission to appeal on paper. An oral hearing of the permission application was sought and fixed for 21 February 2002. Prior to that hearing the claimants' solicitors wrote a letter to the court in which they observed that the application was made eight months out of time, and that no reasons for the delay had been given. This letter was not placed before the judge at the hearing, at which he granted permission to appeal the March 2001 order on the basis that it could not be said that the appeal had no real prospect of success. The fact that the application was so long out of time was apparently overlooked. The substantive appeal was in due course fixed to be heard on 5 December 2002.

7. At the hearing of the appeal the judge took of his own motion the point at the beginning of the submissions in reply that an extension of time for appealing had never been sought. After hearing submissions, he gave a short judgment which had the effect of bringing the proceedings to an end, without any judgment being given on the merits. In due course an order was drawn up on 12 December 2002 which simply directed that the appeal be dismissed and that the claimants' costs be added to the security.

8. Because of the procedural conundrum surrounding the question of the proper destination of any further appeal, it is necessary to consider the terms of the judge's oral judgment.

9. After setting out the procedural history, Judge Appleton said that it was only at the latest hearing that it was realised that relevant procedural provisions had

not been observed. He referred to CPR 52.4(2) (which requires an appellant to file an appellant's notice at the appeal court within 14 days of the relevant decision of the lower court) and CPR 52.6 which provides:

'(1) An application to vary the time limit for filing an appeal notice must be made to the appeal court;

(2) The parties may not agree to extend any date of time limit set by–
 (a) these Rules;
 (b) the relevant practice directions; or
 (c) an order of the appeal court or the lower court.'

10. He also referred to paragraph 5.2 of the Practice Direction to CPR Part 52 which provides that:

'If an appellant requires an extension of time for filing his notice then application must be made in the appellant's notice. The notice should state the reason for the delay and the steps taken prior to the application being made.'

11. The judge then referred to the decision of this court in *Sayers v Clarke Walker* [2002] EWCA Civ 645; [2002] 1 WLR 3095, which prescribes that if an application is made for an extension of time for appealing after the original prescribed time for appealing has expired, in cases of any complexity the court should follow the checklist contained in CPR 3.9 when deciding whether to exercise its discretion to grant an extension of time for appealing.

12. The judge said that on this occasion an extension of time for appealing was not sought on the appeal notice. He added that CPR 3.9 prescribed that any application for relief must be supported by evidence, of which there was none. He said he had come to the conclusion, regrettable though it was, that there was no way round the problem for the defendant.

13. He then touched briefly on the merits, and indicated that there appeared to be force in the defendant's arguments, but he concluded his judgment by saying:

'It just occurs to me, if there is anything to be salvaged from the, as it were, wreckage of failure to comply with the rules, that if there is a sound argument then whenever the court in this particular case or with these particular parties is being asked to make an order the arguments can be revisited, but regrettable as it is, this has been an oversight on the part of the defendant's advisers which I simply, in the light of the Court of Appeal's guidance in *Sayers v Clarke Walker*, cannot see any way round. For these reasons the appeal is bound to fail.'

14. The judge clearly thought that he was making an order dismissing the appeal, because he told the defendants' counsel that any application for permission to appeal would have to be made to this court. As we have said, his order was subsequently drawn up in those terms. When the Notice of Appeal

was filed in this court, however, a question was raised whether the appeal properly lay to the High Court or to the Court of Appeal. On 13 May 2003 Brooke LJ adjourned the paper application for permission to appeal to be heard on notice with the appeal to follow if permission was granted. He also gave the following directions:

> 'The court will first consider whether it or the High Court has jurisdiction to hear the application.
>
> If it decides the High Court has jurisdiction one judge of the court .... will immediately sit as a High Court judge (under section 9 of the Supreme Court Act) and hear the application, with the appeal to follow if permission is granted.'

He said that he was directing this course because of the procedural complexities to which the matter gave rise.

15. The parties did not themselves address these procedural complexities until prompted to do so by a note prepared by Deputy Master di Mambro which was sent to them by a direction of the court last week. In response to this note the defendant contended that her appeal was directed at Judge Appleton's refusal to exercise his discretion to waive the irregularity pursuant to CPR 3.10 and thereafter to apply the criteria contained in CPR 3.9 in determining whether or not to grant an extension of time. In that case the appeal would lie to the High Court because it would be a first appeal, not a second appeal (*Foenander v Bond Lewis & Co* [2001] EWCA Civ 759; [2002] 1 WLR 525).

16. The claimants for their part suggested that there were at least four different ways of analysing the judge's decision:

(i) The judge dismissed the appeal on the grounds that permission to appeal should not have been granted. They accept that this analysis can arguably be criticised because the judge never determined the actual substance of the appeal.

(ii) The judge refused to entertain an application for an extension of time. They rejected this analysis on the grounds that the judge's substantive reason for doing what he did was that there had been no such application and there was no evidence on which he could entertain an application.

(iii) The judge revoked his grant of permission to appeal pursuant to CPR 3.1(7). In that case there would be no scope for Mrs Turner to appeal against his decision, since the refusal of permission to appeal by a first appeal court is not susceptible to appeal to a second appeal court.

(iv) The judge set aside his grant of permission to appeal pursuant to the exceptional powers conferred on an appeal court by CPR Part 52.9(1)(b).

17. Mr Fadipe, who appeared for the claimants, suggested that the fourth analysis was correct (although he conceded that there was much to say in favour of the third). He cited in support of his approach a passage in the judgment of Sedley LJ in *Hartsmere Borough Council v Harty* [2001] EWCA Civ 128, in which he said:

> '... (if) the Judge was misled by an Appellant, not necessarily deliberately, into giving permission to appeal, that may well be a compelling reason within the Rule. It must ... involve showing (a) that the materials put before the judge were inaccurate or incomplete; (b) that these deficiencies had a bearing upon the grounds on which permission to appeal was given; and (c) very importantly, that but for them permission to appeal would not have been given.'

18. We have had the opportunity of considering the transcript of the proceedings before the judge. When he observed that no application had been made to extend the time limit for appealing, Mr Say, who appeared for the defendant, said that he made that application 'if it is necessary'. The judge told him that he could not, since such an application had to be supported by evidence. After debating this question for a while, Mr Say drew the judge's attention to CPR 3.10 which provides that:

> 'Where there has been an error of procedure such as a failure to comply with a rule or practice direction–
> (a)   the error does not invalidate any step taken in the proceedings unless the court so orders; and
> (b)   the court may make an order to remedy the error.'

Mr Say submitted that the purpose of CM 3.10 was to catch a situation like this where there had been a procedural irregularity but the justice of the case required that it should be overlooked.

19. Although the judge does not mention CM 3.10 in his judgment, it is clear that he rejected Mr Say's submission on the basis that the requirement to file evidence in support of an application for an extension of time was in his view mandatory, and that a failure to file evidence was irremediable.

20. The judge certainly did not refuse permission to appeal: his judgment shows that he considered that the underlying point at issue was arguably a good one. Nor did he dismiss the appeal on the merits. Whether the correct analysis is that he decided he had no jurisdiction to hear the appeal (it now not being open to the defendant, for want of evidence, to apply to extend the time for appealing), or that he decided, without expressly saying so, not to grant the extension of time informally sought at the hearing, the result is the same. This was not an order made by a judge on hearing the appeal, such that any appeal could only lie to this court as a second appeal. It was an order of the type discussed in *Foenander v Bond Lewis* [2001] EWCA Civ 759; [2002] 1 WLR 525 which is

susceptible of appeal as a first appeal to the next higher court in the hierarchy. For these reasons we told the parties at the hearing that the application for permission to appeal should therefore be heard by a High Court judge.

21. This is at least the third occasion this year in which difficulties over appeal routes have arisen because insufficient attention was paid to that question when the order of a court was drawn up. In *Hackney v Driscoll (No 1)* [2003] EWCA Civ 614 it was not clear whether an order made by a circuit judge was made by a judge of the county court at first instance, or by a circuit judge in an appeal court. In *Fowler de Pledge* [2003] EWCA Civ 703 it was not clear whether a circuit judge sitting as a first appeal court had directed that a matter should be heard by another circuit judge as an appeal by way of rehearing, or as a rehearing of the original application. In the present case not nearly enough attention was paid by either the judge or by counsel to the true nature of the order that was made.

22. As a result, a lot of avoidable trouble and expense was caused before the correct appeal route was ascertained. We hope that every effort may be made in future to ensure that attention is paid to the precise nature of any order being made, so that the appeal route, if any, can be readily and correctly identified.

(Lord Justice Brooke then considered the application as a High Court judge pursuant to section 9(1)(a) of the Supreme Court Act 1981 and directed that the application be heard by the Court of Appeal pursuant to CPR 52.14(1)(b). He said that the compelling reason for taking this course was that there had already been excessive delay in this matter and that it was appropriate that it should be heard immediately by a three-judge Court of Appeal. There follows the judgment of the Court of Appeal on the substantive appeal).

23. Mr Say accepted that there was no evidence before the judge, and no evidence before this court, to support the application for an extension of time. He said, however, that this was a procedural irregularity which could be waived pursuant to CPR 3.10, as could the failure to apply for an extension of time for appealing, whether on the original notice of appeal or by subsequent amendment. He submitted that we would not be able to understand the very unusual features of this case unless we first understood the argument which the district judge's order had shut his client out from advancing on her counterclaim.

24. She wished to contend in paragraphs 3–5 of her draft defence and counterclaim that the original credit agreement was not 'properly executed', and that the consequence of three of the matters of which complaint was made was that section 127(3) of the 1974 Act gave the court no discretion to enforce the agreement. She therefore sought a declaration that it was unenforceable. As to the other two matters, she accepted that the court had a discretion pursuant to section 127(1) of the Act whether or not to permit it to be enforced, but she

asserted that the court should in its discretion permit no further enforcement having regard to the payments already made.

25. It is unnecessary for the purposes of this judgment to describe in any detail the complaints she made. Her first three complaints centred round a number of failures to comply with regulation 6 and Schedule 6 to the Consumer Credit (Agreements) Regulations 1983 in relation to the manner in which the figure for credit was stated (or alternatively, not stated).

26. Mr Say argued that it was common ground that the defendant could take this point if there was ever any question of the claimants wishing to enforce their possession order (see *Watchtower Investments Ltd v Payne* [2001] EWCA Civ 1159), and in those circumstances it would be consistent with the overriding objective if the defendant was permitted to take the point now, so that the matter cold be cleared up once and for all. He said that if the defendant was permitted to add to her counterclaim paragraphs 3–5 of the draft defence and paragraph (i) of the prayer (which sought a declaration as to the enforceability of the credit agreement and/or the mortgage deed) that issue could then be heard as a preliminary issue which could not possibly take more than a day to try. If, as he anticipated, the defendant succeeded, this would avoid the need to conduct a hearing on the 'extortionate credit bargain' issue for which a 3-day hearing was being sought.

27. Mr Say said that he would not oppose a condition being imposed on any order the court might make which would have the effect of barring the defendant from claiming restitution of any past payments she had paid in relation to this matter.

28. Against this background he submitted that in the peculiar circumstances of this case the court should overlook the fact that no evidence had been filed in support of the application for an extension of time. He impliedly invited us to permit an amendment of the notice of appeal, so that it included an application for an extension of time, and to consider his application without any evidence. In this context he invited us to presume that his client herself was not at fault, still less that she had deliberately instructed her solicitors not to appeal the district judge's order soon after it was made.

29. In these circumstances Mr Say made the following submissions in relation to the CPR 3.9 check list:
(a) So far as the interests of the administration of justice were concerned, the issue would have to be determined sooner or later and it would be very much better if the point could be determined quickly as a preliminary issue, particularly in the light of the savings in court time that would be achieved if the point is a good one.
(b) The application for relief was not made promptly.

(c) The judge accepted that the failure to comply with the time limit was not intentional, and we were invited to do the same.
(d) In the absence of explanation, we were entitled to assume there was no good explanation for the default.
(e) It was common ground (but see para 31(e) below) that there had been no previous history of non-compliance with other rules, practice directions or court orders.
(f) We were invited to presume that the failure to comply was caused by the defendant's legal representatives.
(g) The trial date for the counterclaim had already been adjourned, and if permission to take this point is granted, and the point is a good one, the projected trial need never take place.
(h) It is accepted that the failure to comply has caused delay to the claimants, but if the defendant is not permitted to claim recovery of money already paid, the claimants will suffer no prejudice because the issue will have to be tried in any event.
(i) The granting of relief would have a beneficial effect for both parties since if the point is a good one the litigation can be brought to an end more swiftly and expeditiously than would otherwise be the case.

30. In response to these submissions Mr Fadipe submitted that rules were there to be obeyed. CPR 52.2 states that the parties to an appeal must comply with the relevant practice direction, and paragraph 5.2 of the Practice Direction (see para 10 above) also uses the mandatory word 'must'. He conceded that CPR 3.10 gave the court the power to waive an irregularity of this kind if it was just to do so, but CPR 3.9 also prescribed that an application for relief 'must' be supported by evidence, so that we would have to waive that requirement, too. He said that we were not entitled to presume that the defendant had not given her solicitors specific instructions that she did not wish to appeal the district judge's order at the time it was made. He also complained that the defendant's solicitors had not honoured their undertaking (see para 5 above) to file an application for permission to appeal out of time.

31. Against this uncompromising background, Mr Fadipe's submissions in relation to the application of CPR 3.9 followed a fairly predictable course. In so far as they differed from Mr Say's submissions, he contended:
(a) That it was not in the interests of the administration of justice that a litigant should be able to obtain an order for an adjournment of a trial on the basis of undertakings given by her solicitors to the court, and that those undertakings should then be ignored. Nor was it in the interests of the administration of justice that the court should overlook the breaches of mandatory rules, since this conduct inevitably led to satellite litigation. The appeal against the March 2001 order was eight months out of time.

508   Case Law

(e) Whilst there was substantial compliance with the directions in the March 2001 order, there was an eight-year delay in applying to set aside the May 1993 order.
(h) The failure to comply has caused the claimants not only delay but also significant costs which may well prove irrecoverable.
(i) Because the trial of the counterclaim is concerned with a quite different issue, and the issue raised by paragraphs 3–5 of the draft defence and counterclaim can be properly raised if his clients ever sought to enforce the possession order, the appeal to Judge Appleton, and indeed the present appeal, is somewhat academic.

32. In our judgment the judge was clearly wrong to hold that he had no power to correct the irregularity pursuant to CPR 3.10. He had already concluded that the appeal had potential merit, and CPR 3.10 unquestionably gave him power to give the defendant permission to amend her notice of appeal (to include an application for an extension of time) and to waive the requirement for evidence if he considered it just to do so. The defendant was clearly at mercy, but if the judge had appreciated the extent of his powers, he would have appreciated not only that he had power to waive the irregularities, but that if the point the defendant was raising was a good one to allow the appeal out of time might well lead to a much more expeditious outcome to the litigation than was otherwise in prospect.

33. He could also have mitigated any potential injustice to the claimants by imposing a condition when granting the appeal to the effect that the defendant was not to be at liberty to claim the recovery of any of the money she had paid to the claimants in the past even if the credit agreement were ultimately held to be unenforceable. The value of the court's power to make conditional orders pursuant to CPR 3.1(2)(a) was illustrated in three cases decided by this court in July 2003: *Price v Price* [2003] EWCA Civ 888; [2003] 3 All ER 911; *Beck v Ministry of Defence* [2003] EWCA Civ 1043 and *Jones v T Mobile (UK) Ltd* [2003] EWCA Civ 1162. In the last of these cases Brooke LJ observed at para 28 that:

> 'This new power to make conditional orders gives a court a greater flexibility to make orders that are both proportionate and just than used to be the case when the court's powers were limited to saying 'yes' or 'no' in response to applications of this kind.'

34. The new CPR regime does not lend itself to the cast-iron rigidity which was reflected in Mr Fadipe's submissions. Of course judges at every level must be astute to correct sloppy practice and to avoid at all costs slipping back to the bad old days when courts took a relaxed attitude to the need for compliance with rules and court orders, so that expensive and time-consuming satellite litigation was only too apt to flourish. But judges must also keep in mind the overriding objective, and be ready to recognise the case where an appropriately

drafted conditional order may achieve justice more effectively than merely saying 'yes' or 'no' to the application that is being made.

35. In our judgment, the interests of the administration of justice clearly demand that the issue raised by paragraphs 3–5 of the draft defence be tried as a discrete issue at an early date. It would not be in anybody's interests to leave the question whether this credit agreement is enforceable at all to hang about in the air until such time as the claimants elect to enforce their possession order. Mrs Turner is at present only paying interest on the loan. If she stopped paying altogether, the claimants would no doubt wish to bring the situation to a head by seeking to enforce their order. It would be very much better if the trial of the issues was now organised in an orderly manner, so that there will be no question of any need for an extensive hearing on the 'extortionate credit bargain' issue if the 'unenforceable credit agreement' point turns out to be a good one. Any injustice that might otherwise be suffered by the claimants due to the dilatoriness of the defendant and her solicitors can be mitigated by imposing the condition we have suggested.

36. We will therefore allow the appeal and permit the defendant to amend her original notice of appeal by adding an application for an extension of time for appealing. Although in theory we could now remit the matter to the circuit judge to allow him to determine the appeal, it would be thoroughly undesirable if we were to do so, given the length of the delays that have taken place since the district judge made his order.

37. We turn therefore to the district judge's order, of which Mr Fadipe has submitted a short note (which has not been submitted to the district judge for approval). It appears that the district judge declined to set the 1993 possession order aside on the basis that he had no jurisdiction to do so, and there was no application for permission to appeal against that order eight years out of time. He does not appear to have been invited to direct the trial of the issues arising on paragraphs 3–5 of the draft defence and counterclaim as discrete issues. Argument ran instead on the appropriateness of setting aside the 1993 possession order and the length of time over which the defendant could counterclaim the recovery of payments made in the past.

38. In our judgment, in view of the way in which the argument has developed on the appeal we are entitled to interfere with the district judge's order not because he was clearly wrong on the matters that he did decide, but because he did not take into account material matters (such as making a conditional order or the desirability of ordering a discrete preliminary issue on the enforceability issue) which could have led him to exercise his discretion differently.

39. In these circumstances we are entitled to exercise our discretion afresh. We will therefore add an additional paragraph (1A) to the district judge's order to the effect that:

'The Defendant may also counterclaim for a declaration as to the enforceability of the credit agreement and/or mortgage deed and/or of specific provisions thereof on the grounds set out in paragraphs 3–5 of the draft defence and counterclaim sent to the court under cover of her solicitor's letter dated 23rd January 2001 on the condition that if the said documents or any of them are held to be unenforceable the defendant is not to be at liberty to claim restitution of any of the monies paid by the claimants prior to the date of this order.'

40. The cost of all this ancillary litigation appears to be almost entirely attributable to the way the defendant's solicitors have handled the matter. If the matter had been put before the district judge in the way that it has been put before us, no doubt he would have made a similar order and all the subsequent expense, which was increased by their failure to appeal timeously or to prepare their application for an extension of time correctly, could have been avoided.

41. In these circumstances, although we are willing to hear argument on the point, we would be disposed to direct that the defendant pay the claimants their costs of the appeals both to Judge Appleton and to this court, such costs to be added to the security. We have been told that the defendant has a legal aid certificate. In these circumstances, on any assessment of the defendant's costs, the costs officer or costs judge should deduct any sums properly to be designated as 'wasted costs' which are attributable to the negligent way in which the appeals against the district judge' order appear to have been conducted under the defendant's certificate.

42. If the parties can agree on the terms of an order whereby the issues arising under paragraphs 3–5 of the draft defence can be expeditiously tried as a preliminary issue before a circuit judge, we will be happy to make such an order when this judgment is handed down.

TANFERN LTD V CAMERON-MACDONALD AND ANOTHER

A2.22

COURT OF APPEAL, CIVIL DIVISION

LORD WOOLF MR, GIBSON and BROOKE LJJ

12 MAY 2000

Practice – Appeal – New provisions governing civil appeals in private law matters – Explanation and guidance – Access to Justice Act 1999 – Access to Justice Act 1999 (Destination of Appeals) Order 2000.

(1) Under new provisions governing civil appeals in private law matters which came into effect on 2 May 2000, an appeal court (i.e. the court hearing the first

appeal from a decision) will, as a general rule, only allow an appeal where the decision of the lower court was wrong, or where it was unjust because of a serious procedural or other irregularity. Moreover, the Court of Appeal will only hear a second appeal if it considers that such an appeal will raise an important point of principle or practice or that there is some other compelling reason to do so. Accordingly, the decision of the 'first instance' judge in what used to be called an 'interlocutory appeal' will assume a much greater importance than under the old procedure in which the 'judge in chambers' conducted a complete rehearing, with an entirely fresh discretion to exercise and the decision of the appeal court, whether a circuit judge or a High Court judge, is in most cases now likely to be final. Those changes will compel litigants and their advisers to pay even greater attention to the need to prepare their cases with appropriate care because they may now find it much more difficult to extricate themselves from the consequences of an ill-prepared case before a judge at first instance in a lower court.

(2) Where, in a claim allocated by a court to the multi-track under CPR 12.7, 14.8 or 26.5, the final decision is given by a district judge or circuit judge in the county court, or a master or district judge of the High Court, an appeal from that decision will, under the new provisions, lie directly to the Court of Appeal. Before those provisions came into effect, an appeal from a county court district judge in such a case would have had to have been brought before the circuit judge.

(3) In the context of multi-track claims, a final decision is one that will finally determine the entire proceedings, subject to any possible appeal and or detailed assessment of costs, whichever way the court decides the issues before it. It includes the assessment of damages or any other final decision made at the conclusion of part of a hearing or trial which has been split into parts and would be a final decision if made at the conclusion of that hearing or trial, but does not include a decision only on costs. Accordingly, if a judge makes a final decision on any aspect of a claim, such as limitation, or on part of a claim which has been directed to be heard separately, that is a final decision within the meaning of art 1(3)[a] of the Access to Justice Act 1999 (Destination of Appeals) Order 2000. However, orders striking out the proceedings or a statement of case, and orders giving summary judgment under CPR Pt 24, are not final decisions because they will not finally determine the entire proceedings whichever way the court decides the issues before it.

[a] Article 1, so far as material, is set out at p 806 c, post

(4) Every order made on appeal must record the name and status of the judge against whom the appeal has been brought. Orders relating to the final decisions of a lower court must also make it clear whether the order was made in the small claims track, the fast track or the multi-track. If it was made in the

latter, the order must state whether it was made in a claim allocated to the multi-track or whether the procedure under CPR Pt 8 was followed.

(5) The new rules and destination arrangements will apply in all cases in which an appeal notice has been filed or an application for permission to appeal has been made on or after 2 May 2000. If an application for permission to appeal has been made to the appeal court before 2 May, and that court gives permission to appeal (whether before or after 2 May), the appeal will be brought and will continue its progress under the old rules. However, where the lower court granted permission to appeal, the appeal will be governed by the old rules only if the notice of appeal was filed at the appeal court before 2 May.

Cases referred to in judgments

A T Poeton (Gloucester) Plating Ltd v Horton (9 May 2000, unreported), CA.

Director General of Fair Trading v Stuart [1991] 1 All ER 129, [1990] 1 WLR 1500, CA.

G v G [1985] 2 All ER 225, [1985] 1 WLR 647, HL.

Swain v Hillman (1999) Times, 4 November, [1999] CA Transcript 1732.

Application for directions

By notice of application dated 27 April 2000, the claimant, Tanfern Ltd, applied for directions in respect of bringing an appeal from the decision of District Judge Ackroyd at Portsmouth County Court on 23 February 2000 dismissing its proceedings for unpaid rent against the defendants, Gregor Cameron-MacDonald and Mona Berit Cameron-MacDonald. The facts are set out in the judgment of Brooke LJ.

Lord Justice Brooke (giving the first judgment at the invitation of Lord Woolf MR).

1. This is an application made by the claimants in curious circumstances. They brought an action against the defendants for unpaid rent in relation to a lease of cafe-restaurant premises in Petersfield which the defendants vacated in August 1996. The arrears of rent amounted to just over £20,000, together with interest of about £7,000 up to 23 February 2000, the date of the hearing in the court below. The claim was originally started in the High Court before being transferred to the county court. It was allocated to the multi-track, and with the consent of the parties District Judge Ackroyd heard the claim and entered judgment for the defendants. His jurisdiction to try a multi-track claim was founded in para 11.1(d) of practice direction 2B, which supplements CPR Pt 2. The district judge then gave permission to appeal.

2. The claimants sought to lodge their appeal at the county court as an appeal to the circuit judge. Their solicitors were advised, however, that the designated civil judge had directed the court office at the Portsmouth County Court that since this was a multi-track case heard by the district judge by consent, the appeal must go to the Court of Appeal. They did not believe that this was correct, and when they sought advice from a lawyer in the Civil Appeals Office, she advised them to go back to the county court. They were also told that if they had tried to lodge an appeal at the Court of Appeal under these circumstances the papers would have been returned to them since the Court of Appeal did not have jurisdiction to hear the appeal.

3. When they raised the matter of the appeal with the county court again, they were told that the designated civil judge had commented on their further letter in these terms:

> 'I still think that the appeal in this case goes direct to the Court of Appeal. CCR 37 R6 deals with appeals from District Judges exercising their usual jurisdiction, and as appears from the notes extends and also covers cases within the concurrent trial jurisdiction of the County Court Judge and the District Judge. But this case does not come into either category: it was a multi-track case being heard by a District Judge with the agreement of the parties, ie he was in effect sitting as in the capacity of a Circuit Judge, and consequently an appeal from his decision cannot be entertained by another Circuit Judge. That is a view shared by other Designated Judges.'

4. They therefore returned to the Court of Appeal in search of a home for their appeal. On this occasion the papers were referred to me, and I directed that the matter should be listed before a two-judge court as soon as possible so that there could be an authoritative judicial ruling as to which level of court the appeal should lie. I also requested the preparation of a bench memorandum by a lawyer in the Civil Appeals Office (to be shown to the claimant's solicitors) which would set out dispassionately the arguments for and against this court having jurisdiction to hear the appeal, since the matter, although important, did not appear to warrant the instruction of an amicus. We are very grateful for the assistance we received, both from this source, and from Mr Emmerson, who appeared for the claimants before us. Although we understand that the county court is now willing to list the matter as a substantive appeal, it appeared to us to be very desirable to give an authoritative ruling on the point.

5. This was a county court matter, and at the relevant time appeals from orders of district judges in the county court were governed by CCR Ord 37, r 6 (as scheduled to the CPR). This provides that:

> '(1) Any party affected by a judgment or final order of the district judge may, except where he has consented to the terms of the order, appeal from the judgment or order to the judge ...'

514 *Case Law*

6. This rule was made under powers created by s 77(1A) of the County Courts Act 1984 which was inserted by Sch 17 to the Courts and Legal Services Act 1990. This subsection enables rules of court to make provision:

> '... for any appeal from the exercise by a district judge, assistant district judge or deputy district judge of any power given to him by virtue of any enactment to be to a judge of a county court.'

7. The situation was different so far as High Court proceedings were concerned. RSC Ord 58, r 2 (as scheduled to the CPR) provided for an appeal from certain decisions of masters or district judges to go to the Court of Appeal. These included a judgment, order or decision of a master given or made at trial on the hearing or determination of any cause, matter, question or issue tried before him (Ord 58, r 2(1)(a)). Ord 58, r 3 was concerned with appeals from district judges in the High Court:

> '(1) An appeal shall lie from any judgment, order or decision of a district judge in any proceeding in any Division in the same circumstances and ... subject to the same conditions as if the judgment, order or decision were given or made by a Master or Registrar in those proceedings in that Division, and the provisions of these rules with respect to appeals shall apply accordingly.'

8. When the Civil Procedure Rules were introduced on 26 April 1999, the practice direction which supplemented Ord 58, r 2 provided in para 1.1 that the provision was 'not intended to alter the route of appeal from a decision of a Master or district judge'. Paragraph 1.2 stated that where, before 26 April 1999, an appeal would have lain from a decision of a master or district judge to a judge under RSC Ord 58, r 1, 'it shall continue to do so under the Civil Procedure Rules'. Paragraph 1.3 of the practice direction stated that:

> 'RSC Order 58, rule 2(1)(a) provides that an appeal lies to the Court of Appeal from a decision of a Master or District Judge made 'at trial ... on the hearing or determination of any cause, matter, question or issue tried before him'. This provision only applies where the parties have given their consent for the Master or District Judge to try a case which has been allocated to the multi-track under Part 26 (see paragraph 4.1 of the Practice Direction on Allocation of Cases to Level of Judiciary— Part 2B).'

9. If this action had been proceeding in a district registry of the High Court, the designated civil judge at Portsmouth would have been correct to decline jurisdiction in these circumstances. These, however, were county court proceedings, and there is nothing in the county court rules to indicate a direct route of appeal from a district judge of the county court to the Court of Appeal in circumstances like these.

10. So far as county court procedure is concerned, the judgment of this court in *Director General of Fair Trading v Stuart* [1991] 1 All ER 129, [1990] 1 WLR 1500 elucidates the position helpfully. In that case the registrar of the Salford County Court (who would now be described as a district judge) granted an injunction, to which the appellant raised no objection, restraining him from conducting any unfair trade practices. The appellant appealed to the Court of Appeal, relying on s 42(2) of the Fair Trading Act 1973 which appeared to prescribe that route of appeal.

11. In his judgment, with which the two other members of the court agreed, Lord Donaldson of Lymington MR mentioned this submission, and said:

> 'We have, of course, given due weight to that submission, but the error lies in failing to appreciate that an appeal to the judge of the county court is in the nature of an internal appeal, and it is only if the litigant wishes to appeal outside the county court, an appeal from the county court to another court, that s 42 comes into play and specifies that the court shall be the Court of Appeal rather than a Divisional Court or the Restrictive Trade Practices Court or any other court.' (See [1991] 1 All ER 129 at 130, [1990] 1 WLR 1500 at 1501–1502.)

12. He added:

> 'So, in summary, the appeal does lie to the judge under Ord 37 because that internal form of appeal within the county court is not the type of appeal to which s 42(2) of the Fair Trading Act 1973 applies. It applies to appeals from the county court to another court and such an appeal can only be brought after the internal remedies have been exhausted by an appeal from the registrar to the judge. I would so declare.' (See [1991] 1 All ER 129 at 130, [1990] 1 WLR 1500 at 1502.)

13. In my judgment, this accurately reflects the status of the appellate regime within the county courts up to 2 May 2000, and there is nothing in any rule or practice direction to suggest that the regime would be any different because on a particular occasion a district judge was exercising the jurisdiction of a circuit judge (see practice direction 2B, para 11.1(d)). This may seem to be an anomalous result, because if the district judge had been exercising similar jurisdiction as a district judge of the High Court the appeal would indeed have lain to this court. It was always likely, however, that there would be some anomalies during the interim period of 12 months between the introduction of a modern, integrated set of Civil Procedure Rules for first instance hearings and the introduction of a similar set of procedures in respect of appeals. This interim period is now at an end, and as will be seen from the second part of this judgment, appeal from the final decision of a district judge exercising jurisdiction in the multi-track in a case of this kind will in future lie direct to this court, whether the action assigned to the multi-track is proceeding in the county court or in the High Court.

14. This is sufficient to dispose of the present matter, which must therefore proceed as an appeal to a circuit judge in the county court, with the costs of this application being costs in the appeal. On 2 May 2000, however, a number of major changes were made to the arrangements for appeals in civil courts, and this judgment provides the opportunity to explain their effect. For the many points of detail, courts and practitioners will of course have to consult the instruments which introduced these changes. These are the Access to Justice Act 1999, CPR Pt 52 (together with rr 27.12–27.13 and CPR Pt 47, section VIII), the practice direction supplementing CPR Pt 52 (PD 52) and the Access to Justice Act 1999 (Destination of Appeals) Order 2000, SI 2000/1071. I have incorporated the effect of the Civil Procedure (Amendment No 2) Rules 2000, SI 2000/940 (the Amendment No 2 rules) and the latest version of PD 52 into this judgment. The general rules relating to appeals in CPR Pt 52 are expressly made subject to any rule, enactment or practice direction which sets out special provisions with regard to any particular category of appeal (r 52.1(4)). In this judgment I am concerned only with appeals in civil proceedings in private law matters. I am not concerned with appeals in public law cases or with appeals in family proceedings.

APPEAL TO NEXT LEVEL IN JUDICIAL HIERARCHY: THE GENERAL RULE

15. As a general rule, appeal lies to the next level of judge in the court hierarchy. Thus in the county court appeal lies from a district judge to a circuit judge, and from a circuit judge to a High Court judge; and in the High Court appeals lie from a master or district judge of the High Court to a High Court judge and from a High Court judge to the Court of Appeal. The court hearing a first appeal is described in CPR Pt 52 as 'the appeal court' (r 52.1(3)(b)), and the court from whose decision an appeal is brought is described as 'the lower court' (r 52.1(3)(c)).

A High Court judge hearing an appeal must have attained the status of a High Court judge or a judge of the Court of Appeal. Although retired judges of this status may hear such appeals, they may not be heard by deputies of lesser status (PD 52, para 8.9(1)).

APPEAL TO NEXT LEVEL IN JUDICIAL HIERARCHY: THE EXCEPTIONS

16. The normal route of appeal will not be followed where a district judge or a circuit judge in the county court, or a master or district judge of the High Court gives the final decision in a multi-track claim allocated by a court to the multi-track under CPR 12.7, 14.8 or 26.5 (the 2000 order, art 4(1)). This exception does not apply to a decision made in a Pt 8 claim (which is treated as allocated to the multi-track pursuant to r 8.9(c)) or a decision in a claim allocated to the multi-track under some other provision, where the normal route of appeal will apply.

17. For this purpose a final decision is one that would finally determine the entire proceedings, subject to any possible appeal or detailed assessment of costs, whichever way the court decided the issues before it (the 2000 order, art 1(2)(c)). A final decision includes the assessment of damages or any other final decision where it is 'made at the conclusion of part of a hearing or trial which has been split up into parts and would, if made at the conclusion of that hearing or trial, be a final decision' (the 2000 order, art 1(3)); it does not include a decision only on costs. This means that if a judge makes a final decision on any aspect of a claim, such as limitation, or on part of a claim which has been directed to be heard separately, this is a final decision within the meaning of this provision. Mr Emmerson told us that there was concern in some quarters that parts of a final decision might be subjected to one avenue of appeal and other parts might have a different avenue of appeal, but the language of the 2000 order, art 1(3) appears to preclude this possibility.

18. Orders striking out the proceedings or a statement of case, and orders giving summary judgment under CPR Pt 24 are not final decisions because they are not decisions that would finally determine the entire proceedings whichever way the court decided the issues before it.

19. The Court of Appeal is the appeal court for appeals against final decisions of the type described above (the 2000 order, art 4(a)). It is also the appeal court where a final decision is taken in specialist proceedings to which r 49(2) applies, whatever level of judge made this final decision (the 2000 order, art 4(b)). These proceedings are admiralty proceedings, arbitration proceedings, commercial and mercantile actions, patents court business, technology and construction court business, proceedings under the Companies Acts 1985 and 1989 and contentious probate proceedings.

PERMISSION TO APPEAL: THE GENERAL RULE

20. As a general rule permission is required for an appeal (CPR 52.3(1)). Permission may be granted either by the lower court at the hearing at which the decision to be appealed was made, or by the appeal court (r 52.3(2)). If an appeal court refuses permission without a hearing, a request may be made for the reconsideration of that decision at an oral hearing (r 52.3(4)). If at that oral hearing the appeal court refuses permission to appeal, then no further right of appeal exists, and that is the end of the matter (the 1999 Act, s 54(4); CPR PD 52, para 4.8). One further new provision needs to be noted: if an appellant is in receipt of services funded by the Legal Services Commission (or legally aided) and permission to appeal has been refused by the appeal court without a hearing, the appellant must send a copy of the reasons the appeal court gave for refusing permission to the relevant office of the Legal Services Commission as soon as it has been received from the court (PD 52, para 4.17).

21. Permission to appeal will only be given where the court considers that an appeal would have a real prospect of success or that there is some other compelling reason why the appeal should be heard (r 52.3(6)). Lord Woolf MR has explained that the use of the word 'real' means that the prospect of success must be realistic rather than fanciful (see *Swain v Hillman* (1999) Times, 4 November, [1999] CA Transcript 1732, para 10).

22. An order giving permission to appeal may limit the issues to be heard. It may also be made subject to conditions (r 52.3(7)). If a court confines its permission to some issues only, it should expressly refuse permission on any remaining issues. Those other issues may then only be raised at the hearing of the appeal with the appeal court's permission. That court and the respondent should be informed of any intention to raise such an issue as soon as practicable after notification of the court's order giving permission to appeal (PD 52, para 4.18).

PERMISSION TO APPEAL: EXCEPTIONS

23. Permission to appeal will not be required where the appeal is against a committal order, a refusal of habeas corpus or a secure accommodation order made under s 25 of the Children Act 1989 (r 52.3(1)(a)). In these cases, where the liberty of the subject is in issue, appeal lies as of right.

24. Permission to appeal is not required for an appeal from a district judge to a circuit judge in relation to a decision made in the small claims track. (By r 52.1(2)(a), CPR Pt 52 does not at present apply to an appeal against an order in the small claims track, although I understand that the position relating to such appeals is currently under review.) If a circuit judge dismisses such an appeal without a hearing because no sufficient ground is shown in the notice of appeal (see PD 27, para 8.6), an appeal against that ruling lies to a High Court judge (the 2000 order, art 3(1): it is not a decision on an appeal falling within art 5). No permission is required for this further appeal.

25. Similarly, permission to appeal is not required for an appeal from a decision made (exceptionally) by a circuit judge on hearing a claim allocated to the small claims track, for which a High Court judge is the appeal court (the 2000 order, art 5 does not apply in these circumstances).

26. Permission to appeal is not required for an appeal from a decision made by an authorised court officer in detailed assessment proceedings to a costs judge or a district judge of the High Court (r 47.21 as substituted by the Amendment No 2 rules). On the other hand, permission to appeal is required from a decision made by a costs judge or a district judge of the High Court in such proceedings to a High Court judge (the 2000 order, art 2), because the exception mentioned in r 52.1(2)(b) applies only to appeals in detailed assessment proceedings against the decision of an authorised court officer, and not to

this higher level of appeal in such proceedings. Where costs are summarily assessed by a judge as part of a final decision in a multi-track claim, then the principles relating to appeals against final decisions in multi-track claims will be applied (see paras 17 and 19 above).

FIRST APPEALS DIVERTED FROM THE NORMAL ROUTE SO AS TO BE HEARD BY THE COURT OF APPEALL

27. If the normal route of a first appeal would be to a circuit judge or to a High Court judge, either the lower court or the appeal court may order the appeal to be transferred to the Court of Appeal if they consider that it would raise an important point of principle or practice or there is some other compelling reason for the Court of Appeal to hear it (r 52.14(1)). This rule refers to first appeals, because what is in question is whether the appeal in question should be heard in the county court or the High Court on the one hand or in the Court of Appeal on the other. By the 2000 order, art 5, all second appeals lie to the Court of Appeal and nowhere else, so that this question could not arise in that context.

28. The Master of the Rolls also has the power to direct that an appeal which would normally be heard by a circuit judge or a High Court judge should be heard instead by the Court of Appeal (the 1999 Act, s 57(1)).

29. In such cases the Master of the Rolls and the Court of Appeal also have the power to remit an appeal to the court in which the original appeal was or would have been brought (r 52.14(2)).

THE APPELLATE APPROACH: THE GENERAL RULE

30. As a general rule, every appeal will be limited to a review of the decision of the lower court. This general rule will be applied unless a practice direction makes different provision for a particular category of appeal, or the court considers that in the circumstances of an individual appeal it would be in the interests of justice to hold a rehearing (r 52.11(1)). The appeal court will only allow an appeal where the decision of the lower court was wrong, or where it was unjust because of a serious procedural or other irregularity in the proceedings in the lower court (r 52.11(3)).

31. This marks a significant change in practice, in relation to what used to be called 'interlocutory appeals' from district judges or masters. Under the old practice, the appeal to a judge was a rehearing in the fullest sense of the word, and the judge exercised his/her discretion afresh, while giving appropriate weight to the way the lower court had exercised its discretion in the matter. Under the new practice, the decision of the lower court will attract much

greater significance. The appeal court's duty is now limited to a review of that decision, and it may only interfere in the quite limited circumstances set out in r 52.11(3).

32. The first ground for interference speaks for itself. The epithet 'wrong' is to be applied to the substance of the decision made by the lower court. If the appeal is against the exercise of a discretion by the lower court, the decision of the House of Lords in *G v G* [1985] 2 All ER 225, [1985] 1 WLR 647 warrants attention. In that case Lord Fraser of Tullybelton said:

> 'Certainly it would not be useful to inquire whether different shades of meaning are intended to be conveyed by words such as 'blatant error' used by Sir John Arnold P in the present case, and words such as 'clearly wrong', 'plainly wrong' or simply 'wrong' used by other judges in other cases. All these various expressions were used in order to emphasise the point that the appellate court should only interfere when it considers that the judge of first instance has not merely preferred an imperfect solution which is different from an alternative imperfect solution which the Court of Appeal might or would have adopted, but has exceeded the generous ambit within which a reasonable disagreement is possible.' (See [1985] 2 All ER 225 at 229, [1985] 1 WLR 647 at 652.)

33. So far as the second ground for interference is concerned, it must be noted that the appeal court only has power to interfere if the procedural or other irregularity which it has detected in the proceedings in the lower court was a serious one, and that this irregularity caused the decision of the lower court to be an unjust decision.

THE NEED FOR A SUITABLE RECORD OF ALL JUDGMENTS

34. This new emphasis on the importance of the decision made at first instance gives added weight to the need for all such decisions to be recorded accurately, so that the appeal court will be able to read a reliable version of the judgment which it is concerned to review. If it is a short judgment, the judge or master may of course dictate it to the parties at dictation speed, to save the cost and delay involved in obtaining a transcript. CPR PD 39 (Miscellaneous Provisions Relating To Hearings), para 6.1, requires a judgment to be recorded unless the judge directs otherwise, and if a judge or master is anxious to spare a party of limited means the cost of obtaining an approved transcript, he or she must take steps to ensure that by some other means there is an incontrovertibly accurate record of the judgment.

35. There is a section of the new practice direction headed 'Suitable record of the judgment' (PD 52, paras 5.12–5.13) which brings conveniently into one place a number of rules and other principles which were previously not always easy to find. Because it is still the case that no reliable record is often produced

to an appeal court of a judgment by a master or district judge, and sometimes of a judgment by a circuit judge, I am setting out in this judgment the parts of that practice direction which apply to civil proceedings. Careful attention must be paid in the future to these matters by all who sit or practise in civil courts, because it will be likely to lead to injustice if an appeal court is expected to review a decision when there is no reliable record of what was said in the lower court. The practice direction reads, so far as is material:

'5.12 Where the judgment to be appealed has been officially recorded by the court, an approved transcript of that record should accompany the appellant's notice. Photocopies will not be accepted for this purpose. However, where there is no officially recorded judgment, the following documents will be acceptable: *Written judgments* (1) Where the judgment was made in writing a copy of that judgment endorsed with the judge's signature. *Note of judgment* (2) When judgment was not officially recorded or made in writing a note of the judgment (agreed between the appellant's and respondent's advocates) should be submitted for approval to the judge whose decision is being appealed. If the parties cannot agree on a single note of the judgment, both versions should be provided to that judge with an explanatory letter. For the purpose of an application for permission to appeal the note need not be approved by the respondent or the lower court judge. *Advocates' notes of judgments where the appellant is unrepresented* (3) When the appellant was unrepresented in the lower court it is the duty of any advocate for the respondent to make his/her note of judgment promptly available, free of charge to the appellant where there is no officially recorded judgment or if the court so directs. Where the appellant was represented in the lower court it is the duty of his/her own former advocate to make his/her note available in these circumstances. The appellant should submit the note of judgment to the appeal court ...

5.13 An appellant may not be able to obtain an official transcript or other suitable record of the lower court's decision within the time within which the appellant's notice must be filed. In such cases the appellant's notice must still be completed to the best of the appellant's ability on the basis of the documentation available. However it may be amended subsequently with the permission of the appeal court.'

THE APPELLATE APPROACH: THE EXCEPTIONS

36. The general rule is set out in r 52.11(1) which starts with the words 'Every appeal will be limited to a review of the decision of the lower court unless ...' I have already set out the exceptions contained in that rule, and I have also mentioned the fact that CPR Pt 52 does not apply to two categories of appeal:

appeals against orders under Pt 27 (the small claims track) and appeals against a decision of an authorised court officer in detailed assessment proceedings.

37. So far as the former is concerned, the only permissible grounds of appeal are that there was a serious irregularity affecting the proceedings or that the court made a mistake of law (r 27.12). As to the latter, on an appeal against a decision of an authorised court officer in detailed assessment proceedings, the court will rehear the proceedings which gave rise to the decision appealed against (r 47.23(a) as substituted by the Amendment No 2 rules). In other words, in such a case the court hearing the appeal will exercise its discretion afresh.

Powers of the Appeal Court: The General Rule

38. The general rule set out in CPR Pt 52 provides that every appeal court has all the powers of the lower court (r 52.10(1)). It also has power to affirm, set aside or vary any order or judgment made or given by the lower court; to refer any claim or issue for determination by the lower court; to order a new trial or hearing and to make a costs order (r 52.10(2)). It may exercise its powers in relation to the whole or part of an order of the lower court (r 52.10(4)). In other words every appeal court, whether a circuit judge or a High Court judge or the Court of Appeal, has been expressly given the same powers in relation to appeals governed by CPR Pt 52. The Court of Appeal also has special powers in an appeal from a claim tried by a jury (r 52.10(3)).

Powers of the Appeal Court: The Exceptions

39. The court hearing an appeal against a decision made in the small claims track may make 'any order it considers appropriate' if it is satisfied that there was a serious irregularity affecting the proceedings or that the lower court made a mistake of law. It also has the power to dismiss an appeal without a hearing (r 27.12). I have already mentioned the fact that a review of the appeal procedures in the small claims track is currently being undertaken, so that courts and practitioners must be alert to any future change to this rule.

40. In an appeal from an authorised court officer in detailed assessment proceedings, the court hearing the appeal may 'make any order and give such directions as it considers appropriate' (r 47.23(b) as substituted by the Amendment No 2 rules).

Second Appeals

41. Parliament is responsible for controlling the expenditure of public resources on the administration of justice (whether in relation to the direct costs of the courts, including the cost of the judiciary, or in relation to expenditure on what

used to be called legal aid). It has now made it clear that it is only in an exceptional case that a second appeal may be sanctioned. Section 55(1) of the 1999 Act provides that:

> 'Where an appeal is made to a county court or the High Court in relation to any matter, and on hearing the appeal the court makes a decision in relation to that matter, no appeal may be made to the Court of Appeal from that decision unless the Court of Appeal considers that—(a) the appeal would raise an *important* point of principle or practice, or (b) there is some other *compelling* reason for the Court of Appeal to hear it.'
> (Emphasis added)

42. This reform introduces a major change to our appeal procedures. It will no longer be possible to pursue a second appeal to the Court of Appeal merely because the appeal is 'properly arguable' or 'because it has a real prospect of success'. The tougher rules introduced by a recent Court of Appeal Practice Direction for 'second tier appeals' related only to cases where a would-be appellant had already lost twice in the courts below (see Practice Direction (Court of Appeal: procedure) [1999] 2 All ER 490 at 499, [1999] 1 WLR 1027 at 1036, para 2.19.1). The new statutory provision is even tougher – the relevant point of principle or practice must be an important one – and it has effect even if the would-be appellant won in the lower court before losing in the appeal court. The decision of the first appeal court is now to be given primacy unless the Court of Appeal itself considers that the appeal would raise an important point of principle or practice, or that there is some other compelling reason for it to hear this second appeal.

43. All courts are familiar with the litigant, often an unrepresented litigant, who will never take 'no' for an answer, however unpromising his/her cause. Under the new appeals regime, however, such litigants must appreciate that the general rule will be that the decision of the appeal court on the first appeal will be the final decision. If they wish to pursue the matter further, and to incur the often quite heavy costs involved in paying the court fee and preparing the appeal papers, the Court of Appeal may dismiss their application quite shortly, saying that the appeal raises no important point of principle or practice, and that there is no other compelling reason for the court to hear the appeal.

44. The reason for this significant change of appellate policy can be found in the 1997 review of the business of the Court of Appeal (Civil Division). This review reported that over the previous decade there had been a substantial increase in the number of cases coming to the Court of Appeal. Its authors believed that if there had to be an appeal in a civil case this should normally be the end of the matter. This principle reflected the need for certainty, reasonable expense and proportionality, and they said that there must be special circumstances if there was to be more than one level of appeal. Elsewhere in their report they had said that judges of the quality of Lords Justices of Appeal were

a scarce and valuable resource, and that it was important that they were used effectively and only on work which was appropriate to them (Review of the Court of Appeal (Civil Division), pp 10, 26 and 22).

45. It is clear that in the 1999 Act Parliament not only accepted the report's analysis of the problems confronting the Court of Appeal but that it also adopted even tougher measures than those recommended by the review to ensure that second appeals would in future become a rarity and that the judges of this court would be freed to devote more of their time and energy in hearing first appeals in more substantive matters which either their court or a lower court had assessed as having a realistic prospect of success.

46. These new arrangements are likely to impose great burdens on the staff and lawyers in the Court of Appeal, unless the status of the order being appealed against is completely clear on its face. Every order made on appeal must therefore record the name and status of the judge against whom the appeal was brought. Orders relating to final decisions of a lower court must also make it clear whether the order was made in the small claims track, the fast track or the multi-track, and if it was made in the multi-track, it must state whether it was made in a claim allocated to the multi-track or whether the Pt 8 procedure was followed. If these steps are taken, it will be possible for the Civil Appeals Office to ascertain without undue difficulty whether the Court of Appeal possesses jurisdiction, and whether this is a first appeal or a second appeal, simply by reading the order under challenge.

TRANSITIONAL ARRANGEMENTS

47. The new rules (and the new destination arrangements) will apply in all cases in which an appeal notice has been filed or an application for permission to appeal has been made on or after 2 May 2000. If an application for permission to appeal has been made to the appeal court before 2 May, and that court gives permission to appeal (whether before or after 2 May) the appeal will be brought and will continue its progress under the old rules (see the Civil Procedure (Amendment) Rules 2000, SI 2000/221, r 39, as amended by the Amendment No 2 rules, r 2, and the 2000 order, art 6). Rule 2 of the Amendment No 2 rules, which came into effect on 2 May 2000, reads:

> 'In the Civil Procedure (Amendment) Rules 2000, rule 39 (transitional provisions) is amended to read—"39. Where a person has filed a notice of appeal or applied for permission to appeal before 2nd May 2000—(a) rule 19 of these Rules shall not apply to the appeal to which that notice or application relates; and (b) the rules of court relating to appeals in force immediately before 2nd May 2000 shall apply to that appeal as if they had not been revoked".'

48. Mr Emmerson suggested to us that the language of these transitional arrangements also appeared to embrace an application for permission to appeal to the lower court which had either been granted before 2 May, although no notice of appeal had been filed at the appeal court before that date, or which had been made before, but granted after, that date. Although the language of these provisions might appear to allow for that interpretation of the rule, I am satisfied that on its proper construction, when viewed in the context of a rule which begins with a reference to the filing of the notice of appeal, the words 'applied for permission to appeal' must be taken to refer to an application for permission made to the appeal court before 2 May. In other words, if the lower court granted permission, the notice of appeal must have been filed at the appeal court before 2 May for the old rules to continue to apply to the appeal. If it did not grant permission, or refused permission, before 2 May, an application for permission must have been made to the appeal court before 2 May if the old rules are to be applied to the appeal.

49. In a judgment on security of costs delivered three days ago, on 9 May 2000, in *A T Poeton (Gloucester) Plating Ltd v Horton* (unreported) Morritt LJ was clearly not made aware of the Amendment No 2 rules. If he had been told about this rule, he would no doubt have held that because Mr Horton had filed a notice of appeal before 2 May 2000 the provisions of RSC Ord 59 applied to that appeal as if they had not been revoked. This judgment should therefore not be followed.

Conclusion

50. I have explained these changes, and their effect, in some detail because in many ways they mark the most significant changes in the arrangements for appeals in civil proceedings in this country for over 125 years. In future the decision of the 'first instance' judge in what used to be called an 'interlocutory appeal' will assume a much greater importance than it ever did in the days when the 'judge in chambers' conducted a complete rehearing, with an entirely fresh discretion to exercise. And the decision of the 'appeal court', whether a circuit judge or a High Court judge, is in most cases now likely to be final. These changes will compel litigants and their advisers to pay even greater attention to the need to prepare their cases with appropriate care, because they may find it much more difficult to extricate themselves from the consequences of an ill-prepared case before a judge at first instance in a lower court.

Lord Justice Gibson. I agree.

Lord Woolf MR. I also agree.

Direction accordingly.

Kate O'Hanlon Barrister

UNILEVER PLC V CHEFARO PROPRIETARIES LTD AND OTHER APPEALS

A2.23

[1995] I All ER 587

COURT OF APPEAL, CIVIL DIVISION

SIR THOMAS BINGHAM MR. MANN and SAVILLE LJJ

14, 23 NOVEMBER 1994

Court of Appeal – Appeal – Expedited appeal – Practice – Guidelines – Categories of appeal which will be considered favourably for expedited hearing.

The Court of Appeal is, in general, sparing in its grant of applications for the expedited hearing of appeals and imposes a high threshold which a party must cross before an application will be granted. However, the court will consider favourably applications in the following categories: (1) appeals against committal orders, particularly if the adverse finding is challenged or the sentence is short; (2) cases in which children are likely to suffer extraordinary prejudice (ie prejudice beyond that almost inevitably consequent on involvement in proceedings) if a decision is delayed; (3) cases under the Hague Convention; (4) asylum appeals concerning return to third countries, where the right to return may be jeopardised by delay; (5) cases in which the execution of a possession order is imminent and which appear to have some merit; (6) cases in which a decision is about to be taken or implemented which will be irrevocable or confer rights on third parties; (7) cases in which publication of allegedly unlawful material is imminent; (8) appeals against judicial decisions made in the course of continuing proceedings. The court also recognises the need to try to arrange expedited hearings where it appears that, without such expedition: (i) a party may lose its livelihood, business or home or suffer irreparable loss or extraordinary hardship; (ii) the appeal will become futile; (iii) the resolution of numerous cases turning on the outcome of a case under appeal will be unreasonably delayed, or the orderly management of class or multi-party litigation in a lower court will be disrupted; (iv) widespread divergencies of practice are likely to continue, with the prospect of multiple appeals until the correct practice is laid down; (v) there would be serious detriment to good public administration or to the interests of members of the public not concerned in the instant appeal. In all cases the court will expect the parties involved to approach it as soon as they learn of the order which it is sought to challenge and in fixing the date for a hearing (a) the court will give weight not to the wishes of the parties to the appeal but to the interests of other parties adversely affected by the order and (b) the greater the expedition ordered, the less regard can usually be had to the parties' preferences concerning dates. Expedition will not ordinarily be granted unless the party seeking it is willing, if need be, to change counsel. In an appropriate case the respondent also may have to change counsel; this possible adverse consequence will cause the court to lean against making an order save in a clear case. In granting an application for expedition, the court may seek to mitigate the disruption caused to other parties by giving procedural directions not normally given, with a view to ensuring that the appeal is heard in the minimum time necessary to achieve a just result.

Notes

For appeals to the Court of Appeal in general, see 37 *Halsbury's Laws* (4th edn) para 677.

Case referred to in judgment

Biogen Inc v Medeva plc [1994] CA Transcript 1309

Applications for expedited hearings of appeals

UNILEVER PLC V CHEFARO PROPRIETARIES LTD

The defendants, Chefaro Proprietaries Ltd, applied for an expedited hearing of their appeal from the decision of Jacob J delivered on 30 March 1994 granting an injunction to the plaintiffs, Unilever plc, restraining the defendants from selling a product which infringed a patent held by the plaintiffs, and ordering an inquiry into damages. The facts are set out in the judgment of the court.

CHIRON CORP AND ORS V ORGANON TEKNIKA LTD AND ORS

The defendants, (1) Organon Teknika Ltd, (2) Organon Teknika NV, (3) Akzo Pharma International BV, (4) Akzo Pharma BV, (5) United Biomedical Inc, and (6) Murex Diagnostics Ltd (formerly known as BCW Operations Ltd), in four separate actions brought by the plaintiffs, Chiron Corp, Ortho Diagnostic Systems Inc and Ortho Diagnostic Systems Ltd, applied for an expedited hearing of their appeals from the decisions of Aldous J delivered on 5 October 1993 and 27 May 1994 upholding the validity of the plaintiffs' patent for a method of identifying the Hepatitis C virus and holding that the defendants had infringed the patent. The facts are set out in the judgment of the court.

HENDERSON AND ORS V MERRETT SYNDICATES LTD AND ORS

The plaintiffs, (1) Ian McIntosh Henderson and others, (2) William Hallam-Eames and others, and (3) Elise Heckman Hughes and others, applied for an expedited hearing of their appeal from the decision of Gatehouse J delivered on 14 October 1994 determining on the trial of a preliminary issue that certain claims brought by the plaintiffs against the defendants, Merrett Syndicates Ltd and other underwriting agencies, Stephen Roy Merrett and Ernst & Whinney, were statute-barred. The facts are set out in the judgment of the court.

BROWN V KMR SERVICES LTD

The plaintiff, Richard Kevin Brown, in an action brought against KMR Services Ltd, applied for an expedited hearing of his cross-appeal from the decision of Gatehouse J ([1994] 4 All ER 385) delivered on 13 April 1994 in which the judge held that the defendant was liable to the plaintiff for breach of contract, but that the damages payable by the defendant should be reduced by 30%. The facts are set out in the judgment of the court.

Cur adv vul

23 November 1994. The following judgment of the court was delivered.

Sir Thomas Bingham MR. There is, almost inevitably, a time-lag between the date an appeal is set down and the date it is heard. Such a time-lag is almost inevitable because, when set down, an appeal is not usually ready to be heard. There are procedural steps to be taken before the appeal is ready for hearing and a slot must be found for the case in the court's calendar. In an ideal world the time-lag would not be lengthy and the court would hear the appeal as soon as it was ready to be heard.

Over the past years the court's backlog of unheard appeals has increased and the time-lag between setting-down and hearing has steadily lengthened. This has prompted parties who fear that delay will be prejudicial to their interests to apply for the hearing of their appeal to be expedited. The Civil Division's Review of the Legal Year 1992–93 contained this passage:

> 'These waiting periods, understandably, prompt parties to apply to the Court asking that the hearing of their appeals be expedited. If compelling grounds are shown, such applications may be granted; but it has always to be remembered that the expedition of one appeal inevitably means the deferment of another.'

The Review of the Legal Year 1993–94 also referred to this matter:

> 'Delay in the hearing of appeals not infrequently causes loss, hardship, inconvenience and anxiety to one or both of the parties. Faced with a long wait before their appeals can be heard, parties unsurprisingly apply to the Court for the hearing of their cases to be expedited. They can often advance strong grounds for expedition. But the expedition of one appeal inevitably means the postponement of the date at which another appeal can be heard, and the Court cannot order expedition of all the appeals it would wish. On occasion, the Court has resolved this problem by

ordering that a hearing be expedited but imposing strict pre-determined limits on the time allowed for oral argument of the appeal.'

Since most appeals are scheduled to be heard on dates fixed well in advance, and since court sittings are so far as possible planned a long time ahead, the expediting of an appeal other than the shortest is likely to have one or other of two possible consequences, usually both. One is that a fixture already made for the hearing of another appeal has to be cancelled. The other is that the hearing of another appeal, which may well have been awaiting hearing for about 18 months, has to be deferred. Both these consequences are highly distasteful both to the court and to the parties in the displaced appeal or appeals. This in turn has had two consequences. One is that the court has in general been sparing in its grant of applications for expedition. Since it cannot grant all the applications it would wish, it has imposed a high threshold which a party must cross before its application will be granted. The second is that where the threshold is crossed and an expedited hearing is ordered, the court will in fixing the date for that hearing give weight not to the wishes of the parties to that appeal but to the interests of other parties adversely affected by the order. It will, for instance, do its utmost to avoid cancelling a fixture which has already been cancelled on a previous occasion. The greater the expedition ordered, the less regard can usually be had to the parties' preferences concerning dates. Expedition will not ordinarily be granted unless the party seeking it is willing, if need be, to change counsel. In an appropriate case the respondent also may have to change counsel; this possible adverse consequence will cause the court to lean against making an order save in a clear case. In granting an application for expedition, the court may seek to mitigate the disruption caused to other parties by giving procedural directions not currently given in the ordinary run of cases with a view to ensuring that the appeal is heard in the minimum time necessary to achieve a just result.

In recent weeks over 40 applications for expedition have been lodged with the Civil Appeals Office. Few of these are devoid of merit. But few can be granted without gross disruption to other parties. Perhaps because the principles on which the court works are not well understood, there appears to be a tendency for parties to apply for expedition in the hope that the application may be granted but in the belief that if it is not they are no worse off. This is understandable, but it imposes a heavy burden on those whose task it is to read and rule on such applications, particularly where rulings once given are the subject of question and argument.

With a view to making known the broad principles governing the court's practice, four applications have been referred to the court for argument and decision. But before turning to these cases we attempt to describe the court's practice. No statement can cover the novel, the unexpected and the exceptional, and no two cases are identical. So the practice must be understood and followed with a measure of flexibility and in recognition that no statement can be exhaustive. But it is in our view possible to give a reliable indication of the principles the court is likely to apply. We therefore give this judgment of the court.

Some appeals are so urgent that justice can only be done if the appeal is heard either immediately or within days. In this category we put: (1) appeals against committal orders, particularly if the adverse finding is challenged or the sentence is short; (2) cases in which children are likely to suffer extraordinary prejudice (ie prejudice beyond that almost inevitably consequent on involvement in proceedings) if a decision is delayed; (3) cases under the Convention on the Civil Aspects of International Child Abduction (The Hague, 25 October 1980; TS 66 (1986); Cm 33; Cmnd 8281); (4) asylum appeals concerning return to third countries, where the right to return may be jeopardised by delay; (5) cases in which the execution of a possession order is imminent and which appear to have some merit; (6) cases in which a decision is about to be taken or implemented which will be irrevocable or confer rights on third parties; (7) cases in which publication of allegedly unlawful material is imminent; (8) appeals against judicial decisions made in the course of continuing proceedings.

In all these cases, not least (5), the court will expect the parties involved to approach it as soon as they learn of the order which it is sought to challenge. When the approach is left until the eleventh hour, or the necessary materials are not provided, it may well prove impracticable to arrange a hearing.

The court recognises the need to try and arrange expedited hearings where it appears that, without such expedition: (1) a party may lose its livelihood, business or home or suffer irreparable loss or extraordinary hardship; (2) the appeal will become futile; (3) the resolution of numerous cases turning on the outcome of a case under appeal will be unreasonably delayed, or the orderly management of class or multi-party litigation in a lower court will be disrupted; (4) widespread divergencies of practice are likely to continue, with the prospect of multiple appeals until the correct practice is laid down; (5) there would be serious detriment to good public administration or to the interests of members of the public not concerned in the instant appeal.

Where these criteria are not satisfied, the court will not ordinarily grant an expedited hearing of appeals on preliminary issues, or substantial interlocutory appeals (even where this means loss of a trial date), or appeals concerning the construction of a standard document.

Unilever plc v Chefaro Proprietaries Ltd

In this action Unilever sued Chefaro for infringing Unilever's patent by selling product A. Chefaro challenged the validity of the patent and denied infringement. In a judgment given on 30 March 1994 Jacob J upheld the validity of the patent and found that sale of product A infringed it. By the time of the trial Chefaro were no longer selling product A but were by then selling product B, a similar but different product. Unilever claim that product B also infringes their patent and have issued further proceedings, due to be heard by Jacob J at a second trial due to be held on 22 March 1995. At present Chefaro are not restrained from selling product B, since the injunction which Jacob J granted at the end of the first trial was so expressed as to exclude product B. Chefaro have, however, appealed against Jacob J's decision on validity and infringement and the parties agree that whichever party loses in the second trial is likely to appeal.

Chefaro seek expedition of the hearing of their appeal against the judge's existing decision. They point out that if their appeal on validity succeeds, the second action will inevitably fall. An inquiry into damages under the first judgment is currently proceeding which would be rendered unnecessary if the appeal succeeds. Attention is drawn to the existence of another action in which Unilever are claiming damages against a third party for infringement of this same patent.

Unilever do not oppose expedition but suggest there is no reason for ordering it. If the appeal against the judge's first decision is heard before his second hearing there is (they say) a risk of two appeals instead of one combined appeal. The present injunction is not restricting Chefaro's exploitation of product B. It is standard practice for an inquiry into damages to proceed pending appeal, and if their appeal succeeds Chefaro will be compensated for the costs thrown away. Nothing will be gained by expedition if the appeal does not succeed. The third party action is at an early stage and currently dormant.

In our judgment Chefaro show no grounds to justify an order for expedition. They do not begin to satisfy any of the criteria outlined above. The application will be refused. The costs of the application will be costs in the appeal. In fixing the existing appeal the court will be ready to take account of the probability that this appeal will be enlarged by joinder of an appeal against the decision (whatever it is) in the second action.

CHIRON CORP V ORGANON TEKNIKA LTD

In this case the defendants in four closely related actions appeal against decisions of Aldous J on 5 October 1993 and 27 May 1994. By those decisions the judge upheld the validity of the plaintiffs' patent as amended and found that the defendants had infringed it. The patent relates to the Hepatitis C virus. The plaintiffs claim to have found a means of identifying that virus, an essential step towards countering or neutralising its effect. The invention is of obvious importance to the blood transfusion services. The appeals are estimated to last five weeks. The parties seek a hearing beginning in June 1995. They suggest that it will be helpful to the court if the counsel and scientific adviser who acted at the trial are available.

Both parties are keen that the hearing of the appeals should be expedited. It is said that the decision is of great commercial importance to the parties, and also to other operators in the field, as was recognised when an order for a speedy trial was earlier made. Although an injunction has been sought, such injunction (if granted) may be suspended pending appeal (in which event the suspension itself may be the subject of appeal). Since the blood transfusion services currently use both competing products it is desirable, given the life-saving service they perform, that they learn where they stand as soon as possible. The defendants contend that doubt has been cast on the judge's reasoning in these cases by the court's recent decision in *Biogen Inc v Medeva plc* [1994] CA Transcript 1309 and complain that the plaintiffs are relying on the decision in these cases to obtain patent protection in Holland (where the court has relied on the decision) and Germany.

We accept that these appeals affect interests much wider than those of the immediate parties, and that serious inconvenience and expense will be caused if widespread reliance is placed on Aldous J's decisions in these cases and they are later reversed. For these reasons we regard a measure of expedition as appropriate. But it is impracticable, given the court's existing and prospective commitments, to schedule these appeals for five weeks beginning in June 1995. We shall accordingly direct that the appeals be fixed, with a time estimate of five weeks, beginning on Tuesday, 3 October 1995. Skeleton arguments should not be exchanged but should be served serially so that the respondents' is responsive to the appellants'. Save that both skeleton arguments should reach this court not less than 21 days before the hearing date, we leave it to counsel to agree on the timetable. There will be liberty to apply to the registrar in the unlikely event of difficulty. The costs of this application will be costs in the appeals.

HENDERSON V MERRETT SYNDICATES LTD

These actions are fixed to be heard in the Commercial Court on 27 March 1995. The trial is estimated to last 20 weeks. There are, in all, nearly 2,000 claimants. These are the first in a series of cases which have been called the long-tail cases because they relate to run-off contracts made some years ago and reinsurance to close years which have in some cases long since passed. The trial of these long-tail cases has been the subject of an orderly programme laid down by the Commercial Court, and the programme cannot be maintained if these actions are not tried in March 1995.

In response to a number of the claims pleaded in these Merrett actions the defendants pleaded a defence of limitation. The legal merit of this defence was the subject of a preliminary issue determined, in favour of the defendants, by Gatehouse J on 14 October 1994. The plaintiffs appeal against that decision with the leave of the judge, which he unhesitatingly gave. He also thought it highly desirable that the appeal be considered by this court at the very earliest opportunity and urged the plaintiffs to move the court to that end. This they did. It is not in doubt that the decision on this limitation issue fundamentally affects the scope of the trial in March 1995 and hence the preparatory work needed for that trial.

In our judgment this application very plainly meets the criteria we have set out. There is a very strong case for an early hearing. We direct (1) that the appeal be listed for two days beginning on 19 December 1994; (2) that the parties endeavour to agree a succinct summary of the facts giving rise to the issue of law which is the subject of appeal; (3) that the parties serve skeleton arguments on each other serially, not by way of exchange, so that the respondents' is responsive to the appellants'; (4) that a timetable for service of skeleton arguments be agreed between the parties, but so as to ensure that all skeleton arguments (and the agreed statement of facts) reach the court not less than five clear days before the fixed date; (5) that there be liberty to apply to the registrar in the unlikely event of difficulty; (6) that the costs of this application be costs in the appeal.

BROWN V KMR SERVICES LTD

A number of actions have been brought in which Lloyd's names (or former names) claim damages and an indemnity against their former members' agents on the ground that the agents were negligent in advising the names which syndicates to join and remain members of and what premium limit to impose on such syndicates. Plainly, names vary widely in their knowledge and understanding of the market, and the action reasonably required of an agent to discharge his duty of care to the names may depend on the extent to which the name may choose or reasonably be expected to look after himself.

In the hope that it would promote settlement of other cases the Commercial Court ordered that two actions be tried, the plaintiff names being chosen as broadly representative of the more sophisticated and the less sophisticated of the claimant names. These were not in the strict sense test actions, but it was hoped that the decision in these actions would be of practical assistance in resolving others. The actions were heard together and on 13 April 1994 Gatehouse J ([1994] 4 All ER 385) gave judgment in favour of both names. The agents do not challenge the decision in favour of the less sophisticated name, but do appeal against the decision in favour of Mr Brown, the more sophisticated name. He himself has cross-appealed. In the absence of an order for expedition, his appeal would be heard in about January 1996. It is estimated to last for six to seven days.

It is not suggested that Mr Brown's appeal, viewed in isolation, has any particular claim to expedition. The essential ground of the application is that other claimant names do not know where they stand, and the Commercial Court has declined to fix further actions, until the outcome of the agents' appeal and Mr Brown's cross-appeal in his case are known. There are a significant number of other actions awaiting the outcome of this appeal.

We would wish, if we properly could, to direct a hearing of the appeal and the cross-appeal in this case within the next few months but we do not think the grounds shown are sufficiently strong to justify us in doing so. We do, however, consider a measure of expedition to be justified and we do not consider that a delay until June 1995 will cause serious prejudice to these parties; we hope that prejudice to other parties may be mitigated if trial dates (after June 1995) are allotted to other cases in this category on the understanding that, depending on the outcome of the appeal, they might be ineffective.

The appeal and cross-appeal will be fixed for 19 to 20 June 1995 with an estimate of six to seven days.

We invite counsel to agree a timetable for serial delivery of skeleton arguments in the appeal and the cross-appeal, all of these to reach the court not later than 14 days before the fixed date. There will be liberty to apply to the registrar in the unlikely event of difficulty. The costs of this application will be costs in the appeal and the cross-appeal.

Orders accordingly.

L I Zysman Esq Barrister.

Index

abuse of process
  striking out appeal notice   5.1, A2.17
admiralty claims
  routes of appeal   3.21
  See also **specialist proceedings**
alternative dispute resolution
  compulsory   7.3
  costs
    consequences of turning down   4.112
    sanctions   7.4, 7.5
  CPR   7.1–2
  encouragement to use   7.1
  mediation   7.2, 7.4, 7.6
  overriding objective   7.1
  power of court   7.3
  public bodies   7.4, 7.5
  sanctions for refusal   7.4
amendments
  appellant's notice   1.7, 4.53, 6.19
    applications   4.55–7
    Court of Appeal   4.103
    fee payable   4.56
    new grounds   4.57
    objection by respondent   4.57
    permission   1.7, 4.53, 4.55–7, 6.19
    skeleton argument   1.7
ancillary orders
  judicial review proceedings   3.44
  permission to appeal   3.35
  routes of appeal   3.35, A2.7
appeal
  exercise of discretion. *See*
    exercise of discretion appeals
  first   1.5
  hearing. *See* **hearing of appeal**
  interlocutory   2.4, 4.72
    fresh evidence   2.4, 2.64, 2.66, A2.6
  irregularity of decision. *See*
    grounds for appeal, irregularity
  meaning   1.3

appeal – *contd*
  reopening. *See* **reopening appeals**
  routes. *See* **routes of appeal**
  second. *See* **second appeals**
  unopposed   6.53
appeal bundles   4.102, 6.12, 6.13
  avoidance of duplication   6.13
  binding   6.13
  core bundle   6.28
  Court of Appeal   4.102, 6.13
  disposal   6.50
  filed with appellant's notice   1.7
  format and presentation   6.13
  identification   6.13
  indices   6.13
  inter-solicitor correspondence   6.13
  labels   6.13
  new documents   6.13
  pagination   6.13
  rejection   6.13
  respondent's   4.38, 6.36–7
  revision   6.27
  sanctions for non-compliance   6.13
  service   6.24
  staples removed   6.13
  statements of case   4.28, 6.13
  supplemental   6.36–7
appeal court
  appealing decision of   1.4, 1.5
  applications for incidental
    remedy   4.52, 6.6
  costs orders   1.5
  exercise of discretion   2.61
    See also **exercise of discretion**
    appeals
  extension of time. *See* **extension**
    of time applications
  meaning   1.3
  second appeals. *See* **second**
    appeals

Index

appeal notice
  amendment. *See* **amendments**
  extension of time. *See* **extension of time applications**
  See also **appellant's notice; respondent's notice**
  appeal questionnaire   4.107, 4.108, 6.25
    fees on filing   4.107
    time estimates   6.26
appellant
  bankruptcy of   5.6
appellant's notice   1.7
  amendment. *See* **amendments**
  appeal bundle. *See* **appeal bundles**
  appeal questionnaire   4.107, 4.108, 6.25, 6.26
  contents   4.2, 4.28
  documentation   4.28, 4.102, 6.7, 6.12
    appeal questionnaire   4.107, 4.108, 6.25, 6.26
    chronology   6.16
    Court of Appeal   6.8
    glossary of terms   6.16
    list of persons   6.16
    order to be appealed   4.3, 4.101, 6.10
    record of judgment   6.17, A2.21
    skeleton arguments   6.15, 6.16, 6.43
    small claims appeals   6.9, 6.14
    time estimate   6.26
  See also **appeal bundles**
  extension of time   4.44, 4.45–9, 6.4
    Court of Appeal   6.5–6
  See also **extension of time applications**
  filing   4.2, 4.27
  Form N161   4.30, 6.1
  Form N244   6.6
  grounds for appeal   1.7, 6.2
  human rights claim   6.3
  index to notes   4.2
  permission to appeal request in   4.25
  sealing   1.8, 4.104, 6.18
  service   1.8, 4.27, 4.104, 6.18
    certificate of service   6.18, 8.30
    contempt of court   4.27
    Court of Appeal   1.8
    dispensing with   6.18
  setting aside   4.58, 4.60, A2.2, A2.11
  skeleton arguments   6.15
    content   6.16
    supplementary   6.43
  statement of case   4.28, 6.13
  stay of execution and   4.50, A2.9

appellant's notice – *contd*
  striking out   4.58, 4.61
    abuse of process   5.1, A2.17
  time limits   1.7, 4.27, 4.43, 6.4
    Court of Appeal   4.100
  variation of time application   4.42, A2.20
appendix of documents
  Scottish cases   8.64
applications
  dismissal by consent   6.52
  disposing by consent   6.51
  Form N244   6.6, 6.19
  within respondent's notice   6.34
arbitration proceedings
  index to notes   4.2
  routes of appeal   3.21
  special provisions for appeals   4.7
assessment of costs
  detailed   1.2, 1.11
    authorised appeal officer   2.2, 3.32, 4.65
    CPR exclusion   1.2
  routes of appeal   1.11, 3.31
  summary   1.11, 3.31, 4.112, 6.38
assignment of appeals to Court of Appeal   3.36–8, 4.114–15, A2.21
  criteria for transfer   3.37, 4.114
  important point of principle   3.37, 4.96, 4.114
  powers of transfer   4.115
asylum appeals
  social security payments   A2.18
authorised costs officer
  appealing decision of   2.2, 3.32, 4.65
authorities
  Court of Appeal appeal   6.42
  former   2.15
  House of Lords appeal   8.58
bail
  index to notes   4.2
  power of appeal court   4.68
bankruptcy of party
  appellant   5.6
  House of Lords appeal   8.71
bundle of authorities   6.42, 8.58
bundles of documents
  Court of Appeal   4.102, 6.13
  supplemental to respondent's notice   4.38

bundles of documents – *contd*
  See also **appeal bundles**

case management
  index to notes 4.2
  past costs 4.70, A2.4, A2.5
  permission to appeal decisions 4.17
  powers of appeal court 4.69–70
case stated appeals
  index to notes 4.2
  respondent's skeleton arguments 4.40
CEDR Solve 7.6
  address 7.7
change of circumstances
  change of fact 2.75, 2.76
  change of law 2.75
  CPR 2.79–80
  finality of legislation and 2.77
  grounds for appeal 2.73–80
  rehearings 2.78, 2.79
  review not rehearing 2.78
  RSC 2.73–7, 2.79
change of solicitor 5.2–3
  index to notes 4.2
children
  consent orders 6.54, 6.56
  structured settlements 6.57
circuit judge
  fast track claims 3.8, 3.9, 3.10, 3.11
  Part 8 claims 3.14, 3.15, 3.16
  small claims 3.2, 3.5
circumstance change. *See* **change of circumstances**
circumstances in which appeal allowed. *See* **grounds for appeal**
Civil Procedure Rules 1.1
  ADR 7.1–2
  exclusions 1.2
  main features 1.7
  new regime guidance 2.3–5, 2.7, A2.21
  Practice Direction 1.7
  scope and interpretation 4.5
  See also **overriding objective**
clinical negligence
  credibility of witnesses 2.46
co-operating parties
  private law 2.35
  statutory appeals 2.33–5
committal order appeals
  Court of Appeal 3.18
  Destination of Appeals Order 3.18
  index to notes 4.2
  no permission required 3.17

committal order appeals – *contd*
  routes of appeal 3.17–18
  suspended 3.17
committal proceedings 4.9
companies
  fair trial right 2.85
  routes of appeal 3.21
compulsory purchase orders 8.5
consent
  dismissal by
    appeals 6.52
    applications 6.52
  disposal by
    appeals 6.51
    applications 6.51
    index to notes 4.2
    Practice Direction 4.83
consent orders
  appeals against 5.5
  children 6.54, 6.55
  patients 6.54, 6.56
contempt of court
  Destination of Appeals Order 3.18
  routes of appeal 3.18
  service of appellant's notice 4.27
contentious probate claims
  routes of appeal 3.21
core bundles 6.28
costs
  authorised officer decision 2.2, 3.32, 4.65
  Court of Appeal 3.34, 4.2, 4.112
  detailed assessment
    authorised appeal officer 2.2, 3.32, 4.65
  CPR exclusion 1.2
  routes of appeal 1.11
  High Court judge 3.33, 3.34
  House of Lords
    money in security fund 8.78–81
    petitions for leave 8.27
    submission on 8.72, 8.73
    taxation 8.76–81
  Part 36 offers and payments 4.92
  past 4.70, A2.4, A2.5
  permission to appeal 3.33
  respondent's 4.2
  routes of appeal 3.31–4
  sanctions for ADR refusal 7.4, 7.5
  security for 4.2, 4.59, A2.4, A2.8, A2.9
    petition of appeal 8.32
  summary assessment 4.112, 6.38
  routes of appeal 1.11, 3.31

538 Index

costs orders
  appeal against   1.5
  failure to give reasons   2.26
county courts
  family proceedings   3.40
  reopening decisions   4.122
  routes of appeal from   1.9
  to Court of Appeal   1.9
  to single High Court Judge   1.9
Court of Appeal
  alternative dispute resolution   7.3, 7.6
  appeal bundles. *See* **appeal bundles**
  appeal notices
    amendment   4.103
    filing   4.100
    sealing   1.8, 4.104, 6.18
    service   4.104
    supporting documentation   4.102, 6.8
  appeal questionnaire   4.107, 4.108, 6.25, 6.26
  appeals in   1.8–12
  assignment of appeals to   3.36–8, 4.114–15, A2.21
  bundle of authorities   6.42
  bundles of documents   4.102, 6.13
  Civil Division   5.7
  committal order   3.18
  composition   4.2, 4.110
  compulsory ADR   7.3
  core bundles   6.28
  costs claims   3.34
  costs in   4.2, 4.112
  CPR   4.98
  directions, request for   6.41, A2.21
  dismissal list of hearings   5.8
  documentation
    appellant's supporting documents   4.102, 6.8
    bundle of authorities   6.42
    bundles of documents   4.102, 6.13
    core bundles   6.28
    disposal of bundles   6.50
    See also **appeal bundles**
  enforcement of order   5.9
  evidence in support   4.105
  exercise of powers   4.118–19
  expedited hearings   4.2, 4.111, A2.22
  extension of time
    application   6.5–6
    filing respondent's notice   6.31
  family proceedings   3.42, 4.113
  fast track claims   3.9, 3.10, 3.12

Court of Appeal – *contd*
  filing of documents   4.101, 6.31
  hearings   4.111
  index to notes   4.2
  judgment
    agreed orders following   6.47
    applications for leave to appeal   6.49
    corrections to draft   6.48
    reserved   6.45, 6.46, A2.16
  judicial review appeals   4.116–17
  jurisdiction   A2.8
  leave to appeal to House of Lords   8.5–8
  listing in   4.111
    dismissal list of hearings   5.8
    short-warned list   4.2, 6.39
    special fixtures list   6.40
  master   4.119
    Civil Division   5.7
    and deputy masters   4.2
  mediation scheme   7.6
  original order to be filed   4.3, 4.101, 4.111, 6.10
  Part 36 offers and payments   4.91, 6.11
  permission to appeal. *See* **permission to appeal**
  persons exercising powers of   4.118–19
  points of principle   3.37, 4.96, 4.114
  Practice Direction   1.8, 4.98, 4.99
  reopening appeals   4.121
  request for directions   6.41, A2.21
  reserved judgments, handing down
    attendance of advocates   6.46
    availability before   6.45, A2.16
  respondent's notice   4.109
  routes of appeal   1.9–12
  sealing appeal notice   1.8, 4.104, 6.18
  second appeals to   4.93–5
    CPR   4.93
    meaning   4.94
    original order and   4.3, 4.101, 6.10
  security for costs orders   A2.8
  service of appeal notice   1.8, 4.104
  short warned list   4.2, 6.39
  skeleton arguments   4.106
  small claims   3.5, 3.7
  special fixtures list   6.40
  three-judge court   4.110
  time limits   4.100
    filing respondent's notice   6.31
  transcript of judgment to be appealed   4.3, 4.101, 4.111, 6.10

Index 539

Court of Justice of the European
  Communities. *See* European
  Court of Justice
Court of Sessions
  appeal to House of Lords   8.16
courts
  appeal. *See* **appeal court** *and
    individual courts*
  lower. *See* **lower court** *and
    individual courts*
Crown proceedings
  service of appellant's notice   4.27

death of party
  House of Lords appeal   8.70
Destination of Appeals Order   3.1, 3.18,
                             3.43, 4.2, A2.21
  committal proceedings   3.18
  contempt of court   3.18
  index to notes   4.2
  insolvency proceedings   3.43
disclosure
  Part 36 offers and payments   4.89–91,
                                          6.11
  private and family life right and   2.88
discontinuance of proceedings
  lower court   5.4
discretion
  exercise by appeal court   2.61
  See also **exercise of discretion
    appeals**
dismissal by consent
  appeals   6.52
  applications   6.52
disposal by consent
  appeals   6.51
  applications   6.51
  index to notes   4.2
  Practice Direction   4.83
district judge
  fast track claims   3.10
  Part 8 claims   3.15
divorce
  index to notes   4.2
  See also **family proceedings**
documentation
  appeal bundle. *See* **appeal bundles**
  appeal questionnaire   4.107, 4.108, 6.25,
                                          6.26
  appellant's notice, with   4.28, 4.102, 6.7,
                                          6.12
    Court of Appeal   6.8
    skeleton arguments   6.15, 6.16, 6.43

documentation – *contd*
  appellant's notice, with – *contd*
    small claims appeals   6.9, 6.14
    time estimate   6.26
  appendix of documents   8.37–42
    lodgment   8.43–4
    Scottish cases   8.64
  authorities
    Court of Appeal appeals   6.42
    House of Lords appeals   8.58
  bundle of authorities   6.42
  chronology   6.16
  core bundles   6.28
  glossary of terms   6.16
  House of Lords
    appendix of documents   8.37–42,
                                  8.43–4, 8.64
    authorities   8.58
    lodgment   8.43–4
    numbers of documents   8.66
    statement of facts and issues   8.35–6,
                                       8.43–4
  list of persons   6.16
  order to be appealed   4.3, 4.101, 6.10
  petition for leave/petition of
    appeal. *See* **House of Lords**
  prayers   6.44
  record of judgment   6.17, A2.21
  respondent's
    service   6.37
    skeleton arguments   6.32, 6.33, 6.35
    supplemental bundle   6.36–7
  skeleton arguments
    appellant's   6.15, 6.16, 6.43
    respondent's   6.32, 6.33, 6.35
    supplementary   6.43
  statement of facts and issues   8.35–6
    lodgment   8.43–4
  time estimates   6.26

education appeals
  co-operating parties   2.33
enforcement
  Court of Appeal order   5.9
  final decision, application   1.11
  House of Lords   8.82
  judgment order   8.82
error of law   2.28–31
  absence of evidence   2.19–20, 2.22
  appeal ground   2.17–20
  failure to give reasons   2.23–7, 4.78
  failure to resolve conflicts of
    evidence   2.28–31

540 Index

error of law – *contd*
  nature   2.17–18
  perverse decisions   2.21–2
  scope   2.17–18
European Convention on Human Rights
  right to fair trial   2.83, 2.84–90, 4.67
European Court of Human Rights   9.1, 9.2–3, 9.5
  admissibility criteria   9.6
  anonymity of applicants   9.7
  application form   9.7
  exhaustion precondition   9.7
  friendly settlement   9.8
  individual applications   9.6
  institution of proceedings   9.8
  judgments
    binding force   9.8
    execution   9.8
    reasons   9.8
    'taken into account'   9.4
  jurisdiction   9.6
  Practice Direction   9.8
  Rules of Court   9.7
European Court of Justice   9.1, 9.2
  Advocate-General   9.13
  Art 234 reference procedure   9.10, 9.11
  establishment   9.9
  'exceptional urgency' test   9.15
  failure to give reasons   2.26
  interpretation of Treaty   9.10
  Luxembourg precedent   9.9
  Practice Direction (Part 68)   9.12
  preliminary rulings   9.10
  procedures   9.13–14
  terms of reference   9.12
evidence
  conflicting expert opinions   2.31, 2.41
  Court of Appeal   4.105
  disclosure
    Part 36 offers and payments   4.89–90, 4.91, 6.11
    private and family life right and   2.88
  expert witnesses   2.20, 2.31, 2.41
  failure to resolve conflicts   2.28–31
  fresh/new. *See* **fresh evidence**
  reviewing record of   2.44
  to support applications   4.105
  to support finding of fact   2.20
    absence of   2.19–20, 2.22
'exceptional urgency' test
  European Court of Justice   9.15

exercise of discretion appeals   2.56–61, 4.80
  discretion of appeal court   2.61
  gross miscarriage of justice   2.57
  interference by appeal court   2.56–60
  irrelevant material considered   2.58, 25.59
  relevant material not considered   2.58, 25.59
expedited hearings
  Court of Appeal   4.2, 4.111, A2.22
  House of Lords   8.28
  index to notes   4.2
  requests for   4.111
expert witnesses   2.20
  conflicts between   2.31, 2.41
  present in lower court   2.40–1
extension of time application   1.5, 4.19, 4.29, A2.7
  appealing order   3.35, A2.7
  Court of Appeal   6.5–6
  degree of prejudice   4.46, A2.15
  examination on merits   4.46
  factors taken into account   4.46
  family cases   4.48
  filing appellant's notice   6.4
  filing respondent's notice   4.36, 6.31
  fresh evidence   A2.10
  House of Lords petition   8.67
  index to notes   4.2
  overriding objective   4.46
  reasons for delay   4.46, A2.15
  refusal, appeals against   4.47
  respondent's notice   4.36, 6.31
  respondent's views   4.45

facts
  absence of evidence to support   2.19–20, 2.22
  incorrect basis of fact   2.32–5
  primary, inferences drawn from   2.47–54
  See also **findings of fact, appeals against**
failure to give reasons   2.23–7, 4.78
  costs orders   2.27
  European Court jurisprudence   2.26
  See also **duty to give reasons**
failure to resolve conflicts of evidence   2.28–31
  central issues   2.28, 2.29
fair trial, right to   2.83, 2.84–91
  application of right   2.86
  bias or irregularity   4.67
  companies   2.85
  CPR compliance   2.87, 2.89

Index

fair trial, right to – *contd*
- disclosure and — 2.88
- retrial order — 4.67

family mediation — 7.6

family proceedings
- appeal court — 3.41
- county courts — 3.40
- Court of Appeal — 3.42, 4.113
- CPR 52 and — 4.1
- extension of time application — 4.48
- High Court judge — 3.41, 3.42
- index to notes — 4.2
- judicial review, appeals in proceedings for — 3.44
- permission to appeal — 3.40
- routes of appeal — 3.39–42

fast track claims
- circuit judge — 3.8, 3.9, 3.10, 3.11
- Court of Appeal — 3.9, 3.10, 3.12
- district judge — 3.10
- High Court judge — 3.11, 3.12
- permission to appeal — 3.8, 3.9, 3.11
- routes of appeal — 3.8–12

fees
- amendment of appeal notice — 4.56
- on filing appeal questionnaire — 4.107

final appeals
- reopening — 4.120

final decision
- enforcement application — 1.11
- meaning — 1.3

final decision appeals
- index to notes — 4.2
- point of law — 1.12, 4.81

final orders
- appeals from — 4.8

findings of fact, appeals against
- appellate caution — 2.50, 4.79
- immigration appeals — 2.55
- index to notes — 4.2
- inferences drawn from primary facts — 2.47–54
- legal standard application — 2.50–1
- oral evidence — 2.53
- pre-CPR practice — 2.36–46
- presumption that lower court correct — 2.36
- basis — 2.37–41
- displacement of — 2.42–7
- expert witnesses — 2.40–1
- failure to take account of material matters — 2.42–7
- witnesses — 2.38–9

findings of fact, appeals against – *contd*
- primary facts — 2.47–54
- respect for lower court — 2.54

first appeal — 1.5

Form N161. *See* **appellant's notice**

Form N162. *See* **respondent's notice**

Form N244 — 6.6, 6.19

fraud
- credibility of witnesses — 2.45

fresh evidence — 1.7, 2.7, A2.10
- failure to produce at lower court — 2.71
- final decisions — 2.64, 2.65
- ground for appeal — 2.62–72, 4.84–6
- hearing on merits — 2.65, 2.66, A2.6
- index to notes — 4.2
- interim decision — 2.70, A2.6
- interlocutory decisions — 2.64, 2.66, A2.6
- overriding objective and — 2.68, 2.69, 2.70
- permission of court — 2.67, 2.68, A2.10
- public law cases — 2.72
- rehearings — 2.69
- retrial — 4.66
- review — 2.71
- special grounds — 2.67, 2.68, 2.69, 4.85

further evidence. *See* **fresh evidence**

grounds for appeal — 211–16
- in appellant's notice — 1.7, 6.2
- application to all courts — 2.12, 2.15
- change of circumstances — 2.73–80
  - change of fact — 2.75, 2.76
  - change of law — 2.75
  - CPR — 2.79–80
  - finality of legislation and rehearings — 2.77
  - review not rehearing — 2.78, 2.79
  - RSC — 2.78
- changing — 2.73–7, 2.79
- error of law — 4.86
  - absence of evidence — 2.19–20, 2.22
  - failure to give reasons — 2.23–7, 4.78
  - failure to resolve conflicts of evidence — 2.28–31
  - nature — 2.17–18
  - perverse decisions — 2.21–2
  - scope — 2.17–18
- failure to give reasons — 2.23–7, 4.78
  - costs orders — 2.27
  - European Court jurisprudence — 2.26
- failure to resolve conflicts of evidence — 2.28–31
- fresh evidence — 2.62–72, 4.84–6
- incorrect basis of fact — 2.32–5

grounds for appeal – contd
index to notes	4.2
irregularity	1.7, 2.11, 2.13, A2.13
resulting in injustice	2.81–3, 4.75, 4.76
serious	2.81–3, 4.76
new grounds	4.18
not in appellant's notice	1.7
perverse decision	2.21–2
point of law	1.12n2, 4.81
See also error of law	
precedents	4.88
serious irregularity	
causing injustice	4.75, 4.76
procedural	2.81–3
statutory	2.32–5
co-operating parties	2.33
unfairness, incorrect basis of fact	2.32–5
unjust decision	2.11, 2.13
wrong decision of lower court	2.11, 2.13, 2.14, 4.76, A2.12
exercise of discretion	2.14, 4.80
failure to give reasons	2.23–7, 4.78
former authorities	2.15
perverse decision	2.21–2
'wrong'	2.14
See also error of law	

handed down judgments
index to notes	4.2
reserved judgments	6.45, 6.46, A2.16

hearing of appeal
in Court of Appeal	4.111
CPR	4.71
directions, request for	6.41, A2.21
index to notes	4.2
interlocutory appeals	2.4, 4.72
nature of	4.72
oral evidence	4.77
prayers	6.44
rehearing	4.72, 4.74–5
request for directions	6.41, A2.21
reserved judgments	
attendance of advocates	6.46
availability before hand down	6.45, A2.16
review	4.74
review of decision	4.72
short-warned list	4.2, 6.39
special fixtures list	6.40

High Court
appeals to House of Lords	8.9–15
reopening appeals	4.121
writ of habeas corpus	8.15

High Court judge
costs	3.33, 3.34
family proceedings	3.41, 3.42
fast track claims	3.11, 3.12
Part 8 claims	3.16
small claims	3.6, 3.7

House of Lords
allocation of time	8.60
appeals to	8.1–4
from Court of Appeal	8.5–8
from Court of Sessions	8.16
from High Court	8.9–15
appearance for respondent	8.31
appellant's case	8.45, 8.46
appendix of documents	8.37
agreement between parties	8.41
contents	8.39
format	8.40
lodgment	8.43–4
Scottish cases	8.64
submission of lists	8.41
bankruptcy of party	8.71
bill of costs	
extension of time applications	8.77
failure to lodge	8.81
lodgment	8.76
bound volumes	8.55–7
cases	
appellant's	8.45, 8.46
exchange	8.49
lodgment	8.49
respondent's	8.45, 8.47
separate and joint	8.46
conjoinder of appeals	8.50, 8.52–3
consolidation of appeals	8.50–1, 8.53
costs	
bill of costs	8.76–81
money in security fund	8.78–81
submission on	8.72, 8.73
taxation of	8.76–81
cross appeals	8.54
death of party	8.70
documentation	
authorities	8.58
bound volumes	8.55–7
lodgment. *See* lodgment of documents	
numbers of documents	8.66
See also individual documents *eg* cases	
enforcement of judgment order	8.82
exchange of cases	8.49
extension of time petition	8.67

House of Lords – *contd*
  Human Rights Act 8.34
  incidental petitions 8.68
  incompatibility of legislation
    with EHRC 8.34
  index to notes 4.2
  judgment
    drafts of orders 8.74
    enforcement of order 8.82
    final order 8.74
    form of 8.73
  'leapfrog' appeals 8.9
  leave to appeal
    application from High Court 8.10–13
    applications, consideration of 8.3
    Court of Appeal hearing 8.6
    refusal by Court of Appeal 8.7
    Scottish cases 8.62
    See also petition for leave
  leave to appeal certificate
    application for 8.10–12
    refusal of 8.12
  leave to cross appeal 8.8
  legal aid 8.33
  lodgment of documents
    appendix of documents 8.43–4
    bill of costs 8.76
    bound volumes 8.55–7
    cases 8.49
    statement of facts and issues 8.43–4
  notice of hearing 8.59
  petition of appeal
    certificate of service 8.30
    prescribed contents and style 8.29
    Scottish appeals 8.29
    Scottish cases 8.63
    service on respondent 8.30
  petition for extension of time 8.67
  petition for leave
    Appeal Committee 8.21, 8.26
    appearance 8.19
    consideration of 8.21
    contents 8.18
    costs 8.27
    expedition 8.28
    format 8.18
    from Court of Appeal 8.7
    from High Court 8.13, 8.14
    legal aid 8.20
    objects of respondent 8.25
    petition allowed 8.23
    petition dismissed 8.22
    procedures 8.17–27

House of Lords – *contd*
  petition for leave – *contd*
    public funding 8.20
    referral to hearing 8.26
    terms 8.24
    time limit for lodging 8.17
    Practice Direction 8.2
    procedures 8.2, 8.84
    public funding 8.33
    respondent
      appearance for 8.31
      cross appeals 8.54
      objections to petition for leave 8.25
    respondent's case 8.45, 8.47
    Scottish cases 8.61–6
      appendix of documents 8.64
    security for costs 8.32
    standing orders 8.2
    statement of facts and issues 8.35–6
      lodgment 8.43–4
    withdrawal before setting down 8.69
      costs 8.81
    writ of habeas corpus 8.15
human rights
  appellant's notice 6.3
  bias or irregularity 4.67
  companies 2.85
  declaration of incompatibility 4.27
  fair trial, right to 2.83, 2.84–90, 4.67
  House of Lords appeal 8.34
  overriding objective and 2.89, 2.90
  private and family life 2.88

immigration appeals
  co-operating parties 2.33
  fear of persecution A2.14
  finding of facts 2.55
  racial discrimination A2.14
  striking out action A2.17
incidental remedies applications 4, 52, 6.6
inferences
  drawn from primary facts 2.47–54
injustice
  irregularity resulting in 2.81–3, 4.75, 4.76
insolvency proceedings
  Destination of Appeals Order 3.43
  locus standi A2.11
  routes of appeal 3.43
intellectual property claims
  routes of appeal 3.21
interlocutory appeals 2.4, 4.72
  fresh evidence 2.4, 2.64, 2.66, A2.6

544 Index

irregularity
  appeal ground   2.11, 2.13, 2.81–3, 4.75,
        4.76
  of judge's decision   1.7
  resulting in injustice   2.81–3, 4.75, 4.76
irrelevant material
  taken into consideration by lower
    court   2.58

judgment of appeal
  agreed orders following   6.47
  application for leave to appeal   6.49
  draft
    contents   6.47
    corrections   6.48
  reserved judgments
    attendance of advocates   6.46
    availability before hand down   6.45, A2.16
judicial review
  appeals in Court of Appeal   4.116–17
  appeals in proceedings for   3.44
  index to notes   4.2
  permission to appeal, of   4.16
  time limit for appellant's notice   1.7

'leapfrog' appeals   8.9
leave to appeal to House of Lords
  applications
    consideration of   8.3
    Court of Appeal hearing   8.6
    from High Court   8.10–13
    refusal by Court of Appeal   8.7
  certificate
    application for   8.10–12
    refusal of   8.12
  Court of Appeal
    appeal from   8.5–8
    applications hearing   8.6, 8.7
  petitions
    from Court of Appeal   8.7
    from High Court   8.13, 8.14
    to House of Lords   8.7
  refusal by Court of Appeal   8.7
  Scottish cases   8.62
  See also **petition for leave to appeal**
legal aid
  House of Lords appeal   8.33
lower court   1.6
  discontinuance of proceedings   5.4
  enforcement of Court of Appeal order   5.9

lower court – *contd*
  meaning   1.3
  presumption that correct   2.36
    basis   2.37–41
    displacement of   2.42–7
    expert witnesses   2.40–1
    failure to take account of
      material matters   2.42–7
    witnesses   2.38–9
  wrong decision ground for appeal   2.11, 2.13, 2.14, 4.76, A2.12
  error of law. *See* **error of law**
  exercise of discretion   2.14, 4.80
  failure to give reasons   2.23–7, 4.78
  former authorities   2.15
  perverse decision   2.21–2
  'wrong'   2.14

masters
  Court of Appeal Civil Division   5.7
  and deputy masters   4.2
  dismissal list of hearings   5.8
  and district judges   4.2
  index to notes   4.2
mediation   7.2
  costs   7.4
  Court of Appeal scheme   7.6
  family matters   7.6
  reasonable prospect of success   7.4
multi-track claims
  appeal court   3.21
  appeals in proceedings for
    judicial review   3.44
  oral hearing request   3.25
  permission to appeal   3.24
  routes of appeal   3.20–5

new evidence. *See* **fresh evidence**
notice of discontinuance   5.4

order to be appealed   4.3
  record of   6.17, A2.21
  status of   4.4
  transcript of judgment   4.3, 4.101, 4.111, 6.10
orders
  ancillary. *See* **ancillary orders**
  final, appeals from   4.8
  index to notes   4.2
overriding objective
  alternative dispute resolution   7.1
  extension of time application   4.46
  fresh evidence   2.68, 2.69, 2.70

overriding objective – *contd*
  human rights   2.89, 2.90

Part 7 claims
  routes of appeal   3.20
Part 8 claims
  circuit judge   3.14, 3.15, 3.16
  district judge   3.15
  High Court judge   3.16
  oral hearing request   3.15
  permission to appeal   3.14, 3.16
  routes of appeal   3.12–16, 3.13–16
  second appeal   3.15
Part 36 offers and payments
  compromise of appeal   4.92
  costs of appeal   4.92
  index to notes   4.2
  non-disclosure   4.89–90, 6.11
  removal of reference to   4.91, 6.11
patents claims
  routes of appeal   3.21
patients
  consent orders   6.54, 6.56
  structured settlements   6.57
payment into court
  index to notes   4.2
  See also **Part 36 offers and payments**
permission to amend appeal notice   4.53, 4.55–7, 6.19
  fee payable   4.56
permission to appeal
  ancillary orders   3.35
  appellant's notice   4.25
  case management decisions   4.17
  committal order   3.17
  conditional   4.2, 4.23, 4.58
    imposition of conditions   4.62, A2.5
  costs   3.33
    of respondent   6.23, A2.12
  Court of Appeal   A2.8
  CPR   4.12
  extension of time   4.19, A2.15
  family proceedings   3.40
  fast track claims   3.8, 3.9, 3.11
  grant, judicial review of   4.16
  index to notes   4.2
  judge giving   1.7
  judicial review and   4.16
  limited   4.2, 4.22, 6.22
  multi-track claims   3.24
  new grounds of appeal   4.18
  notice of hearing   4.21

permission to appeal – *contd*
  oral hearing   6.20, A2.19
  Part 8 claims   3.14, 3.16
  point of principle   3.37, 4.96, 4.114
  precedent   4.24
  publicly funded applicant   6.21
  refusal   4.2
    after hearing   1.7
    at oral hearing   4.15
    judge who refused, at appeal   4.87
    judicial review of   4.16
    notification of decision   6.20
    oral hearing request   4.20, 6.20, A2.19, A2.20
    on paper   4.2, 4.20, A2.19
    renewal to oral hearing   4.2
    without hearing   1.7, 6.20
  requirement   1.7, 4.14
  respondent's submissions   4.31, 6.23, A2.12
  restrictions   1.4
  setting aside   4.2, 4.60, A2.2, A2.3
    precedent   4.63
  small claims   3.3, 3.7
  specialist proceedings   3.24
permission to change grounds   4.86
perverse decision
  decision not permissible option   2.22
  grounds for appeal   2.21–2
petition for leave to appeal
  Appeal Committee   8.21, 8.26
  appearance   8.19
  consideration of   8.21
  contents   8.18
  costs   8.27
  expedition   8.28
  format   8.18
  from Court of Appeal   8.7
  from High Court   8.13, 8.14
  legal aid   8.20
  objects of respondent   8.25
  petition allowed   8.23
  petition dismissed   8.22
  procedures   8.17–27
  public funding   8.20
  referral to hearing   8.26
  terms   8.24
  time limit for lodging   8.17
planning appeals
  co-operating parties   2.33
points of principle
  assigned to Court of Appeal   3.37, 4.96, 4.114

possession proceedings	A2.20
index to notes	4.2
special provisions for appeals	4.6
powers of appeal court	4.65, A2.21
bail	4.68
case management	4.69–70
compulsory ADR	7.3
CPR	4.64
fresh evidence admission	4.85
index to notes	4.2
retrial order	
bias or irregularity	4.67
on new evidence	4.66
Practice Direction	4.11
compliance with	4.10
index to notes	4.2
prayers	6.44
primary facts	2.47–54
probate	
routes of appeal	3.21
public bodies	
adverse costs sanctions	7.4, 7.5
alternative dispute resolution	7.4, 7.5
public funding	
House of Lords appeal	8.20, 8.33
permission to appeal application	6.21
petition for leave	8.20
questionnaire, appeal	4.107, 4.108, 6.25
fees on filing	4.107
time estimates	6.26
re-opening decisions	4.2
reasons for decision	
duty to give	2.23–7, 4.82
European Court jurisprudence	2.26
failure to give. See **failure to give reasons**	
orders for costs	2.27
refusal of permission to appeal	4.2
after hearing	1.7
at oral hearing	4.15
judge who refused acting at appeal	4.87
judicial review of	4.16
notification of decision	6.20
oral hearing request	4.20, 6.20, A2.19, A2.20
on paper	4.2, 4.20, A2.19
renewal to oral hearing	4.2
without hearing	1.7, 6.20
rehearing	1.7, 4.72, 4.74–5
of appeal	2.10

rehearing – *contd*	
before same/different judge	2.8–9
change of circumstances	2.78, 2.79
fresh evidence	2.69, 4.85
inadequately reasoned lower court decision	2.6
index to notes	4.2
in interests of justice	2.5–7
interlocutory appeals	2.4, 2.64, 2.66, A2.6
no decision from lower court	2.7
of original application	2.10
review compared	2.1–10
Rules of Supreme Court	2.7
reopening appeals	
county court decisions	4.122
Court of Appeal	4.121
Court of Appeal decisions	4.121
final appeals	4.120
High Court decisions	4.121
reserved judgments, hand down	
attendance of advocates	6.45
availability before	6.45, A2.16
respondents	
application to House of Lords	8.8
costs	4.33, 6.23, A2.12
cross appeals	
House of Lords	8.54
permission	4.34
extension of time views	4.45, A2.15
leave to cross appeal	8.8
meaning	1.3
objections	
to amendment of appeal notice	4.57
to House of Lords petition	8.25
permission to appeal application and	6.23, A2.12
role	4.33
petition of appeal appearance	8.31
service on	1.8, 4.27, 4.104, 6.18
petition of appeal	8.30
skeleton arguments	4.35, 4.36, 4.40, 6.32, 6.33, 6.35
respondent's notice	4.31, 6.29
applications within	6.34
costs	4.2
Court of Appeal	4.109
extension of time required	4.36
failure to file	4.39
filing	4.31
form N162	1.7, 4.41
index to notes	4.2

respondent's notice – *contd*
  notification of intention to file   6.33
  permission request   4.31, 4.34
  permission to cross appeal   4.34
  service   4.35, 6.37
  skeleton arguments   4.2, 4.35, 4.36, 4.40, 6.32, 6.33, 6.35
  supporting documents   4.37, 4.38
    service of   6.37
    skeleton arguments   4.2, 4.35, 4.36, 4.40, 6.32, 6.33, 6.35
    supplemental bundle   6.36–7
  time limit for filing   4.31, 6.30
    Court of Appeal   6.31
    extension of time   6.31
retrial
  index to notes   4.2
  new evidence   4.66
  power to order   4.2
review   2.1, 4.74
  change of circumstances grounds   2.78
  fresh evidence   2.71, 4.85
  index to notes   4.2
  new regime guidance   2.3–5, 2.7, A2.21
  rehearing compared   2.1–10
  Rules of Supreme Court   2.7
routes of appeal   2.12
  admiralty claims   3.21
  ancillary orders   3.35, A2.7
  arbitration claims   3.21
  assessment of costs   1.11, 3.31
  committal order   3.17–18
  Companies Acts proceedings   3.21
  contempt of court   3.18
  contentious probate claims   3.21
  costs   3.31–4
  Destination of Appeals Order   3.1
  family proceedings   3.39–42
  fast track claims   3.8–12
  flowcharts   4.2
  from county court   1.9
  index to notes   4.2
  insolvency proceedings   3.43
  intellectual property claims   3.21
  meaning   1.3
  multi-track claims   3.20–5
  normal route inappropriate   1.12
  Part 7 claims   3.20
  Part 8 claims   3.12–16
  patents claims   3.21
  probate claims   3.21
  second appeals   3.26–30
  small claims   3.2–7

routes of appeal – *contd*
  specialist proceedings   3.21
  Technology and Construction Court claims   3.21
  to Court of Appeal   1.9–12
  track to which claim allocated   1.9, 1.10
Rules of Supreme Court
  change of circumstances ground   2.73–7, 2.79
  rehearings   2.7
  review   2.7
Scottish appeals
  Court of Sessions to House of Lords   8.16
  House of Lords   8.16, 8.61–6
    appendix of documents   8.64
    leave to appeal   8.62
    petition of appeal   8.63
Sealing of appeal notice   1.8, 4.104, 6.18
second appeals   1.4, 1.6
  appeal court   1.4, 1.5
  appellate policy   3.29–30
  index to notes   4.2
  meaning   1.3, 4.94
  original order and   4.3, 4.101, 6.10
  Part 8 claims   3.15
  routes of appeal   3.26–30
  small claims   3.5
  to Court of Appeal   4.93–5
security for costs   A2.4, A2.8, A2.9
  of appeal   4.59
  index to notes   4.2
  petition of appeal   8.32
service of documents
  appellant's notice   4.27, 4.104, 6.18
    certificate of service   6.18, 8.30
    contempt of court   4.27
    Court of Appeal   1.8
    dispensing with   6.18
  certificate of service   6.18, 8.30
  petition of appeal   8.30
  respondent's documents
    respondent's notice   4.35, 6.37
    skeleton arguments   6.37
    supplemental bundle   6.37
setting aside
  appellant's notice   4.58, 4.60, A2.2, A2.11
  permission to appeal   4.60, A2.2, A2.3
  precedent   4.63
short-warned list   6.39
  index to notes   4.2

Index

skeleton arguments
  amendment 1.7
  appellant's 6.15, 6.16, 6.43
  content 6.16, 6.33
  cost of preparing 6.16
  Court of Appeal 4.106
  respondent's 4.2, 4.35, 4.36, 4.40, 6.32, 6.33, 6.35
  supplementary 6.43
small claims
  appellant's supporting documents 6.9, 6.14
  circuit judge 3.2, 3.5
  Court of Appeal 3.5, 3.7
  documents 3.4, 6.9, 6.14
  High Court judge 3.6, 3.7
  index to notes 4.2
  permission to appeal 3.3, 3.7
  routes of appeal 3.2–7
  second appeal 3.5
Social Security
  urgent case payment to asylum seeker A2.18
solicitor, change of 5.2–3
  index to notes 4.2
special fixtures list 6.40
specialist proceedings
  appeals in proceedings for judicial review 3.44
  oral hearing request 3.25, A2.20
  permission to appeal 3.24
  routes of appeal 3.21, 3.21–5
statement of case
  in appeal bundle 4.28, 6.13
  in chapter form 6.13
statement of facts and issues
  House of Lords 8.35–6, 8.43–4
  lodgment 8.43–4
statutory appeals
  grounds 2.32–5
  index to notes 4.2
stay of execution
  appellant's notice and 4.50, A2.9
  application for incidental remedy 4.52, 6.6
  House of Lords and 8.7
stay of proceedings 4.49
  in lower court 4.51, A2.1
stays
  index to notes 4.2
striking out
  abuse of process 5.1, A2.17
  appeal notice 4.58, 4.61, 5.1, A2.17

striking out – *contd*
  decision 1.3
  index to notes 4.2
structured settlements
  children 6.57
  patients 6.57
summary assessment of costs 4.112, 6.38
supplemental bundle
  respondent's 6.36–7
  service 6.37
supplementary skeleton arguments 6.43

Technology and Construction Court claims
  routes of appeal 3.21
terminology 1.3
three-judge court 4.110
time estimates
  in appeal questionnaire 6.26
time limits 4.43–4
  appellant's notice 1.7, 4.27, 4.43, 4.100, 6.4
  appellant's notice filing 6.4
  Court of Appeal 4.100
  extension of time. *See* **extension of time application**
  filing appellant's notice 1.7
  respondent's notice 6.30, 6.31
  variation of time application 4.42, A2.20
transfer of appeals to Court of Appeal 3.36–8, 4.114–15, A2.21
  criteria for transfer 3.37, 4.114
  important point of principle 3.37, 4.96, 4.114
  index to notes 4.2
  powers of transfer 4.115
trustee in bankruptcy 5.6

UK College of Family Mediators 7.6
unjust decision ground 2.11, 2.13
unopposed appeals 6.53

variation of time
  appeal notice filing 4.42, A2.20

witnesses
  credibility 2.45
  experts 2.20, 2.31, 2.40–1
  impression as to demeanour 2.43
writ of habeas corpus
  appeals to House of Lords 8.15

wrong decision of lower court 2.11, 2.13, 2.14, 4.76, A2.12
error of law. *See* **error of law**
exercise of discretion 2.14, 4.80
failure to give reasons 2.23–7, 4.78

wrong decision of lower court – *contd*
former authorities 2.15
perverse decision 2.21–2
'wrong' 2.14